Contents

ARISTOTLE   315

HELLENISTIC AND ROMAN PHILOSOPHY   463

EPICURUS   467

LUCRETIUS   491

Preface

The philosophers of ancient Greece have fascinated thinking persons for centuries, and their writings have been one of the key influences on the development of Western civilization. Beginning with the fragmentary statements of the Pre-Socratics, moving to the all-embracing systems of Plato and Aristotle, and culminating in the practical advice of the Hellenistic writers, Greek philosophers have defined the questions and suggested many of the answers for subsequent generations. As the great Greek statesman, Pericles, sagely predicted, "Future ages will wonder at us, as the present age wonders at us now."

This volume in the *Philosophic Classics* series includes the writings of the most important Greek philosophers, along with selections from some of their Roman followers. In choosing texts for this volume, I have tried to follow the editorial principles established by Walter Kaufmann in his 2 volume *Philosophic Classics* (1961) on which this current series is based: (1) to use complete works or, where more appropriate, complete sections of works (2) in clear translations (3) of texts central to the thinker's philosophy or widely accepted as part of the "canon." To make the works more accessible to students, most footnotes treating textual matters (variant readings, etc.) have been omitted and all Greek words have been transliterated and put in angle brackets. In addition, each thinker is introduced by a brief essay composed of three sections: (1) biographical (a glimpse of the life), (2) philosophical (a résumé of the philosopher's thought), and (3) bibliographical (suggestions for further reading).

WHAT'S NEW IN THIS EDITION?

- New translations of Plato's *Meno, Symposium, Republic, Parmenides, Theaetetus,* and *Timeus* from the acclaimed Focus Philosophical Library Series.
- Additional material from Plato's *Republic* on censorship and how democracy can lead to tyranny.
- New translation of Aristotle's *Categories* and *On Interpretation* from the Loeb Classics Series.
- New translations of Aristotle's *Physics, Metaphysics,* and *On the Soul* by Joe Sachs.
- New reading from Aristotle's *Poetics* from the Focus Series.
- New translation of Lucretius's *On the Nature of Things,* from the Focus Series.
- Updated bibliographies reflecting the most recent scholarship on each thinker and philosophical school.
- To allow for all these changes, the nonessential speeches from Plato's *Symposium* have been dropped.

Those who use this first volume in a one-term course in ancient philosophy will find more material here than can easily fit a normal semester. But this embarrassment of riches gives teachers some choice and, for those who offer the same course year after year, an opportunity to change the menu.

*   *   *

I would like to thank the many people who assisted me in this volume, including the library staff of Whitworth College, especially Hans Bynagle, Gail Fielding, and Jeanette Langston; my colleagues F. Dale Bruner, who made helpful suggestions on all the introductions, Barbara Filo, who helped make selections for artwork, and Ronald Pyle, who made suggestions about Aspasia; Stephen Davis, Claremont McKenna College; Jerry H. Gill, The College of St. Rose; Rex Hollowell, Spokane Falls Community College; Stanley Obitts, Westmont College; and Charles Young, The Claremont Graduate School, who each read some of the introductions and gave helpful advice; my production editor Shiny Rajesh of Integra, my project manager, Sarah Holle of Prentice Hall; and my former acquisitions editors, Mical Moser, Ross Miller, Karita France, Angela Stone, and Ted Bolen. I would also like to acknowledge the following reviewers: Marianina Alcott, San Jose State University; James W. Allard, Montana State University; David Apolloni, Augsberg College; Robert C. Bennett, El Centro College; Sarah Borden, Wheaton College; Herbert L. Carson, Ferris State University; Stuart Dalton, Monmouth College; Mark Hébert, Austin College; John Hurley, Central Connecticut State University; Helen S. Lang, Trinity College; Scott MacDonald, University of Iowa; Nick More, Westminster College; Paul Newberry, California State University—Bakersfield; David F.T. Rodier, American University; Reginald Savage, North Carolina State University; Gregory Schultz, Wisconsin Lutheran College; Stephen Scott, Eastern Washington University; Daniel C. Shartin, Worcester State College; Ted Toadvine, Emporia State University; Donald Phillip Verene, Emory University; Tamara Welsh, University of Tennessee—Chattanooga; Robert M. Wieman, Ohio University; and Sarah Worth, Allegheny College.

I am especially thankful to my wife, Joy Lynn Fulton Baird, and to our children, Whitney, Sydney, and Soren, who have supported me in this enterprise. Finally, I would like to thank Stanley R. Obitts and Robert N. Wennberg, who first introduced me to the joys of philosophy. It is to them that this volume is dedicated.

Forrest E. Baird
Professor of Philosophy
Whitworth University
Spokane, WA 99251
email: fbaird@whitworth.edu

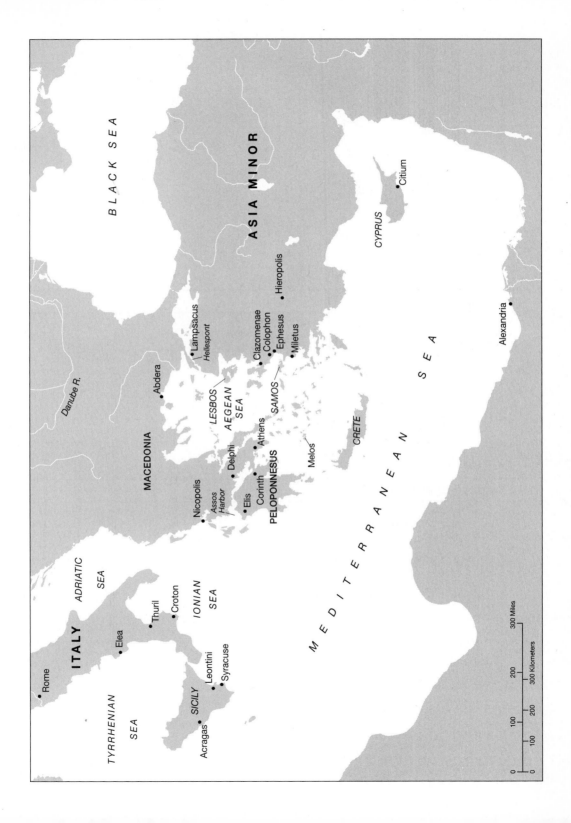

BLACK SEA

ASIA MINOR

CYPRUS

Citium

Alexandria

Lampsacus
Hellespont

Clazomenae
Colophon
Ephesus
Miletus

Hieropolis

Abdera

LESBOS

AEGEAN
SEA

SAMOS

MEDITERRANEAN

SEA

Athens

Delphi

Melos

CRETE

MACEDONIA

Nicopolis
Assos
Harbor

Elis
Corinth

PELOPONNESUS

ADRIATIC

SEA

IONIAN

SEA

ITALY

Rome

Elea

Thurii

Croton

Leontini
Syracuse

SICILY

Acragas

TYRRHENIAN

SEA

Danube R.

0   100   200   300 Miles

0   100   200   300 Kilometers

Philosophers In This Volume

600 B.C.	500 B.C	400 B.C.	300 B.C.	200 B.C.

Thales
Anaximander
Anaximenes
Pythagoras
Xenophanes
Heraclitus
Anaxagoras
Protagoras
Parmenides
Empedocles
Critias
Aspasia
Gorgias
Socrates
Zeno of Elea
Democritus

Plato
Aristotle
Pyrrho

Epicurus
Zeno of Citium
Cleanthes

Other Important Figures

Zoroaster
Lao Tzu
Ezekial
Buddah
Confucius
Pericles
Sophocles
Herodotus
Euripides
Thucydides
Hippocrates
Aristophanes
Ezra

Nehemiah
Alexander the Great
Euclid

A Sampling of Major Events

Jerusalem falls to Babylonians
Battle of Marathon
Parthenon built
Peloponnesian War

Punic Wars and rise
of Rome
Wall of
China

600 B.C.	500 B.C	400 B.C.	300 B.C.	200 B.C.

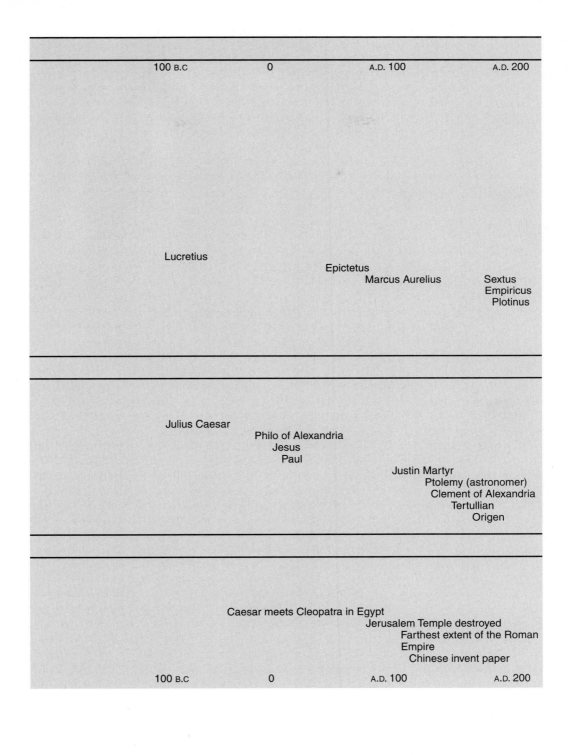

100 B.C	0	A.D. 100	A.D. 200

Lucretius

Epictetus

Marcus Aurelius

Sextus
Empiricus
Plotinus

Julius Caesar

Philo of Alexandria
Jesus
Paul

Justin Martyr
Ptolemy (astronomer)
Clement of Alexandria
Tertullian
Origen

Caesar meets Cleopatra in Egypt
Jerusalem Temple destroyed
Farthest extent of the Roman
Empire
Chinese invent paper

100 B.C	0	A.D. 100	A.D. 200

BEFORE SOCRATES

Something unusual happened in Greece and the Greek colonies of the Aegean Sea some twenty-five hundred years ago. Whereas the previous great cultures of the Mediterranean had used mythological stories of the gods to explain the operations of the world and of the self, some of the Greeks began to discover new ways of explaining things. Instead of reading their ideas into, or out of, ancient scriptures or poems, they began to use reason, contemplation, and sensory observation to make sense of reality.

The story, as we know it, began with the Greeks living on the coast of Asia Minor (present-day Turkey). These colonists, such as Thales, tried to find the one common element in the diversity of nature. Subsequent thinkers, such as Anaximenes, sought not only to find this one common element, but also to find the process by which one form changes into another. Other thinkers, such as Pythagoras, turned to the nature of form itself rather than the basic stuff that takes on a particular form. These lovers of wisdom, or *philosophers*, came to very different conclusions and often spoke disrespectfully of one another. Some held the universe to be one, while others insisted that it must be many. Some believed that human knowledge was capable of understanding virtually everything about the world, while others thought that it was not possible to have any knowledge at all. But despite all their differences, there is a thread of continuity, a continuing focus: the *human* attempt to understand the world, using *human* reason. This fact distinguishes these philosophers from the great minds that preceded them.

There are excellent reasons for beginning a study of philosophy with these men and then proceeding to Socrates and Plato. This, after all, is how Western

1

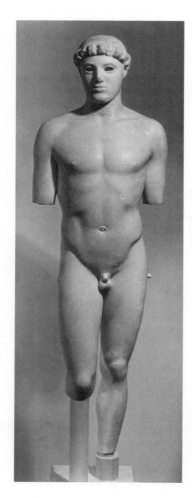

The Kritos Boy (Statue from the Acropolis attributed to Kritos.) Ca. 480 B.C. Just as the philosophers of classical Greece focused on human reason and its ability to know, the artists of the same period examined the human body in its idealized form. *(Athens, Acropolis Museum. Photographer: Alison Frantz.)*

philosophy did begin, and we can still recapture something of the excitement of this new way of thinking as we move from the bald statements of Thales to the all-embracing questions of Socrates, and thence to Plato's efforts to fuse criticism with construction.

If dissatisfaction with facile answers is the starting point of philosophic thought, the fragments of the Pre-Socratics are especially appropriate for a beginning. Not one of their works has survived complete—all we have are scattered quotations and reports from later writers. As a result, Pre-Socratic thought has a mysterious quality. Cryptic passages and forceful aphorisms, whose original context is lost, stimulate the imagination. Instead of looking for "the" answer, one is fascinated by a wealth of possible answers. And in the effort to show why some suggested answers are untenable, one develops critical faculties.

Some fragments may remind readers of archaic statues—heads with broken noses, torsos without heads or arms—pieces so perfect in form that one has no regrets at the loss of the whole and may even believe that the complete work could not have been as fascinating.

For all that, most interest in the Pre-Socratics is motivated by the fact that these thinkers furnish the backdrop for the thought of Socrates, Plato, and Aristotle—this is why one lumps them together as the "Pre-Socratics." But this magnificent succession of thinkers deserves more respect. Though often enigmatic and at times oracular, the Pre-Socratics are distinguished above all by their appeal to reason. And through the appeal to reason, each thinker makes it possible for successors to exercise criticism, to amend, to develop alternatives, to move beyond.

The Pre-Socratics' influence on Plato was so great that a study of their thought is essential to understanding many passages in his dialogues and his intentions; many problems were suggested to him by Heraclitus, the Eleatics, and the Pythagoreans—and, of course, by his originality. Aristotle studied the Pre-Socratics closely and discussed them at length in the first book of his *Metaphysics* (reprinted in this volume). Of the later Greek philosophers, it has often been remarked that the Stoics were particularly influenced by Heraclitus, and the Epicureans by Democritus. Elements of Orphism, an early Greek religious movement, also found their way into the ideas of the Pre-Socratics—most obviously, but by no means only, into Pythagoreanism—and hence into Plato and, later, into Christianity. In fact, a few of the fragments survived only as quotations in the works of early Christian writers.

*   *   *

What follows is only a selection. There is no such thing as a complete roster of the Pre-Socratics. The so-called Sophists were Socrates' contemporaries, but Protagoras and Gorgias were older than he and had acquired reputations before he came along and challenged them; and they are included here. After all, it was partly in response to their teaching that Socrates' thought was developed. Among the older writers, it is arguable who was, and who was not, a philosopher. Various poets, for example, are occasionally included among the Pre-Socratics. Not counting the Sophists, the present selection concentrates on eleven major figures. They might conveniently be arranged into four groups: (1) the three great Milesians (Thales, Anaximander, and Anaximenes); (2) the three great independents—figures who came from different places and stood for quite different principles (Pythagoras, Xenophanes, and Heraclitus); (3) the two great monists (Parmenides and Zeno of Elea); and, finally, (4) the three great pluralists (Empedocles, Anaxagoras, and Democritus). The only major name missing in this list is Leucippus, founder of the atomistic philosophy, who is included with his better-known follower, Democritus.

If we were to offer all the fragments of these figures, we would have to include such unhelpful items as the following, each given in its entirety: "The joint connects two things"; "as when fig juice binds white milk"; "having kneaded together barley-meal with water" (Empedocles, fragments 32, 33, 34). Instead, the following selections were chosen to give an idea of each thinker's main teachings, as far as possible in his own words, and to provide some sense of his way of thinking and feeling. In short, the selections should give us the essence of thinkers who still have the power to astonish students across roughly twenty-five hundred years.

*   *   *

For a comprehensive work on the Pre-Socratics, see Volumes I and II of W.K.C. Guthrie's authoritative *The History of Greek Philosophy,* six volumes, (Cambridge: Cambridge University Press, 1962–1981). John Burnet, *Early Greek Philosophy* (1892; reprinted New York: Meridian, 1960); John Mansley Robinson, *An Introduction to Early Greek Philosophy* (Boston: Houghton Mifflin, 1968); Jonathan Barnes, *The Pre-Socratic Philosophers* (London: Routledge & Kegan Paul, 1982); and Edward Hussey, *The Presocratics* (Indianapolis, IN: Hackett, 1995) are standard secondary sources, while the relevant sections of W.T. Jones, *The Classical Mind* (New York: Harcourt, Brace & World, 1969); Frederick Copleston, *A History of Philosophy: Volume I, Greece & Rome, Part I* (Garden City, NY: Doubleday, 1962); Friedo Ricken, *Philosophy of the Ancients,* translated by Eric Watkins (Notre Dame, IN: University of Notre Dame Press, 1991); J.V. Luce, *An Introduction to Greek Philosophy* (New York: Thames and Hudson, 1992); Catherine Osborne, *Presocratic Philosophy: A Very Short Introduction* (Oxford: Oxford University Press, 2004); and Anthony Kenny, *Ancient Philosophy: A New History of Western Philosophy* (Oxford: Oxford University Press, 2004) provide basic introductions. Robert S. Brumbaugh, *The Philosophers of Greece* (Albany, NY: SUNY Press, 1981), is an accessible introduction with pictures, charts, and maps. Francis MacDonald Cornford, *Principium Sapientiae: The Origins of Greek Philosophical Thought* (Cambridge: Cambridge University Press, 1952), and Werner Jaeger, *The Theology of the Early Greek Philosophers* (Oxford: Clarendon Press, 1947) are both classic works that discuss the movement from mythology to philosophy, while Kathryn Morgan, *Myth and Philosophy from the Presocratics to Plato* (Cambridge: Cambridge University Press, 2000) is a more recent study on the subject. More recent works and references include Christopher C. Shields, ed., *The Blackwell Guide to Ancient Philosophy* (London: Blackwell, 2002); David Roochnik, *Retrieving the Ancients* (London: Blackwell, 2004); Nigel Wilson, ed., *Encyclopedia of Ancient Greece* (London: New York: Routledge, 2005); and Patricia Curd and Daniel Graham, eds., *The Oxford Handbook of Presocratic Philosophy* (Oxford: Oxford University Press, 2008). For collections of essays, see David J. Furley and R.E. Allen, eds., *Studies in Presocratic Philosophy,* two volumes (New York: Humanities Press, 1970–1975); A.P.D. Mourelatos, ed., *The Pre-Socratics* (Princeton: Princeton University Press, 1993); Gregory Vlastos, ed., *Studies in Greek Philosophy, Volume I: The Presocratics* (Princeton: Princeton University Press, 1995); Terence Irwin, ed., *Philosophy Before Socrates* (Hamden, CT: Garland Publishing, 1995); Mary Louise Gill and Pierre Pellegrin, eds., *A Companion to Ancient Philosophy* (London: Blackwell, 2004); and Patricia F. O'Grady, *Meet the Philosophers of Ancient Greece* (Burlington, VT: Ashgate, 2005).

In addition to the general sources listed here, the individual articles in Paul Edwards, ed., *The Encyclopedia of Philosophy* (New York: Macmillan, 1967) and Edward Craig, ed., *Routledge Encyclopedia of Philosophy* (New York: Routledge, 1998) are frequently useful. Consult the following books for these specific thinkers:

THALES: Patricia Frances O'Grady, *Thales of Miletus: The Beginning of Western Science and Philosophy* (Burlington, VT: Ashgate, 2002).

ANAXIMANDER: Charles H. Kahn, *Anaximander and the Origins of Greek Cosmology* (New York: Columbia University Press, 1960).

PYTHAGORAS: Walter Burkert, *Lore and Science in Ancient Pythagoreanism*, translated by Edwin L. Minar, Jr. (Cambridge, MA: Harvard University Press, 1972); and Arnold Hermann, *To Think Like God: Pythagoras and Parmenides— The Origins of Philosophy* (Las Vegas, NV: Parmenides Publishing, 2004).

HERACLITUS: G.S. Kirk, *Heraclitus: The Cosmic Fragments* (Cambridge: Cambridge University Press, 1954); and Charles H. Kahn, *The Art and Thought of Heraclitus* (Cambridge: Cambridge University Press, 1979).

PARMENIDES: Leonardo Tarán, *Parmenides: A Text with Translation, Commentary, and Critical Essays* (Princeton: Princeton University Press, 1965); A.P.D. Mourelatos, *The Route of Parmenides* (New Haven, CT: Yale University Press, 1970); David Gallop, *Parmenides of Elea* (Toronto: University of Toronto Press, 1984); Patricia Curd, *The Legacy of Parmenides* (Princeton: Princeton University Press, 1998); Néstor-Luis Cordero, *By Being, It Is: The Thesis of Parmenides* (Las Vegas, NV: Parmenides Publishing, 2004); and Scott Austin, *Parmenides and the History of Dialectic* (Las Vegas, NV: Parmenides Publishing, 2007).

ZENO OF ELEA: Wesley C. Salmon, ed., *Zeno's Paradoxes* (Indianapolis, IN: Bobbs-Merrill, 1970); Adolf Grünbaum, *Modern Science and Zeno's Paradoxes* (Middletown, CT: Wesleyan University Press, 1967); and J.A. Faris, *The Paradoxes of Zeno* (Avebury, UK: Ashegate, 1996).

EMPEDOCLES: Denis O'Brien, *Empedocles' Cosmic Cycle* (Cambridge: Cambridge University Press, 1969); and M.R. Wright, *Empedocles: The Extant Fragments* (Indianapolis, IN: Hackett, 1995).

ANAXAGORAS: Malcolm Schofield, *An Essay on Anaxagoras* (Cambridge: Cambridge University Press, 1980).

DEMOCRITUS (ATOMISM): Cyril Bailey, *The Greek Atomists and Epicurus* (Oxford: Clarendon Press, 1928; reprinted New York: Russell and Russell, 1964).

SOPHISTS: G.B. Kerferd, *The Sophistic Movement* (Cambridge: Cambridge University Press, 1981); and Ugo Zilioli, *Protagoras and the Challenge of Relativism: Plato's Subtlest Enemy* (Burlington, VT: Ashgate, 2007).

Much of the critical work on the Pre-Socratics is found only in journal articles. The Philosophers' Index offers a way to locate such articles. (Please note that some of the books on specific thinkers assume some knowledge of Ancient Greek and can be very technical.)

*   *   *

All of the fragments and most of the paraphrases in the following texts were collected by a nineteenth-century German scholar, Hermann Diels (and later modified by Walther Kranz), in *Die Fragmente der Vorsokratiker* (Berlin: Weidmann, most recent edition, 1967). Diels assembled the original Greek texts and furnished German translations for all the fragments. He also collected and printed, but did not translate, reports of ancient authors about the lives, works, and ideas of the Pre-Socratics.

Kathleen Freeman published *An Ancilla to the Pre-Socratic Philosophers: A Complete Translation of the Fragments in Diels, Die Fragmente der Vorsokratiker* (Cambridge, MA: Harvard University Press, 1947). Like Diels-Kranz, she translated only the fragments, not the ancient paraphrases and reports about the philosophers' lives and works. G.S. Kirk, J.E. Raven, and M. Schofield translated many of these previously untranslated items in *The Presocratic Philosophers: A Critical History with a Selection of Texts,* 2nd edition (Cambridge: Cambridge University Press, 1983). Almost all the translations I have used are either those of Freeman (marked with an *F*) or those of Kirk, Raven, and Schofield (marked with a *K*). In a few cases the translation is Kaufmann's (marked with a *WK*) or the older first edition (1957) of Kirk and Raven (so indicated in the notes). Some of the translations have been modified by Kaufmann or myself (and are marked with an *). After direct quotations, the symbols (*K, F,* and *WK*) are preceded by the number that the fragment bears in the fifth edition of Diels-Kranz's standard work. (Freeman's numbering is the same as that of Diels-Kranz.) After paraphrases, the ancient works in which the paraphrases occur are cited briefly (along with the abbreviation and number from one of the above sources).

For discussions of the fragments and the paraphrases, see the Kirk, Raven, and Schofield's work as well as Richard D. McKirahan Jr., *Philosophy Before Socrates* (Indianapolis, IN: Hackett, 1994).

*   *   *

Sources of the fragments:

THALES: 1. Plato, Theaetetus 174a; K 72; 2. Aristotle, *Politics* A11, 1259a; K 73; 3. Herodotus I, 75; K 66; 4. Aristotle, *Metaphysics* A3, 983b; W.D. Ross's translation; 5. Heraclitus Homericus, *Quaest. Hom.* 22; K 87. These may not really have been Thales' reasons; 6. Seneca, *Qu. Nat.* III, 14; K 88; 7. Aristotle, *De Anima* A2, 405a; K 89; 8. Aristotle, *De Anima* A5, 411a; K 91.

ANAXIMANDER: 1. Suda s.v.; K 95. Some of this has been disputed; 2. Themistius, *Or.* 26; K 96; 3. Simplicius, *Physics* 24; K 101A and 119. Some scholars believe that the quotation begins earlier and comprises the whole sentence; 4. Ps.-Plutarch, *Strom.* 2; K 121; 5. *Ibid.;* K 122A; 6. Hippolytus, *Ref.* I, 6, 3; K 122B; 7. Aetius II, 20; K 126; 8. Aetius V, 19; K 133; 9. Ps.-Plutarch, *Strom.* 2; K 134; 10. Plutarch, *Symp.* VIII, 730E; K 137.

ANAXIMENES: 1. Diogenes Laertius II, 3; K 138; 2. Augustine, *City of God,* VIII, 2; K 146; 3. Aristotle, *Metaphysics,* A3, 984a5; K 139; 4. Simplicius, *Physics,* 24, 26; K 140; 5. Ps.-Plutarch, Strom. 3; K 148; 6. Hippolytus, *Ref.* I, 7, 1; K 141; 7. Cicero, *de natura deorum* I, 10, 26; K 144; 8. Aristotle, *Meteor.* B7, 365b6; K159.

PYTHAGORAS: 1. Herodotus IV, 95; K 257; 2. Porphyry, *V.P.* 9; K 266; 3. Iustinus *ap.* Pomp. Trog. *Hist. Phil. Epit.* XX, 4, 14; K 272; 4. Aetius I, 3, 8; 1st edition K 280; 5. Proclus, *In Eucl.,* p. 426 Friedl; 1st edition K 281; 6. Diogenes Laertius VIII, 36; Xenophanes, fragment 7; K 260; 7. Herodotus II, 123; 1st edition K 270; 8. Porphyry, *Vita Pythagorae* 19; 1st edition K 271; 9. Eudemus *ap.* Simplic. *Phys.,* 732, 30; 1st edition K 272. The doctrine of the eternal recurrence of the same events at gigantic intervals was revived in modern times by Friedrich Nietzsche; cf. Walter Kaufmann, *Nietzsche* (Princeton: Princeton University Press, 1950; Cleveland, OH: Meridian Books, 1956), Chapter 11, "Overman and Eternal Recurrence"; 10–27. Iamblichus, *Protr.* 21; 1st edition K 275. These were some of the rules of the sect founded by Pythagoras. The numbers of the rules in K are given in parentheses after each paragraph; 28. Procl., *In Eucl.,* p. 65 Friedl.; 1st edition K 277; 29. Diogenes Laertius VIII, 8; 1st edition K 278.

XENOPHANES: 1. Diogenes Laertius IX, 18; K 161; 2. 11; WK; 3. 14; WK; 4. 15; WK; 5. 16; WK; 6. 23; F*; 7. 24; F; 8. 25; F*; 9. 26; F; 10. 27; F*; 11. 34; K 186; 12. 18; WK.

HERACLITUS: 1. Diogenes Laertius IX, 6; K 191; 2. *Ibid.,* IX, 5; K 192. Some scholars have questioned the claim about the three parts of his book; indeed, some have doubted that he wrote any book at all; 3. 89; WK; 4. 113; F; 5. 1; K 194; 6. 2; K 195; 7. 50; K 196; 8. 55; K 197; 9. 101a; F; 10. 7; F; 11. 107; K 198; 12. 60; K 200; 13. 6; F; 14. 49a; F*; 15. 91; F; 16. 12; K 214; 17. 61; K 199; 18. 111; K 201; 19. 8; F*; 20. 53; K 212; 21. 80; K 211; 22. 36; K 229; 23. 62; WK; 24. 27; F*; 25. 52; F; 26. 40; WK; 27. 42; WK; 28. 57; WK; 29. 5; F*; 30. 14; WK; 31. 96; WK. To appreciate the full measure of this heresy, one should recall Sophocles' *Antigone* and Homer's *Iliad.*; 32. 102; K 206; 33. 79; F; 34. 76; F*; 35. 66; F; 36. 30; K 217; 37. 9; F*; 38. 97; F; 39. 4; F*; 40. 110; F*; 41. 112; F*; 42. 116; WK; 43. 118; K 230; 44. 117; K 231; 45. 29; WK; 46. 44; K 249; 47. 49; F*; 48. 121; F*; 49. 101; WK; 50. 18; WK; 51. 119; WK; 52. 123; WK; 53. 92; F*; 54. 93; K 244.

PARMENIDES: 1. 1 (Lines 1–32); K 288; 2. 2; K 291; 3. 3; K 292. K construes the literal meaning as: "the same thing exists for thinking and for being"; Freeman's "For it is the same thing to think and to be" is based on Diels' *Denn (das Seiende) denken und sein ist dasselbe*. This much-discussed sentence seems to be continuous with the preceding two fragments; 4. 4; K 313; 5. 5; K 289; 6. 6; K 293. Freeman renders the final words: "in everything there is a way of opposing stress." Either way, many interpreters believe that Parmenides here alludes to Heraclitus; 7. 7; K 294; 8. 8; F*; 9. 9; Kranz takes <*epei*> with the previous line and translates: "For nothing is possible which does not come under either of the two" (i.e., everything belongs to one or the other of the two categories light and night); F*; 10–14. 10–14; F.

ZENO OF ELEA: 1. Plato, *Parmenides* 128c; F.M. Cornford's translation; 2. Plato, *Phaedrus* 261d; R. Hackforth's translation; 3. Simplicius, *Physics* 139, 18–19; WK; 4. Simplicius, *Physics* 109, 34; WK; 5. Simplicius, *Physics* 140, 30; WK; 6. Aristotle, *Topics* 160b 7; WK. Evidently the stage setting of the argument is a race course. On this ground it is better to call the argument by this name, instead of "The Dichotomy," as is often done in the literature, keeping "The Stadium" as the generally accepted name of the fourth argument; 7. Aristotle, *Physics* 233a 21; WK; 8. Aristotle, *Physics* 239b 11; WK; 9. Aristotle, *Physics* 263a 5; WK; 10. Simplicius, *Physics* 1013, 4ff; WK; 11. Aristotle, *Physics* 239b 14; P.H. Wicksteed's translation, edited by F.M. Cornford; 12. Aristotle, *Physics* 239b 1, 30; Wicksteed's translation; 13. Aristotle, *Physics* 239b 33; Wicksteed's translation; 14. Aristotle, *Physics* 209a 23; WK; 15. Simplicius, *Physics* 1108, 18; WK.

EMPEDOCLES: 1. Simplicius, *Physics* 25, 19; K 335; 2. Aristotle, *Metaphysics* A3, 984a; 3–36. The fragments in this section are all from F. I have numbered them consecutively to make it easier to follow. The Diels-Freeman numbering follows each paragraph.

ANAXAGORAS: 1. Diogenes Laertius II, 7–15; K 459; 2. Strabo 14, p. 645 Cas.; K 463; 3. Diogenes Laertius I, 16; K 466; 4–23. 1–19, 21 (Opening sentences from his book *On Natural Science*); F.

DEMOCRITUS (AND LEUCIPPUS): 1. Simplicius, *Physics* 28, 4; 1st edition of K 539; 2. Diogenes Laertius X, 13; K 540; 3. Cicero, *Academica* pr. II, 37, 118; K 541; 4. Diogenes Laertius IX, 34; K 542; 5. *Ibid.,* IX, 35; K 544; 6. Aristotle, *De Gen. et Corr.,* A 8, 325a; K 545; 7. Simplicius, *De Caelo* 242, 18; K 557; 8. Dionysius *ap.* Eusebium P.E. XIV, 23, 3; K 561; 9. Hyppolytus *Ref.* I, 13, 2; K 565; 10. Diogenes Laertius IX, 45; K 566; cf. "the only extant saying of Leucippus himself," K 569, Fr. 2, Aetius I, 25, 4: "Nothing occurs at random, but everything for a reason and by necessity"; 11. Aristotle, *On Democritus ap.* Simplicium *De Caelo* 295, 11; K 583; 12. Aristotle, *De Anima,* A2, 405a; K 585; 13. Aristotle, *De Sensu* 4, 442a; K 587; 14. Aetius IV, 8; K 588; 15. Theophrastus, *De Sensu* 50; R 589; 16. 7 (from "On the Forms"); F; 17. 8 (from "On the Forms"); F; 18. 9; F; 19. 10; F; 20. 11 (from "The Canon"); F; 21. 156; F; 22-27. The fragments in this section are all from F. I have numbered them consecutively to make it easier to follow. The Diels-Freeman numbering follows each paragraph.

PROTAGORAS: 1. 1 (from "Truth" or "Refutatory Arguments"); F; 2. 3 (from a treatise entitled "Great Logus"); F; 3. 4 (from "On the Gods"); F; 4. 6b; F; 5. 9; F; 6. 10; F; 7. 11; F.

GORGIAS: 1. 3, Sextus, from *On Not-being or on Nature;* F.

CRITIAS: 1. Stobaeus, *Selections* 3.29.11, from Milton C. Nahm, *Selections from Early Greek Philosophy* (Englewood Cliffs, NJ: Prentice Hall, 1964); 2. *Ibid.*, 3.37.15; 3. Sextus Empiricus, translated as *Against the Physicists* 1.54, by R. C. Bury in *Sextus Empiricus,* 3.31 sq. (London: W. Heinemann, 1936). From The Loeb Classical Library. Reprinted by permission of the President and Fellows of Harvard College; 4. Pseudo-Dionysus, *Art of Rhetoric* 6.2.277.10, from Nahm, *op. cit.*

The Milesians

THALES
fl. ca. 585 B.C.

Thales lived in Miletus in Ionia (on the west coast of present-day Turkey) and is said to have been so scientifically skilled that he accurately predicted the eclipse of the sun on May 28, 585 B.C. He was a contemporary of the Hebrew prophet Jeremiah, of the Persian prophet Zoroaster, of the Indian sage Gautama Siddhartha (the Buddha), and of the Chinese philosophers Confucius and Lao-Tze.

Thales has traditionally been considered the first Western philosopher (though some scholars now claim that this honor belongs to Anaximander). Thales was apparently the first to ask the question, "What is the basic 'stuff' of the universe?" According to Aristotle, Thales claimed that this basic stuff was water. This claim involves three vital assumptions: (1) that the fundamental explanation of the universe must be one in number, (2) that this one reality must be a "thing," and (3) that this one thing must have within itself the ability to move and change. Later thinkers disputed Thales' choice of the universe's basic "stuff," but his bold theory encouraged them and helped them develop their own philosophical programs.

Like many other Pre-Socratics, Thales was by no means a philosopher only. He was also a statesman, an astronomer, a geometer, and a sage. The first three fragments that follow deal with Thales' life. Number one is probably the world's oldest "absent-minded professor" story, while numbers two and three appear to be defenses designed to show how practical Thales could be. The remaining fragments are reports on Thales' ideas. There are no known writings by Thales himself.

[1]* A witty and attractive Thracian servant-girl is said to have mocked Thales for falling into a well while he was observing the stars and gazing upwards; declaring that

---

*The numbers in brackets serve the purposes of this volume. See the "Sources of the Fragments" section on page 6 for the source of each fragment.

Miletus, Ionia, in Asia Minor (present-day Turkey), was once an important port city at the mouth of the Maeander River. However, the slow-moving river (from which we get the term "meander") carried silt from the interior mountains, moving the coastline five miles west. Today, the low-lying parts of the ruins are still flooded in the spring. It is not hard to see how Thales, who lived here, might think that "when water is compacted and changes into slime it becomes earth." *(Forrest E. Baird)*

he was eager to know the things in the sky, but that what was behind him and just by his feet escaped his notice.

[2] When they reproached him because of his poverty, as though philosophy were no use, it is said that, having observed through his study of the heavenly bodies that there would be a large olive-crop, he raised a little capital while it was still winter, and paid deposits on all the olive presses in Miletus and Chios, hiring them cheaply because no one bid against him. When the appropriate time came there was a sudden rush of requests for the presses; he then hired them out on his own terms and so made a large profit, thus demonstrating that it is easy for philosophers to be rich, if they wish, but that it is not in this that they are interested.

[3] When he came to the Halys river, Croesus then, as I say, put his army across by the existing bridges; but, according to the common account of the Greeks, Thales the Milesian transferred the army for him. For it is said that Croesus was at a loss how his army should cross the river, since these bridges did not yet exist at this period; and that Thales, who was present in the army, made the river, which flowed on the left hand of the army, flow on the right hand also. He did so in this way: beginning upstream of the army he dug a deep channel, giving it a crescent shape, so that it should flow round the back of where the army was encamped, being diverted in this way from its old course by the channel, and passing the camp should flow into its old course once more. The result was that as soon as the river was divided it became fordable in both of its parts.

*   *   *

[4] Thales . . . says the principle is water (for which reason he declared that the earth rests on water), getting the notion perhaps from seeing that the nutriment of all things is moist, and that heat itself is generated from the moist and kept alive by it . . . , and from the fact that the seeds of all things have a moist nature, and that water is the origin of the nature of moist things.

[5] Moist natural substance, since it is easily formed into each different thing, is accustomed to undergo very various changes: that part of it which is exhaled is made into air, and the finest part is kindled from air into aether, while when water is compacted and changes into slime it becomes earth. Therefore Thales declared that water, of the four elements, was the most active, as it were, as cause.

[6] He [Thales] said that the world is held up by water and rides like a ship, and when it is said to "quake" it is actually rocking because of the water's movement.

[7] Thales, too, seems, from what they relate, to have supposed that the soul was something kinetic, if he said that the [Magnesian] stone possesses soul because it moves iron.

[8] Some say that it [soul] is intermingled in the universe, for which reason, perhaps, Thales also thought that all things are full of gods.

ANAXIMANDER
ca. 610–ca. 546 B.C.

Anaximander was born in Miletus about 610 B.C., and he died around 546 B.C. During his lifetime, Nebuchadnezzar conquered Jerusalem and the prophet Ezekiel was exiled to Babylon. Anaximander traveled extensively and was so highly regarded by his fellow Milesians that he was honored with the leadership of a new colony. He may have been the first Greek to write a book of prose.

Anaximander seems to have accepted Thales' three basic assumptions (summed up in the statement that the universe must be one changeable thing), but he differed with Thales on the nature of the "stuff" underlying the "many" that we observe. In place of Thales' water, Anaximander introduced the concept of the <apeiron>—the unlimited, boundless, infinite, or indefinite—as the fundamental principle of the world. This notion was a step up in philosophical sophistication—a metaphysical principle rather than an empirically observed material thing. This idea of a basic "stuff," with properties different from anything in the observable world, has survived to the present.

Anaximander also developed a rudimentary concept of natural law—the idea that all growing things in the natural world develop according to an identical pattern. He invented the idea of models, drawing what is considered to be the first geographical map. But what has fascinated all subsequent students of philosophy, more than anything else, is the one sentence, or half-sentence, quoted by Simplicius in fragment [3] which follows. This remark, the oldest known piece of Western philosophy, has elicited a large body of literature, including a forty-eight-page essay by Martin Heidegger.

[1] Anaximander son of Praxiades, of Miletus, philosopher, was a kinsman, pupil, and successor of Thales. He first discovered the equinox and solstices and hour-indicators, and that the earth lies in the center. He introduced the gnomon [a vertical rod whose shadow indicates the sun's direction and height] and in general made known an outline of geometry. He wrote *On Nature, Circuit of the Earth* and *On the Fixed Stars and a Celestial Globe,* and some other works.

[2] [Anaximander] was the first of the Greeks whom we know who ventured to produce a written account on nature.

* * *

[3] Of those who say that it is one, moving, and infinite, Anaximander, son of Praxiades, a Milesian, the successor and pupil of Thales, said that the principle and element of existing things was the *<apeiron>* [indefinite, or infinite], being the first to introduce this name of the material principle. He says that it is neither water nor any other of the so-called elements, but some other *<apeiron>* nature, from which come into being all the heavens and the worlds in them. And the source of coming-to-be for existing things is that into which destruction, too, happens "according to necessity; for they pay penalty and retribution to each other for their injustice according to the assessment of time," as he describes it in these rather poetical terms. It is clear that he, seeing the changing of the four elements into each other, thought it right to make none of these the substratum, but something else besides these; and he produces coming-to-be not through the alteration of the element, but by the separation off of the opposites through the eternal motion.

[4] He says that that which is productive from the eternal of hot and cold was separated off at the coming-to-be of this world, and that a kind of sphere of flame from this was formed round the air surrounding the earth, like bark around a tree. When this was broken off and shut off in certain circles, the sun and moon and stars were formed.

[5] He says that the earth is cylindrical in shape, and that its depth is a third of its width.

[6] Its shape is curved, round, similar to the drum of a column; of its flat surfaces we walk on one, and the other is on the opposite side.

[7] Anaximander [says the sun] is a circle twenty-eight times the size of the earth, like a chariot wheel, with its [rim] hollow and full of fire, and showing the fire at a certain point through an aperture as though through the nozzle of a bellows.

[8] Anaximander said that the first living creatures were born in moisture, enclosed in thorny barks; and that as their age increased they came forth on to the drier part and, when the bark had broken off, they lived a different kind of life for a short time.

[9] Further he says that in the beginning man was born from creatures of a different kind; because other creatures are soon self-supporting, but man alone needs prolonged nursing. For this reason he would not have survived if this had been his original form.

[10] Therefore they [the Syrians] actually revere the fish as being of similar race and nurturing. In this they philosophize more suitably than Anaximander; for he declares, not that fishes and men came into being in the same parents, but that originally men came into being inside fishes, and that, having been nurtured there—like sharks—and having become adequate to look after themselves, they then came forth and took to the land.

ANAXIMENES
fl. 546 B.C.?

Very little is known about the life of Anaximenes, except that he was a Milesian and a younger contemporary of Anaximander. Anaximenes proposed air as the basic world principle. While at first this thesis may seem a step backwards from the more comprehensive (like Anaximander's unlimited) to the less comprehensive particular (like Thales' water), Anaximenes added an important point. He explained a *process* by which the underlying one (air) becomes the observable many: By rarefaction, air becomes fire, and, by condensation, air becomes, successively, wind, water, and earth. Observable qualitative differences (fire, wind, water, earth) are the result of quantitative changes, that is, of how densely packed is the basic principle. This view is still held by scientists.

[1] Anaximenes, son of Eurystratus of Miletus, was a pupil of Anaximander. . . . He said that the material principle was air and the infinite; and that the stars move, not under the earth, but around it. He used simple and unsuperfluous Ionic speech. He was active, according to what Apollodorus says, around the time of the capture of Sardis [by Cyrus in 546/5 B.C.?], and died in the 63rd Olympiad.

[2] He [Anaximander] left Anaximenes as his disciple and successor, who attributed all the causes of things to infinite air, and did not deny that there were gods, or pass them over in silence; yet he believed not the air was made by them, but that they arose from air.

*   *   *

[3] Anaximenes and Diogenes make air, rather than water, the material principle above the other simple bodies.

[4] Anaximenes, son of Eurystratus, of Miletus, a companion of Anaximander, also says, like him, that the underlying nature is one and infinite, but not undefined as Anaximander said but definite, for he identifies it as air; and it differs in its substantial nature by rarity and density. Being made finer it becomes fire, being made thicker it becomes wind, then cloud, then (when thickened still more) water, then earth, then

stones; and the rest come into being from these. He, too, makes motion eternal, and says that change, also, comes about through it.

[5] And all things are produced by a kind of condensation, and again rarefaction, of this [air]. Motion, indeed, exists from everlasting; he says that when the air melts, there first of all comes into being the earth, quite flat—therefore it accordingly rides on the air; and sun and moon and the remaining heavenly bodies have their source of generation from earth. At last, he declares the sun to be earth, but that through the rapid motion it obtains heat in great sufficiency.

[6] Anaximenes . . . said that infinite air was the principle, from which the things that are becoming, and that are, and that shall be, and gods and things divine, all come into being, and the rest from its products. The form of air is of this kind: whenever it is most equable it is invisible to sight, but is revealed by the cold and the hot and the damp and by movement. It is always in motion; for things that change do not change unless there be movement. Through becoming denser or finer it has different appearances; for when it is dissolved into what is finer it becomes fire, while winds, again, are air that is becoming condensed, and cloud is produced from air by felting. When it is condensed still more, water is produced; with a further degree of condensation earth is produced, and when condensed as far as possible, stones. The result is that the most influential components of generation are opposites, hot and cold.

[7] Afterwards, Anaximenes determined that air is a god, and that it comes into being, and is measureless and infinite and always in motion; as though either formless air could be a god . . . or mortality did not attend upon everything that has come into being.

[8] Anaximenes says that the earth, through being drenched and dried off, breaks asunder, and is shaken by the peaks that are thus broken off and fall in. Therefore earthquakes happen in periods both of drought and again of excessive rains; for in droughts, as has been said, it dries up and cracks, and being made over-moist by the waters it crumbles apart.

Three Solitary Figures

PYTHAGORAS
ca. 571–ca. 497 B.C.

Pythagoras was a contemporary of the Hebrew prophets Haggai and Zechariah, as well as of the Buddha, who had his enlightenment about 521 B.C. Born on the island of Samos, just off the coast of Asia Minor and very close to Miletus, Pythagoras moved to southern Italy, where the Greeks had colonies, and settled at Croton, on the Bay of Tarentum.

Pythagoras was soon associated with so many legends that few scholars dare to say much about his life, his personality, or even his teachings, without adding that we cannot be sure our information is accurate. That there was a man named Pythagoras who founded the sect called the Pythagoreans, we need not doubt: Among the witnesses to his historicity was his younger contemporary, Heraclitus, who thought ill of him (see Heraclitus, section D, following). Nevertheless, it is notoriously difficult to distinguish between the teachings of Pythagoras himself and those of his followers, the Pythagoreans.

Today he is best known for the so-called Pythagorean theorem in geometry (fragment [5] following). But his interest in mathematics went far beyond this theorem. Although the Egyptians and others had been interested in mathematics for its practical uses in building, commerce, and so on, Pythagoras was interested in mathematics for its own sake. And while the Milesians searched for the *stuff* of all things, Pythagoras (or the Pythagoreans) focused on the *form* of all things. He claimed that "things are numbers," that mathematical formulas and ratios explain the physical world. (Those who think this odd might ponder the contemporary physicist's assertion that an electron is a "probability cloud.")

Pythagoras was also interested in religious salvation and established a proto-monastic religious order with strict rules of conduct (see fragments [10–27] following). His religion and his philosophy might seem disconnected to us, but for Pythagoras the two were inseparable. Like Plato after him, he believed that the study of mathematics could convert the soul from the world of the senses to the contemplation of the eternal. The religious sect Pythagoras founded still existed in Plato's time, 150 years later, and decisively influenced Plato's thought—an influence, in fact, second only to that of Plato's revered teacher, Socrates.

The following Pythagorean ideas especially influenced Plato: the dualism of body and soul and the conception of the body (*soma* in Greek) as the tomb (*sema* in Greek) of the soul; the belief in the immortality of the soul; the doctrine of the transmigration of souls; the idea that knowledge and a philosophic life are required for the salvation of the soul; the notion that one might design a society that would be an instrument of salvation for its members; the admission of women to this society; the suggestion that all members of this society should hold their property in common; and, finally, the division of humankind into three basic types—tradesmen being the lowest class; those in whom the competitive spirit and ambition are highly developed, a little higher; and those who prefer contemplation, the highest. In fact, the whole of Plato's thought, from his earliest to his latest works, can be understood as a gradual and sustained departure from the heritage of Socrates to that of Pythagoras.

[1] As I have heard from the Greeks who live on the Hellespont and the Black Sea, this Salmoxis was a man, who was a slave in Samos, the slave in fact of Pythagoras son of Mnesarchus. . . .

[2] Aristoxenus says that at the age of forty, seeing that the tyranny of Polycrates was too intense . . . he made his departure for Italy [to Croton].

[3] Three hundred of the young men [followers of Pythagoras], bound to each other by oath like a brotherhood, lived segregated from the rest of the citizens, as if to form a secret band of conspirators, and brought the city [Croton] under their control.

*   *   *

[4] Ten is the very nature of number. All Greeks and all barbarians alike count up to ten, and having reached ten revert again to the unit. And again, Pythagoras maintains, the power of the number ten lies in the number four, the tetrad. This is the reason: If one starts at the unit and adds the successive numbers up to four, one will make up the number ten; and if one exceeds the tetrad, one will exceed ten, too. If, that is, one takes the unit, adds two, then three, and then four, one will make up the number ten. . . . So the Pythagoreans used to invoke the tetrad as their most binding oath: "Nay, by him that gave to our generation the tetractys, which contains the fount and root of eternal nature."

[5] The square of the hypotenuse of a right-angled triangle is equal to the sum of the squares on the sides enclosing the right angle. [The text of the next sentence is corrupt, but the sense is:] If we pay any attention to those who like to recount ancient history, we may find some of them referring this theorem to Pythagoras, and saying that he sacrificed an ox in honor of his discovery.

[6] On the subject of reincarnation, Xenophanes bears witness in an elegy which begins: "Now I will turn to another tale and show the way." What he says about Pythagoras runs thus: "Once they say that he was passing by when a puppy was being whipped, and he took pity and said: Stop, do not beat it; for it is the soul of a friend that I recognized when I heard it giving tongue."

[7] Moreover, the Egyptians are the first to have maintained the doctrine that the soul of man is immortal and that, when the body perishes, it enters into another animal that is being born at the time, and when it has been the complete round of the creatures of the dry land and of the sea and of the air it enters again into the body of a man at birth; and its cycle is completed in three thousand years. There are some Greeks who have adopted this doctrine, some in former times and some in later, as if it were their own invention; their names I know but refrain from writing down.

[8] None the less the following became universally known: first that he maintains that the soul is immortal; next, that it changes into other kinds of living things; also that events recur in certain cycles, and that nothing is ever absolutely new; and finally, that all living things should be regarded as akin. Pythagoras seems to have been the first to bring these beliefs into Greece.

[9] If one were to believe the Pythagoreans that events recur in an arithmetical cycle, and that I shall be talking to you again sitting as you are now, with this pointer in my hand, and that everything else will be just as it is now, then it is plausible to suppose that the time, too, will be the same as now.

*   *   *

[10] Let the rules to be pondered be these:

[11] When you are going out to a temple, worship first, and on your way neither say nor do anything else connected with your daily life. (1)

[12] On a journey neither enter a temple nor worship at all, not even if you are passing the very doors. (2)

[13] Sacrifice and worship without shoes on. (3)

[14] Turn aside from highways and walk by footpaths. . . . (4)

[15] Follow the gods and restrain your tongue above all else. . . . (6)

[16] Stir not the fire with iron. . . . (8)

[17] Help a man who is loading freight, but not one who is unloading. (10)

[18] Putting on your shoes, start with the right foot; washing your feet, with the left. (11)

[19] Speak not of Pythagorean matters without light. (12)

[20] Never step over a cross-bar. (13)

[21] When you are out from home, look not back, for the furies come after you. . . . (14)

[22] Do not wear a ring. . . . (22)

[23] Do not look in a mirror beside a lamp. . . . (23)

[24] Eat not the heart. . . . (30)

[25] Spit upon the trimmings of your hair and finger-nails. . . . (32)

[26] Abstain from beans. . . . (37)

[27] Abstain from living things. (39)

[28] Pythagoras turned geometrical philosophy into a form of liberal education by seeking its first principles in a higher realm of reality.

[29] Life, he said, is like a festival; just as some come to the festival to compete, some to ply their trade, but the best people come as spectators, so in life the slavish men go hunting for fame or gain, the philosophers for the truth.

XENOPHANES
ca. 570–ca. 478 B.C.

A contemporary of Pythagoras, Xenophanes was from Colophon on the mainland of Asia Minor, a few miles inland and approximately fifty miles north of Miletus and about fifteen miles north of Ephesus. He traveled a great deal, reciting his poetry, of which only a few fragments survive. At one time he was thought to have been Parmenides' teacher and the founder of the Eleatic school, no doubt because of his conception of one unmoving god—a notion readily associated with Parmenides' idea of being. But this connection is now generally rejected, and Xenophanes is seen rather as an essentially solitary figure.

Little of his work has come down to us, but the little that has is unforgettable. Xenophanes challenges Homer's and Hesiod's anthropomorphic conception of the gods and invites skepticism about the ability of humans to know the divine.

[1] Xenophanes, son of Dexios, or, according to Apollodorus, of Orthomenes, of Colophon . . . being expelled from his native land, passed his time in Zancle in Sicily and in Catana. . . . He wrote in epic metre, also elegiacs and iambics, against Hesiod and Homer, reproving them for what they said about the gods. But he himself also recited his own original poems. He is said to have held contrary opinions to Thales and Pythagoras, and to have rebuked Epimenides, too. He had an extremely long life, as he himself somewhere says: "Already there are seven and sixty years tossing my thought up and down the land of Greece; and from my birth there were another twenty-five to add to these, if I know how to speak truly about these things."

[2] Homer and Hesiod ascribed to the gods whatever is infamy and reproach among men: theft and adultery and deceiving each other.

[3] Mortals suppose that the gods are born and have clothes and voices and shapes like their own.

[4] But if oxen, horses, and lions had hands or could paint with their hands and fashion works as men do, horses would paint horse-like images of gods and oxen ox-like ones, and each would fashion bodies like their own.

[5] The Ethiopians consider the gods flat-nosed and black; the Thracians blue-eyed and red-haired.

[6] There is one god, among gods and men the greatest, not at all like mortals in body or mind.

[7] He sees as a whole, thinks as a whole, and hears as a whole.

[8] But without toil he moves everything by the thought of his mind.

[9] He always remains in the same place, not moving at all, nor is it fitting for him to change his position at different times.

[10] Everything comes from earth and returns to earth in the end.

[11] No man knows or ever will know the truth about the gods and about everything I speak of: for even if one chanced to say the complete truth, yet oneself knows it not; but seeming is wrought over all things.

[12] Not from the beginning have the gods revealed all things to mortals, but by long seeking men find what is better.

HERACLITUS
fl. 500 B.C.

Little is known about the life of Heraclitus except that he lived in Ephesus (just north of Miletus) and flourished around 500 B.C. He may have come from an aristocratic family, since his writings indicate a clear contempt for common people. The mystery of his life, together with the obscurity of his writings, led the ancients to call him the "dark philosopher." His surviving epigrammatic fragments, though often paradoxical and elusive, are immensely suggestive, invite frequent rereading, and haunt the mind. In the sayings of Heraclitus, as in no previous philosopher, one encounters the personality of the thinker. After twenty-five centuries, he still evokes instant antipathy in some and the highest admiration in others. Influential admirers include Hegel, Nietzsche, and Bergson.

Whereas Thales considered water the basic principle, and Anaximenes believed it was air, Heraclitus saw the fundamental "world stuff" in fire. Fire seems to have been associated in his mind with change, strife, and war. He may also have been influenced by the Persians and their conception of a fiery judgment (see fragment [35], following). Fire, or the process of change itself, is the "one" truth <*Logos*> that teaches those few who will listen.

Plato referred to Heraclitus frequently and named one of his dialogues after Heraclitus' follower, Cratylus. One of the speakers in the dialogue *Cratylus* speaks of "the opinion of Heraclitus that all things flow," and the phrase, "all things flow" <*panta rhei*> has often been called the quintessence of Heracliteanism. With some slight oversimplification, one can say that Plato was convinced by Heraclitus that in this sensible world all things are in flux and, if this sensible world is all there is, no rational discourse is possible. This led Plato to the conclusion that there must be another world beyond the world of sense experience—a realm utterly free from change, motion, and time. At that point Plato was probably influenced not only by the Pythagoreans, but also by Parmenides, the next great Pre-Socratic.

A. THE MAN

[1] Antisthenes, in his *Successions,* quotes as a sign of his [Heraclitus'] arrogance that he resigned the hereditary "kingship" to his brother.

[2] The book said to be his is called *On Nature,* from its chief content, and is divided into three discourses: On the Universe, Politics, Theology. He dedicated it and placed it in the temple of Artemis, as some say, having purposely written it rather obscurely so that only those of rank and influence should have access to it, and it should not be easily despised by the populace. . . . The work had so great a reputation that from it arose disciples, those called Heracliteans.

B. LOGOS* AND SENSES

[3] Those awake have one ordered universe in common, but in sleep every man turns away to one of his own.

[4] The thinking faculty is common to all.

[5] Of the Logos, which is as I describe it, men always prove to be uncomprehending, both before they have heard it and when once they have heard it. For although all things happen according to this Logos, men are like people of no experience, even when they experience such words and deeds as I explain, when I distinguish each thing according to its constitution and declare how it is; but the rest of men fail to notice what they do after they wake up just as they forget what they do when asleep.

[6] Therefore it is necessary to follow the common; but although the Logos is common the many live as though they had a private understanding.

[7] Listening not to me but to the Logos, it is wise to agree that all things are one.

[8] The things of which there is seeing and hearing and perception, these do I prefer.

[9] The eyes are more exact witnesses than the ears.

[10] If all existing things turned to smoke, the nose would be the discriminating organ.

[11] Evil witnesses are eyes and ears for men, if they have souls that do not understand their language.

*The term <*Logos*>, left untranslated in this section, is sometimes rendered as "reason," sometimes as "word" (as in the first sentence of the Gospel of John: "In the beginning was the Word"); and it may also denote a rational principle in the world.

C. COSMOS

[12] The path up and down is one and the same.

[13] The sun is new each day.

[14] In the same river we both step and do not step, we are and are not.

[15] It is not possible to step twice into the same river.

[16] Upon those that step into the same rivers different and different waters flow.

[17] Sea is the most pure and polluted water: for fishes it is drinkable and salutary, but for men undrinkable and deleterious.

[18] Disease makes health pleasant and good, hunger satiety, weariness rest.

[19] What is in opposition is in concert, and from what differs comes the most beautiful harmony.

[20] War is the father of all and king of all, and some he shows as gods, others as men; some he makes slaves, others free.

[21] It is necessary to know that war is common and right is strife, and that all things happen by strife and necessity.

[22] For souls it is death to become water; for water, death to become earth; from earth, water comes-to-be, and from water, soul.

[23] Immortals are mortal, mortals immortal, living each other's death, dying each other's life.

[24] After death things await men which they do not expect or imagine.

[25] Time is a child playing a game of draughts; the kingship is in the hands of a child.

D. RELIGION AND FIRE

[26] Being a polymath does not teach understanding: else Hesiod would have had it and Pythagoras; also Xenophanes and Hekataeus.

[27] Homer deserves to be thrown out of the contests and whipped, and Archilochus, too.

[28] The most popular teacher is Hesiod. Of him people think he knew most—he who did not even know day and night: They are one.

[29] They purify themselves by staining themselves with other blood, as if one stepped into mud to wash off mud. But a man would be thought mad if one of his fellowmen saw him do that. Also, they talk to statues as one might talk with houses, in ignorance of the nature of gods and heroes.

[30] The consecrations of the mysteries, as practiced among men, are unholy.

[31] Corpses should be thrown away more than dung.

[32] To god all things are beautiful and good and just, but men have supposed some things to be unjust, others just.

[33] Man is called childish compared with divinity, just as a boy compared with a man.

[34] Fire lives the death of earth, and air the death of fire; water lives the death of air, earth that of water.

[35] Fire, having come upon them, will judge and seize upon [condemn] all things.

[36] This world-order [the same of all] did none of gods or men make, but it always was and is and shall be: an ever-living fire, kindling in measures and going out in measures.

E. MEN AND MORALS

[37] Asses prefer chaff to gold.

[38] Dogs bark at those whom they do not recognize.

[39] If happiness lay in bodily pleasures, we should call oxen happy when they find vetch to eat.

[40] It is not good for men to obtain all they wish.

[41] Sane thinking is the greatest virtue, and wisdom is speaking the truth and acting according to nature, paying heed.

[42] All men are granted what is needed for knowing oneself and sane thinking.

[43] A dry soul is wisest and best.

[44] A man when he is drunk is led by an unfledged boy, stumbling and not knowing where he goes, having his soul moist.

[45] The best choose one above all else: everlasting fame above mortals. The majority are contented like well-fed cattle.

[46] The people must fight on behalf of the law as though for the city wall.

[47] One man to me is ten thousand if he is the best.

[48] The Ephesians would do well to hang themselves, every adult man, and leave their city to adolescents, since they expelled Hermodorus, the worthiest man among them, saying: Let us not have even one worthy man; but if we do, let him go elsewhere and live among others!

F. EPILOGUE

[49] I sought myself.

[50] If one does not expect the unexpected one will not find it, for it is not reached by search or trail.

[51] Character is man's fate.

[52] Nature loves hiding.

[53] The Sybil, uttering her unlaughing, unadorned, unincensed words with raving mouth, reaches out over a thousand years with her voice, through the god.

[54] The lord whose oracle is in Delphi neither speaks out nor conceals, but gives a sign.

The Monists

PARMENIDES
fl. ca. 485 B.C.?

Parmenides, a younger contemporary of Heraclitus and an older contemporary of Socrates, lived in Elea in southern Italy. According to Plato's dialogue of the same name (*Parmenides,* reprinted in part in this volume), Parmenides visited Athens when he was about sixty-five, accompanied by his chief pupil, Zeno, then nearly forty, and conversed with the still "quite young" Socrates. Whether the visit to Athens really took place, we do not know; that Socrates met Parmenides is not likely; that they did not have the conversation reported in the dialogue is absolutely clear, for that discussion presupposes Plato's earlier work.

According to Parmenides, there are two ways of inquiry. The first asserts that whatever is (i.e., being), "is and cannot not-be" (see fragment [2] following). This is the path of truth that leads us to see that being is one and cannot be created, destroyed, or changed. (If any of these alterations in being were possible, being would no longer be what "is" and would become what "is not"—but by definition there *is* no "is not" from which being could arise or into which being could change.) Being must be one seamless unchanging whole. The other path of inquiry, the path of opinion, which claims that something arises from not-being, is not only impossible, it is unthinkable.

Parmenides, the philosopher of changeless being, has often been contrasted with Heraclitus, the philosopher of change and becoming. But it should not be overlooked that both are one in repudiating the wisdom of tradition and of common sense. Both claim that things may not be what they seem to be. One is as radical as the other.

Plato was greatly impressed by Parmenides' thought and freely acknowledged his debt to the Eleatic philosopher. In the Platonic *Parmenides,* the character "Parmenides" instructs the young Socrates, while in most dialogues Socrates bests or teaches others. Plato's dichotomies—of knowledge/belief and of

Bronze charioteer from the monument
dedicated by Polyzalus of Gela at
Delphi, ca. 475 B.C. Delphi, Museum.
*(Alison Frantz Photographic
Collection, American School of
Classical Studies at Athens.)*

unchanging, eternal, timeless reality/ever-changing, temporal appearance—were
derived from Parmenides. However, Plato did not accept Parmenides' idea that
reality is one, devoid of any plurality: Plato occupied the "real" world with a
number of unchanging, eternal forms.

The following fragments are part of a poem which, after an imposing prologue, distinguishes the ways of knowledge and belief, of being and nonbeing.

[1] The mares that carry me as far as my heart ever aspires sped me on, when they
had brought and set me on the far-famed road of the god, which bears the man who

knows over all cities. On that road was I borne, for that way the wise horses bore me, straining at the chariot, and maidens led the way. And the axle in the naves gave out the whistle of a pipe, blazing, for it was pressed hard on either side by the two well-turned wheels as the daughters of the Sun made haste to escort me, having left the halls of Night for the light, and having thrust the veils from their heads with their hands.

There are the gates of the paths of Night and Day, and a lintel and a stone threshold enclose them. They themselves, high in the air, are blocked with great doors, and avenging Justice holds the alternate bolts. Her the maidens beguiled with gentle words and cunningly persuaded to push back swiftly from the gates the bolted bar. And the gates created a yawning gap in the door frame when they flew open, swinging in turn in their sockets the bronze-bound pivots made fast with dowels and rivets. Straight through them, on the broad way, did the maidens keep the horses and the chariot.

And the goddess greeted me kindly, and took my right hand in hers, and addressed me with these words: "Young man, you who come to my house in the company of immortal charioteers with the mares which bear you, greetings. No ill fate has sent you to travel this road—far indeed does it lie from the steps of men but right and justice. It is proper that you should learn all things, both the unshaken heart of well-rounded truth, and the opinions of mortals, in which there is no true reliance. But nonetheless you shall learn these things too, how what is believed would have to be assuredly, pervading all things throughout."

[2] Come now, and I will tell you (and you must carry my account away with you when you have heard it) the only ways of enquiry that are to be thought of. The one, that [it] is and that it is impossible for [it] not to be, is the path of Persuasion (for she attends upon Truth); the other, that [it] is not and that it is needful that [it] not be, that I declare to you is an altogether indiscernible track: for you could not know what is not—that cannot be done—nor indicate it.

[3] For the same thing is there both to be thought of and to be.

[4] But look at things which, though far off, are securely present to the mind; for you will not cut off for yourself what is from holding to what is, neither scattering everywhere in every way in order [i.e., cosmic order] nor drawing together.

[5] It is a common point from which I start; for there again and again I shall return.

[6] What is there to be said and thought needs must be; for it is there for being, but nothing is not. I bid you ponder that, for this is the first way of enquiry from which I hold you back, but then from that on which mortals wander knowing nothing, two-headed; for helplessness guides the wandering thought in their breasts, and they are carried along, deaf and blind at once, dazed, undiscriminating hordes, who believe that to be and not to be are the same and not the same, and the path taken by them is backward-turning.

[7] For never shall this be forcibly maintained, that things that are not are, but you must hold back your thought from this way of enquiry, nor let habit, born of much experience, force you down this way, by making you use an aimless eye or an ear and a tongue full of meaningless sound: judge by reason the strife-encompassed refutation spoken by me.

[8] Only one way remains; that it is. To this way there are very many sign-posts: that being has no coming-into-being and no destruction, for it is whole of limb, without motion, and without end. And it never was, nor will be, because it is now, a whole all together, one, continuous; for what creation of it will you look? How, whence sprung? Nor shall I allow you to speak or think of it as springing from not-being; for it is neither

expressible nor thinkable that what-is-not is. Also, what necessity impelled it, if it did spring from nothing, to be produced later or earlier? Thus it must be absolutely, or not at all. Nor will the force of credibility ever admit that anything should come into being, beside being itself, out of not-being. So far as that is concerned, justice has never released *(being)* from its fetters and set it free either to come into being or to perish, but holds it fast. The decision on these matters depends on the following: it is, or it is not. It is therefore decided, as is inevitable: ignore the one way as unthinkable and inexpressible (for it is no true way) and take the other as the way of being and reality. How could being perish? How could it come into being? If it came into being, it is not, and so too if it is about-to-be at some future time. Thus coming-into-being is quenched, and destruction also into the unseen.

Nor is being divisible, since it is all alike. Nor is there anything there which could prevent it from holding together, nor any lesser thing, but all is full of being. Therefore it is altogether continuous; for being is close to being.

But it is motionless in the limits of mighty bonds, without beginning, without cease, since becoming and destruction have been driven very far away, and true conviction has rejected them. And remaining the same in the same place, it rests by itself and thus remains there fixed; for powerful necessity holds it in the bonds of a limit, which constrains it round about, because it is decreed by divine law that being shall not be without boundary. For it is not lacking; but if it were *(spatially infinite),* it would be lacking everything.

To think is the same as the thought that it is; for you will not find thinking without being to which it refers. For nothing else either is or shall be except being, since fate has tied it down to be a whole and motionless; therefore all things that mortals have established, believing in their truth, are just a name: becoming and perishing, being and not-being, and change of position, and alteration of bright color.

But since there is a *(spatial)* limit, it is complete on every side, like the mass of a well-rounded sphere, equally balanced from its center in every direction; for it is not bound to be at all either greater or less in this direction or that; nor is there not-being which could check it from reaching to the same point, nor is it possible for being to be more in this direction, less in that, than being, because it is an inviolate whole. For, in all directions equal to itself, it reaches its limits uniformly.

At this point I cease my reliable theory <*Logos*> and thought, concerning Truth; from here onwards you must learn the opinions of mortals, listening to the deceptive order of my words.

They have established *(the custom of)* naming two forms, one of which ought not to be *(mentioned):* that is where they have gone astray. They have distinguished them as opposite in form, and have marked them off from another by giving them different signs: on one side the flaming fire in the heavens, mild, very light *(in weight),* the same as itself in every direction, and not the same as the other. This *(other)* also is by itself and opposite: dark night, a dense and heavy body. This world-order I describe to you throughout as it appears with all its phenomena, in order that no intellect of mortal men may outstrip you.

[9] But since all things are named light and night, and names have been given to each class of things according to the power of one or the other, everything is full equally of light and invisible night, as both are equal, because to neither of them belongs any share (of the other).

[10] You shall know the nature of the heavens, and all the signs in the heavens, and the destructive works of the pure bright torch of the sun, and whence they came into

being. And you shall learn of the wandering works of the round-faced moon, and its nature; and you shall know also the surrounding heaven, whence it sprang and how necessity brought and constrained it to hold the limits of the stars.

[11] *(I will describe)* how earth and sun and moon, and the aether common to all, and the Milky Way in the heavens, and outermost Olympus, and the hot power of the stars, hastened to come into being.

[12] For the narrower rings were filled with unmixed fire, and those next to them with night, but between (these) rushes the portion of flame. And in the center of these is the goddess who guides everything; for throughout she rules over cruel birth and mating, sending the female to mate with the male, and conversely again the male with the female.

[13] First of all the gods she devised Love.

[14] *(The moon):* Shining by night with a light not her own, wandering round the earth.

ZENO OF ELEA
fl. ca. 465 B.C.

All the ancient authorities agree that Zeno of Elea was a pupil and associate of Parmenides. Zeno is noted for his writings in defense of Parmenides' concept of the One. Zeno showed the paradoxes that result from the theses of plurality held by philosophers like Pythagoras. Zeno's paradoxes were designed to prove that plurality and change are not possible.

Zeno's puzzles have fascinated philosophers, logicians, and mathematicians ever since, and never more than in our own time: Probably more has been written on his paradoxes in the last hundred years than in the preceding two thousand. (See the suggestions for further reading in the introduction to the Pre-Socratics.) Much of this work is cheerfully unconcerned with the connection, if any, between the writers' "Zeno" and Zeno himself. Reading the critics could give one extravagant notions of the reasoning powers of this remote Greek. Hence one will probably be surprised by reading what Zeno actually said in the fragments that follow.

The fragments have been arranged into four broad arguments: against plurality, against motion, against space, and, in a slightly different vein, against the reliability of sense experience (in the paradox of the millet seed). These paradoxes are all designed to show that Parmenides is correct: Being is one seamless unchanging whole.

The four paradoxes against motion are perhaps the most famous—and the most difficult to resolve. These paradoxes clearly bring out the discrepancy between logic and experience. For example, the second of the paradoxes logically concludes that Achilles cannot catch a tortoise—but it *seems* so obvious to experience that he can. Either there is something wrong with Zeno's logic (which is, of course, what modern discussions of the paradox have tried to show), or else experience is illusory. Zeno maintained that his logic was valid and that he had demonstrated that Parmenides was right: Change is impossible.

[1] [Zeno's] book is in fact a sort of defence of Parmenides' argument against those who try to make fun of it by showing that his supposition, that there is a One, leads to many absurdities and contradictions. This book, then, is a retort against those who assert a plurality. It pays them back in the same coin with something to spare, and aims at showing that, on a thorough examination, their own supposition that there is a plurality leads to even more absurd consequences than the hypothesis of the One.

[2] [Zeno] of Elea has an art of speaking, such that he can make the same things appear to his audience like and unlike, or one and many, or again at rest and in motion. . . .

A. ARGUMENTS AGAINST PLURALITY

[3] He [Zeno] showed earlier [i.e., prior to the arguments following in fragments 6–11] that nothing has size because each of the many is self-identical and one.

[4] For if it [something having no size] were added to another, it would make it [the latter] no larger. For having no size, it could not contribute anything by way of size when added. And thus the thing added would be nothing. If indeed when [something is] subtracted from another, the latter is not reduced, nor again increased when [something is] added [to it], it is clear that what is added or subtracted is nothing.

[5] If there are many, they must be just so many as they are, neither more nor fewer. But if they are just so many as they are, they must be finite [in number]. If there are many, the existents are infinite [in number]: for there are always other [existents] between existents, and again others between these. And thus the existents are infinite [in number].

B. ARGUMENTS AGAINST MOTION

THE RACE COURSE

[6] For we have many arguments contrary to (common) beliefs, whose solution is yet difficult, like Zeno's that it is impossible to move or to traverse the race course.

[7] For this reason Zeno's argument too assumes falsely that it is impossible to traverse or to come in contact with each one of an infinite number [of things] in a finite time.

[8] The first [of Zeno's arguments against motion "which cause difficulty to those who try to solve the problems they raise"] says that there is no motion, because the moving [body] must reach the midpoint before it gets to the end.

[9] In the same way one should reply to those who pose [literally, "ask"] Zeno's argument, claiming that it is always necessary to traverse the half [i.e., to traverse any given distance we must first traverse its first half], and these [i.e., half-distances] are infinitely numerous, while it is impossible to traverse an infinity. . . .

[10] If there is motion, the moving object must traverse an infinity in a finite [time]: and this is impossible. Hence motion does not exist. He demonstrates his hypothesis thus: The moving object must move a certain stretch. And since every stretch is infinitely divisible, the moving object must first traverse half the stretch it is moving, and then the whole; but before the whole of the half, half of that and, again, the half of that. If then these halves are infinite, since, whatever may be the given [stretch] it is possible to halve it, and [if, further,] it is impossible to traverse the infinity [of these stretches] in a finite time . . . it follows that it is impossible to traverse any given length in a finite time.

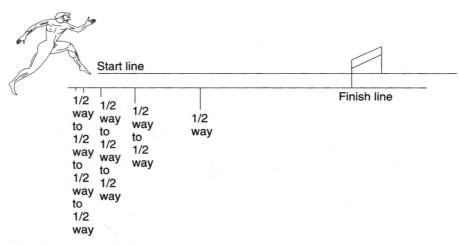

Start line

1/2 way to 1/2 way to 1/2 way to 1/2 way to 1/2 way

1/2 way to 1/2 way to 1/2 way to 1/2 way

1/2 way to 1/2 way to 1/2 way

1/2 way

Finish line

Before the runner can reach the finish line, he must first get halfway there. But before he can get halfway there, he must get halfway to the halfway point, and so on. Zeno concludes that the runner, with only a finite amount of time, could never traverse this infinite number of halfway to halfway points.

THE ACHILLES

[11] The second [of Zeno's arguments against motion] is what is known as "the Achilles," which purports to show that the slowest will never be overtaken in its course by the swiftest, inasmuch as, reckoning from any given instant, the pursuer, before he can catch the pursued, must reach the point from which the pursued started at that instant, and so the slower will always be some distance in advance of the swifter.

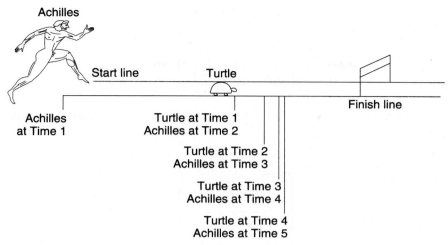

Achilles, the famous Greek athlete, and a turtle are racing toward the finish line. When they begin [at time 1], the turtle has a head start. A few seconds later [at time 2] Achilles has reached the point where the turtle *was* at the start of the race. But the turtle has moved forward slightly. Achilles continues running and a moment later [at time 3] reaches the point where the turtle *was* [at time 2]. Achilles continues to get closer and closer to the turtle, but he always arrives at a point where the turtle *was* a split-second before. Hence, Zeno concludes, Achilles can never catch the turtle.

THE ARROW

[12] The third [of Zeno's arguments against motion is] that the arrow is stationary while on its flight. . . . Since a thing is at rest when it has not shifted in any degree out of a place equal to its own dimensions, and since at any given instant during the whole of its supposed motion the supposed moving thing is in the place it occupies at that instant, the arrow is not moving at any time during its flight.

THE STADIUM

[13] The fourth [of Zeno's arguments against motion] supposes a number of objects all equal with each other in dimensions, forming two equal trains and arranged so that one train stretches from one end of a racecourse to the middle of it, and the other from the middle to the other end. Then, if you let the two trains, moving in opposite directions but at the same rate, pass each other, Zeno undertakes to show that half of the time they occupy in passing each other is equal to the whole of it. . . . This is his demonstration. Let there be a number of objects *AAAA,* equal in number and bulk to those that compose the two trains but stationary in the middle of the stadium. Then let the objects *BBBB,* in number and dimension equal to the *A*s, form one of the trains stretching from the middle of the *A*s in one direction; and from the inner end of the *B*s let *CCCC* stretch in the opposite direction, being the equal in number, dimension, and rate of movement to the *B*s.

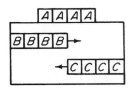

Then when they cross, the first *B* and the first *C* will simultaneously reach the extreme *A*'s in contrary directions.

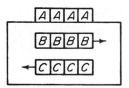

Now during this process, the first *C* has passed all the *B*s, whereas the first *B* has only passed half the *A*s, and therefore only taken half the time; for it takes an equal time (the minimal time) for the *C* to pass one *B* as for the *B* to pass one *A*. But during this same half-time the first *B* has also passed all the *C*'s (though the first *B* takes as long, says Zeno, to pass a *C* as an *A*) because measured by their progress through the *A*s the *B*s and *C*s have had the same time in which to cross each other. Such is his argument. . . .

C. ARGUMENT AGAINST SPACE

[14] If place is something that exists, where will it be? The difficulty raised by Zeno requires some answer. For if *everything* that exists has a place, it is clear that place too will have a place, and so on without limit.

D. THE PARADOX OF THE MILLET SEED

[15] "Tell me, Protagoras," [Zeno] said, "does a single millet seed, or the ten-thousandth part of a seed, make a noise when they fall?" When Protagoras said they did not, he said: "Does the bushel then make a noise when it falls or not?" When Protagoras said this did, Zeno said: "Is there not then some ratio of the bushel to one seed and to a ten-thousandth of a seed?" When Protagoras said there was, Zeno said: "But then must not the respective noises stand to one another in the same ratios? For as the sounding bodies are to one another, so must be the sounds they make. This being so, if the bushel of millet makes a noise, then the single millet seed must also make a noise, and so must the ten-thousandth of a millet seed."

The Pluralists

EMPEDOCLES
ca. 484—424 B.C.

The philosophers who came after the Eleatics, down to Plato and Aristotle, were concerned with showing how change *was* possible. The first three philosophers to attempt this are sometimes lumped together as the "Pluralists," for each of them tried to explain change by invoking several ultimate principles.

The first of these was Empedocles from Acragas on the south coast of Sicily. Born of an aristocratic family, he opposed tyranny and reputedly refused the crown of his native town. Like the more legendary Pythagoras, he fused scientific thought with religious concerns and left others with the impression he had performed miracles. Again like Pythagoras, he spoke both of the transmigration of souls and of himself as a god. He is said to have ended his life by leaping into the crater of Mount Etna.

Empedocles wrote two poems, "On Nature" and "Purifications." The former is said to have been divided into two books, totaling two thousand lines, of which fewer than four hundred have survived. According to Diogenes Laertius, the two poems together came to five thousand lines; if so, less than one-fifth of the "Purifications" has come down to us.

Empedocles was the first great synthesizer of the history of philosophy. Around 450 B.C., a full century before Aristotle's summation, Empedocles tried to find a place in his thought for all the major contributions of his predecessors. By explaining generation and destruction, if not all change, in terms of mixture and separation, Empedocles sought to reconcile Heraclitus' insistence on the reality of change with the Eleatic claim that generation and destruction are unthinkable. Going back to the Greeks' traditional belief in four elements, he found a place for Thales' water, Anaximenes' air, and Heraclitus' fire, and he added earth as the fourth. In addition to these four elements, which Aristotle would later call "material causes," Empedocles postulated two "efficient causes": strife (Heraclitus's great principle) and love. He envisaged four successive ages: an age of love or perfect mixture in the beginning; then gradual separation as strife enters; then complete separation as strife rules; finally, as love enters again, a gradual remixture.

[1] Empedocles of Acragas was born not long after Anaxagoras, and was an emulator and associate of Parmenides, and even more of the Pythagoreans.

[2] Anaxagoras of Clazomenae, though older than Empedocles, was later in his philosophical activity.

*   *   *

[3] For limited are the means of grasping *(i.e., the organs of sense-perception),* which are scattered throughout their limbs, and many are the miseries that press in and blunt the thoughts. And having looked at (only) a small part of existence during their lives, doomed to perish swiftly like smoke, they are carried aloft and wafted away, believing only that upon which as individuals they chance to hit as they wander in all directions; but every man preens himself on having found the Whole: so little are these things to be seen by men or to be heard, or to be comprehended by the mind! But you, since you have come here into retirement, shall learn—not more than mortal intellect can attain.

[4] I shall tell you another thing: there is no creation of substance in any one of mortal existences, nor any end in execrable death, but only mixing and exchange of what has been mixed; and the name "substance" [*<physis>* "nature"] is applied to them by mankind. (8)

[5] But men, when these *(the Elements)* have been mixed in the form of a man and come into the light, or in the form of a species of wild animals, or plants, or birds, then say that this has "come into being"; and when they separate, this men call sad fate *(death).* The terms that right demands they do not use; but through custom I myself also apply these names. (9)

[6] From what in no wise exists, it is impossible for anything to come into being; and for being to perish completely is incapable of fulfillment and unthinkable; for it will always be there, wherever anyone may place it on any occasion. (12)

[7] Nor is there any part of the whole that is empty or overfull. (13)

[8] No part of the whole is empty; so whence could anything additional come? (14)

[9] I shall tell of a double *(process):* at one time it increased so as to be a single one out of many; at another time again it grew apart so as to be many out of one. There is a double creation of mortals and a double decline: the union of all things causes the birth and destruction of the one *(race of mortals),* the other is reared as the elements grow apart, and then flies asunder. And these *(elements)* never cease their continuous exchange, sometimes uniting under the influence of love, so that all become one, at other times again each moving apart through the hostile force of hate. Thus, in so far as they have the power to grow into one out of many, and again, when the one grows apart and many are formed, in this sense they come into being and have no stable life; but in so far as they never cease their continuous exchange, in this sense they remain always unmoved *(unaltered)* as they follow the cyclic process.

But come, listen to my discourse! For be assured, learning will increase your understanding. As I said before, revealing the aims of my discourse, I shall tell you of a double process. At one time it increased so as to be a single one out of many; at another time it grew apart so as to be many out of one—fire and water and earth and the boundless height of air, and also execrable hate apart from these, of equal weight in all directions, and love in their midst, their equal in length and breadth. Observe her with your mind, and do not sit with wondering eyes! She it is who is believed to be implanted in mortal limbs also; through her they think friendly thoughts and perform harmonious actions, calling her joy and Aphrodite. No mortal man has perceived her as she moves in and out among them. But *you* must listen to the undeceitful progress of my argument.

All these *(elements)* are equal and of the same age in their creation; but each presides over its own office, and each has its own character, and they prevail in turn in the course of time. And besides these, nothing else comes into being, nor does anything cease. For if they had been perishing continuously, they would be no more; and what could increase the whole? And whence could it have come? In what direction could it perish, since nothing is empty of these things? No, but these things alone exist, and running through one another they become different things at different times, and are ever continuously the same. (17)

[10] This process is clearly to be seen throughout the mass of mortal limbs: sometimes through love all the limbs which the body has as its lot come together into one, in the prime of flourishing life; at another time again, sundered by evil feuds, they wander severally by the breakers of the shore of life. Likewise too with shrub-plants and fish in their watery dwelling, and beasts with mountain lairs and diver-birds that travel on wings. (20)

[11] But come, observe the following witness to my previous discourse, lest in my former statements there was any substance of which the form was missing. Observe the sun, bright to see and hot everywhere, and all the immortal things *(heavenly bodies)* drenched with its heat and brilliant light; and the rain, dark and chill over everything; and from the earth issue forth things based on the soil and solid. But in *(the reign of)* wrath they are all different in form and separate, while in *(the reign of)* love they come together and long for one another. For from these *(elements)* come all things that were and are and will be; and trees spring up, and men and women, and beasts and birds and water-nurtured fish, and even the long-lived gods who are highest in honor. For these *(elements)* alone exist, but by running through one another they become different; to such a degree does mixing change them. (21)

[12] For all these things—beaming sun and earth and heaven and sea—are connected in harmony with their own parts: all those *(parts)* which have been sundered from them and exist in mortal limbs. Similarly all those things which are suitable for mixture are made like one another and united in affection by Aphrodite. But those things which differ most from one another in origin and mixture and the forms in which they are molded are completely unaccustomed to combine, and are very baneful because of the commands of hate, in that hate has wrought their origin. (22)

[13] . . . Touching on summit after summit, not to follow a single path of discourse to the end. (24)

[14] For what is right can well be uttered even twice. (25)

[15] In turn they get the upper hand in the revolving cycle, and perish into one another and increase in the turn appointed by fate. For they alone exist, but running through one another they become men and the tribes of other animals, sometimes uniting under the influence of love into one ordered whole, at other times again each moving apart through the hostile force of hate, until growing together into the whole which is one, they are quelled. Thus in so far as they have the power to grow into one

out of many, and again, when the one grows apart and many are formed, in this sense they come into being and have no stable life; but in so far as they never cease their continuous exchange, in this sense they remain always unmoved *(unaltered)* as they follow the cyclic process. (26)

[16] *(The sphere under the dominion of love):* Therein are articulated neither the swift limbs of the sun, nor the shaggy might of earth, nor the sea: so firmly is it *(the whole)* fixed in a close-set secrecy, a rounded Sphere enjoying a circular solitude. (27)

[17] But he *(God)* is equal in all directions to himself and altogether eternal, a rounded sphere enjoying a circular solitude. (28)

[18] For there do not start two branches from his back; *(he has)* no feet, no swift knees, no organs of reproduction; but he was a sphere, and in all directions equal to himself. (29)

[19] But I will go back to the path of song which I formerly laid down, drawing one argument from another: that *(path which shows how)* when hate has reached the bottommost abyss of the eddy, and when love reaches the middle of the whirl, then in it *(the whirl)* all these things come together so as to be one—not all at once, but voluntarily uniting, some from one quarter, others from another. And as they mixed, there poured forth countless races of mortals. But many things stand unmixed side by side with the things mixing—all those which hate *(still)* aloft checked, since it had not yet faultlessly withdrawn from the whole to the outermost limits of the circle, but was remaining in some places, and in other places departing from the limbs *(of the sphere)*. But in so far as it went on quietly streaming out, to the same extent there was entering a benevolent immortal inrush of faultless love. And swiftly those things became mortal which previously had experienced immortality, and things formerly unmixed became mixed, changing their paths. And as they mixed, there poured forth countless races of mortals, equipped with forms of every sort, a marvel to behold. (35)

[20] As they came together, hate returned to the outermost. (36)

[21] There whirls round the earth a circular borrowed light. (45)

[22] It is the earth that makes night by coming in the way of the *(sun's)* rays. (48)

[23] Sea, the sweat of earth. (55)

[24] Limbs wandered alone. (58)

[25] Creatures with rolling gait and innumerable hands. (60)

[26] The way everything breathes in and out is as follows: all have tubes of flesh, empty of blood, which extend over the surface of the body; and at the mouths of these tubes the outermost surface of the skin is perforated with frequent pores, so as to keep in the blood while a free way is cut for the passage of the air. Thus, when the thin blood flows back from here, the air, bubbling, rushes in in a mighty wave; and when the blood leaps up *(to the surface)*, there is an expiration of air. As when a girl, playing with a water-catcher of shining brass—when, having placed the mouth of the pipe on her well-shaped hand, she dips the vessel into the yielding substance of silvery water, still the volume of air pressing from inside on the many holes keeps out the water, until she uncovers the condensed stream *(of air)*. Then at once when the air flows out, the water flows in, in an equal quantity. Similarly, when water occupies the depths of the brazen vessel, and the opening or passage is stopped by the human flesh *(hand)*, and the air outside, striving to get in, checks the water, by controlling the surface at the entrance of the noisy strainer until she lets go with her hand: then again, in exactly the opposite way from what happened before, as the air rushes in, the water flows out in equal volume. Similarly when the thin blood, rushing through the limbs, flows back into the interior, straightway a stream of air flows

in with a rush; and when the blood flows up again, again there is a breathing-out in equal volume. (100)

[27] If you press them deep into your firm mind, and contemplate them with good will and a studious care that is pure, these things will all assuredly remain with you throughout your life; and you will obtain many other things from them; for these things of themselves cause each *(element)* to increase in the character, according to the way of each man's nature. But if you intend to grasp after different things such as dwell among men in countless numbers and blunt their thoughts, miserable *(trifles),* certainly these things will quickly desert you in the course of time, longing to return to their own original kind. For all things, be assured, have intelligence and a portion of thought. (110)

[28] You shall learn all the drugs that exist as a defence against illness and old age; for you alone will I accomplish all this. You shall check the force of the unwearying winds which rush upon the earth with their blasts and lay waste the culti-vated fields. And again, if you wish, you shall conduct the breezes back again. You shall create a seasonable dryness after the dark rain for mankind, and again you shall create after summer drought the streams that nourish the trees and *(which will flow in the sky).* And you shall bring out of Hades a dead man restored to strength. (111)

KATHARMOI (PURIFICATIONS)

[29] Friends, who dwell in the great town on the city's heights, looking down on yellow Agrigentum, you who are occupied with good deeds, who are harbors treating foreigners with respect, and who are unacquainted with wickedness: greeting! I go about among you as an immortal god, no longer a mortal, held in honor by all, as I seem *(to them to deserve),* crowned with fillets and flowing garlands. When I come to them in their flourishing towns, to men and women, I am honored; and they follow me in thou-sands, to inquire where is the path of advantage, some desiring oracles, while others ask to hear a word of healing for their manifold diseases, since they have long been pierced with cruel pains. (112)

[30] But why do I lay stress on these things, as if I were achieving something as great in that I surpass mortal men who are liable to many forms of destruction? (113)

[31] Friends, I know that truth is present in the story that I shall tell; but it is actually very difficult for men, and the impact of conviction on their minds is unwelcome. (114)

[32] There is an oracle of necessity, an ancient decree of the gods, eternal, sealed fast with broad oaths, that when one of the divine spirits whose portion is long life sinfully stains his own limbs with bloodshed, and following hate has sworn a false oath—these must wander for thrice ten thousand seasons far from the company of the blessed, being born throughout the period into all kinds of mortal shapes, which exchange one hard way of life for another. For the mighty air chases them into the sea, and the sea spews them forth on to the dry land, and the earth *(drives them)* towards the rays of the blazing sun; and the sun hurls them into the eddies of the Aether. One *(Element)* receives them from the other, and all loathe them. Of this number am I too, now, a fugitive from heaven and a wanderer, because I trusted in raging Hate. (115)

[33] For by now I have been born boy, girl, plant, bird, and dumb sea-fish. (117)

[34] I wept and wailed when I saw the unfamiliar land *(at birth).* (118)

[35] How great the honor, how deep the happiness from which *(I am exiled)!* (119)

[36] Will ye not cease from this harsh-sounding slaughter? Do you not see that you are devouring one another in the thoughtlessness of your minds? (136)

ANAXAGORAS
ca. 500–ca. 428 B.C.

Anaxagoras came from Clazomenae on the coast of Asia Minor, not far northwest of Colophon (Xenophanes' home) and Ephesus (Heraclitus' home). He was the first of the Greek philosophers to move to Athens, where he became a good friend of Pericles, the great statesman, who gave his name to the whole epoch. The dates are uncertain, but Anaxagoras may have been born about 500 B.C. and have come to Athens around 480. He lived in Athens in the time of its greatest glory, a contemporary of the classical tragedians Aeschylus, Sophocles, and Euripides. Anaxagoras was the first philosopher to be tried and condemned on a charge of heresy or impiety. He was saved by Pericles and went into exile at Lampsacus, a Milesian colony on the Hellespont, where he died about 428/7 B.C., a year after Pericles.

Anaxagoras taught that everything consists of an infinite number of particles or seeds, and that in all things there is a portion of everything. Hair could not come from what is not hair, nor could flesh come from what is not flesh. The names we apply to things are determined by the preponderance of certain seeds in them—for example, hair seeds or flesh seeds. Like Empedocles, he added to such "material causes" an "efficient cause" to account for the motion and direction of things; however, unlike Empedocles' two, Anaxagoras added only one "efficient cause," which was mind, <*nous*> in Greek. The introduction of mind led Aristotle to hail Anaxagoras as the only sober man among the Pre-Socratics; yet Aristotle found fault with Anaxagoras for not making more use of this new principle to explain natural events.

[1] He is said to have been twenty years old at the time of Xerxes' crossing, and to have lived to seventy-two. . . . He began to be a philosopher at Athens in the archonship of Callias [456/5 B.C.], at the age of twenty, as Demetrius Phalereus tells us in his *Register of Archons,* and is said to have spent thirty years there. . . . There are different accounts given of his trial. Sotion, in his *Succession of Philosophers,* says that he was prosecuted by Cleon for impiety, because he claimed that the sun was a red-hot mass of metal, and that after Pericles, his pupil, had made a speech in his defense, he was fined five talents and exiled. Satyrus, in his *Lives,* on the other hand, says that the charge was brought by Thucydides in his political campaign against Pericles; and he adds that the charge was not only for

impiety but for Medism [Persian leanings] as well; and he was condemned to death in absence. . . . Finally he withdrew to Lampsacus, and there died. It is said that when the rulers of the city asked him what privilege he wished to be granted, he replied that the children should be given a holiday every year in the month in which he died. The custom is preserved to the present day. When he died, the Lampsacenes buried him with full honors.

[2] Anaxagoras, the natural philosopher, was a distinguished Clazomenion, an associate of Anaximenes of Miletus; and his own pupils included Archelaus the natural philosopher and Euripides the poet.

[3] Those who wrote only one book include Melissus, Parmenides, and Anaxagoras.

* * *

[4] All Things were together, infinite in number and in smallness. For the Small also was infinite. And since all were together, nothing was distinguishable because of its smallness. For Air and Aether dominated all things, both of them being infinite. For these are the most important *(Elements)* in the total mixture, both in number and in size.

[5] Air and Aether are separated off from the surrounding multiplicity, and that which surrounds is infinite in number.

[6] For in Small there is no Least, but only a Lesser: for it is impossible that Being should Not-Be, and in Great there is always a Greater. And it is equal in number to the small, but each thing is to itself both great and small.

[7] Conditions being thus, one must believe that there are many things of all sorts in all composite products, and the seeds of all Things, which contain all kinds of shapes and colors and pleasant savors. And men too were fitted together, and all other creatures which have life. And the men possessed both inhabited cities and artificial works [cultivated fields] just like ourselves, and they had sun and moon and the rest, just as we have, and the earth produced for them many and diverse things, of which they collected the most useful, and now use them for [or, "in"] their dwellings. This I say concerning Separation, that it must have taken place not only with us, but elsewhere.

Before these things were separated off, all things were together, nor was any color distinguishable, for the mixing of all Things prevented this, *(namely)* the mixing of moist and dry, and hot and cold, and bright and dark, and there was a great quantity of earth in the mixture, and seeds infinite in number, not at all like one another. For none of the other things either is like any other. And as this was so, one must believe that all Things were present in the Whole.

[8] These things being thus separated off, one must understand that all things are in no wise less or more (for it is not possible for them to be more than All), but all things are forever equal *(in quantity)*.

[9] And since there are equal *(quantitative)* parts of Great and Small, so, too, similarly in everything there must be everything. It is not possible *(for them)* to exist apart, but all things contain a portion of everything. Since it is not possible for the Least to exist, it cannot be isolated, nor come into being by itself; but as it was in the beginning, so now, all things are together. In all things there are many things, and of the things separated off, there are equal numbers in *(the categories)* Great and Small.

[10] So that the number of the things separated off cannot be known either in thought or in fact.

[11] The things in the one Cosmos are not separated off from one another with an axe, neither the Hot from the Cold, nor the Cold from the Hot.

[12] Thus these things circulate and are separated off by force and speed. The speed makes the force. Their speed is not like the speed of any of the Things now existing among mankind, but altogether many times as fast.

[13] How can hair come from not-hair, and flesh from not-flesh?

[14] In everything there is a portion of everything except Mind; and some things contain Mind also.

[15] Other things all contain a part of everything, but Mind is infinite and self-ruling, and is mixed with no Thing, but is alone by itself. If it were not by itself, but were mixed with anything else, it would have had a share of all Things, if it were mixed with anything; for in everything there is a portion of everything, as I have said before. And the things mixed *(with Mind)* would have prevented it, so that it could not rule over any Thing in the same way as it can being alone by itself. For it is the finest of all Things, and the purest, and has complete understanding of everything, and has the greatest power. All things which have life, both the greater and the less, are ruled by Mind. Mind took command of the universal revolution, so as to make *(things)* revolve at the outset. And at first things began to revolve from some small point, but now the revolution extends over a greater area, and will spread even further. And the things which were mixed together, and separated off, and divided, were all understood by Mind. And whatever they were going to be, and whatever things were then in existence that are not now, and all things that now exist and whatever shall exist—all were arranged by Mind, as also the revolution now followed by the stars, the sun and moon, and the Air and Aether which were separated off. It was this revolution which caused the separation off. And dense separates from rare, and hot from cold, and bright from dark, and dry from wet. There are many portions of many things. And nothing is absolutely separated off or divided the one from the other except Mind. Mind is all alike, both the greater and the less. But nothing else is like anything else, but each individual thing is and was most obviously that of which it contains the most.

[16] And when Mind began the motion, there was a separating-off from all that was being moved; and all that Mind set in motion was separated *(internally);* and as things were moving and separating off *(internally),* the revolution greatly increased this *(internal)* separation.

[17] Mind, which ever Is, certainly still exists also where all other things are, *(namely)* in the multiple surrounding *(mass)* and in the things which were separated off before, and in the things already separated off [things that have been either aggregated or separated].

[18] The dense and moist and cold and dark *(Elements)* collected here, where now is Earth, and the rare and hot and dry went outwards to the furthest part of the Aether.

[19] From these, while they are separating off, Earth solidifies; for from the clouds, water is separated off, and from the water, earth, and from the earth, stones are solidified by the cold; and these rush outward rather than the water.

[20] The Greeks have an incorrect belief on Coming into Being and Passing Away. No Thing comes into being or passes away, but it is mixed together or separated from existing Things. Thus they would be correct if they called coming into being "mixing," and passing away "separation-off."

[21] It is the sun that endows the moon with its brilliance.

[22] We give the name Iris to the reflection of the sun on the clouds. It is therefore the sign of a storm, for the water which flows round the cloud produces wind or forces out rain.

[23] Through the weakness of the sense-perceptions, we cannot judge truth.

DEMOCRITUS
ca. 460–ca. 370 B.C.

LEUCIPPUS
fifth century B.C.

Democritus of Abdera, on the coast of Thrace, was probably born in 460 B.C. He wrote over sixty works, of which several hundred fragments survive. Together with Leucippus, a virtually unknown figure who was supposedly his teacher, Democritus was the prime exponent of the philosophy known as *atomism*. While Leucippus's work has perished, we have many reports about the Democritean form of atomistic philosophy.

Atomism accepted Parmenides' idea that being must be one seamless whole but posited an infinite number of such "one's." According to Democritus, the world is made up of tiny "un-cutables" <*atomos*> that move within the "void" (corresponding to Parmenides' non-being). These atoms combine in different patterns to form the material objects of the observable world. Democritus applied this understanding of reality to human beings as well. Both the soul and the body are made up of atoms. Perception occurs when atoms from objects outside the person strike the sense organs inside the person, which in turn strike the atoms of the soul further inside. Death, in turn, is simply the dissipation of the soul atoms when the body atoms no longer hold them together.

Such an understanding of the person seems to eliminate all possibility of freedom of choice and, indeed, the only known saying of Leucippus is "Nothing happens at random; everything happens out of reason and by necessity." Such a position would seem to eliminate all ethics: If you *must* act a certain way, it seems futile to talk about what you *ought* to do (since, as Kant later said, "*ought* implies *can*"). Yet Democritus wrote a great deal on ethics, including a book of ethical maxims called the *Gnomae*.

The fragments that follow are grouped into two sections: first, the ancient reports about Leucippus and Democritus; then the metaphysical and epistemological fragments.

Democritus's philosophy is important for at least two reasons. First, while atomism represents still another pluralistic answer to Parmenides, and while Leucippus was a Pre-Socratic, nevertheless Democritus was actually a slightly younger contemporary of Socrates and an older contemporary of Plato. Hence, Democritus's atomistic materialism may be viewed as an important alternative to Plato's idealism. Second, Democritus's thought continued to have an impact, being taken up first by Epicurus and then, in Roman times, by Lucretius.

A. ANCIENT REPORTS ON ATOMISM

[1] Leucippus of Elea or Miletus (both accounts are current) had associated with Parmenides in philosophy, but in his view of reality he did not follow the same path as Parmenides and Xenophanes but rather, it seems, the opposite path. For while they regarded the whole as one, motionless, uncreated, and limited, and forbade even the search for what is not, he posited innumerable elements in perpetual motion—namely the atoms—and held that the number of their shapes was infinite, on the ground that there was no reason why any atom should be of one shape rather than another; for he observed too that coming-into-being and change are incessant in the world. Further he held that not-being exists as well as being, and the two are equally the causes of things coming-into-being. The nature of atoms he supposed to be compact and full; that, he said, was being, and it moved in the void, which he called not-being and held to exist no less than being. In the same way his associate, Democritus of Abdera, posited as principles the full and the void.

[2] Apollodorus in the *Chronicles* says that Epicurus was instructed by Nausiphanes and Praxiphanes; but Epicurus himself denies this, saying in the letter to Eurylochus that he instructed himself. He and Hemarchus both maintain that there never was a philosopher Leucippus, who some (including Apollodorus the Epicurean) say was the teacher of Democritus.

[3] Leucippus postulated atoms and void, and in this Democritus resembled him, though in other respects he was more productive.

[4] Democritus . . . met Leucippus and, according to some, Anaxagoras also, whose junior he was by forty years. . . . As he himself says in the *Little World-system,* he was a young man in the old age of Anaxagoras, being forty years younger.

[5] Demetrius in his *Homonyms* and Antisthenes in his *Successions* say that he [Democritus] traveled to Egypt to visit the priests and learn geometry, and that he went also to Persia to visit the Chaldaeans, and to the Red Sea. Some say that he associated with the "naked philosophers" in India; also that he went to Ethiopia.

[6] Leucippus thought he had arguments which would assert what is consistent sense-perception and not do away with coming into being or perishing or motion, or the plurality of existents. He agrees with the appearances to this extent, but he concedes, to those who maintain the One [the Eleatics], that there would be no motion without void, and says that the void is non-existent, and that no part of what is is non-existent—for what is in the strict sense is wholly and fully being. But such being, he says, is not one; there is an infinite number, and they are invisible because of the smallness of the particles. They move in the void (for there *is* void), and when they come together they cause coming to be, and when they separate they cause perishing.

[7] They [Leucippus, Democritus, and Epicurus] said that the first principles were infinite in number, and thought they were indivisible atoms and impassible owing to their compactness, and without any void in them; divisibility comes about because of the void in compound bodies.

[8] To this extent they differed, that one [Epicurus] supposed that all atoms were very small, and on that account imperceptible; the other, Democritus, that there are some atoms that are very large.

[9] Democritus holds the same view as Leucippus about the elements, full and void . . . he spoke as if the things that are were in constant motion in the void; and there are innumerable worlds which differ in size. In some worlds there is no sun and moon, in others they are larger than in our world, and in others more numerous. The intervals between the worlds are unequal; in some parts there are more worlds, in others fewer; some are increasing, some at their height, some decreasing; in some parts they are arising, in others failing. They are destroyed by collision, one with another. There are some worlds devoid of living creatures or plants or any moisture.

[10] Everything happens according to necessity; for the cause of the coming-into-being of all things is the whirl, which he calls necessity.

[11] As they [the atoms] move, they collide and become entangled in such a way as to cling in close contact to one another, but not so as to form one substance of them in reality of any kind whatever; for it is very simple-minded to suppose that two or more could ever become one. The reason he gives for atoms staying together for a while is the intertwining and mutual hold of the primary bodies; for some of them are angular, some hooked, some concave, some convex, and indeed with countless other differences; so he thinks they cling to each other and stay together until such time as some stronger necessity comes from the surrounding and shakes and scatters them apart.

[12] Democritus says that the spherical is the most mobile of shapes; and such is mind and fire.

[13] Democritus and the majority of natural philosophers who discuss perception are guilty of a great absurdity; for they represent all perception as being by touch.

[14] Leucippus, Democritus, and Epicurus say that perception and thought arise when images enter from outside; neither occurs to anybody without an image impinging.

[15] Democritus explains sight by the visual image, which he describes in a peculiar way; the visual image does not arise directly in the pupil, but the air between the eye and the object of sight is contracted and stamped by the object seen and the seer; for from everything there is always a sort of effluence proceeding. So this air, which is solid and variously colored, appears in the eye, which is moist (?); the eye does not admit the dense part, but the moist passes through.

B. METAPHYSICAL AND EPISTEMOLOGICAL FRAGMENTS

[16] We know nothing about anything really, but opinion is for all individuals an inflowing (? of the atoms).

[17] It will be obvious that it is impossible to understand how in reality each thing is.

[18] Sweet exists by convention, bitter by convention, color by convention; atoms and void (alone) exist in reality. . . . We know nothing accurately in reality, but *(only)* as it changes according to the bodily condition, and the constitution of those things that flow upon *(the body)* and impinge upon it.

[19] It has often been demonstrated that we do not grasp how each thing is or is not.

[20] There are two sorts of knowledge, one genuine, one bastard (or *"obscure"*). To the latter belong all the following: sight, hearing, smell, taste, touch. The real is separated from this. When the bastard can do no more—neither see more minutely, nor hear, nor smell, nor taste, nor perceive by touch—and a finer investigation is needed, then the genuine comes in as having a tool for distinguishing more finely.

[21] Naught exists just as much as Aught.

C. FRAGMENTS ON ETHICS

[22] Pleasure and absence of pleasure are the criteria of what is profitable and what is not. (4)

[23] Nature and instruction are similar; for instruction transforms the man, and in transforming, creates his nature. (33)

[24] *(To live badly is)* not to live badly, but to spend a long time dying. (160)

[25] But the gods are the givers of all good things, both in the past and now. They are not, however, the givers of things which are bad, harmful or non-beneficial, either in the past or now, but men themselves fall into these through blindness of mind and lack of sense. (175)

[26] The criterion of the advantageous and disadvantageous is enjoyment and lack of enjoyment. (188)

[27] Cheerfulness is created for men through moderation of enjoyment and harmoniousness of life. Things that are in excess or lacking are apt to change and cause great disturbance in the soul. Souls which are stirred by great divergences are neither stable nor cheerful. Therefore one must keep one's mind on what is attainable, and be content with what one has, paying little heed to things envied and admired, and not dwelling on them in one's mind. Rather must you consider the lives of those in distress, reflecting on their intense sufferings, in order that your own possessions and condition may seem great and enviable, and you may, by ceasing to desire more, cease to suffer in your soul. For he who admires those who have, and who are called happy by other mortals, and who dwells on them in his mind every hour, is constantly compelled to undertake something new and to run the risk, through his desire, of doing something irretrievable among those things which the laws prohibit. Hence one must not seek the latter, but must be content with the former, comparing one's own life with that of those in worse cases, and must consider oneself fortunate, reflecting on their sufferings, in being so much better off than they. If you keep to this way of thinking, you will live more serenely, and will expel those not-negligible curses in life, envy, jealousy and spite. (191)

Three Sophists

PROTAGORAS
ca. 490–ca. 420 B.C.

Protagoras, like Democritus, came from Abdera, on the Thracian coast. An ancient story relates that he was at first a porter and that Democritus of Abdera saw him, admired his poise, and decided to instruct him; but this story's truth is doubtful. Protagoras reflected on language and developed a system of grammar. Having settled in Athens, where he taught the youth, he won the respect of Pericles, who commissioned him to frame laws for the new colony of Thurii, in Italy. At age seventy he was accused and convicted of atheism and is said to have left for Sicily and to have drowned at sea.

Protagoras is primarily known for his claim that "of all things the measure is Man. . . . " In the dialogues *Protagoras* and *Theaetetus* (the relevant sections from the latter are reprinted in this volume), Plato takes Protagoras to mean that each person, not humanity as a whole, is the measure of all things and so attacks Protagoras's relativism.

Protagoras was the first of those traveling teachers of philosophy and rhetoric who became known as "Sophists." Sophists were not as interested in metaphysical theories as they were in the skill of <arete>, or "excellence," in the sense of bettering oneself. Many conservative Greeks, such as Aristophanes, considered proper speech and good manners the inherited characteristics of the upper classes. The Sophists, however, taught such skills for a fee—to the consternation of the aristocracy.

Plato considered it his task to oppose these men, and since his dialogues survived and most of their writings did not, his highly polemical pictures of the Sophists have been widely accepted as fair portraits. The very name "Sophist" has become a reproach. Yet one should not uncritically accept Plato's image of the Sophists. Although many disagree with Sophist conclusions, their questioning of conventions, especially in ethics, and their critique of the limits of knowledge represent a milestone in the history of thought.

[1] Of all things the measure is Man, of the things that are, that they are, and of the things that are not, that they are not.

[2] Teaching needs endowment and practice. Learning must begin in youth.

[3] About the gods, I am not able to know whether they exist or do not exist, nor what they are like in form; for the factors preventing knowledge are many: the obscurity of the subject, and the shortness of human life.

[4] To make the weaker cause the stronger.

[5] When his sons, who were fine young men, died within eight days, he (Pericles) bore it without mourning. For he held on to his serenity, from which every day he derived great benefit in happiness, freedom from suffering, and honor in the people's eyes—for all who saw him bearing his griefs valiantly thought him great-souled and brave and superior to themselves, well knowing their own helplessness in such a calamity.

[6] Art without practice, and practice without art, are nothing.

[7] Education does not take root in the soul unless one goes deep.

GORGIAS
fl. ca. 427 B.C.

After Protagoras, Gorgias was probably the most renowned Sophist. Gorgias came from Leontini, in southern Sicily. His dates are uncertain, but he is said to have died at the age of 108, possibly as late as 375 B.C. He first came to Athens on a mission from his Sicilian countrymen, enlisting (successfully) Athenian help against Syracuse. While in Athens, he taught the art of persuasion to Isocrates, the famous rhetorician.

Like Protagoras, Gorgias is a character in Plato's dialogue bearing his name. Also like Protagoras, Gorgias held views—in this case on the impossibility of knowledge—that Plato found unacceptable. The following selections constitute the single philosophic fragment that has come down to us (a long quotation in Sextus Empiricus) and three very short pieces that may help fill out the picture of Gorgias.

[1]   I. Nothing exists.
      (a) Not-Being does not exist.
      (b) Being does not exist.

       i. as everlasting.
      ii. as created.
     iii. as both.
     iv. as One.
      v. as Many.
  (c) A mixture of Being and Not-Being does not exist.
 II. If anything exists, it is incomprehensible.
III. If it is comprehensible, it is incommunicable.

  I. Nothing exists. If anything exists, it must be either Being or Not-Being, or both Being and Not-Being.
   (a) It cannot be Not-Being, for Not-Being does not exist; if it did, it would be at the same time Being and Not-Being, which is impossible.
   (b) It cannot be Being, for Being does not exist. If Being exists, it must be either everlasting, or created, or both.
      i. It cannot be everlasting; if it were, it would have no beginning, and therefore would be boundless; if it is boundless, then it has no position, for if it had position it would be contained in something, and so it would no longer be boundless, for that which contains is greater than that which is contained, and nothing is greater than the boundless. It cannot be contained by itself, for then the thing containing and the thing contained would be the same, and Being would become two things—both position and body—which is absurd. Hence if Being is everlasting, it is boundless; if boundless, it has no position ("is nowhere"); if without position, it does not exist.
      ii. Similarly, Being cannot be created; if it were, it must come from something, either Being or Not-Being, both of which are impossible.
     iii. Similarly, Being cannot be both everlasting and created, since they are opposite. Therefore Being does not exist.
     iv. Being cannot be one, because if it exists it has size, and is therefore infinitely divisible; at least it is threefold, having length, breadth, and depth.
      v. It cannot be many, because the many is made up of an addition of ones, so that since the one does not exist, the many do not exist either.
   (c) A mixture of Being and Not-Being is impossible. Therefore since Being does not exist, nothing exists.
 II. If anything exists, it is incomprehensible. If the concepts of the mind are not realities, reality cannot be thought; if the thing thought is white, then white is thought about; if the thing thought is non-existent, then non-existence is thought about; this is equivalent to saying that "existence, reality, is not thought about, cannot be thought." Many things thought about are not realities: we can conceive of a chariot running on the sea, or a winged man. Also, since things seen are the objects of sight, and things heard are the objects of hearing, and we accept as real things seen without their being heard, and vice versa; so we would have to accept things thought without their being seen or heard; but this would mean believing in things like the chariot racing on the sea. Therefore reality is not the object of thought, and cannot be comprehended by it. Pure mind, as opposed to sense-perception, or even as an equally valid criterion, is a myth.

III. If anything is comprehensible, it is incommunicable. The things which exist are perceptibles; the objects of sight are apprehended by sight, the objects of hearing by hearing, and there is no interchange; so that these sense-perceptions cannot communicate with one another. Further, that with which we communicate is speech, and speech is not the same thing as the things that exist, the perceptibles; so that we communicate not the things which exist, but only speech; just as that which is seen cannot become that which is heard, so our speech cannot be equated with that which exists, since it is outside us. Further, speech is composed from the percepts which we receive from without, that is, from perceptibles; so that it is not speech which communicates perceptibles, but perceptibles which create speech. Further, speech can never exactly represent perceptibles, since it is different from them, and perceptibles are apprehended each by the one kind of organ, speech by another. Hence, since the objects of sight cannot be presented to any other organ but sight, and the different sense-organs cannot give their information to one another, similarly speech cannot give any information about perceptibles. Therefore, if anything exists and is comprehended, it is incommunicable.

CRITIAS
ca. 460–403 B.C.

Critias was an Athenian politician, born sometime around 460 B.C. Little is known of his origin except that he was a cousin to Plato's mother. As a young man, Critias was a follower of Socrates—a point used later against Socrates. For Critias became one of the "Thirty Tyrants," the opponents of democracy, and he was known as an especially harsh ruler. According to Xenophon,* Socrates' accusers at his trial made much of the connection. The implication was that Socrates' teaching had led Critias to his excesses. Critias himself was killed in battle during the civil war of 403 B.C. between the oligarchs and the democrats.

Critias was not, strictly speaking, a Sophist, as he was not a paid teacher. Yet his ideas (and perhaps his activities) represented the implications of sophistic ideas. Where Protagoras proclaimed a kind of agnosticism regarding the gods, Critias argued that the gods were invented by a clever person to enforce the law of the state. Where Gorgias implied that "truth" cannot be known, Critias asserted that the gods are a human invention, "the truth concealed under words untrue." Anticipating the

---

*See Xenophon, *Recollections of Socrates,* translated by Anna S. Benjamin (New York: Macmillan, 1965)

work of Thomas Hobbes some 2,000 years later, Critias posited a primordial "state of nature" where everyone is at war with everyone. Penal laws are not adequate to control this anarchy, hence the need for the invention of the gods.

[1] More men are good by training than by nature.

[2] A worthy character is steadier than the law. For never could an orator pervert [a worthy character] but he often confuses the law this way, that way, and so often brings it to ruin.

[3] Critias, one of the Tyrants at Athens, seems to belong to the company of the atheists when he says that the ancient lawgivers invented God as a kind of overseer of the right and wrong actions of men, in order to make sure that nobody injured his neighbors privily through fear of vengeance at the hands of the Gods; and his statement runs thus:

> A time there was when anarchy did rule
> The lives of men, which then were like the beasts',
> Enslaved to force; nor was there then reward
> For good men, nor for wicked punishment.
> Next, as I deem, did men establish laws
> For punishment, that justice might be lord
> Of all mankind, and Insolence enchain'd;
> And whosoever did sin was penalized.
> Next, as the laws did hold men back from deeds
> Of open violence, but still such deeds
> Were done in secret,—then, as I maintain,
> Some shrewd man first, a man in counsel wise,
> Discovered unto men the fear of Gods,
> Thereby to frighten sinners should they sin
> E'en secretly in deed, or word, or thought.
> Hence was it that he brought in Deity,
> Telling how God enjoys an endless life,
> Hears with his mind and sees, and taketh thought
> And heeds things, and his nature is divine,
> So that he hearkens to men's every word
> And has the power to see men's every act.
> E'en if you plan in silence some ill deed,
> The Gods will surely mark it; for in them
> Wisdom resides. So, speaking words like these,
> Most cunning doctrine did he introduce,
> The truth concealing under speech untrue.
> The place he spoke of as God's abode
> Was that whereby be could affright men most,
> The place from which, he knew, both terrors came
> And easements unto men of toilsome life
> To wit the vault above, wherein do dwell
> The lightnings, be beheld, and awesome claps
> Of thunder, and the starry face of heaven,
> Fair-spangled by that cunning craftsman Time,
> Whence, too, the meteor's glowing mass doth speed
> And liquid rain descends upon the earth.
> Such were the fears wherewith he hedged men round,
> And so to God he gave a fitting home,

By this his speech, and in a fitting place,
And thus extinguished lawlessness by laws.

. . . .

Thus first did some man, as I deem, persuade
Men to suppose a race of Gods exists.

[4] For a man, once he is born, nothing but death is sure; while he lives it is certain that he cannot move out of the way of ruin. . . .

Epilogue I:
Two Views of Athens

THUCYDIDES
ca. 460–ca. 400 B.C.

While philosophy actually began on the Ionian coast of Asia Minor (in modern Turkey), with the fifth century B.C. the center of philosophical inquiry became the city-state of Athens. The Persian Empire overran the Ionian colonies, forcing Greek philosophers there to flee to Athens. In 499 B.C. the remaining Greeks in Ionia, supported by Athens, rebelled against their Persian overlords. The Persian king, Darius, used the unsuccessful rebellion as a pretext to attack the Greek mainland. The Persian Wars, as they are now known, lasted about fifty years, though most of the fighting took place between 490 and 479 B.C. While the specifics of the war are fascinating—and the names of major battles such as those at Marathon and Thermopylae are still famous today—we do not have space to treat them. (See the suggested readings for descriptions of the war.) The upshot of the conflict, however, was astounding: The vastly outnumbered Greeks, led by the Athenians, defeated the Persians.

In the years following the Persian Wars, Athens blossomed. Artists, sculptors, architects, playwrights, poets, and philosophers found a haven there. Democracy encouraged participation in government; the Parthenon, one of the most famous buildings in the world, was built (beginning in 447 B.C.); Aeschylus (525–456 B.C.), Sophocles (ca. 496–406 B.C.), Euripides (ca. 485–406 B.C.), and Aristophanes (ca. 450–ca. 385 B.C.), invented theater as we know it; sculptors such as Myron produced magnificent statues like the *Discus Thrower* (ca. 450 B.C.); Hippocrates (ca. 460–ca. 377 B.C.) developed the concept of compassionate medicine (the "Hippocratic Oath" is still taken by physicians today); Thucydides (ca. 460–ca. 400 B.C.) introduced the concept of factual history; while the man whose name is synonymous with the age, Pericles (ca. 495–429 B.C.), presided wisely over the state.

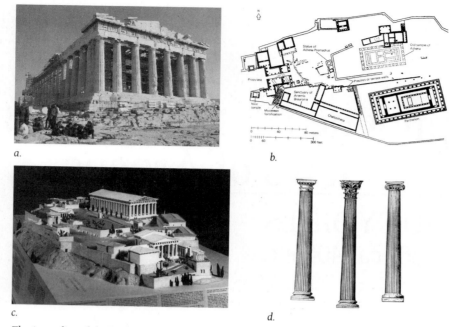

a. *b.*

c. *d.*

The Acropolis and the Parthenon

a. The Parthenon, Athens, built 477–438 B.C. The Parthenon, dedicated to Athena, patron deity of Athens, was at one period rededicated to the Christian Virgin Mary and then later became a Turkish mosque. In 1687 a gunpowder explosion created the ruin we see today. The Doric shell remains as a monument to ancient architectural engineering expertise and to a sense of classical beauty and order. *(Forrest E. Baird)*

b. Restored plan of the Acropolis, 400 B.C. The history of the Acropolis is as varied as the style and size of the temples and buildings constructed atop the ancient site. *(Pearson Education/PH College)*

c. This model of the Acropolis of Athens recreates the complexity of fifth century B.C. public space, which included centers for worship, public forum, and entertainment. *(Royal Ontario Museum, Toronto)*

d. Doric, Ionic, and Corinthian columns with their characteristic capitals. *(Library of Congress)*

However, the Golden Age of Athens did not last long. Beginning in 431, the Athenians entered into a conflict with the Spartans, their allies in the Persian Wars. At the end of the first year of the Peloponnesian Wars (named for the Peloponnesian Peninsula, southwest of Athens, where Sparta was located), Pericles gave a famous speech at the funeral of the slain Athenians. The speech, reprinted here (as recorded by Thucydides, translated by Richard Crawley) movingly defends Athenian democracy and shows Athenians at their best.

Shortly after this speech, the tide of war turned against the Athenians. Ensconced behind safe walls, the Athenians had hoped to wait out the Spartans. But plague hit the city in 429 B.C. and among its victims was Pericles himself. Without the wise leadership of Pericles, the Athenians made a series of political and military blunders that eventually led to their defeat at the hands of the Spartans in 404 B.C. But before this, during the war, the Athenians had attempted to force all other Greek city-states to join them against the Spartans. In 416 B.C., the Athenians even sent a military delegation to neutral Melos demanding that the Melians submit or be destroyed. The Melians refused the ultimatum and the Athenians responded by killing all the men and selling the women and children as slaves. Thucydides' unwaveringly honest description of the Melian conference (given here complete) shows a side of the Athenians not visible in Pericles' oration and helps to explain why and how these democrats and lovers of ideas and arts could later execute Socrates.

*   *   *

General histories of this period include Russell Meiggs, *The Athenian Empire* (Oxford: Clarendon Press, 1972); Simon Hornblower, *The Greek World, 479–323 B.C.* (London: Methuen, 1983); Joint Association of Classical Teachers, *The World of Athens: An Introduction to Classical Athenian Culture* (Cambridge: Cambridge University Press, 1984); Charles W. Fornara and Loren J. Samons II, *Athens from Cleisthenes to Pericles* (Berkeley: University of California Press, 1991); J.F. Lazenby, *The Defence of Greece, 490–479 B.C.* (Warminster, England: Aris & Phillips, 1993) and Paul Cartledge, *The Cambridge Illustrated History of Ancient Greece* (Cambridge: Cambridge University Press, 1998). For discussions of the Athenian city-state, see Malcolm F. McGregor, *The Athenians and Their Empire* (Vancouver, BC: University of British Columbia Press, 1987); David Stockton, *The Classical Athenian Democracy* (Oxford: Oxford University Press, 1990); Roger Just, *Women in Athenian Law and Life* (London Routledge, 1991); and Jennifer Tolbert Roberts, *Athens on Trial: The Antidemocratic Tradition in Western Thought* (Princeton: Princeton University Press, 1997). A.R. Burns, *Persia and the Greeks,* 2nd ed. (Stanford, CA: Stanford University Press, 1984) gives a description of the Persian Wars while Donald Kagan, *The Outbreak of the Peloponnesian War* (Ithaca, NY: Cornell University Press, 1969) and G.E.M. de Ste. Croix, *The Origins of the Peloponnesian War* (Ithaca, NY: Cornell University Press, 1972) discuss the Peloponnesian War. For a commentary on Thucydides' history of the Peloponnesian War, see David Cartwright, *A Historical Commentary on Thucydides* (Ann Arbor: University of Michigan Press, 1997).

The classical work, *Twelve Lives,* by Plutarch is a good place to begin a study of Pericles. More recent works include Charles Alexander Robinson, *Athens in the Age of Pericles* (Norman: OK: University of Oklahoma Press, 1959); Rex Warner, *Pericles the Athenian* (Boston: Little, Brown, 1963); and Donald Kagan, *Pericles of Athens and the Birth of Democracy* (New York: Free Press, 1991). For discussions of Thucydides as a historian and as a person, see Francis Macdonald Cornford, *Thucydides Mythistoricus* (London: Routledge, 1965); Peter R. Pouncey, *The Necessities of War: A Study of Thucydides' Pessimism* (New York: Columbia University Press, 1980); Marc Cogan, *The Human Thing: The Speeches and Principles of Thucydides' History* (Chicago: University of Chicago Press, 1981); Simon Hornblower, *Thucydides* (Baltimore: Johns Hopkins University Press, 1987); and Clifford Orwin, *The Humanity of Thucydides* (Princeton: Princeton University Press, 1997). For a discussion of Pericles' Oration, see S. Collins and D. Stauffer, *Empire and the Ends of Politics* (Newburyport, MA: Focus, 1999).

PERICLES' FUNERAL ORATION

BOOK II, CHAPTER 6: THE FUNERAL ORATION OF PERICLES

After the bodies have been laid in the earth, a man chosen by the state, of approved wisdom and eminent reputation, pronounces over them an appropriate panegyric; after which all retire. Such is the manner of the burying; and throughout the whole of the war, whenever the occasion arose, the established custom was observed. Meanwhile these were the first that had fallen, and Pericles, son of Xanthippus, was chosen to pronounce their eulogium. When the proper time arrived, he advanced from the sepulchre to an elevated platform in order to be heard by as many of the crowd as possible, and spoke as follows:

FUNERAL ORATION

Most of my predecessors in this place have commended him who made this speech part of the law, telling us that it is well that it should be delivered at the burial of those who fall in battle. For myself, I should have thought that the worth which had displayed itself in deeds would be sufficiently rewarded by honours also shown by deeds; such as you now see in this funeral prepared at the people's cost. And I could have wished that the reputations of many brave men were not to be imperilled in the mouth of a single individual, to stand or fall according as he spoke well or ill. For it is hard to speak properly upon a subject where it is even difficult to convince your hearers that you are speaking the truth. On the one hand, the friend who is familiar with every fact of the story may think that some point has not been set forth with that fullness which he wishes and knows it to deserve; on the other, he who is a stranger to the matter may be led by envy to suspect exaggeration if he hears anything above his own nature. For men can endure to hear others praised only so long as they can severally persuade themselves of their own ability to equal the actions recounted: when this point is passed, envy comes in and with it incredulity. However, since our ancestors have stamped this custom with their approval, it becomes my duty to obey the law and to try to satisfy your several wishes and opinions as best I may.

I shall begin with our ancestors: it is both just and proper that they should have the honour of the first mention on an occasion like the present. They dwelt in the country without break in the succession from generation to generation, and handed it down free to the present time by their valour. And if our more remote ancestors deserve praise, much more do our own fathers, who added to their inheritance the empire which we now possess, and spared no pains to be able to leave their acquisitions to us of the present generation. Lastly, there are few parts of our dominions that have not been augmented by those of us here, who are still more or less in the vigour of life; while the mother country has been furnished by us with everything that can enable her to depend on her own resources whether for war or for peace. That part of our history which tells

Thucydides, *The Peloponnesian War,* translated by Richard Crawley.

of the military achievements which gave us our several possessions, or of the ready valour with which either we or our fathers stemmed the tide of Hellenic or foreign aggression, is a theme too familiar to my hearers for me to dilate on, and I shall therefore pass it by. But what was the road by which we reached our position, what the form of government under which our greatness grew, what the national habits out of which it sprang; these are questions which I may try to solve before I proceed to my panegyric upon these men; since I think this to be a subject upon which on the present occasion a speaker may properly dwell, and to which the whole assemblage, whether citizens or foreigners, may listen with advantage.

Our constitution does not copy the laws of neighbouring states; we are rather a pattern to others than imitators ourselves. Its administration favours the many instead of the few; this is why it is called a democracy. If we look to the laws, they afford equal justice to all in their private differences; if no social standing, advancement in public life falls to reputation for capacity, class considerations not being allowed to interfere with merit; nor again does poverty bar the way, if a man is able to serve the state, he is not hindered by the obscurity of his condition. The freedom which we enjoy in our government extends also to our ordinary life. There, far from exercising a jealous surveillance over each other, we do not feel called upon to be angry with our neighbour for doing what he likes, or even to indulge in those injurious looks which cannot fail to be offensive, although they inflict no positive penalty. But all this case in our private relations does not make us lawless as citizens. Against this fear is our chief safeguard, teaching us to obey the magistrates and the laws, particularly such as regard the protection of the injured, whether they are actually on the statute book, or belong to that code which, although unwritten, yet cannot be broken without acknowledged disgrace.

Further, we provide plenty of means for the mind to refresh itself from business. We celebrate games and sacrifices all the year round, and the elegance of our private establishments forms a daily source of pleasure and helps to banish the spleen; while the magnitude of our city draws the produce of the world into our harbour, so that to the Athenian the fruits of other countries are as familiar a luxury as those of his own.

If we turn to our military policy, there also we differ from our antagonists. We throw open our city to the world, and never by alien acts exclude foreigners from any opportunity of learning or observing, although the eyes of an enemy may occasionally profit by our liberality; trusting less in system and policy than to the native spirit of our citizens; while in education, where our rivals from their very cradles by a painful discipline seek after manliness, at Athens we live exactly as we please, and yet are just as ready to encounter every legitimate danger. In proof of this it may be noticed that the Lacedaemonians do not invade our country alone, but bring with them all their confederates; while we Athenians advance unsupported into the territory of a neighbour, and fighting upon a foreign soil usually vanquish with ease men who are defending their homes. Our united force was never yet encountered by any enemy, because we have at once to attend to our marine and to dispatch our citizens by land upon a hundred different services; so that, wherever they engage with some such fraction of our strength, a success against a detachment is magnified into a victory over the nation, and a defeat into a reverse suffered at the hands of our entire people. And yet if with habits not of labour but of ease, and courage not of art but of nature, we are still willing to encounter danger, we have the double advantage of escaping the experience of hardships in anticipation and of facing them in the hour of need as fearlessly as those who are never free from them.

Nor are these the only points in which our city is worthy of admiration. We cultivate refinement without extravagance and knowledge without effeminacy; wealth we employ more for use than for show, and place the real disgrace of poverty not in owning to the fact but in declining the struggle against it. Our public men have, besides politics, their private affairs to attend to, and our ordinary citizens, though occupied with the pursuits of industry, are still fair judges of public matters; for, unlike any other nation, regarding him who takes no part in these duties not as unambitious but as useless, we Athenians are able to judge at all events if we cannot originate, and, instead of looking on discussion as a stumbling-block in the way of action, we think it an indispensable preliminary to any wise action at all. Again, in our enterprises we present the singular spectacle of daring and deliberation, each carried to its highest point, and both united in the same persons; although usually decision is the fruit of ignorance, hesitation of reflection. But the palm of courage will surely be adjudged most justly to those, who best know the difference between hardship and pleasure and yet are never tempted to shrink from danger. In generosity we are equally singular, acquiring our friends by conferring, not by receiving, favours. Yet, of course, the doer of the favour is the firmer friend of the two, in order by continued kindness to keep the recipient in his debt; while the debtor feels less keenly from the very consciousness that the return he makes will be a payment, not a free gift. And it is only the Athenians, who, fearless of consequences, confer their benefits not from calculations of expediency, but in the confidence of liberality.

In short, I say that as a city we are the school of Hellas; while I doubt if the world can produce a man who, where he has only himself to depend upon, is equal to so many emergencies, and graced by so happy a versatility, as the Athenian. And that this is no mere boast thrown out for the occasion, but plain matter of fact, the power of the state acquired by these habits proves. For Athens alone of her contemporaries is found when tested to be greater than her reputation, and alone gives no occasion to her assailants to blush at the antagonist by whom they have been worsted, or to her subjects to question her title by merit to rule. Rather, the admiration of the present and succeeding ages will be ours, since we have not left our power without witness, but have shown it by mighty proofs; and far from needing a Homer for our panegyrist, or other of his craft whose verses might charm for the moment only for the impression which they gave to melt at the touch of fact, we have forced every sea and land to be the highway of our daring, and everywhere, whether for evil or for good, have left imperishable monuments behind us. Such is the Athens for which these men, in the assertion of their resolve not to lose her, nobly fought and died; and well may every one of their survivors be ready to suffer in her cause.

Indeed if I have dwelt at some length upon the character of our country, it has been to show that our stake in the struggle is not the same as theirs who have no such blessings to lose, and also that the panegyric of the men over whom I am now speaking might be by definite proofs established. That panegyric is now in a great measure complete; for the Athens that I have celebrated is only what the heroism of these and their like have made her, men whose fame, unlike that of most Hellenes, will be found to be only commensurate with their deserts. And if a test of worth be wanted, it is to be found in their closing scene, and this not only in the cases in which it set the final seal upon their merit, but also in those in which it gave the first intimation of their having any. For there is justice in the claim that steadfastness in his country's battles should be as a cloak to cover a man's other imperfections; since the good action has blotted out the bad, and his merit as a citizen more than outweighed his demerits as an individual. But none of these allowed either wealth with its prospect of future enjoyment to unnerve his spirit, or poverty with its hope of a day of freedom and riches to tempt him to shrink from danger. No, holding that vengeance upon their enemies was more to be desired than any personal blessings, and reckoning this to be the most glorious of hazards, they joyfully determined to accept the risk, to make sure of their vengeance, and to let their wishes wait; and while committing to hope the uncertainty of final success, in the business before them they thought fit to act boldly and trust in themselves. Thus choosing to die resisting, rather than to live submitting, they fled only from dishonour, but met danger face to face, and after one brief moment, while at the summit of their fortune, escaped, not from their fear, but from their glory.

So died these men as became Athenians. You, their survivors, must determine to have as unfaltering a resolution in the field, though you may pray that it may have a happier issue. And not contented with ideas derived only from words of the advantages which are bound up with the defence of your country, though these would furnish a valuable text to a speaker even before an audience so alive to them as the present, you must yourselves realize the power of Athens, and feed your eyes upon her from day to day, till love of her fills your hearts; and then, when all her greatness shall break upon you, you must reflect that it was by courage, sense of duty, and a keen feeling of honour in action that men were enabled to win all this, and that no personal failure in an enterprise could make them consent to deprive their country of their valour, but they laid it at her feet as the most glorious contribution that they could offer. For this offering of their lives made in common by them all they each of them individually received that renown which never grows old, and for a sepulchre, not so much that in which their bones have been deposited, but that noblest of shrines wherein their glory is laid up to be eternally remembered upon every occasion on which deed or story shall call for its commemoration. For heroes have the whole earth for their tomb; and in lands far from their own, where the column with its epitaph declares it, there is enshrined in every breast a record unwritten with no tablet to preserve it, except that of the heart. These take as your model and, judging happiness to be the fruit of freedom and freedom of valour, never decline the dangers of war. For it is not the miserable that would most justly be unsparing of their lives; these have nothing to hope for: it is rather they to whom continued life may bring reverses as yet unknown, and to whom a fall, if it came, would be most tremendous in its consequences. And surely, to a man of spirit, the degradation of cowardice must be immeasurably more grievous than the unfelt death which strikes him in the midst of his strength and patriotism!

Comfort, therefore, not condolence, is what I have to offer to the parents of the dead who may be here. Numberless are the chances to which, as they know, the life of man is subject; but fortunate indeed are they who draw for their lot a death so glorious as that which has caused your mourning, and to whom life has been so exactly measured as to terminate in the happiness in which it has been passed. Still I know that this is a hard saying, especially when those are in question of whom you will constantly be reminded by seeing in the homes of others blessings of which once you also boasted: for grief is felt not so much for the want of what we have never known, as for the loss of that to which we have been long accustomed. Yet you who are still of an age to beget children must bear up in the hope of having others in their stead; not only will they help you to forget those whom you have lost, but will be to the state at once a reinforcement and a security; for never can a fair or just policy be expected of the citizen who does not, like his fellows, bring to the decision the interests and apprehensions of a father. While those of you who have passed your prime must congratulate yourselves with the thought that the best part of your life was fortunate, and that the brief span that remains will be cheered by the fame of the departed. For it is only the love of honour that never grows old; and honour it is, not gain, as some would have it, that rejoices the heart of age and helplessness.

Turning to the sons or brothers of the dead, I see an arduous struggle before you. When a man is gone, all are wont to praise him, and should your merit be ever so transcendent, you will still find it difficult not merely to overtake, but even to approach their renown. The living have envy to contend with, while those who are no longer in our path are honoured with a goodwill into which rivalry does not enter. On the other hand, if I must say anything on the subject of female excellence to those of you who will now be in widowhood, it will be all comprised in this brief exhortation. Great will be your glory in not falling short of your natural character; and greatest will be hers who is least talked of among the men, whether for good or for bad.

My task is now finished. I have performed it to the best of my ability, and in word, at least, the requirements of the law are now satisfied. If deeds be in question, those who are here interred have received part of their honours already, and for the rest, their children will be brought up till manhood at the public expense: the state thus offers a valuable prize, as the garland of victory in this race of valour, for the reward both of those who have fallen and their survivors. And where the rewards for merit are greatest, there are found the best citizens.

And now that you have brought to a close your lamentations for your relatives, you may depart.

THE MELIAN CONFERENCE

BOOK V, CHAPTER 17: THE ATHENIAN DESTRUCTION OF MELOS

The next summer Alcibiades sailed with twenty ships to Argos and seized the suspected persons still left of the Lacedæmonian [Spartan] faction to the number of three hundred, whom the Athenians forthwith lodged in the neighboring islands of their empire. The Athenians also made an expedition against the isle of Melos with thirty ships of their own, six Chian, and two Lesbian vessels, sixteen hundred heavy infantry, three hundred archers, and twenty mounted archers from Athens, and about fifteen hundred heavy infantry from the allies and the islanders. The Melians are a colony of Lacedæmonian that would not submit to the Athenians like the other islanders, and at first remained neutral and took no part in the struggle, but afterwards upon the Athenians using violence and plundering their territory, assumed an attitude of open hostility. Cleomedes son of Lycomedes, and Tisias, son of Tisimachus, the generals, encamping in their territory with the above armament, before doing any harm to their land, sent envoys to negotiate. These the Melians did not bring before the people, but bade them state the object of their mission to the magistrates and the few; upon which the Athenian envoys spoke as follows:

ATHENIANS: Since the negotiations are not to go on before the people, in order that we may not be able to speak straight on without interruption, and deceive the ears of the multitude by seductive arguments which would pass without refutation (for we know that this is the meaning of our being brought before the few), what if you who sit there

Thucydides, *The Peloponnesian War*, translated by Richard Crawley.

were to pursue a method more cautious still? Make no set speech yourselves, but take us up at whatever you do not like, and settle that before going any farther. And first tell us if this proposition of ours suits you.

The Melian commissioners answered:

MELIANS: To the fairness of quietly instructing each other as you propose there is nothing to object; but your military preparations are too far advanced to agree with what you say, as we see you are come to be judges in your own cause, and that all we can reasonably expect from this negotiation is war, if we prove to have right on our side and refuse to submit, and in the contrary case, slavery.

ATHENIANS: If you have met to reason about presentiments of the future, or for anything else than to consult for the safety of your state upon the facts that you see before you, we will give over; otherwise we will go on.

MELIANS: It is natural and excusable for men in our position to turn more ways than one both in thought and utterance. However, the question in this conference is, as you say, the safety of our country; and the discussion, if you please, can proceed in the way which you propose.

ATHENIANS: For ourselves, we shall not trouble you with specious pretences—either of how we have a right to our empire because we overthrew the Mede, or are now attacking you because of wrong that you have done us—and make a long speech which would not be believed; and in return we hope that you, instead of thinking to influence us by saying that you did not join the Lacedæmonianians, although their colonists, or that you have done us no wrong, will aim at what is feasible, holding in view the real sentiments of us both; since you know as well as we do that right, as the world goes, is only in question between equals in power, while the strong do what they can and the weak suffer what they must.

MELIANS: As we think, at any rate, it is expedient—we speak as we are obliged, since you enjoin us to let right alone and talk only of interest—that you should not destroy what is our common protection, the privilege of being allowed in danger to invoke what is fair and right, and even to profit by arguments not strictly valid if they can be got to pass current. And you are as much interested in this as any, as your fall would be a signal for the heaviest vengeance and an example for the world to meditate upon.

ATHENIANS: The end of our empire, if end it should, does not frighten us: a rival empire like Lacedæmonian, even if Lacedæmonian was our real antagonist, is not so terrible to the vanquished as subjects who by themselves attack and overpower their rulers. This, however, is a risk that we are content to take. We will now proceed to show you that we are come here in the interest of our empire, and that we shall say what we are now going to say, for the preservation of your country; as we would fain exercise that empire over you without trouble, and see you preserved for the good of us both.

MELIANS: And how, pray, could it turn out as good for us to serve as for you to rule?

ATHENIANS: Because you would have the advantage of submitting before suffering the worst, and we should gain by not destroying you.

MELIANS: So that you would not consent to our being neutral, friends instead of enemies, but allies of neither side.

ATHENIANS: No; for your hostility cannot so much hurt us as your friendship will be an argument to our subjects of our weakness, and your enmity of our power.

MELIANS: Is that your subjects' idea of equity, to put those who have nothing to do with you in the same category with peoples that are most of them your own colonists, and some conquered rebels?

ATHENIANS: As far as right goes they think one has as much of it as the other, and that if any maintain their independence it is because they are strong, and that if we do not molest them it is because we are afraid; so that besides extending our empire we should gain in security by your subjection; the fact that you are islanders and weaker than others rendering it all the more important that you should not succeed in baffling the masters of the sea.

MELIANS: But do you consider that there is no security in the policy which we indicate? For here again if you debar us from talking about justice and invite us to obey your interest, we also must explain ours, and try to persuade you, if the two happen to coincide. How can you avoid making enemies of all existing neutrals who shall look at our case and conclude from it that one day or another you will attack them? And what is this but to make greater the enemies that you have already, and to force others to become so who would otherwise have never thought of it?

ATHENIANS: Why, the fact is that continentals generally give us but little alarm; the liberty which they enjoy will long prevent their taking precautions against us; it is rather islanders like yourselves, outside our empire, and subjects smarting under the yoke, who would be the most likely to take a rash step and lead themselves and us into obvious danger.

MELIANS: Well then, if you risk so much to retain your empire, and your subjects to get rid of it, it were surely great baseness and cowardice in us who are still free not to try everything that can be tried, before submitting to your yoke.

ATHENIANS: Not if you are well advised, the contest not being an equal one, with honour as the prize and shame as the penalty, but a question of self-preservation and of not resisting those who are far stronger than you are.

MELIANS: But we know that the fortune of war is sometimes more impartial than the disproportion of numbers might lead one to suppose; to submit is to give ourselves over to despair, while action still preserves for us a hope that we may stand erect.

ATHENIANS: Hope, danger's comforter, may be indulged in by those who have abundant resources, if not without loss at all events without ruin; but its nature is to be extravagant, and those who go so far as to put their all upon the venture see it in its true colours only when they are ruined; but so long as the discovery would enable them to guard against it, it is never found wanting. Let not this be the case with you, who are weak and hang on a single turn of the scale; nor be like the vulgar, who, abandoning such security as human means may still afford, when visible hopes fail them in extremity, turn to invisible, to prophecies and oracles, and other such inventions that delude men with hopes to their destruction.

MELIANS: You may be sure that we are as well aware as you of the difficulty of contending against your power and fortune, unless the terms be equal. But we trust that the gods may grant us fortune as good as yours, since we are just men fighting against unjust, and that what we want in power will be made up by the alliance of the Lacedæmonianians, who are bound, if only for very shame, to come to the aid of their kindred. Our confidence, therefore, after all is not so utterly irrational.

ATHENIANS: When you speak of the favour of the gods, we may as fairly hope for that as yourselves; neither our pretensions nor our conduct being in any way contrary to what men believe of the gods, or practise among themselves. Of the gods we believe, and of men we know, that by a necessary law of their nature they rule wherever they can. And it is not as if we were the first to make this law, or to act upon it when made: we found it existing before us, and shall leave it to exist for ever after us; all we do is to make use of it, knowing that you and everybody else, having the same power as we have, would do the same as we do. Thus, as far as the gods are concerned, we have no fear and no reason to fear that we shall be at a disadvantage. But when we come to your notion about the Lacedæmonianians, which leads you to believe that shame will make them help you, here we bless your simplicity but do not envy your folly. The Lacedæmonian, when their own interests or their country's laws are in question, are the worthiest men alive; of their conduct towards others much might be said, but no clearer idea of it could be given than by shortly saying that of all the men we know they are most conspicuous in considering what is agreeable honourable, and what is expedient just. Such a way of thinking does not promise much for the safety which you now unreasonably count upon.

MELIANS: But it is for this very reason that we now trust to their respect for expediency to prevent them from betraying the Melians, their colonists, and thereby losing the confidence of their friends in Hellas and helping their enemies.

ATHENIANS: Then you do not adopt the view that expediency goes with security, while justice and honour cannot be followed without danger; and danger the Lacedæmonianians generally court as little as possible.

MELIANS: But we believe that they would be more likely to face even danger for our sake, and with more confidence than for others, as our nearness to Peloponnese makes it easier for them to act, and our common blood insures our fidelity.

ATHENIANS: Yes, but what an intending ally trusts to, is not the goodwill of those who ask his aid, but a decided superiority of power for action; and the Lacedæmonianians look to this even more than others. At least, such is their distrust of their home resources that it is only with numerous allies that they attack a neighbour; now is it likely that while we are masters of the sea they will cross over to an island?

MELIANS: But they would have others to send. The Cretan sea is a wide one, and it is more difficult for those who command it to intercept others, than for those who wish to elude them to do so safely. And should the Lacedæmonianians miscarry in this, they would fall upon your land, and upon those left of your allies whom Brasidas did not reach; and instead of places which are not yours, you will have to fight for your own country and your own confederacy.

ATHENIANS: Some diversion of the kind you speak of you may one day experience, only to learn as others have done, that the Athenians never once yet withdrew from a siege for fear of any. But we are struck by the fact, that after saying you would consult for the safety of your country, in all this discussion you have mentioned nothing which men might trust in and think to be saved by. Your strongest arguments depend upon hope and the future, and your actual resources are too scanty, as compared with those arrayed against you, for you to come out victorious. You will therefore show great blindness of judgment, unless, after allowing us to retire, you can find some counsel more prudent than this. You will surely not be caught by that idea of disgrace, which in dangers that are disgraceful, and at the same time too plain to be mistaken, proves so fatal to mankind; since in too many cases the very men that have their eyes perfectly open to what they are rushing into, let the thing called disgrace, by the mere influence of a seductive name, lead them on to a point at which they become so enslaved by the phrase as in fact to fall wilfully into hopeless disaster, and incur disgrace more disgraceful as the companion of error, than when it comes as the result of misfortune. This, if you are well advised, you will guard against; and you will not think it dishonourable to submit to the greatest city in Hellas, when it makes you the moderate offer of becoming its tributary ally, without ceasing to enjoy the country that belongs to you; nor when you have the choice given you between war and security, will you be so blinded as to choose the worse. And it is certain that those who do not yield to their equals, who keep terms with their superiors, and are moderate towards their inferiors, on the whole succeed best. Think over the matter, therefore, after our withdrawal, and reflect once and again that it is for your country that you are consulting, that you have not more than one, and that upon this one deliberation depends its prosperity or ruin.

The Athenians now withdrew from the conference; and the Melians, left to themselves, came to a decision corresponding with what they had maintained in the discussion, and answered, "Our resolution, Athenians, is the same as it was at first. We will not in a moment deprive of freedom a city that has been inhabited these seven hundred years; but we put our trust in the fortune by which the gods have preserved it until now, and in the help of men that is, of the Lacedæmonianians; and so we will try and save ourselves. Meanwhile we invite you to allow us to be friends to you and foes to neither party, and to retire from our country after making such a treaty as shall seem fair to us both."

Such was the answer of the Melians. The Athenians now departing from the conference said, "Well, you alone, as it seems to us, judging from these resolutions, regard what is future as more certain than what is before your eyes, and what is out of sight, in your eagerness, as already coming to pass; and as you have staked most on, and trusted most in, the Lacedæmonianians, your fortune, and your hopes, so will you be most completely deceived."

The Athenian envoys now returned to the army; and the Melians showing no signs of yielding, the generals at once betook themselves to hostilities, and drew a line of circumvallation round the Melians, dividing the work among the different states. Subsequently the Athenians returned with most of their army, leaving behind them a certain number of their own citizens and of the allies to keep guard by land and sea. The force thus left stayed on and besieged the place.

About the same time the Argives invaded the territory of Phlius and lost eighty men cut off in an ambush by the Phliasians and Argive exiles. Meanwhile the Athenians at Pylos took so much plunder from the Lacedæmonianians that the latter, although they still refrained from breaking off the treaty and going to war with Athens, yet proclaimed that any of their people that chose might plunder the Athenians. The Corinthians also commenced hostilities with the Athenians for private quarrels of their own; but the rest of the Peloponnesians stayed quiet. Meanwhile the Melians attacked by night and took the part of the Athenian lines over against the market, and killed some of the men, and brought in corn and all else that they could find useful to them, and so returned and kept quiet, while the Athenians took measures to keep better guard in future.

Summer was now over. The next winter the Lacedæmonianians intended to invade the Argive territory, but arriving at the frontier found the sacrifices for crossing unfavourable, and went back again. This intention of theirs gave the Argives suspicions of certain of their fellow-citizens, some of whom they arrested; others, however, escaped them. About the same time the Melians again took another part of the Athenian lines which were but feebly garrisoned. Reinforcements afterwards arriving from Athens in consequence, under the command of Philocrates, son of Demeas, the siege was now pressed vigorously; and some treachery taking place inside, the Melians surrendered at discretion to the Athenians, who put to death all the grown men whom they took, and sold the women and children for slaves, and subsequently sent out five hundred colonists and inhabited the place themselves.

Epilogue II: Aspasia

ASPASIA
fl. ca. 430 B.C.

A thoughtful reader of ancient philosophy will ask: Where are the women? Why are women's voices missing in the "canon" of Western philosophy. The case of Aspasia helps answer that question and sheds some light on the culture of ancient Athens in general and the role of women in particular.

The details of Aspasia's life are sketchy at best and can only be culled from sources that may not be entirely reliable. So far as we know, Aspasia was born in Miletus, sometime between 470 and 460 B.C. Apparently, she was educated in music and conversation as a *hetaira,* a high-class paid companion. In fact, the name "Aspasia" means "greeting with affection" or "welcome" and may have been a "professional" name. As a *hetaira,* Aspasia was allowed to interact with men more freely than most Athenian women. While outside the home a wife would rarely engage in conversation with a man, Aspasia interacted with important men. At some point around 445 B.C., the leader Pericles fell in love with Aspasia. Her background as a Milesian made it impossible for them to marry, and so she became his companion and bore him a son (also named Pericles). Following Pericles' death in 429 B.C., Aspasia apparently became the companion to an uneducated sheep merchant, Lysicles, and helped him become a political leader in Athens. Following this, we have no information about her life.

Much has been made of Aspasia's connection with Pericles. In his *Lives,* Plutarch blames Aspasia for convincing Pericles to start a war (see fragment 2 following) and tells how Pericles saved Aspasia when she was on trial (fragment 3). Aristophanes spoke disdainfully of Aspasia's companions as "Aspasia's whores." But Aspasia was more than Pericles' mistress. She apparently engaged in political discussions with Pericles and his colleagues. According to several sources,

Apasia Receives the Most Illustrious Men of Athens (Aspasie s'entretenant avec les hommes les plus illustres d' Athènes), 1806, by Nicolas-Andre Monsiau (1755–1837). As a "hetaira," or high-class paid companion, Aspasia was allowed to interact with men more freely than most Athenian women. She apparently engaged in political discussions with Pericles and other notable Athenian men (as depicted in this romantic painting). (*Musée des Beaux-Arts, Chambery, France. ©Reunion des Musées Nationaux/Art Resource, N.Y.*)

Socrates called on her wisdom (see, for example, fragments 4–6) and Plato used Aspasia as a character in his dialogue *Menexenus*. There have even been claims that Aspasia was in some sense Socrates' teacher and that she was the ghost writer for some of Pericles' speeches—such as the Funeral Oration given above.

The problems for those who would understand Aspasia and assess her ideas and influence are that those who mentioned her always had a definite bias and there are no surviving copies of what she herself said. Plutarch seems intent on praising Pericles and blaming Aspasia for Pericles' mistakes. Plato uses the character of "Aspasia" to criticize rhetoric. Cratinus, Eupolis, and Aristophanes all mock Aspasia in their comedies. Apparently, Socrates' follower, Aeschines of Sphettos, wrote a dialogue that put Aspasia in a more positive light, but only a few fragments survive. Aspasia was important enough to be frequently mentioned but was apparently not valued enough to be accurately recorded. With such a lack of reliable information, people over the centuries have understood Aspasia however they wanted. As Madeleine Henry says in her book on Aspasia,

> When we need Aspasia to be a chaste muse and teacher, she is there; when we need a grand horizontal, she is there; when we need a protofeminist, she is there also. Recent essays refigure Aspasia in the history of rhetoric and the sophistic movement.
>
> Her status as the only female from classical Greece to have enjoyed a substantial *bios* has overloaded the mortal historical actor with a burden she is unable to bear. Because we continue to define classical Athens as a time and place of immense

importance in world civilization and because we cannot help but continue to redefine classical Athens in our own image, we continue to redefine Aspasia.*

The best source for the study of Aspasia is Madeline Henry, *Prisoner of
History: Aspasia of Miletus and Her Biographical Tradition* (Oxford: Oxford
University Press, 1995). Information about Aspasia can also be found in Mary
Ellen Waithe, *A History of Women Philosophers, Volume I: Ancient Women
Philosophers, 600 B.C.–500 A.D.* (Dordrecht, Netherlands: Kluwer Academic
Publishers, 1987). For the role of women in ancient Greece and Rome, see J.B.
Bury and Russell Meiggs, *A History of Greece* (New York: St. Martin's, 1975);
Sarah Pomeroy, *Goddesses, Whores, Wives, and Slaves* (New York: Schocken,
1975); Eva Cantarella, *Pandora's Daughters* (Baltimore: Johns Hopkins
University Press, 1981); Eva Keuls, *The Reign of the Phallus* (New York: Harper
& Row, 1985); and Elaine Fantham et al., *Women in the Classical World: Image
and Text* (Oxford: Oxford University Press, 1994). For a source book of topically
arranged translations of ancient texts related to women, see Mary R. Lefkowitz
and Maureen B. Fant, *Women's Life in Greece and Rome* (Baltimore: Johns
Hopkins University Press, 1982). For a collection of essays, see Pauline Schmitt
Pantel, ed., *A History of Women in the West, Volume I: From Ancient Goddesses to
Christian Saints* (Cambridge, MA: Harvard University Press, 1992).

*   *   *

[1] Aspasia, some say, was courted and caressed by Pericles because of her
knowledge and skill in politics. Socrates himself would sometimes go to visit her, and
some of his acquaintance with him; and those who frequented her company would carry
their wives with them to listen to her. Her occupation was anything but creditable, her
house being a home for young courtesans. Eschines tells us, also, that Lysicles, a sheep-
dealer, a man of low birth and character, by keeping Aspasia company after Pericles'
death, came to be a chief man in Athens. And in Plato's *Menexenus,* though we do not
take the introduction as quite serious, still this much seems to be historical: that she had
the repute of being resorted to by many of the Athenians for instruction in the art of
speaking. Pericles' inclination for her seems, however, to have rather proceeded from
the passion of love . . . He loved her with wonderful affection; every day, both as he
went out and as he came in from the market place, he saluted and kissed her.**

[2] Pericles was charged with having proposed to the assembly the war against
the Samians at the request of Aspasia as a favor to the Milesians. For the two states were
at war for the possession of Priene. The Samians, getting the better [of the fight],
refused to lay down their arms and to have the controversy between them decided by
arbitration before the Athenians. Pericles, therefore, fitting out a fleet, went and broke
up the oligarchical government at Samos. And taking fifty of the principal men of the
town as hostages, and as many of their children, [Pericles] sent them to be kept on the
isle of Lemnos. Some say each one of the hostages offered [Pericles] a talent apiece for
himself, and that those who were anxious not to have a democracy offered many other
presents. Moreover, Pisuthnes the Persian, one of the king's lieutenants, bearing some

---

*Madeline Henry, *Prisoner of History: Aspasia of Miletus and Her Biographical Tradition* (Oxford:
Oxford University Press, 1995), p. 128.

**Plutarch, *Lives,* Pericles [Dryden translation, with my modifications].

goodwill to the Samians, sent [Pericles] ten thousand pieces of gold to excuse the city. Pericles, however, would receive none of these. Instead he followed the course with the Samians which he thought fit and set up a democracy among them and then sailed back to Athens.*

[3] About the same time, Aspasia was indicted for impiety, based on a charge from Hermippus, the comic poet, who also alleged that she received into her house free-born women for the uses of Pericles . . . At the trial, according to Aeschines, Pericles shed many tears, personally pleading to the jurors, and begged off Aspasia.**

[4] Socrates: "I will introduce Aspasia to you, and she will explain the whole matter to you with more knowledge than I possess. I think that the wife who is a good partner in the household contributes just as much as her husband to its good; because the incomings for the most part are the result of the husband's exertions, but the outgoings are controlled mostly by the wife's dispensation. If both do their part well, the estate is increased; if they act incompetently, it is diminished. If you think you want to know about other branches of knowledge, I fancy I can show you people who acquit themselves creditably in any one of them."***

[5] Socrates: "[Aspasia] said that good matchmakers were shrewd in arranging marriages for men if they reported good qualities truthfully and refused to praise men falsely; for the deceived parties hate each other and the matchmaker as well. I am convinced that this is correct and I believe I cannot say anything in praise of you without verifying it first."†

[6] . . . In Aeschines of Sphettos' dialogue, Socrates shows that Aspasia spoke with Xenophon's wife and Xenophon himself:

"Tell me, please, wife of Xenophon, if your neighbour had a better piece of gold jewelry than you, would you prefer hers or your own?"

"Hers," said the wife.

"So—if she should have a dress or other feminine ornament more expensive than you have, would you prefer hers or yours?"

"Hers, naturally," said the wife.

"So now: what if that woman had a better husband than you? Would you prefer hers or your own?"

Here the woman blushed. Aspasia, however, began to interrogate Xenophon himself.††

*Ibid.
**Ibid.
***Xenophon, *Works on Socrates, Economics,* translated by E.C. Marchant (Cambridge, MA: Harvard University Press, 1923), Book III, Line 14.
†Xenophon, *Recollections of Socrates,* translated by Anna S. Benjamin (New York: Macmillan, 1965), Book II, Chapter 6, Line 36.
††Fragment 31 of Aeschines' *Aspasia* preserved in Cicero's *de Inventione Rhetorica 1.31.51ff,* from Madeleine M. Henry, *op.cit.,* p. 44.

SOCRATES
470–399 B.C.
PLATO
428/7–348/7 B.C.

Socrates has fascinated and inspired men and women for over two thousand years. All five of the major "schools" of ancient Greece (Academics, Peripatetics, Epicureans, Stoics, and Cynics) were influenced by his thought. Some of the early Christian thinkers, such as Justin Martyr, considered him a "proto-Christian," while others, such as St. Augustine (who rejected this view) still expressed deep admiration for Socrates' ethical life. More recently, existentialists have found in Socrates' admonition "know thyself" an encapsulation of their thought, and opponents of unjust laws have seen in Socrates' trial a blueprint for civil disobedience. In short, Socrates is one of the most admired men who ever lived.

The Athens into which Socrates was born in 470 B.C. was a city still living in the flush of its epic victory over the Persians, and it was bursting with new ideas. The playwrights Euripides and Sophocles were young boys, and Pericles, the great Athenian democrat, was still a young man. The Parthenon's foundation was laid when Socrates was twenty-two, and its construction was completed fifteen years later.

Socrates was the son of Sophroniscus, a sculptor, and of Phaenarete, a midwife. As a boy, Socrates received a classical Greek education in music, gymnastics, and grammar (or the study of language), and he decided early on to become a sculptor like his father. Tradition says he was a gifted artist who fashioned impressively simple statues of the Graces. He married a woman named Xanthippe, and together they had three children. He took an early interest in the developing science of the Milesians, and then he served for a time in the army.

When he was a middle-aged man, Socrates' friend, Chaerephon, asked the oracle at Delphi "if there was anyone who was wiser than Socrates." For once the mysterious oracle gave an unambiguous answer: "No one." When Socrates heard of the incident, he was confused. He knew that he was not a wise man. So he set out to find a wiser man to prove the answer wrong. Socrates later described the method and results of his mission:

> So I examined the man—I need not tell you his name, he was a politician—but this was the result. Athenians. When I conversed with him I came to see that, though a great many persons, and most of all he himself, thought that he was wise, yet he was not wise. Then I tried to prove to him that he was not wise, though he fancied that he was. By so doing I made him indignant, and many of the bystanders. So when I went away, I thought to myself, "I am wiser than this man: neither of us knows anything that is really worth knowing, but he thinks that he has knowledge when he has not, while I, having no knowledge, do not think that I have. I seem, at any rate, to be a little wiser than he is on this point: I do not think that I know what I do not know." Next I went to another man who was reputed to be still wiser than the last, with exactly the same result. And there again I made him, and many other men, indignant. (*Apology* 21c)

As Socrates continued his mission by interviewing the politicians, poets, and artisans of Athens, young men followed along. They enjoyed seeing the authority figures humiliated by Socrates' intense questioning. Those in authority, however, were not amused. Athens was no longer the powerful, self-confident city of 470 B.C., the year of Socrates' birth. An exhausting succession of wars with Sparta (the Peloponnesian Wars) and an enervating series of political debacles had left the city narrow in vision and suspicious of new ideas and of dissent. In 399 B.C., Meletus and Anytus brought an indictment of impiety and corrupting the youth against Socrates. As recorded in the *Apology,* the Athenian assembly found him guilty by a vote of 281 to 220 and sentenced him to death. His noble death is described incomparably in the closing pages of the *Phaedo* by Plato.

Socrates wrote nothing, and our knowledge of his thought comes exclusively from the report of others. The playwright Aristophanes (455–375 B.C.) satirized Socrates in his comedy *The Clouds.* His caricature of Socrates as a cheat and charlatan was apparently so damaging that Socrates felt compelled to offer a rebuttal before the Athenian assembly (see the *Apology,* following). The military general Xenophon (ca. 430–350 B.C.) honored his friend Socrates in his *Apology of Socrates,* his *Symposium,* and, later, in his *Memorabilia* ("Recollections of Socrates"). In an effort to defend his dead friend's memory, Xenophon's writings illumine Socrates' life and character. Though born fifteen years after the death of Socrates, Aristotle (384–322 B.C.) left many fascinating allusions to Socrates in his philosophic works, as did several later Greek philosophers. But the primary source of our knowledge of Socrates comes from one of those young men who followed him: Plato.

*   *   *

Plato was probably born in 428/7 B.C. He had two older brothers, Adeimantus and Glaucon, who appear in Plato's *Republic,* and a sister, Potone. Though he may have known Socrates since childhood, Plato was probably nearer twenty when he came under the intellectual spell of Socrates. The death of Socrates made an enormous impression on Plato and contributed to his call to bear witness to posterity of "the best, . . . the wisest and most just" person that he knew (*Phaedo,* 118). Though Plato was from a distinguished family and might have followed his relatives into politics, he chose philosophy.

Following Socrates' execution, the twenty-eight-year-old Plato left Athens and traveled for a time. He is reported to have visited Egypt and Cyrene—though some scholars doubt this. During this time he wrote his early dialogues on Socrates' life and teachings. He also visited Italy and Sicily, where he became the friend of Dion, a relative of Dionysius, the tyrant of Syracuse, Sicily.

On returning to Athens from Sicily, Plato founded a school, which came to be called the Academy. One might say it was the world's first university, and it endured as a center of higher learning for nearly one thousand years, until the Roman emperor Justinian closed it in A.D. 529. Except for two later trips to Sicily, where he unsuccessfully sought to institute his political theories, Plato spent the rest of his life at the Athenian Academy. Among his students was Aristotle. Plato died at eighty in 348/7 B.C.

Plato's influence was best described by the twentieth-century philosopher Alfred North Whitehead when he said, "The safest general characterization of the European philosophical tradition is that it consists of a series of footnotes to Plato."

*   *   *

It is difficult to separate the ideas of Plato from those of his teacher, Socrates. In virtually all of Plato's dialogues, Socrates is the main character, and it is possible that in the early dialogues Plato is recording his teacher's actual words. But in the later dialogues, "Socrates" gives Plato's views—views that, in some cases, in fact, the historical Socrates denied.

The first four dialogues presented in this text describe the trial and death of Socrates and are arranged in narrative order. The first, the *Euthyphro,* takes place as Socrates has just learned of the indictment against him. He strikes up a conversation with a "theologian" so sure of his piety that he is prosecuting his own father for murder. The dialogue moves on, unsuccessfully, to define piety. Along the way, Socrates asks a question that has vexed philosophers and theologians for centuries: Is something good because the gods say it is, or do the gods say it is good because it is?

The next dialogue, the *Apology,* is generally regarded as one of Plato's first, and as eminently faithful to what Socrates said at his trial on charges of impiety and corruption of youth. The speech was delivered in public and heard by a large audience; Plato has Socrates mention that Plato was present; and there is no need to doubt the historical veracity of the speech, at least in essentials. There are two breaks in the narrative: one after Socrates' defense (during which the Athenians vote "guilty") and one after Socrates proposes an alternative to the death penalty (during which the Athenians decide on death). This dialogue includes Socrates' famous characterization of his mission and purpose in life.

In the *Crito,* Plato has Crito visit Socrates in prison to assure him that his escape from Athens has been well prepared and to persuade him to consent to leave. Socrates argues that one has an obligation to obey the state even when it orders one to suffer wrong. That Socrates, in fact, refused to leave is certain; that he used the arguments Plato ascribes to him is less certain. In any case, anyone who has read the *Apology* will agree that after his speech Socrates could not well escape.

The moving account of Socrates' death is given at the end of the *Phaedo,* the last of our group of dialogues. There is common agreement that this dialogue was written much later than the other three and that the earlier part of the dialogue, with its Platonic doctrine of Forms and immortality, uses "Socrates" as a vehicle for Plato's own ideas. These ideas owe much to Pythagoreanism, which exerted an ever-increasing influence on Plato's thought. (See the introduction to the Pythagorean selections, pages 00–00.) These first four dialogues are given in the F.J. Church translation.

Like the *Phaedo,* the *Meno, Symposium,* and *Republic* were written during Plato's "middle period," when he had returned from Sicily to Athens and had established the Academy. The *Meno* gives a fine and faithful picture of Socrates practicing the art of dialogue; it also marks the point at which Plato moves beyond his master. This dialogue answers the question, "Can virtue be taught?" and treats the issues of knowledge and belief. The translation is by George Anastaplo and Laurence Berns.

The *Symposium* represents the high point of Plato's literary skill. In this collection of speeches on love, Plato uses several styles of speaking, including some light-hearted banter. The *Symposium* is a work of art and surely makes no claim to historic accuracy, except for Alcibiades' speech on Socrates. As for the rest, we need not believe that Aristophanes, for example, really told the fanciful myth ascribed to him here. (Some commentators see Plato paying Aristophanes back for his earlier ridicule of Socrates.) Our selection includes the key speeches by Aristophanes, Socrates, and Alcibides. While they different dramatically, all three serve to explicate Plato's idea that love is the desire for that which we lack. The translation is by Avi Sharon.

Note that when reading the *Symposium,* a modern reader should keep in mind that among some—but by no means all—Greek intellectuals, homosexuality was not only accepted, it was considered a superior form of love. Since women were rarely educated, it was thought that only with males could a man move beyond "inferior" physical attraction to reach the heights of love.

There are few books in Western civilization that have had the impact of Plato's *Republic*—aside from the Bible, perhaps none. Like the Bible, there are also few books whose interpretation and evaluation have differed so widely. Apparently it is a description of Plato's ideal society: a utopian vision of the just state, possible only if philosophers were kings. But some (see the following suggested readings) claim that its purpose is not to give a model of the ideal state, but to show the impossibility of such a state and to convince aspiring philosophers to shun politics. Evaluations of the *Republic* have also varied widely: from the criticisms of Karl Popper, who denounced the *Republic* as totalitarian, to the admiration of more traditional interpreters, such as Francis MacDonald Cornford and Gregory Vlastos.

Given the importance of this work and the diversity of opinions concerning its point and value, it was extremely difficult to decide which sections of the *Republic* to include in this series. I chose to include the introduction and the discussion of justice from Books I and II, the descriptions of the guardians and of the "noble lie" from Book III, the discussions of the virtues and the soul in Book IV, the presentations of the guardians' qualities and life-styles in Book V, and the key sections on knowledge (including the analogy of the line and the myth of the cave) from the end of Book VI and the beginning of Book VII. I admit that space constraints have forced me to exclude important sections. Ideally, the selections chosen will whet the student's appetite to read the rest of this classic. The translation is by Joe Sachs.

The *Parmenides* marks a move in the development of Plato's thought—from positive philosophy to critical issues. The *Parmenides* is remarkable for the honesty with which Plato attacks the problems with his own doctrine of Forms. The second half is a lengthy and confusing series of "lessons" designed (apparently) to show that "unity is." This part is omitted because it is the most abstruse and difficult work Plato ever wrote. The translation is by Albert Keith Whitaker.

The *Theaetetus* deals with the problem of knowledge and contains an interesting discussion of some of the ideas of Protagoras, the Sophist. Throughout the dialogue, Socrates assumes that knowledge leads to goodness, so a clear understanding of knowledge is vitally important. However, no conclusion about the nature of knowledge is reached—only agreement about what it is *not*. Still, this lack of knowledge about knowledge is nonetheless valuable, Socrates claims, because they have at least learned not to claim knowledge when they do not possess it. The translation is by Joe Sachs.

The brief section from the *Timaeus* presents Plato's account of creation. It is given in the translation by Peter Kalkavage.

Finally, the material from the *Laws,* translated by Benjamin Jowett, introduces what will becme a long series of attempts in Western philosophy to prove the existence of God.

*   *   *

For studies of Socrates, see the classic A.E. Taylor, *Socrates: The Man and His Thought* (London: Methuen, 1933); the second half of Volume III of W.K.C. Guthrie, *The History of Greek Philosophy* (Cambridge: Cambridge University Press, 1969); Hugh H. Benson, *Essays on the Philosophy of Socrates* (Oxford: Oxford University Press, 1992); Anthony Gottlieb, *Socrates* (London: Routledge, 1999); Christopher Taylor's pair of introductions, *Socrates* and *Socrates: A Very Short Introduction* (both Oxford: Oxford University Press, 1999 and 2000); Nalin Ranasingle, *The Soul of Socrates* (Ithaca, NY: Cornell University Press, 2000); Thomas C. Brickhouse and Nicholas D. Smith, *The Philosophy of Socrates* (Boulder, CO: Westview, 2000); James A. Colaiaco, *Socrates Against Athens* (London: Routledge, 2001); and Thomas C. Brickhouse and Nicholas D. Smith, *The Trial and Execution of Socrates: Sources and Controversies* (Oxford: Oxford University Press, 2002). For collections of essays, see Gregory Vlastos, ed., *The Philosophy of Socrates* (Garden City, NY: Doubleday, 1971); Hugh H. Benson, ed., *Essays on the Philosophy of Socrates* (Oxford: Oxford University Press, 1992); Terence Irwin, ed., *Socrates and His Contemporaries* (Hamden, CT: Garland Publishing, 1995); the multi-volume William J. Prior, ed., *Socrates* (Oxford: Routledge, 1996); and Lindsay Judson and Vassilis Karasmanis, eds., *Remembering Socrates: Philosophical Essays* (Oxford: Oxford University Press, 2006). For discussions of the similarities and differences between the historical Socrates and the "Socrates" of the Platonic dialogues, see Gregory Vlastos, *Socrates: Ironist and Moral Philosopher* (Ithaca, NY: Cornell University Press, 1991), especially Chapters 2 and 3.

Books about Plato are legion. Once again the work of W.K.C. Guthrie is sensible, comprehensive, yet readable. See Volumes IV and V of his *The History of Greek Philosophy* (Cambridge: Cambridge University Press, 1975 and 1978). Paul Shorey, *What Plato Said* (Chicago: Chicago University Press, 1933), and G.M.A. Grube, *Plato's Thought* (London: Methuen, 1935) are classic treatments of Plato, while Robert Brumbaugh, *Plato for a Modern Age* (New York: Macmillan, 1964); I.M. Crombie, *An Examination of Plato's Doctrines,* two volumes (New York: Humanities Press, 1963–1969); R.M. Hare, *Plato* (Oxford: Oxford University Press, 1982); David J. Melling, *Understanding Plato* (Oxford: Oxford University Press, 1987); Bernard Williams, *Plato* (London: Routledge, 1999); and Julius Moravcsik, *Plato and Platonism* (Oxford: Basil Blackwell, 2000) are more recent studies. For collections of essays, see Gregory Vlastos, ed., *Plato: A Collection of Critical Essays,* two volumes (Garden City, NY: Doubleday, 1971); Richard Kraut, ed., *The Cambridge Companion to Plato* (Cambridge: Cambridge University Press, 1991); Nancy Tuana, ed., *Feminist Interpretations of Plato* (College Park: Pennsylvania State University Press, 1994); Terence Irwin, ed., *Plato's Ethics* and *Plato's Metaphysics and Epistemology* (both Hamden, CT: Garland Publishing, 1995); Gregory Vlastos, ed., *Studies in Greek Philosophy, Volume II: Socrates, Plato, and Their Tradition* (Princeton: Princeton University Press, 1995); Nicholas D. Smith, ed., *Plato: Critical Assessments* (London: Routledge, 1998); Gail Fine, ed., *Plato* (Oxford: Oxford University

Press, 2000); Gerald A. Press, ed., *Who Speaks for Plato?* (Lanham, MD: Rownan and Littlefield, 2000); and Gail Fine, *The Oxford Handbook of Plato* (Oxford: Oxford University Press, 2008). C.D.C. Reeve, *Socrates in the Apology* (Indianapolis, IN: Hockett, 1989); Jane M. Day, ed., *Plato's Meno in Focus* (Oxford: Routledge, 1994); Robert G. Turnbull, *The Parmenides and Plato's Late Philosophy* (Toronto: University of Toronto Press, 1998); Samuel C. Rickless, *Plato's Forms in Transition: A Reading of the* Parmenides (Cambridge: Cambridge University Press, 2006); Dominic Scott, ed., *Plato's* Meno (Cambridge: Cambridge University Press, 2006); Cristina Ionescu, *Plato's* Meno: *An Interpretation* (Lanham, MD: Lexington Books, 2007); Paul Stern, *Knowledge and Politics in Plato's* Theaetetus (Cambridge: Cambridge University Press, 2008); and Andrea Tschemplik, *Knowledge and Self-Knowledge in Plato's* Theaetetus (Lanham, MD: Lexington Books, 2008) give insights on their respective dialogues. For further reading on the *Republic,* see Nicholas P. White, *A Companion to Plato's* Republic (Indianapolis, IN: Hackett, 1989); Julia Annas, *An Introduction to Plato's* Republic (Oxford: Clarendon Press, 1981); Nickolas Pappas, *Routledge Guidebook to Plato and the* Republic (Oxford: Routledge, 1995); Daryl Rice, *A Guide to Plato's* Republic (Oxford: Oxford University Press, 1997); Richard Kraut, ed., *Plato's* Republic: *Critical Essays* (Lanham, MD: Rowan & Littlefield, 1997); Sean Sayers, *Plato's* Republic: *An Introduction* (New York: Columbia University Press, 2000); Stanley Rosen, *Plato's* Republic (New Haven, CT: Yale University Press, 2005); Luke Purshouse, *Plato's* Republic: *A Reader's Guide* (London: Continuum, 2006); and G.R.F. Ferrari, ed., *The Cambridge Companion to Plato's* Republic (Cambridge: Cambridge University Press, 2007). Terence Irwin, *Plato's Ethics* (Oxford: Oxford University Press, 1995) and Gabriela Roxana Carone, *Plato's Cosmology and Its Ethical Dimensions* (Cambridge: Cambridge Univesity Press, 2005) examine several dialogues while exploring Plato's ethical thought. Finally, for unusual interpretations of Plato and his work, see Werner Jaeger, *Paideia,* Vols. II and III, translated by Gilbert Highet (New York: Oxford University Press, 1939–1943); Karl R. Popper, *The Open Society and Its Enemies; Volume I: The Spell of Plato* (Princeton: Princeton University Press, 1962); and Allan Bloom's interpretive essay in Plato, *Republic,* translated by Allan Bloom (New York: Basic Books, 1968).

EUHYPHRO

Characters

Socrates
Euthyphro
Scene—The Hall of the King*

2   EUTHYPHRO: What in the world are you doing here in the king's hall, Socrates? Why have you left your haunts in the Lyceum? You surely cannot have a suit before him, as I have.

---

*The anachronistic title "king" was retained by the magistrate who had jurisdiction over crimes affecting the state religion.

Plato, *Euthyphro,* translated by F.J. Church (New York: Macmillan/Library of the Liberal Arts, 1963).

SOCRATES: The Athenians, Euthyphro, call it an indictment, not a suit.

EUTHYPHRO: What? Do you mean that someone is prosecuting you? I cannot   b
believe that you are prosecuting anyone yourself.

SOCRATES: Certainly I am not.

EUTHYPHRO: Then is someone prosecuting you?

SOCRATES: Yes.

EUTHYPHRO: Who is he?

SOCRATES: I scarcely know him myself, Euthyphro; I think he must be some
unknown young man. His name, however, is Meletus, and his district Pitthis, if you can
call to mind any Meletus of that district—a hook-nosed man with lanky hair and rather
a scanty beard.

EUTHYPHRO: I don't know him, Socrates. But tell me, what is he prosecuting you for?

SOCRATES: What for? Not on trivial grounds, I think. It is no small thing for so   c
young a man to have formed an opinion on such an important matter. For he, he says,
knows how the young are corrupted, and who are their corrupters. He must be a wise
man who, observing my ignorance, is going to accuse me to the state, as his mother, of   d
corrupting his friends. I think that he is the only one who begins at the right point in his
political reforms; for his first care is to make the young men as good as possible, just as
a good farmer will take care of his young plants first, and, after he has done that, of the
others. And so Meletus, I suppose, is first clearing us away who, as he says, corrupt the   3
young men growing up; and then, when he has done that, of course he will turn his
attention to the older men, and so become a very great public benefactor. Indeed, that is
only what you would expect when he goes to work in this way.

EUTHYPHRO: I hope it may be so, Socrates, but I fear the opposite. It seems to me
that in trying to injure you, he is really setting to work by striking a blow at the foundation of the state. But how, tell me, does he say that you corrupt the youth?

SOCRATES: In a way which sounds absurd at first, my friend. He says that I am a   b
maker of gods; and so he is prosecuting me, he says, for inventing new gods and for not
believing in the old ones.

EUTHYPHRO: I understand, Socrates. It is because you say that you always have a
divine guide. So he is prosecuting you for introducing religious reforms; and he is going
into court to arouse prejudice against you, knowing that the multitude are easily preju-
diced about such matters. Why, they laugh even at me, as if I were out of my mind,
when I talk about divine things in the assembly and tell them what is going to happen;   c
and yet I have never foretold anything which has not come true. But they are resentful
of all people like us. We must not worry about them; we must meet them boldly.

SOCRATES: My dear Euthyphro, their ridicule is not a very serious matter. The
Athenians, it seems to me, may think a man to be clever without paying him much
attention, so long as they do not think that he teaches his wisdom to others. But as soon
as they think that he makes other people clever, they get angry, whether it be from   d
resentment, as you say, or for some other reason.

EUTHYPHRO: I am not very anxious to test their attitude toward me in this matter.

SOCRATES: No, perhaps they think that you are reserved, and that you are not anxious to teach your wisdom to others. But I fear that they may think that I am; for my
love of men makes me talk to everyone whom I meet quite freely and unreservedly, and
without payment. Indeed, if I could I would gladly pay people myself to listen to me. If
then, as I said just now, they were only going to laugh at me, as you say they do at you,
it would not be at all an unpleasant way of spending the day—to spend it in court, joking and laughing. But if they are going to be in earnest, then only prophets like you can
tell where the matter will end.

EUTHYPHRO: Well, Socrates, I dare say that nothing will come of it. Very likely you will be successful in your trial, and I think that I shall be in mine.

SOCRATES: And what is this suit of yours, Euthyphro? Are you suing, or being sued?

EUTHYPHRO: I am suing.

SOCRATES: Whom?

4   EUTHYPHRO: A man whom people think I must be mad to prosecute.

SOCRATES: What? Has he wings to fly away with?

EUTHYPHRO: He is far enough from flying; he is a very old man.

SOCRATES: Who is he?

EUTHYPHRO: He is my father.

SOCRATES: Your father, my good man?

EUTHYPHRO: He is indeed.

SOCRATES: What are you prosecuting him for? What is the accusation?

EUTHYPHRO: Murder, Socrates.

b   SOCRATES: Good heavens, Euthyphro! Surely the multitude are ignorant of what is right. I take it that it is not everyone who could rightly do what you are doing; only a man who was already well advanced in wisdom.

EUTHYPHRO: That is quite true, Socrates.

SOCRATES: Was the man whom your father killed a relative of yours? But, of course, he was. You would never have prosecuted your father for the murder of a stranger?

EUTHYPHRO: You amuse me, Socrates. What difference does it make whether the murdered man were a relative or a stranger? The only question that you have to ask is, did the murderer kill justly or not? If justly, you must let him alone; if unjustly, you

c   must indict him for murder, even though he share your hearth and sit at your table. The pollution is the same if you associate with such a man, knowing what he has done, without purifying yourself, and him too, by bringing him to justice. In the present case the murdered man was a poor laborer of mine, who worked for us on our farm in Naxos. While drunk he got angry with one of our slaves and killed him. My father therefore bound the man hand and foot and threw him into a ditch, while he sent to Athens to ask the priest what he should do. While the messenger was gone, he entirely neglected the man, thinking that he was a murderer, and that it would be no great matter, even if he were to die. And that was exactly what happened; hunger and cold and his bonds killed

d   him before the messenger returned. And now my father and the rest of my family are indignant with me because I am prosecuting my father for the murder of this murderer. They assert that he did not kill the man at all; and they say that, even if he had killed him over and over again, the man himself was a murderer, and that I ought not to concern

e   myself about such a person because it is impious for a son to prosecute his father for murder. So little, Socrates, do they know the divine law of piety and impiety.

SOCRATES: And do you mean to say, Euthyphro, that you think that you understand divine things and piety and impiety so accurately that, in such a case as you have stated, you can bring your father to justice without fear that you yourself may be doing something impious?

EUTHYPHRO: If I did not understand all these matters accurately, Socrates, I should

5   not be worth much—Euthyphro would not be any better than other men.

SOCRATES: Then, my dear Euthyphro, I cannot do better than become your pupil and challenge Meletus on this very point before the trial begins. I should say that I had always thought it very important to have knowledge about divine things; and that now, when he says that I offend by speaking carelessly about them, and by introducing

b   reforms, I have become your pupil. And I should say, "Meletus, if you acknowledge

Euthyphro to be wise in these matters and to hold the correct belief, then think the same of me and do not put me on trial; but if you do not, then bring a suit, not against me, but against my master, for corrupting his elders—namely, myself whom he corrupts by his teaching, and his own father whom he corrupts by admonishing and punishing him." And if I did not succeed in persuading him to release me from the suit or to indict you in my place, then I could repeat my challenge in court.

EUTHYPHRO: Yes, by Zeus! Socrates, I think I should find out his weak points if he were to try to indict me. I should have a good deal to say about him in court long before I spoke about myself.

SOCRATES: Yes, my dear friend, and knowing this I am anxious to become your pupil. I see that Meletus here, and others too, seem not to notice you at all, but he sees through me without difficulty and at once prosecutes me for impiety. Now, therefore, please explain to me what you were so confident just now that you knew. Tell me what are righteousness and sacrilege with respect to murder and everything else. I suppose that piety is the same in all actions, and that impiety is always the opposite of piety, and retains its identity, and that, as impiety, it always has the same character, which will be found in whatever is impious.

EUTHYPHRO: Certainly, Socrates, I suppose so.

SOCRATES: Tell me, then, what is piety and what is impiety?

EUTHYPHRO: Well, then, I say that piety means prosecuting the unjust individual who has committed murder or sacrilege, or any other such crime, as I am doing now, whether he is your father or your mother or whoever he is; and I say that impiety means not prosecuting him. And observe, Socrates, I will give you a clear proof, which I have already given to others, that it is so, and that doing right means not letting off unpunished the sacrilegious man, whosoever he may be. Men hold Zeus to be the best and the most just of the gods; and they admit that Zeus bound his own father, Cronos, for wrongfully devouring his children; and that Cronos, in his turn, castrated his father for similar reasons. And yet these same men are incensed with me because I proceed against my father for doing wrong. So, you see, they say one thing in the case of the gods and quite another in mine.

SOCRATES: Is not that why I am being prosecuted, Euthyphro? I mean, because I find it hard to accept such stories people tell about the gods? I expect that I shall be found at fault because I doubt those stories. Now if you who understand all these matters so well agree in holding all those tales true, then I suppose that I must yield to your authority. What could I say when I admit myself that I know nothing about them? But tell me, in the name of friendship, do you really believe that these things have actually happened?

EUTHYPHRO: Yes, and more amazing things, too, Socrates, which the multitude do not know of.

SOCRATES: Then you really believe that there is war among the gods, and bitter hatreds, and battles, such as the poets tell of, and which the great painters have depicted in our temples, notably in the pictures which cover the robe that is carried up to the Acropolis at the great Panathenaic festival? Are we to say that these things are true, Euthyphro?

EUTHYPHRO: Yes, Socrates, and more besides. As I was saying, I will report to you many other stories about divine matters, if you like, which I am sure will astonish you when you hear them.

SOCRATES: I dare say. You shall report them to me at your leisure another time. At present please try to give a more definite answer to the question which I asked you just now. What I asked you, my friend, was, What is piety? and you have not explained it to me to my satisfaction. You only tell me that what you are doing now, namely, prosecuting your father for murder, is a pious act.

EUTHYPHRO: Well, that is true, Socrates.

SOCRATES: Very likely. But many other actions are pious, are they not, Euthyphro?

EUTHYPHRO: Certainly.

SOCRATES: Remember, then, I did not ask you to tell me one or two of all the many pious actions that there are; I want to know what is characteristic of piety which makes all pious actions pious. You said, I think, that there is one characteristic which makes all pious actions pious, and another characteristic which makes all impious actions impious. Do you not remember?

EUTHYPHRO: I do.

SOCRATES: Well, then, explain to me what is this characteristic, that I may have it to turn to, and to use as a standard whereby to judge your actions and those of other men, and be able to say that whatever action resembles it is pious, and whatever does not, is not pious.

EUTHYPHRO: Yes, I will tell you that if you wish, Socrates.

SOCRATES: Certainly I do.

EUTHYPHRO: Well, then, what is pleasing to the gods is pious, and what is not pleasing to them is impious.

SOCRATES: Fine, Euthyphro. Now you have given me the answer that I wanted. Whether what you say is true, I do not know yet. But, of course, you will go on to prove that it is true.

EUTHYPHRO: Certainly.

SOCRATES: Come, then, let us examine our statement. The things and the men that are pleasing to the gods are pious, and the things and the men that are displeasing to the gods are impious. But piety and impiety are not the same; they are as opposite as possible—was not that what we said?

EUTHYPHRO: Certainly.

SOCRATES: And it seems the appropriate statement?

EUTHYPHRO: Yes, Socrates, certainly.

SOCRATES: Have we not also said, Euthyphro, that there are quarrels and disagreements and hatreds among the gods?

EUTHYPHRO: We have.

SOCRATES: But what kind of disagreement, my friend, causes hatred and anger? Let us look at the matter thus. If you and I were to disagree as to whether one number were more than another, would that make us angry and enemies? Should we not settle such a dispute at once by counting?

EUTHYPHRO: Of course.

SOCRATES: And if we were to disagree as to the relative size of two things, we should measure them and put an end to the disagreement at once, should we not?

EUTHYPHRO: Yes.

SOCRATES: And should we not settle a question about the relative weight of two things by weighing them?

EUTHYPHRO: Of course.

SOCRATES: Then what is the question which would make us angry and enemies if we disagreed about it, and could not come to a settlement? Perhaps you have not an answer ready; but listen to mine. Is it not the question of the just and unjust, of the honorable and the dishonorable, of the good and the bad? Is it not questions about these matters which make you and me and everyone else quarrel, when we do quarrel, if we differ about them and can reach no satisfactory agreement?

EUTHYPHRO: Yes, Socrates, it is disagreements about these matters.

SOCRATES: Well, Euthyphro, the gods will quarrel over these things if they quarrel at all, will they not?

EUTHYPHRO: Necessarily.

SOCRATES: Then, my good Euthyphro, you say that some of the gods think one   e
thing just, the others another; and that what some of them hold to be honorable or good, others hold to be dishonorable or evil. For there would not have been quarrels among them if they had not disagreed on these points, would there?

EUTHYPHRO: You are right.

SOCRATES: And each of them loves what he thinks honorable, and good, and just; and hates the opposite, does he not?

EUTHYPHRO: Certainly.

SOCRATES: But you say that the same action is held by some of them to be just, and by others to be unjust; and that then they dispute about it, and so quarrel and fight   8
among themselves. Is it not so?

EUTHYPHRO: Yes.

SOCRATES: Then the same thing is hated by the gods and loved by them; and the same thing will be displeasing and pleasing to them.

EUTHYPHRO: Apparently.

SOCRATES: Then, according to your account, the same thing will be pious and impious.

EUTHYPHRO: So it seems.

SOCRATES: Then, my good friend, you have not answered my question. I did not ask you to tell me what action is both pious and impious; but it seems that whatever is pleasing to the gods is also displeasing to them. And so, Euthyphro, I should not be sur-   b
prised if what you are doing now in punishing your father is an action well pleasing to Zeus, but hateful to Cronos and Uranus, and acceptable to Hephaestus, but hateful to Hera; and if any of the other gods disagree about it, pleasing to some of them and displeasing to others.

EUTHYPHRO: But on this point, Socrates, I think that there is no difference of opinion among the gods: they all hold that if one man kills another unjustly, he must be punished.

SOCRATES: What, Euthyphro? Among mankind, have you never heard disputes   c
whether a man ought to be punished for killing another man unjustly, or for doing some other unjust deed?

EUTHYPHRO: Indeed, they never cease from these disputes, especially in courts of justice. They do all manner of unjust things; and then there is nothing which they will not do and say to avoid punishment.

SOCRATES: Do they admit that they have done something unjust, and at the same time deny that they ought to be punished, Euthyphro?

EUTHYPHRO: No, indeed, that they do not.

SOCRATES: Then it is not the case that there is nothing which they will not do and say. I take it, they do not dare to say or argue that they must not be punished if they have done something unjust. What they say is that they have not done anything unjust, is it not so?   d

EUTHYPHRO: That is true.

SOCRATES: Then they do not disagree over the question that the unjust individual must be punished. They disagree over the question, who is unjust, and what was done and when, do they not?

EUTHYPHRO: That is true.

SOCRATES: Well, is not exactly the same thing true of the gods if they quarrel about justice and injustice, as you say they do? Do not some of them say that the others e   are doing something unjust, while the others deny it? No one, I suppose, my dear friend, whether god or man, dares to say that a person who has done something unjust must not be punished.

EUTHYPHRO: No, Socrates, that is true, by and large.

SOCRATES: I take it, Euthyphro, that the disputants, whether men or gods, if the gods do disagree, disagree over each separate act. When they quarrel about any act, some of them say that it was just, and others that it was unjust. Is it not so?

EUTHYPHRO: Yes.

9   SOCRATES: Come, then, my dear Euthyphro, please enlighten me on this point. What proof have you that all the gods think that a laborer who has been imprisoned for murder by the master of the man whom he has murdered, and who dies from his imprisonment before the master has had time to learn from the religious authorities what he should do, dies unjustly? How do you know that it is just for a son to indict his father and to prosecute him for the murder of such a man? Come, see if you can make it clear

b   to me that the gods necessarily agree in thinking that this action of yours is just; and if you satisfy me, I will never cease singing your praises for wisdom.

EUTHYPHRO: I could make that clear enough to you, Socrates; but I am afraid that it would be a long business.

SOCRATES: I see you think that I am duller than the judges. To them, of course, you will make it clear that your father has committed an unjust action, and that all the gods agree in hating such actions.

EUTHYPHRO: I will indeed, Socrates, if they will only listen to me.

c   SOCRATES: They will listen if they think that you are a good speaker. But while you were talking, it occurred to me to ask myself this question: suppose that Euthyphro were to prove to me as clearly as possible that all the gods think such a death unjust, how has he brought me any nearer to understanding what piety and impiety are? This particular act, perhaps, may be displeasing to the gods, but then we have just seen that piety and impiety cannot be defined in that way; for we have seen that what is displeasing to the

d   gods is also pleasing to them. So I will let you off on this point, Euthyphro; and all the gods shall agree in thinking your father's action wrong and in hating it, if you like. But shall we correct our definition and say that whatever all the gods hate is impious, and whatever they all love is pious; while whatever some of them love, and others hate, is either both or neither? Do you wish us now to define piety and impiety in this manner?

EUTHYPHRO: Why not, Socrates?

SOCRATES: There is no reason why I should not, Euthyphro. It is for you to consider whether that definition will help you to teach me what you promised.

e   EUTHYPHRO: Well, I should say that piety is what all the gods love, and that impiety is what they all hate.

SOCRATES: Are we to examine this definition, Euthyphro, and see if it is a good one? Or are we to be content to accept the bare statements of other men or of ourselves without asking any questions? Or must we examine the statements?

EUTHYPHRO: We must examine them. But for my part I think that the definition is right this time.

SOCRATES: We shall know that better in a little while, my good friend. Now con-

10 sider this question. Do the gods love piety because it is pious, or is it pious because they love it?

EUTHYPHRO: I do not understand you, Socrates.

SOCRATES: I will try to explain myself: we speak of a thing being carried and carrying, and being led and leading, and being seen and seeing; and you understand that all such expressions mean different things, and what the difference is.

EUTHYPHRO: Yes, I think I understand.

SOCRATES: And we talk of a thing being loved, of a thing loving, and the two are different?

EUTHYPHRO: Of course.

SOCRATES: Now tell me, is a thing which is being carried in a state of being carried because it is carried, or for some other reason?

EUTHYPHRO: No, because it is carried.

SOCRATES: And a thing is in a state of being led because it is led, and of being seen because it is seen?

EUTHYPHRO: Certainly.

SOCRATES: Then a thing is not seen because it is in a state of being seen: it is in a state of being seen because it is seen; and a thing is not led because it is in a state of being led: it is in a state of being led because it is led; and a thing is not carried because it is in a state of being carried: it is in a state of being carried because it is carried. Is my meaning clear now, Euthyphro? I mean this: if anything becomes or is affected, it does not become because it is in a state of becoming: it is in a state of becoming because it becomes; and it is not affected because it is in a state of being affected: it is in a state of being affected because it is affected. Do you not agree?

EUTHYPHRO: I do.

SOCRATES: Is not that which is being loved in a state either of becoming or of being affected in some way by something?

EUTHYPHRO: Certainly.

SOCRATES: Then the same is true here as in the former cases. A thing is not loved by those who love it because it is in a state of being loved; it is in a state of being loved because they love it.

EUTHYPHRO: Necessarily.

SOCRATES: Well, then, Euthyphro, what do we say about piety? Is it not loved by all the gods, according to your definition?

EUTHYPHRO: Yes.

SOCRATES: Because it is pious, or for some other reason?

EUTHYPHRO: No, because it is pious.

SOCRATES: Then it is loved by the gods because it is pious; it is not pious because it is loved by them?

EUTHYPHRO: It seems so.

SOCRATES: But, then, what is pleasing to the gods is pleasing to them, and is in a state of being loved by them, because they love it?

EUTHYPHRO: Of course.

SOCRATES: Then piety is not what is pleasing to the gods, and what is pleasing to the gods is not pious, as you say, Euthyphro. They are different things.

EUTHYPHRO: And why, Socrates?

SOCRATES: Because we are agreed that the gods love piety because it is pious, and that it is not pious because they love it. Is not this so?

EUTHYPHRO: Yes.

SOCRATES: And that what is pleasing to the gods because they love it, is pleasing to them by reason of this same love, and that they do not love it because it is pleasing to them.

EUTHYPHRO: True.

SOCRATES: Then, my dear Euthyphro, piety and what is pleasing to the gods are different things. If the gods had loved piety because it is pious, they would also have loved what is pleasing to them because it is pleasing to them; but if what is pleasing to them had been pleasing to them because they loved it, then piety, too, would have been piety because they loved it. But now you see that they are opposite things, and wholly different from each other. For the one is of a sort to be loved because it is loved, while the other is loved because it is of a sort to be loved. My question, Euthyphro, was, What is piety? But it turns out that you have not explained to me the essential character of piety; you have been content to mention an effect which belongs to it—namely, that all

b   the gods love it. You have not yet told me what its essential character is. Do not, if you please, keep from me what piety is; begin again and tell me that. Never mind whether the gods love it, or whether it has other effects: we shall not differ on that point. Do your best to make clear to me what is piety and what is impiety.

EUTHYPHRO: But, Socrates, I really don't know how to explain to you what is in my mind. Whatever statement we put forward always somehow moves round in a circle, and will not stay where we put it.

SOCRATES: I think that your statements, Euthyphro, are worthy of my ancestor

c   Daedalus.* If they had been mine and I had set them down, I dare say you would have made fun of me, and said that it was the consequence of my descent from Daedalus that the statements which I construct run away, as his statues used to, and will not stay where they are put. But, as it is, the statements are yours, and the joke would have no point. You yourself see that they will not stay still.

EUTHYPHRO: Nay, Socrates, I think that the joke is very much in point. It is not my

d   fault that the statement moves round in a circle and will not stay still. But you are the Daedalus, I think; as far as I am concerned, my statements would have stayed put.

SOCRATES: Then, my friend, I must be a more skillful artist than Daedalus; he only used to make his own works move, while I, you see, can make other people's works move, too. And the beauty of it is that I am wise against my will. I would rather that our statements had remained firm and immovable than have all the wisdom of Daedalus and

e   all the riches of Tantalus to boot. But enough of this. I will do my best to help you to explain to me what piety is, for I think that you are lazy. Don't give in yet. Tell me, do you not think that all piety must be just?

EUTHYPHRO: I do.

12   SOCRATES: Well, then, is all justice pious, too? Or, while all piety is just, is a part only of justice pious, and the rest of it something else?

EUTHYPHRO: I do not follow you, Socrates.

SOCRATES: Yet you have the advantage over me in your youth no less than your wisdom. But, as I say, the wealth of your wisdom makes you complacent. Exert yourself, my good friend: I am not asking you a difficult question. I mean the opposite of what the poet [Stasinus] said, when he wrote:

b   "You shall not name Zeus the creator, who made all things: for where there is fear there also is reverence."

Now I disagree with the poet. Shall I tell you why?

EUTHYPHRO: Yes.

SOCRATES: I do not think it true to say that where there is fear, there also is reverence. Many people who fear sickness and poverty and other such evils seem to me to have fear, but no reverence for what they fear. Do you not think so?

EUTHYPHRO: I do.

*Daedalus' statues were reputed to have been so lifelike that they came alive.

SOCRATES: But I think that where there is reverence there also is fear. Does any man feel reverence and a sense of shame about anything, without at the same time dreading and fearing the reputation of wickedness?

EUTHYPHRO: No, certainly not.

SOCRATES: Then, though there is fear wherever there is reverence, it is not correct to say that where there is fear there also is reverence. Reverence does not always accompany fear; for fear, I take it, is wider than reverence. It is a part of fear, just as the odd is a part of number, so that where you have the odd you must also have number, though where you have number you do not necessarily have the odd. Now I think you follow me?

EUTHYPHRO: I do.

SOCRATES: Well, then, this is what I meant by the question which I asked you. Is there always piety where there is justice? Or, though there is always justice where there is piety, yet there is not always piety where there is justice, because piety is only a part of justice? Shall we say this, or do you differ?

EUTHYPHRO: No, I agree. I think that you are right.

SOCRATES: Now observe the next point. If piety is a part of justice, we must find out, I suppose, what part of justice it is? Now, if you had asked me just now, for instance, what part of number is the odd, and what number is an odd number, I should have said that whatever number is not even is an odd number. Is it not so?

EUTHYPHRO: Yes.

SOCRATES: Then see if you can explain to me what part of justice is piety, that I may tell Meletus that now that I have been adequately instructed by you as to what actions are righteous and pious, and what are not, he must give up prosecuting me unjustly for impiety.

EUTHYPHRO: Well, then, Socrates, I should say that righteousness and piety are that part of justice which has to do with the careful attention which ought to be paid to the gods; and that what has to do with the careful attention which ought to be paid to men is the remaining part of justice.

SOCRATES: And I think that your answer is a good one, Euthyphro. But there is one little point about which I still want to hear more. I do not yet understand what the careful attention is to which you refer. I suppose you do not mean that the attention which we pay to the gods is like the attention which we pay to other things. We say, for instance, do we not, that not everyone knows how to take care of horses, but only the trainer of horses?

EUTHYPHRO: Certainly.

SOCRATES: For I suppose that the skill that is concerned with horses is the art of taking care of horses.

EUTHYPHRO: Yes.

SOCRATES: And not everyone understands the care of dogs, but only the huntsman.

EUTHYPHRO: True.

SOCRATES: For I suppose that the huntsman's skill is the art of taking care of dogs.

EUTHYPHRO: Yes.

SOCRATES: And the herdsman's skill is the art of taking care of cattle.

EUTHYPHRO: Certainly.

SOCRATES: And you say that piety and righteousness are taking care of the gods, Euthyphro?

EUTHYPHRO: I do.

SOCRATES: Well, then, has not all care the same object? Is it not for the good and benefit of that on which it is bestowed? For instance, you see that horses are benefited and improved when they are cared for by the art which is concerned with them. Is it not so?

EUTHYPHRO: Yes, I think so.

c   SOCRATES: And dogs are benefited and improved by the huntsman's art, and cattle by the herdsman's, are they not? And the same is always true. Or do you think care is ever meant to harm that which is cared for?

EUTHYPHRO: No, indeed; certainly not.

SOCRATES: But to benefit it?

EUTHYPHRO: Of course.

SOCRATES: Then is piety, which is our care for the gods, intended to benefit the gods, or to improve them? Should you allow that you make any of the gods better when you do a pious action?

EUTHYPHRO: No indeed; certainly not.

SOCRATES: No, I am quite sure that that is not your meaning, Euthyphro. It was for

d   that reason that I asked you what you meant by the careful attention which ought to be paid to the gods. I thought that you did not mean that.

EUTHYPHRO: You were right, Socrates. I do not mean that.

SOCRATES: Good. Then what sort of attention to the gods will piety be?

EUTHYPHRO: The sort of attention, Socrates, slaves pay to their masters.

SOCRATES: I understand; then it is a kind of service to the gods?

EUTHYPHRO: Certainly.

SOCRATES: Can you tell me what result the art which serves a doctor serves to produce? Is it not health?

EUTHYPHRO: Yes.

e   SOCRATES: And what result does the art which serves a ship-wright serve to produce?

EUTHYPHRO: A ship, of course, Socrates.

SOCRATES: The result of the art which serves a builder is a house, is it not?

EUTHYPHRO: Yes.

SOCRATES: Then tell me, my good friend: What result will the art which serves the gods serve to produce? You must know, seeing that you say that you know more about divine things than any other man.

EUTHYPHRO: Well, that is true, Socrates.

SOCRATES: Then tell me, I beg you, what is that grand result which the gods use our services to produce?

EUTHYPHRO: There are many notable results, Socrates.

14   SOCRATES: So are those, my friend, which a general produces. Yet it is easy to see that the crowning result of them all is victory in war, is it not?

EUTHYPHRO: Of course.

SOCRATES: And, I take it, the farmer produces many notable results; yet the principal result of them all is that he makes the earth produce food.

EUTHYPHRO: Certainly.

SOCRATES: Well, then, what is the principal result of the many notable results which the gods produce?

EUTHYPHRO: I told you just now, Socrates, that accurate knowledge of all these

b   matters is not easily obtained. However, broadly I say this: if any man knows that his words and actions in prayer and sacrifice are acceptable to the gods, that is what is pious; and it preserves the state, as it does private families. But the opposite of what is acceptable to the gods is sacrilegious, and this it is that undermines and destroys everything.

SOCRATES: Certainly, Euthyphro, if you had wished, you could have answered my

c   main question in far fewer words. But you are evidently not anxious to teach me. Just now, when you were on the very point of telling me what I want to know, you stopped short. If you had gone on then, I should have learned from you clearly enough by this time what piety is. But now I am asking you questions, and must follow wherever you lead me; so tell me, what is it that you mean by piety and impiety? Do you not mean a science of prayer and sacrifice?

EUTHYPHRO: I do.

SOCRATES: To sacrifice is to give to the gods, and to pray is to ask of them, is it not?

EUTHYPHRO: It is, Socrates.

SOCRATES: Then you say that piety is the science of asking of the gods and giving   d
to them?

EUTHYPHRO: You understand my meaning exactly, Socrates.

SOCRATES: Yes, for I am eager to share your wisdom, Euthyphro, and so I am all attention; nothing that you say will fall to the ground. But tell me, what is this service of the gods? You say it is to ask of them, and to give to them?

EUTHYPHRO: I do.

SOCRATES: Then, to ask rightly will be to ask of them what we stand in need of   e
from them, will it not?

EUTHYPHRO: Naturally.

SOCRATES: And to give rightly will be to give back to them what they stand in need of from us? It would not be very skillful to make a present to a man of something that he has no need of.

EUTHYPHRO: True, Socrates.

SOCRATES: Then piety, Euthyphro, will be the art of carrying on business between gods and men?

EUTHYPHRO: Yes, if you like to call it so.

SOCRATES: But I like nothing except what is true. But tell me, how are the gods benefited by the gifts which they receive from us? What they give is plain enough. Every good thing that we have is their gift. But how are they benefited by what we give   15
them? Have we the advantage over them in these business transactions to such an extent that we receive from them all the good things we possess, and give them nothing in return?

EUTHYPHRO: But do you suppose, Socrates, that the gods are benefited by the gifts which they receive from us?

SOCRATES: But what *are* these gifts, Euthyphro, that we give the gods?

EUTHYPHRO: What do you think but honor and praise, and, as I have said, what is acceptable to them.

SOCRATES: Then piety, Euthyphro, is acceptable to the gods, but it is not profitable   b
to them nor loved by them?

EUTHYPHRO: I think that nothing is more loved by them.

SOCRATES: Then I see that piety means that which is loved by the gods.

EUTHYPHRO: Most certainly.

SOCRATES: After that, shall you be surprised to find that your statements move about instead of staying where you put them? Shall you accuse me of being the Daedalus that makes them move, when you yourself are far more skillful than Daedalus was, and make them go round in a circle? Do you not see that our statement has come round to where it was before? Surely you remember that we have already seen that piety   c
and what is pleasing to the gods are quite different things. Do you not remember?

EUTHYPHRO: I do.

SOCRATES: And now do you not see that you say that what the gods love is pious? But does not what the gods love come to the same thing as what is pleasing to the gods?

EUTHYPHRO: Certainly.

SOCRATES: Then either our former conclusion was wrong or, if it was right, we are wrong now.

EUTHYPHRO: So it seems.

SOCRATES: Then we must begin again and inquire what piety is. I do not mean to give in until I have found out. Do not regard me as unworthy; give your whole mind to the question, and this time tell me the truth. For if anyone knows it, it is you; and you are a Proteus whom I must not let go until you have told me. It cannot be that you would ever have undertaken to prosecute your aged father for the murder of a laboring man unless you had known exactly what piety and impiety are. You would have feared to risk the anger of the gods, in case you should be doing wrong, and you would have been afraid of what men would say. But now I am sure that you think that you know exactly what is pious and what is not; so tell me, my good Euthyphro, and do not conceal from me what you think.

EUTHYPHRO: Another time, then, Socrates. I am in a hurry now, and it is time for me to be off.

SOCRATES: What are you doing, my friend! Will you go away and destroy all my hopes of learning from you what is pious and what is not, and so of escaping Meletus? I meant to explain to him that now Euthyphro has made me wise about divine things, and that I no longer in my ignorance speak carelessly about them or introduce reforms. And then I was going to promise him to live a better life for the future.

APOLOGY

Characters

Socrates

Meletus

Scene—The Court of Justice

SOCRATES: I do not know what impression my accusers have made upon you, Athenians. But I do know that they nearly made me forget who I was, so persuasive were they. And yet they have scarcely spoken one single word of truth. Of all their many falsehoods, the one which astonished me most was their saying that I was a clever speaker, and that you must be careful not to let me deceive you. I thought that it was most shameless of them not to be ashamed to talk in that way. For as soon as I open my mouth they will be refuted, and I shall prove that I am not a clever speaker in any way at all— unless, indeed, by a clever speaker they mean someone who speaks the truth. If that is their meaning, I agree with them that I am an orator not to be compared with them.

Plato, *Apology*, translated by F.J. Church (New York: Macmillan/Library of the Liberal Arts, 1963).

My accusers, I repeat, have said little or nothing that is true, but from me you shall hear the whole truth. Certainly you will not hear a speech, Athenians, dressed up, like theirs, with fancy words and phrases. I will say to you what I have to say, without artifice, and I shall use the first words which come to mind, for I believe that what I have to say is just; so let none of you expect anything else. Indeed, my friends, it would hardly be right for me, at my age, to come before you like a schoolboy with his concocted phrases. But there is one thing, Athenians, which I do most earnestly beg and entreat of you. Do not be surprised and do not interrupt with shouts if in my defense I speak in the same way that I am accustomed to speak in the market place, at the tables of the money-changers, where many of you have heard me, and elsewhere. The truth is this: I am more than seventy, and this is the first time that I have ever come before a law court; thus your manner of speech here is quite strange to me. If I had really been a stranger, you would have forgiven me for speaking in the language and the manner of my native country. And so now I ask you to grant me what I think I have a right to claim. Never mind the manner of my speech— it may be superior or it may be inferior to the usual manner. Give your whole attention to the question, whether what I say is just or not? That is what is required of a good judge, as speaking the truth is required of a good orator.

c

d

18

I have to defend myself, Athenians, first against the older false accusations of my old accusers, and then against the more recent ones of my present accusers. For many men have been accusing me to you, and for very many years, who have not spoken a word of truth; and I fear them more than I fear Anytus* and his associates, formidable as they are. But, my friends, the others are still more formidable, since they got hold of most of you when you were children and have been more persistent in accusing me untruthfully, persuading you that there is a certain Socrates, a wise man, who speculates about the heavens, who investigates things that are beneath the earth, and who can make the worse argument appear the stronger. These men, Athenians, who spread abroad this report are the accusers whom I fear; for their hearers think that persons who pursue such inquiries never believe in the gods. Besides they are many, their attacks have been going on for a long time, and they spoke to you when you were most ready to believe them, since you were all young, and some of you were children. And there was no one to answer them when they attacked me. The most preposterous thing of all is that I do not even know their names: I cannot tell you who they are except when one happens to be a comic poet. But all the rest who have persuaded you, from motives of resentment and prejudice, and sometimes, it may be, from conviction, are hardest to cope with. For I cannot call any one of them forward in court to cross-examine him. I have, as it were, simply to spar with shadows in my defense, and to put questions which there is no one to answer. I ask you, therefore, to believe that, as I say, I have been attacked by two kinds of accusers—first, by Meletus** and his associates, and, then, by those older ones of whom I have spoken. And, with your leave, I will defend myself first against my old accusers, since you heard their accusations first, and they were much more compelling than my present accusers are.

b

c

d

e

Well, I must make my defense, Athenians, and try in the short time allowed me to remove the prejudice which you have been so long a time acquiring. I hope that I may

19

---

*Anytus is singled out as politically the most influential member of the prosecution. He had played a prominent part in the restoration of the democratic regime at Athens.

**Apparently, in order to obscure the political implications of the trial, the role of chief prosecutor was assigned to Meletus, a minor poet with fervent religious convictions. Anytus was evidently ready to make political use of Meletus' convictions without entirely sharing his fervor, for in the same year as this trial Meletus also prosecuted Andocides for impiety, but Anytus came to Andocides' defense.

manage to do this, if it be best for you and for me, and that my defense may be successful; but I am quite aware of the nature of my task, and I know that it is a difficult one. Be
the outcome, however, as is pleasing to god, I must obey the law and make my defense.

b   Let us begin from the beginning, then, and ask what is the accusation that has
given rise to the prejudice against me, on which Meletus relied when he brought his
indictment. What is the prejudice which my enemies have been spreading about me? I
must assume that they are formally accusing me, and read their indictment. It would run
somewhat in this fashion: "Socrates is guilty of engaging in inquiries into things
beneath the earth and in the heavens, of making the weaker argument appear the
c   stronger, and of teaching others these same things." That is what they say. And in the
comedy of Aristophanes* you yourselves saw a man called Socrates swinging around in
a basket and saying that he walked on air, and sputtering a great deal of nonsense about
matters of which I understand nothing at all. I do not mean to disparage that kind of
knowledge if there is anyone who is wise about these matters. I trust Meletus may never
be able to prosecute me for that. But the truth is, Athenians, I have nothing to do with
d   these matters, and almost all of you are yourselves my witnesses of this. I beg all of you
who have ever heard me discussing, and they are many, to inform your neighbors and
tell them if any of you have ever heard me discussing such matters at all. That will show
e   you that the other common statements about me are as false as this one.

But the fact is that not one of these is true. And if you have heard that I undertake
20   to educate men, and make money by so doing, that is not true either, though I think that
it would be a fine thing to be able to educate men, as Gorgias of Leontini, and Prodicus
of Ceos, and Hippias of Elis do. For each of them, my friends, can go into any city, and
persuade the young men to leave the society of their fellow citizens, with any of whom
they might associate for nothing, and to be only too glad to be allowed to pay money for
the privilege of associating with themselves. And I believe that there is another wise
man from Paros residing in Athens at this moment. I happened to meet Callias, the son
of Hipponicus, a man who has spent more money on sophists than everyone else put
b   together. So I said to him (he has two sons), "Callias, if your two sons had been foals or
calves, we could have hired a trainer for them who would have trained them to excel in
doing what they are naturally capable of. He would have been either a groom or a
farmer. But whom do you intend to take to train them, seeing that they are men? Who
understands the excellence which a man and citizen is capable of attaining? I suppose
that you must have thought of this, because you have sons. Is there such a person or
not?" "Certainly there is," he replied. "Who is he," said I, "and where does he come
c   from, and what is his fee?" "Evenus, Socrates," he replied, "from Paros, five minae."
Then I thought that Evenus was a fortunate person if he really understood this art and
could teach so cleverly. If I had possessed knowledge of that kind, I should have been
conceited and disdainful. But, Athenians, the truth is that I do not possess it.

Perhaps some of you may reply: "But, Socrates, what is the trouble with you?
What has given rise to these prejudices against you? You must have been doing something out of the ordinary. All these rumors and reports of you would never have arisen if
you had not been doing something different from other men. So tell us what it is, that
d   we may not give our verdict arbitrarily." I think that that is a fair question, and I will try
to explain to you what it is that has raised these prejudices against me and given me this
reputation. Listen, then. Some of you, perhaps, will think that I am joking, but I assure
you that I will tell you the whole truth. I have gained this reputation, Athenians, simply

---

*The Clouds. The basket was satirically assumed to facilitate Socrates' inquiries into things in the
heavens.

by reason of a certain wisdom. But by what kind of wisdom? It is by Just that wisdom which is perhaps human wisdom. In that, it may be, I am really wise. But the men of whom I was speaking just now must be wise in a wisdom which is greater than human wisdom, or else I cannot describe it, for certainly I know nothing of it myself, and if any man says that I do, he lies and speaks to arouse prejudice against me. Do not interrupt me with shouts, Athenians, even if you think that I am boasting. What I am going to say is not my own statement. I will tell you who says it, and he is worthy of your respect. I will bring the god of Delphi to be the witness of my wisdom, if it is wisdom at all, and of its nature. You remember Chaerephon. From youth upwards he was my comrade; and also a partisan of your democracy, sharing your recent exile* and returning with you. You remember, too, Chaerephon's character–how impulsive he was in carrying through whatever he took in hand. Once he went to Delphi and ventured to put this question to the oracle—I entreat you again, my friends, not to interrupt me with your shouts—he asked if there was anyone who was wiser than I. The priestess answered that there was no one. Chaerephon himself is dead, but his brother here will witness to what I say.

e

21

Now see why I tell you this. I am going to explain to you how the prejudice against me has arisen. When I heard of the oracle I began to reflect: What can the god mean by this riddle? I know very well that I am not wise, even in the smallest degree. Then what

b

The *Thólos* at Delphi with the *Sanctuary of Apollo* in the background. Socrates' friend, Chaerophon, went to the famous oracle at Delphi to ask if there was anyone wiser than Socrates. The oracle, who usually gave very cryptic answers, responded with a simple "no." This led Socrates on a quest to find someone wiser than himself—a quest which resulted in Socrates making a number of influential enemies. *(Forrest E. Baird)*

*During the totalitarian regime of The Thirty, which remained in power for eight months (404 B.C.), five years before the trial.

can he mean by saying that I am the wisest of men? It cannot be that he is speaking falsely, for he is a god and cannot lie. For a long time I was at a loss to understand his meaning. Then, very reluctantly, I turned to investigate it in this manner: I went to a man who was reputed to be wise, thinking that there, if anywhere, I should prove the answer wrong, and meaning to point out to the oracle its mistake, and to say, "You said that I was the wisest of men, but this man is wiser than I am." So I examined the man—I need not tell you his name, he was a politician—but this was the result, Athenians. When I conversed with him I came to see that, though a great many persons, and most of all he himself, thought that he was wise, yet he was not wise. Then I tried to prove to him that he was not wise, though he fancied that he was. By so doing I made him indignant, and many of the bystanders. So when I went away, I thought to myself, "I am wiser than this man: neither of us knows anything that is really worth knowing, but he thinks that he has knowledge when he has not, while I, having no knowledge, do not think that I have. I seem, at any rate, to be a little wiser than he is on this point: I do not think that I know what I do not know." Next I went to another man who was reputed to be still wiser than the last, with exactly the same result. And there again I made him, and many other men, indignant.

Then I went on to one man after another, realizing that I was arousing indignation every day, which caused me much pain and anxiety. Still I thought that I must set the god's command above everything. So I had to go to every man who seemed to possess any knowledge, and investigate the meaning of the oracle. Athenians, I must tell you the truth; I swear, this was the result of the investigation which I made at the god's command: I found that the men whose reputation for wisdom stood highest were nearly the most lacking in it, while others who were looked down on as common people were much more intelligent. Now I must describe to you the wanderings which I undertook, like Herculean labors, to prove the oracle irrefutable. After the politicians, I went to the poets, tragic, dithyrambic, and others, thinking that there I should find myself manifestly more ignorant than they. So I took up the poems on which I thought that they had spent most pains, and asked them what they meant, hoping at the same time to learn something from them. I am ashamed to tell you the truth, my friends, but I must say it. Almost any one of the bystanders could have talked about the works of these poets better than the poets themselves. So I soon found that it is not by wisdom that the poets create their works, but by a certain instinctive inspiration, like soothsayers and prophets, who say many fine things, but understand nothing of what they say. The poets seemed to me to be in a similar situation. And at the same time I perceived that, because of their poetry, they thought that they were the wisest of men in other matters too, which they were not. So I went away again, thinking that I had the same advantage over the poets that I had over the politicians.

Finally, I went to the artisans, for I knew very well that I possessed no knowledge at all worth speaking of, and I was sure that I should find that they knew many fine things. And in that I was not mistaken. They knew what I did not know, and so far they were wiser than I. But, Athenians, it seemed to me that the skilled artisans had the same failing as the poets. Each of them believed himself to be extremely wise in matters of the greatest importance because he was skillful in his own art: and this presumption of theirs obscured their real wisdom. So I asked myself, on behalf of the oracle, whether I would choose to remain as I was, without either their wisdom or their ignorance, or to possess both, as they did. And I answered to myself and to the oracle that it was better for me to remain as I was.

From this examination, Athenians, has arisen much fierce and bitter indignation, and as a result a great many prejudices about me. People say that I am "a wise man." For the bystanders always think that I am wise myself in any matter wherein I refute another. But, gentlemen, I believe that the god is really wise, and that by this oracle he meant that human wisdom is worth little or nothing. I do not think that he meant that Socrates was wise. He only made use of my name, and took me as an example, as though he would say to men, "He among you is the wisest who, like Socrates, knows that his wisdom is really worth nothing at all." Therefore I still go about testing and examining every man whom I think wise, whether he be a citizen or a stranger, as the god has commanded me. Whenever I find that he is not wise, I point out to him, on the god's behalf, that he is not wise. I am so busy in this pursuit that I have never had leisure to take any part worth mentioning in public matters or to look after my private affairs. I am in great poverty as the result of my service to the god.

Besides this, the young men who follow me about, who are the sons of wealthy persons and have the most leisure, take pleasure in hearing men cross-examined. They often imitate me among themselves; then they try their hands at cross-examining other people. And, I imagine, they find plenty of men who think that they know a great deal when in fact they know little or nothing. Then the persons who are cross-examined get angry with me instead of with themselves, and say that Socrates is an abomination and corrupts the young. When they are asked, "Why, what does he do? What does he teach?" they do not know what to say. Not to seem at a loss, they repeat the stock charges against all philosophers, and allege that he investigates things in the air and under the earth, and that he teaches people to disbelieve in the gods, and to make the worse argument appear the stronger. For, I suppose, they would not like to confess the truth, which is that they are shown up as ignorant pretenders to knowledge that they do not possess. So they have been filling your ears with their bitter prejudices for a long time, for they are ambitious, energetic, and numerous; and they speak vigorously and persuasively against me. Relying on this, Meletus, Anytus, and Lycon have attacked me. Meletus is indignant with me on behalf of the poets, Anytus on behalf of the artisans and politicians, and Lycon on behalf of the orators. And so, as I said at the beginning, I shall be surprised if I am able, in the short time allowed me for my defense, to remove from your minds this prejudice which has grown so strong. What I have told you, Athenians, is the truth: I neither conceal nor do I suppress anything, trivial or important. Yet I know that it is just this outspokenness which rouses indignation. But that is only a proof that my words are true, and that the prejudice against me, and the causes of it, are what I have said. And whether you investigate them now or hereafter, you will find that they are so.

What I have said must suffice as my defense against the charges of my first accusers. I will try next to defend myself against Meletus, that "good patriot," as he calls himself, and my later accusers. Let us assume that they are a new set of accusers, and read their indictment, as we did in the case of the others. It runs thus: Socrates is guilty of corrupting the youth, and of believing not in the gods whom the state believes in, but in other new divinities. Such is the accusation. Let us examine each point in it separately. Meletus says that I am guilty of corrupting the youth. But I say, Athenians, that he is guilty of playing a solemn joke by casually bringing men to trial, and pretending to have a solemn interest in matters to which he has never given a moment's thought. Now I will try to prove to you that this is so.

Come here, Meletus. Is it not a fact that you think it very important that the young should be as good as possible?

MELETUS: It is.

SOCRATES: Come, then, tell the judges who improves them. You care so much,* you must know. You are accusing me, and bringing me to trial, because, as you say, you

---

*Throughout the following passage, Socrates plays on the etymology of the name "Meletus" as meaning "the man who cares."

have discovered that I am the corrupter of the youth. Come now, reveal to the gentlemen who improves them. You see, Meletus, you have nothing to say; you are silent. But don't you think that this is shameful? Is not your silence a conclusive proof of what I say—that you have never cared? Come, tell us, my good man, who makes the young better?

MELETUS: The laws.

e   SOCRATES: That, my friend, is not my question. What man improves the young, who begins by knowing the laws?

MELETUS: The judges here, Socrates.

SOCRATES: What do you mean, Meletus? Can they educate the young and improve them?

MELETUS: Certainly.

SOCRATES: All of them? Or only some of them?

MELETUS: All of them.

SOCRATES: By Hera, that is good news! Such a large supply of benefactors! And

25   do the members of the audience here improve them, or not?

MELETUS: They do.

SOCRATES: And do the councilors?

MELETUS: Yes.

SOCRATES: Well, then, Meletus, do the members of the assembly corrupt the young or do they again all improve them?

MELETUS: They, too, improve them.

SOCRATES: Then all the Athenians, apparently, make the young into good men except me, and I alone corrupt them. Is that your meaning?

MELETUS: Certainly, that is my meaning.

SOCRATES: You have discovered me to be most unfortunate. Now tell me: do you think that the same holds good in the case of horses? Does one man do them harm and

b   everyone else improve them? On the contrary, is it not one man only, or a very few— namely, those who are skilled with horses—who can improve them, while the majority of men harm them if they use them and have anything to do with them? Is it not so, Meletus, both with horses and with every other animal? Of course it is, whether you and Anytus say yes or no. The young would certainly be very fortunate if only one man corrupted them, and everyone else did them good. The truth is, Meletus, you prove conclu-

c   sively that you have never thought about the young in your life. You exhibit your carelessness in not caring for the very matters about which you are prosecuting me.

Now be so good as to tell us, Meletus, is it better to live among good citizens or bad ones? Answer, my friend. I am not asking you at all a difficult question. Do not the bad harm their associates and the good do them good?

MELETUS: Yes.

d   SOCRATES: Is there anyone who would rather be injured than benefitted by his companions? Answer, my good man; you are obliged by the law to answer. Does anyone like to be injured?

MELETUS: Certainly not.

SOCRATES: Well, then, are you prosecuting me for corrupting the young and making them worse, voluntarily or involuntarily?

MELETUS: For doing it voluntarily.

SOCRATES: What, Meletus? Do you mean to say that you, who are so much younger than I, are yet so much wiser than I that you know that bad citizens always do

e   evil, and that good citizens do good, to those with whom they come in contact, while I am so extraordinarily ignorant as not to know that, if I make any of my companions evil, he will probably injure me in some way? And you allege that I do this voluntarily? You will not make me believe that, nor anyone else either, I should think. Either I do not corrupt the young at all or, if I do, I do so involuntarily, so that you are lying in either case. 26 And if I corrupt them involuntarily, the law does not call upon you to prosecute me for an error which is involuntary, but to take me aside privately and reprove and educate me. For, of course, I shall cease from doing wrong involuntarily, as soon as I know that I have been doing wrong. But you avoided associating with me and educating me; instead you bring me up before the court, where the law sends persons, not for education, but for punishment.

The truth is, Athenians, as I said, it is quite clear that Meletus has never cared at all about these matters. However, now tell us, Meletus, how do you say that I corrupt the b young? Clearly, according to your indictment, by teaching them not to believe in the gods the state believes in, but other new divinities instead. You mean that I corrupt the young by that teaching, do you not?

MELETUS: Yes, most certainly I mean that.

SOCRATES: Then in the name of these gods of whom we are speaking, explain c yourself a little more clearly to me and to these gentlemen here. I cannot understand what you mean. Do you mean that I teach the young to believe in some gods, but not in the gods of the state? Do you accuse me of teaching them to believe in strange gods? If that is your meaning, I myself believe in some gods, and my crime is not that of complete atheism. Or do you mean that I do not believe in the gods at all myself, and that I teach other people not to believe in them either?

MELETUS: I mean that you do not believe in the gods in any way whatever.

SOCRATES: You amaze me, Meletus! Why do you say that? Do you mean that I believe neither the sun nor the moon to be gods, like other men? d

MELETUS: I swear he does not, judges. He says that the sun is a stone, and the moon earth.

SOCRATES: My dear Meletus, do you think that you are prosecuting Anaxagoras? You must have a very poor opinion of these men, and think them illiterate, if you imagine that they do not know that the works of Anaxagoras of Clazomenae are full of these doctrines. And so young men learn these things from me, when they can often buy them in the theater for a drachma at most, and laugh at Socrates were he to pretend that these e doctrines, which are very peculiar doctrines, too, were his own. But please tell me, do you really think that I do not believe in the gods at all?

MELETUS: Most certainly I do. You are a complete atheist.

SOCRATES: No one believes that, Meletus, not even you yourself. It seems to me, Athenians, that Meletus is very insolent and reckless, and that he is prosecuting me simply out of insolence, recklessness, and youthful bravado. For he seems to be testing me, by asking me a riddle that has no answer. "Will this wise Socrates," he says to himself, 27 "see that I am joking and contradicting myself? Or shall I deceive him and everyone else who hears me?" Meletus seems to me to contradict himself in his indictment: it is as if he were to say, "Socrates is guilty of not believing in the gods, but believes in the gods." This is joking.

Now, my friends, let us see why I think that this is his meaning. You must answer me, Meletus, and you, Athenians, must remember the request which I made to you at b the start, and not interrupt me with shouts if I talk in my usual manner.

Is there any man, Meletus, who believes in the existence of things pertaining to men and not in the existence of men? Make him answer the question, gentlemen, without these interruptions. Is there any man who believes in the existence of horsemanship and not in the existence of horses? Or in flute playing, and not in flute players? There is not, my friend. If you will not answer, I will tell both you and the judges. But you must answer my next question. Is there any man who believes in the existence of divine things and not in the existence of divinities?

MELETUS: There is not.

SOCRATES: I am very glad that these gentlemen have managed to extract an answer from you. Well then, you say that I believe in divine things, whether they be old or new, and that I teach others to believe in them. At any rate, according to your statement, I believe in divine things. That you have sworn in your indictment. But if I believe in divine things, I suppose it follows necessarily that I believe in divinities. Is it not so? It is. I assume that you grant that, as you do not answer. But do we not believe that divinities are either gods themselves or the children of the gods? Do you admit that?

MELETUS: I do.

SOCRATES: Then you admit that I believe in divinities. Now, if these divinities are gods, then, as I say, you are joking and asking a riddle, and asserting that I do not believe in the gods, and at the same time that I do, since I believe in divinities. But if these divinities are the illegitimate children of the gods, either by the nymphs or by other mothers, as they are said to be, then, I ask, what man could believe in the existence of the children of the gods, and not in the existence of the gods? That would be as absurd as believing in the existence of the offspring of horses and asses, and not in the existence of horses and asses. You must have indicted me in this manner, Meletus, either to test me or because you could not find any act of injustice that you could accuse me of with truth. But you will never contrive to persuade any man with any sense at all that a belief in divine things and things of the gods does not necessarily involve a belief in divinities, and in the gods.

But in truth, Athenians, I do not think that I need say very much to prove that I have not committed the act of injustice for which Meletus is prosecuting me. What I have said is enough to prove that. But be assured it is certainly true, as I have already told you, that I have aroused much indignation. That is what will cause my condemnation if I am condemned; not Meletus nor Anytus either, but that prejudice and resentment of the multitude which have been the destruction of many good men before me, and I think will be so again. There is no prospect that I shall be the last victim.

Perhaps someone will say: "Are you not ashamed, Socrates, of leading a life which is very likely now to cause your death?" I should answer him with justice, and say: "My friend, if you think that a man of any worth at all ought to reckon the chances of life and death when he acts, or that he ought to think of anything but whether he is acting justly or unjustly, and as a good or a bad man would act, you are mistaken. According to you, the demigods who died at Troy would be foolish, and among them Achilles, who thought nothing of danger when the alternative was disgrace. For when his mother—and she was a goddess—addressed him, when he was resolved to slay Hector, in this fashion, 'My son, if you avenge the death of your comrade Patroclus and slay Hector, you will die yourself, for fate awaits you next after Hector.' When he heard this, he scorned danger and death; he feared much more to live a coward and not to avenge his friend. 'Let me punish the evildoer and afterwards die,' he said, 'that I may not remain here by the beaked ships jeered at, encumbering the earth.'"* Do you suppose that he thought of danger or of death? For this, Athenians, I believe to be the truth. Wherever a man's station is, whether he has chosen it of his own will, or whether he has

*Homer, *Iliad,* xviii, 96, 98.

been placed at it by his commander, there it is his duty to remain and face the danger without thinking of death or of any other thing except disgrace.

When the generals whom you chose to command me, Athenians, assigned me my station during the battles of Potidaea, Amphipolis, and Delium, I remained where they stationed me and ran the risk of death, like other men. It would be very strange conduct on my part if I were to desert my station now from fear of death or of any other thing when the god has commanded me—as I am persuaded that he has done—to spend my life in searching for wisdom, and in examining myself and others. That would indeed be a very strange thing. Then certainly I might with justice be brought to trial for not believing in the gods, for I should be disobeying the oracle, and fearing death and thinking myself wise when I was not wise. For to fear death, my friends, is only to think ourselves wise without really being wise, for it is to think that we know what we do not know. For no one knows whether death may not be the greatest good that can happen to man. But men fear it as if they knew quite well that it was the greatest of evils. And what is this but that shameful ignorance of thinking that we know what we do not know? In this matter, too, my friends, perhaps I am different from the multitude. And if I were to claim to be at all wiser than others, it would be because, not knowing very much about the other world, I do not think I know. But I do know very well that it is evil and disgraceful to do an unjust act, and to disobey my superior, whether man or god. I will never do what I know to be evil, and shrink in fear from what I do not know to be good or evil. Even if you acquit me now, and do not listen to Anytus' argument that, if I am to be acquitted, I ought never to have been brought to trial at all, and that, as it is, you are bound to put me to death because, as he said, if I escape, all your sons will be utterly corrupted by practicing what Socrates teaches. If you were therefore to say to me, "Socrates, this time we will not listen to Anytus. We will let you go, but on the condition that you give up this investigation of yours, and philosophy. If you are found following these pursuits again, you shall die." I say, if you offered to let me go, on these terms, I should reply: "Athenians, I hold you in the highest regard and affection, but I will be persuaded by the god rather than you. As long as I have breath and strength I will not give up philosophy and exhorting you and declaring the truth to every one of you whom I meet, saying, as I am accustomed, 'My good friend, you are a citizen of Athens, a city which is very great and very famous for its wisdom and power—are you not ashamed of caring so much for the making of money and for fame and prestige, when you neither think nor care about wisdom and truth and the improvement of your soul?'" If he disputes my words and says that he does care about these things, I shall not at once release him and go away: I shall question him and cross-examine him and test him. If I think that he has not attained excellence, though he says that he has, I shall reproach him for undervaluing the most valuable things, and overvaluing those that are less valuable. This I shall do to everyone whom I meet, young or old, citizen or stranger, but especially to citizens, since they are more closely related to me. This, you must recognize, the god has commanded me to do. And I think that no greater good has ever befallen you in the state than my service to the god. For I spend my whole life in going about and persuading you all to give your first and greatest care to the improvement of your souls, and not till you have done that to think of your bodies or your wealth. And I tell you that wealth does not bring excellence, but that wealth, and every other good thing which men have, whether in public or in private, comes from excellence. If then I corrupt the youth by this teaching, these things must be harmful. But if any man says that I teach anything else, there is nothing in what he says. And therefore, Athenians, I say, whether you are persuaded by Anytus or not, whether you acquit me or not, I shall not change my way of life; no, not if I have to die for it many times.

Do not interrupt me, Athenians, with your shouts. Remember the request which I made to you, and do not interrupt my words. I think that it will profit you to hear them. I am going to say something more to you, at which you may be inclined to protest, but do not do that. Be sure that if you put me to death, I who am what I have told you that I am, you will do yourselves more harm than me. Meletus and Anytus can do me no harm: that

d   is impossible, for I am sure it is not allowed that a good man be injured by a worse. He may indeed kill me, or drive me into exile, or deprive me of my civil rights. Perhaps Meletus and others think those things great evils. But I do not think so. I think it is a much greater evil to do what he is doing now, and to try to put a man to death unjustly. And now, Athenians, I am not arguing in my own defense at all, as you might expect me to do, but rather in yours in order you may not make a mistake about the gift of the god

e   to you by condemning me. For if you put me to death, you will not easily find another who, if I may use a ludicrous comparison, clings to the state as a sort of gadfly to a horse that is large and well-bred but rather sluggish because of its size, so that it needs to be aroused. It seems to me that the god has attached me like that to the state, for I am con-

31   stantly alighting upon you at every point to arouse, persuade, and reproach each of you all day long. You will not easily find anyone else, my friends, to fill my place; and if you are persuaded by me, you will spare my life. You are indignant, as drowsy persons are when they are awakened, and, of course, if you are persuaded by Anytus, you could easily kill me with a single blow, and then sleep on undisturbed for the rest of your lives, unless the god in his care for you sends another to arouse you. And you may easily see

b   that it is the god who has given me to your city; for it is not human, the way in which I have neglected all my own interests and allowed my private affairs to be neglected for so many years, while occupying myself unceasingly in your interests, going to each of you privately, like a father or an elder brother, trying to persuade him to care for human excellence. There would have been a reason for it, if I had gained any advantage by this, or if I had been paid for my exhortations; but you see yourselves that my accusers, though they accuse me of everything else without shame, have not had the shamelessness to say

c   that I ever either exacted or demanded payment. To that they have no witness. And I think that I have sufficient witness to the truth of what I say—my poverty.

Perhaps it may seem strange to you that, though I go about giving this advice privately and meddling in others' affairs, yet I do not venture to come forward in the assembly and advise the state. You have often heard me speak of my reason for this, and

d   in many places: it is that I have a certain divine guide, which is what Meletus has caricatured in his indictment. I have had it from childhood. It is a kind of voice which, whenever I hear it, always turns me back from something which I was going to do, but never urges me to act. It is this which forbids me to take part in politics. And I think it does well to forbid me. For, Athenians, it is quite certain that, if I had attempted to take part in politics, I should have perished at once and long ago without doing any good

e   either to you or to myself. And do not be indignant with me for telling the truth. There is no man who will preserve his life for long, either in Athens or elsewhere, if he firmly opposes the multitude, and tries to prevent the commission of much injustice and ille-

32   gality in the state. He who would really fight for justice must do so as a private citizen, not as a political figure, if he is to preserve his life, even for a short time.

I will prove to you that this is so by very strong evidence, not by mere words, but by what you value more—actions. Listen, then, to what has happened to me, that you may know that there is no man who could make me consent to commit an unjust act from the fear of death, but that I would perish at once rather than give way. What I am going to tell you may be commonplace in the law court; nevertheless, it is true. The only

b   office that I ever held in the state, Athenians, was that of councilor. When you wished to

try the ten admirals who did not rescue their men after the battle of Arginusae as a group, which was illegal, as you all came to think afterwards, the executive committee was composed of members of the tribe Antiochis, to which I belong.* On that occasion I alone of the committee members opposed your illegal action and gave my vote against you. The orators were ready to impeach me and arrest me; and you were clamoring and urging them on with your shouts. But I thought that I ought to face the danger, with law   c
and justice on my side, rather than join with you in your unjust proposal, from fear of imprisonment or death. That was when the state was democratic. When the oligarchy came in, The Thirty sent for me, with four others, to the council-chamber, and ordered us to bring Leon the Salaminian from Salamis, that they might put him to death. They were in the habit of frequently giving similar orders to many others, wishing to implicate as many as possible in their crimes. But then I again proved, not by mere words, but by my actions, that, if I may speak bluntly, I do not care a straw for death; but that I do   d
care very much indeed about not doing anything unjust or impious. That government with all its power did not terrify me into doing anything unjust. When we left the council-chamber, the other four went over to Salamis and brought Leon across to Athens; I went home. And if the rule of The Thirty had not been overthrown soon afterwards, I should very likely have been put to death for what I did then. Many of you will be my   e
witnesses in this matter.**

Now do you think that I could have remained alive all these years if I had taken part in public affairs, and had always maintained the cause of justice like a good man, and had held it a paramount duty, as it is, to do so? Certainly not, Athenians, nor could any other man. But throughout my whole life, both in private and in public, whenever I   33
have had to take part in public affairs, you will find I have always been the same and have never yielded unjustly to anyone; no, not to those whom my enemies falsely assert to have been my pupils. But I was never anyone's teacher. I have never withheld myself from anyone, young or old, who was anxious to hear me converse while I was making my investigation; neither do I converse for payment, and refuse to converse without   b
payment. I am ready to ask questions of rich and poor alike, and if any man wishes to answer me, and then listen to what I have to say, he may. And I cannot justly be charged with causing these men to turn out good or bad, for I never either taught or professed to teach any of them any knowledge whatever. And if any man asserts that he ever learned or heard anything from me in private which everyone else did not hear as well as he, be sure that he does not speak the truth.

Why is it, then, that people delight in spending so much time in my company? You have heard why, Athenians. I told you the whole truth when I said that they delight in   c
hearing me examine persons who think that they are wise when they are not wise. It is certainly very amusing to listen to. And, as I have said, the god has commanded me to examine men, in oracles and in dreams and in every way in which the divine will was ever declared to man. This is the truth, Athenians, and if it were not the truth, it would be

---

*The Council was the administrative body in Athens. Actual administrative functions were performed by an executive committee of the Council, and the members of this committee were recruited from each tribe in turn. The case Socrates is alluding to was that of the admirals who were accused of having failed to rescue the crews of ships that sank during the battle of Arginusae. The six admirals who were actually put on trial were condemned as a group and executed.

**There is evidence that Meletus was one of the four who turned in Leon. Socrates' recalling this earlier lapse from legal procedure is probably also a thrust at Anytus. The Thirty successfully implicated so many Athenians in their crimes that an amnesty was declared, which Anytus strongly favored, in order to enlist wider support for the restored democracy. Thus those who were really implicated could now no longer be prosecuted legally, but Socrates is himself being illegally prosecuted (as he now goes on to suggest) because he was guilty of having associated with such "pupils" as Critias, who was a leader of The Thirty.

easily refuted. For if it were really the case that I have already corrupted some of the
d   young men, and am now corrupting others, surely some of them, finding as they grew
older that I had given them bad advice in their youth, would have come forward today to
accuse me and take their revenge. Or if they were unwilling to do so themselves, surely
their relatives, their fathers or brothers, or others, would, if I had done them any harm,
have remembered it and taken their revenge. Certainly I see many of them in court. Here
e   is Crito, of my own district and of my own age, the father of Critobulus; here is Lysanias
of Sphettus, the father of Aeschines; here is also Antiphon of Cephisus, the father of
Epigenes. Then here are others whose brothers have spent their time in my company—
Nicostratus, the son of Theozotides and brother of Theodotus—and Theodotus is dead,
so he at least cannot entreat his brother to be silent; here is Paralus, the son of
34   Demodocus and the brother of Theages; here is Adeimantus, the son of Ariston, whose
brother is Plato here; and Aeantodorus, whose brother is Aristodorus. And I can name
many others to you, some of whom Meletus ought to have called as witnesses in the
course of his own speech; but if he forgot to call them then, let him call them now—I will
yield the floor to him—and tell us if he has any such evidence. No, on the contrary, my
friends, you will find all these men ready to support me, the corrupter who has injured
b   their relatives, as Meletus and Anytus call me. Those of them who have been already corrupted might perhaps have some reason for supporting me, but what reason can their relatives have who are grown up, and who are uncorrupted, except the reason of truth and
justice that they know very well that Meletus is lying, and that I am speaking the truth?

Well, my friends, this, and perhaps more like this, is pretty much all I have to offer
in my defense. There may be some one among you who will be indignant when he
c   remembers how, even in a less important trial than this, he begged and entreated the
judges, with many tears, to acquit him, and brought forward his children and many of his
friends and relatives in court in order to appeal to your feelings; and then finds that I shall
do none of these things, though I am in what he would think the supreme danger. Perhaps
he will harden himself against me when he notices this; it may make him angry, and he
may cast his vote in anger. If it is so with any of you—I do not suppose that it is, but in
d   case it should be so—I think that I should answer him reasonably if I said: "My friend, I
have relatives, too, for, in the words of Homer, I am 'not born of an oak or a rock'* but of
flesh and blood." And so, Athenians, I have relatives, and I have three sons, one of them
nearly grown up, and the other two still children. Yet I will not bring any of them forward
e   before you and implore you to acquit me. And why will I do none of these things? It is
not from arrogance, Athenians, nor because I lack respect for you—whether or not I can
face death bravely is another question—but for my own good name, and for your good
name, and for the good name of the whole state. I do not think it right, at my age and with
my reputation, to do anything of that kind. Rightly or wrongly, men have made up their
35   minds that in some way Socrates is different from the multitude of men. And it will be
shameful if those of you who are thought to excel in wisdom, or in bravery, or in any
other excellence, are going to act in this fashion. I have often seen men of reputation
behaving in an extraordinary way at their trial, as if they thought it a terrible fate to be
killed, and as though they expected to live for ever if you did not put them to death. Such
b   men seem to me to bring shame upon the state, for any stranger would suppose that the
best and most eminent Athenians, who are selected by their fellow citizens to hold office,
and for other honors, are no better than women. Those of you, Athenians, who have any
reputation at all ought not to do these things, and you ought not to allow us to do them.

*Homer, *Odyssey,* xix, 163.

You should show that you will be much more ready to condemn men who make the state ridiculous by these pathetic performances than men who remain quiet.

But apart from the question of reputation, my friends, I do not think that it is right to entreat the judge to acquit us, or to escape condemnation in that way. It is our duty to teach and persuade him. He does not sit to give away justice as a favor, but to pronounce judgment; and he has sworn, not to favor any man whom he would like to favor, but to judge according to law. And, therefore, we ought not to encourage you in the habit of breaking your oaths; and you ought not to allow yourselves to fall into this habit, for then neither you nor we would be acting piously. Therefore, Athenians, do not require me to do these things, for I believe them to be neither good nor just nor pious; especially, do not ask me to do them today when Meletus is prosecuting me for impiety. For were I to be successful and persuade you by my entreaties to break your oaths, I should be clearly teaching you to believe that there are no gods, and I should be simply accusing myself by my defense of not believing in them. But, Athenians, that is very far from the truth. I do believe in the gods as no one of my accusers believes in them; and to you and to the god I commit my cause to be decided as is best for you and for me.

(He is found guilty by 281 votes to 220.)

I am not indignant at the verdict which you have given, Athenians, for many reasons. I expected that you would find me guilty; and I am not so much surprised at that as at the numbers of the votes. I certainly never thought that the majority against me would have been so narrow. But now it seems that if only thirty votes had changed sides, I should have escaped. So I think that I have escaped Meletus, as it is; and not only have I escaped him, for it is perfectly clear that if Anytus and Lycon had not come forward to accuse me, too, he would not have obtained the fifth part of the votes, and would have had to pay a fine of a thousand drachmae.

So he proposes death as the penalty. Be it so. And what alternative penalty shall I propose to you, Athenians?* What I deserve, of course, must I not? What then do I deserve to pay or to suffer for having determined not to spend my life in ease? I neglected the things which most men value, such as wealth, and family interests, and military commands, and public oratory, and all the civic appointments, and social clubs, and political factions, that there are in Athens; for I thought that I was really too honest a man to preserve my life if I engaged in these affairs. So I did not go where I should have done no good either to you or to myself. I went, instead, to each one of you privately to do him, as I say, the greatest of benefits, and tried to persuade him not to think of his affairs until he had thought of himself and tried to make himself as good and wise as possible, nor to think of the affairs of Athens until he had thought of Athens herself; and to care for other things in the same manner. Then what do I deserve for such a life? Something good, Athenians, if I am really to propose what I deserve; and something good which it would be suitable for me to receive. Then what is a suitable reward to be given to a poor benefactor who requires leisure to exhort you? There is no reward, Athenians, so suitable for him as receiving free meals in the prytaneum. It is a much more suitable reward for him than for any of you who has won a victory at the Olympic games with his horse or his chariots. Such a man only makes you seem happy, but I make you really happy; he is not in want, and I am. So if I am to propose the penalty which I really deserve, I propose this—free meals in the prytaneum.

---

*For certain crimes no penalty was fixed by Athenian law. Having reached a verdict of guilty, the court had still to decide between the alternative penalties proposed by the prosecution and the defense.

Perhaps you think me stubborn and arrogant in what I am saying now, as in what I said about the entreaties and tears. It is not so, Athenians. It is rather that I am convinced that I never wronged any man voluntarily, though I cannot persuade you of that, since we have conversed together only a little time. If there were a law at Athens, as there is elsewhere, not to finish a trial of life and death in a single day, I think that I could have persuaded you; but now it is not easy in so short a time to clear myself of great prejudices. But when I am persuaded that I have never wronged any man, I shall certainly not wrong myself, or admit that I deserve to suffer any evil, or propose any evil for myself as a penalty. Why should I? Lest I should suffer the penalty which Meletus proposes when I say that I do not know whether it is a good or an evil? Shall I choose instead of it something which I know to be an evil, and propose that as a penalty? Shall I propose imprisonment? And why should I pass the rest of my days in prison, the slave of successive officials? Or shall I propose a fine, with imprisonment until it is paid? I have told you why I will not do that. I should have to remain in prison, for I have no money to pay a fine with. Shall I then propose exile? Perhaps you would agree to that. Life would indeed be very dear to me if I were unreasonable enough to expect that strangers would cheerfully tolerate my discussions and arguments when you who are my fellow citizens cannot endure them, and have found them so irksome and odious to you that you are seeking now to be relieved of them. No, indeed, Athenians, that is not likely. A fine life I should lead for an old man if I were to withdraw from Athens and pass the rest of my days in wandering from city to city, and continually being expelled. For I know very well that the young men will listen to me wherever I go, as they do here. If I drive them away, they will persuade their elders to expel me; if I do not drive them away, their fathers and other relatives will expel me for their sakes.

Perhaps someone will say, "Why cannot you withdraw from Athens, Socrates, and hold your peace?" It is the most difficult thing in the world to make you understand why I cannot do that. If I say that I cannot hold my peace because that would be to disobey the god, you will think that I am not in earnest and will not believe me. And if I tell you that no greater good can happen to a man than to discuss human excellence every day and the other matters about which you have heard me arguing and examining myself and others and that an unexamined life is not worth living, then you will believe me still less. But that is so, my friends, though it is not easy to persuade you. And, what is more, I am not accustomed to think that I deserve anything evil. If I had been rich, I would have proposed as large a fine as I could pay: that would have done me no harm. But I am not rich enough to pay a fine unless you are willing to fix it at a sum within my means. Perhaps I could pay you a mina, so I propose that. Plato here, Athenians, and Crito, and Critobulus, and Apollodorus bid me propose thirty minae, and they guarantee its payment. So I propose thirty minae. Their security will be sufficient to you for the money.

(He is condemned to death.)

You have not gained very much time, Athenians, and at the price of the slurs of those who wish to revile the state. And they will say that you put Socrates, a wise man, to death. For they will certainly call me wise, whether I am wise or not, when they want to reproach you. If you had waited for a little while, your wishes would have been fulfilled in the course of nature; for you see that I am an old man, far advanced in years, and near to death. I am saying this not to all of you, only to those who have voted for my death. And to them I have something else to say. Perhaps, my friends, you think that I have been convicted because I was wanting in the arguments by which I could have

Despite refuting his accusers (as recorded in the *Apology*). Socrates was found guilty of impiety toward the gods and of corrupting the youth. He was sentenced to die by drinking the poison hemlock. *(Corbis-Bettmann)*

persuaded you to acquit me, if I had thought it right to do or to say anything to escape punishment. It is not so. I have been convicted because I was wanting, not in arguments, but in impudence and shamelessness—because I would not plead before you as you would have liked to hear me plead, or appeal to you with weeping and wailing, or say e and do many other things which I maintain are unworthy of me, but which you have been accustomed to from other men. But when I was defending myself, I thought that I ought not to do anything unworthy of a free man because of the danger which I ran, and I have not changed my mind now. I would very much rather defend myself as I did, and die, than as you would have had me do, and live. Both in a lawsuit and in war, there are some things which neither I nor any other man may do in order to escape from death. In 39 battle, a man often sees that he may at least escape from death by throwing down his arms and falling on his knees before the pursuer to beg for his life. And there are many other ways of avoiding death in every danger if a man is willing to say and to do anything. But, my friends, I think that it is a much harder thing to escape from wickedness than from death, for wickedness is swifter than death. And now I, who am old and slow, b have been overtaken by the slower pursuer: and my accusers, who are clever and swift, have been overtaken by the swifter pursuer—wickedness. And now I shall go away, sentenced by you to death; they will go away, sentenced by truth to wickedness and injustice. And I abide by this award as well as they. Perhaps it was right for these things to be so. I think that they are fairly balanced.

And now I wish to prophesy to you, Athenians, who have condemned me. For I c am going to die, and that is the time when men have most prophetic power. And I prophesy to you who have sentenced me to death that a far more severe punishment than you have inflicted on me will surely overtake you as soon as I am dead. You have done this thing, thinking that you will be relieved from having to give an account of your lives. But I say that the result will be very different. There will be more men who will call you to account, whom I have held back, though you did not recognize it. And they will be harsher toward you than I have been, for they will be younger, and you will be more indignant with them. For if you think that you will restrain men from reproaching you for not living as you should, by putting them to death, you are very much mistaken. That way of escape is neither possible nor honorable. It is much more honorable and much easier not to suppress others, but to make yourselves as good as you can. This is my parting prophecy to you who have condemned me.

d

e

With you who have acquitted me I should like to discuss this thing that has happened, while the authorities are busy, and before I go to the place where I have to die. So, remain with me until I go: there is no reason why we should not talk with each other while it is possible. I wish to explain to you, as my friends, the meaning of what has happened to me. An amazing thing has happened to me, judges—for I am right in calling you judges.* The prophetic guide has been constantly with me all through my life till now, opposing me even in trivial matters if I were not going to act rightly. And now you yourselves see what has happened to me—a thing which might be thought, and which is sometimes actually reckoned, the supreme evil. But the divine guide did not oppose me when I was leaving my house in the morning, nor when I was coming up here to the court, nor at any point in my speech when I was going to say anything; though at other times it has often stopped me in the very act of speaking. But now, in this matter, it has never once opposed me, either in my words or my actions. I will tell you what I believe to be the reason. This thing that has come upon me must be a good; and those of us who think that death is an evil must needs be mistaken. I have a clear proof that that is so; for my accustomed guide would certainly have opposed me if I had not been going to meet with something good.

40

b

c

And if we reflect in another way, we shall see that we may well hope that death is a good. For the state of death is one of two things: either the dead man wholly ceases to be and loses all consciousness or, as we are told, it is a change and a migration of the soul to another place. And if death is the absence of all consciousness, and like the sleep of one whose slumbers are unbroken by any dreams, it will be a wonderful gain. For if a man had to select that night in which he slept so soundly that he did not even dream, and had to compare with it all the other nights and days of his life, and then had to say how many days and nights in his life he had spent better and more pleasantly than this night, I think that a private person, nay, even the Great King of Persia himself, would find them easy to count, compared with the others. If that is the nature of death, I for one count it a gain. For then it appears that all time is nothing more than a single night. But if death is a journey to another place, and what we are told is true—that all who have died are there—what good could be greater than this, my judges? Would a journey not be worth taking, at the end of which, in the other world, we should be delivered from the pretended judges here and should find the true judges who are said to sit in judgment below, such as Minos and Rhadamanthus and Aeacus and Triptolemus, and the other demigods who were just in their own lives? Or what would you not give to converse with Orpheus and Musaeus and Hesiod and Homer? I am willing to die many times if this be true. And for my own part I should find it wonderful to meet there Palamedes, and Ajax the son of

d

e

41

b

---

*The form of address hitherto has always been "Athenians," or "my friends." The "judges" in an Athenian court were simply the members of the jury.

Telamon, and the other men of old who have died through an unjust judgment, and to compare my experiences with theirs. That I think would be no small pleasure. And, above all, I could spend my time in examining those who are there, as I examine men here, and in finding out which of them is wise, and which of them thinks himself wise when he is not wise. What would we not give, my judges, to be able to examine the leader of the great expedition against Troy, or Odysseus, or Sisyphus, or countless other   c
men and women whom we could name? It would be an inexpressible happiness to converse with them and to live with them and to examine them. Assuredly there they do not put men to death for doing that. For besides the other ways in which they are happier than we are, they are immortal, at least if what we are told is true.

And you too, judges, must face death hopefully, and believe this one truth, that no evil can happen to a good man, either in life or after death. His affairs are not neglected by the gods; and what has happened to me today has not happened by chance. I am persuaded   d
that it was better for me to die now, and to be released from trouble; and that was the reason why the guide never turned me back. And so I am not at all angry with my accusers or with those who have condemned me to die. Yet it was not with this in mind that they accused me and condemned me, but meaning to do me an injury. So far I may blame them.   e

Yet I have one request to make of them. When my sons grow up, punish them, my friends, and harass them in the same way that I have harassed you, if they seem to you to care for riches or for any other thing more than excellence; and if they think that they are something when they are really nothing, reproach them, as I have reproached you, for not caring for what they should, and for thinking that they are something when really they are nothing. And if you will do this, I myself and my sons will have received   42
justice from you.

But now the time has come, and we must go away—I to die, and you to live. Which is better is known to the god alone.

CRITO

Characters

Socrates

Crito

Scene—The Prison of Socrates

SOCRATES: Why have you come at this hour, Crito? Is it not still early?   43
CRITO: Yes, very early.
SOCRATES: About what time is it?
CRITO: It is just daybreak.
SOCRATES: I wonder that the jailer was willing to let you in.
CRITO: He knows me now, Socrates; I come here so often, and besides, I have given him a tip.
SOCRATES: Have you been here long?

Plato, *Crito*, translated by F.J. Church (New York: Macmillan/Library of the Liberal Arts, 1963).

CRITO: Yes, some time.

b   SOCRATES: Then why did you sit down without speaking? Why did you not wake me at once?

CRITO: Indeed, Socrates, I wish that I myself were not so sleepless and sorrowful. But I have been wondering to see how soundly you sleep. And I purposely did not wake you, for I was anxious not to disturb your repose. Often before, all through your life, I have thought that your temperament was a happy one; and I think so more than ever now when I see how easily and calmly you bear the calamity that has come to you.

c   SOCRATES: Nay, Crito, it would be absurd if at my age I were disturbed at having to die.

CRITO: Other men as old are overtaken by similar calamities, Socrates; but their age does not save them from being disturbed by their fate.

SOCRATES: That is so; but tell me why are you here so early? Crito. I am the bearer of sad news, Socrates; not sad, it seems, for you, but for me and for all your friends, both sad and hard to bear; and for none of them, I think, is it as hard to bear as it is for me.

SOCRATES: What is it? Has the ship come from Delos, at the arrival of which I am
d   to die?

CRITO: No, it has not actually arrived, but I think that it will be here today, from the news which certain persons have brought from Sunium, who left it there. It is clear from their report that it will be here today; and so, Socrates, tomorrow your life will have to end.

44   SOCRATES: Well, Crito, may it end well. Be it so, if so the gods will. But I do not think that the ship will be here today,

CRITO: Why do you suppose not?

SOCRATES: I will tell you. I am to die on the day after the ship arrives, am I not?*

CRITO: That is what the authorities say.

SOCRATES: Then I do not think that it will come today, but tomorrow. I am counting on a dream I had a little while ago in the night, so it seems to be fortunate that you did not wake me.

CRITO: And what was this dream?

SOCRATES: A fair and beautiful woman, clad in white, seemed to come to me, and
b   call me and say, "O Socrates—On the third day shall you fertile Phthia reach."**

CRITO: What a strange dream, Socrates!

SOCRATES: But its meaning is clear, at least to me, Crito.

CRITO: Yes, too clear, it seems. But, O my good Socrates, I beg you for the last time to listen to me and save yourself. For to me your death will be more than a single disaster; not only shall I lose a friend the like of whom I shall never find again, but many persons who do not know you and me well will think that I might have saved you if I
c   had been willing to spend money, but that I neglected to do so. And what reputation could be more disgraceful than the reputation of caring more for money than for one's friends? The public will never believe that we were anxious to save you, but that you yourself refused to escape.

SOCRATES: But, my dear Crito, why should we care so much about public opinion? Reasonable men, of whose opinion it is worth our while to think, will believe that we acted as we really did.

---

*Criminals could not be put to death while the sacred ship was away on its voyage.
**Homer, *Iliad,* ix, 363.

CRITO: But you see, Socrates, that it is necessary to care about public opinion, too.   d
This very thing that has happened to you proves that the multitude can do a man not the
least, but almost the greatest harm, if he is falsely accused to them.

SOCRATES: I wish that the multitude were able to do a man the greatest harm, Crito,
for then they would be able to do him the greatest good, too. That would have been fine.
But, as it is, they can do neither. They cannot make a man either wise or foolish: they act
wholly at random.

CRITO: Well, as you wish. But tell me this, Socrates. You surely are not anxious   e
about me and your other friends, and afraid lest, if you escape, the informers would say
that we stole you away, and get us into trouble, and involve us in a great deal of expense,
or perhaps in the loss of all our property, and, it may be, bring some other punishment
upon us besides? If you have any fear of that kind, dismiss it. For of course we are   45
bound to run these risks, and still greater risks than these, if necessary, in saving you. So
do not, I beg you, refuse to listen to me.

SOCRATES: I am anxious about that, Crito, and about much besides.

CRITO: Then have no fear on that score. There are men who, for no very large
sum, are ready to bring you out of prison into safety. And then, you know, these informers are cheaply bought, and there would be no need to spend much upon them. My fortune is at your service, and I think that it is adequate; and if you have any feeling about   b
making use of my money, there are strangers in Athens whom you know, ready to use
theirs; and one of them, Simmias of Thebes, has actually brought enough for this very
purpose. And Cebes and many others are ready, too. And therefore, I repeat, do not
shrink from saving yourself on that ground. And do not let what you said in the court—
that if you went into exile you would not know what to do with yourself—stand in your
way; for there are many places for you to go to, where you will be welcomed. If you
choose to go to Thessaly, I have friends there who will make much of you and protect   c
you from any annoyance from the people of Thessaly.

And besides, Socrates, I think that you will be doing what is unjust if you abandon your life when you might preserve it. You are simply playing into your enemies'
hands; it is exactly what they wanted—to destroy you. And what is more, to me you
seem to be abandoning your children, too. You will leave them to take their chance in
life, as far as you are concerned, when you might bring them up and educate them. Most   d
likely their fate will be the usual fate of children who are left orphans. But you ought
not to bring children into the world unless you mean to take the trouble of bringing
them up and educating them. It seems to me that you are choosing the easy way, and not
the way of a good and brave man, as you ought, when you have been talking all your life
long of the value that you set upon human excellence. For my part, I feel ashamed both   e
for you and for us who are your friends. Men will think that the whole thing which has
happened to you—your appearance in court to face trial, when you need not have
appeared at all; the very way in which the trial was conducted; and then last of all this,
the crowning absurdity of the whole affair—is due to our cowardice. It will look as if
we had shirked the danger out of miserable cowardice; for we did not save you, and you   46
did not save yourself, when it was quite possible to do so if we had been good for anything at all. Take care, Socrates, lest these things be not evil only, but also dishonorable
to you and to us. Reflect, then, or rather the time for reflection is past; we must make up
our minds. And there is only one plan possible. Everything must be done tonight. If we
delay any longer, we are lost. Socrates, I implore you not to refuse to listen to me.

SOCRATES: My dear Crito, if your anxiety to save me be right, it is most valuable;   b
but if not, the greater it is the harder it will be to cope with. We must reflect, then, whether

we are to do as you say or not; for I am still what I always have been—a man who will accept no argument but that which on reflection I find to be truest. I cannot cast aside my former arguments because this misfortune has come to me. They seem to me to be as true as ever they were, and I respect and honor the same ones as I used to. And if we have no better argument to substitute for them, I certainly shall not agree to your proposal, not even though the power of the multitude should scare us with fresh terrors, as children are scared with hobgoblins, and inflict upon us new fines and imprisonments, and deaths. What is the most appropriate way of examining the question? Shall we go back first to what you say about opinions, and ask if we used to be right in thinking that we ought to pay attention to some opinions, and not to others? Were we right in saying so before I was condemned to die, and has it now become apparent that we were talking at random and arguing for the sake of argument, and that it was really nothing but playful nonsense? I am anxious, Crito, to examine our former argument with your help, and to see whether my present circumstance will appear to me to have affected its truth in any way or not; and whether we are to set it aside, or to yield assent to it. Those of us who thought at all seriously always used to say, I think, exactly what I said just now, namely, that we ought to respect some of the opinions which men form, and not others. Tell me, Crito, I beg you, do you not think that they were right? For you in all probability will not have to die tomorrow, and your judgment will not be biased by that circumstance. Reflect, then, do you not think it reasonable to say that we should not respect all the opinions of men but only some, nor the opinions of all men but only of some men? What do you think? Is not this true?

CRITO: It is.

SOCRATES: And we should respect the good opinions, and not the worthless ones?

CRITO: Yes.

SOCRATES: But the good opinions are those of the wise, and the worthless ones those of the foolish?

CRITO: Of course.

SOCRATES: And what did we say about this? Does a man who is in training, and who is serious about it, pay attention to the praise and blame and opinion of all men, or only of the one man who is a doctor or a trainer?

CRITO: He pays attention only to the opinion of the one man.

SOCRATES: Then he ought to fear the blame and welcome the praise of this one man, not of the multitude?

CRITO: Clearly.

SOCRATES: Then he must act and exercise, and eat and drink in whatever way the one man who is his director, and who understands the matter, tells him; not as others tell him?

CRITO: That is so.

SOCRATES: Good. But if he disobeys this one man, and disregards his opinion and his praise, and respects instead what the many say, who understand nothing of the matter, will he not suffer for it?

CRITO: Of course he will.

SOCRATES: And how will he suffer? In what way and in what part of himself?

CRITO: Of course in his body. That is disabled.

SOCRATES: You are right. And, Crito, to be brief, is it not the same in everything? And, therefore, in questions of justice and injustice, and of the base and the honorable, and of good and evil, which we are now examining, ought we to follow the opinion of the many and fear that, or the opinion of the one man who understands these matters (if we can find him), and feel more shame and fear before him than before all other men? For if we do not follow him, we shall corrupt and maim that part of us which, we used to say, is improved by justice and disabled by injustice. Or is this not so?

CRITO: No, Socrates, I agree with you.

SOCRATES: Now, if, by listening to the opinions of those who do not understand, we disable that part of us which is improved by health and corrupted by disease, is our life worth living when it is corrupt? It is the body, is it not?   e

CRITO: Yes.

SOCRATES: Is life worth living with the body corrupted and crippled?

CRITO: No, certainly not.

SOCRATES: Then is life worth living when that part of us which is maimed by injustice and benefited by justice is corrupt? Or do we consider that part of us, whatever it is, which has to do with justice and injustice to be of less consequence than our body?   48

CRITO: No, certainly not.

SOCRATES: But more valuable?

CRITO: Yes, much more so.

SOCRATES: Then, my good friend, we must not think so much of what the many will say of us; we must think of what the one man who understands justice and injustice, and of what truth herself will say of us. And so you are mistaken, to begin with, when you invite us to regard the opinion of the multitude concerning the just and the honorable and the good, and their opposites. But, it may be said, the multitude can put us to death?

CRITO: Yes, that is evident. That may be said, Socrates.   b

SOCRATES: True. But, my good friend, to me it appears that the conclusion which we have just reached is the same as our conclusion of former times. Now consider whether we still hold to the belief that we should set the highest value, not on living, but on living well?

CRITO: Yes, we do.

SOCRATES: And living well and honorably and justly mean the same thing: do we hold to that or not?

CRITO: We do.

SOCRATES: Then, starting from these premises, we have to consider whether it is just or not for me to try to escape from prison, without the consent of the Athenians. If   c
we find that it is just, we will try; if not, we will give up the idea. I am afraid that considerations of expense, and of reputation, and of bringing up my children, of which you talk, Crito, are only the opinions of the many, who casually put men to death, and who would, if they could, as casually bring them to life again, without a thought. But reason, which is our guide, shows us that we can have nothing to consider but the question which I asked just now—namely, shall we be acting justly if we give money and thanks to the men who are to aid me in escaping, and if we ourselves take our respective parts in my escape? Or shall we in truth be acting unjustly if we do all this? And if we find   d
that we should be acting unjustly, then we must not take any account either of death, or of any other evil that may be the consequence of remaining here, where we are, but only of acting unjustly.

CRITO: I think that you are right, Socrates. But what are we to do?

SOCRATES: Let us examine this question together, my friend, and if you can contradict anything that I say, do so, and I shall be persuaded. But if you cannot, do not go   e
on repeating to me any longer, my dear friend, that I should escape without the consent of the Athenians. I am very anxious to act with your approval and consent. I do not want you to think me mistaken. But now tell me if you agree with the premise from which I start, and try to answer my questions as you think best.   49

CRITO: I will try.

SOCRATES: Ought we never to act unjustly voluntarily? Or may we act unjustly in some ways, and not in others? Is it the case, as we have often agreed in former times,

that it is never either good or honorable to act unjustly? Or have all our former conclusions been overturned in these few days; and did we at our age fail to recognize all
b   along, when we were seriously conversing with each other, that we were no better than children? Is not what we used to say most certainly the truth, whether the multitude agrees with us or not? Is not acting unjustly evil and shameful in every case, whether we incur a heavier or a lighter punishment as the consequence? Do we believe that?

CRITO: We do.

SOCRATES: Then we ought never to act unjustly?

CRITO: Certainly not.

SOCRATES: If we ought never to act unjustly at all, ought we to repay injustice with injustice, as the multitude thinks we may?

c   CRITO: Clearly not.

SOCRATES: Well, then, Crito, ought we to do evil to anyone?

CRITO: Certainly I think not, Socrates.

SOCRATES: And is it just to repay evil with evil, as the multitude thinks, or unjust?

CRITO: Certainly it is unjust.

SOCRATES: For there is no difference, is there, between doing evil to a man and acting unjustly?

CRITO: True.

SOCRATES: Then we ought not to repay injustice with injustice or to do harm to
d   any man, no matter what we may have suffered from him. And in conceding this, Crito, be careful that you do not concede more than you mean. For I know that only a few men hold, or ever will hold, this opinion. And so those who hold it and those who do not have no common ground of argument; they can of necessity only look with contempt on each other's belief. Do you therefore consider very carefully whether or not you agree with me and share my opinion. Are we to start in our inquiry from the premise that it is never right either to act unjustly, or to repay injustice with injustice, or to avenge ourselves on any man who harms us, by harming him in return? Or do you disagree with
e   me and dissent from my premise? I myself have believed in it for a long time, and I believe in it still. But if you differ in any way, explain to me how. If you still hold to our former opinion, listen to my next point.

CRITO: Yes, I hold to it, and I agree with you. Go on.

SOCRATES: Then, my next point, or rather my next question, is this: Ought a man to carry out his just agreements, or may he shuffle out of them?

CRITO: He ought to carry them out.

SOCRATES: Then consider. If I escape without the state's consent, shall I be injur-
50   ing those whom I ought least to injure, or not? Shall I be abiding by my just agreements or not?

CRITO: I cannot answer your question, Socrates. I do not understand it.

SOCRATES: Consider it in this way. Suppose the laws and the commonwealth were to come and appear to me as I was preparing to run away (if that is the right phrase to describe my escape) and were to ask, "Tell us, Socrates, what have you in your mind to
b   do? What do you mean by trying to escape but to destroy us, the laws and the whole state, so far as you are able? Do you think that a state can exist and not be overthrown, in which the decisions of law are of no force, and are disregarded and undermined by private individuals?" How shall we answer questions like that, Crito? Much might be said, especially by an orator, in defense of the law which makes judicial decisions supreme. Shall I reply,
c   "But the state has injured me by judging my case unjustly?" Shall we say that?

CRITO: Certainly we will, Socrates.

SOCRATES: And suppose the laws were to reply, "Was that our agreement? Or was it that you would abide by whatever judgments the state should pronounce?" And if we were surprised by their words, perhaps they would say, "Socrates, don't be surprised by our words, but answer us; you yourself are accustomed to ask questions and to answer them. What complaint have you against us and the state, that you are trying to destroy us? Are we not, first of all, your parents? Through us your father took your mother and brought you into the world. Tell us, have you any fault to find with those of us that are the laws of marriage?" "I have none," I should reply. "Or have you any fault to find with those of us that regulate the raising of the child and the education which you, like others, received? Did we not do well in telling your father to educate you in music and athletics?" "You did," I should say. "Well, then, since you were brought into the world and raised and educated by us, how, in the first place, can you deny that you are our child and our slave, as your fathers were before you? And if this be so, do you think that your rights are on a level with ours? Do you think that you have a right to retaliate if we should try to do anything to you? You had not the same rights that your father had, or that your master would have had if you had been a slave. You had no right to retaliate if they ill-treated you, or to answer them if they scolded you, or to strike them back if they struck you, or to repay them evil with evil in any way. And do you think that you may retaliate in the case of your country and its laws? If we try to destroy you, because we think it just, will you in return do all that you can to destroy us, the laws, and your country, and say that in so doing you are acting justly—you, the man who really thinks so much of excellence? Or are you too wise to see that your country is worthier, more to be revered, more sacred, and held in higher honor both by the gods and by all men of understanding, than your father and your mother and all your other ancestors; and that you ought to reverence it, and to submit to it, and to approach it more humbly when it is angry with you than you would approach your father; and either to do whatever it tells you to do or to persuade it to excuse you; and to obey in silence if it orders you to endure flogging or imprisonment, or if it sends you to battle to be wounded or to die? That is just. You must not give way, nor retreat, nor desert your station. In war, and in the court of justice, and everywhere, you must do whatever your state and your country tell you to do, or you must persuade them that their commands are unjust. But it is impious to use violence against your father or your mother; and much more impious to use violence against your country." What answer shall we make, Crito? Shall we say that the laws speak the truth, or not?

CRITO: I think that they do.

SOCRATES: "Then consider, Socrates," perhaps they would say, "if we are right in saying that by attempting to escape you are attempting an injustice. We brought you into the world, we raised you, we educated you, we gave you and every other citizen a share of all the good things we could. Yet we proclaim that if any man of the Athenians is dissatisfied with us, he may take his goods and go away wherever he pleases; we give that privilege to every man who chooses to avail himself of it, so soon as he has reached manhood, and sees us, the laws, and the administration of our state. No one of us stands in his way or forbids him to take his goods and go wherever he likes, whether it be to an Athenian colony or to any foreign country, if he is dissatisfied with us and with the state. But we say that every man of you who remains here, seeing how we administer justice, and how we govern the state in other matters, has agreed, by the very fact of remaining here, to do whatsoever we tell him. And, we say, he who disobeys us acts unjustly on three counts: he disobeys us who are his parents, and he disobeys us who reared him, and he disobeys us after he has agreed to obey us, without persuading us

52   that we are wrong. Yet we did not tell him sternly to do whatever we told him. We offered him an alternative; we gave him his choice either to obey us or to convince us that we were wrong; but he does neither.

"These are the charges, Socrates, to which we say that you will expose yourself if you do what you intend; and you are more exposed to these charges than other Athenians." And if I were to ask, "Why?" they might retort with justice that I have bound myself by the agreement with them more than other Athenians. They would say,

b   "Socrates, we have very strong evidence that you were satisfied with us and with the state. You would not have been content to stay at home in it more than other Athenians unless you had been satisfied with it more than they. You never went away from Athens to the festivals, nor elsewhere except on military service; you never made other journeys like other men; you had no desire to see other states or other laws; you were contented

c   with us and our state; so strongly did you prefer us, and agree to be governed by us. And what is more, you had children in this city, you found it so satisfactory. Besides, if you had wished, you might at your trial have offered to go into exile. At that time you could have done with the state's consent what you are trying now to do without it. But then you gloried in being willing to die. You said that you preferred death to exile. And now you do not honor those words: you do not respect us, the laws, for you are trying to

d   destroy us; and you are acting just as a miserable slave would act, trying to run away, and breaking the contracts and agreement which you made to live as our citizen. First, therefore, answer this question. Are we right, or are we wrong, in saying that you have agreed not in mere words, but in your actions, to live under our government?" What are we to say, Crito? Must we not admit that it is true?

CRITO: We must, Socrates.

SOCRATES: Then they would say, "Are you not breaking your contracts and agree-

e   ments with us? And you were not led to make them by force or by fraud. You did not have to make up your mind in a hurry. You had seventy years in which you might have gone away if you had been dissatisfied with us, or if the agreement had seemed to you unjust. But you preferred neither Sparta nor Crete, though you are fond of saying that they are well governed, nor any other state, either of the Greeks or the Barbarians. You

53   went away from Athens less than the lame and the blind and the crippled. Clearly you, far more than other Athenians, were satisfied with the state, and also with us who are its laws; for who would be satisfied with a state which had no laws? And now will you not abide by your agreement? If you take our advice, you will, Socrates; then you will not make yourself ridiculous by going away from Athens.

"Reflect now. What good will you do yourself or your friends by thus transgress-

b   ing and breaking your agreement? It is tolerably certain that they, on their part, will at least run the risk of exile, and of losing their civil rights, or of forfeiting their property. You yourself might go to one of the neighboring states, to Thebes or to Megara, for instance—for both of them are well governed—but, Socrates, you will come as an enemy to these governments, and all who care for their city will look askance at you, and think that you are a subverter of law. You will confirm the judges in their opinion,

c   and make it seem that their verdict was a just one. For a man who is a subverter of law may well be supposed to be a corrupter of the young and thoughtless. Then will you avoid well-governed states and civilized men? Will life be worth having, if you do? Will you associate with such men, and converse without shame—about what, Socrates? About the things which you talk of here? Will you tell them that excellence and justice and institutions and law are the most valuable things that men can have? And do you not

d   think that that will be a disgraceful thing for Socrates? You ought to think so. But you will leave these places; you will go to the friends of Crito in Thessaly. For there is found the greatest disorder and license, and very likely they will be delighted to hear of the ludicrous way in which you escaped from prison, dressed up in peasant's clothes, or in some other disguise which people put on when they are running away, and with your appearance altered. But will no one say how you, an old man, with probably only a few more years to live, clung so greedily to life that you dared to break the highest laws? Perhaps not, if you do not annoy them. But if you do, Socrates, you will hear much that will make you blush. You will pass your life as the flatterer and the slave of all men; and what will you be doing but feasting in Thessaly?* It will be as if you had made a journey to Thessaly for a banquet. And where will be all our old arguments about justice and excellence then? But you wish to live for the sake of your children? You want to bring them up and educate them? What? Will you take them with you to Thessaly, and bring them up and educate them there? Will you make them strangers to their own country, that you may bestow this benefit of exile on them too? Or supposing that you leave them in Athens, will they be brought up and educated better if you are alive, though you are not with them? Yes, your friends will take care of them. Will your friends take care of them if you make a journey to Thessaly, and not if you make a journey to Hades? You ought not to think that, at least if those who call themselves your friends are worth anything at all.

"No, Socrates, be persuaded by us who have reared you. Think neither of children nor of life, nor of any other thing before justice, so that when you come to the other world you may be able to make your defense before the rulers who sit in judgment there. It is clear that neither you nor any of your friends will be happier, or more just, or more pious in this life, if you do this thing, nor will you be happier after you are dead. Now you will go away a victim of the injustice, not of the laws, but of men. But if you repay evil with evil, and injustice with injustice in this shameful way, and break your agreements and covenants with us, and injure those whom you should least injure, yourself and your friends and your country and us, and so escape, then we shall be angry with you while you live, and when you die our brothers, the laws in Hades, will not receive you kindly; for they will know that on earth you did all that you could to destroy us. Listen then to us, and let not Crito persuade you to do as he says."

Be sure, my dear friend Crito, that this is what I seem to hear, as the worshippers of Cybele seem, in their passion, to hear the music of flutes; and the sound of these arguments rings so loudly in my ears, that I cannot hear any other arguments. And I feel sure that if you try to change my mind you will speak in vain. Nevertheless, if you think that you will succeed, speak.

CRITO: I have nothing more to say, Socrates.

SOCRATES: Then let it be, Crito, and let us do as I say, since the god is our guide.

*The Athenians disdained the Thessalians as heavy eaters and drinkers.

PHAEDO

Characters
Phaedo (The Narrator)
Apollodorus
Cebes
Echecrates
Crito
Socrates
Simmias
The Servent of the Eleven
Scene—The Prison of Socrates

57   ECHECRATES: Were you with Socrates yourself, Phaedo, on that day when he drank the poison in the prison, or did you hear the story from someone else?

PHAEDO: I was there myself, Echecrates.

ECHECRATES: Then what was it that our master said before his death, and how did he die? I should be very glad if you would tell me. None of our citizens go very much to

b   Athens now; and no stranger has come from there for a long time who could give us any definite account of these things, except that he drank the poison and died. We could learn nothing beyond that.

58   PHAEDO: Then have you not heard about the trial either, how that went?

ECHECRATES: Yes, we were told of that, and we were rather surprised to find that he did not die till so long after the trial. Why was that, Phaedo?

PHAEDO: It was an accident, Echecrates. The stern of the ship, which the Athenians send to Delos, happened to have been crowned on the day before the trial.

ECHECRATES: And what is this ship?

PHAEDO: It is the ship, as the Athenians say, in which Theseus took the seven

b   youths and the seven maidens to Crete, and saved them from death, and himself was saved. The Athenians made a vow then to Apollo, the story goes, to send a sacred mission to Delos every year, if they should be saved; and from that time to this they have always sent it to the god, every year. They have a law to keep the city pure as soon as the mission begins, and not to execute any sentence of death until the ship has returned

c   from Delos; and sometimes, when it is detained by contrary winds, that is a long while. The sacred mission begins when the priest of Apollo crowns the stern of the ship; and, as I said, this happened to have been done on the day before the trial. That was why Socrates lay so long in prison between his trial and his death.

ECHECRATES: But tell me about his death, Phaedo. What was said and done, and which of his friends were with our master? Or would not the authorities let them be there? Did he die alone?

d   PHAEDO: Oh, no; some of them were there, indeed several.

ECHECRATES: It would be very good of you, if you are not busy, to tell us the whole story as exactly as you can.

Plato, *Phaedo,* translated by F.J. Church (New York: Macmillan/Library of the Liberal Arts, 1951).

PHAEDO: No, I have nothing to do, and I will try to relate it. Nothing is more pleasant to me than to recall Socrates to my mind, whether by speaking of him myself or by listening to others.

ECHECRATES: Indeed, Phaedo, you will have an audience like yourself. But try to tell us everything that happened as precisely as you can.

PHAEDO: Well, I myself was strangely moved on that day. I did not feel that I was being present at the death of a dear friend; I did not pity him, for he seemed to me happy, Echecrates, both in his bearing and in his words, so fearlessly and nobly did he die. I could not help thinking that the gods would watch over him still on his journey to the other world, and that when he arrived there it would be well with him, if it was ever well with any man. Therefore I had scarcely any feeling of pity, as you would expect at such a mournful time. Neither did I feel the pleasure which I usually felt at our philosophical discussions; for our talk was of philosophy. A very singular feeling came over me, a strange mixture of pleasure and of pain, when I remembered that he was presently to die. All of us who were there were in much the same state, laughing and crying by turns, particularly Apollodorus. I think you know the man and his ways.

ECHECRATES: Of course I do.

PHAEDO: Well, he did not restrain himself at all, and I myself and the others were greatly agitated too.

ECHECRATES: Who were there, Phaedo?

PHAEDO: Of native Athenians, there was this Apollodorus, and Critobulus, and his father Crito, and Hermogenes, and Epigenes, and Aeschines, and Antisthenes. Then there was Ctesippus the Paeanian, and Menexenus, and some other Athenians. Plato I believe was ill.

ECHECRATES: Were any strangers there?

PHAEDO: Yes, there was Simmias of Thebes, and Cebes, and Phaedondes; and Eucleides and Terpsion from Megara.

ECHECRATES: But Aristippus and Cleombrotus, were they present?

PHAEDO: No, they were not. They were said to be in Aegina.

ECHECRATES: Was anyone else there?

PHAEDO: No, I think that these were all.

ECHECRATES: Then tell us about your conversation.

PHAEDO: I will try to relate the whole story to you from the beginning. On the previous days I and the others had always met in the morning at the court where the trial was held, which was close to the prison; and then we had gone in to Socrates. We used to wait each morning until the prison was opened, conversing, for it was not opened early. When it was opened we used to go in to Socrates, and we generally spent the whole day with him. But on that morning we met earlier than usual; for the evening before we had learned, on leaving the prison, that the ship had arrived from Delos. So we arranged to be at the usual place as early as possible. When we reached the prison, the porter, who generally let us in, came out to us and bade us wait a little, and not to go in until he summoned us himself: "For the Eleven," he said, "are releasing Socrates from his fetters and giving directions for his death today." In no great while he returned and bade us enter. So we went in and found Socrates just released, and Xanthippe—you know her—sitting by him, holding his child in her arms. When Xanthippe saw us, she wailed aloud, and cried, in her woman's way, "This is the last time, Socrates, that you will talk with your friends, or they with you." And Socrates glanced at Crito, and said, "Crito, let her be taken home." So some of Crito's servants led her away weeping bitterly and beating her breast. But Socrates sat up on the bed, and bent his leg and rubbed it with his hand, and while he was rubbing it said to us, How strange a thing is what men call pleasure! How wonderful is its relation to pain, which seems to be the opposite of it! They will not come to a man together; but if he pursues the one and gains it, he is

c   almost forced to take the other also, as if they were two distinct things united at one end.

And I think, said he, that if Aesop had noticed them he would have composed a fable about them, to the effect that God had wished to reconcile them when they were quarrelling, and that, when he could not do that, he joined their ends together; and that therefore whenever the one comes to a man, the other is sure to follow. That is just the case with me. There was pain in my leg caused by the chains, and now, it seems, pleasure is come following the pain.

Cebes interrupted him and said, By the bye, Socrates, I am glad that you reminded me. Several people have been inquiring about your poems, the hymn to

d   Apollo, and Aesop's fables which you have put into meter, and only a day or two ago Evenus asked me what was your reason for writing poetry on coming here, when you had never written a line before. So if you wish me to be able to answer him when he asks me again, as I know that he will, tell me what to say.

Then tell him the truth, Cebes, he said. Say that it was from no wish to pose as a

e   rival to him, or to his poems. I knew that it would not be easy to do that. I was only testing the meaning of certain dreams and acquitting my conscience about them, in case they should be bidding me make this kind of music. The fact is this. The same dream used often to come to me in my past life, appearing in different forms at different times, but always saying the same words, "Socrates, work at music and compose it." Formerly

61   I used to think that the dream was encouraging me and cheering me on in what was already the work of my life, just as the spectators cheer on different runners in a race. I supposed that the dream was encouraging me to create the music at which I was working already, for I thought that philosophy was the highest music, and my life was spent in philosophy. But then, after the trial, when the feast of the god delayed my death, it occurred to me that the dream might possibly be bidding me create music in the popu-

b   lar sense, and that in that case I ought to do so, and not to disobey. I thought that it would be safer to acquit my conscience by creating poetry in obedience to the dream before I departed. So first I composed a hymn to the god whose feast it was. And then I turned such fables of Aesop as I knew, and had ready to my hand, into verse, taking those which came first; for I reflected that a man who means to be a poet has to use fiction and not facts for his poems; and I could not invent fiction myself.

c   Tell Evenus this, Cebes, and bid him farewell from me; and tell him to follow me as quickly as he can, if he is wise. I, it seems, shall depart today, for that is the will of the Athenians.

And Simmias said, What strange advice to give Evenus, Socrates! I have often met him, and from what I have seen of him I think that he is certainly not at all the man to take it, if he can help it.

What, he said, is not Evenus a philosopher?

Yes, I suppose so, replied Simmias.

Then Evenus will wish to die, he said, and so will every man who is worthy of having any part in this study. But he will not lay violent hands on himself; for that, they

d   say, is wrong. And as he spoke he put his legs off the bed on to the ground, and remained sitting thus for the rest of the conversation.

Then Cebes asked him, What do you mean, Socrates, by saying that it is wrong for a man to lay violent hands on himself, but that the philosopher will wish to follow the dying man?

What, Cebes? Have you and Simmias been with Philolaus, and not heard about these things?

Nothing very definite, Socrates.

Well, I myself only speak of them from hearsay, yet there is no reason why I should not tell you what I have heard. Indeed, as I am setting out on a journey to the other world, what could be more fitting for me than to talk about my journey and to consider what we imagine to be its nature? How could we better employ the interval between this and sunset?

Then what is their reason for saying that it is wrong for a man to kill himself, Socrates? It is quite true that I have heard Philolaus say, when he was living at Thebes, that it is not right; and I have heard the same thing from others, too, but I never heard anything definite on the subject from any of them.

You must be of good cheer, said he, possibly you will hear something some day. But perhaps you will be surprised if I say that this law, unlike every other law to which mankind is subject, is absolute and without exception; and that it is not true that death is better than life only for some persons and at some times. And perhaps you will be surprised if I tell you that these men, for whom it would be better to die, may not do themselves a service, but that they must await a benefactor from without.

Oh indeed, said Cebes, laughing quietly, and speaking in his native dialect.

Indeed, said Socrates, so stated it may seem strange, and yet perhaps a reason may be given for it. The reason which the secret teaching* gives, that man is in a kind of prison, and that he may not set himself free, nor escape from it, seems to me rather profound and not easy to fathom. But I do think, Cebes, that it is true that the gods are our guardians, and that we men are a part of their property. Do you not think so?

I do, said Cebes.

Well then, said he, if one of your possessions were to kill itself, though you had not signified that you wished it to die, should you not be angry with it? Should you not punish it, if punishment were possible?

Certainly, he replied.

Then in this way perhaps it is not unreasonable to hold that no man has a right to take his own life, but that he must wait until God sends some necessity upon him, as has now been sent upon me.

Yes, said Cebes, that does seem natural. But you were saying just now that the philosopher will desire to die. Is not that a paradox, Socrates, if what we have just been saying, that God is our guardian and that we are his property, be true? It is not reasonable to say that the wise man will be content to depart from this service, in which the gods, who are the best of all rulers, rule him. He will hardly think that when he becomes free he will take better care of himself than the gods take of him. A fool perhaps might think so, and say that he would do well to run away from his master; he might not consider that he ought not to run away from a good master, but that he ought to remain with him as long as possible, and so in his thoughtlessness he might run away. But the wise man will surely desire to remain always with one who is better than himself. But if this be true, Socrates, the reverse of what you said just now seems to follow. The wise man should grieve to die, and the fool should rejoice.

I thought Socrates was pleased with Cebes' insistence. He looked at us, and said, Cebes is always examining arguments. He will not be convinced at once by anything that one says.

*[The Esoteric system of the Pythagoreans.]

Yes, Socrates, said Simmias, but I do think that now there is something in what Cebes says. Why should really wise men want to run away from masters who are better than themselves, and lightly quit their service? And I think Cebes is aiming his argument at you, because you are so ready to leave us, and the gods, who are good rulers, as you yourself admit.

b   You are right, he said. I suppose you mean that I must defend myself against your charge, as if I were in a court of justice.

That is just our meaning, said Simmias.

Well then, he replied, let me try to make a more successful defense to you than I did to the judges at my trial. I should be wrong, Cebes and Simmias, he went on, not to

c   grieve at death, if I did not think that I was going to live both with other gods who are good and wise, and with men who have died and who are better than the men of this world. But you must know that I hope that I am going to live among good men, though I am not quite sure of that. But I am as sure as I can be in such matters that I am going to live with gods who are very good masters. And therefore I am not so much grieved at death; I am confident that the dead have some kind of existence, and, as has been said of old, an existence that is far better for the good than for the wicked.

Well, Socrates, said Simmias, do you mean to go away and keep this belief to

d   yourself, or will you let us share it with you? It seems to me that we too have an interest in this good. And it will also serve as your defense, if you can convince us of what you say.

I will try, he replied. But I think Crito has been wanting to speak to me. Let us first hear what he has to say.

Only, Socrates, said Crito, that the man who is going to give you the poison has

e   been telling me to warn you not to talk much. He says that talking heats people, and that the action of the poison must not be counteracted by heat. Those who excite themselves sometimes have to drink it two or three times.

Let him be, said Socrates; let him mind his own business, and be prepared to give me the poison twice, or, if need be, thrice.

I knew that would be your answer, said Crito, but the man has been importunate.

Never mind him, he replied. But I wish now to explain to you, my judges, why it seems to me that a man who has really spent his life in philosophy has reason to be of

64   good cheer when he is about to die, and may well hope after death to gain in the other world the greatest good. I will try to show you, Simmias and Cebes, how this may be.

The world, perhaps, does not see that those who rightly engage in philosophy study only dying and death. And, if this be true, it would be surely strange for a man all through his life to desire only death, and then, when death comes to him, to be vexed at it, when it has been his study and his desire for so long.

Simmias laughed, and said: Indeed, Socrates, you make me laugh, though I am

b   scarcely in a laughing humor now. If the multitude heard that, I fancy they would think that what you say of philosophers is quite true; and my countrymen would entirely agree with you that philosophers are indeed eager to die, and they would say that they know full well that philosophers deserve to be put to death.

And they would be right, Simmias, except in saying that they know it. They do

c   not know in what sense the true philosopher is eager to die, or what kind of death he deserves, or in what sense he deserves it. Let us dismiss them from our thoughts, and converse by ourselves. Do we believe death to be anything?

We do, replied Simmias.

And do we not believe it to be the separation of the soul from the body? Does not death mean that the body comes to exist by itself, separated from the soul, and that the soul exists by herself, separated from the body? What is death but that?

It is that, he said.

Now consider, my good friend, if you and I are agreed on another point which I   d think will help us to understand the question better. Do you think that a philosopher will care very much about what are called pleasures, such as the pleasures of eating and drinking?

Certainly not, Socrates, said Simmias.

Or about the pleasures of sexual passion?

Indeed, no.

And, do you think that he holds the remaining cares of the body in high esteem? Will he think much of getting fine clothes, and sandals, and other bodily adornments, or   e will he despise them, except so far as he is absolutely forced to meddle with them?

The real philosopher, I think, will despise them, he replied.

In short, said he, you think that his studies are not concerned with the body? He stands aloof from it, as far as he can, and turns toward the soul?

I do.

Well then, in these matters, first, it is clear that the philosopher releases his soul   65 from communion with the body, so far as he can, beyond all other men?

It is.

And does not the world think, Simmias, that if a man has no pleasure in such things, and does not take his share in them, his life is not worth living? Do not they hold that he who thinks nothing of bodily pleasures is almost as good as dead?

Indeed you are right.

But what about the actual acquisition of wisdom? If the body is taken as a companion in the search for wisdom, is it a hindrance or not? For example, do sight and hear-   b ing convey any real truth to men? Are not the very poets forever telling us that we neither hear nor see anything accurately? But if these senses of the body are not accurate or clear, the others will hardly be so, for they are all less perfect than these, are they not?

Yes, I think so, certainly, he said.

Then when does the soul attain truth? he asked. We see that, as often as she seeks to investigate anything in company with the body, the body leads her astray.

True.   c

Is it not by reasoning, if at all, that any real truth becomes manifest to her?

Yes.

And she reasons best, I suppose, when none of the senses, whether hearing, or sight, or pain, or pleasure, harasses her; when she has dismissed the body, and released herself as far as she can from all intercourse or contact with it, and so, coming to be as much alone with herself as is possible, strives after real truth.

That is so.

And here too the soul of the philosopher very greatly despises the body, and flies   d from it, and seeks to be alone by herself, does she not?

Clearly.

And what do you say to the next point, Simmias? Do we say that there is such a thing as absolute justice, or not?

Indeed we do.

And absolute beauty, and absolute good?

Of course.

Have you ever seen any of them with your eyes?

Indeed I have not, he replied.

e   Did you ever grasp them with any bodily sense? I am speaking of all absolutes, whether size, or health, or strength; in a word, of the essence or real being of everything. Is the very truth of things contemplated by the body? Is it not rather the case that the man who prepares himself most carefully to apprehend by his intellect the essence of each thing which he examines will come nearest to the knowledge of it?

Certainly.

And will not a man attain to this pure thought most completely if he goes to each thing, as far as he can, with his mind alone, taking neither sight nor any other sense

66   along with his reason in the process of thought, to be an encumbrance? In every case he will pursue pure and absolute being, with his pure intellect alone. He will be set free as far as possible from the eye and the ear and, in short, from the whole body, because intercourse with the body troubles the soul, and hinders her from gaining truth and wisdom. Is it not he who will attain the knowledge of real being, if any man will?

Your words are admirably true, Socrates, said Simmias.

b   And, he said, must not all this cause real philosophers to reflect, and make them say to each other, It seems that there is a narrow path which will bring us safely to our journey's end, with reason as our guide. As long as we have this body, and an evil of that sort is mingled with our souls, we shall never fully gain what we desire; and that is truth. For

c   the body is forever taking up our time with the care which it needs; and, besides, whenever diseases attack it, they hinder us in our pursuit of real being. It fills us with passions, and desires, and fears, and all manner of phantoms, and much foolishness; and so, as the say-

d   ing goes, in very truth we can never think at all for it. It alone and its desires cause wars and factions and battles; for the origin of all wars is the pursuit of wealth, and we are forced to pursue wealth because we live in slavery to the cares of the body. And therefore, for all these reasons, we have no leisure for philosophy. And last of all, if we ever are free from the body for a time, and then turn to examine some matter, it falls in our way at every step of the inquiry, and causes confusion and trouble and panic, so that we cannot see the

e   truth for it. Verily we have learned that if we are to have any pure knowledge at all, we must be freed from the body; the soul by herself must behold things as they are. Then, it seems, after we are dead, we shall gain the wisdom which we desire, and for which we say we have a passion, but not while we are alive, as the argument shows. For if it be not possible to have pure knowledge while the body is with us, one of two things must be true:

67   either we cannot gain knowledge at all, or we can gain it only after death. For then, and not till then, will the soul exist by herself, separate from the body. And while we live, we shall come nearest to knowledge, if we have no communion or intercourse with the body beyond what is absolutely necessary, and if we are not defiled with its nature. We must live pure from it until God himself releases us. And when we are thus pure and released from its follies, we shall dwell, I suppose, with others who are pure like ourselves, and we

b   shall of ourselves know all that is pure; and that may be the truth. For I think that the impure is not allowed to attain to the pure. Such, Simmias, I fancy must needs be the language and the reflections of the true lovers of knowledge. Do you not agree with me?

Most assuredly I do, Socrates.

And, my friend, said Socrates, if this be true, I have good hope that, when I reach the place whither I am going, I shall there, if anywhere, gain fully that which we have sought so earnestly in the past. And so I shall set forth cheerfully on the journey that is appointed

c   me today, and so may every man who thinks that his mind is prepared and purified.

That is quite true, said Simmias.

And does not the purification consist, as we have said, in separating the soul from the body, as far as is possible, and in accustoming her to collect and rally herself together from the body on every side, and to dwell alone by herself as much as she can, both now and hereafter, released from the bondage of the body?   d

Yes, certainly, he said.

Is not what we call death a release and separation of the soul from the body?

Undoubtedly, he replied.

And the true philosopher, we hold, is alone in his constant desire to set his soul free? His study is simply the release and separation of the soul from the body, is it not?

Clearly.

Would it not be absurd then, as I began by saying, for a man to complain at death   e coming to him, when in his life he has been preparing himself to live as nearly in a state of death as he could? Would not that be absurd?

Yes, indeed.

In truth, then, Simmias, he said, the true philosopher studies to die, and to him of all men is death least terrible. Now look at the matter in this way. In everything he is at enmity with his body, and he longs to possess his soul alone. Would it not then be most unreasonable if he were to fear and complain when he has his desire, instead of   68 rejoicing to go to the place where he hopes to gain the wisdom that he has passionately longed for all his life, and to be released from the company of his enemy? Many a man has willingly gone to the other world, when a human love or wife or son has died, in the hope of seeing there those whom he longed for, and of being with them: and will a man who has a real passion for wisdom, and a firm hope of really finding   b wisdom in the other world and nowhere else, grieve at death, and not depart rejoicing? Nay, my friend, you ought not to think that, if he be truly a philosopher. He will be firmly convinced that there and nowhere else will he meet with wisdom in its purity. And if this be so, would it not, I repeat, be very unreasonable for such a man to fear death?

Yes, indeed, he replied, it would.

Does not this show clearly, he said, that any man whom you see grieving at the   c approach of death is after all no lover of wisdom, but a lover of his body? He is also, most likely, a lover either of wealth, or of honor, or, it may be, of both.

Yes, he said, it is as you say.

Well then, Simmias, he went on, does not what is called courage belong especially to the philosopher?

Certainly I think so, he replied.

And does not temperance, the quality which even the world calls temperance, and which means to despise and control and govern the passions—does not temperance belong only to such men as most despise the body, and pass their lives in philosophy?

Of necessity, he replied.   d

For if you will consider the courage and the temperance of other men, said he, you will find that they are strange things.

How so, Socrates?

You know, he replied, that all other men regard death as one of the great evils to which mankind is subject?

Indeed they do, he said.

And when the brave men of them submit to death, do not they do so from a fear of still greater evils?

Yes.

Then all men but the philosopher are brave from fear and because they are afraid. Yet it is rather a strange thing for a man to be brave out of fear and cowardice.

Indeed it is.

e

And are not the orderly men of them in exactly the same case? Are not they temperate from a kind of intemperance? We should say that this cannot be; but in them this state of foolish temperance comes to that. They desire certain pleasures, and fear to lose

69   them; and so they abstain from other pleasures because they are mastered by these. Intemperance is defined to mean being under the dominion of pleasure, yet they only master certain pleasures because they are mastered by others. But that is exactly what I said just now—that, in a way, they are made temperate from intemperance.

It seems to be so.

My dear Simmias, I fear that virtue is not really to be bought in this way, by bartering pleasure for pleasure, and pain for pain, and fear for fear, and the greater for the

b   less, like coins. There is only one sterling coin for which all these things ought to be exchanged, and that is wisdom. All that is bought and sold for this and with this, whether courage, or temperance, or justice, is real; in one word, true virtue cannot be without wisdom, and it matters nothing whether pleasure, and fear, and all other such things are present or absent. But I think that the virtue which is composed of pleasures and fears bartered with one another, and severed from wisdom, is only a shadow of true

c   virtue, and that it has no freedom, nor health, nor truth. True virtue in reality is a kind of purifying from all these things; and temperance, and justice, and courage, and wisdom itself are the purification. And I fancy that the men who established our mysteries had a very real meaning: in truth they have been telling us in parables all the time that whoso-

d   ever comes to Hades uninitiated and profane will lie in the mire, while he that has been purified and initiated shall dwell with the gods. For "the thyrsusbearers are many," as they say in the mysteries, "but the inspired few." And by these last, I believe, are meant only the true philosophers. And I in my life have striven as hard as I was able, and have left nothing undone, that I might become one of them. Whether I have striven in the right way, and whether I have succeeded or not, I suppose that I shall learn in a little while, when I reach the other world, if it be the will of god.

That is my defense, Simmias and Cebes, to show that I have reason for not being

e   angry or grieved at leaving you and my masters here. I believe that in the next world, no less than in this, I shall meet with good masters and friends, though the multitude are incredulous of it. And if I have been more successful with you in my defense than I was with my Athenian judges, it is well.

When Socrates had finished, Cebes replied to him, and said, I think that for the

70   most part you are right, Socrates. But men are very incredulous of what you have said of the soul. They fear that she will no longer exist anywhere when she has left the body, but that she will be destroyed and perish on the very day of death. They think that the moment that she is released and leaves the body, she will be dissolved and vanish away like breath or smoke, and thenceforward cease to exist at all. If she were to exist some-

b   where as a whole, released from the evils which you enumerated just now, we should have good reason to hope, Socrates, that what you say is true. But it will need no little persuasion and assurance to show that the soul exists after death, and continues to possess any power or wisdom.

True, Cebes, said Socrates; but what are we to do? Do you wish to converse about these matters and see if what I say is probable?

I for one, said Cebes, should gladly hear your opinion about them.

I think, said Socrates, that no one who heard me now, even if he were a comic poet, would say that I am an idle talker about things which do not concern me. So, if you wish it, let us examine this question.   c

Let us consider whether or not the souls of men exist in the next world after death, thus. There is an ancient belief, which we remember, that on leaving this world they exist there, and that they return hither and are born again from the dead. But if it be true that the living are born from the dead, our souls must exist in the other world; otherwise they could not be born again. It will be a sufficient proof that this is so if we can really   d prove that the living are born only from the dead. But if this is not so, we shall have to find some other argument.

Exactly, said Cebes.

Well, said he, the easiest way of answering the question will be to consider it not in relation to men only, but also in relation to all animals and plants, and in short to all things that are generated. Is it the case that everything which has an opposite is gener-   e ated only from its opposite? By opposites I mean the honorable and the base, the just and the unjust, and so on in a thousand other instances. Let us consider then whether it is necessary for everything that has an opposite to be generated only from its own opposite. For instance, when anything becomes greater, I suppose it must first have been less and then become greater?

Yes.

And if a thing becomes less, it must have been greater, and afterward become   71 less?

That is so, said he.

And further, the weaker is generated from the stronger, and the swifter from the slower?

Certainly.

And the worse is generated from the better, and the more just from the more unjust?

Of course.

Then it is sufficiently clear to us that all things are generated in this way, opposites from opposites?

Quite so.

And in every pair of opposites, are there not two generations between the two   b members of the pair, from the one to the other, and then back again from the other to the first? Between the greater and the less are growth and diminution, and we say that the one grows and the other diminishes, do we not?

Yes, he said.

And there is division and composition, and cold and hot, and so on. In fact, is it not a universal law, even though we do not always express it in so many words, that opposites are generated always from one another, and that there is a process of generation from one to the other?

It is, he replied.

Well, said he, is there an opposite to life, in the same way that sleep is the oppo   c site of being awake?

Certainly, he answered.

What is it?

Death, he replied.

Then if life and death are opposites, they are generated the one from the other: they are two, and between them there are two generations. Is it not so?

Of course.

Now, said Socrates, I will explain to you one of the two pairs of opposites of which I spoke just now, and its generations, and you shall explain to me the other. Sleep
d   is the opposite of waking. From sleep is produced the state of waking, and from the state of waking is produced sleep. Their generations are, first, to fall asleep; secondly, to awake. Is that clear? he asked.

Yes, quite.

Now then, said he, do you tell me about life and death. Death is the opposite of life, is it not?

It is.

And they are generated the one from the other?

Yes.

Then what is that which is generated from the living?

The dead, he replied.

And what is generated from the dead?

I must admit that it is the living.

Then living things and living men are generated from the dead, Cebes?
e   Clearly, said he.

Then our souls exist in the other world? he said.

Apparently.

Now of these two generations the one is certain? Death I suppose is certain enough, is it not?

Yes, quite, he replied.

What then shall we do? said he. Shall we not assign an opposite generation to correspond? Or is nature imperfect here? Must we not assign some opposite generation to dying?

I think so, certainly, he said.

And what must it be?

To come to life again.

72   And if there be such a thing as a return to life, he said, it will be a generation from the dead to the living, will it not?

It will, certainly.

Then we are agreed on this point: namely, that the living are generated from the dead no less than the dead from the living. But we agreed that, if this be so, it is a sufficient proof that the souls of the dead must exist somewhere, whence they come into being again.

I think, Socrates, that that is the necessary result of our premises.

And I think, Cebes, said he, that our conclusion has not been an unfair one. For if
b   opposites did not always correspond with opposites as they are generated, moving as it were round in a circle, and there were generation in a straight line forward from one opposite only, with no turning or return to the other, then, you know, all things would come at length to have the same form and be in the same state, and would cease to be generated at all.

What do you mean? he asked.

It is not at all hard to understand my meaning, he replied. If, for example, the one opposite, to go to sleep, existed without the corresponding opposite, to wake up, which
c   is generated from the first, then all nature would at last make the tale of Endymion meaningless, and he would no longer be conspicuous; for everything else would be in the same state of sleep that he was in. And if all things were compounded together and never separated, the Chaos of Anaxagoras would soon be realized. Just in the same way,

my dear Cebes, if all things in which there is any life were to die, and when they were dead were to remain in that form and not come to life again, would not the necessary result be that everything at last would be dead, and nothing alive? For if living things   d were generated from other sources than death, and were to die, the result is inevitable that all things would be consumed by death. Is it not so?

It is indeed, I think, Socrates, said Cebes; I think that what you say is perfectly true.

Yes, Cebes, he said, I think it is certainly so. We are not misled into this conclusion. The dead do come to life again, and the living are generated from them, and the souls of the dead exist; and with the souls of the good it is well, and with the souls of the   e evil it is evil.

And besides, Socrates, rejoined Cebes, if the doctrine which you are fond of stating, that our learning is only a process of recollection, be true, then I suppose we must have learned at some former time what we recollect now. And that would be impossible unless our souls had existed somewhere before they came into this human form. So that   73 is another reason for believing the soul immortal.

But, Cebes, interrupted Simmias, what are the proofs of that? Recall them to me; I am not very clear about them at present.

One argument, answered Cebes, and the strongest of all, is that if you question men about anything in the right way, they will answer you correctly of themselves. But they would not have been able to do that unless they had had within themselves knowl-   b edge and right reason. Again, show them such things as geometrical diagrams, and the proof of the doctrine is complete.*

And if that does not convince you, Simmias, said Socrates, look at the matter in another way and see if you agree then. You have doubts, I know, how what is called knowledge can be recollection.

Nay, replied Simmias, I do not doubt. But I want to recollect the argument about recollection. What Cebes undertook to explain has nearly brought your theory back to me and convinced me. But I am nonetheless ready to hear you undertake to explain it.

In this way, he returned. We are agreed, I suppose, that if a man remembers any-   c thing, he must have known it at some previous time.

Certainly, he said.

And are we agreed that when knowledge comes in the following way, it is recollection? When a man has seen or heard anything, or has perceived it by some other sense, and then knows not that thing only, but has also in his mind an impression of some other thing, of which the knowledge is quite different, are we not right in saying   d that he remembers the thing of which he has an impression in his mind?

What do you mean?

I mean this. The knowledge of a man is different from the knowledge of a lyre, is it not?

Certainly.

And you know that when lovers see a lyre, or a garment, or anything that their favorites are wont to use, they have this feeling. They know the lyre, and in their mind they receive the image of the youth whose the lyre was. That is recollection. For instance, someone seeing Simmias often is reminded of Cebes; and there are endless examples of the same thing.

Indeed there are, said Simmias.

*[For an example of this see Meno 82a–86b (pp. 160–66 in this volume).]

e   Is not that a kind of recollection, he said; and more especially when a man has this feeling with reference to things which the lapse of time and inattention have made him forget?

Yes, certainly, he replied.

Well, he went on, is it possible to recollect a man on seeing the picture of a horse, or the picture of a lyre? Or to recall Simmias on seeing a picture of Cebes?

Certainly.

And it is possible to recollect Simmias himself on seeing a picture of Simmias?

74   No doubt, he said.

Then in all these cases there is recollection caused by similar objects, and also by dissimilar objects?

There is.

But when a man has a recollection caused by similar objects, will he not have a further feeling and consider whether the likeness to that which he recollects is defective in any way or not?

He will, he said.

Now see if this is true, he went on. Do we not believe in the existence of equality— not the equality of pieces of wood or of stones, but something beyond that—equality in the abstract? Shall we say that there is such a thing, or not?

b   Yes indeed, said Simmias, most emphatically we will.

And do we know what this abstract equality is?

Certainly, he replied.

Where did we get the knowledge of it? Was it not from seeing the equal pieces of wood, and stones, and the like, which we were speaking of just now? Did we not form from them the idea of abstract equality, which is different from them? Or do you think that it is not different? Consider the question in this way. Do not equal pieces of wood and stones appear to us sometimes equal and sometimes unequal, though in fact they remain the same all the time?

Certainly they do.

c   But did absolute equals ever seem to you to be unequal, or abstract equality to be inequality?

No, never, Socrates.

Then equal things, he said, are not the same as abstract equality?

No, certainly not, Socrates.

Yet it was from these equal things, he said, which are different from abstract equality, that you have conceived and got your knowledge of abstract equality?

That is quite true, he replied.

And that whether it is like them or unlike them?

Certainly.

d   But that makes no difference, he said. As long as the sight of one thing brings another thing to your mind, there must be recollection, whether or no the two things are like.

That is so.

Well then, said he, do the equal pieces of wood, and other similar equal things, of which we have been speaking, affect us at all this way? Do they seem to us to be equal, in the way that abstract equality is equal? Do they come short of being like abstract equality, or not?

Indeed, they come very short of it, he replied.

Are we agreed about this? A man sees something and thinks to himself, "This e   thing that I see aims at being like some other thing, but it comes short and cannot be like that other thing; it is inferior"; must not the man who thinks that have known at some previous time that other thing, which he says that it resembles, and to which it is inferior?

He must.

Well, have we ourselves had the same sort of feeling with reference to equal things, and to abstract equality?

Yes, certainly.

Then we must have had knowledge of equality before we first saw equal things,   75 and perceived that they all strive to be like equality, and all come short of it.

That is so.

And we are agreed also that we have not, nor could we have, obtained the idea of equality except from sight or touch or some other sense; the same is true of all the senses.

Yes, Socrates, for the purposes of the argument that is so.

At any rate, it is by the senses that we must perceive that all sensible objects strive   b to resemble absolute equality, and are inferior to it. Is not that so?

Yes.

Then before we began to see, and to hear, and to use the other senses, we must have received the knowledge of the nature of abstract and real equality; otherwise we could not have compared equal sensible objects with abstract equality, and seen that the former in all cases strive to be like the latter, though they are always inferior to it?

That is the necessary consequence of what we have been saying, Socrates.

Did we not see, and hear, and possess the other senses as soon as we were born?

Yes, certainly.

And we must have received the knowledge of abstract equality before we had   c these senses?

Yes.

Then, it seems, we must have received that knowledge before we were born?

It does.

Now if we received this knowledge before our birth, and were born with it, we knew, both before and at the moment of our birth, not only the equal, and the greater, and the less, but also everything of the same kind, did we not? Our present reasoning does not refer only to equality. It refers just as much to absolute good, and absolute   d beauty, and absolute justice, and absolute holiness; in short, I repeat, to everything which we mark with the name of the real, in the questions and answers of our dialectic. So we must have received our knowledge of all realities before we were born.

That is so.

And we must always be born with this knowledge, and must always retain it throughout life, if we have not each time forgotten it, after having received it. For to know means to receive and retain knowledge, and not to have lost it. Do not we mean by forgetting, the loss of knowledge, Simmias?

Yes, certainly, Socrates, he said.   e

But, I suppose, if it be the case that we lost at birth the knowledge which we received before we were born, and then afterward, by using our senses on the objects of sense, recovered the knowledge which we had previously possessed, then what we call learning is the recovering of knowledge which is already ours. And are we not right in calling that recollection?

Certainly.

For we have found it possible to perceive a thing by sight, or hearing, or any other   76 sense, and thence to form a notion of some other thing, like or unlike, which had been forgotten, but with which this thing was associated. And therefore, I say, one of two things must be true. Either we are all born with this knowledge and retain it all our life;

or, after birth, those whom we say are learning are only recollecting, and our knowledge is recollection.

Yes indeed, that is undoubtedly true, Socrates.

Then which do you choose, Simmias? Are we born with knowledge or do we rec-
b   ollect the things of which we have received knowledge before our birth?

I cannot say at present, Socrates.

Well, have you an opinion about this question? Can a man who knows give an account of what he knows, or not? What do you think about that?

Yes, of course he can, Socrates.

And do you think that everyone can give an account of the ideas of which we have been speaking?

I wish I did, indeed, said Simmias, but I am very much afraid that by this time tomorrow there will no longer be any man living able to do so as it should be done.

c   Then, Simmias, he said, you do not think that all men know these things?

Certainly not.

Then they recollect what they once learned?

Necessarily.

And when did our souls gain this knowledge? It cannot have been after we were born men.

No, certainly not.

Then it was before?

Yes.

Then, Simmias, our souls existed formerly, apart from our bodies, and possessed intelligence before they came into man's shape.

Unless we receive this knowledge at the moment of birth, Socrates. That time still remains.

d   Well, my friend, and at what other time do we lose it? We agreed just now that we are not born with it; do we lose it at the same moment that we gain it, or can you suggest any other time?

I cannot, Socrates. I did not see that I was talking nonsense.

Then, Simmias, he said, is not this the truth? If, as we are forever repeating, beauty,
e   and good, and the other ideas really exist, and if we refer all the objects of sensible per-
ception to these ideas which were formerly ours, and which we find to be ours still, and compare sensible objects with them, then, just as they exist, our souls must have existed before ever we were born. But if they do not exist, then our reasoning will have been thrown away. Is it so? If these ideas exist, does it not at once follow that our souls must have existed before we were born, and if they do not exist, then neither did our souls?

Admirably put, Socrates, said Simmias. I think that the necessity is the same for
77   the one as for the other. The reasoning has reached a place of safety in the common proof of the existence of our souls before we were born and of the existence of the ideas of which you spoke. Nothing is so evident to me as that beauty, and good, and the other ideas which you spoke of just now have a very real existence indeed. Your proof is quite sufficient for me.

But what of Cebes? said Socrates. I must convince Cebes too.

I think that he is satisfied, said Simmias, though he is the most skeptical of men in argument. But I think that he is perfectly convinced that our souls existed before we were born.

But I do not think myself, Socrates, he continued, that you have proved that the
b   soul will continue to exist when we are dead. The common fear which Cebes spoke of, that she [the soul] may be scattered to the winds at death, and that death may be the end

of her existence, still stands in the way. Assuming that the soul is generated and comes together from some other elements, and exists before she ever enters the human body, why should she not come to an end and be destroyed, after she has entered into the body, when she is released from it?

You are right, Simmias, said Cebes. I think that only half the required proof has been given. It has been shown that our souls existed before we were born; but it must also be shown that our souls will continue to exist after we are dead, no less than that they existed before we were born, if the proof is to be complete.   c

That has been shown already, Simmias and Cebes, said Socrates, if you will combine this reasoning with our previous conclusion, that all life is generated from death. For if the soul exists in a previous state and if, when she comes into life and is born, she can only be born from death, and from a state of death, must she not exist after death too, since she has to be born again? So the point which you speak of has been already proved.   d

Still I think that you and Simmias would be glad to discuss this question further. Like children, you are afraid that the wind will really blow the soul away and disperse her when she leaves the body, especially if a man happens to die in a storm and not in a calm.   e

Cebes laughed and said, Try and convince us as if we were afraid, Socrates; or rather, do not think that we are afraid ourselves. Perhaps there is a child within us who has these fears. Let us try and persuade him not to be afraid of death, as if it were a bugbear.

Socrates' Prison, near the Acropolis, Athens. The traditional site of the prison where Socrates was held while awaiting execution. *(Forrest E. Baird)*

You must charm him every day, until you have charmed him away, said Socrates.

78   And where shall we find a good charmer, Socrates, he asked, now that you are leaving us?

Hellas is a large country, Cebes, he replied, and good men may doubtless be found in it; and the nations of the Barbarians are many. You must search them all through for such a charmer, sparing neither money nor labor; for there is nothing on which you could spend money more profitably. And you must search for him among yourselves too, for you will hardly find a better charmer than yourselves.

That shall be done, said Cebes. But let us return to the point where we left off, if you will.

b   Yes, I will: why not?

Very good, he replied.

Well, said Socrates, must we not ask ourselves this question? What kind of thing is liable to suffer dispersion, and for what kind of thing have we to fear dispersion? And then we must see whether the soul belongs to that kind or not, and be confident or afraid about our own souls accordingly.

That is true, he answered.

c   Now is it not the compound and composite which is naturally liable to be dissolved in the same way in which it was compounded? And is not what is uncompounded alone not liable to dissolution, if anything is not?

I think that that is so, said Cebes.

And what always remains in the same state and unchanging is most likely to be uncompounded, and what is always changing and never the same is most likely to be compounded, I suppose?

Yes, I think so.

Now let us return to what we were speaking of before in the discussion, he said.
d   Does the being, which in our dialectic we define as meaning absolute existence, remain always in exactly the same state, or does it change? Do absolute equality, absolute beauty, and every other absolute existence, admit of any change at all? Or does absolute existence in each case, being essentially uniform, remain the same and unchanging, and never in any case admit of any sort or kind of change whatsoever?

It must remain the same and unchanging, Socrates, said Cebes.

And what of the many beautiful things, such as men, and horses, and garments, and the like, and of all which bears the names of the ideas, whether equal, or beautiful,
e   or anything else? Do they remain the same or is it exactly the opposite with them? In short, do they never remain the same at all, either in themselves or in their relations?

These things, said Cebes, never remain the same.

79   You can touch them, and see them, and perceive them with the other senses, while you can grasp the unchanging only by the reasoning of the intellect. These latter are invisible and not seen. Is it not so?

That is perfectly true, he said.

Let us assume then, he said, if you will, that there are two kinds of existence, the one visible, the other invisible.

Yes, he said.

And the invisible is unchanging, while the visible is always changing.

Yes, he said again.

b   Are not we men made up of body and soul?

There is nothing else, he replied.

And which of these kinds of existence should we say that the body is most like, and most akin to?

The visible, he replied; that is quite obvious.

And the soul? Is that visible or invisible?

It is invisible to man, Socrates, he said.

But we mean by visible and invisible, visible and invisible to man; do we not?

Yes; that is what we mean.

Then what do we say of the soul? Is it visible or not visible?

It is not visible.

Then is it invisible?

Yes.

Then the soul is more like the invisible than the body; and the body is like the visible.

That is necessarily so, Socrates.

c

Have we not also said that, when the soul employs the body in any inquiry, and makes use of sight, or hearing, or any other sense—for inquiry with the body means inquiry with the senses—she is dragged away by it to the things which never remain the same, and wanders about blindly, and becomes confused and dizzy, like a drunken man, from dealing with things that are ever changing?

Certainly.

But when she investigates any question by herself, she goes away to the pure, and eternal, and immortal, and unchangeable, to which she is akin, and so she comes to be ever with it, as soon as she is by herself, and can be so; and then she rests from her wanderings and dwells with it unchangingly, for she is dealing with what is unchanging. And is not this state of the soul called wisdom?

d

Indeed, Socrates, you speak well and truly, he replied.

Which kind of existence do you think from our former and our present arguments that the soul is more like and more akin to?

e

I think, Socrates, he replied, that after this inquiry the very dullest man would agree that the soul is infinitely more like the unchangeable than the changeable.

And the body?

That is like the changeable.

Consider the matter in yet another way. When the soul and the body are united, nature ordains the one to be a slave and to be ruled, and the other to be master and to rule. Tell me once again, which do you think is like the divine, and which is like the mortal? Do you not think that the divine naturally rules and has authority, and that the mortal naturally is ruled and is a slave?

80

I do.

Then which is the soul like?

That is quite plain, Socrates. The soul is like the divine, and the body is like the mortal.

Now tell me, Cebes, is the result of all that we have said that the soul is most like the divine, and the immortal, and the intelligible, and the uniform, and the indissoluble, and the unchangeable; while the body is most like the human, and the mortal, and the unintelligible, and the multiform, and the dissoluble, and the changeable? Have we any other argument to show that this is not so, my dear Cebes?

b

We have not.

Then if this is so, is it not the nature of the body to be dissolved quickly, and of the soul to be wholly or very nearly indissoluble?

Certainly.

c

You observe, he said, that after a man is dead, the visible part of him, his body, which lies in the visible world and which we call the corpse, which is subject to dissolution and decomposition, is not dissolved and decomposed at once? It remains as it was for a considerable time, and even for a long time, if a man dies with his body in good condition and in the vigor of life. And when the body falls in and is embalmed,

d like the mummies of Egypt, it remains nearly entire for an immense time. And should it decay, yet some parts of it, such as the bones and muscles, may almost be said to be immortal. Is it not so?

Yes.

And shall we believe that the soul, which is invisible, and which goes hence to a place that is like herself, glorious, and pure, and invisible, to Hades, which is rightly called the unseen world, to dwell with the good and wise God, whither, if it be the will of God, my soul too must shortly go—shall we believe that the soul, whose nature is so

e glorious, and pure, and invisible, is blown away by the winds and perishes as soon as she leaves the body, as the world says? Nay, dear Cebes and Simmias, it is not so. I will tell you what happens to a soul which is pure at her departure, and which in her life has had no intercourse that she could avoid with the body, and so draws after her, when she dies, no taint of the body, but has shunned it, and gathered herself into herself, for such has been her constant study—and that only means that she has loved wisdom rightly,

81 and has truly practiced how to die. Is not this the practice of death?

Yes, certainly.

Does not the soul, then, which is in that state, go away to the invisible that is like herself, and to the divine, and the immortal, and the wise, where she is released from error, and folly, and fear, and fierce passions, and all the other evils that fall to the lot of men, and is happy, and for the rest of time lives in very truth with the gods, as they say that the initiated do? Shall we affirm this, Cebes?

Yes, certainly, said Cebes.

b But if she be defiled and impure when she leaves the body, from being ever with it, and serving it and loving it, and from being besotted by it and by its desires and pleasures, so that she thinks nothing true but what is bodily and can be touched, and seen, and eaten, and drunk, and used for men's lusts; if she has learned to hate, and tremble at,

c and fly from what is dark and invisible to the eye, and intelligible and apprehended by philosophy—do you think that a soul which is in that state will be pure and without alloy at her departure?

No, indeed, he replied.

She is penetrated, I suppose, by the corporeal, which the unceasing intercourse and company and care of the body has made a part of her nature.

Yes.

And, my dear friend, the corporeal must be burdensome, and heavy, and earthy, and visible; and it is by this that such a soul is weighed down and dragged back to the

d visible world, because she is afraid of the invisible world of Hades, and haunts, it is said, the graves and tombs, where shadowy forms of souls have been seen, which are the phantoms of souls which were impure at their release and still cling to the visible; which is the reason why they are seen.

That is likely enough, Socrates.

That is likely, certainly, Cebes; and these are not the souls of the good, but of the evil, which are compelled to wander in such places as a punishment for the wicked lives that they have lived; and their wanderings continue until, from the desire for the corpo-

e real that clings to them, they are again imprisoned in a body.

And, he continued, they are imprisoned, probably, in the bodies of animals with habits similar to the habits which were theirs in their lifetime.

What do you mean by that, Socrates?

I mean that men who have practiced unbridled gluttony, and wantonness, and drunkenness probably enter the bodies of asses and suchlike animals. Do you not think so?   82

Certainly that is very likely.

And those who have chosen injustice, and tyranny, and robbery enter the bodies of wolves, and hawks, and kites. Where else should we say that such souls go?

No doubt, said Cebes, they go into such animals.

In short, it is quite plain, he said, whither each soul goes; each enters an animal with habits like its own.

Certainly, he replied, that is so.

And of these, he said, the happiest, who go to the best place, are those who have practiced the popular and social virtues which are called temperance and justice, and   b which come from habit and practice, without philosophy or reason.

And why are they the happiest?

Because it is probable that they return into a mild and social nature like their own, such as that of bees, or wasps, or ants; or, it may be, into the bodies of men, and that from them are made worthy citizens.

Very likely.

But none but the philosopher or the lover of knowledge, who is wholly pure when   c he goes hence, is permitted to go to the race of the gods; and therefore, my friends, Simmias and Cebes, the true philosopher is temperate and refrains from all the pleasures of the body, and does not give himself up to them. It is not squandering his substance and poverty that he fears, as the multitude and the lovers of wealth do; nor again does he dread the dishonor and disgrace of wickedness, like the lovers of power and honor. It is not for these reasons that he is temperate.

No, it would be unseemly in him if he were, Socrates, said Cebes.

Indeed it would, he replied, and therefore all those who have any care for their   d souls, and who do not spend their lives in forming and molding their bodies, bid farewell to such persons, and do not walk in their ways, thinking that they know not whither they are going. They themselves turn and follow whithersoever philosophy leads them, for they believe that they ought not to resist philosophy, or its deliverance and purification.

How, Socrates?

I will tell you, he replied. The lovers of knowledge know that when philosophy receives the soul, she is fast bound in the body, and fastened to it; she is unable to con-   e template what is, by herself, or except through the bars of her prison house, the body; and she is wallowing in utter ignorance. And philosophy sees that the dreadful thing about the imprisonment is that it is caused by lust, and that the captive herself is an   83 accomplice in her own captivity. The lovers of knowledge, I repeat, know that philosophy takes the soul when she is in this condition, and gently encourages her, and strives to release her from her captivity, showing her that the perceptions of the eye, and the ear, and the other senses are full of deceit, and persuading her to stand aloof from the senses and to use them only when she must, and exhorting her to rally and gather her-   b self together, and to trust only to herself and to the real existence which she of her own self apprehends, and to believe that nothing which is subject to change, and which she perceives by other faculties, has any truth, for such things are visible and sensible, while what she herself sees is apprehended by reason and invisible. The soul of the true philosopher thinks that it would be wrong to resist this deliverance from captivity, and therefore she holds aloof, so far as she can, from pleasure, and desire, and pain, and   c fear; for she reckons that when a man has vehement pleasure, or fear, or pain, or desire, he suffers from them not merely the evils which might be expected, such as sickness or some loss arising from the indulgence of his desires; he suffers what is the greatest and last of evils, and does not take it into account.

What do you mean, Socrates? asked Cebes.

I mean that when the soul of any man feels vehement pleasure or pain, she is forced at the same time to think that the object, whatever it be, of these sensations is the most distinct and truest, when it is not. Such objects are chiefly visible ones, are they not?

They are.

d   And is it not in this state that the soul is most completely in bondage to the body?

How so?

Because every pleasure and pain has a kind of nail, and nails and pins her to the body, and gives her a bodily nature, making her think that whatever the body says is true. And so, from having the same fancies and the same pleasures as the body, she is obliged, I suppose, to come to have the same ways, and way of life: she must always be

e   defiled with the body when she leaves it, and cannot be pure when she reaches the other world; and so she soon falls back into another body and takes root in it, like seed that is sown. Therefore she loses all part in intercourse with the divine, and pure, and uniform.

That is very true, Socrates, said Cebes.

It is for these reasons then, Cebes, that the real lovers of knowledge are temperate

84   and brave; and not for the world's reasons. Or do you think so?

No, certainly I do not.

Assuredly not. The soul of a philosopher will consider that it is the office of philosophy to set her free. She will know that she must not give herself up once more to the bondage of pleasure and pain, from which philosophy is releasing her, and, like Penelope, do a work, only to undo it continually, weaving instead of unweaving her web. She gains for herself peace from these things, and follows reason and ever abides

b   in it, contemplating what is true and divine and real, and fostered up by them. So she thinks that she should live in this life, and when she dies she believes that she will go to what is akin to and like herself, and be released from human ills. A soul, Simmias and Cebes, that has been so nurtured and so trained will never fear lest she should be torn in pieces at her departure from the body, and blown away by the winds, and vanish, and utterly cease to exist.

c   At these words there was a long silence. Socrates himself seemed to be absorbed in his argument, and so were most of us. Cebes and Simmias conversed for a little by themselves. When Socrates observed them, he said: What? Do you think that our reasoning is incomplete? It still offers many points of doubt and attack, if it is to be examined thoroughly. If you are discussing another question, I have nothing to say. But if you have any

d   difficulty about this one, do not hesitate to tell me what it is, and, if you are of the opinion that the argument should be stated in a better way, explain your views yourselves, and take me along with you if you think that you will be more successful in my company.

Simmias replied: Well, Socrates, I will tell you the truth. Each of us has a difficulty, and each has been pushing on the other and urging him to ask you about it. We were anxious to hear what you have to say; but we were reluctant to trouble you, for we were afraid that it might be unpleasant to you to be asked questions now.

Socrates smiled at this answer and said, Dear me! Simmias; I shall find it hard to

e   convince other people that I do not consider my fate a misfortune when I cannot convince even you of it, and you are afraid that I am more peevish now than I used to be. You seem to think me inferior in prophetic power to the swans, which, when they find

that they have to die, sing more loudly than they ever sang before, for joy that they are   85
about to depart into the presence of God, whose servants they are. The fear which men
have of death themselves makes them speak falsely of the swans, and they say that the
swan is wailing at its death, and that it sings loud for grief. They forget that no bird
sings when it is hungry, or cold, or in any pain; not even the nightingale, nor the swallow, nor the hoopoe, which, they assert, wail and sing for grief. But I think that neither   b
these birds nor the swan sing for grief. I believe that they have a prophetic power and
foreknowledge of the good things in the next world, for they are Apollo's birds; and so
they sing and rejoice on the day of their death, more than in all their life. And I believe
that I myself am a fellow slave with the swans, and consecrated to the service of the
same God, and that I have prophetic power from my master no less than they, and that I
am not more despondent than they are at leaving this life. So, as far as vexing me goes,
you may talk to me and ask questions as you please, as long as the Eleven of the
Athenians* will let you.

Good, said Simmias; I will tell you my difficulty, and Cebes will tell you why he   c
is dissatisfied with your statement. I think, Socrates, and I daresay you think so too, that
it is very difficult, and perhaps impossible, to obtain clear knowledge about these matters in this life. Yet I should hold him to be a very poor creature who did not test what is
said about them in every way, and persevere until he had examined the question from
every side, and could do no more. It is our duty to do one of two things. We must learn,
or we must discover for ourselves, the truth of these matters; or, if that be impossible,   d
we must take the best and most irrefragable of human doctrines and, embarking on that,
as on a raft, risk the voyage of life, unless a stronger vessel, some divine word, could be
found, on which we might take our journey more safely and more securely. And now,
after what you have said, I shall not be ashamed to put a question to you; and then I shall
not have to blame myself hereafter for not having said now what I think. Cebes and I
have been considering your argument, and we think that it is hardly sufficient.

I daresay you are right, my friend, said Socrates. But tell me, where is it insufficient?   e

To me it is insufficient, he replied, because the very same argument might be used
of a harmony, and a lyre, and its strings. It might be said that the harmony in a tuned lyre
is something unseen, and incorporeal, and perfectly beautiful, and divine, while the lyre
and its strings are corporeal, and with the nature of bodies, and compounded, and   86
earthly, and akin to the mortal. Now suppose that, when the lyre is broken and the
strings are cut or snapped, a man were to press the same argument that you have used,
and were to say that the harmony cannot have perished and that it must still exist, for it
cannot possibly be that the lyre and the strings, with their mortal nature, continue to
exist, though those strings have been broken, while the harmony, which is of the same   b
nature as the divine and the immortal, and akin to them, has perished, and perished
before the mortal lyre. He would say that the harmony itself must still exist somewhere,
and that the wood and the strings will rot away before anything happens to it. And I
think, Socrates, that you too must be aware that many of us believe the soul to be most
probably a mixture and harmony of the elements by which our body is, as it were,
strung and held together, such as heat and cold, and dry and wet, and the like, when they
are mixed together well and in due proportion. Now if the soul is a harmony, it is clear   c
that, when the body is relaxed out of proportion, or overstrung by disease or other evils,
the soul, though most divine, must perish at once, like other harmonies of sound and of
all works of art, while what remains of each body must remain for a long time, until it

*[Officials whose duty it was to superintend executions.]

d   be burned or rotted away. What then shall we say to a man who asserts that the soul, being a mixture of the elements of the body, perishes first at what is called death?

Socrates looked keenly at us, as he often used to do, and smiled. Simmias' objection is a fair one, he said. If any of you is readier than I am, why does he not answer? e   For Simmias looks like a formidable assailant. But before we answer him, I think that we had better hear what fault Cebes has to find with my reasoning, and so gain time to consider our reply. And then, when we have heard them both, we must either give in to them, if they seem to harmonize, or, if they do not, we must proceed to argue in defense of our reasoning. Come, Cebes, what is it that troubles you and makes you doubt?

I will tell you, replied Cebes. I think that the argument is just where it was, and still 87   open to our former objection. You have shown very cleverly and, if it is not arrogant to say so, quite conclusively that our souls existed before they entered the human form. I don't retract my admission on that point. But I am not convinced that they will continue to exist after we are dead. I do not agree with Simmias' objection, that the soul is not stronger and more lasting than the body: I think that it is very much superior in those respects. "Well, then," the argument might reply, "do you still doubt, when you see that b   the weaker part of a man continues to exist after his death? Do you not think that the more lasting part of him must necessarily be preserved for as long?" See, therefore, if there is anything in what I say; for I think that I, like Simmias, shall best express my meaning in a figure. It seems to me that a man might use an argument similar to yours to prove that a weaver, who had died in old age, had not in fact perished, but was still alive somewhere, on the ground that the garment which the weaver had woven for himself and c   used to wear had not perished or been destroyed. And if anyone were incredulous, he might ask whether a human being, or a garment constantly in use and wear, lasts the longest; and on being told that a human being lasts much the longest, he might think that he had shown beyond all doubt that the man was safe, because what lasts a shorter time than the man had not perished. But that, I suppose, is not so, Simmias; for you too must examine what I say. Everyone would understand that such an argument was simple non- d   sense. This weaver wove himself many such garments and wore them out; he outlived them all but the last, but he perished before that one. Yet a man is in no wise inferior to his cloak, or weaker than it, on that account. And I think that the soul's relation to the body may be expressed in a similar figure. Why should not a man very reasonably say in just the same way that the soul lasts a long time, while the body is weaker and lasts a shorter time? But, he might go on, each soul wears out many bodies, especially if she e   lives for many years. For if the body is in a state of flux and decay in the man's lifetime, and the soul is ever repairing the worn-out part, it will surely follow that the soul, on perishing, will be clothed in her last robe, and perish before that alone. But when the soul has perished, then the body will show its weakness and quickly rot away. So as yet we 88   have no right to be confident, on the strength of this argument, that our souls continue to exist after we are dead. And a man might concede even more than this to an opponent who used your argument; he might admit not only that our souls existed in the period before we were born, but also that there is no reason why some of them should not continue to exist in the future, and often come into being, and die again, after we are dead; for the soul is strong enough by nature to endure coming into being many times. He might grant that, without conceding that she suffers no harm in all these births, or that b   she is not at last wholly destroyed at one of the deaths; and he might say that no man knows when this death and dissolution of the body, which brings destruction to the soul, will be, for it is impossible for any man to find out that. But if this is true, a man's confidence about death must be an irrational confidence, unless he can prove that the soul is wholly indestructible and immortal. Otherwise everyone who is dying must fear that his soul will perish utterly this time in her separation from the body.

It made us all very uncomfortable to listen to them, as we afterward said to each   c
other. We had been fully convinced by the previous argument; and now they seemed to overturn our conviction, and to make us distrust all the arguments that were to come, as well as the preceding ones, and to doubt if our judgment was worth anything, or even if certainty could be attained at all.

ECHECRATES: By the gods, Phaedo, I can understand your feelings very well. I   d
myself felt inclined while you were speaking to ask myself, "Then what reasoning are we to believe in future? That of Socrates was quite convincing, and now it has fallen into discredit." For the doctrine that our soul is a harmony has always taken a wonderful hold of me, and your mentioning it reminded me that I myself had held it. And now I must begin again and find some other reasoning which shall convince me that a man's soul does not die with him at his death. So tell me, I pray you, how did Socrates pursue   e
the argument? Did he show any signs of uneasiness, as you say that you did, or did he come to the defense of his argument calmly? And did he defend it satisfactorily or not? Tell me the whole story as exactly as you can.

PHAEDO: I have often, Echecrates, wondered at Socrates; but I never admired him   89
more than I admired him then. There was nothing very strange in his having an answer. What I chiefly wondered at was, first, the kindness and good nature and respect with which he listened to the young men's objections; and, secondly, the quickness with which he perceived their effect upon us; and, lastly, how well he healed our wounds, and rallied us as if we were beaten and flying troops, and encouraged us to follow him, and to examine the reasoning with him.

ECHECRATES: How?

PHAEDO: I will tell you. I was sitting by the bed on a stool at his right hand, and his seat was a good deal higher than mine. He stroked my head and gathered up the hair   b
on my neck in his hand—you know he used often to play with my hair—and said, Tomorrow, Phaedo, I daresay you will cut off these beautiful locks.

I suppose so, Socrates, I replied.

You will not, if you take my advice.

Why not? I asked.

You and I will cut off our hair today, he said, if our argument be dead indeed, and we cannot bring it to life again. And I, if I were you, and the argument were to escape   c
me, would swear an oath, as the Argives did, not to wear my hair long again until I had renewed the fight and conquered the argument of Simmias and Cebes.

But Heracles himself, they say, is not a match for two, I replied.

Then summon me to aid you, as your Iolaus, while there is still light.

Then I summon you, not as Heracles summoned Iolaus, but as Iolaus might summon Heracles.

It will be the same, he replied. But first let us take care not to make a mistake.

What mistake? I asked.

The mistake of becoming misologists, or haters of reasoning, as men become misan-   d
thropists, he replied; for to hate reasoning is the greatest evil that can happen to us. Misology and misanthropy both come from similar causes. The latter arises out of the implicit and irrational confidence which is placed in a man who is believed by his friend to be thoroughly true and sincere and trustworthy, and who is soon afterward discovered to be a bad man and untrustworthy. This happens again and again; and when a man has had this experience many times, particularly at the hands of those whom he has believed to be his   e

nearest and dearest friends, and he has quarreled with many of them, he ends by hating all men and thinking that there is no good at all in anyone. Have you not seen this happen?

Yes, certainly, said I.

Is it not discreditable? he said. Is it not clear that such a man tries to deal with men without understanding human nature? Had he understood it he would have known that, in fact, good men and bad men are very few indeed, and that the majority of men are neither one nor the other.

What do you mean? I asked.

Just what is true of extremely large and extremely small things, he replied. What is rarer than to find a man, or a dog, or anything else which is either extremely large or extremely small? Or again, what is rarer than to find a man who is extremely swift or slow, or extremely base or honorable, or extremely black or white? Have you not noticed that in all these cases the extremes are rare and few, and that the average specimens are abundant and many?

Yes, certainly, I replied.

And in the same way, if there were a competition in wickedness, he said, don't you think that the leading sinners would be found to be very few?

That is likely enough, said I.

Yes, it is, he replied. But this is not the point in which arguments are like men; it was you who led me on to discuss this point. The analogy is this. When a man believes some reasoning to be true, though he does not understand the art of reasoning, and then soon afterward, rightly or wrongly, comes to think that it is false, and this happens to him time after time, he ends by disbelieving in reasoning altogether. You know that persons who spend their time in disputation, come at last to think themselves the wisest of men, and to imagine that they alone have discovered that there is no soundness or certainty anywhere, either in reasoning or in things, and that all existence is in a state of perpetual flux, like the currents of the Euripus, and never remains still for a moment.

Yes, I replied, that is certainly true.

And, Phaedo, he said, if there be a system of reasoning which is true, and certain, and which our minds can grasp, it would be very lamentable that a man who has met with some of these arguments which at one time seem true and at another false should at last, in the bitterness of his heart, gladly put all the blame on the reasoning, instead of on himself and his own unskillfulness, and spend the rest of his life in hating and reviling reasoning, and lose the truth and knowledge of reality.

Indeed, I replied, that would be very lamentable.

First then, he said, let us be careful not to admit into our souls the notion that all reasoning is very likely unsound; let us rather think that we ourselves are not yet sound. And we must strive earnestly like men to become sound, you, my friends, for the sake of all your future life, and I, because of my death. For I am afraid that at present I can hardly look at death like a philosopher; I am in a contentious mood, like the uneducated persons who never give a thought to the truth of the question about which they are disputing, but are only anxious to persuade their audience that they themselves are right. And I think that today I shall differ from them only in one thing. I shall not be anxious to persuade my audience that I am right, except by the way; but I shall be very anxious indeed to persuade myself. For see, my dear friend, how selfish my reasoning is. If what I say is true, it is well to believe it. But if there is nothing after death, at any rate I shall pain my friends less by my lamentations in the interval before I die. And this ignorance will not last forever—that would have been an evil—it will soon come to an end. So prepared, Simmias and Cebes, he said, I come to the argument. And you, if you take my advice, will think not of Socrates, but of the truth; and you will agree with me if you think that what I say is true; otherwise you will oppose me with every argument that you have; and be careful that, in my anxiety to convince you, I do not deceive both you and myself, and go away, leaving my sting behind me, like a bee.

Now let us proceed, he said. And first, if you find I have forgotten your arguments, repeat them. Simmias, I think, has fears and misgivings that the soul, being of the nature of a harmony, may perish before the body, though she is more divine and nobler than the body. Cebes, if I am not mistaken, conceded that the soul is more enduring than the body; but he said that no one could tell whether the soul, after wearing out many bodies many times, did not herself perish on leaving her last body, and whether death be not precisely this—the destruction of the soul; for the destruction of the body is unceasing. Is there anything else, Simmias and Cebes, which we have to examine?

They both agreed that these were the questions.

Do you reject all our previous conclusions, he asked, or only some of them?

Only some of them, they replied.

Well, said he, what do you say of our doctrine that knowledge is recollection, and that therefore our souls must necessarily have existed somewhere else, before they were imprisoned in our bodies?

I, replied Cebes, was convinced by it at the time in a wonderful way; and now there is no doctrine to which I adhere more firmly.

And I am of that mind too, said Simmias; and I shall be very much surprised if I ever change it.

But, my Theban friend, you will have to change it, said Socrates, if this opinion of yours, that a harmony is a composite thing, and that the soul is a harmony composed of the elements of the body at the right tension, is to stand. You will hardly allow yourself to assert that the harmony was in existence before the things from which it was to be composed? Will you do that?

Certainly not, Socrates.

But you see that that is what your assertion comes to when you say that the soul existed before she came into the form and body of man, and yet that she is composed of elements which did not yet exist? Your harmony is not like what you compare it to: the lyre and the strings and the sounds, as yet untuned, come into existence first; and the harmony is composed last of all, and perishes first. How will this belief of yours accord with the other?

It will not, replied Simmias.

And yet, said he, an argument about harmony is hardly the place for a discord.

No, indeed, said Simmias.

Well, there is a discord in your argument, he said. You must choose which doctrine you will retain—that knowledge is recollection or that the soul is a harmony.

The former, Socrates, certainly, he replied. The latter has never been demonstrated to me; it rests only on probable and plausible grounds, which make it a popular opinion. I know that doctrines which ground their proofs on probabilities are impostors and that they are very apt to mislead, both in geometry and everything else, if one is not on one's guard against them. But the doctrine about recollection and knowledge rests upon a foundation which claims belief. We agreed that the soul exists before she ever enters the body, as surely as the essence itself which has the name of real being exists. And I am persuaded that I believe in this essence rightly and on sufficient evidence. It follows therefore, I suppose, that I cannot allow myself or anyone else to say that the soul is a harmony.

And, consider the question in another way, Simmias, said Socrates. Do you think that a harmony or any other composition can exist in a state other than the state of the elements of which it is composed?

Certainly not.

Nor, I suppose, can it do or suffer anything beyond what they do and suffer?

He assented.

A harmony therefore cannot lead the elements of which it is composed; it must follow them?

He agreed.

And much less can it be moved, or make a sound, or do anything else in opposition to its parts.

Much less, indeed, he replied.

Well, is not every harmony by nature a harmony according as it is adjusted?

I don't understand you, he replied.

If it is tuned more, and to a greater extent, he said, supposing that to be possible, will it not be more a harmony, and to a greater extent, while if it is tuned less, and to a smaller extent, will it not be less a harmony, and to a smaller extent?

Certainly.

Well, is this true of the soul? Can one soul be more a soul, and to a greater extent, or less a soul, and to a smaller extent, than another, even in the smallest degree?

Certainly not, he replied.

Well then, he replied, please tell me this; is not one soul said to have intelligence and virtue and to be good, while another is said to have folly and vice and to be bad? And is it not true?

Yes, certainly.

What then will those who assert that the soul is a harmony say that the virtue and the vice which are in our souls are? Another harmony and another discord? Will they say that the good soul is in tune, and that, herself a harmony, she has within herself another harmony, and that the bad soul is out of tune herself, and has no other harmony within her?

I, said Simmias, cannot tell. But it is clear that they would have to say something of the kind.

But it has been conceded, he said, that one soul is never more or less a soul than another. In other words, we have agreed that one harmony is never more, or to a greater extent, or less, or to a smaller extent a harmony than another. Is it not so?

Yes, certainly.

And the harmony which is neither more nor less a harmony, is not more or less tuned. Is that so?

Yes.

And has that which is neither more nor less tuned a greater, or a less, or an equal share of harmony?

An equal share.

Then, since one soul is never more nor less a soul than another, it has not been more or less tuned either?

True.

Therefore it can have no greater share of harmony or of discord?

Certainly not.

And, therefore, can one soul contain more vice or virtue than another, if vice be discord and virtue harmony?

By no means.

Or rather, Simmias, to speak quite accurately, I suppose that there will be no vice in any soul if the soul is a harmony. I take it there can never be any discord in a harmony which is a perfect harmony.

Certainly not.

Neither can a soul, if it be a perfect soul, have any vice in it?

No; that follows necessarily from what has been said.

Then the result of this reasoning is that all the souls of all living creatures will be equally good if the nature of all souls is to be equally souls.

Yes, I think so, Socrates, he said.

And do you think that this is true, he asked, and that this would have been the fate of our argument, if the hypothesis that the soul is a harmony had been correct?

No, certainly not, he replied.

Well, said he, of all the parts of a man, should you not say that it was the soul, and particularly the wise soul, which rules?

I should.

Does she yield to the passions of the body or does she oppose them? I mean this. When the body is hot and thirsty, does not the soul drag it away and prevent it from drinking, and when it is hungry does she not prevent it from eating? And do we not see her opposing the passions of the body in a thousand other ways?

Yes, certainly.

But we have also agreed that, if she is a harmony, she can never give a sound contrary to the tensions, and relaxations, and vibrations, and other changes of the elements of which she is composed; that she must follow them, and can never lead them?

Yes, he replied, we certainly have.

Well, now, do we not find the soul acting in just the opposite way, and leading all the elements of which she is said to consist, and opposing them in almost everything all through life, and lording it over them in every way, and chastising them, sometimes severely, and with a painful discipline, such as gymnastics and medicine; and sometimes lightly, sometimes threatening and sometimes admonishing the desires and passions and fears, as though she were speaking to something other than herself, as Homer makes Odysseus do in the *Odyssey,* where he says that

He smote upon his breast, and chid his heart:
"Endure, my heart, e'en worse hast thou endured." [XX.17]

Do you think that when Homer wrote that, he supposed the soul to be a harmony and capable of being led by the passions of the body, and not of a nature to lead them and be their lord, being herself far too divine a thing to be like a harmony?

Certainly, Socrates, I think not.

Then, my excellent friend, it is quite wrong to say that the soul is a harmony. For then, you see, we should not be in agreement either with the divine poet Homer or with ourselves.

That is true, he replied.

Very good, said Socrates; I think that we have contrived to appease our Theban Harmonia with tolerable success. But how about Cadmus, Cebes? he said. How shall we appease him, and with what reasoning?

I daresay that you will find out how to do it, said Cebes. At all events you have argued that the soul is not a harmony in a way which surprised me very much. When Simmias was stating his objection, I wondered how anyone could possibly dispose of his argument; and so I was very much surprised to see it fall before the very first onset of yours. I should not wonder if the same fate awaited the argument of Cadmus.

My good friend, said Socrates, do not be overconfident, or some evil eye will overturn the argument that is to come. However, that we will leave to God; let us, like Homer's heroes, "advancing boldly," see if there is anything in what you say. The sum of what you seek is this. You require me to prove to you that the soul is indestructible and immortal; for if it be not so, you think that the confidence of a philosopher, who is confident in death, and who believes that when he is dead he will fare infinitely better in the other world than if he had lived a different sort of life in this world, is a foolish and idle confidence. You say that to show that the soul is strong and godlike, and that she existed before we were born men, is not enough; for that does not necessarily prove her immortality, but only that she lasts a long time, and has existed an enormous while, and

d   has known and done many things in a previous state. Yet she is not any the more immortal for that; her very entrance into man's body was, like a disease, the beginning of her destruction. And, you say, she passes this life in misery, and at last perishes in what we call death. You think that it makes no difference at all to the fears of each one of us, whether she enters the body once or many times; for everyone but a fool must fear

e   death, if he does not know and cannot prove that she is immortal. That, I think, Cebes, is the substance of your objection. I state it again and again on purpose, that nothing may escape us, and that you may add to it or take away from it anything that you wish.

Cebes replied: No, that is my meaning. I don't want to add or to take away anything at present.

Socrates paused for some time and thought. Then he said, It is not an easy question that you are raising, Cebes. We must examine fully the whole subject of the causes of gen-

96   eration and decay. If you like, I will give you my own experiences, and if you think that you can make use of anything that I say, you may employ it to satisfy your misgivings.

Indeed, said Cebes, I should like to hear your experiences.

Listen, then, and I will tell you, Cebes, he replied. When I was a young man, I had a passionate desire for the wisdom which is called Physical Science. I thought it a splendid thing to know the causes of everything; why a thing comes into being, and why

b   it perishes, and why it exists. I was always worrying myself with such questions as, Do living creatures take a definite form, as some persons say, from the fermentation of heat and cold? Is it the blood, or the air, or fire by which we think? Or is it none of these, but the brain which gives the senses of hearing and sight and smell, and do memory and opinion come from these, and knowledge from memory and opinion when in a state of

c   quiescence? Again, I used to examine the destruction of these things, and the changes of the heaven and the earth, until at last I concluded that I was wholly and absolutely unfitted for these studies. I will prove that to you conclusively. I was so completely blinded by these studies that I forgot what I had formerly seemed to myself and to others to know quite well; I unlearned all that I had been used to think that I understood; even the

d   cause of man's growth. Formerly I had thought it evident on the face of it that the cause of growth was eating and drinking, and that, when from food flesh is added to flesh, and bone to bone, and in the same way to the other parts of the body their proper elements, then by degrees the small bulk grows to be large, and so the boy becomes a man. Don't you think that my belief was reasonable?

I do, said Cebes.

Then here is another experience for you. I used to feel no doubt, when I saw a tall

e   man standing by a short one, that the tall man was, it might be, a head the taller, or, in the same way, that one horse was bigger than another. I was even clearer that ten was more than eight by the addition of two, and that a thing two cubits long was longer by half its length than a thing one cubit long.

And what do you think now? asked Cebes.

I think that I am very far from believing that I know the cause of any of these things. Why, when you add one to one, I am not sure either that the one to which one is

97   added has become two, or that the one added and the one to which it is added become,

by the addition, two. I cannot understand how, when they are brought together, this union, or placing of one by the other, should be the cause of their becoming two, whereas, when they were separated, each of them was one, and they were not two. Nor, again, if you divide one into two, can I convince myself that this division is the cause of one becoming two; for then a thing becomes two from exactly the opposite cause. In the former case it was because two units were brought together, and the one was added to the other; while now it is because they are separated, and the one divided from the other. Nor, again, can I persuade myself that I know how one is generated; in short, this method does not show me the cause of the generation or destruction or existence of anything. I have in my own mind a confused idea of another method, but I cannot admit this one for a moment.

But one day I listened to a man who said that he was reading from a book of Anaxagoras, which affirmed that it is Mind which orders and is the cause of all things. I was delighted with this theory; it seemed to me to be right that Mind should be the cause of all things, and I thought to myself, If this is so, then Mind will order and arrange each thing in the best possible way. So if we wish to discover the cause of the generation or destruction or existence of a thing, we must discover how it is best for that thing to exist, or to act, or to be acted on. Man therefore has only to consider what is best and fittest for himself, or for other things, and then it follows necessarily that he will know what is bad; for both are included in the same science. These reflections made me very happy: I thought that I had found in Anaxagoras a teacher of the cause of existence after my own heart, and I expected that he would tell me first whether the earth is flat or round, and that he would then go on to explain to me the cause and the necessity, and tell me what is best, and that it is best for the earth to be of that shape. If he said that the earth was in the center of the universe, I thought that he would explain that it was best for it to be there; and I was prepared not to require any other kind of cause, if he made this clear to me. In the same way I was prepared to ask questions about the sun, and the moon, and the stars, about their relative speeds, and revolutions, and changes; and to hear why it is best for each of them to act and be acted on as they are acted on. I never thought that, when he said that things are ordered by Mind, he would introduce any reason for their being as they are, except that they are best so. I thought that he would assign a cause to each thing, and a cause to the universe, and then would go on to explain to me what was best for each thing, and what was the common good of all. I would not have sold my hopes for a great deal: I seized the books very eagerly, and read them as fast as I could, in order that I might know what is best and what is worse.

All my splendid hopes were dashed to the ground, my friend, for as I went on reading I found that the writer made no use of Mind at all, and that he assigned no causes for the order of things. His causes were air, and ether, and water, and many other strange things. I thought that he was exactly like a man who should begin by saying that Socrates does all that he does by Mind, and who, when he tried to give a reason for each of my actions, should say, first, that I am sitting here now, because my body is composed of bones and muscles, and that the bones are hard and separated by joints, while the muscles can be tightened and loosened, and, together with the flesh and the skin which holds them together, cover the bones; and that therefore, when the bones are raised in their sockets, the relaxation and contraction of the muscles make it possible for me now to bend my limbs, and that that is the cause of my sitting here with my legs bent. And in the same way he would go on to explain why I am talking to you: he would assign voice, and air, and hearing, and a thousand other things as causes; but he would e   quite forget to mention the real cause, which is that since the Athenians thought it right to condemn me, I have thought it right and just to sit here and to submit to whatever sentence they may think fit to impose. For, by the dog of Egypt, I think that these muscles

99   and bones would long ago have been in Megara or Boeotia, prompted by their opinion of what is best, if I had not thought it better and more honorable to submit to whatever penalty the state inflicts, rather than escape by flight. But to call these things causes is too absurd! If it were said that without bones and muscles and the other parts of my body I could not have carried my resolutions into effect, that would be true. But to say

b   that they are the cause of what I do, and that in this way I am acting by Mind, and not from choice of what is best, would be a very loose and careless way of talking. It simply means that a man cannot distinguish the realcause from that without which the cause cannot be the cause, and this it is, I think, which the multitude, groping about in the dark, speaks of as the cause, giving it a name which does not belong to it. And so one man surrounds the earth with a vortex, and makes the heavens sustain it. Another

c   represents the earth as a flat kneading trough, and supports it on a basis of air. But they never think of looking for a power which is involved in these things being disposed as it is best for them to be, nor do they think that such a power has any divine strength. They expect to find an Atlas who is stronger and more immortal and abler to hold the world together, and they never for a moment imagine that it is the binding force of good which really binds and holds things together. I would most gladly learn the nature of that kind

d   of cause from any man, but I wholly failed either to discover it myself or to learn it from anyone else. However, I had a second string to my bow, and perhaps, Cebes, you would like me to describe to you how I proceeded in my search for the cause.

I should like to hear very much indeed, he replied.

When I had given up inquiring into real existence, he proceeded, I thought that I must take care that I did not suffer as people do who look at the sun during an eclipse.

e   For they are apt to lose their eyesight, unless they look at the sun's reflection in water or some such medium. That danger occurred to me. I was afraid that my soul might be completely blinded if I looked at things with my eyes, and tried to grasp them with my

100   senses. So I thought that I must have recourse to conceptions, and examine the truth of existence by means of them. Perhaps my illustration is not quite accurate. I am scarcely prepared to admit that he who examines existence through conceptions is dealing with mere reflections, any more than he who examines it as manifested in sensible objects. However, I began in this way. I assumed in each case whatever principle I judged to be strongest; and then I held as true whatever seemed to agree with it, whether in the case of the cause or of anything else, and as untrue whatever seemed not to agree with it. I should like to explain my meaning more clearly; I don't think you understand me yet.

Indeed I do not very well, said Cebes.

b   I mean nothing new, he said; only what I have repeated over and over again, both in our conversation today and at other times. I am going to try to explain to you the kind of cause at which I have worked, and I will go back to what we have so often spoken of, and begin with the assumption that there exists an absolute beauty, and an absolute good, and an absolute greatness, and so on. If you grant me this, and agree that they exist, I hope to be able to show you what my cause is, and to discover that the soul is immortal.

c   You may assume that I grant it you, said Cebes; go on with your proof.

Then do you agree with me in what follows? he asked. It appears to me that if anything besides absolute beauty is beautiful, it is so simply because it partakes of absolute beauty, and I say the same of all phenomena. Do you allow that kind of cause?

I do, he answered.

Well then, he said, I do no longer recognize nor can I understand these other wise causes: if I am told that anything is beautiful because it has a rich color, or a goodly form, or the like, I pay no attention, for such language only confuses me; and in a simple and plain, and perhaps a foolish way, I hold to the doctrine that the thing is only made beautiful by the presence or communication, or whatever you please to call it, of absolute beauty—I do not wish to insist on the nature of the communication, but what I am sure of is that it is absolute beauty which makes all beautiful things beautiful. This seems to me to be the safest answer that I can give myself or others; I believe that I shall never fail if I hold to this; it is a safe answer to make to myself or anyone else, that it is absolute beauty which makes beautiful things beautiful. Don't you think so?

I do.

And it is largeness that makes large things large, and larger things larger, and smallness that makes smaller things smaller?

Yes.

And if you were told that one man was taller than another by a head, and that the shorter man was shorter by a head, you would not accept the statement. You would protest that you say only that the greater is greater by size, and that size is the cause of its being greater; and that the less is only less by smallness, and that smallness is the cause of its being less. You would be afraid to assert that a man is greater or smaller by a head, lest you should be met by the retort, first, that the greater is greater, and the smaller smaller, by the same thing, and secondly, that the greater is greater by a head, which is a small thing, and that it is truly marvelous that a small thing should make a man great. Should you not be afraid of that?

Yes, indeed, said Cebes, laughing.

And you would be afraid to say that ten is more than eight by two, and that two is the cause of the excess; you would say that ten was more than eight by number, and that number is the cause of the excess? And in just the same way you would be afraid to say that a thing two cubits long was longer than a thing one cubit long by half its length, instead of by size, would you not?

Yes, certainly.

Again, you would be careful not to affirm that, if one is added to one, the addition is the cause of two, or, if one is divided, that the division is the cause of two? You would protest loudly that you know of no way in which a thing can be generated, except by participation in its own proper essence; and that you can give no cause for the generation of two except participation in duality; and that all things which are to be two must participate in duality, while whatever is to be one must participate in unity. You would leave the explanation of these divisions and additions and all such subtleties to wiser men than yourself. You would be frightened, as the saying is, at your own shadow and ignorance, and would hold fast to the safety of our principle, and so give your answer. But if anyone should attack the principle itself, you would not mind him or answer him until you had considered whether the consequences of it are consistent or inconsistent, and when you had to give an account of the principle itself, you would give it in the same way, by assuming some other principle which you think the strongest of the higher ones, and so go on until you had reached a satisfactory resting place. You would not mix up the first principle and its consequences in your argument, as mere disputants do, if you really wish to discover anything of existence. Such persons will very likely not spend a single word or thought upon that, for they are clever enough to be able to please themselves entirely, though their argument is a chaos. But you, I think, if you are a philosopher, will do as I say.

Very true, said Simmias and Cebes together.

ECHECRATES: And they were right, Phaedo. I think the clearness of his reasoning, even to the dullest, is quite wonderful.

PHAEDO: Indeed, Echecrates, all who were there thought so too.

ECHECRATES: So do we who were not there, but who are listening to your story. But how did the argument proceed after that?

PHAEDO: They had admitted that each of the Ideas exists and that Phenomena take
b   the names of the Ideas as they participate in them. Socrates, I think, then went on to ask:

If you say this, do you not, in saying that Simmias is taller than Socrates and shorter than Phaedo, say that Simmias possesses both the attribute of tallness and the attribute of shortness?

I do.

But you admit, he said, that the proposition that Simmias is taller than Socrates is
c   not exactly true, as it is stated; Simmias is not really taller because he is Simmias, but because of his height. Nor again is he taller than Socrates because Socrates is Socrates, but because of Socrates' shortness compared with Simmias' tallness.

True.

Nor is Simmias shorter than Phaedo because Phaedo is Phaedo, but because of Phaedo's tallness compared with Simmias' shortness.

That is so.

Then in this way Simmias is called both short and tall, when he is between the two; he exceeds the shortness of one by the excess of his height, and gives the other a
d   tallness exceeding his own shortness. I daresay you think, he said, smiling, that my language is like a legal document for precision and formality. But I think that it is as I say.

He agreed.

I say it because I want you to think as I do. It seems to me not only that absolute greatness will never be great and small at once, but also that greatness in us never admits smallness, and will not be exceeded. One of two things must happen: either the greater will
e   give way and fly at the approach of its opposite, the less, or it will perish. It will not stand its ground, and receive smallness, and be other than it was, just as I stand my ground, and receive smallness, and remain the very same small man that I was. But greatness cannot endure to be small, being great. Just in the same way again smallness in us will never become nor be great; nor will any opposite, while it remains what it was, become or be at
103   the same time the opposite of what it was. Either it goes away or it perishes in the change.

That is exactly what I think, said Cebes.

Thereupon someone—I am not sure who—said,

But surely is not this just the reverse of what we agreed to be true earlier in the argument, that the greater is generated from the less, and the less from the greater, and, in short, that opposites are generated from opposites? But now it seems to be denied that this can ever happen.

Socrates inclined his head to the speaker and listened. Well and bravely remarked,
b   he said, but you have not noticed the difference between the two propositions. What we said then was that a concrete thing is generated from its opposite; what we say now is that the absolute opposite can never become opposite to itself, either when it is in us, or when it is in nature. We were speaking then of things in which the opposites are, and we named them after those opposites; but now we are speaking of the opposites them-
c   selves, whose inherence gives the things their names; and they, we say, will never be generated from each other. At the same time he turned to Cebes and asked, Did his objection trouble you at all, Cebes?

No, replied Cebes; I don't feel that difficulty. But I will not deny that many other things trouble me.

Then we are quite agreed on this point, he said. An opposite will never be opposite to itself.

No never, he replied.

Now tell me again, he said; do you agree with me in this? Are there not things which you call heat and cold?

Yes.

Are they the same as snow and fire?

No, certainly not.

Heat is different from fire, and cold from snow?   d

Yes.

But I suppose, as we have said, that you do not think that snow can ever receive heat, and yet remain what it was, snow and hot: it will either retire or perish at the approach of heat.

Certainly.

And fire, again, will either retire or perish at the approach of cold. It will never endure to receive the cold and still remain what it was, fire and cold.

True, he said.   e

Then, it is true of some of these things that not only the idea itself has a right to its name for all time, but that something else too, which is not the idea, but which has the form of the idea wherever it exists, shares the name. Perhaps my meaning will be clearer by an example. The odd ought always to have the name of odd, ought it not?

Yes, certainly.

Well, my question is this. Is the odd the only thing with this name, or is there something else which is not the same as the odd, but which must always have this name,   104
together with its own, because its nature is such that it is never separated from the odd? There are many examples of what I mean: let us take one of them, the number three, and consider it. Do you not think that we must always call it by the name of odd, as well as by its own name, although the odd is not the same as the number three? Yet the nature of the number three, and of the number five, and of half the whole series of numbers, is   b
such that each of them is odd, though none of them is the same as the odd. In the same way the number two, and the number four, and the whole of the other series of numbers, are each of them always even, though they are not the same as the even. Do you agree or not?

Yes, of course, he replied.

Then see what I want to show you. It is not only opposite ideas which appear not to admit their opposites; things also which are not opposites, but which always contain opposites, seem as if they would not admit the idea which is opposite to the idea that they   c
contain: they either perish or retire at its approach. Shall we not say that the number three would perish or endure anything sooner than become even while it remains three?

Yes, indeed, said Cebes.

And yet, said he, the number two is not the opposite of the number three.

No, certainly not.

Then it is not only the ideas which will not endure the approach of their opposites; there are some other things besides which will not endure such an approach.

That is quite true, he said.

Shall we determine, if we can, what is their nature? he asked.

Certainly.

Will they not be those things, Cebes, which force whatever they are in to have   d
always not its own idea only, but the idea of some opposite as well?

What do you mean?

Only what we were saying just now. You know, I think, that whatever the idea of three is in, is bound to be not three only, but odd as well.

Certainly.

Well, we say that the opposite idea to the form which produces this result will never come to that thing.

Indeed, no.

But the idea of the odd produces it?

Yes.

And the idea of the even is the opposite of the idea of the odd?

Yes.

e   Then the idea of the even will never come to three?

Certainly not.

So three has no part in the even?

None.

Then the number three is uneven?

Yes.

So much for the definition which I undertook to give of things which are not opposites, and yet do not admit opposites; thus we have seen that the number three does not admit the even, though it is not the opposite of the even, for it always brings with it the

105   opposite of the even, and the number two does not admit the odd, nor fire cold, and so on. Do you agree with me in saying that not only does the opposite not admit the opposite, but also that whatever brings with it an opposite of anything to which it goes never admits the opposite of that which it brings? Let me recall this to you again; there is no harm in repetition. Five will not admit the idea of the even, nor will the double of five—

b   ten—admit the idea of the odd. It is not itself an opposite, yet it will not admit the idea of the odd. Again, one and a half, a half, and the other numbers of that kind will not admit the idea of the whole, nor again will such numbers as a third. Do you follow and agree?

I follow you and entirely agree with you, he said.

Now begin again, and answer me, he said. And imitate me; do not answer me in the terms of my question: I mean, do not give the old safe answer which I have already spoken of, for I see another way of safety, which is the result of what we have been say-

c   ing. If you ask me, what is that which must be in the body to make it hot, I shall not give our old safe and stupid answer, and say that it is heat; I shall make a more refined answer, drawn from what we have been saying, and reply, fire. If you ask me, what is that which must be in the body to make it sick, I shall not say sickness, but fever; and again to the question what is that which must be in number to make it odd, I shall not reply oddness, but unity, and so on. Do you understand my meaning clearly yet?

Yes, quite, he said.

Then, he went on, tell me, what is that which must be in a body to make it alive?

A soul, he replied.

d   And is this always so?

Of course, he said.

Then the soul always brings life to whatever contains her?

No doubt, he answered.

And is there an opposite to life, or not?

Yes.

What is it?

Death.

And we have already agreed that the soul cannot ever receive the opposite of what she brings?

Yes, certainly we have, said Cebes.

Well; what name did we give to that which does not admit the idea of the even?

The uneven, he replied.

And what do we call that which does not admit justice or music?

The unjust, and the unmusical.

Good; and what do we call that which does not admit death?

The immortal, he said.

And the soul does not admit death?

No.

Then the soul is immortal?

It is.

Good, he said. Shall we say that this is proved? What do you think?

Yes, Socrates, and very sufficiently.

Well, Cebes, he said, if the odd had been necessarily imperishable, must not three have been imperishable?

106

Of course.

And if cold had been necessarily imperishable, snow would have retired safe and unmelted, whenever warmth was applied to it. It would not have perished, and it would not have stayed and admitted the heat.

True, he said.

In the same way, I suppose, if warmth were imperishable, whenever cold attacked fire, the fire would never have been extinguished or have perished. It would have gone away in safety.

Necessarily, he replied.

And must we not say the same of the immortal? he asked. If the immortal is imperishable, the soul cannot perish when death comes upon her. It follows from what we have said that she will not ever admit death, or be in a state of death, any more than three, or the odd itself, will ever be even, or fire, or the heat itself which is in fire, cold. But, it may be said, Granted that the odd does not become even at the approach of the even; why, when the odd has perished, may not the even come into its place? We could not contend in reply that it does not perish, for the uneven is not imperishable; if we had agreed that the uneven was imperishable, we could have easily contended that the odd and three go away at the approach of the even; and we could have urged the same contention about fire and heat and the rest, could we not?

b

c

Yes, certainly.

And now, if we are agreed that the immortal is imperishable, then the soul will be not immortal only, but also imperishable; otherwise we shall require another argument.

d

Nay, he [Cebes] said, there is no need of that, as far as this point goes; for if the immortal, which is eternal, will admit of destruction, what will not?

And all men would admit, said Socrates, that God, and the essential form of life, and all else that is immortal, never perishes.

All men, indeed, he said; and, what is more, I think, all gods would admit that.

Then if the immortal is indestructible, must not the soul, if it be immortal, be imperishable?

e

Certainly, it must.

Then, it seems, when death attacks a man, his mortal part dies, but his immortal part retreats before death, and goes away safe and indestructible.

It seems so.

Then, Cebes, said he, beyond all question the soul is immortal and imperishable, and our souls will indeed exist in the other world.

107

I, Socrates, he replied, have no more objections to urge; your reasoning has quite satisfied me. If Simmias, or anyone else, has anything to say, it would be well for him to say it now; for I know not to what other season he can defer the discussion if he wants to say or to hear anything touching this matter.

No, indeed, said Simmias; neither have I any further ground for doubt after what you have said. Yet I cannot help feeling some doubts still in my mind; for the subject of our conversation is a vast one, and I distrust the feebleness of man.

You are right, Simmias, said Socrates, and more than that, you must re-examine our original assumptions, however certain they seem to you; and when you have analyzed them sufficiently, you will, I think, follow the argument, as far as man can follow it; and when that becomes clear to you, you will seek for nothing more.

That is true, he said.

But then, my friends, said he, we must think of this. If it be true that the soul is immortal, we have to take care of her, not merely on account of the time which we call life, but also on account of all time. Now we can see how terrible is the danger of neglect. For if death had been a release from all things, it would have been a godsend to the wicked; for when they died they would have been released with their souls from the body and from their own wickedness. But now we have found that the soul is immortal, and so her only refuge and salvation from evil is to become as perfect and wise as possible. For she takes nothing with her to the other world but her education and culture; and these, it is said, are of the greatest service or of the greatest injury to the dead man at the very beginning of his journey thither. For it is said that the genius, who has had charge of each man in his life, proceeds to lead him, when he is dead, to a certain place where the departed have to assemble and receive judgment and then go to the world below with the guide who is appointed to conduct them thither. And when they have received their deserts there, and remained the appointed time, another guide brings them back again after many long revolutions of ages. So this journey is not as Aeschylus describes it in the *Telephus,* where he says that "a simple way leads to Hades." But I think that the way is neither simple nor single; there would have been no need of guides had it been so; for no one could miss the way if there were but one path. But this road must have many branches and many windings, as I judge from the rites of burial on earth.* The orderly and wise soul follows her leader and is not ignorant of the things of that world; but the soul which lusts after the body flutters about the body and the visible world for a long time, as I have said, and struggles hard and painfully, and at last is forcibly and reluctantly dragged away by her appointed genius. And when she comes to the place where the other souls are, if she is impure and stained with evil, and has been concerned in foul murders, or if she has committed any other crimes that are akin to these and the deeds of kindred souls, then everyone shuns her and turns aside from meeting her, and will neither be her companion nor her guide, and she wanders about by herself in extreme distress until a certain time is completed, and then she is borne away by force to the habitation which befits her. But the soul that has spent her life in purity and temperance has the gods for her companions and guides, and dwells in the place which befits her. There are many wonderful places in the earth; and neither its nature nor its size is what those who are wont to describe it imagine, as a friend has convinced me.

What do you mean, Socrates? said Simmias. I have heard a great deal about the earth myself, but I have never heard the view of which you are convinced. I should like to hear it very much.

*[Sacrifices were offered to the gods of the lower world in places where three roads met.]

Well, Simmias, I don't think that it needs the skill of Glaucus to describe it to you, but I think that it is beyond the skill of Glaucus to prove it true. I am sure that I could not do so; and besides, Simmias, even if I knew how, I think that my life would come to an end before the argument was finished. But there is nothing to prevent my describing to you what I believe to be the form of the earth and its regions.

Well, said Simmias, that will do.

In the first place then, said he, I believe that the earth is a spherical body placed in the center of the heavens, and that therefore it has no need of air or of any other force to support it; the equiformity of the heavens in all their parts, and the equipoise of the earth itself, are sufficient to hold it up. A thing in equipoise placed in the center of what is equiform cannot incline in any direction, either more or less; it will remain unmoved and in perfect balance. That, said he, is the first thing that I believe.

And rightly, said Simmias.

Also, he proceeded, I think that the earth is of vast extent, and that we who dwell between the Phasis and the pillars of Heracles inhabit only a small portion of it, and dwell round the sea, like ants or frogs round a marsh; and I believe that many other men dwell elsewhere in similar places. For everywhere on the earth there are many hollows of every kind of shape and size, into which the water and the mist and the air collect; but the earth itself lies pure in the purity of the heavens, wherein are the stars, and which men who speak of these things commonly call ether. The water and the mist and the air, which collect into the hollows of the earth, are the sediment of it. Now we dwell in these hollows though we think that we are dwelling on the surface of the earth. We are just like a man dwelling in the depths of the ocean who thought that he was dwelling on its surface and believed that the sea was the heaven, because he saw the sun and the stars through the water; but who was too weak and slow ever to have reached the water's surface, and to have lifted his head from the sea, and come out from his depths to our world, and seen, or heard from one who had seen, how much purer and fairer our world was than the place wherein he dwelt. We are just in that state; we dwell in a hollow of the earth, and think that we are dwelling on its surface; and we call the air heaven, and think it to be the heaven wherein the stars run their courses. But the truth is that we are too weak and slow to pass through to the surface of the air. For if any man could reach the surface, or take wings and fly upward, he would look up and see a world beyond, just as the fishes look forth from the sea, and behold our world. And he would know that that was the real heaven, and the real light, and the real earth, if his nature were able to endure the sight. For this earth, and its stones, and all its regions have been spoiled and corroded, as things in the sea are corroded by the brine: nothing of any worth grows in the sea, nor, in short, is there anything therein without blemish, but, wherever land does exist, there are only caves, and sand, and vast tracts of mud and slime, which are not worthy even to be compared with the fair things of our world. But you would think that the things of that other world still further surpass the things of our world. I can tell you a tale, Simmias, about what is on the earth that lies beneath the heavens, which is worth your hearing.

Indeed, Socrates, said Simmias, we should like to hear your tale very much.

Well, my friend, he said, this is my tale. In the first place, the earth itself, if a man could look at it from above, is like one of those balls which are covered with twelve pieces of leather, and is marked with various colors, of which the colors that our painters use here are, as it were, samples. But there the whole earth is covered with them, and with others which are far brighter and purer ones than they. For part of it is purple of marvelous beauty, and part of it is golden, and the white of it is whiter than chalk or snow. It is made up of the other colors in the same way, and also of colors which are more beautiful than any that we have ever seen. The very hollows in it, that are filled with water and d air, have themselves a kind of color, and glisten amid the diversity of the others, so that its form appears as one unbroken and varied surface. And what grows in this fair earth— its trees and flowers and fruit—is more beautiful than what grows with us in the same proportion; and so likewise are the hills and the stones in their smoothness and trans-

e parency and color. The pebbles which we prize in this world, our cornelians, and jaspers, and emeralds, and the like, are but fragments of them, but there all the stones are as our precious stones, and even more beautiful still. The reason of this is that they are pure and not corroded or spoiled, as ours are, with the decay and brine from the sediment that collects in the hollows and brings to the stones and the earth and all animals and plants . . .

111 deformity and disease. All these things, and with them gold and silver and the like, adorn the real earth; and they are conspicuous from their multitude and size, and the many places where they are found; so that he who could behold it would be a happy man. Many creatures live upon it; and there are men, some dwelling inland, and others round the air, as we dwell round the sea, and others in islands encircled by the air, which lie

b near the continent. In a word, they use the air as we use water and the sea, and the ether as we use the air. The temperature of their seasons is such that they are free from disease, and live much longer than we do; and in sight, and hearing, and smell, and the other senses, they are as much more perfect than we, as air is purer than water, and ether than air. Moreover, they have sanctuaries and temples of the gods, in which the gods dwell in

c very truth; they hear the voices and oracles of the gods, and see them in visions, and have intercourse with them face to face; and they see the sun and moon and stars as they really are; and in other matters their happiness is of a piece with this.

   That is the nature of the earth as a whole, and of what is upon it; and everywhere on its globe there are many regions in the hollows, some of them deeper and more open

d than that in which we dwell; and others also deeper, but with narrower mouths; and others again shallower and broader than ours. All these are connected by many channels beneath the earth, some of them narrow and others wide; and there are passages by which much water flows from one of them to another, as into basins, and vast and never-failing rivers of both hot and cold water beneath the earth, and much fire, and great rivers of fire, and many rivers of liquid mud, some clearer and others more turbid, like

e the rivers of mud which precede the lava stream in Sicily, and the lava stream itself. These fill each hollow in turn, as each stream flows round to it. All of them are moved up and down by a certain oscillation which is in the earth and which is produced by a natural cause of the following kind. One of the chasms in the earth is larger than all the

112 others, and pierces right through it, from side to side. Homer describes it in the words—

   Far away, where is the deepest depth beneath the earth. [*Iliad* VIII.14]

   And elsewhere he and many others of the poets have called it Tartarus. All the rivers flow into this chasm and out of it again; and each of them comes to be like the soil

b through which it flows. The reason why they all flow into and out of the chasm is that the liquid has no bottom or base to rest on; it oscillates and surges up and down, and the air and wind around it do the same, for they accompany it in its passage to the other side of the earth, and in its return; and just as in breathing the breath is always in process of

c being exhaled and inhaled, so there the wind, oscillating with the water, produces terrible and irresistible blasts as it comes in and goes out. When the water retires with a rush to what we call the lower parts of the earth, it flows through to the regions of those streams and fills them, as if it were pumped into them. And again, when it rushes back hither from those regions, it fills the streams here again, and then they flow through the

d channels of the earth and make their way to their several places, and create seas, and lakes, and rivers, and springs. Then they sink once more into the earth, and after making, some a long circuit through many regions, and some a shorter one through fewer, they fall again into Tartarus, some at a point much lower than that at which they rose, and others only a little lower; but they all flow in below their point of issue. And some of them burst forth again on the side on which they entered; others again on the opposite side; and there are some which completely encircle the earth, twining round it, like snakes, once or perhaps oftener, and then fall again into Tartarus, as low down as they e can. They can descend as far as the center of the earth from either side but no farther. Beyond that point on either side they would have to flow uphill.

These streams are many, and great, and various; but among them all are four, of which the greatest and outermost, which flows round the whole of the earth, is called Oceanus. Opposite Oceanus, and flowing in the reverse direction, is Acheron, which runs through desert places and then under the earth until it reaches the Acherusian lake, whither 113 the souls of the dead generally go, and after abiding there the appointed time, which for some is longer and for others shorter, are sent forth again to be born as animals. The third river rises between these two, and near its source falls into a vast and fiery region and forms a lake larger than our sea, seething with water and mud. Thence it goes forth turbid and muddy round the earth, and after many windings comes to the end of the Acherusian b lake, but it does not mingle with the waters of the lake; and after many windings more beneath the earth, it falls into the lower part of Tartarus. This is the river that men name Pyriphlegethon; and portions of it are discharged in the lava streams, wherever they are found on the earth. The fourth river is on the opposite side; it is said to fall first into a terrible and savage region, of which the color is one dark blue. It is called the Stygian stream, and the lake which its waters create is called Styx. After falling into the lake and receiving c strange powers in its waters, it sinks into the earth, and runs winding about in the opposite direction to Pyriphlegethon, which it meets in the Acherusian lake from the opposite side. Its waters, too, mingle with no other waters; it flows round in a circle and falls into Tartarus opposite to Pyriphlegethon. Its name, the poets say, is Cocytus.

Such is the nature of these regions; and when the dead come to the place whither d each is brought by his genius, sentence is first passed on them according as their lives have been good and holy, or not. Those whose lives seem to have been neither very good nor very bad go to the river Acheron, and, embarking on the vessels which they find there, proceed to the lake. There they dwell, and are punished for the crimes which they have committed, and are purified and absolved; and for their good deeds they are rewarded, each according to his deserts. But all who appear to be incurable from the e enormity of their sins—those who have committed many and great sacrileges, and foul and lawless murders, or other crimes like these—are hurled down to Tartarus by the fate which is their due, whence they never come forth again. Those who have committed sins which are great, but not too great for atonement, such, for instance, as those who have used violence toward a father or a mother in wrath and then repented of it for the rest of their lives, or who have committed homicide in some similar way, have also to 114 descend into Tartarus; but then when they have been there a year, a wave casts them forth, the homicides by Cocytus, and the parricides and matricides by Pyriphlegethon; and when they have been carried as far as the Acherusian lake they cry out and call on those whom they slew or outraged, and beseech and pray that they may be allowed to b come out into the lake, and be received as comrades. And if they prevail, they come out, and their sufferings cease; but if they do not, they are carried back to Tartarus, and thence into the rivers again, and their punishment does not end until they have prevailed on those whom they wronged: such is the sentence pronounced on them by their judges.

But such as have been pre-eminent for holiness in their lives are set free and released
c   from this world, as from a prison; they ascend to their pure habitation and dwell on the
earth's surface. And those of them who have sufficiently purified themselves with philosophy live thenceforth without bodies and proceed to dwellings still fairer than these,
which are not easily described, and of which I have not time to speak now. But for all
these reasons, Simmias, we must leave nothing undone, that we may obtain virtue and
wisdom in this life. Noble is the prize, and great the hope.

d   A man of sense will not insist that these things are exactly as I have described
them. But I think that he will believe that something of the kind is true of the soul and
her habitations, seeing that she is shown to be immortal, and that it is worth his while to
stake everything on this belief. The venture is a fair one, and he must charm his doubts
with spells like these. That is why I have been prolonging the fable all this time. For

e   these reason a man should be of good cheer about his soul if in his life he has renounced
the pleasures and adornments of the body, because they were nothing to him, and
because he thought that they would do him not good but harm; and if he has instead
earnestly pursued the pleasures of learning, and adorned his soul with the adornment of

115   temperance, and justice, and courage, and freedom, and truth, which belongs to her and
is her own, and so awaits his journey to the other world, in readiness to set forth whenever fate calls him. You, Simmias and Cebes, and the rest will set forth at some future
day, each at his own time. But me now, as a tragic poet would say, fate calls at once; and
it is time for me to betake myself to the bath. I think that I had better bathe before I
drink the poison, and not give the women the trouble of washing my dead body.

b   When he had finished speaking Crito said, Be it so, Socrates. But have you any
commands for your friends or for me about your children, or about other things? How
shall we serve you best?

Simply by doing what I always tell you, Crito. Take care of your own selves, and
you will serve me and mine and yourselves in all that you do, even though you make no
promises now. But if you are careless of your own selves, and will not follow the path
of life which we have pointed out in our discussions both today and at other times, all

c   your promises now, however profuse and earnest they are, will be of no avail.

We will do our best, said Crito. But how shall we bury you?

As you please, he answered; only you must catch me first and not let me escape
you. And then he looked at us with a smile and said, My friends, I cannot convince Crito
that I am the Socrates who has been conversing with you and arranging his arguments

d   in order. He thinks that I am the body which he will presently see a corpse, and he asks
how he is to bury me. All the arguments which I have used to prove that I shall not
remain with you after I have drunk the poison, but that I shall go away to the happiness
of the blessed, with which I tried to comfort you and myself, have been thrown away on
him. Do you therefore be my sureties to him, as he was my surety at the trial, but in a
different way. He was surety for me then that I would remain; but you must be my
sureties to him that I shall go away when I am dead, and not remain with you; then he

e   will feel my death less; and when he sees my body being burned or buried, he will not
be grieved because he thinks that I am suffering dreadful things; and at my funeral he
will not say that it is Socrates whom he is laying out, or bearing to the grave, or burying.
For, dear Crito, he continued, you must know that to use words wrongly is not only a
fault in itself, it also creates evil in the soul. You must be of good cheer, and say that you

116   are burying my body; and you may bury it as you please and as you think right.

With these words he rose and went into another room to bathe. Crito went with
him and told us to wait. So we waited, talking of the argument and discussing it, and

The Death of Socrates, 1787, by Jacques-Louis David (1748–1825). (*Oil on canvas, 51 × 77-1/4 inches. The Metropolitan Museum of Art, Wolfe Fund, 1931. Catharine Lorillard Wolfe Collection. [31.45]*)

then again dwelling on the greatness of the calamity which had fallen upon us: it seemed as if we were going to lose a father and to be orphans for the rest of our lives.   b
When he had bathed, and his children had been brought to him—he had two sons quite little, and one grown up—and the women of his family were come, he spoke with them in Crito's presence, and gave them his last instructions; then he sent the women and children away and returned to us. By that time it was near the hour of sunset, for he had been a long while within. When he came back to us from the bath he sat down, but not much was said after that. Presently the servant of the Eleven came and stood before him   c
and said, "I know that I shall not find you unreasonable like other men, Socrates. They are angry with me and curse me when I bid them drink the poison because the authorities make me do it. But I have found you all along the noblest and gentlest and best man that has ever come here; and now I am sure that you will not be angry with me, but with those who you know are to blame. And so farewell, and try to bear what must be as   d
lightly as you can; you know why I have come." With that he turned away weeping, and went out.

Socrates looked up at him and replied, Farewell, I will do as you say. Then he turned to us and said, How courteous the man is! And the whole time that I have been here, he has constantly come in to see me, and sometimes he has talked to me, and has been the best of men; and now, how generously he weeps for me! Come, Crito, let us obey him; let the poison be brought if it is ready, and if it is not ready, let it be prepared.

Crito replied: But, Socrates, I think that the sun is still upon the hills; it has not   e
set. Besides, I know that other men take the poison quite late, and eat and drink heartily, and even enjoy the company of their chosen friends, after the announcement has been made. So do not hurry; there is still time.

Socrates replied: And those whom you speak of, Crito, naturally do so, for they think that they will be gainers by so doing. And I naturally shall not do so, for I think that I should gain nothing by drinking the poison a little later, but my own contempt for so greedily saving a life which is already spent. So do not refuse to do as I say.

Then Crito made a sign to his slave who was standing by; and the slave went out, and after some delay returned with the man who was to give the poison, carrying it prepared in a cup. When Socrates saw him, he asked, You understand these things, my good man, what have I to do?

You have only to drink this, he replied, and to walk about until your legs feel heavy, and then lie down; and it will act of itself.

With that he handed the cup to Socrates, who took it quite cheerfully, Echecrates, without trembling, and without any change of color or of feature, and looked up at the man with that fixed glance of his, and asked, What say you to making a libation from this draught? May I, or not?

We only prepare so much as we think sufficient, Socrates, he answered.

I understand, said Socrates. But I suppose that I may, and must, pray to the gods that my journey hence may be prosperous. That is my prayer; may it be so. With these words he put the cup to his lips and drank the poison quite calmly and cheerfully.

Till then most of us had been able to control our grief fairly well; but when we saw him drinking and then the poison finished, we could do so no longer: my tears came fast in spite of myself, and I covered my face and wept for myself; it was not for him, but at my own misfortune in losing such a friend. Even before that Crito had been unable to restrain his tears, and had gone away; and Apollodorus, who had never once ceased weeping the whole time, burst into a loud wail and made us one and all break down by his sobbing, except Socrates himself.

What are you doing, my friends? he exclaimed. I sent away the women chiefly in order that they might not behave in this way; for I have heard that a man should die in silence. So calm yourselves and bear up.

When we heard that, we were ashamed, and we ceased from weeping. But he walked about, until he said that his legs were getting heavy, and then he lay down on his back, as he was told. And the man who gave the poison began to examine his feet and legs from time to time. Then he pressed his foot hard and asked if there was any feeling in it, and Socrates said, No; and then his legs, and so higher and higher, and showed us that he was cold and stiff. And Socrates felt himself and said that when it came to his heart, he should be gone. He was already growing cold about the groin, when he uncovered his face, which had been covered, and spoke for the last time. Crito, he said, I owe a cock to Asclepius; do not forget to pay it.*

It shall be done, replied Crito. Is there anything else that you wish? He made no answer to this question; but after a short interval there was a movement, and the man uncovered him, and his eyes were fixed. Then Crito closed his mouth and his eyes.

Such was the end, Echecrates, of our friend, a man, I think, who was the wisest and justest, and the best man I have ever known.

---

*[Asclepius was the Greek god of healing. When one recovered from an illness it was customary to offer a cock as a sacrifice, so Socrates' last words imply that death is a kind of healing. See, for instance 66b ff., 67c.]

MENO

Characters
Socrates
Meno
A Slave of Meno
Anytus
Scene—Athens

MENO: Can you tell me, Socrates, whether virtue is something teachable? Or is it   70
not teachable, but something that comes from practice? Or is it something neither from
practice nor from learning, but something that comes to human beings by nature, or
some other way?

SOCRATES: Meno, it used to be that Thessalians were well-reputed among the
Greeks and were admired both for horsemanship and for wealth, but now, it seems to
me, they are to be admired for wisdom also; and not least of them the fellow citizens of   b
your comrade, Aristippus, the Larissians. And the one responsible for this happening to
you is Gorgias. For when he came to the city, he captivated the foremost men among the
Aleudai as lovers of wisdom, of whom your lover Aristippus is one, and the foremost of
the other Thessalians too. And in particular this is the habit to which he has habituated
you, namely, of answering both fearlessly and magnificently whenever anyone asks you
anything, as is fitting for those who know; inasmuch, indeed, as he makes himself avail-   c
able to any Greek who wants to question him about whatever one might wish to ask, and
there is no one whom he does not answer. But hereabouts, dear Meno, the opposite con-   71
dition prevails: it's as if some sort of drought of wisdom has come about, and there
seems to be a danger that wisdom has left these parts for yours. And so, if you are willing to ask anyone hereabouts such a question, there is no one who will not laugh and
say, "Stranger, I seem to be in danger of your thinking me to be someone who is
blessed—to know about virtue, whether it is something teachable or in what way it
comes about. But I am so far from knowing about virtue, whether it is something teachable or not teachable, that I happen not to know at all what that thing virtue itself is."

And I myself, Meno, am in this condition, too. I share the poverty of my fellow   b
citizens in this matter and blame myself for not knowing about virtue at all. And how
could I know what sort of thing something is, if I do not know what it is? Or does it
seem possible to you that someone who has no cognizance of Meno at all, who he is,
could know whether he is handsome or rich or well-born, or the opposite of these? Does
it seem possible to you?

MENO: Not to me. But do you, Socrates, truly not know what virtue is, and is this   c
really what we should report about you back home?

SOCRATES: Not only that, comrade, but also that I never yet happened to meet anyone else who, in my opinion, did know.

MENO: What? You didn't happen to meet Gorgias when he was here?

SOCRATES: I did.

Plato, *Plato's Meno*, translated by George Anastaplo and Laurence Berns (Newburyport, MA: Focus
Philosophical Library, 2004). Reprinted by permission of Focus Publishing/R. Pullins Company.

MENO: Really– did he not seem to you to know?

SOCRATES: I'm not a very good rememberer, Meno, so I'm not able to say at present how he seemed to me then. But, perhaps, he did know, and you know what he used to say. Then, remind me how he said it. Or, if you wish, speak yourself, for you, surely, share his opinion.

MENO: I do.

SOCRATES: Then let's let him go, since, in fact, he is not here. But you yourself, by the gods, Meno, what do you declare virtue to be? Speak and don't be begrudging, so that I will have fabricated a most fortunate falsehood if it becomes evident that you and Gorgias do know, while I've stated that I never happened to come across anyone who knew.

MENO: But it's not hard to tell, Socrates. First, then, if it's the virtue of a man you want, it's easy to say that this is the virtue of a man: to be sufficient to carry on the affairs of the city and while carrying them on to do well by his friends and harm to his enemies and to take care that he not suffer any such thing himself. And if it's the virtue of a woman you want, that's not hard to go through, in that she needs to manage the household well, conserving what is inside and being obedient to her man. And the virtue of a child is different, both female and male, and of an elderly man, and, if you want, of a freeman or, if you want, of a slave. And there are a great many other virtues, so that there is no difficulty in speaking about what virtue is. For according to each activity and each time of life relative to each task for each of us there is a virtue, and in the same way, I suppose, Socrates, there is also a vice.

SOCRATES: I seem to have hit upon some great good fortune, Meno, if, while seeking one virtue I have discovered a sort of swarm of virtues gathered about you. But, Meno, following up this image about swarms, if after you had been asked by me about the very being of a bee, just what it is, and you were saying that there are many and of all sorts, what would you answer me if I asked you: "Then are you saying that they are many and of all sorts and different from one another in this by which they are bees? Or that it is not this in which they differ, but in something else, such as beauty or size or something else of this sort?" Tell me, what would you answer after being questioned in this way?

MENO: I would answer this, that they do not differ, one from the other, in that by which they are bees.

SOCRATES: If then I were to say after that: "Tell me further, Meno, this very thing in which they do not differ but are all the same thing, what do you say that is?" You could, I suppose, tell me what it is?

MENO: I could.

SOCRATES: And so too, surely, about the virtues: even if they are many and of all sorts, still they all have some one and the same form through which they are virtues and upon which one would somehow do well to focus one's gaze, that is, the one answering him who has asked him to clarify that, namely, what does virtue happen to be. Or do you not understand what I'm saying?

MENO: It seems to me that I do understand. Yet somehow I don't grasp what is being asked as well as I would like.

SOCRATES: Is it about virtue only that you think in this way, Meno, that there is one for a man and another for a woman and the others; or do you think the same way about health and about size and about strength? Does the health of a man seem to you to be one thing and the health of a woman another? Or is it the same form everywhere, if it is indeed health, whether it exists in a man or in anyone else whatever?

MENO: Health, at any rate, does seem to me to be the same both for a man and for a woman.

SOCRATES: And not then also size and strength? If a woman is really strong, will she not be strong by the same form and by the same strength? For "by the same" I mean this: strength does not differ with respect to being strength whether it exists in a man or in a woman. Or does it seem to you that there is some difference?

MENO: Not to me.

SOCRATES: And will virtue differ in some way, with respect to its being virtue,   73
whether it exists in a child or in an old man or in a woman or in a man?

MENO: It somehow seems to me, at any rate, Socrates, that this is no longer like those others.

SOCRATES: But why? Were you not saying that the virtue of a man is to manage a city well, and that of a woman, a household?

MENO: I was.

SOCRATES: Then can one manage a city well, or a household, or anything else whatever, if one does not manage it moderately and justly?

MENO: Surely not.

SOCRATES: Then if people really manage justly and moderately, will they manage   b
by justice and moderation?

MENO: Necessarily.

SOCRATES: Then both need the same things, if they really intend to be good, both the woman and the man, namely, justice and moderation.

MENO: So it appears.

SOCRATES: What about a child and an old man? If they should be licentious and unjust, could they ever become good?

MENO: Surely not.

SOCRATES: But if they are moderate and just?

MENO: Yes.

SOCRATES: Then all human beings are good in the same way; for it is from the   c
same things that they happen to become good.

MENO: It seems likely.

SOCRATES: They would surely not be good in the same way if they didn't have the same virtue.

MENO: Surely not.

SOCRATES: Since, therefore, virtue is the same for all, try to say and to recollect what that very thing is which Gorgias, and you with him, affirm it to be.

MENO: What else than to be able to rule over human beings—if indeed you are seeking some one thing concerning all of them?

SOCRATES: But certainly I do seek that. But then, is the virtue of both a child,   d
Meno, and a slave the same, for the two of them to be able to rule the master, and does it seem to you that he who rules would still be a slave?

MENO: It does not at all seem so to me, Socrates.

SOCRATES: Since, my very good man, it is not likely. Then also observe the following: "to be able to rule," you say. Shall we not add to that "justly, but not unjustly"?

MENO: I, at any rate, think so. For justice, Socrates, is virtue.

SOCRATES: Is it virtue, Meno, or some particular virtue?   e

MENO: How do you mean that?

SOCRATES: Just as about anything else whatever. For example, about roundness, if you want, I would say that it is a particular shape, not just simply that it is shape. The reason I would speak in this way is that there are also other shapes.

MENO: What you say is quite right, for I too say that there is not only justice, but that there are also other virtues.

74   SOCRATES: What are these? Tell me. Just as I too could tell you that there are also other shapes, if you were to order me to do so, you too then tell me other virtues.

MENO: Well then, courage seems to me, at any rate, to be a virtue, and moderation, and wisdom, and magnificence, and a great many others.

SOCRATES: Again, Meno, we have suffered the same thing. Although seeking one, we have found many virtues, but in another way than we did just now. But the one which exists throughout all of these we are not able to find out.

MENO: No, for I am somehow not able to grasp, Socrates, as you seek it, one
b   virtue from all, as I can in the other cases.

SOCRATES: That is likely. But I am quite willing, if I am able, to help us advance. For you understand, I suppose, that this is how it holds for everything. If someone were to ask you this, which I was just now speaking of, "What is shape, Meno?"—and if you were to say to him that it is roundness, and if he were to say to you what I did, "Is roundness shape, or a particular shape?", you would surely say that it is a particular shape.

MENO: Certainly, I would.

c   SOCRATES: Is it not because of this, that there are also other shapes?

MENO: Yes.

SOCRATES: And if he were to ask you further what sorts of shapes, you would tell him?

MENO: I would.

SOCRATES: And again, if he were to ask you about color in the same way, what it is, and you said that it is white, and after that the questioner took it up, asking, "Is the white color a particular color?", you would say that it is a particular color because there also happen to be other colors?

MENO: I would.

SOCRATES: And if then he ordered you to tell other colors, would you speak of
d   others that happen to be colors no less than white is?

MENO: Yes.

SOCRATES: If then he, just as I, was following up the argument and said, "We always arrive at many, but this is not what I'm seeking. But since you address these many by some one name and you say of none of them that they are not shape, even those that are opposite to one another, what is this that comprises the round or the
e   straight, which indeed you name shape, and you affirm that the round is no more shape than the straight?" Or is this not the way that you speak?

MENO: I do.

SOCRATES: Whenever you do speak in this way, do you then affirm that the round is no more round than straight and that the straight is no more straight than round?

MENO: Certainly not, Socrates.

SOCRATES: But, indeed, you do affirm that the round is no more a shape than the straight, the one no more than the other.

MENO: You speak the truth.

SOCRATES: Whatever then is this of which this is the name: shape? Try to say. If
75   then you had said to someone questioning in this way either about shape or about color, "But I don't understand what you want, fellow, nor do I know what you mean," probably he would have wondered and said, "You do not understand that what I am seeking is that which is the same over all of these?" Or would you not be able to tell about these things, Meno, if someone had asked you: "What is it that is over the round and the straight and the others, and is the same over all of those things which you, indeed, call shapes?" Try to say it, so that you can get some serious practice for the answer about virtue.

MENO: No, but you say it, Socrates.   b

SOCRATES: You want me to gratify you?

MENO: I certainly do.

SOCRATES: Will you then also be willing to tell me about virtue?

MENO: I will.

SOCRATES: Well then, one must be for it; for it is a worthy endeavor.

MENO: By all means.

SOCRATES: Come then, let us try to tell you what shape is. See then whether you can accept it to be the following: for us, indeed, let this be shape: it is that which alone, of all the things that are, which always happens to accompany color. Is that sufficient for you, or do you somehow seek it in some other way? For I would be content if you   c could tell me about virtue in this way.

MENO: But this is really simple-minded, Socrates.

SOCRATES: How do you mean that?

MENO: That shape is, in some way, according to your argument, that which always accompanies color. Very well; but if, indeed, someone should declare that he does not know color but is at a loss about it in the same way that he is about shape, what do you suppose you would have answered him?

SOCRATES: The truth is what I would have answered. And if the questioner were one of those wise men with a bent for strife and contention, I would tell him, "That's   d what I said. And if I don't speak correctly, it's your task to take up the argument and refute it." But if, being friends as both I and you are now, they should want to have a discussion with one another, then surely a somehow more gentle and more dialectical way of answering is required. And it is perhaps more dialectical to answer not only with the truth, but also through those things which he who is being questioned could agree that he knows. I too, indeed, will try to speak to you in this way. For, tell me, is there something you call an end? I mean this sort of thing, like a limit or an extremity—all these, I   e say, are the same thing, though perhaps Prodicus would differ from us; but you, at any rate, do call something as having been limited or ended. This is the sort of thing I want to say, nothing fancy.

MENO: But I do so call it that, and I think I do understand what you mean.

SOCRATES: And what then? Is there something you call a plane surface, and some-   76 thing else again you call a solid, as, for example, in geometry?

MENO: I do so call them.

SOCRATES: Therefore, you could immediately understand what I mean about shape. For I say this about every shape: that at which the solid ends, that is shape; what I could say, in summing it up, is that shape is the limit of a solid.

MENO: And about color, what do you say, Socrates?

SOCRATES: You are outrageous, Meno. You pose troublesome problems for an old man to answer, but you yourself are unwilling to recollect and say whatever Gorgias   b says virtue is.

MENO: But whenever you tell me this, Socrates, I'll tell you that.

SOCRATES: Even someone who is blindfolded could know, Meno, from conversing with you that you are handsome and still have lovers.

MENO: Why indeed?

SOCRATES: Because you do nothing but impose commands in your arguments, the very thing that spoiled people do, so as to tyrannize as long as they are in their prime. And at the same time it is likely that you've noticed about me, that I have a weakness for   c beautiful people. So I will gratify you and I will answer.

MENO: By all means then, gratify me.

SOCRATES: Then do you want me to answer in the style of Gorgias, by which you might be, as much as possible, able to follow?

MENO: I do want it. And why not?

SOCRATES: Then don't you people say, as does Empedocles, that there are certain effluences from the things that are?

MENO: Very much so.

SOCRATES: And there are certain passageways into which and through which the effluences pass?

MENO: Yes, by all means.

d   SOCRATES: And that some of the effluences fit some of the passageways and others are too small or too large?

MENO: That is so.

SOCRATES: Then there is also something that you call sight?

MENO: I do.

SOCRATES: From these very agreements, as Pindar says, "understand what I mean." For color is an effluence of shapes commensurate with sight and perceptible.

MENO: You seem to me, Socrates, to have put this answer in the best possible way.

SOCRATES: Perhaps because it was said in accordance with the way in which you have been habituated. At the same time, I suppose, you consider that from this you
e   could also say what sound is, and smell, and many other things of this sort.

MENO: By all means.

SOCRATES: For it is a tragical answer, Meno, and therefore satisfies you more than the one about shape.

MENO: It does.

SOCRATES: But it is not better, son of Alexidemus, but, as I persuade myself, the other one is. And I think it would not seem so to you, if it were not necessary, as you were saying yesterday, for you to leave before the Mysteries, but were both to stay around and to be initiated.

77   MENO: But I would stay around, Socrates, if you would tell me about many other such things.

SOCRATES: But I certainly will in no way fall short of zeal, both for your sake and for my own, in talking about such things; but I do fear that I will not be able to talk about many such. But come now, you too try to pay back your promise to me in saying about virtue as a whole, what it is, and stop making many out of one, as those who like to jeer say each time about those who break something, but rather, leaving it whole and
b   healthy, tell me what virtue is. The patterns, at any rate, you have got from me.

MENO: Well then, it seems to me, Socrates, that virtue is just what the poet says, "both to rejoice and to be capable in beautiful things." I too say that this is virtue: to desire beautiful things and to be capable of providing them for oneself.

SOCRATES: Then do you mean that he who desires beautiful things is someone who desires good things?

MENO: Most certainly.

SOCRATES: Then are you saying that there are some people who desire bad things
c   and others who desire good things? Does it not seem to you, my very good man, that everyone desires good things?

MENO: Not to me.

SOCRATES: But some desire bad things?

MENO: Yes.

SOCRATES: Supposing that the bad things are good, you mean, or even, while recognizing that they are bad, they nevertheless do desire them?

MENO: Both, it seems to me.

SOCRATES: Then does it really seem to you, Meno, that someone who recognizes that the bad things are bad, nevertheless desires them?

MENO: Certainly.

SOCRATES: What do you mean by "desires"? That they should become his?

MENO: Become his; what else could it be?

SOCRATES: Does he believe that the bad things benefit him whose they become, or does he recognize that bad things harm him whom they come to be with?   d

MENO: There are some who believe the bad things benefit, and others who recognize that they harm.

SOCRATES: Do those who believe that bad things benefit also seem to you to recognize that bad things are bad?

MENO: This does not seem to me to be so at all.

SOCRATES: Therefore it is clear that those who do not recognize bad things as bad do not desire bad things, but they desire those things which they were supposing to be good, the very things which are, in fact, bad; so that not recognizing bad things to be bad and supposing them to be good, it is clear that they desire good things. Is it not so?   e

MENO: These, at any rate, probably do.

SOCRATES: What then? Those who desire bad things, as you affirm, but who believe that the bad things harm him to whom they come to belong, they surely recognize that they are harmed by them?

MENO: Necessarily.   78

SOCRATES: But do not these men think that those being harmed are miserable to the extent that they are being harmed?

MENO: This too is necessary.

SOCRATES: And are not the miserable ill-fated?

MENO: I, anyway, think they are.

SOCRATES: Now is there anyone who wishes to be miserable and ill-fated?

MENO: It does not seem so to me, Socrates.

SOCRATES: Therefore, no one, Meno, wishes for bad things, if indeed he does not wish to be this sort of person. For what else is it to be miserable than both to desire and to acquire bad things?

MENO: I dare say you speak the truth, Socrates, and no one wishes bad things for himself.   b

SOCRATES: Then were you saying just now that virtue is to wish for good things and to be capable of them?

MENO: I sure did say it.

SOCRATES: Then from what has just been said, does not the wishing pertain to everyone, and in this respect no one is better than anyone else?

MENO: So it appears.

SOCRATES: But it is clear that if one man is better than another it would be by being more excellent in capability.

MENO: Certainly so.

SOCRATES: This, therefore, as it seems, is, according to your argument, virtue: a power of providing good things for oneself.   c

MENO: It seems to me, Socrates, altogether to hold in just the way you now understand it.

SOCRATES: Now let us see in this, too, whether what you say is true, for you could perhaps be speaking well. Do you affirm that to be able to provide oneself with good things is virtue?

MENO: I do.

SOCRATES: Are not both health and wealth the kinds of things that you call goods?

MENO: And to acquire gold, I mean, and silver, and honors in a city and offices.

SOCRATES: You don't mean, I suppose, that some things other than this kind are the good things?

d   MENO: No, but I mean everything of this kind.

SOCRATES: Very well; to provide oneself with gold and silver, then, is virtue, as declares Meno, the ancestral guest-friend of the Great King. Do you add the words "justly" and "piously" to this providing, Meno, or does it make no difference to you, but even if someone should provide himself with these things unjustly, would you still call these doings virtue?

MENO: Surely not, Socrates.

SOCRATES: But vice.

MENO: By all means, surely

SOCRATES: Therefore it seems likely that one should add justice or moderation or e   piety, or some other piece of virtue, to this providing. And, if not, it will not be virtue, even though it were a thoroughgoing provision of the good things.

MENO: For how could virtue come to be without these things?

SOCRATES: And not procuring gold and silver, whenever it is not just, either for oneself or for another, is not this lack of provision also virtue?

MENO: So it appears.

SOCRATES: Therefore, the providing of goods such as these could be virtue no more than the lack of a way of providing them; but it is likely that whatever comes 79   about with justice will be virtue and that whatever comes about without anything of this sort will be vice.

MENO: It seems to me that it must be necessarily as you say.

SOCRATES: Then did we not affirm a little while ago that each piece of these things was virtue, justice and moderation and everything of this sort?

MENO: Yes.

SOCRATES: So, Meno, are you making fun of me?

MENO: How indeed is that, Socrates?

SOCRATES: Because just now when you were requested by me not to shatter virtue or to change it into small coin, and I gave you patterns in accordance with which it was to be b   answered, yet you paid no attention to this and tell me that virtue is to be able to provide good things for oneself along with justice. And this, you declare, is a piece of virtue?

MENO: I do.

SOCRATES: Then it follows from what you agree to, that to act, whatever one might do, with a piece of virtue, this is virtue. For you affirm that justice and each of these is a piece of virtue. Why then do I say this? Because when I begged you to talk about virtue as a whole, you fell far short of saying what it is, but you declared that c   every action is a virtue whenever it is done with some piece of virtue, just as if you had said what the whole, virtue, is and it was immediately recognized by me, even if you were to change it into pieces of small change. Now what you need, again from the beginning, it seems to me, my dear Meno, is the same question, What is virtue?—if every action with a piece of virtue could be virtue. For this is what it means whenever someone says that every action accompanied by justice is virtue. Does it not seem to you that the same question is required again, or do you rather suppose that someone knows what a piece of virtue is, without knowing virtue itself?

MENO: It does not seem so to me.

SOCRATES: For, if you also remember, when I had just answered you about shape,   d
we, I think, rejected the kind of answer that tries to answer through those things that are still being sought and are not yet agreed upon.

MENO: And we were right in rejecting it, Socrates.

SOCRATES: Therefore, my very good man, while what virtue is as a whole is still being sought, do not suppose that in answering through its pieces you will in any way clarify it, or anything else, by speaking of it in this same way, but consider that you will   e
be in need again of the very same question. What is this virtue that you speak about as you speak? Or does it seem to you that I'm not saying anything?

MENO: You seem to me to speak rightly.

SOCRATES: Then answer again, from the beginning: what do you affirm virtue to be, both you and your comrade?

MENO: Socrates, I certainly used to hear, even before meeting you, that you never do anything else than exist in a state of perplexity yourself and put others in a state of per-   80
plexity. And now you seem to me to be bewitching me and drugging me and simply subduing me with incantations, so that I come to be full of perplexity. And you seem to me, if it is even appropriate to make something of a joke, to be altogether, both in looks and in other respects, like the flat torpedo-fish of the sea. For, indeed, it always makes anyone who approaches and touches it grow numb, and you seem to me now to have done that very sort of thing to me, making me numb. For truly, both in soul and in mouth, I am numb and have nothing with which I can answer you. And yet thousands of times I have made a   b
great many speeches about virtue, and before many people, and done very well, in my own opinion anyway; yet now I'm altogether unable to say what it is. And it seems to me that you are well-advised not to sail away or emigrate from here: for, if you, a foreigner in a different city, were to do this sort of thing, you would probably be arrested as a sorcerer.

SOCRATES: You are a clever rogue, Meno, and you almost deceived me.

MENO: What are you getting at, Socrates?

SOCRATES: I'm aware of why you portrayed me in a likeness.   c

MENO: Why, indeed, do you suppose?

SOCRATES: So that I would make a likeness of you in return. And I know this about all beautiful people, that they delight in having images made of them; it pays for them. Because, I suppose, even the images of beautiful people are beautiful. But I will not make an image of you in return. And I—if the torpedo-fish itself is numb in its way even as it also makes others numb—I am like it: but if not, not. For it is not while being well-provided myself that I make others unprovided or perplexed; but it is while I myself, more than anyone, am unprovided or perplexed, that I make others unprovided or perplexed. And now   d
about virtue, I do not know what it is; but you, of course, perhaps, did know it earlier, before you came into contact with me, but now you are certainly like one who does not know. Nevertheless, I am willing to look with you and seek together for whatever it is.

MENO: And in what way will you seek, Socrates, for that which you know nothing at all about what it is? What sort of thing among those things which you do not know are you proposing to seek for yourself? Or, even if, at best, you should happen upon it, how will you know it is that which you did not know?

SOCRATES: I understand the sort of thing you want to say, Meno. Do you not see   e
how inclined to strife this argument you are drawing out is, that it is not possible for a human being to seek either what he knows or what he does not know? For he could not

seek for what he knows, because he knows it and then there's no need of any seeking for this sort of person; nor could he seek for what he does not know, because then he does not know what he is seeking.

81   MENO: Doesn't this argument seem to you to have been said beautifully, Socrates?

SOCRATES: No, not to me.

MENO: Can you say in what way?

SOCRATES: I can. For I have heard from both men and women wise about things divine—

MENO: What was the account they gave?

SOCRATES: A true one, it seems to me, and a beautiful one.

MENO: What is it, and who are those who say it?

SOCRATES: Those who say it are among those priests and priestesses who have made it their concern to be able to give an account about those things they have taken in hand. And Pindar speaks too and many others of those poets who are divine. And what they say is this– but look whether they seem to you to speak the truth—for they declare the human soul to be immortal, and that at one time it comes to an end, which indeed they call dying, and again, at another time, it comes into being, but it is never destroyed. Indeed, because of this, one is required to live through one's life as piously as possible.

For those from whom

Persephone has accepted redemption for the ancient affliction, of these in the ninth year she sends the souls above again to the upper sun. From them glorious kings grow up, men with sweeping strength and greatest wisdom, and for the rest of time they are called holy heroes by mankind.

Inasmuch as the soul is immortal and has been born many times and has seen all things both here and in the house of Hades, there is nothing which it has not learned. So that there is nothing wondrous about its also being able to recollect about virtue and about other things, which it already knew before. For inasmuch as all nature is akin and the soul has learned all things, there is nothing to prevent someone who recollects (which people call learning) one thing only from discovering all other things, so long as he is brave and does not grow tired of seeking. For seeking and learning therefore consist wholly in recollection. So then one must not be persuaded by this contentious argument. For it would make us lazy and is pleasant only for fainthearted people to hear, but the other argument makes us both ready to work and to seek. Trusting in this one to be true, I am willing with you to seek for whatever virtue is.

MENO: Yes, Socrates. But how do you mean this: that we do not learn, but that what we call learning is recollection? Can you teach me how this can be?

82   SOCRATES: And after I just now said, Meno, that you are a clever rogue, you ask me now if I can teach you—I who deny that teaching is anything but recollection—in order that I may straightway be shown up to be contradicting myself.

MENO: No, by Zeus, Socrates, I was not looking to that when I spoke, but it was just by habit. But if you somehow can point out to me that it is as you say, point it out.

SOCRATES: But it's not easy, nevertheless I'm willing to make the effort for your sake. But call over one of these many followers of yours here for me, whichever you want, so that in him I'll be able to exhibit things for you.

MENO: By all means. You, come here.

SOCRATES: He is Greek, then, and speaks Greek?

MENO: By all means, very much so; he was born in the house.

SOCRATES: Now then turn your mind to which of the two ways he seems to you to exhibit, recollecting or learning from me.

MENO: Of course, I'll turn my mind to it.

SOCRATES: Now tell me, Boy, do you know that a square area is this sort of thing?

[Socrates begins to draw figures in the sand at his feet. He points to the square ABCD.]

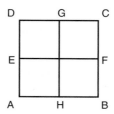

BOY: I do.

SOCRATES: Then a square area has all these lines, being four in number, equal?   c

BOY: Certainly.

SOCRATES: Does it not also have these lines here, through the middle [of each side of the square] equal? *[The lines* EF *and* GH.*]*

BOY: Yes.

SOCRATES: Then could not this sort of area be larger or smaller?

BOY: Certainly.

SOCRATES: If then this side were two feet and this other side two feet, how many feet would the whole be? Look at it this way: if this side were two feet and this other side only one foot, would not the area be once times two feet?

BOY: Yes.

SOCRATES: But as this other side is also two feet, does it not become twice two?   d

BOY: It does.

SOCRATES: Therefore, it becomes two times two feet?

BOY: Yes.

SOCRATES: How many, then, are the two times two feet? After you have calculated it, tell me.

BOY: Four, Socrates.

SOCRATES: Then could there not come to be another area two times as large as this one, and of the same sort, having all its lines equal, just as this one?

BOY: Yes.

SOCRATES: How many feet, then, will it be?

BOY: Eight.

SOCRATES: Come then, try to tell me how large each line of that area will be. For   e the line of this one is two feet. What then is the line of that area two times as large?

BOY: It is clear, Socrates, that the line is two times as large.

SOCRATES: Do you see, Meno, that I am not teaching him anything, but all that I do is ask questions? And now he supposes that he knows what sort of line it is from which the eight-foot area will come to be. Or does it not seem so to you?

MENO: It does to me.

SOCRATES: Does he know then?

MENO: Surely not.

SOCRATES: For he supposes that it comes from the double line?

MENO: Yes.

SOCRATES: Watch him now recollecting in order, just as one should recollect.

[To the boy] And you, tell me: do you affirm that from the double line the double area comes to be? I mean this sort of thing: let it be an area that is not long on this side and short on the other, but equal on every side, just like this one here.

83

BOY: It does to me.

SOCRATES: Then does this line *[AB]* become double of that if we add another of the same length here *[BJ—see diagram below]*?

BOY: Certainly.

SOCRATES: From this line then, you affirm, there will be the eight-foot area, when-ever four lines of that length come to be?

b

BOY: Yes.

SOCRATES: Then let us fill out the drawing from this line with four equal lines. *[Socrates adds lines JK, KL, and LD to make the square AJKL.]* Then would not this one here be what you affirm is the eight-foot area?

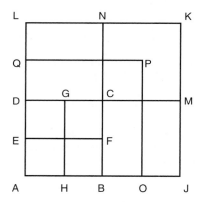

BOY: Certainly.

SOCRATES: Then in this one here there are four areas.

[Socrates has drawn in the lines CM and CN to the diagram above to complete the squares he wishes to point out.]

BOY: Yes.

SOCRATES: How many then does it become? Is it not four times as great?

BOY: How not?

SOCRATES: Then is the area which is four times as great a double-area?

BOY: No, by Zeus!

SOCRATES: But how many times as much is it?

BOY: Four times as much.

SOCRATES: Therefore, Boy, from the double line, not the double area, but the four-fold area comes into being.

c

BOY: You speak the truth.

SOCRATES: For four times an area of four feet is sixteen feet. Isn't it?

BOY: Yes.

SOCRATES: And from what sort of line does the eight-foot area come to be? Doesn't the fourfold area come from this line *[AJ]*?

BOY: I say so.

SOCRATES: And the four-foot area came from this half-line right here *[AB]*?

BOY: Yes.

SOCRATES: Very well. Is not the eight-foot area double of this one and half of that one? Will it not be from a line greater than this one but less than this one here? Or not?

BOY: It seems so to me.   d

SOCRATES: Fine. Keep answering this very thing, what seems so to you. And tell me, is not this line *[AB]*, as we said, two feet and that line *[AJ]* four?

BOY: Yes.

SOCRATES: It must be, therefore, that the line of the eight-foot area is greater than this two-foot line *[AB]*, but less than the four-foot line *[AJ]*.

BOY: It must.

SOCRATES: Try now to say what size you affirm it to be.   e

BOY: Three feet.

SOCRATES: Then if it is to be three feet, let's take of this line one half in addition and it will be three feet *[AO]*? For the feet of this one is two *[AB]* and that of the other is one *[BO]*; and the same way here these are two *[AD]* and the other is one *[DQ]*; and this area of which you spoke comes into being.

BOY: Yes.

SOCRATES: Then whenever it is three feet this way and three feet that way does the whole area become three times three feet *[square AOPQ above]*?

BOY: It appears so.

SOCRATES: And how many feet are three times three?

BOY: Nine.

SOCRATES: And how many feet was the required double area to be?

BOY: Eight.

SOCRATES: Therefore, in no way does the eight-foot area come to be from the three-feet line.

BOY: Surely not.

SOCRATES: But from what sort of line? Try to tell us precisely: and if you don't   84 want to count, show us rather, from what sort of line.

BOY: But, by Zeus, Socrates, I, for one, do not know.

SOCRATES: Are you considering again, Meno, how far it is that he has now gone in his recollecting? That, at first, he did not know what the line of the eight-foot area is, just as now he does not yet know, but, however that may be, then he thought he knew it, and boldly answered as one who knows, and he did not believe that he was unprovided and perplexed. But now, at this time, he believes that he is unprovided and perplexed,   b and just as he does not know, he does not think that he knows.

MENO: You speak the truth.

SOCRATES: Then is he not better off now, about the thing which he did not know?

MENO: This too seems to me so.

SOCRATES: Then by making him unprovided and perplexed and numbing him, just like the torpedo-fish, have we in any way harmed him?

MENO: It does not seem so to me.

SOCRATES: Then, at any rate, we have done something useful for the work at hand, as is fitting for discovering how things are. For now he, not knowing, can even carry on the search gladly, whereas then he could easily think that both before many people and   c many times he could speak well about the double area, how it required having the line that was double in length.

MENO: It seems likely.

SOCRATES: Well, do you think that before he would have tried to seek for or to learn that which he thought he knew while he did not know—before he fell down into perplexity and want and came to believe that he did not know, and longed to know?

MENO: It does not seem so to me, Socrates.

SOCRATES: Did he benefit, then, from being numbed?

MENO: It seems so to me.

SOCRATES: Look, now, at what he will discover from this perplexity and want, searching along with me, while I do nothing but ask questions and do not teach. And watch out for whether you might discover me somehow teaching and explaining things to him instead of asking for his own opinions about the matter.

[Socrates rubs out the previous figure and starts again.]

[To the boy] For you, tell me: Is not this our four-foot area? *[ABCD below.]* Do you understand?

BOY: I do.

SOCRATES: And can we not add here another area equal to it? *[BFEC.]*

BOY: Yes.

SOCRATES: And this third one equal to each of these? *[DCHJ.]*

BOY: Yes.

SOCRATES: Then can we add this one in the corner so as to fill it out? *[CEGH.]*

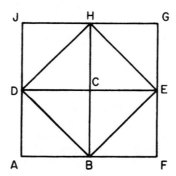

BOY: Certainly.

SOCRATES: Then would it not come about that there are these four equal areas?

BOY: Yes.

SOCRATES: What then? How many times more does this whole area *[AFGJ]* become than that one *[ABCD]*?

BOY: Four times.

SOCRATES: But what we needed was the double area. Or don't you remember?

BOY: I certainly do.

SOCRATES: Is this not, then, a line going from corner to corner and cutting each of these areas in two? *[Lines BE, EH, HD, and DB above.]*

BOY: Yes.

SOCRATES: Then do not these four equal lines come about containing this area here? *[Square BEHD.]*

BOY: They sure do.

SOCRATES: Look now: what size is this area?

BOY: I don't understand.

SOCRATES: Has not each of these inside lines *[i.e.,* BE, EH, HD, *and* DB*]* cut off half of each of these four areas or not?

BOY: Yes.

SOCRATES: Then how many areas of this size *[ABCD]* are there in this area *[*BEHD*]*?

BOY: Four.

SOCRATES: And how many in this area here *[ABCD]*?

BOY: Two.

SOCRATES: And what is the relation of the four to the two?

BOY: Double.

SOCRATES: Then how many feet does this area *[*BEHD*]* become?   b

BOY: Eight feet.

SOCRATES: From what kind of line?

BOY: From this one *[*DB*]*.

SOCRATES: From the one stretching from corner to corner of the four-foot area?

BOY: Yes.

SOCRATES: The Sophists call this line the diagonal; so that if diagonal is its name, it would be from the diagonal, as you, Meno's boy, declare, that the double area would come to be.

BOY: By all means, Socrates.

SOCRATES: What does it seem to you, Meno? Is there any opinion which he gave in his answers that was not his own?

MENO: No, they were all his own.   c

SOCRATES: And yet he did not know, as we were saying a little while ago.

MENO: You speak the truth.

SOCRATES: Still, these opinions were in him, were they not?

MENO: Yes.

SOCRATES: Then in someone who does not know about that which he does not know, there are true opinions about those things which he does not know?

MENO: So it appears.

SOCRATES: And now those very opinions have just been stirred up in him, like a dream. But if someone were to ask him these same questions many times and in different ways, you know that he will finally understand them no less precisely than anyone else.   d

MENO: It seems likely.

SOCRATES: Then with no one teaching, but someone only asking questions, he will understand, he himself taking up the knowledge again out of himself?

MENO: Yes.

SOCRATES: And his taking up knowledge again that is in himself, is this not recollecting?

MENO: Certainly.

SOCRATES: Then concerning the knowledge which he now has, is it not either that at some time he acquired it or that he always had it?

MENO: Yes.

SOCRATES: Then if he always had it, he was also always one who knows; but, if he acquired it at some time, he could not have acquired it in his present life. Or has some-one taught him how to do geometry? For then he will do these same things with all of   e geometry and all the other subjects of learning. Is there then any one who has taught him all these things? For you, I guess, are just the man to know, especially since he was born and raised in your house.

MENO: But I know that no one ever taught him.

SOCRATES: Does he have these opinions or not?

MENO: Necessarily, Socrates, it appears so.

SOCRATES: But if he did not acquire them in his present life, is this not now clear
86 that he had them and learned them in some other time?

MENO: So it appears.

SOCRATES: Then was this the time when he was not a human being?

MENO: Yes.

SOCRATES: If then both during the time in which he is and the time in which he is
not a human being, true opinions will exist within him, which after being aroused by
questioning become matters of knowledge, then will not his soul for all time be in a condition of having learned? For it is clear that for all time he is, or he is not, a human being.

MENO: So it appears.

b   SOCRATES: Then if the truth about the things which are is always in our soul, the
soul would be immortal, so that you must be bold about what you now happen not to
know, that is, what is not remembered, to try to seek and to recollect it?

MENO: You seem to me to speak well, Socrates, I don't know how.

SOCRATES: And so do I to myself, Meno. And for the rest of the points I would not
assert myself altogether confidently on behalf of my argument; but that in supposing
one ought to seek what one does not know we would be better, more able to be brave
c   and less lazy than if we supposed that which we do not know we are neither capable of
discovering nor ought to seek—on behalf of that I would surely battle, so far as I am
able, both in word and in deed.

MENO: That, too, you seem to me to speak well, Socrates.

SOCRATES: Do you want us, then, since we are of one mind that one ought to seek
for what one does not know, to try to seek in common for what virtue is?

MENO: By all means. Not, Socrates, but that I would with most pleasure both look for
and hear about that which I asked about at first, whether one ought to undertake it as being
d   itself teachable, or as by nature, or as in whatever way virtue comes to human beings.

SOCRATES: Yet, Meno, if I were ruling not only myself, but you too, we would not
first look at whether virtue is something teachable or not teachable before we first
sought what it itself is: but, since you don't even try to rule yourself, in order indeed that
you might be free, you both try to rule me and do rule me, I will yield to you—for what
e   can I do? It seems, then, that we must look into what sort of thing something is, something about which we don't yet know what it is. If you won't do anything else, at least
relax your rule a little for me and agree to examine it hypothetically, whether it is teachable or whatever. And I mean by "hypothetically" the following: just as geometers often
look at things whenever someone asks them, for example, about a figure, whether this
87   triangular figure is able to be inscribed in this circle, someone might say: "I don't yet
know if this is that sort of figure, but I think I have, as it were, a certain hypothesis useful for the problem, as follows: If this is the sort of figure which, after someone applies
it to the given line of itself, falls short by that sort of figure like the one which has been
itself applied, then one thing seems to me to result; and some other thing results if, on
b   the other hand, it is impossible for this to fall out. So then it is on the hypothesis of the
inscription of the figure in the circle that I am willing to tell you whether the result is
impossible or not." In this way then, about virtue too—since we know neither what it is,
nor what sort of thing it is—let us look hypothetically at it, whether it is teachable or not
teachable, speaking in the following way: If virtue is some sort of thing among those
things that have regard to the soul, would it be teachable or not teachable? First, then, if
it's the kind of thing that is different from, or like, knowledge, is it teachable or not, or,

as we were just now saying it, is it recollectable?—let it make no difference to us about   c
whatever name we use—but is it teachable? Or is this, at any rate, clear to everyone, that
a human being is taught nothing else than knowledge?

MENO: It seems so to me.

SOCRATES: And if virtue is some kind of knowledge, it is clear that it could be
taught.

MENO: For how not?

SOCRATES: Well, we are rid of this quickly, that if virtue is one sort of thing it is
teachable, if it is another sort, it is not.

MENO: Certainly.

SOCRATES: And after this, it seems likely, that whether virtue is knowledge or the
kind of thing that is different from knowledge should be looked into.

MENO: It seems to me, anyway, that this should be looked into after that.   d

SOCRATES: Well, what then? Do we not affirm that virtue is a good thing in itself,
and does this same hypothesis remain with us, that it is a good thing in itself?

MENO: By all means.

SOCRATES: Then, if there is something good and it is something else separated
from knowledge, it may be that virtue would not be some sort of knowledge; but if there
is nothing good which knowledge does not encompass, then we would be right in suspecting what we suspected, that it is some sort of knowledge.

MENO: That is so.

SOCRATES: And surely it is by means of virtue that we are good?   e

MENO: Yes.

SOCRATES: And if we are good, we are beneficent: for all good things are beneficial.
Are they not?

MENO: Yes.

SOCRATES: Now virtue, too, is beneficial?

MENO: Necessarily, from what has been agreed to.

SOCRATES: Now let us see, taking them up one by one, what sorts of things are
beneficial for us: health, we affirm, and strength, and beauty and, surely, wealth: these
and these kinds of things we say are beneficial. Do we not?

MENO: Yes.   88

SOCRATES: But these same things, we affirm, sometimes also harm; or do you
affirm it otherwise than this?

MENO: No, but this way.

SOCRATES: Now look, what directs each of these things whenever it benefits us
and whenever it harms? Then is it not that whenever right usage directs, it benefits; but
when not, it harms?

MENO: Certainly.

SOCRATES: Now, then, let us look also at those things that pertain to the soul. Is
there something that you call moderation, as well as justice and courage and readiness-
to-learn and memory and magnificence, and all such kinds of things?

MENO: I do.

SOCRATES: Now look at whether any of these things seem to you to be not knowl-   b
edge, but something other than knowledge; whether they don't sometimes harm and
sometimes benefit? For example, courage, if the courage is not prudence, but some sort
of boldness—is it not the case that when a human being is bold without intelligence that
he is harmed and whenever with intelligence he is benefited?

MENO: Yes.

SOCRATES: Then is it also the same with moderation and readiness to learn; when they are learned and trained for with intelligence, they are beneficial, but without intelligence, harmful?

MENO: Very much so.

c   SOCRATES: Then, in sum, all the things undertaken and endured by the soul when directed by prudence come to end in happiness, but when controlled by thoughtlessness in the opposite?

MENO: It seems likely.

SOCRATES: If then virtue is something in the soul and is itself necessarily beneficial, it must be prudence: since, indeed, all things that pertain to the soul are, themselves

d   in themselves neither beneficial nor harmful, but when prudence or thoughtlessness is added to them, they become harmful or beneficial. According to this argument, indeed, virtue being beneficial, it must be some kind of prudence.

MENO: It seems so to me.

SOCRATES: And plainly also the other things we were just now talking about, wealth and those kinds of things, are sometimes good and sometimes harmful. Then just as prudence directing the rest of the soul makes the things of the soul beneficial and thoughtlessness makes them harmful, in this way again does not the soul, by rightly using and directing these things too, make them beneficial, but if not rightly makes them harmful?

MENO: Certainly.

SOCRATES: And does the thoughtful soul direct rightly, but the thoughtless mistakenly?

MENO: That is so.

SOCRATES: Then is it possible to speak in just this way about everything, that for a human being all other things depend upon the soul, but the things of the soul itself

89   depend upon prudence, if they are going to be good: and by this argument the beneficial would be prudence: and do we affirm that virtue is beneficial?

MENO: Certainly.

SOCRATES: Therefore, do we affirm that prudence is virtue, either virtue altogether or some part of it?

MENO: It seems to me, Socrates, that the things which have been said have been finely said.

SOCRATES: Then if this is how it is, the good could not be good by nature.

MENO: It doesn't seem so to me.

b   SOCRATES: For even if this somehow were so, this too would follow: if the good were to become so by nature, we would, I guess, have people who recognized those among the youth with good natures, whom, after we took them from those who had revealed them, we would guard on the Acropolis, setting our seal on them much more than we do with gold, so that no one could corrupt them, and that when they should come of age, they could become useful to their cities.

MENO: That is surely likely, Socrates.

c   SOCRATES: Since, then, the good become good not by nature, then is it by learning?

MENO: It now seems to me to be necessary: and it is clear, Socrates, according to the hypothesis, that if virtue is indeed knowledge, it is teachable.

SOCRATES: Perhaps, by Zeus; but maybe we did not agree rightly about this?

MENO: And yet it did seem just now to have been said rightly.

SOCRATES: But it ought not to seem to have been said rightly only just now, but also in the present time and in the time to come, if there's going to be some soundness about it.

MENO: What then is this? What are you seeing that bothers you about it and makes you doubt that virtue is knowledge?

SOCRATES: I will tell you, Meno. For that it is teachable, if, indeed, it is knowledge, I don't take back as not being said rightly; but that it may not be knowledge, see whether I seem to you to be reasonable in my doubt about that. For tell me this: if anything whatever is teachable, and not only virtue, are there not necessarily also teachers and learners of it?

MENO: It seems so to me.

SOCRATES: Then, again, on the contrary, that of which there would be neither teachers nor learners, would we not liken it rightly if we should liken it to what is not teachable?

MENO: That is so. But does it seem to you that there are no teachers of virtue?

SOCRATES: I've sought, surely, many times, whether there might be some teachers of it and, trying everything, I'm not able to find out. And yet I share the search with many people, and especially those whom I suppose to be most experienced in this matter. And now indeed, Meno, just at the right moment, Anytus here has sat down beside us, to whom we should give a share in the search. And it would be fitting for us to give him a share: for Anytus here, first of all, is the son of a father both wealthy and wise, Anthemion, who became wealthy not by chance, nor from some gift, like the one who has just recently received Polycrates' goods, Ismenias the Theban, but acquired it by his own wisdom and diligence. Then, in other respects too, he did not seem to be a haughty citizen, nor puffed up and offensive, but an orderly and well-mannered man. Then he brought up and educated our man here well, as the majority of the Athenians judge; they elect him, at any rate, to the highest offices. Now it is only just to search for teachers of virtue with such men, whether there are or are not any and whoever they might be.

[To Anytus] You, then, Anytus, do search along with us, both with me and your guest-friend, Meno, here, whether in this matter there might be any teachers. And look at it this way: if we should want Meno here to become a good doctor, to whom would we send him as teachers? Would it not be to the doctors?

ANYTUS: Certainly.

SOCRATES: And what if we should want him to become a good shoemaker, would we not send him to the shoemakers?

ANYTUS: Yes.

SOCRATES: So, too, with the others?

ANYTUS: Certainly.

SOCRATES: Now tell me again about these same cases, in this way. To the doctors, we say, we would send him rightly, if we were to send him, wanting him to become a doctor. Now whenever we say that, do we also say this, that we would be sensible, if we sent him to those who claim to practice the art, rather than to those who don't, and because they practice the art charge fees for it, who have declared themselves to be teachers for anyone who wants to come and learn? Then, if we had looked to these things, would we not be right in sending him?

ANYTUS: Yes.

SOCRATES: Then do not these same things hold for flute-playing and the rest? It's very foolish of those who want to make someone a flute-player to be unwilling to send him to those who undertake to teach the art and who charge a fee for it, but who make trouble by having the student seek to learn from those who neither pretend to be teachers nor have any student in that very subject which we consider the one for which we would send someone to learn from them. Does this not seem very unreasonable to you?

ANYTUS: Yes, by Zeus, to me it does, and stupid as well.

SOCRATES: Finely spoken. Then now it should be possible for you to deliberate in
91   common with me about this guest-friend of ours, Meno here. For he, Anytus, has been
saying to me for some time now that he desires that wisdom and virtue by which people
manage both households and cities finely, and take care of their own parents, and know
how to receive and to send off both citizens and foreigners hospitably, in a way worthy of
b   a good man. Then in order to learn this virtue, consider to whom, if we sent him, we
would rightly send him. Or, is it clear, indeed, according to the argument just made, it
should be to those who undertake to be teachers of virtue and have professed themselves
publicly to any Greek who wants to learn, and have fixed fees that they charge for it?

ANYTUS: And just who are these people you speak of, Socrates?

SOCRATES: Surely you too know that these are those whom people call Sophists.

c   ANYTUS: By Heracles, watch what you're saying, Socrates. May such madness not
seize any of my own people, neither my family nor my friends, neither fellow-citizen nor
foreigner, so as to be debased by going to them, since it is evident that these men are the
debasement and corruption of those who associate with them.

SOCRATES: How do you mean that, Anytus? Then do these alone of those who
claim to know some way of doing good differ by so much from the others, that they not
only do not benefit whatever one hands over to them, but even, on the contrary, ruin it?

d   And for these services they openly consider themselves entitled to demand money? Now
I cannot believe you: for I know one man, Protagoras, who acquired more money from
this wisdom of his than Phidias, who produced such manifestly beautiful works, and any
ten other sculptors. And yet how portentous what you say is, considering that those who
work on old shoes and mend clothes would not be able to get away, for thirty days, with
e   giving back the clothes and shoes in more miserable condition than they received them,
but if they ever did such things, they would soon die of hunger. And yet Protagoras hid it
from the whole of Greece for forty years that he was corrupting his associates and sending them back more miserable than he received them. For I think when he died he was
nearly seventy years old, after being in his art for forty years. And in all this time, up to
92   this very day, he has not ceased to be well thought of; and not only Protagoras, but very
many others as well, some born before him and others still alive now. Then, indeed,
should we declare, according to your argument, that they knowingly deceived and ruined
the youth, or that it had been hidden from themselves too? And shall we deem those
whom some declare to be the wisest of human beings to be so mad?

ANYTUS: They are far from being mad, Socrates; but much more so are the youth
b   who give them money, and even more than these are the relatives who turn them over to
them, but most of all are the cities that permit them to come in and don't drive them out,
whether it's some foreigner that undertakes to do something of this sort, or a fellow citizen.

SOCRATES: Has any one of the Sophists wronged you, Anytus, that you should be
so hard on them?

ANYTUS: No, by Zeus, I never associated with any of them, and I would not allow
anyone else of my people to do so.

SOCRATES: Then you are altogether without experience of these men?

ANYTUS: I am and may I remain so.

c   SOCRATES: How then, my daemonic one, could you know about this business,
whether there is anything good or worthless in that of which you are altogether without
experience?

ANYTUS: Easily: I still know what these people are, whether I am without experience of them or not.

SOCRATES: You are perhaps a diviner, Anytus, for how else, I might wonder, do you
know about them, from what you yourself say about them. But we are not searching for

those from whose company Meno would become worthless after he came to them,—for these, if you want, let them be the Sophists—but tell us, and do your hereditary comrade here a good turn by telling him, to whom to go in so great a city as this so that he might become worthy of mention in the virtue I was just now going through.

ANYTUS: Why don't you tell him?

SOCRATES: Well, I did say who I thought were teachers of these things; but it happened that I made no sense, as you say. And perhaps there is something to what you say. But you now, in your turn, tell him to whom among the Athenians he should go. Tell him the name of anyone you want.

ANYTUS: Why should one hear the name of just one man? For of any Athenian gentleman he should happen to meet, there is none who will not make him better than the Sophists would, if he is willing to listen.

SOCRATES: Did these gentlemen become such spontaneously, and yet without learning from anyone are they nevertheless able to teach others what they themselves did not learn?

ANYTUS: I claim that they too learned from those who were gentlemen before them: or don't you think that there have been many good men in this city?

SOCRATES: I, too, do think, Anytus, that there are good men in politics here, and before now there have been men no worse than they are, but have they also been good teachers of this virtue of theirs? For this is what our discussion happens to be about: not whether or not there are good men here, nor whether there have been such before, but we have for some time been looking into whether virtue is teachable. And in looking into this, we look into the following, whether the good men, both those now and those before, knew how to hand over to another the virtue in which they were good, or whether this is not something able to be handed over or to be received by any human being from another. This is what I and Meno have for some time been seeking. Now, look at it this way, out of your own argument: would you not affirm that Themistocles was a good man?

ANYTUS: I would, even the best of all.

SOCRATES: And therefore that he was a good teacher, if anyone was a teacher of his own virtue?

ANYTUS: I suppose so, if he wanted to be.

SOCRATES: But do you think that he would not have wanted any others to become gentlemen, and especially his own son? Or do you think he begrudged him getting it, and purposely did not pass on the virtue in which he himself was good? Or haven't you heard that Themistocles had his son Cleophantus taught to be a good horseman. He could even stay on horses while standing upright and hurl javelins from horses while upright; and he accomplished many other marvelous things in which his father had him educated and made him skilled; there were so many things for which he depended on good teachers. Haven't you heard about them from your elders?

ANYTUS: I've heard.

SOCRATES: So then no one could have charged his son with having a nature that was bad.

ANYTUS: Perhaps not.

SOCRATES: And what about this? Have you ever heard from anyone, either young or old, that Cleophantus, the son of Themistocles, became a good and wise man in those very things in which his father did?

ANYTUS: Surely not.

SOCRATES: Then are we to suppose that he wanted to educate his son in those other things, but in that wisdom in which he was himself wise, not to make him any better than his neighbors, if indeed virtue really is, as we were saying, teachable?

ANYTUS: Perhaps not, by Zeus.

SOCRATES: Here then is just such a teacher of virtue, whom you also agree to be
94   among the best of those from former times. But let us look into another one, Aristides,
the son of Lysimachus. Do you not agree that he was good?

ANYTUS: I certainly do, in every way.

SOCRATES: Then did he too not give his son, Lysimachus, the finest education of
the Athenians, in all those things for which he had teachers, and does he seem to you to
have made him a better man than anyone else? For you, I suppose, have been in his
company, and see what sort of man he is. And, if you want, there is Pericles, so magnif-
b   icently wise a man; do you know that he brought up two sons, Paralus and Xanthippus?

ANYTUS: I do.

SOCRATES: He certainly taught them, as you also know, to be no worse horsemen
than any Athenian, and educated them in music and gymnastics and everything else that
could be had by art to be inferior to no one; and did he not want to make them good
men? I would think he wanted to, but it was not something teachable. And lest you think
c   that only a few and the lowest Athenians are incapable in this affair, consider that
Thucydides also brought up two sons, Melesias and Stephanus, and he educated them
well both in other things and to be the finest wrestlers in Athens—he turned over the
one to Xanthias, and the other to Eudorus; and they were, I guess, reputed to be the
finest wrestlers of that time—or don't you remember?

ANYTUS: I do, by hearsay.

SOCRATES: Then is it clear that he would never, on the one hand, where it was
d   required to go to considerable expense to teach, teach his own sons those things; but, on
the other hand, where it was not required to spend a lot of money, to make them good
men, fail to teach them, if that was something teachable? Or perhaps Thucydides was a
low person and did not have many friends among Athenians and the allies? Yet he was
from a great house and capable of great things in his city and among the other Greeks,
so that if this thing were teachable, he would have found out who was going to make his
e   sons good, either one of his countrymen, or some foreigner, if he himself had no leisure
time because of his tending to the city. But, I fear, Anytus, my comrade, that virtue may
not be something teachable.

ANYTUS: Socrates, it seems to me that you easily speak badly of people. Now I
could give you some advice, if you're willing to be persuaded by me, to be careful:
95   since it is perhaps easier to do harm to people than to benefit them in other cities too,
and in this city that is certainly so. But I suppose you know that yourself.

SOCRATES: Meno, Anytus seems angry to me, and I don't wonder at it: for, first of
all, he supposes me to be speaking badly about those men, and then he also believes
himself to be one of them. But if he should ever know what sort of thing talking badly
is, he will cease being angry, yet now he does not know. But you, tell me, are there not
men among your people who are gentlemen too?

MENO: Certainly.

b   SOCRATES: What then? Are these men willing to offer themselves as teachers
to the youth, and to agree both that they are teachers and that virtue is something
teachable?

MENO: No, by Zeus, Socrates, for sometimes you can hear from them that it is
something teachable, and sometimes that it is not.

SOCRATES: Should we affirm then that these men, about whom there is no agreement on this very thing, are teachers of this subject?

MENO: It does not seem so to me, Socrates.

SOCRATES: Well, what then? Do these Sophists, who alone proclaim it, seem to you to be teachers of virtue?

MENO: Now that is something I admire most in Gorgias, Socrates, that you would never hear him promising this, but he even laughs at the others whenever he hears them promising that. But he does think that there is a need to make men speak skillfully.

SOCRATES: Then the Sophists do not seem to you to be teachers?

MENO: I cannot say, Socrates. For I too undergo the very thing that most people do: sometimes it seems to me they are and sometimes not.

SOCRATES: Do you know that it seems so not only to you and to the other political men, that some times they think this is teachable and other times not; but do you know that Theognis the poet, too, says these same things?

MENO: In which verses?

SOCRATES: In his elegiacs, where he says:

> Drink and eat with them, and with them sit,
> And gratify them whose power is great.
> For from good men you will be taught good things.
> But if you mingle with the bad, you will simply lose
> Even the mind you have.

Do you see that in these verses he speaks of virtue as being something teachable?

MENO: It does appear so.

SOCRATES: But in other verses, he changes course a bit: "And if it was able to be done," he says, "and intelligence could be put into a man,"—he says something like that—many and great fees would they bear off, those who could do this," and,

> Never would a bad man be born from a good father,
> Being persuaded by sober speech. But by teaching
> You will never make the bad man good.

Do you understand that he is saying opposite things about the same things to himself again?

MENO: It appears so.

SOCRATES: Can you tell me then of any other subject whatever where these who affirm that they are teachers are not only not acknowledged by others to be teachers but are not even recognized as understanding it themselves, being regarded instead as worthless in the very subject in which they declare themselves to be teachers—while, on the other hand, those who are acknowledged gentlemen sometimes declare it to be teachable and, at other times, not? Could you declare that people who are so confused by any subject are, in any authoritative sense, teachers of it?

MENO: By Zeus, I certainly could not.

SOCRATES: Then if neither the Sophists nor those who are themselves gentlemen are teachers of the subject, is it clear that there could not be any other teachers of it?

MENO: It does not seem so to me.

SOCRATES: And if there are no teachers, there are no learners?

MENO: It seems to me to be as you say.

SOCRATES: And have we agreed that this subject, of which there were neither teachers nor learners, is not teachable?

MENO: We have agreed.

SOCRATES: Then of virtue there appear to be no teachers anywhere?

MENO: That is so.

SOCRATES: And if no teachers, then no learners?

MENO: It appears not.

SOCRATES: Therefore virtue could not be something teachable?

d   MENO: It's not likely, if we were looking at it correctly. So that I really wonder, Socrates, whether perhaps there are no good men, or what could be the way of generation for good men to come to be?

SOCRATES: There is a danger, Meno, that I and you are both sort of worthless men, and that Gorgias has not sufficiently educated you, nor Prodicus me. So that, above all,

e   we should apply our minds to our very selves, and seek whoever will make us better in some one particular way: and I say this, first focusing my gaze on the search just made, how ridiculously it has escaped us that it is not only when knowledge is directing that human beings act rightly and well in their affairs, and perhaps that is why knowing in what sort of way men become good has also escaped us.

MENO: How do you mean this, Socrates?

SOCRATES: In this way: that good men are required to be beneficent; we have

97   agreed rightly that this could not be otherwise. Is that not so?

MENO: Yes.

SOCRATES: And that they will be beneficent whenever they direct our affairs rightly, I suppose we were right in agreeing to this too?

MENO: Yes.

SOCRATES: But that it is not possible to direct rightly, if one is not prudent, in this we are like those who have not rightly agreed.

MENO: How, indeed, do you mean "rightly"?

SOCRATES: I'll tell you. If someone who knows the road to Larissa, or any other place you want, went there and directed others, would he not direct them rightly and well?

MENO: Certainly.

b   SOCRATES: And what if someone is right in his opinion about what the road is, but has not gone there, nor knows the road, would he not also direct them rightly?

MENO: Certainly.

SOCRATES: And just as long as he would have right opinion about those things of which another has knowledge, himself supposing what is the truth, but not prudently knowing it, he will be no worse a guide than he who prudently knows it.

MENO: No worse, I agree.

SOCRATES: True opinion, therefore, is no worse a guide to right action than prudence. And this is what just now we were leaving aside in our examination about what

c   sort of thing virtue might be, when we said that only prudence directs action rightly, whereas true opinion does so too.

MENO: That is likely.

SOCRATES: Right opinion, therefore, is no less beneficial than knowledge.

MENO: To this extent, Socrates, that he who has knowledge would always hit the mark, whereas he who has right opinion would sometimes hit it, and sometimes not.

SOCRATES: How do you mean that? Would not he that always has right opinion always hit on it, just so long as his opinions were right?

MENO: Necessarily, it appears to me. So that I wonder, Socrates, this being so,

d   that knowledge is always so much more honored than right opinion, and why one of them is so different from the other.

SOCRATES: Do you know then why you wonder, or should I tell you?

MENO: Certainly, tell me.

SOCRATES: Because you have never applied your mind to the statues of Daedalus. But perhaps there are none among you.

MENO: With a view to what do you say this?

SOCRATES: Because if they have not been tied down, they make their escape and run away; but if they are tied down, they stay put.

MENO: Well, what about it?

SOCRATES: To have acquired one of his works that has been let loose is not worth very much, like acquiring a runaway slave, for he does not stay put; but one that is tied down is worth a great deal. For his works are very beautiful. With a view to what, then, do I say this? With a view to true opinions. For true opinions too, for as long a time as they should stay put, are a fine thing and accomplish all kinds of good things. Yet much of the time they are not willing to stay put, but run away out of the human soul; so that they are not worth much until someone should bind them with causes by reasoning. And this, my comrade Meno, is recollection, as we agreed before. And whenever they have been bound, first they become knowledge and then steadfast. And this is why knowledge is worth more than right opinion, and, by its binding, knowledge differs from and excels right opinion.

MENO: By Zeus, Socrates, it is like something of this sort.

SOCRATES: And yet, I too speak, not as one who knows, but as one who makes images and conjectures. But I certainly do not think I am making images or guessing this, that right opinion and knowledge are different things. But if there is anything I could affirm that I know, and there are few I could affirm—one of those, at any rate, which I could set down that I know is this.

MENO: And you are right, Socrates, in saying this.

SOCRATES: What then? Is the following not rightly said, that true opinion directing the work of each action brings it to completion no worse than knowledge?

MENO: In this, too, you seem to me to speak the truth.

SOCRATES: Then right opinion will be no worse, nor less beneficial, in actions than knowledge, nor the man having right opinion than the one having knowledge.

MENO: That is so.

SOCRATES: And we did agree that the good man is beneficent.

MENO: Yes.

SOCRATES: Now then, since not only through knowledge can men be good and beneficial to their cities, if they would, but also through right opinion; and neither of these two is natural to human beings, neither knowledge nor true opinion, nor are they acquired—or does it seem to you that either of them is by nature?

MENO: Not to me.

SOCRATES: Then since they are not by nature, neither could the good men be such by nature.

MENO: Surely not.

SOCRATES: Since they are not such by nature, we looked next into whether it is something teachable.

MENO: Yes.

SOCRATES: Then did it not seem to be teachable, if virtue is prudence?

MENO: Yes.

SOCRATES: And if it should be something teachable, it would be prudence?

MENO: Certainly.

SOCRATES: And if there should be teachers, it would be teachable, but if there are not, not teachable?

MENO: Quite so.

SOCRATES: But surely we have agreed that there are no teachers of it?

MENO: That is so.

SOCRATES: We have agreed, therefore, that it is neither teachable nor prudence?

MENO: Certainly.

SOCRATES: But surely we agree that it is a good thing?

MENO: Yes.

SOCRATES: And what directs rightly is beneficial and good?

MENO: Certainly.

99 SOCRATES: And these two things only direct rightly: true opinion and knowledge, which the human being who directs rightly has. For things which turn out rightly from some sort of chance do not come about through human direction. But those things, through which a human being is a director to what is right, are these two, true opinion and knowledge.

MENO: This is the way it seems to me.

SOCRATES: Then since it is not something teachable, virtue indeed does not come into being consequent to knowledge?

MENO: It appears not.

b SOCRATES: Therefore of two things which are good and beneficial, one of them has been let off, and in political action it could not be knowledge that directs.

MENO: It seems not, to me.

SOCRATES: It is not, therefore, by any wisdom or by being wise that such men direct their cities, Themistocles and those like him and those about whom Anytus here was just speaking. And, indeed, this is why they are unable to make others such as they are themselves, inasmuch as it is not through knowledge that they are the kind of men they are.

MENO: It is likely to be just as you say, Socrates.

SOCRATES: Then if not by knowledge, what remains, indeed, comes to be by good judgment based on opinion, which is what political men use when they straighten out c their cities. They are not in a different situation with respect to prudent understanding than soothsayers or inspired diviners. For these, too, when they are inspired, do say true things, very many of them, but they do not know what they say.

MENO: It probably is that way.

SOCRATES: Then, Meno, do these men deserve to be called divine who, having no intelligence, set straight many great matters in the things that they do and say?

MENO: Certainly.

SOCRATES: We could, therefore, rightly call divine those about whom we were just now speaking, soothsayers and diviners and all poetic people; and the political people d are not least of those whom we might affirm to be divine and divinely inspired, being inspired and possessed by the god, whenever by their speaking they set straight many great affairs, without knowing those things about which they speak.

MENO: Certainly.

SOCRATES: And women too, surely, Meno, call good men divine. And the Laconians, whenever they praise any good man, say, "This man's divine."

e MENO: And it appears, Socrates, that they speak rightly. And yet, perhaps Anytus here is annoyed with you for speaking this way.

SOCRATES: That doesn't matter to me. We will, Meno, indeed converse with him again. But now, if we in this whole account both searched rightly and were speaking rightly, virtue would be neither by nature, nor something teachable, but has come by divine dispensation without intelligence in those to whom it might come, unless there

should be that sort of man among the political men who could also make someone else   100
politic. And if there should be one, he could almost be said to be among the living what
Homer said Tiresias was among the dead, saying about him that "he alone of those in
Hades has his wits about him, but the others flit about as shadows." The same would hold
here too, such a man would be as a true thing alongside shadows, in regard to virtue.

MENO: You have spoken most beautifully, it seems to me, Socrates.   b

SOCRATES: Then from this reasoning, Meno, virtue appears to have come to us by
divine dispensation, for those to whom it may come. But we shall know what is clear
about it when, before we seek whatever way virtue comes to human beings, we will first
undertake to seek what virtue, itself in itself, is. Now it's time for me to go, but you persuade your guest-friend Anytus here too about those very same things that you yourself
have been persuaded, so that he may be more gentle: for if you do persuade him, you   c
will also confer upon the Athenians a benefit.

SYMPOSIUM* (in part)

Characters
Socrates
Agathon
Phaedrus
Pausanias
Aristophanes
Eryximachus
Alcibides
Scene—Agathon's home

ARISTOPHANES' SPEECH

It seems to me that mankind still hasn't learned the power of Love, not in the least. If we   188
had we'd have built him the most impressive temples with altars laden with offerings
from the richest sacrifices. But right now he receives none of these honors, though he
deserves them more than anyone else. For there is no other god who loves the human
race the way he does. He supports us and heals those wounds which stand in the way of
our greatest happiness. So let me try and convey to you the extent of Love's influence,
and perhaps one day you will do the same for someone else. But first you must come to   b
understand the true nature of mankind, how we looked at the very start of things and
what we have suffered over time.

*Apollodorus, a devoted follower of Socrates, narrates the entire dialogue to a group of anonymous companions.

Plato, *Symposium* (189c–193d, 201d–end: 223d), translated by Avi Sharon (Newburyport, MA: Focus Philosophical Library, 1997). Reprinted by permission of Focus Publishing/R. Pullins Company.

Long ago both our nature and form were quite different from what they are now. First, in those days there were three kinds of human beings, not just two, male and female, the kinds you see today. The third type, which combined the other two into one, is now extinct and only its name, "androgyne," survives. In name and nature this third gender partook of both man (*andros*) and woman (*gyne*). Today, however, only the

c   name is left and people use it mostly as an insult.

Even more unusual, however, all three types of these aboriginal humans were compounds, two bodies joined together front to front with their backs and sides forming a circle. Each one had four arms, four legs and two identical faces upon a rounded neck. There was just one head apiece with the two faces looking out in both directions. Everyone had two backs, arched and facing outward, which joined together at head and

d   hips. They had four ears and two sets of sexual organs and all the other parts in duplicate, just as you would imagine from what I've already said. With their four arms dangling at their sides, they walked in an upright position, just as we do now, in any direction they chose. But if they wanted to run at full speed they would stiffen and extend all eight of their limbs and twirl round and round like gymnasts doing cartwheels.

If you want to know why they looked so unusual, just consider who their parents were. The ones who were made up of two males joined together were sons of Father

e   Helios. Those compounded of two females were daughters of Mother Earth. The Androgynes, that hybrid of male and female, were children of the Moon, since the Moon shares in both the Sun and the Earth. Since all three types took after their spherical parents, they too were round and travelled in circles. They were also very strong and terribly ambitious. In fact, once they even dared to attack Zeus and the other gods on

189   Mount Olympus. Some scholars even argue that Homer's story about Ephialtes and
b   Otus was originally about these arrogant youngsters and how they clambered up to heaven to try and topple the gods.

When this happened, Zeus and the rest of the Olympians huddled in council to decide what action to take. Their hands were tied. They couldn't simply annihilate the entire human race with a lightning stroke as they'd done to the race of giants. For if all humans were killed, no one would be left to worship the gods and deliver up the savory sacrificial smoke. But nor could the gods allow mankind to go unpunished. There

c   seemed to be no solution. However, after brooding over the matter closely, Zeus rose slowly from his throne to speak among the gods:

"My fellow Olympians," he said. "I have found a way. Surely we cannot destroy mankind completely, but if we could somehow weaken them to the point that they would have to refrain from such wanton behavior in the future, that would be best. I have decided to slice each of them in two. In this way, at one stroke, we can easily halve their strength while we double their numbers, thus doubling the amount of pious devo-

d   tion we collect from them. After the operation they will have only two legs on which to get about. And should they continue to misbehave, if they refuse to lead a life of peace and quiet, I will cut them in half once more. When that day comes they will have to make their way by hopping around on one leg!"

With these words he chopped every human in two, from top to bottom, the way you cut apples to preserve them or slice an egg with a strand of hair. As Zeus cut each in half he called on Apollo to twist their heads around to face the horrible gash. For he felt that our forefathers would learn greater restraint if they were forced to contemplate their wounds all day long. Zeus' last command to Apollo was to suture up their wounds. So Apollo rotated each of their heads until they faced the incision. Then he drew the loose flaps of skin from their sides in toward the center, as if he were drawing a purse closed with a string. Leaving a tiny opening in the middle of the stomach, he tied the

remaining folds of skin there into a knot, creating the navel. Then he smoothed out all   e
the ripples on the surface and gave shape to the chest using the same tool that cobblers
use to smooth the wrinkles in shoe-leather. In the end he left a few creases around the
stomach to remind us of our ancient undoing.

When our original nature had thus been cut in two, each half immediately began
to long for its complementary half. They all scattered, casting their arms around each
other, knitting themselves together and trying to bond and become one again. As soon
as one fragment found his missing half he refused to be separated from his companion
for any reason whatsoever. In time, however, they began to die off from hunger and idle-
ness. When one of the two passed away the surviving half would seek out another shard
and couple with it. Sometimes that half was female, sometimes it was male. It didn't
matter. The race was dying out.

Finally Zeus took pity on their wretched condition and came up with another
tactic. He decided to move their sexual organs from the back to the front. For until then,
these parts, like all the others, were on our backs and we produced offspring not by   190
depositing seed inside one another, but by scattering it on the ground, the way cicadas
do. Zeus, therefore, decided to transfer our genitals to the front so that birth might take
place through intercourse between the male and the female. His hope was that, under
this new arrangement, when a man embraced a woman, the act might result in conception and birth. And if a man were to embrace another man, the two might at least get
some satisfaction from the act and then cease their affections, turn back to their work
and look to their other needs in life.

You can see then from this history how deeply ingrained is our desire to love. It is
Love that draws together the severed halves of our original state as we desperately try to
make one out of two, to heal the human condition. For each of us is but the tally of some   b
other half and, like flat-fish, we all exhibit the puckered scars of having been sliced in two.

That's why we are all perpetually in search of the perfect fit, the love of our life,
our missing half. All of those men who were split off from the combined male-female
gender (the type we called androgynous) spend their lives chasing after women. Most of
them happen to be adulterers and so are the women who come from this group.
However, women who were severed from the all-female type have no interest in men.
Their desires are directed only toward other women and it's from this antique hybrid
that lesbians have come. Finally, all those cut from the all-male group are drawn always
to other men. Once severed from another man, they naturally fall in love with men, and,   c
as I see it, they are the finest sort we know. They are inherently more manly and robust.
Only a fool would argue that such boys are without shame. These lads choose this path
not out of any shamelessness but, on the contrary, because of their courage and manliness, the very same qualities which they look for in their mates. Conclusive proof of this
lies in the fact that these are the very same young men who later on in life choose to
become politicians. And then, when these youngsters grow to manhood, they in turn
become attracted to young boys. In fact, if our customs didn't force them to do otherwise, they'd choose to have nothing at all to do with marriage and children. They would
be happy to live out their lives together never bothering about women. In this last group
belong those men who love boys and those boys who feel affection for men, the two   d
inclining toward and relishing their own kinds and characteristics.

Now, whenever someone happens upon his matching half, whatever the gender,
it's an amazing thing to witness. The lucky couple is suddenly enclouded by such a
degree of affection and intimacy and love that they will refuse to be separated for even
a moment. Yet these same two people, though they may spend their entire lives together,
will never be able to explain just what it is that they hope to get from one another.

Surely it isn't the pleasure of sex alone that causes them to take such joy in being with each other. Each of us must desire something more, something which he can't put into words. Yet we all have a prophetic sense of what we want and express this wish some-

e   times in riddles. For instance, imagine if Hephaestus were to come with his bag of tools and stand over them as they lie there together. Hephaestus would ask:

"What is it you two mortals really want from one another?" They'd be stunned of course, and wouldn't know how to respond. So Hephaestus would continue:

"Is this what you want, to lie here together, day and night, and never be apart? For if that is your wish I can weld the two of you together, solder you into a single form.

191   Then for as long as you live you will share this one life together, and when you die you will be carried in a single bier to Hades. Consider well if this is your desire, if this is the fate you long for."

Can you imagine? Would anyone refuse? Could he wish for anything else? Who wouldn't realize that he'd finally been offered what he had long desired: for two to be joined forever into one, lover and beloved together in love? For long ago we were united and whole, but now we are lonely and incomplete. Love alone inspires in us that wild craving to come together and to restore our original state. Once upon a time we were united as one, but now, because of our misdeeds, we've been divided and scattered by the gods, just as the Arcadians were dispersed by the Spartans. And now we must go about always in fear that if we misbehave we could be cut in two once more. If that hap-

b   pens we'd appear in profile all the time, with our noses sliced down the middle, like

c   those figures in relief on tombstones and coins. Therefore we should urge all men to be obedient and deal piously with the gods and to keep Love forever as our guide and leader. If anyone opposes Love, he will be deemed an enemy of the gods. But if we become Love's friends he will help us find and love those youngsters who were truly meant for us, our own matching halves—a very rare achievement these days.

Now Eryximachus, I don't want you to think that I've been making fun of Pausanias

d   and Agathon all this time. Perhaps both of them do belong to that group which was once entirely male by nature. But never mind that. What I'm saying applies to everyone, men and women alike. The way for us all to find genuine happiness is to bring love to its most fitting conclusion, and we can do this, each of us, by finding the love of our lives and achieving a more perfect union. That, my friends, is the goal, and we must try to approach it as best we can. We must all try to win the favor of the boy who is our surest match.

And if we are to sing a hymn of praise to the god who can bestow this heavenly

e   gift, then we must sing a song of Love. For not only will Love grant us this great bless-ing, leading us to the person who will complement us today, but he promises us also the greatest of hopes for the future. For if we treat the gods with due reverence, Love may restore us to our original state and by healing all our wounds, he will make us blessed, whole and happy.

*   *   *

DIOTIMA AND SOCRATES

199ᵇ   SOCRATES: When I was a young boy I had a discussion with a woman named Diotima, a priestess from Mantinea. Diotima was famous for her expertise in all areas of Love, in addition to her many other accomplishments. She was the one who for ten years kept the plague from reaching the city of Athens simply by persuading our citizens to perform the proper rituals. This woman taught me all I know about Love, and if you wish, I could try and repeat for you the instruction she offered me many years ago. I'll start from the conclusions which Agathon and I have just reached together and then, if I can, I'll go on from there alone. The important thing, Agathon, is just as you explained before: first one must give a detailed account of the nature of Love before one turns to his good works and benefits. The best way for me to offer such an account will be to repeat the same set of questions which that wise old woman put to me long ago. And, as a matter of fact, Diotima had me acting out the same role which Agathon was playing just a moment ago with me. That's right, there I was stubbornly insisting to Diotima that Love was a handsome god, attracted to all sorts of beautiful things. But then, using the same arguments which I used just now with Agathon, Diotima compelled me to admit, by my own logic, that Love was neither beautiful nor good:

"Diotima, do you mean to tell me that Love is ugly and bad?"

"Bite your tongue, Socrates! How could you say such a thing? Is it because you think that anything which isn't beautiful must therefore be ugly?"

"Well, yes."

"Then you must also think that a simple lack of knowledge is the same as total ignorance, or have you never considered that there might be something in between the extremes of wisdom and ignorance?"

"What could that be?"

"Why, correct opinion, of course. Surely you've noticed how some people often have the right opinion about a certain matter but are unable to explain their opinion or justify it with an argument. They don't actually possess knowledge about the topic in question, because you must be able to explain anything that you truly know and understand. But you couldn't call it ignorance either, since total ignorance has nothing to do with the truth. Correct opinion, therefore, must stand somewhere in between complete knowledge and utter ignorance.

"That seems reasonable."

"Then stop insisting that everything which is 'not beautiful' must therefore be 'ugly,' or that everything which is 'not good' must therefore be 'bad.' And once you've conceded that Love is neither 'good' nor 'beautiful,' don't go thinking that he must therefore be 'bad' and 'ugly' The truth is he's somewhere in between these two extremes."

"Very well, Diotima, but everyone agrees that he's a most magnificent god."

"Who says that? Do you mean the scholars, or are you counting non-experts as well?"

"I mean everyone, absolutely everyone."

"But Socrates, how could the very people who deny he's a god at all say that he's a 'magnificent' one?"

"Who do you mean by that?"

"You for one, and I'm another."

"But Diotima, that's blasphemy. How could you?"

"Very easily. Don't you believe that all of the gods are beautiful and happy, or are you one of those who deny it?"

"Not I, Diotima, certainly not I."

"And someone is happy when he happens to possess good and beautiful things?"

"Indeed."

"And yet just a minute ago you agreed with me when I said that Love desires good and beautiful things because he lacks and does not possess them."

"I did, didn't I."

"Then how could Love be a god, yet not possess anything good or beautiful?"

200   "Then I suppose he can't be a god after all."

"So you admit it, Socrates. You too are one of those who deny that Love is a god."

"But if he's not a god, what is he? A mortal?"

"Of course not, Socrates."

"Then what? What else could he be?"

"He is somewhere in between the two, just as we were saying earlier. He stands in
b   the middle, between mortals and immortals."

"Then he is . . . "

"A great spirit, Socrates. He is a spirit of the threshold, one of those who shuttle
between men and gods."

"But what do these spirits do?"

"They work as messengers and translators, moving between human beings and
the immortal gods. They carry our prayers and sacrifices up to the heavens and fetch
down the replies and commands of the gods. They fill up the space between heaven and
earth and help bind the whole universe together, enabling gods and men to connect.
They also assist in the art of prophecy and work with priests to perform sacrifices and
rituals, singing magical songs and incantations. Since there is normally little hope of
c   even the slightest association between gods and mortals, we depend upon these spiritual
intermediaries quite a bit. In fact, the only communication between us and the immortals, whether in dreams or awake, is made possible by these go-between spirits. And if
anyone acquires any real expertise in this area, he tends to develop a very spiritual disposition, while skill in nearly all of the other professions renders a man coarse and
materialistic. There are many such spirits, Socrates, and of all different sorts. Love is
just one of them."

"But who were his parents?"

"Now that's a long story, Socrates, but if you insist:

d   "Once upon a time all of the gods were invited to Zeus' mansion to celebrate the
birth of Aphrodite. One of the guests was Wherewithal, the handsome young son of the
goddess Wit. Also in attendance at the gala was the goddess Want, a rather needy divine
who was in the habit of arriving long after the meal had been served in order to scav-
enge for leftovers at the rear of the mansion. Now, during the party Wherewithal
became quite drunk on nectar (they hadn't discovered wine yet), and staggered outside
into Zeus' extensive gardens where he collapsed dead asleep. When Want, peering into
the garden in search of a scrap of food, caught sight of the handsome Wherewithal lying
there asleep, she suddenly felt impelled by her general lack of resources to lay down
e   beside him and conceive of Love. And that, Socrates, is the reason why Love, the god,
is Aphrodite's servant and is always by her side, for he was conceived on her first birth-
day. It also explains why Love is constantly drawn to beautiful things, for Aphrodite is
the very essence of beauty.

"Therefore, a direct descendant of both Wherewithal and Want, Love has not fallen
far from the tree. His mother's son, he is ever wanting and, although some may find this
hard to believe, he is not the least bit delicate or handsome. On the contrary, he is a vagrant
with tough, parched skin. He is always barefoot and homeless, sleeping under a roof of
sky or in the doorways of strangers. Sometimes you can hear him snoring in ditches by the
side of the road. In all this he takes after his poor mother and is always in need.

"From Wherewithal, his father, Love gets his cleverness and ingenuity and a passion for everything beautiful or good. He is a genius at magic and an expert in the use of

Amor and Psyche, a Roman copy ca 150 B.C. after a Greek statue. Caught in a tender embrace, the two youthful figures. Eros and Psyche, symbolize both love and the human soul. While his friends describe Eros as a young, beautiful god (as this statue depicts), Socrates presents a very different picture. *(Musei Capitolini, Rome, Italy. Alinari/Art Resource, N.Y.)*

words and herbs. He has a notorious reputation as a daring and ferocious hunter and is always devising clever snares for us. Endlessly resourceful, he is constantly on the trail of truth and wisdom.

"By nature he is neither mortal nor god but drifts continuously between the two. On some days he blooms like a plant and is in full flower, only to wilt and die that very evening. But straightaway he revives, thanks to his father's influence. Now and then he'll come into some money, but it's always trickling away, so Love is never either completely with or without resources. Moreover, he has a middling intellect, possessing neither divine omniscience nor untrammeled ignorance. The reason is that gods and those few men whom we consider to be truly wise never feel any love or desire for wisdom since they already possess it. And the same holds true for the ignorant: they too have no desire for wisdom, but in their case it is due to their willingness to remain just as dumb as the day they started. This golden rule always applies: if someone doesn't think he needs something, he will not want it, since he cannot want what he doesn't think he needs. Do you understand?"

201

"But, Diotima, who are the people who actually do become lovers of wisdom, or philosophers, if it's neither the wise nor the ignorant?"

"Isn't it obvious by now, Socrates, that those who love wisdom are not wise or ignorant but the ones in between, like Love himself. In addition, the young god Love loves wisdom because wisdom and knowledge are the most beautiful things we know of, and Love is always drawn to beauty. It follows that Love must be a lover of wisdom and that all lovers of wisdom, that is, all philosophers, like Love himself, are somewhere in between total ignorance and complete omniscience. The cause of his generally in-between state lies in Love's parents: his father, you recall, was wise and resourceful, while his mother, well, his mother was not.

b

"That, in general, is the nature of the spirit we call Love. It doesn't surprise me that you mistook him earlier, Socrates, judging by what you told me before. For you thought that Love always played the role of the beloved, the object of love, rather than the pursuing lover. That's why he struck you as being necessarily quite handsome, since any boy who kindles one's desire must of course be very beautiful and delicate and so on. But the truth is that Love, like most lovers, has a very different appearance, as I've just shown."

c

"All right Diotima, I can accept that. But if you're right, what does he do for us? Love, I mean."

"That's your next lesson. So far we have gone over the origin and nature of Love, but he is also, according to you at least, a lover of beautiful things. What would we say then to someone who asked 'why does Love desire beautiful things,' or, more simply, 'when a lover desires beautiful things, what exactly does he desire?'"

"He desires to have them for himself."

"Yes, Socrates, but your answer longs for another question. Try this: 'what exactly will the lover get once he possesses the beautiful things which he desires?'"

d

"I have no ready answer for that."

"Then let's change the question. Put 'good things' in place of 'beautiful things.' A lover of good things, what exactly does he desire?"

"He wants to have them for himself."

"And what will he have once the good things which he desires are his?"

"That's easy. He'll be happy."

"So people are happy when they happen to possess good things; and there is surely no need to go any further and ask why anyone would want to be happy. So your answer is final."

"That's right."

"And this desire for happiness, this love, do you think it's universal, does everyone want to have good things and to have them forever?"

"By all means, we all want this."

"But if everyone loves the same good things, why don't we call everyone lovers? As it is we say that only certain people are in love, while most others are not."

"I wonder about that myself, Diotima."

"Well, there's really nothing to wonder about. The fact is we always tend to single out one particular kind of love, the sexual kind, and designate it by the word which really belongs to the whole range of passionate activities associated with love. Then we are forced to employ other terms to describe all of our other passions."

"Like what, for instance?"

"Well, like this. Take the word 'art.' It's a very broad term which covers all forms of creating some special work which had no existence before that. We use the word 'art' to describe all such creative works and we call the people who create these works 'artists.'"

"That's correct."

"But we have so impoverished the meaning of the word 'artist' that today we usually apply this title only to those who work in a single art form, the art of painting, which deals with color and line. But in fact, anyone who creates any work of art is really an 'artist' though only one group today is given the name 'artist,' a word which ought really to apply to any creative person, regardless of the medium in which he works."

"True."

"The same goes for Love. The love and desire to be happy, which we all share, is everyone's first and most demanding god. This universal passion for happiness, in the most general sense, is what Love embodies. Yet we all feel and express this passion in different ways. Some feel it, for instance, when they do business and make money, others by playing sports, and still others through philosophy. Yet it would sound strange if you said that such people are actually in love or if you called them lovers, which in actual fact they are. For it's only when people devote themselves to one kind of love, sexual love, that we make use of the words 'love,' and 'lover,' words which really ought to belong to the whole spectrum of human action."

"I'm beginning to see your point."

"Good. But there's something else, a theory which argues that all lovers are constantly searching for their missing half, an idea which seems to me dead wrong. For true love is no search for any half or any whole unless that half or whole happens to be good for its own sake. In fact, most people are ready to amputate their arms and legs if they are informed that these parts are somehow bad or diseased. I say that the only people who are truly in love are those who acknowledge something to be good for themselves and who then embrace it and hold it tight. In other words, the only thing that men really love is what's good for them. Do you agree?"

"Definitely."

"So it's simply this, that all men love what is good."

"Yes."

"And loving the good, they want to possess it for themselves."

"Yes, that too."

"And to possess it forever."

"Yes."

"Then our conclusion so far is that Love is each person's desire to acquire the good for himself, and to possess it forever."

"That's correct."

"Good. Now that we've defined love's object, we need to ask how people pursue their objective if they really are in love? How do they exercise this passionate desire which they call love? What is Love's aim and what does it accomplish?"

203   "Indeed, Diotima, that's just what I've come here to learn, and so far you have astonished me by your expertise in the matter."

"I'll tell you then. The aim of Love is to give birth in beauty, in both body and soul."

"To give birth? Come now, Diotima, I'll need a prophet to divine what you mean."

"Then I will try to speak more plainly. You see, Socrates, all human beings are
b   pregnant or fertile in body and soul, and when we reach a certain age it's only natural that we desire to give birth and have children. Now there is something divine about the whole process of human creation, and this is true even of the mere physical exchange between a man and a woman which, as some argue, may be considered a kind of birth. And birth itself by passing on a man's name, can impart a certain immortality to a human being. Therefore, although the body is surely mortal, there is something godlike in both the act of conception and in giving birth as well.

"Technically, however, it is impossible for the soul to conceive in the presence of anything ugly. Ugliness, after all, is totally out of tune with the numinous, and in this
c   divine rite there can be no threat of discord. Beauty, on the other hand, is very much in harmony with the divine. In fact, it is the beauty of any single individual which attracts the lover to begin with, thus enabling conception and birth to go on. Therefore, instead of those other gods, Moira and Eilethuia, who normally preside over childbirth, the goddess Beauty must take her stand in their place.

"Because of this, whenever the lover, pregnant or potent with desire, approaches any beautiful body he begins to relax and in a shudder of delight, spills over with his potency and conceives. On the other hand, should the lover meet with an unattractive specimen he will turn away in disgust, shrivel up and shrink back in pain. In this case,
d   needless to say, impregnation will not occur. In fact, the man may even suffer some discomfort from having to go on bearing the burden of his potency. But later on, if he should only chance upon a beautiful physique, he will experience a sudden fluttering within and achieve the most glorious relief from the pangs of his swollen and congested potency. As you can see, Socrates, Love is not interested in beauty alone."

"What then?"

"Love is interested in conception and birth in beauty."

"I suppose."

"No, Socrates, this much is certain, though maybe you are wondering what all this has to do with giving birth? The point is that birth and reproduction bring us as
e   close as we ever get to godhead. That is, by forever reproducing ourselves generation after generation, we seem to go on forever, as if we were actually immortal. And, given our earlier conclusion, you remember, that love is the desire which each of us has for the permanent possession of the good, it follows that we must all desire permanence, or immortality, along with goodness. Love, then, is really the desire we all have to live forever and be immortal."

All of this was taught to me by Diotima when she lectured on Love. Then one day she asked me:

204   "Socrates, what do you think is the cause of Love and desire? Haven't you ever noticed how animals often make the wildest noises and go into such a tormented state when the desire to reproduce seizes hold of them. Birds and beasts become sick with the yearning to mate, and then they seem so terribly driven to nurture and protect their

young. In fact, for the sake of their children the weakest animals are ready to battle the strongest, and sometimes they do damage to their own health, starving themselves to feed their brood. Perhaps humans do this because we understand the benefits involved, but what could cause animals and birds to behave in such a fashion? Why are they so strangely affected by Love?"

b

"I have no idea."

"Now Socrates, how can you ever hope to become an expert on the subject if you can't even begin to answer that?"

"But that's why I'm here in the first place, Diotima, because I know that I lack the right teachers. Please go on. Explain to me what causes this and anything else that has to do with Love."

c

"Well, if you remain convinced by our previous argument, that the object and end of love is immortality, then the answer is simple, for the same theory applies to animals as well as humans. Our mortal nature seeks, as best it can, to live forever and never die. The only way to achieve this is through birth, by endlessly replacing the old, dying generation with a new and lasting one. For all mortal things, Socrates, are forever coming and going, passing on and being replaced. And though every human being may be said to remain the same person from infancy to old age, nevertheless each is undergoing constant alteration, for he is continuously suffering both the ravages and revisions of time. All kinds of decay and renewal take place in his skin, his hair, his bones and blood, in his whole body for that matter, and not only in his body, but in his soul, too. His thoughts and ways and beliefs, his pleasures, pains, and fears, nothing remains the same. New elements are always appearing as old ones disappear.

"And you could say the same of our intelligence. One day we learn something new and the next day we forget it. And not only does this apply to knowledge itself, but each single scintilla of wit in our heads is forever coming and going. In fact, when we study, what we are trying to do is replenish information which has somehow disappeared. For knowledge leaks out in a process called forgetting and must continually be reacquired by means of study, which replaces whatever was lost with a fresh memory of it. When the knowledge which was displaced has been replaced by drill and repetition, it seems as if nothing has changed, since the new knowledge looks just like the old. Only by such constant discipline do our minds manage to retain anything at all.

d

"This is the way all fleeting, mortal things are preserved and maintained. For no man could remain the same forever. Only the gods can do that. Therefore, every so often we must take what is aged and worn out and replace it with something new, yet something which resembles whatever has passed away. By this process, and only by this process, can ephemeral mortality share in the eternity of the gods, in body and mind and everything else. So don't be surprised when you see how we all instinctively place such great value on our children. For the love and care which all parents show toward their offspring is just an expression of this all-consuming desire for immortality."

e

"Well, I suppose you're right, Diotima, I mean, you're the expert. But can this really be the way it is?"

Then, like a consummate sophist she said:

205

"Trust me, Socrates. If you have any doubts, just consider the way men pursue honor. All of that wild activity would seem utterly pointless if you didn't keep in mind that man's pursuit of immortality is a matter of life and death. Look at the extraordinary behavior of all those who've tried to make a name for themselves, hoping to win endless and undying glory. For such a prize most people would risk dangers greater than they would for their own children. No sum of money would be too large, no labors too trying.

Even death itself would not be too high a price to pay for such repute. Come now, surely you don't think that Alcestis would have sacrificed herself to save Admetus, that Achilles would have died to avenge Patroclus' murder, or that your own Kodros would have given up his life and throne, if each of them hadn't felt certain that, by their actions, they would go down in history, as in fact they have, as immortal examples of courage and virtue? Of course not. Every hero begins his labors with the hope, one day, of winning lasting glory

b   and undying repute. And the more heroic they are, the more impressive their labors. Doesn't that begin to suggest to you how large and universal is the desire we all have for immortality?

"Now, getting back to our earlier discussion. Any man whose potency is strictly physical will probably confine himself to the pursuit of women and will express his love in that activity alone. He'll find a mate and fall in love in the hope of acquiring, through his children, undying repute and happiness. He will seek glory in the name that will be carried on by his descendants to the very end of time, or so he hopes. However, those

c   who are potent in their souls, and there are some who have greater mental than physical potency, will one day become pregnant with what the soul eventually conceives and gives birth to. And what is that, you ask? Wisdom and all the rest of the virtues, which the poets have begotten, along with all those artists who are true creators. But the finest creation, the most important kind of wisdom, is that which concerns the proper managing of both cities and households: good judgment and a sense of right.

"Now then, when anyone, from his early youth, has been potent with these virtues in his soul, a bachelor I mean, when this young man reaches the age where he yearns to be a father and to have his own children, he must seek out a beautiful body in which to give birth, since he would never father a child on any ugly mate. Being full of seed, he will find himself irresistibly drawn to physical beauty, never to its opposite, and he will be even more delighted if he should find that the body which he decides on has a soul which is also beautiful and noble and gifted. At this point he will gladly embrace this

d   lovely combination of mind and body. Indeed, the mere sight of such a boy should fill him with ideas and eloquence on the subject of virtue, on what a good man is like and on how one may become so, and soon he will begin to teach the youngster all he knows.

"After having chosen his partner, the older lover will conceive and give birth to all of the virtuous ideas and stories which he had been pregnant with for so long. Then, after the birth, and whenever his beloved is away, he will recall and cherish his precious progeny, the conversations they had together. But when the two of them are together, they will share the labor of raising their brood of thoughts. These couples tend to have a much closer relation to such spiritual offspring than we do with our own human children. Moreover, the bond of affection between the parents themselves tends to be much stronger than ours because the children which they've produced and share are more beautiful and immortal than our own. Given the choice, we would all rather produce

e   offspring of this sort than the merely physical kind. Why, just look at how we envy those great poets, Homer and Hesiod. How we admire their spiritual creations, the noble children they've left behind. Such children, being immortal themselves, bring their parents endless glory and perpetual repute. Consider Lykourgos and his Spartan offspring, those laws which, when the Persians invaded our borders, saved not only Sparta but virtually all of Greece. Then there's your own Solon who won such esteem in Athens for giving birth to the laws there. And there are countless other examples in Greece and abroad of those who have engendered every kind of virtue by giving birth to so many beautiful works and ideas. Many of these men are honored to this day and some are even worshiped in sanctuaries because of their immortal progeny. Surely no father of merely human offspring could claim such honors.

"Now it is here, Socrates, that we must decide whether you are to continue on your journey into the mysteries of Love. For I'm still not sure if you're ready for the final revelation, the goal for which all of this discussion has been a mere preview. Nevertheless, I will conduct you further and offer you every support. Try to follow me as best you can.

206

"To proceed in the correct way one must start at an early age, learning while still a boy to admire every sort of physical beauty. The initiate must first be encouraged, under the proper guidance, to fall in love with a single beautiful person and in such company to give birth to fine ideas and conversation. Soon, however, he must come to realize that the beauty of this one body is brother to the beauty of any other, and in time he will realize that, as far as physical beauty is concerned, the beauty inherent in all the world's beautiful bodies is really one and the same. As soon as this is understood, the initiate will become a lover of all beautiful bodies without distinction, and his obsessive attraction to any single boy should begin to diminish and will soon seem trivial.

b

"At this point the lover must begin to transfer his love of beauty from the body to the soul. He must learn to value mental beauty so highly that, even if his young partner happens to be quite ugly, so long as he has a beautiful mind, that should be enough to kindle his feelings of love and incline him to cherish the boy and to try and give birth in his company to the sort of rich conversation which improves a young man. If he does this correctly our lover may then proceed to the next level, where he will glimpse the beauty of many different laws and customs. And in time he will see, even here, that the beauty inherent in all of these different institutions is really one and the same. At this point he will have come to regard physical beauty as truly unimportant.

c

"The next stage will take the initiate from the study of law and ethics to the various branches of the sciences. Here he will learn of the beauty of knowledge itself and he will see before his eyes not just a single instance of beauty, but beauty abounding. He would have to be terribly immature if, at this stage, he were still obsessed or attracted by the beauty of just one boy or the goodness of any one law. For here the lover will turn, in his boundless love of wisdom, to gaze upon the vast ocean of beauty and, intent on this, he will give birth to countless beautiful ideas and speeches. Then, after he has been restored and strengthened by this sight he will be ready to contemplate a most singular kind of knowledge, the knowledge of such Beauty that . . .

d

"Now here, Socrates, you must try as hard as you can to stay with me:

e

"A man who has been led this far into the mysteries of love, who has contemplated, step by step, all of the different kinds of beauty in the proper ascending order, as he reaches the end of his journey, approaching the true goal of Love, he will now see a truly wonderful sight: a vision of the very nature and Form of the Beautiful. And it will be eternal and infinite, not something that is born and dies or waxes and wanes, but whole and independent. Not something beautiful in this way but ugly in that, or beautiful at one time but ugly at another, or beautiful to one man but not to another. During this vision, Beauty will not appear to him as a face or a hand or any other part of the human body. It will not appear as any single argument or branch of knowledge. It will not appear as any being we know on earth or in heaven. What he will see is Beauty, in itself and by itself, alone, endless and whole. And only then will he understand how all beautiful things derive their beauty from this alone, and that while all beautiful things may come and go and change, this Beauty will neither grow nor diminish nor suffer any change, but will remain always one and the same.

207

"Anyone who starts by loving boys in the proper way and later tries to catch sight of this singular Beauty is already within striking distance of the goal. The steps by which the lover must proceed, either alone or with guidance, are these: First, begin with the

b

beauty you can see in someone's body and fall in love with that. Then, as if you were climbing the steps of a ladder, continue one rung up and there you will fall in love with physical beauty in general. Take another step up and you will reach the beauty of law and custom and from there it is just one more rung to reach the beauty of the different branches of knowledge. Then, finally, ascend to the very top of the ladder, to the recog-

c nition and study of that ultimate knowledge which is the knowledge of Beauty itself.

"What else could make life truly worthwhile, Socrates, if not the constant gazing upon and relishing of such a sight? Glimpse it once and all of those things which once seemed beautiful to you, gold and fancy clothing and handsome boys, they will all seem utterly meaningless. As it stands now, when you and so many others see a beautiful boy a subtle fire suddenly goes racing through your limbs and you try to hunt the lad down. You would gladly go without food and drink if you could survive off the sight of this boy alone. But just try to imagine if instead you could actually see Beauty itself, per-fect, pure, undilute Beauty, untainted by human flesh or color or any other mortal non-sense, just Beauty itself, singular and divine. Don't you think that such a life would be

d the only one truly worth living? A lifetime spent gazing upon beauty in the mind's eye

e and being there with it. Remember that it is only there, in the mind, looking at the Beautiful in the only way it can truly be seen that one may give birth not to images or copies of virtue, but to true virtue, virtue itself, since one is actually there, in touch with Beauty and Truth itself. The man who could give birth to and nourish true virtue in this way would certainly be dear to the gods. If anyone could reach immortal godhead, Socrates, he would be the one."

"And that," said Socrates, "was what Diotima taught me and what I try to teach others. I am convinced that there is no better ally than Love for those who want life immortal. Therefore I myself revere and practice keenly all that has to do with Love, and I counsel everyone I know to do the same. That's why I offer the highest praise I can muster, today and every day, to the power and daring of Love. You may take this for my eulogy of the god, Phaedrus, or call it whatever you like."

ALCIBIADES' ENTRANCE

The applause began as soon as Socrates had finished speaking. Aristophanes alone held back, struggling amid the noise to answer Socrates' criticism of his earlier remarks.

208 The celebration came to a sudden halt, however, with a loud banging at the outer door and the high-pitched voice of a flute-girl wafting above a noisy, drunken crowd.

"Go and see who it is," said Agathon to one of his servants. "If he's a friend, you may invite him in. If not, tell him we are through with the drinking and that the party is over."

Moments later the voice of Alcibiades was echoing in the hallway. He was obvi-

b ously drunk, crying out like a bull: "Where's Agathon, I want Agathon."

c A throng of admirers guided Alcibiades inside. Suddenly there he was, framed in the doorway, crowned with a leafy garland of violets and ivy, over-topped by a wreath of ribbons in his hair.

"G-Good evening, gentlemen," Alcibiades began. "How about letting a real drinker join the party, or should I just crown Agathon with these ribbons and leave? That's my only reason for coming, you know. I couldn't yesterday, but now I'm here to hand over these ribbons, to transfer them, from my own head, to the head, I don't mind saying it, of the cleverest, most handsome young man in Athens. What's this? You're laughing at me? You think I'm drunk, don't you! Well, go ahead and laugh. I know it's the truth at least. So what do you say? Can I join you on these terms? Who'll down a cup with me?"

Everyone shouted for him to come in, especially Agathon, who beckoned him over to his couch. As his troops carried him in, Alcibiades drunkenly began to unwind the ribbons from his hair. With all the colors dangling before his eyes, he hadn't noticed Socrates, who'd moved to the other side of Agathon's couch during the ruckus. Alcibiades stumbled toward the two of them and fell onto the couch. He embraced Agathon, then affectionately began to decorate the playwright's head with the ribbons.

"Pull off his sandals so he can lie here with the two of us," Agathon announced to his servants.

"Lovely," Alcibiades smiled, "but who's our third?" And as he spoke he twisted round to look. When he saw it was Socrates he sprang to his feet, crying out:

"Heracles, what's this? How long have you been hiding there? You're always angling for a surprise attack, turning up when and where I least expect you! What do you want from me now? I suppose you tried to avoid sitting by Aristophanes or some other comedian, and in that mysterious way of yours you manage to end up next to the most beautiful man in the room!"

"Please, Agathon," Socrates cried out, "you must help me. This young man's attentions have gotten to be quite a problem. Ever since we fell in together I haven't been free to look at or speak to another soul, and if I do he burns with jealousy. He starts to scream and barely keeps his hands to himself. I'm afraid he'll explode again tonight. Please, Agathon, try to settle things between us, and if he gets violent, you'll have to protect me. I'm terrified by this turbulent passion he seems to have conceived for me. "

"There'll be no truce here, Agathon," grumbled Alcibiades. "I'll get my revenge for this another time. But you'll have to give me back some of those ribbons. Now I have to give some to Socrates. I must crown that extraordinary head or else he'll scold me for giving you this garland on only your first victory when I've never yet offered one to him, even though he's won every speaking contest there is." Alcibiades retrieved some of the ribbons, arranged them gently around Socrates' head, and lay back down.

From there he spoke again: "My friends, you look too sober! You're miles behind me in drink and until you catch up, I elect myself Commissioner of Wine. Bring me the largest cup you've got. No, wait! You there, bring me that contraption on the floor." Alcibiades saw a pitcher which could hold about half a gallon of wine. He had them fill it to the rim, then he drank it down, immediately signaling them to fill it again for Socrates.

"I know my tactics are useless against him," Alcibiades admitted to them all. "Even if he swallowed as much as you asked, Socrates never appears drunk."

The servant filled the pot with wine and Socrates emptied it.

Then Eryximachus interrupted: "Will someone please explain what is going on here? Alcibiades, are we to have no toast or song to accompany the drinking? Are we simply to drink without decorum like the thirsty rabble?"

"O Eryximachus, noblest son of the soberest sire, good evening," Alcibiades sang.

"Yes, yes," muttered Eryximachus. "But with what method are we to proceed?"

"With whatever method you prescribe, Eryximachus, for by all means we must follow your advice. After all, as Homer says, *A doctor's worth a thousand men.*"

"Then listen to this idea, Alcibiades," Eryximachus began. "We all agreed, before you arrived, that each of us, couch by couch, would compose the finest speech he could in praise of Love. You alone are left, and since you've drained your cup, it's time you gave thanks to the god. After you finish you may propose a topic for Socrates, there on your right, then he may do the same for his neighbor, and so on as we circle the room."

e   "A fine idea, Eryximachus," answered Alcibiades, "but do you really think it's fair to set the babbling of a drunk alongside your sober disquisitions? And besides, Socrates is the real problem. I mean, I certainly hope you didn't believe a word he just said about me, did you? Why it's just the reverse. He's the one who gives me a beating whenever I praise anyone other than him, god or man."

"Hold your tongue!" Socrates cried out.

"Damn it, I speak the truth," Alcibiades insisted. "I'm never allowed to praise anyone else when you're around."

210   "Well then," Eryximachus reasoned, "if that's the case, why don't you make a speech in praise of Socrates."

"Really?" asked Alcibiades, looking tempted. "Should I? Should I just lay into the man and get my revenge right here in front of everyone?"

"Now wait a minute," Socrates interrupted, "just what do you have in mind? You want to praise me and mock me at the same time?

b   "I'll tell only the truth," Alcibiades answered, "if you'll allow it."

"If it's the truth you'll tell," Socrates parried, "not only do I allow it, I urge you to continue."

"Right away," said Alcibiades. "But make me one promise. If I say anything that's not true I want you to stop me right there and point it out. I don't want anyone to think I'm creating some fiction. However, if I don't get everything down in the order it hap-

c   pened, don't be surprised. It would be quite a task for anyone, especially someone in my condition, to number up a fluent and orderly account of all your outlandish ways."

ALCIBIADES' SPEECH

Now, gentlemen, let me begin my hymn to Socrates with a comparison we'll all recognize. He'll complain that I'm just mocking him, but I'm not trying to be funny here: I want the truth. I say that Socrates is the spitting image of those statues of Silenoi you see lying around the sculptors' workshops with a flute or a pan-pipe in their hands.

d   You all know the kind of work I mean: they're made of hollow plaster with a seam down the side. It's there that the two halves come apart, revealing the tiny statuettes of the gods hidden in their bellies. Otherwise he reminds me of the satyr Marsyas. No one could deny that you resemble these statues, you least of all, Socrates. But the resemblance isn't just skin deep.

You're also as wildly arrogant as those Satyrs, Socrates, are you not? If you want to dispute the charges I'll call my witnesses. But perhaps there is one difference between the two of you: Satyrs play the flute and Marsyas made use of an old reed pipe

e   to charm his listeners, the same instrument they use to play his songs today. And it was Marsyas, by the way, who taught Olympus all the songs he knew. Whether the finest musician or a wrinkled old flute-girl plays his melodies the effect is the same: the music charms the listener and makes clear which members of the audience are ready to receive the god and his mysteries. But Socrates is far more gifted than old Marsyas. For

211   Socrates can charm you without any musical instruments at all, just by his talk. Come now. I know that none of you here ever listens to a word of what our finest orators rant

on about. But if anyone listens to Socrates speak or hears even a third-hand report of what he says, you're immediately spellbound by the man's words. Is that not so?

In fact, if I told you what effect his words have on me, and I can feel it even as I speak, I'm sure you'd think I was thoroughly smashed. But it's true: as soon as he starts   b
in I feel like a wild man, a shivering, shaking corybant. My heart starts pounding and tears go streaming down my face. And I'm not alone in this. Sure, Pericles and the other orators have the finest skills, but they have never achieved the same effect. They don't start a chill at the base of my spine or make me resent my entire way of life. But this Marsyas here does it in every conversation we have. He leads me to think that my life,   c
as it is now, simply isn't worth living. You can't deny it, Socrates. In fact, I'm sure that if I gave him half the chance he'd perform for you all right here. His method is simple: he traps me, forcing me to admit that I ignore the things I need most while I busy myself with politics here in Athens. Whenever he begins a conversation I refuse to listen. I cake my ears with wax and run as if he were some Siren that could seize me and hold me till I was wrinkled and gray.

And yet only Socrates has ever made me feel something which all of you thought me incapable of: shame. That's right. Only when I'm with him do I ever feel ashamed, knowing that I can't refute the advice he offers me. But then, as soon as I'm out of his   d
sight, I slink back to my comfortable habits and give in to my craving to please the crowd. I flee like a runaway slave, and when I meet him later on in the street I redden with remorse for all the promises I made to him and broke. Sometimes I think I'd be happier if he were dead. Yet if he actually were to die I would probably be even more miserable than I am right now. I just don't know what to do with the man.

Such are the effects which this Satyr's music has on me and many others. Now   e
listen to several other ways in which he resembles a Satyr and you may begin to glimpse the extent of his powers. You'll realize that not one of you has really understood him until now. But, since I've begun, I may as well go on to uncover the rest of his secrets.

I suppose you all know that Socrates has a passion for handsome boys and is always following them around in a daze. You've probably also heard how he claims to be utterly ignorant, that he doesn't know a thing. Well, isn't that just like a Silenus, with his clay patina keeping those holy statuettes out of sight? But just try to imagine, my fellow drinkers, what a wise and temperate man lies beneath that superficial disguise? Believe me, he couldn't give a damn whether a boy is beautiful or rich or famous or any   212
of the things that most people care about. I tell you he has contempt for all of that, and he thinks that we ourselves are totally worthless. In public his whole life is one endless game of irony. In fact, I doubt whether any of you has ever caught him in his real state. But I did once, and it was then I got a look under that outer covering at those little stat-ues hidden inside, and they were golden and divine, radiant and beautiful and so amaz-   b
ing that I had no choice but to do whatever Socrates asked of me.

Now I was certain, at the time, that Socrates had fallen in love with me and I counted this a godsend. For I thought that merely by offering to satisfy any of Socrates' desires I would be able to learn all that he knew. I'm sure you all remember how confi-dent I used to be in my good looks. So I dismissed my attendant and arranged a date with Socrates. Here I have to confess the whole truth, so pay attention. And, Socrates, you stop me if I tell them anything that didn't actually happen.*

---

*Much of the comedy in this speech lies in the intentional inversion of the roles of lover and beloved. The gorgeous young Alcibiades is here shown chasing the unwashed Socrates around Athens. This reversal is part and parcel of the Socratic method itself, whereby Socrates can be both the lover or pursuer of the Athenian youth as well as the object of their longing, insofar as he embodies their youthful desire for knowledge.

So there we were, just the two of us, alone at last. I was sure that he would jump
c   at the chance to whisper all the things that lovers say when they're alone: I was so
excited. But it didn't turn out that way at all. Socrates just spoke to me in his usual tone
and left at the end of the day. The next time I decided to invite him to the gym. I thought
that after taking a fall or two together in the buff, things might really get going between
us. So we worked out and wrestled together a number of times with no one else in sight.
But once again, I couldn't get anywhere with him.

Finally, since nothing else had worked, I decided on a frontal attack. I was not
d   about to retreat so late in a battle which I'd begun. Besides, I wanted to know where
things stood between us. So I invited Socrates to my house for dinner, as if I, the young
Alcibiades, were chasing after this old man. And even then he played hard to get,
although he finally conceded and accepted the invitation. That first night he asked if he
could leave immediately after having finished his dinner and I was too embarrassed to
try and stop him. However, the next time we dined I had armed myself with a plan: I
started a conversation with him just after the meal and kept him talking late into the
e   night. This time, when he asked to leave I insisted, since it was so late, that he just spend
the night at my house. He thought about it for a moment, nodded assent and then lay
right down on the couch facing mine, where he'd eaten his dinner, and immediately fell
asleep. No one else was in the room.

Now, this much I could have told anyone, but I wouldn't say another word if, as
the saying goes, there were no truth in wine, whether the servants hear or not. And secondly, it just wouldn't be right to end my praise of Socrates without mentioning one of
his proudest accomplishments. But the problem is, well, it's like what they say about
snake-bite: you can only discuss it among people who have actually suffered it them-
213 selves, because they're the only ones who could understand the pain you felt or forgive
the horrible things you said and did. Well, it's something much stronger than a snake
that's bitten me, and he bit me in the most sensitive part, I mean my heart or my soul or
whatever we ought to call it. Yes, I've been pricked and stung by this man's philosophy,
and its fang-like grip on young and talented souls is much fiercer than any snake's,
causing us to do and say the most amazing things. All of you here: Phaedrus and
Agathon, Eryximachus, Aristodemus, Pausanias and Aristophanes. I leave Socrates out.
Every one of you has shared in this madness, this Dionysiac frenzy of philosophy, so
you alone can hear what followed. Only you could forgive me for what I did then and
for what I'm now about to say. But as for the servants and anyone who's too foolish or
b   immature for initiation into the mystery: close tight the doors of your ears.

So, gentlemen. The lights were out; the servants had left. "No more beating
around the bush," I thought. "I'll tell him straight out what I have in mind." So I shook
him gently and whispered, "Socrates, are you asleep?"

"No," he grumbled.

"Do you know what I think?"

"What is it?"

"I think you're the only worthwhile lover I've ever had, and yet look how shy you
c   are with me! Let me explain how I see the situation. I think it would be ridiculous of me
d   not to gratify any desire you might have. Please take me or my money or that of my
friends; anything at all. For my greatest hope is to become the best that I possibly can,
and only you can help me do that. Please Socrates, I'm not afraid. I'd be far more
ashamed of what one sensible person would say if I didn't take you as my lover than
what the whole city would say if I did."

When Socrates heard this he replied with his typical mock-modesty:

"My dear Alcibiades, You are hardly the beginner you claim to be if what you say about me is true. If this beauty you see in me really does have the power to make you a better man, then my beauty must be quite stupendous, one which makes your own fade in comparison. And if that's the case then I'd be trading gold for bronze, hardly a fair exchange. As I see it, you are behaving like a glutton, demanding more than your share, offering me the mere appearance of beauty in return for true beauty, the thing itself. But maybe you ought to reconsider, my gifted friend, for you could be wrong. I may be of no use to you at all. For as you well know, your mind's sight grows keen only when the sharpness of your eyes begins to wane, and you're still a long way from that."

Frustrated in this, my last attempt, I finally lost control: "That's the last straw, Socrates. I have nothing more to say. Now it's up to you to judge what's best for the both of us."

"Now there you're talking sense," he said smiling. "In the future we will consider things jointly and do whatever seems best for you and me together."

Hearing this I naively thought that I'd hit the target, that I'd wounded him with my shafts. I didn't want to allow him the chance to say another word so I got up, wrapped my cloak around him (it was winter then) slipped beneath it myself and wrapped my arms around this truly extraordinary, miraculous man. We spent the whole night lying there together just like that. Isn't that right, Socrates? But in spite of all my efforts, this insolent man turned me down, scorned my beauty, flouting the one thing which I truly prided myself on, gentlemen of the jury, since that is what you are in fact. You've been empanelled here to pass judgment upon Socrates' monstrous arrogance.

You've got to believe me. I swear by the gods and goddesses together: my night with Socrates was as chaste as if I'd spent it with my own father or older brother!

You can imagine how I felt the next morning. I was humiliated of course, but at the same time I couldn't help but admire his courage and self-control. I'd never dreamt of meeting a man so strong, with such self-restraint. How could I bring myself to hate him? On the contrary, I was sure that I couldn't go on without his company. But how could I entice him back? I knew that he was less vulnerable to money than Ajax was to a steel blade. The one way I could have snared him had already proven a failure. I was totally without hope, wandering around in the most abject misery which anyone has ever experienced.

Now all this had taken place some time before Athens' invasion of Potidaea, an expedition on which both Socrates and I served and where we were messmates together. While I was stationed there I noticed that no one in the army endured the hardships of the campaign better than Socrates, not even myself. For instance, when we got cut off in the bush, which happens often when you're in the field, no one stood up to hunger the way he did, and yet he was the only one who really enjoyed the food when we had any. And though he had no real interest in drinking, if we forced him to he would outdrink us all. And incredibly, no one ever managed to get him drunk, but we'll put him to the test again tonight.

In addition, he had an almost inhuman ability to resist the cold, and the winters up north can be abominable. I remember once there was a bitter frost which kept the whole camp indoors. We only went out if we were forced to, and then only after we had bundled ourselves in everything we could find, tying extra straps of leather and sheepskin around our boots. But Socrates went out in that frigid weather wearing the same old cloak he always wore, and in his bare feet he marched faster over the frozen ground than

e

214

b

c

the other soldiers did in their boots. Soon the men began to think that Socrates was try-
d   ing to ridicule them. He provoked quite a bit of controversy up in Potidaea.

In fact, *the hero's next great labor* occurred during the same campaign. One
morning at dawn Socrates began to dwell on some question. He walked outside to the
field to be alone and stood there trying to figure it out. When the answer didn't come he
e   didn't give up but kept right on standing there in the very same spot. By midday, word
had reached the other soldiers. They refused to believe that Socrates had been standing
motionless all day long, thinking. In the evening, after dinner, several recruits from
Ionia moved their bunks outside to sleep where it was cooler (it was summer now).
Their real motive, obviously, was to keep watch on Socrates, to see if he would go on
standing there all night. And sure enough, he stood in that same spot until dawn the next
215   day, and when the sun came up, Socrates greeted it with a prayer and walked away.

You should also keep in mind his conduct during the heat and press of battle. For
though I was the one who was decorated for bravery during that campaign it was
Socrates, alone of the whole battalion, who intervened to save my life. You see, I'd been
wounded in a skirmish when Socrates found me and refused to leave me behind, pulling
me from certain death and rescuing my shield as well. Now Socrates, you know that I
b   explained to everyone how the prize really belonged to you, so you can't blame me for
my conduct then or say that I'm lying now. It was the generals, looking to my reputation
in Athens, who insisted on giving me the citation. And, as a matter of fact, you were
even more avid for me to have it than they were.

Finally, there was the retreat from Delium.* Here I was in the cavalry with
Socrates marching under foot. Our troops had just begun to scatter in retreat when I
c   came upon Socrates and the general Laches. I called out to them both, urging them not
to give up hope. Socrates looked so much more composed than Laches that the whole
scene made me think of something Aristophanes once wrote: Socrates was walking
along just like he does here in Athens, swaggering and looking from side to side. He
was watching everyone, friend or foe, with the most extreme calm. It was clear, even
d   from a distance, that if any of the enemy approached him, they'd have a very tough fight
ahead. It was Socrates' noble bearing that day which saved both him and Laches, I'm
sure of it. For generally you try to keep a good distance between yourself and such res-
olute men in battle. It's the men who run haphazardly in retreat that you tend to pursue.

Now I could go on and on like this, but why not let this last point suffice.
Although it's true that Socrates shares some characteristics with other men, as a whole
he is utterly unique. He is like no one else, past or present, and that's the most extraordinary thing of all. For you could easily get some idea of what Achilles must have been
e   like by comparing him to Brasidas or some other great contemporary. Or you might
compare Nestor or Antenor or any great orator from myth to our own Pericles and, proceeding in this way, you could find a clear model or precedent for each one of us. But
not for him. Socrates is so strange, so different, he and his ideas are so unusual, that
wherever you may look you will find no one, living or dead, who even remotely resembles him. So you'd be wise to follow me in comparing him not to any other human
216   being, but placing him among Silenoi and Satyrs. And the same could be said about his
style of speaking.

---

*On its way back to Athens after setting up a garrison in the town of Delium in 424 B.C., the Athenian
army was attacked by a Boeotian force. The courageous manner in which Socrates met the assault is
described further in the dialogue called Laches.

I should have mentioned this at the beginning, how even his speeches and conversations are like those hollow statues of Silenoi. What I mean is, when you listen to his arguments, at first they seem totally ridiculous, since he's always using words as coarse as the skin of the most bestial Satyr. He is continually talking about pack-asses and blacksmiths and cobblers and tanners, and is constantly making the same old points in the same tired phrases. A fool or anyone who's simply unfamiliar with his peculiar style of interrogation would probably just laugh at his ideas. But if the student could only see these same ideas when they are lying open like those statuettes. That is, if he only looked beneath their surface, he'd begin to find that no other arguments make any sense. He'd see that no other conversations are so divine or so rich in images of virtue. Indeed, such conversations are of the most singular importance for anyone who has any hope of becoming a good man.

b

Well, gentlemen, that's all I have to say: My speech in praise of Socrates. There's some blame in it too, where I describe how rudely Socrates treated me—and not just me, but Charmides, too, and Euthydemus and many others. He deceives us all by making us think he is in love with us, when suddenly you realize that you're the one in love with him. So Agathon, consider yourself warned. Learn from our mistakes and be careful with Socrates. Don't wait too long and, like that fool in the proverb, learn your lesson only after you've suffered it.

c

A Seated Man at a Greek Symposium. Red-figure vase. 460–450 B.C. Today the term "symposium" usually means a scholarly meeting; in ancient Greece it meant a drinking party (as depicted on this vase—and in the dialogue). *(Catalogue No. 431545, Department of Anthropology, Smithsonian Institution)*

THE FINAL SCENE

d   When Alcibiades had finished everyone broke out in laughter at how candidly he'd spoken, for he seemed to be still quite fond of Socrates, who commented:

"I see you've sobered up by now, Alcibiades. Otherwise you would never have been able to wrap yourself about so cunningly, trying to conceal from us all the real motive of your speech. And then you go and put it at the end, as if it were some minor point! Come now, all night long you've been trying to rouse up a quarrel between Agathon and me because you think that I ought to love you and no one else. Meanwhile, Agathon here is to remain your prize and yours alone. But now your Satyro-Silenic e   game is over. Agathon my dear, let's keep him from victory. You and I must take special care not to let anyone set the two of us at odds."

"You know, Socrates," Agathon joined in "I do think you are right. And I take his lying down here in the middle of this couch as an obvious attempt to separate us two. But in this he will not succeed. I will come over there right now and lie down next to you."

217   "Please do," said Socrates. "There's room here on this side."

"By God, he's at it again," Alcibiades fumed. "He always has to outdo me. Socrates, you might at least allow me to share the man with you. Let's compromise: why not let Agathon lie here between the two of us."

"Impossible," Socrates pointed out. "Don't you see. You just finished praising me b   and now it's my turn to speak in praise of the man to my right. But if Agathon sits between us it will be his turn to praise me all over again before I get a chance to praise him just once. So leave him alone, you rascal. Don't begrudge the man my praise, for I want very much to speak on his behalf."

"I am very sorry, Alcibiades," Agathon chimed in. "But Socrates is right. I cannot remain in this seat any longer. I simply must change places so that I can hear Socrates c   speak in praise of me."

"There he goes again," Alcibiades moaned. "With Socrates around no one else has a chance with the handsome ones. Did you see how easily he convinced Agathon to join him?"

But just as Agathon was starting towards Socrates' couch, a great sea of revellers poured in through the front door which a departing guest had left standing open. The crowd filled the room with chatter and in the ensuing chaos all cups were filled and the drinking started again. When this happened, Eryximachus and Phaedrus got up to leave along with some others. Aristodemus, however, had fallen asleep and was unconscious for what must have been quite some time. At least that's what he had assumed, since the nights were always so long at that time of year. He woke with the cock-crow, just before d   dawn, and saw that everyone else had either fallen asleep or gone home. The only people still awake were Agathon, Aristophanes and Socrates. The three of them were drinking from an oversize jug of wine which they were passing from right to left. Socrates was evidently carrying on a discussion with the two poets, but Aristodemus couldn't remember the whole argument. He was still groggy, he told me, and had missed the beginning of the conversation. But he did say that the gist of it, or at least what Socrates was forcing the two poets to admit, was the idea that one and the same man must know how to compose both tragedy and comedy, and that a good tragic poet must, of necessity, be a good comic poet as well. Of course, they were both being led around to Socrates' point of view, but in the end they were too exhausted to stay awake. Aristophanes was the first one to go under, and a short time later, right around daybreak,

Agathon fell asleep as well. Once he'd put the two of them to bed, Socrates got to his feet and walked out the door with Aristodemus, as usual, following behind. From there Socrates made his way in the morning sun straight to the Lyceum to wash up. He then   218
spent the entire day as he would any other, and went home in the evening to rest.

REPUBLIC* (in part)

Characters
Socrates
Glaucon
Adeimantus
Cephalus
Polemarchus
Thrasymachus
Cleitophon
Scene—Cephalus' home at Pireus

BOOK I

*   *   *

SOCRATES: And when Thrasymachus many times, even while we were in the mid-   336^b
dle of our conversation, was making motions to take over the argument, he was prevented by those sitting by him, who wanted to hear the argument out. But when we
paused as I said this, he could no longer keep still, but having gathered himself to spring
like a wild animal, he launched himself at us as if to tear us to pieces. Both I and
Polemarchus were quaking in fear, and he, snarling into our midst, said: "What drivel   c
are you people full of now, Socrates? And why do you act like idiots kowtowing to each
other? But if you truly want to know what's just, don't merely ask and then, as befits

---

*The only speaker in the dialogue is Socrates. He begins recounting a conversation he had on the occasion of a foreign religious festival that took place just outside Athens. Between the day and night portions of the festivities, a group of young men latches on to Socrates, who could be expected to provide entertaining talk. Polemarchus takes the group to his house, where they meet his father Cephalus, a very old man preoccupied with making amends before his death for any injustices in his life. Socrates asks him what he understands justice to be and begins to examine the implications of his answer. [We pick up the conversation as Thrasymachus, a well-known sophist, breaks in to the conversation.]

Plato, *Republic* (Book I, 336b–349b, 350d–354b; Book II, 357a–362c, 368e–376e; Book III, 386b–d, 387b–388e, 412b–417b; Book IV, 427c–445e; Book V, Complete: 449–480a; Book VI–VII, 502c–521b; Book VIII, 562a–563e), translated by Joe Sachs (Newburyport, MA: Focus Philosophical Library, 2007). Reprinted by permission of Focus Publishing/R. Pullins Company.

someone with a passion for honor, cross-examine whenever anybody answers, knowing that it's easier to ask than to answer, but also answer yourself and tell what you claim

d   the just thing is. And don't give me any of that about how it's the needful or the beneficial or the profitable or the gainful or the advantageous, but tell me clearly and precisely what you mean, since I won't stand for it if you talk in such empty words."

And I was flabbergasted when I heard this, and was afraid as I looked at him, and it seemed to me that if I had not seen him before he saw me I would have been struck dumb.* But as it was, just as he was beginning to be driven wild by the argument I

e   looked at him first, and so I was able to answer him, and said, trembling a little, "Don't be rough on us, Thrasymachus. If we're mistaken in any point in the examination of the argument, I and this fellow here, you can be assured that we're going astray unwillingly. For don't even imagine, when, if we were looking for gold, we wouldn't be willing to kowtow to each other in the search and ruin our chances of finding it, that when we're looking for justice, a thing more valuable than much gold, we'd be so senseless as to defer to each other and not be as serious as possible about bringing it to light. Don't so

337   much as imagine that, friend. But I imagine we don't have the power to find it. So it's much more fitting anyway for us to be pitied by you clever people instead of being roughed up."

And hearing this, he burst out laughing with great scorn and said "Oh Heracles, this is that routine irony of Socrates. I knew about this, and I kept telling these people before that you wouldn't be willing to answer, but you'd be ironic and do everything else but answer if anyone asked you anything."

"That's because you're wise, Thrasymachus," I said, "so you know very well that

b   if you asked anyone how much twelve is, and in asking demanded of him in advance, 'don't give me any of that, fellow, about how twelve is two times six or three times four or six times two or four times three, since I won't stand for such drivel from you,' it was clear to you, I imagine, that no one could answer someone who interrogated him that way. But if he said to you, 'Thrasymachus, how do you mean it? That I must give none of the answers you prohibited in advance? Not even, you strange fellow, if it happens to be one of these, but instead I have to say something other than the truth? Or how do you

c   mean it?' What would you say to him about that?"

"Oh sure," he said, "as if this was like that."

"Nothing prevents it," I said. "But then even if it isn't like it, but appears to be to someone who is asked such a question, do you imagine he'll any the less answer the question the way it appears to him, whether we forbid it or not?"

"So what else," he said; "are you going to do the same thing? Are you going to give any of those answers I banned?" "I wouldn't be surprised," I said, "if it seemed that way to me when I had examined it."

d   "Then what if I show you a different answer about justice," he said, "beyond all these, better than they are? What penalty would you think you deserve to suffer?"

"What other penalty," I said, "than the one it's fitting for someone who doesn't have knowledge to suffer? And it's fitting, no doubt, for him to learn from someone who has knowledge. So I think I too deserve to suffer this penalty."

"You're amusing," he said, "but in addition to learning, pay a penalty in money too."

"Okay, whenever I get any," I said.

"He's got it," said Glaucon. "So as far as money's concerned, Thrasymachus, speak up, since all of us will chip in for Socrates."

---

*[A popular superstition, that if a wolf sees you first, you become dumb.]

"I imagine you will," he said, "so Socrates can go on with his usual routine: he won't answer but when somebody else answers he'll grab hold of his statement and cross-examine him."

"Most skillful one," I said, "how could anyone give an answer who in the first place doesn't know and doesn't claim to know, and then too, even if he supposes something about these things, would be banned from saying what he believes by no inconsiderable man? So it's more like it for you to speak, since you do claim to know and to have something to say. So don't do anything else but gratify me by answering, and don't be grudging about teaching Glaucon here as well as the others."

And when I'd said these things, Glaucon and the others kept begging him not to do otherwise. And Thrasymachus was obviously longing to speak in order to be well thought of, believing that he had an answer of overwhelming beauty. But he made a pretense of battling eagerly for me to be the one that answered. But making an end of this, he gave way, and then said, "This is the wisdom of Socrates; he himself is not willing to teach, but he goes around learning from others and doesn't even pay them any gratitude."

"In saying that I learn from others," I said, "you tell the truth, Thrasymachus, but when you claim that I don't pay for it in full with gratitude, you lie, for I pay all that is in my power. I have the power only to show appreciation, since I don't have money. And how eagerly I do this, if anyone seems to me to speak well, you'll know very well right away when you answer, for I imagine you'll speak well."

"Then listen," he said. "I assert that what's just is nothing other than what's advantageous to the stronger. So why don't you show appreciation? But you won't be willing to."

"First I need to understand what you mean," I said, "since now I don't yet know. You claim that what's advantageous to the stronger is just. Now whatever do you mean by this, Thrasymachus? For I'm sure you're not saying this sort of thing: that if Polydamas the no-holdsbarred wrestler is stronger than we are, and bull's meat is advantageous to him for his body, this food would also be advantageous, and at the same time just, for us who are weaker than he is."

"You're nauseating, Socrates," he said, "and you grab hold of the statement in the way that you can do it the most damage."

"Not at all, most excellent man," I said, "just say more clearly what you mean."

"So you don't know," he said, "that some cities are run tyrannically, some democratically, and some aristocratically?"

"How could I not?"

"And so this prevails in strength in each city, the ruling part?"

"Certainly."

"And each ruling power sets up laws for the advantage of itself, a democracy setting up democratic ones, a tyranny tyrannical ones, and the others likewise. And having set them up, they declare that this, what's advantageous for them, is just for those who are ruled, and they chastise someone who transgresses it as a lawbreaker and a person doing injustice. So this, you most skillful one, is what I'm saying, that the same thing is just in all cities, what's advantageous to the established ruling power. And this surely prevails in strength, so the conclusion, for someone who reasons correctly, is that the same thing is just everywhere, what's advantageous to the stronger."

"Now," I said, "I understand what you mean. But whether it's true or not, I'll try to learn. So you too answer that the advantageous is just, Thrasymachus, even though you made a prohibition for me that I could not give this answer, though there is added to it 'for the stronger.' "

"A small addendum, no doubt," he said.

"It's not clear yet whether it's a big one. But it is clear that whether you're speaking the truth needs to be examined. For since you're saying and I'm agreeing that what's just is something advantageous, but you're making an addition and claiming it to be that of the stronger, while I don't know that, it needs to be examined."

"So examine it," he said.

"That will be done," I said. "Now tell me, do you not claim, though, that it's also just to obey the rulers?"

"I do."

c   "And are the rulers in each city infallible, or the sort of people who also make mistakes?"

"By all means," he said, "they're surely the sort of people who also make mistakes."

"So when they try to set up laws, they set up some correctly and certain others incorrectly?"

"I certainly imagine so."

"Then to set them up correctly is to set up laws that are advantageous to themselves, and incorrectly, disadvantageous ones? Or how do you mean it?"

"That's the way."

"But whatever they set up needs to be done by those who are ruled, and this is what is just?"

"How could it be otherwise?"

d   "Then according to your statement, not only is it just to do what's advantageous to the stronger, but also to do the opposite, what's disadvantageous."

"What do you mean?" he said.

"What you mean, it seems to me; but let's examine it better. Wasn't it agreed that when the rulers command those who are ruled to do certain things they're sometimes completely mistaken about what's best for themselves, but what the rulers command is just for those who are ruled to do? Wasn't this agreed?"

"I certainly imagine so," he said.

e   "Well then," I said, "imagine also that it was agreed by you that doing what's disadvantageous for those who rule and are stronger is just, whenever the rulers unwillingly command things that are bad for themselves, while you claim that for the others to do those things which they commanded is just. So then, most wise Thrasymachus, doesn't it turn out necessarily in exactly this way, that it's just to do the opposite of what you say? For what's disadvantageous to the stronger is without doubt commanded to the weaker to do."

340   "By Zeus, yes, Socrates," said Polemarchus, "most clearly so."

"If you're going to be a witness for him," Cleitophon interjected.

"And what need is there for a witness? Thrasymachus himself agrees that the rulers sometimes command things that are bad for themselves, and that for the others to do these things is just."

"That's because Thrasymachus set it down, Polemarchus, that doing what's ordered by the rulers is just."

"Because he also set it down, Cleitophon, that what's advantageous to the b   stronger is just. And having set down both these things, he agreed next that sometimes the stronger order things that are disadvantageous to themselves for those who are weaker and ruled to do. And from these agreements what's advantageous to the stronger would be no more just than what's disadvantageous."

"But," said Cleitophon, "he meant that the advantage of the stronger is what the stronger believes is advantageous to himself; this is what needs to be done by the weaker, and he set this down as what's just."

"But he didn't say it that way," said Polemarchus.

"It makes no difference, Polemarchus," I said, "but if Thrasymachus says it this way now, let's accept it this way from him. And tell me, Thrasymachus, was this what you wanted to say the just is, what seems to the stronger to be the advantage of the stronger, whether it might be advantageous or not? Shall we say you mean it that way?"

"That least of all," he said. "Do you imagine that I call someone who makes a mistake stronger when he's making a mistake?"

"I did imagine that you were saying that," I said, "when you agreed that the rulers are not infallible but are even completely mistaken about some things."

"That's because you're a liar who misrepresents things in arguments, Socrates. To start with, do you call someone who's completely mistaken about sick people a doctor on account of that very thing he's mistaken about? Or call someone skilled at arithmetic who makes a mistake in doing arithmetic, at the time when he's making it, on account of this mistake? I imagine instead that we talk that way in a manner of speaking, saying that the doctor made a mistake, or the one skilled at arithmetic made a mistake, or the grammarian. But I assume that each of these, to the extent that this is what we address him as, never makes a mistake, so that in precise speech, since you too are precise in speech, no skilled worker makes a mistake. For it's by being deficient in knowledge that the one who makes a mistake makes it, in respect to which he is not a skilled worker. So no one who's a skilled worker or wise or a ruler makes a mistake at the time when he is a ruler, though everyone would say that the doctor made a mistake or the ruler made a mistake. Take it then that I too was answering you just now in that sort of way. But the most precise way of speaking is exactly this, that the one who rules, to the extent that he is a ruler, does not make mistakes, and in not making a mistake he sets up what is best for himself, and this needs to be done by the one who is ruled. And so I say the very thing I've been saying from the beginning is just, to do what's advantageous to the stronger."

"Okay, Thrasymachus," I said. "I seem to you to misrepresent things by lying?"

"Very much so," he said.

"Because you imagine that I asked the question the way I did out of a plot to do you harm in the argument?"

"I know that very well," he said. "And it's not going to do you any good, because you couldn't do me any harm without it being noticed, and without being unnoticed you wouldn't have the power to do violence with the argument."

"I wouldn't even try, blessed one," I said. "But in order that this sort of thing doesn't happen to us again, distinguish the way you mean someone who rules and is stronger, whether it's the one who is so called or the one in precise speech whom you just now mentioned, for whose advantage, since he's stronger, it will be just for the weaker to act."

"The one who's a ruler in the most precise speech," he said. "Do harm to that and misrepresent it by lies if you have any power to—I ask for no mercy from you—but you won't be able to."

"Do you imagine," I said, "that I'm crazy enough to try to shave a lion or misrepresent Thrasymachus by lies?"

"You certainly tried just now," he said, "but you were a zero even at that."

"That's enough of this sort or thing," I said. "But tell me, the doctor in precise speech that you were just now talking about, is he a moneymaker or a healer of the sick? And speak about the one who is a doctor."

"A healer of the sick," he said.

"And what about a helmsman? Is the one who's a helmsman in the correct way a ruler of sailors or a sailor?"

d   "A ruler of sailors."

"I assume there's no need to take into account that he does sail in the ship, and no need for him to be called a sailor, since it's not on account of sailing that he's called a helmsman, but on account of his art and his ruling position among the sailors."

"That's true," he said.

"Then for each of the latter there's something advantageous?"

"Certainly."

"And isn't art by its nature for this," I said, "for seeking and providing what's advantageous in each case?"

"For that," he said.

"Then is there any advantage for each of the arts other than to be as complete as possible?"

e   "In what sense are you asking this?"

"In the same sense," I said, "as, if you were to ask me whether it's sufficient for a body to be a body or whether it needs something extra, I'd say 'Absolutely it needs something extra, and it's for that reason that the medical art has now been discovered, because a body is inadequate and isn't sufficient to itself to be the sort of thing it is. So it's for this reason, in order that it might provide the things that are advantageous for the body, that the art was devised.' Would I seem to you to be speaking correctly in saying this," I said, "or not?"

342   "It's correct," he said.

"What then? Is the medical art itself—or any other art—inadequate, and is it the case that it has need of some extra virtue? Just as eyes need sight and ears need hearing and for these reasons there is need of some art applied to them that will consider and provide what's advantageous for these things, is there then in the art itself some inadequacy in it too, and a need for each art to have another art that will consider what's advantageous for it, and for the one that will consider that to have another art in turn of

b   that kind, and this is unending? Or will it consider what's advantageous for itself? Or is there no additional need either for it or for any other art to consider what's advantageous for its inadequacy, because there is no inadequacy or mistake present in any art, nor is it appropriate for an art to look out for the advantage of anything other than that with which the art is concerned, but it itself is without defect and without impurity since it is correct as long as each is the whole precise art that it is. Consider it in that precise speech now: is that the way it is, or is it some other way?"

"That way," he said, "as it appears."

c   "So then," I said, "the medical art considers what's advantageous not for the medical art but for a body."

"Yes," he said.

"And horsemanship considers what's advantageous not for horsemanship but for horses, and neither does any other art consider what's advantageous for itself, since there's no extra need for that, but for that with which the art is concerned."

"So it appears," he said.

"But surely, Thrasymachus, the arts rule over and have power over that with which they're concerned."

He went along with that too, very grudgingly.

d   "Then no sort of knowledge considers or commands what's advantageous for the stronger, but what's advantageous for what's weaker and ruled by it."

He finally agreed with this too, though he tried to make a fight about it, and when he agreed I said, "So does anything else follow except that no doctor, to the extent he is a doctor, considers or commands what's advantageous for a doctor, but instead for someone who's sick? For it was agreed that the doctor is precisely a ruler of bodies but not a moneymaker. Or was that not agreed?"

He said so.

"Then the helmsman too was agreed to be precisely a ruler of sailors but not a sailor?"   e

"It was agreed."

"Then this sort of helmsman and ruler at any rate will not consider and command what's advantageous for a helmsman, but what's advantageous for the sailor who's ruled."

He said so, grudgingly.

"Therefore, Thrasymachus," I said, "neither will anyone else in any ruling position, to the extent he is a ruler, consider or command what's advantageous for himself, but what's advantageous for whatever is ruled, for which he himself is a skilled workman, and looking toward that, and to what's advantageous and appropriate for that, he both says and does everything that he says and does."

Now when we were at this point in the argument, and it was obvious to everyone   343 that the statement about what's just had turned around into its opposite, Thrasymachus, instead of replying, said "Tell me, Socrates, do you have someone nursing you?"

"What?" I said. "Shouldn't you give an answer rather than asking things like that?"

"Well," he said, "she must not be noticing your snotty nose because she's not wiping it when you need her to, if it's her fault you can't tell a sheep from a shepherd."

"Because of what in particular?" I said.

"Because you imagine that shepherds or cattlemen consider the good of the sheep   b or cattle and fatten them up and take care of them looking to anything other than the good of their bosses and of themselves, and so you also believe that the rulers in cities, the ones who truly are rulers, think about those who are ruled in any other way than someone would treat sheep, and that they consider anything, day and night, other than this: how they themselves are going to benefit. And you're so far off about what's just   c and justice and what's unjust and injustice that you don't know that justice and what's just are in fact someone else's good, what's advantageous for the person who's stronger and a ruler, and one's own harm for the person who obeys and is subservient; injustice is the opposite, and rules over those who are truly simpletons and just people, while the ones who are ruled do what's advantageous for the person who's stronger and make him happy by serving him, but themselves not in any way whatsoever.   d

"It needs to be looked at this way, most simple-minded Socrates: a just man has less than an unjust one in every situation. First, in contracts with each other, where the one sort is partnered with the other, nowhere would you find that the one who's just had more in the breaking up of the partnership than the unjust one—only less. Next, in things related to the city, whenever there are any taxes, the one who's just pays more tax on an equal amount of property, the other less, and whenever there are allotments, the former   e gains nothing, the latter a lot. Also, whenever each of the two holds some ruling office it goes without saying for the one who's just, that even if he has no other loss, his household circumstances get into a sorry state from lack of attention, while, on account of being just, he gets no benefit from the public treasury, and on top of that he gets the antagonism of his family and acquaintances when he isn't willing to do them any services contrary to what's just. And for the one who's unjust, it goes without saying that everything is the opposite of this —I mean the person I was just now talking about, the   344 one who has the power to get a lot more than his due. So consider this person if you want to judge by how much more what's unjust is to his private advantage than what's just.

"You'll understand this most easily of all if you go up to the most complete injustice, which makes the one who does the injustice the most happy and the ones the injustice is done to the most miserable if they aren't willing to be unjust too. And this is tyranny, which, by both furtiveness and force, takes away what belongs to others, both the sacred

b and the profane, both the private and the public, not little by little but all at one swoop. When anyone who does injustice in a single portion of that doesn't go undetected, he is punished and has the greatest disgrace—impious men, hijackers, home invaders, cheats, and thieves are names given to those who do the injustice involved in parts of that sort of evildoing—but when someone, in addition to stealing the citizens' money, steals the men

c themselves and makes slaves of them, instead of these disgraceful names he's called happy and blessed, not only by the citizens but by everyone else who hears that his injustice has been total injustice. Those who condemn injustice condemn it not because they're afraid of doing unjust things but because they're afraid of suffering them.

"This is the way, Socrates, that injustice, when it comes on the scene with sufficient strength, is stronger, more free, and more overpowering than justice, and the way that what's just is exactly what I was saying from the beginning, what's advantageous to the stronger, while what's unjust is profitable and advantageous to oneself."

d When he'd said these things, Thrasymachus had it in mind to go away, just like a bath attendant who had sloshed a lot of speech into our ears all at once. But those who were present didn't let him go but forced him to stay and submit to a discussion of the things he'd said.

And I too myself begged him very strongly and said "Thrasymachus, you supernatural being, what sort of speech have you flung at us, that you have it in mind to go away before teaching us adequately or learning whether it's that way or some other? Or

e do you imagine it's a small matter to try to determine the course of a lifetime, by which each of us who leads it would live the most profitable life?"

"Do I imagine it's any different?" said Thrasymachus.

"You seemed to," I said, "or else not to be bothered at all about us, or have any concern whether we'll live worse or better lives for being ignorant of what you claim to know.

345 But, good fellow, be willing to display it to us too—it certainly won't be a bad deposit to your account that you did a good deed for us, so many as we are—because I'm telling you that for my part I'm not persuaded, nor do I suppose that injustice is more of a gain than justice, not even if one gives it its own way and doesn't hinder it from doing what it wants. But, good fellow, let someone be unjust, and let him have the power to do injustice either

b by going undetected or by fighting his way through; he still doesn't persuade me that that's more of a gain than justice. Now perhaps some other one of us, and not I alone, has gotten this impression, so persuade us, blessed one, in an adequate way, that we aren't being counseled correctly when we hold justice at a greater value than injustice."

"And how," he said, "am I going to persuade you? If you're not persuaded by the things I was saying just now, what more am I going to do for you? Or shall I bring the argument and spoon-feed it into your soul?"

"By Zeus," I said, "not that—not you. But first, stick by whatever you say, or if you

c change them make the change openly and don't mislead us. But you see what you're doing now, Thrasymachus—because we still need to examine the things you said before—that after first defining the true doctor, you later supposed there was no longer a need to be on guard in a precise way about the true shepherd, but imagined that, to the extent that he is a shepherd, he fattens up his sheep, not looking toward what's best for the sheep, but, like someone at a banquet about to be feasted, toward a good meal, or else

d toward turning a profit, like a moneymaker instead of a shepherd. But surely nothing is of concern to the art of shepherding other than how it's going to provide what's best for that over which it's appointed—since it's no doubt sufficiently provided for that the things pertaining to the art itself will be best so long as it lacks nothing of being the art of shepherding. That's why I supposed just now that it was necessary for us to agree that every ruling office, to the extent that it is a ruling office, considers what's best for no other thing than the one that's ruled over and cared for, in both political and private rule. And do you imagine that the rulers in cities, the ones who truly are rulers, rule willingly?"

"I don't imagine it, by Zeus," he said, "I know it well."

"Then what about the other kinds of rule, Thrasymachus?" I said.

"Don't you realize that no one willingly desires to rule, but people demand wages on the grounds that there won't be any benefit to them from their ruling but only to the ones that are ruled? Because tell me this much: don't we claim, no doubt, that each of the arts is different in each case in this respect, in having a different power? And so that we may get to a conclusion, blessed one, don't answer contrary to your opinion,"

"They are indeed different in that respect," he said.

"Then does each of these also furnish us with some benefit that's particular to it and not shared by them all, such as health with the medical art, safety in sailing with helmsmanship, and so on with the others?"

"Certainly."

"So then wages too with the wage-earning art? Because that's *its* power—or do you call the medical art and helmsmanship the same? Or if in fact you want to distinguish them with precision, as you set down for our principle, even if someone becomes healthy as a helmsman, because it's advantageous to him to sail on the sea, do you any the more on that account call his skill the medical art?"

"Of course not," he said.

"Nor, I imagine, do you call the wage-earning art medical, even if someone earning wages gets healthy?"

"Of course not."

"And what about the medical art—even if someone who heals someone earns wages do you call his skill the wage-earning art?"

"No," he said.

"Didn't we agree that the benefit of each art is particular to it?"

"So be it," he said.

"Therefore it's clear that whatever sort of benefit all skilled workmen benefit by in common, they get that benefit from using in addition something that's the same, shared by them in common."

"It seems like it," he said.

"Then we're saying that the wages the skilled workmen gain for their benefit come to them from their additional use of the wage-earning art."

He said so grudgingly.

"Therefore it's not from his own art that this benefit, that of getting wages, belongs to each of them, but if one is required to consider it with precision, the medical art produces health and the mercenary art wages, and the house-building art produces a house and the mercenary art following along with it produces wages, and it's this way with all the other arts—each works at its own work and benefits that over which its work is appointed. And if there were no wages attached to it, is there any benefit that the workman would get from his art?"

"It doesn't appear so," he said.

"And does he produce a benefit even on an occasion when he does his work for free?"

"I imagine so."

"Then, Thrasymachus, this is already obvious, that no art nor any ruling function provides for its own benefit, but, the very thing we've been saying for so long, it both provides for and commands the benefit of the one ruled, considering the benefit of that weaker one and not that of the stronger. So it's for these reasons, Thrasymachus my friend, that I was also saying just now that no one willingly desires to rule and deal with 347 straightening out other people's troubles, but people demand wages because the one who's going to do a beautiful job by art never does what's best for himself or commands it when he's commanding in accord with his art, but only for the one ruled, on account of which, as is only fitting, there need to be wages for those who are going to be willing to rule, either money, or honor, or a penalty if one does not rule."

"How do you mean that, Socrates," said Glaucon. "I recognize the two sorts of wages, but I don't understand what you mean by the penalty and how you've declared it to be in the class of wages."

b   "Then you don't understand the wages of the best people," I said, "on account of which the most decent ones rule, when they're willing to rule. Or don't you know that people are said to be passionate for honor and money as a reproach, and it is one?"

"I do," he said.

"So," I said, "that's why good people aren't willing to rule for the sake of either money or honor. They don't want to be called mercenary if they openly get wages for the ruling office, or thieves if they secretly take money from the office themselves. And they don't rule for the sake of honor either, since they aren't passionate for honor. So c   there needs to be a necessity attached to it for them, and a penalty, if they're going to be willing to rule; that's liable to be where it comes from that it's considered shameful to go willingly to rule rather than to await necessity. And the greatest sort of penalty is to be ruled by someone less worthy, if one is not oneself willing to rule. It's on account of fearing this that decent people appear to me to rule, when they do rule, and then they go to rule not as though they were heading for something good or as though they were d   going to have any enjoyment in it, but as though to something necessary, since they have no one better than or similar to themselves to entrust it to. Because, if a city of good men were to come into being, they'd be liable to have a fight over not ruling just as people do now over ruling, and it would become obvious there that the person who is a true ruler in his being is not of such a nature as to consider what's advantageous for himself rather than for the one ruled. So everyone with any discernment would choose to be benefited by someone else rather than to have the trouble of benefiting someone e   else. On this point, then, I by no means go along with Thrasymachus that what's just is what's advantageous for the stronger. But we'll examine this some other time, for what Thrasymachus is saying now seems to me to be much more important, when he claims that the life of someone who's unjust is more powerful than that of someone who's just. Now you, Glaucon," I said, "which way do you choose? And which claim seems to you to be more truly spoken?"

"To me, the one that says the life of the one who's just is more profitable."

348   "Even though you heard all the good things Thrasymachus went through just now," I said, "about that of the one who's unjust?"

"Because I heard them," he said, "but I'm not persuaded."

"Then do you want us to persuade him, if it's in our power to discover a way, that he's not speaking the truth?"

"How could I not want it?" he said.

"Well now," I said, "if we're to address him by spreading out one statement in exchange for another along the length of his speech, about all the good things being just

includes, and he'd reply in turn, and we with another speech, it will be necessary to   b
count up the good points each of us makes in each speech and measure how good they
are, and by that time we'll need some sort of jury of people to judge it. But if, as we
were doing just now, we examine the question based on things we agree with each other
about, we ourselves will be jurors and advocates at the same time."

"Very much so," he said.

"Whichever way you please, then," I said.

"The latter," he said.

"Come now, Thrasymachus," I said, "answer us from the beginning. Do you
claim that complete injustice is more profitable than justice when it's complete?"

"I claim it very much so," he said, "and I've said why."   c

"Well then, how do you speak about them in this respect? I presume you call one
of the pair virtue and the other vice?"

"How could it be otherwise?"

"So you call justice virtue and injustice vice?"

"Yeah, right, you most amusing fellow," he said, "since I also say that injustice is
profitable and justice isn't."

"What then?"

"The opposite," he said.

"Justice is vice?"

"No, just very well bred simplemindedness."

"Then do you call injustice bad character?"   d

"No," he said, "just good judgment."

"And do unjust people seem to you, Thrasymachus, to be intelligent and good?"

"If they're able to be completely unjust," he said, "and have the power to bring
cities and throngs of people under their control. But you probably imagine I'm talking
about pickpockets. Now things like that are profitable too," he said, "so long as one goes
undetected—they're just not worthy of mention compared to what I was talking about
just now."

"On that point," I said, "I'm not unaware of what you want to say, but I did won-   e
der about this one, whether you place injustice in the class of virtue and wisdom, and
justice among their opposites."

"That's exactly the way I place them."

"This is already something harder, my companion," I said, "and it's no longer
easy to have anything one could say about it. For if you placed injustice as being profitable, but still agreed, the way some others do, that it's vice and shameful, we'd have
something to say by speaking in accordance with the things customarily believed, but
now you're obviously going to claim that it's both beautiful and strong, and you'll add   349
to it all the other things that we attribute to what's just, since you even had the nerve to
place it among virtue and wisdom."

"Your premonition is very true," he said.

"But still," I said, "one mustn't shrink from going through the argument to examine it, so long as I get the impression that you're saying exactly what you think. For you
seem to me now, Thrasymachus, without pretense and not joking, but stating what
seems to you about the truth."

"What difference does it make to you," he said, "whether it seems that way to me
or not? Aren't you just cross-examining the argument?"

"No difference," I said.   b

*   *   *

350d   Now Thrasymachus did agree to all these things, though not as easily as I'm telling it now, but being dragged along and grudging it, after sweating a prodigious amount, seeing as how it was also summer. And then I saw something I had never seen before: Thrasymachus blushing. So when we had come to agreement that justice is virtue and wisdom, and injustice vice and stupidity, I said "Okay, let this be the way it now stands according to us, but we were also claiming that injustice is something strong. Or don't you remember, Thrasymachus?"

"I remember," he said, "but what you're saying now isn't good enough for me, and I have something to say about it. But if I were to say it, I know well that you'd claim

e   I was speaking rhetorically. So either let me speak as much as I want or, if you want to ask questions, ask them, and I'll treat you the way people do old women when they're telling stories, and tell you 'okay,' and nod my head or shake it."

"Don't by any means do that contrary to your own opinion," I said.

"Just to please you," he said, "seeing as how you won't let me speak. What else do you want?"

"Nothing, by Zeus," I said; "but if you're going to do that, do it, and I'll ask questions."

"Ask away."

"Well, I'm asking this, the very thing I asked just now, so that we might go

351   through an orderly examination of the argument about exactly what sort of thing justice is in relation to injustice. For it was said, surely, that injustice would be a more powerful and stronger thing than justice, but now," I said, "if justice is in fact wisdom and virtue, it will easily be brought to light, I imagine, as a stronger thing than injustice, seeing as how injustice is stupidity. No one could any longer be ignorant of that. But,

b   Thrasymachus, I don't wish for it to be considered so simply, but in something like the following way: would you claim that a city is unjust that tries to enslave other cities unjustly, and has made slaves of them, and holds them in slavery to itself?"

"How could it be otherwise?" he said. "And the best city will do this the most, since it is also the most completely unjust."

"I understand," I said, "that this was your argument, but I'm considering this about it: will the city that becomes master of a city hold this power without justice, or is it necessary for it to hold it with justice?"

c   "If, as you were saying just now, justice is wisdom," he said, "with justice. But if it's the way I was saying, with injustice."

"I very much admire, Thrasymachus," I said, "the fact that you aren't just nodding or shaking your head but also answering very beautifully."

"Well, I'm doing it to humor you," he said.

"And you're doing it well. Now just humor me this much more and tell me, do you believe that either a city or an army or pirates or thieves or any other group that embarks on anything in common unjustly will have the power to accomplish it if they behave unjustly toward one another?"

"Not at all," he said.

d   "And what if they don't behave unjustly? Won't they accomplish more?"

"Very much so."

"For surely, Thrasymachus, injustice causes factions and hatreds and fights among one another, while justice causes like-mindedness and friendship. Isn't that so?"

"So be it," he said, "so I won't be at odds with you."

"And you're behaving very well, most excellent fellow. But tell me this: if that's the work of injustice, to bring in hatred wherever it's present, won't it also, when it

comes in among the free as well as the enslaved, make them hate each other and form   e
factions and be powerless to act in common with one another?"

"Certainly."

"Then what if it comes to be present in two people? Won't they be at odds and
hate and be enemies of one another as well as of those who are just?"

"They will be," he said.

"Then, you surprising fellow, if injustice comes to be present in one person, will
it lose its power completely, or still have it to no less extent?"

"Let it have it to no less extent," he said.

"Then does it come to light as having some such power as this, in that in which it
comes to be present, whether a particular city, a race of people, an army, or anything
else whatsoever, that first of all injustice makes it powerless to act with itself on account   352
of being in factions and at odds, then also makes it be an enemy to itself and everything
opposed to it and to what is just? Isn't that the way it is?"

"Certainly."

"So even when it's present in one person, I assume, it will do these very same
things that are its workings by its nature: first it will make him powerless to act, being
at faction and not of one mind himself with himself, and then an enemy both to himself
and to those who are just. Right?"

"Yes."

"And, my friend, the gods too are just?"

"So be it."   b

"Therefore, Thrasymachus, someone who's unjust will also be an enemy to the
gods, but someone who's just will be a friend."

"Gorge yourself on the argument fearlessly," he said. "I won't oppose you anyway, so that I won't be hateful to these people here."

"Come on then," I said, "and fill up what's left of the feasting for me by answering just as you are now. Because those who are just have come to light as wiser and better and more empowered to act, while those who are unjust are not able to act in any   c
way with each other, but in fact we aren't speaking the whole truth when we claim that
people who are unjust ever yet acted vigorously in common with one another in anything, since they couldn't have kept their hands off each other if they were completely
unjust, but it's clear that there was a certain justice in them which made them not do
injustice to each other, at least at the same time they were also doing it to those they
were doing it to. It was by means of this justice that they acted in whatever respects they
did act, and they embarked on their unjust deeds as semi-vicious people, since those
who are all-vicious and completely unjust are also completely powerless to act. Now I   d
understand that these things are so, and not the way you set them down at first. But
whether those who are just also live better and are happier than those who are unjust,
the very thing we proposed to consider later, needs to be considered. And now, as it
seems to me at least, they do appear to from the things we've said. Nevertheless, it
needs to be examined still better, since the discussion is not about some random thing,
but about the way one ought to live."

"So examine it," he said.

"I'm examining it," I said, "and tell me, does it seem to you that there is a certain   e
work that belongs to a horse?"

"To me, yes."

"And would you set this down as the work of a horse or of anything else
whatever—what one could do only, or best, with it?"

"I don't understand," he said.

"Try it this way: is there anything else you could see with except eyes?"

"Surely not."

"What then; could you hear with anything except ears?"

"Not at all."

"Then do we justly claim that these things are their work?"

"Certainly."

353   "What about this? Could you cut off a branch from a vine with a dagger or a carving knife or with many other things?"

"How could I not?"

"But with none of these, I imagine, so beautifully as with a pruning knife that's worked up for this use?"

"True."

"Then shall we not set this down as the work of this thing?"

"We certainly shall."

"So now I assume you'd understand better what I was asking just now, when I inquired whether the work of each thing wouldn't be that which only it accomplishes, or which it, compared to other things, accomplishes most beautifully."

b   "I do understand," he said, "and it does seem to me that this is the work of each thing."

"Okay," I said, "and then does it seem to you that there's a virtue for each thing that has some work attached to it? Let's go back to the same examples: we claim there's some work that belongs to eyes?"

"There is."

"So is there also a virtue that belongs to eyes?"

"A virtue too."

"What next? Was there a work belonging to ears?"

"Yes."

"Then a virtue too?"

"A virtue too."

"What then about everything else? Isn't it that way?"

"It's that way."

c   "Keep on. Could eyes ever accomplish their own work beautifully if they didn't have their own particular virtue but vice instead of the virtue?"

"How could they?" he said. "You no doubt mean blindness instead of sight."

"Whatever virtue belongs to them," I said, "since I'm not yet asking about that, but whether with the particular virtue that pertains to their work they're going to do the work they do well, but do it badly with the vice."

"On this point," he said, "you're telling the truth."

"So then ears too, when deprived of their virtue, will accomplish their work badly?"

"Certainly."

d   "And will we put everything else too into the same statement?"

"It seems that way to me."

"Come then, after these things, consider this one. Is there any work belonging to a soul that you couldn't perform with any single other thing there is? Like this, for instance—managing and ruling and deliberating and everything like that—is there anything other than a soul to which we could justly attribute them and claim that they belong to that in particular?"

"Nothing else."

"And next, what about living? Won't we claim that it's work belonging to a soul?"

"Especially that," he said.

"Then do we also claim there's some virtue belonging to a soul?"

"We claim that."

"So, Thrasymachus, will a soul ever accomplish its work well if it's deprived of   e
its own particular virtue, or is that out of its power?"

"Out of its power."

"Therefore it's necessary for a bad soul to rule and manage things badly and for a
good one to do all these things well."

"Necessary."

"And haven't we granted that justice is virtue of soul and injustice vice?"

"We've granted it."

"Therefore the just soul and the just man will live well and the unjust badly."

"So it appears," he said, "according to your argument."

"But surely someone who lives well is blessed and happy and someone who   354
doesn't is the opposite."

"How not?"

"Therefore someone who's just is happy and someone who's unjust is miserable."

"So be it," he said.

"But surely it's not being miserable that's profitable, but being happy."

"How not?"

"Therefore, blessed Thrasymachus, injustice is never more profitable than justice."

"So, Socrates," he said, "let these things be your feast in the festivities for Bendis."

"It's thanks to you, Thrasymachus," I said, "since you have become gentle and
stopped being savage toward me. I haven't feasted myself beautifully, though, but that's   b
on account of myself and not you. Just as greedy eaters are always taking a bite of
what's carried past them, grabbing at it before they've enjoyed the previous dish in full
measure, I too seem to myself to be like that. Before finding the thing we were considering first—what in the world the just thing is—I let go of that to start looking around it
to see whether it's vice and stupidity or wisdom and virtue. And when in turn an argument fell my way later that injustice is more profitable than justice, I couldn't hold back
from going after this one and away from that one. And so it has come to pass that now I   c
know nothing from the conversation, because when I don't know what the just thing is,
I'm hardly going to know whether it happens to be a virtue or not, or whether someone
who has it is unhappy or happy."

BOOK II

Now when I said these things, I imagined I'd be released from discussion, but as it   357
seems, it was just a prologue. For Glaucon is always most courageous in confronting
everything, and in particular he wouldn't stand for Thrasymachus's giving up, but said
"Socrates, do you want to seem to have persuaded us or truly persuade us that in every   b
way it's better to be just than unjust?"

"If it would be up to me," I said, "I'd choose truly."

"Then you're not doing what you want. For tell me, does it seem to you there's a
certain kind of good that we'd take hold of not because we desire its consequences, but
to embrace it itself for its own sake, such as enjoyment and any of the pleasures that are

harmless and from which nothing comes into the succeeding time other than to enjoy having them?"

c

"It seems to me," I said, "that there is such a thing."

"Then what about the kind that we love both itself for its own sake and for the things that come from it, such as thinking and seeing and being healthy? For presumably we embrace such things for both reasons."

"Yes," I said.

"And do you see a third form of good," he said, "in which there's gymnastic exercise, and being given medical treatment when sick, and giving medical treatment, as well as the rest of moneymaking activity? Because we'd say these are burdensome, but

d

for our benefit, and we wouldn't take hold of them for their own sake, but we do for the sake of wages and of all the other things that come from them."

"There is also this third kind," I said, "but what about it?"

"In which of these kinds," he said, "do you put justice?"

358

"I imagine in the most beautiful kind," I said, "which must be loved both for itself and for the things that come from it by someone who's going to be blessedly happy."

"Well it doesn't seem that way to most people," he said, "but to belong to the burdensome kind that ought to be pursued for the sake of the wages and reputation that come from opinion, but ought to be avoided itself on its own account as being something difficult."

"I know it seems that way," I said, "and a while ago it was condemned by Thrasymachus as being that sort of thing, while injustice was praised, but, as it seems, I'm a slow learner."

b

"Come then," he said, "and listen to me, if the same things still seem true to you, because Thrasymachus appears to me to have been charmed by you like a snake, sooner than he needed to be. But to my way of thinking, no demonstration has taken place yet about either one, since I desire to hear what each of them is and what power it has itself by itself when it's present in the soul, and to say goodbye to the wages and the things that come from them.

"So I'm going to do it this way, if that seems good to you too: I'll revive

c

Thrasymachus's argument, and I'll say first what sort of thing people claim justice is and where they say it comes from, and second that everyone who pursues it pursues it unwillingly as something necessary but not good, and third that they do it fittingly since the life of someone who's unjust is much better than that of someone who's just—as *they* say, since it doesn't seem that way to me at all, Socrates, though I'm stumped as

d

my ears are talked deaf when I listen to Thrasymachus and tens of thousands of other people, while I haven't yet heard the argument on behalf of justice, that it's better than injustice, from anyone in the way I want it. I want to hear it itself by itself praised, and I assume that I'd hear this most of all from you.

"That's why I'll strain myself to speak in praise of the unjust life, and as I speak I'll point out to you in what way I want to hear you in turn condemn injustice and praise justice. But see if what I'm saying is to your liking."

"Most of all," I said, "for what would anyone who has any sense enjoy more to

e

talk about and hear about repeatedly?"

"You're speaking most beautifully," he said. "Listen then to what I said I'd talk about first, what sort of thing justice is and where it comes from. People claim that doing injustice is by its nature good and suffering injustice is bad, but that suffering injustice crosses over farther into bad than doing injustice does into good, so that when people both do injustice to and suffer it from each other and get a taste of both, it seems profitable to the ones who don't have the power to avoid the latter and choose

the former to make a contract with each other neither to do injustice nor suffer it. And   359
from then on they begin to set up laws and agreements among themselves and to name
what's commanded by the law both lawful and just, and so this is the origin and being
of justice, being in the middle between what is best, if one could do injustice and not
pay a penalty, and what is worst, if one were powerless to take revenge when suffering   b
injustice. What's just, being at a mean between these two things, is something to be
content with not as something good, but as something honored out of weakness at
doing injustice, since someone with the power to do it and who was truly a man would
never make a contract with anyone neither to do nor suffer injustice. He'd be insane.

"So, Socrates, it's the nature of justice to be this and of this sort, and these are the
sorts of things it comes from by its nature, as the argument goes. The fact that those who
pursue it pursue it unwillingly from a lack of power to do injustice, we might perceive
most clearly if we were to do something like this in our thinking: by giving to each of   c
them, the just and the unjust, freedom to do whatever he wants, we could then follow
along and see where his desire will lead each one. Then we could catch the just person
in the act of going the same route as the unjust one because of greed for more, which is
what every nature, by its nature, seeks as good, though it's forcibly pulled aside by law
to respect for equality.

"The sort of freedom I'm talking about would be most possible if the sort of
power ever came to them that people say came to the ancestor of Gyges the Lydian.   d
They say he was a shepherd working as a hired servant to the one who then ruled Lydia,
when a big storm came up and an earthquake broke open the earth, and there was a
chasm in the place where he was pasturing the sheep. Seeing it and marveling, he went
down and saw other marvels people tell legends about as well as a bronze horse, hol-
lowed out, that had windows in it, and when he stooped down to look through them he
saw a dead body inside that appeared bigger than a human being. And this body had on
it nothing else but a gold ring around its finger, which he took off and went away.   e

"And when the customary gathering of the shepherds came along, so that they
could report each month to the king about his flocks, he too came and had on the ring.
Then while he was sitting with the others, he happened to turn the stone setting of the
ring around toward himself into the inside of his hand, and when this happened he   360
became invisible to those sitting beside him, and they talked about him as though he'd
gone away. He marveled, and running his hand over the ring again he twisted the stone
setting outward, and when he had twisted it he became visible. And reflecting on this,
he tried out whether the ring had this power in it, and it turned out that way for him, to
become invisible when he twisted the stone setting in and visible when he twisted it out.
Perceiving this, he immediately arranged to become one of the messengers attending   b
the king, and went and seduced the king's wife, and with her attacked and killed the
king and took possession of his reign.

"Now if there were a pair of rings of that sort, and a just person put on one while
an unjust person put on the other, it would seem that there could be no one so inflexible
that he'd stand firm in his justice and have the fortitude to hold back and not lay a hand
on things belonging to others, when he was free to take what he wanted from the
marketplace, and to go into houses and have sex with anyone he wanted, and to kill and   c
set loose from chains everyone he wanted, and to do everything he could when he was
the equal of a god among human beings. And in acting this way, he would do nothing
different from the other, but both would go the same route.

"And surely someone could claim this is a great proof that no one is just willingly,
but only when forced to be, on the grounds that it is not for his private good, since wherever each one imagines he'll be able to do injustice he does injustice. Because every

d   man assumes that injustice is much more profitable to him privately than justice, and the one saying the things involved in this sort of argument will claim that he's assuming the truth, because if anyone got hold of such freedom and was never willing to do injustice or lay a hand on things belonging to others, he'd seem to be utterly miserable to those who observed it, and utterly senseless as well, though they'd praise him to each other's faces, lying to one another from fear of suffering injustice.

"So that's the way that part goes. But as for the choice itself of the life of the peo-
e   ple we're talking about, we'll be able to decide it correctly if we set the most just person opposite the most unjust; if we don't, we won't be able to. What then is the way of opposing them? This: we'll take nothing away either from the injustice of the unjust person or from the justice of the just person, but set out each as complete in his own pursuit. First, then, let the unjust one do as clever workmen do; a top helmsman, for instance, or doctor, distinguishes clearly between what's impossible in his art and
361   what's possible, and attempts the latter while letting the former go, and if he still slips up in any way, he's competent to set himself right again. So too, let the unjust person, attempting his injustices in the correct way, go undetected, if he's going to be surpassingly unjust. Someone who gets caught must be considered a sorry specimen, since the ultimate injustice is to seem just when one is not.

"So one must grant the completely unjust person the most complete injustice, and not take anything away but allow him, while doing the greatest injustices, to secure for
b   himself the greatest reputation for justice; and if thereafter he slips up in anything, one must allow him to have the power to set himself right again, and to be competent both to speak so as to persuade if he's denounced for any of his injustices, and to use force for everything that needs force, by means of courage and strength as well as a provision of friends and wealth. And having set him up as this sort, let's stand the just person beside him in our argument, a man simple and well bred, wishing not to seem but be good, as Aeschylus puts it.

c   "So one must take away the seeming, for if he's going to seem to be just there'll be honors and presents for him as one seeming that way. Then it would be unclear whether he would be that way for the sake of what's just or for the sake of the presents and honors. So he must be stripped bare of everything except justice and made to be situated in a way opposite to the one before, for while he does nothing unjust, let him have a reputation for the greatest injustice, in order that he might be put to the acid test for justice: its not being softened by bad reputation and the things that come from that. Let
d   him go unchanged until death, seeming to be unjust throughout life while being just, so that when both people have come to the ultimate point, one of justice and the other of injustice, it can be decided which of the pair is happier."

"Ayayay, Glaucon my friend," I said, "how relentlessly you scrub each of them pure, like a statue, for the decision between the two men."

"As much as is in my power," he said, "and now that the two are that way, there's
e   nothing difficult any more, as I imagine, about going on through in telling the sort of life that's in store for each of them. "So it must be said, and if in fact it's said too crudely, don't imagine I'm saying it, Socrates, but the people who praise injustice in preference to justice.

"They'll say this: that situated the way he is, the just person will be beaten with whips, stretched on the rack, bound in chains, have both eyes burned out, and as an end
362   after suffering every evil he'll be hacked in pieces, and know that one ought to wish not to be but seem just. And therefore the lines of Aeschylus would be much more correct to speak about the unjust person, since they'll claim that the one who is unjust in his being,

inasmuch as he's pursuing a thing in contact with truth and not living with a view to opinion, wishing not to seem but be unjust

> Gathers in the fruit cultivated deep in his heart   b
> From the place where wise counsels breed.

In the first place, he rules in his city as one who seems to be just; next, he takes a wife from wherever he wants, and gives a daughter to whomever he wants; he contracts to go in partnership with whomever he wishes; and besides benefiting from all these things, he gains by not being squeamish about doing injustice. So when he goes into competition both in private and in public, he overcomes his enemies and comes out with more, and since he has more he is rich and does good to his friends and damages his enemies.   c
And to the gods he makes sacrifices in an adequate way and dedicates offerings in a magnificent way, and does much better service to the gods, and to the human beings it pleases him to, than the just person does, so that in all likelihood it's more suitable for him, rather than the just person, to be dearer to the gods.

"In that way, Socrates, they claim that, on the part of both gods and human beings, a better life is provided for the unjust person than for the just."

*   *   *

[Socrates responds to Glaucon and Adeimantus]: "You've experienced something godlike if you haven't been persuaded that injustice is better than justice, though you have the power to speak that way on behalf of it. And you seem to me truly not persuaded, but I gather this from other indications of your disposition, since from your arguments I'd distrust you. But to the degree that I trust you more, I'm that much more stumped as to how I can be of use, and I have no way to help out, since I seem to myself to be powerless. A sign of this for me is that I imagined what I said to Thrasymachus demonstrated that justice is better than injustice, but you didn't let my argument stand. But neither is there any way for me not to help out, since I'm afraid that it would be irreverent to be standing by while justice is being defamed and not help out as long as I'm still breathing and have the power to utter a sound. So what has the most force is for me to come to its defense in whatever way is in my power."   368   b   c

Then Glaucon and the others begged me in every way to help out and not give up the argument, but to track down what each of them is and what the truth is about the sort of benefit that goes with the two of them. So I said exactly what seemed to me the case: "The inquiry we're setting ourselves to is no inconsiderable thing, but for someone sharp-sighted, as it appears to me. So since we aren't clever," I said, "the sort of inquiry for us to make about it seems to me exactly like this: if someone had ordered people who were not very sharp-sighted to read small print from a distance, and then it occurred to someone that maybe the same letters are also somewhere else, both bigger and on something bigger, it would plainly be a godsend, I assume, to read those first and examine the smaller ones by that means, if they were exactly the same."   d

"Certainly," Adeimantus said, "but Socrates, what have you spotted in the inquiry about justice that's of that sort?"   e

"I'll tell you," I said. "There's justice, we claim, of one man, and there's presumably also justice of a whole city?"

"Certainly," he said.

"Isn't a city a bigger thing than one man?"

"It's bigger," he said.

369   "Then maybe more justice would be present in the bigger thing, and it would be easier to understand it clearly. So if you people want to, we'll inquire first what sort of thing it is in cities, and then we'll examine it by that means also in each one of the people, examining the likeness of the bigger in the look of the smaller."

"You seem to me to be saying something beautiful," he said.

"Then if we were to look at a city as it comes into being in speech," I said, "would we see the justice and injustice that belong to it coming into being as well?"

"Probably so," he said.

b   "And then, once it has come into being, is there a hope of seeing what we're looking for more readily?"

"Very much so."

"Does it seem good, then, that we should try to accomplish this? Because I imagine it's not a small task, so you people consider it."

"It's been considered," Adeimantus said. "Don't do anything else."

"Okay," I said. "A city, as I imagine, comes into being because it happens that each of us is not self-sufficient, but needs many things. Or do you imagine a city is founded from any other origin?"

"None at all," he said.

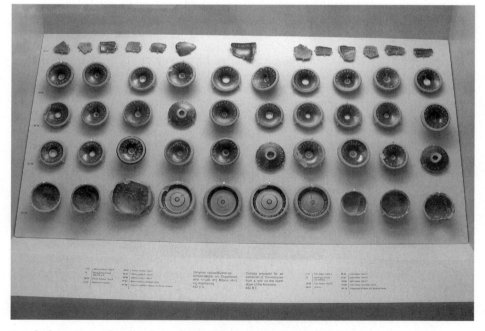

Ostraka from 428 B.C., found on the north side of the Acropolis. These clay disks were used in ostracism voting. Each eligible male Athenian citizen scratched the name of the man he thought most undesirable. The "candidate" with the most votes was obliged to leave Athens for ten years. Given that "each of us is not self-sufficient" (*Republic* 369b) and all are dependent on the community, this was a severe punishment. *(Forrest E. Baird/Hellenic Ministry of Culture)*

"So then when one person associates with another for one use, and with another for another use, since they need many things, and many people assemble in one dwelling place as partners and helpers, to this community we give the name city, don't we?"   c

"Certainly."

"And they share things one with another, if they give or take shares of anything, because each supposes it to be better for himself?"

"Certainly."

"Come then," I said, "and let's make a city from the beginning in our speech. And it seems like what will make it will be our need."

"What else could it be?"

"But surely the first and greatest of needs is the provision of food for the sake of   d being and living."

"Absolutely."

"And second is the need for a dwelling place, and third for clothes and such things."

"That's so."

"Well then," I said, "how big a city will be sufficient to provide this much? Is it anything else than one person as a farmer, another a housebuilder, and some other a weaver? Or shall we add to it a leatherworker or someone who attends to something else for the body?"

"Certainly."

"And the city that's most necessary anyway would consist of four or five men."

"So it appears."   e

"And then what? Should each one of these put in his own work for them all in common, with the farmer, say, who is one, providing food for four and spending four times the time and effort in the provision of food for the others too to share, or paying no attention to that, make a fourth part of this food for himself alone in a fourth part of   370 the time and devote one of the other three to providing for a house, another to a cloak, and the other to shoes, and not have the trouble of sharing things with others but do himself, by himself, the things that are for himself?"

And Adeimantus said, "Probably, Socrates, the first way would be easier than that one."

"And by Zeus, there's nothing strange about that," I said. "For I'm thinking too myself, now that you mention it, that in the first place, each of us doesn't grow up to be   b entirely like each, but differing in nature, with a different person in practice growing toward a different sort of work. Or doesn't it seem that way to you?"

"It does to me."

"Then what? Would someone do a more beautiful job who, being one, worked at many arts, or when one person works at one art?"

"When one person works at one art," he said.

"And I assume this too is clear, that if anyone lets the critical moment in any work go by, it's ruined."

"That's clear."

"Because I don't imagine the thing that's being done is willing to wait for the leisure of the person who's doing it, but it's necessary for the one doing it to keep on the   c track of the thing he's doing, not when the turn comes for a sideline."

"That's necessary."

"So as a result of these things, everything comes about in more quantity, as more beautiful, and with more ease when one person does one thing in accord with his nature and at the right moment, being free from responsibility for everything else."

"Absolutely so."

"So there's need for more than four citizens, Adeimantus, for the provisions we were talking about, since the farmer himself, as seems likely, won't make his own plow,

d   if it's going to be beautifully made, or his pickax, or any of the other tools for farming. And neither will the housebuilder, and there's need of many things for that, and likewise with the weaver and the leatherworker."

"That's true."

"So with carpenters and metalworkers and many such particular kinds of craftsmen coming in as partners in our little city, they'll make it a big one."

"Very much so."

"But it still wouldn't be a very big one if we add cattlemen and shepherds to them,

e   and other herdsmen, so that the farmers would have oxen for plowing, and the housebuilders along with the farmers could use teams of animals for hauling, and the weavers and leatherworkers could use hides and wool."

"It wouldn't be a small city either," he said, "when it had all these."

"But still," I said, "even to situate the city itself in the sort of place in which it won't need imported goods is just about impossible."

"It's impossible."

"Therefore there's still a further need for other people too who'll bring it what it needs from another city."

"There'll be a need."

"And if the courier goes empty-handed, carrying nothing those people need

371   from whom ours will get the things for their own use, he'll leave empty-handed, won't he?"

"It seems that way to me."

"Then they'll need to make not only enough things to be suitable for themselves, but also the kinds and quantity of things suitable for those people they need things from."

"They'll need to."

"So our city will need more of the farmers and other craftsmen."

"More indeed."

"And in particular other couriers no doubt, who'll bring in and carry away each kind of thing, and these are commercial traders aren't they?"

"Yes."

"So we'll also need commercial traders."

"Certainly."

b   "And if the commerce is carried on by sea, there'll be an additional need for many other people gathered together who know the work connected with the sea."

"Very many."

"And how about in the city itself? How are they going to share out with each other the things each sort makes by their work? It was for the sake of this that we even went into partnership and founded the city."

"It's obvious," he said: "by selling and buying."

"So a marketplace will arise out of this for us, and a currency as a conventional medium of exchange?"

"Certainly."

c   "But if, when the farmer or any other workman has brought any of the things he produces into the marketplace, he doesn't arrive at the same time as those who need to exchange things with him, is he going to stay unemployed at his craft sitting in the marketplace?"

"Not at all," he said, "but there are people who, seeing this, take this duty on themselves; in rightly managed cities it's pretty much for the people who are weakest in body and useless for any other work to do. Because there's a need for it, so they stay   d
around the marketplace to give money in exchange to those who need to sell something and to exchange in turn for money with all those who need to buy something."

"Therefore," I said, "this useful service makes for the origin of retail tradesmen in the city. Don't we call people retail tradesmen who are set up in the marketplace providing the service of buying and selling, but call those who travel around to cities commercial traders?"

"Certainly."

"And as I imagine, there are still certain other serviceable people, who don't entirely merit sharing in the partnership for things that involve thinking but have suffi-   e
cient strength of body for labors, so since they sell the use of their strength and call this payment wages, they are called, as I imagine, wage laborers, aren't they?"

"Yes."

"And the wage laborers, as seems likely, are the component that fills up the city?"

"It seems that way to me."

"Well then Adeimantus, has our city already grown to be complete?"

"Maybe."

"Then where in it would the justice and the injustice be? And together with which of the things we examined did they come to be present?"

"I have no idea, Socrates," he said, "unless it's somewhere in some usefulness of   372
these people themselves to each other."

"And maybe you're putting it beautifully," I said. "We need to examine it though and not be shy about it. So first, let's consider what style of life people will lead who've been provided for in this way. Will they do otherwise than produce grain and wine and cloaks and shoes? And when they've built houses, by summer they'll work at most things lightly clad and barefoot, but in winter adequately clothed and in shoes. And   b
they'll nourish themselves by preparing cereal from barley and flour from wheat, baking the latter and shaping the former by hand, and when they've set out fine cakes of barley meal and loaves of wheat bread on some sort of straw or clean leaves, reclining on leafy beds spread smooth with yew and myrtle, they and their children will feast themselves, drinking wine to top it off, while crowned with wreaths and singing hymns to the gods, joining with each other pleasurably, and not producing children beyond   c
their means, being cautious about poverty or war."

And Glaucon broke in, saying "It looks like you're making your men have a feast without any delicacies."

"That's true," I said. "As you say, I forgot that they'll have delicacies too, salt obviously, as well as olives and cheese, and they'll boil up the sorts of roots and greens that are cooked in country places. And as sweets we'll doubtless set out for them some figs and   d
chickpeas and beans, and at the fire they'll roast myrtle berries and acorns, while sipping wine in moderation. And in this way it's likely that, going through life in peace combined with health and dying in old age, they'll pass on another life of this sort to their offspring."

And he said, "And if you were making provisions for a city of pigs, Socrates, what would you fatten them on besides this?"

"But how should they be provided for, Glaucon?" I said.

"With the very things that are customary," he said. "I assume they'll lie back on couches so they won't get uncomfortable, and take their meals from tables, and have   e
exactly those delicacies and sweets that people do now."

"Okay, I understand," I said. "We're examining, it seems, not just how a city comes into being, but a city that lives in luxury. And maybe that's not a bad way to do it, since by examining that kind of city we might quickly spot the way that justice and injustice take root in cities. Now it seems to me though that the true city is the one we've gone over, just as it's a healthy one. But if you want us also to look in turn at an infected city, nothing prevents it. For these things, it seems, aren't sufficient for some people, and neither is this way of life, but couches and tables and the other furnishings will be added, and especially delicacies as well as perfumed ointments and incense and harem girls and pastries, and each of these in every variety. And so it's no longer the necessities we were speaking of at first—houses, cloaks, and shoes—that have to be put in place, but painting and multicolored embroidery have to be set in motion, and gold and ivory and all that sort of thing have to be acquired, don't they?"

"Yes," he said.

373

b   "Isn't there a need then to make the city bigger again? Because that healthy one isn't sufficient any longer, but is already filled with a mass of things and a throng of people, things that are no longer in the cities for the sake of necessity, such as all the hunters as well as the imitators [i.e., artists], many of whom are concerned with shapes and colors, many others with music, and also the poets and their assistants, the reciters, c   actors, dancers, theatrical producers, and craftsmen for all sorts of gear, including makeup for women and everything else. And we'll especially need more providers of services, or doesn't it seem there'll be a need for tutors, wet nurses, nannies, beauticians, barbers, and also delicacy-makers and chefs? Furthermore, there'll be an extra need for pig farmers; this job wasn't present in our earlier city because there was no need for it, but in this one there's the extra need for this too. And there'll be a need for a great multitude of other fattened livestock too, if one is going to eat them. Isn't that so?"

"How could it be otherwise?"

d   "Then won't we be much more in need of doctors when people live this way instead of the earlier way?"

"Very much so."

"And doubtless the land that was sufficient then to feed the people will now have gone from sufficient to small. Or how do we put it?"

"That way," he said.

"Then does something have to be cut off by us from our neighbors' land if we're going to have enough to graze on and plow, and by them in turn from ours if they too e   give themselves over to the unlimited acquisition of money, exceeding the limit of necessities?"

"That's a great necessity, Socrates," he said.

"So what comes after this, Glaucon, is that we go to war? Or how will it be?"

"That way," he said.

"And let's say nothing yet, at any rate," I said, "about whether war accomplishes anything bad or good, but only this much, that we have discovered in its turn the origin of war, in those things out of which most of all cities incur evils both in private and in public, when they do incur them."

"Very much so."

"So, my friend, there's a need for the city to be still bigger, not by a small amount 374   but by a whole army, which will go out in defense of all their wealth and in defense of the things we were just now talking about, and do battle with those who come against them."

"Why's that?" he said. "Aren't they themselves sufficient?"

"Not if it was beautifully done," I said, "for you and all of us to be in agreement when we were shaping the city; surely we agreed, if you recall, that one person has no power to do a beautiful job at many arts."

"What you say is true," he said.

"Then what?" I said. "Does the contest involved in war not seem to you to require art?"   b

"Much of it," he said.

"So is there any need to go to more trouble over leatherworking than over warfare?"

"By no means."

"But that's the very reason we prevented the leatherworker from attempting at the same time to be a farmer or a weaver or a housebuilder, but just be a leatherworker, so that the work of leathercraft would be done beautifully for us, and in the same way we gave out one job to one person for each of the others, the job into which each had grown naturally   c and for which he was going to stay at leisure from the other jobs, working at it throughout life and not letting the critical moments slip by to accomplish it beautifully. But isn't it of the greatest consequence that the things involved in war be accomplished well? Or are they so easy that even some farmer is going to be skilled at warfare at the same time, or a leatherworker or anyone working at any other art whatever, while no one could become sufficiently skillful at playing checkers or dice who didn't practice that very thing from his youth but treated it as a sideline? And someone who picks up a shield or any other weapon   d or implement of war, on that very day is going to be an adequate combatant in heavy-armor fighting or any other sort of battle that's needed in war, when no other implement that's picked up is going to make anyone a craftsman or fighter or even be usable to someone who hasn't gotten any knowledge about it or been supplied with adequate training?"

"Those implements would be worth a lot," he said.

"So then," I said, "to the extent that the work of the guardians is the most impor-   e tant, would it also be in need of the most leisure compared to other pursuits, as well as of the greatest art and care?"

"I certainly imagine so," he said.

"So wouldn't it also need a nature adapted to that very pursuit?"

"How could it not?"

"So it would be our task, likely, if we're going to be capable of it, to pick out which and which sort of natures are adapted to the guarding of the city."

"Ours indeed."

"By Zeus," I said, "it's no light matter we've called down as a curse on ourselves. Still, it's not something to run away from in fear, at least to the extent our power permits."

"Certainly not," he said.   375

"So do you imagine that for guarding" I said, "there's any difference in nature between a pure bred puppy and a well bred young man?"

"What sort of nature are you talking about?"

"For instance, each of the pair, I suppose, needs to be sharp at perceiving things, nimble at pursuing what it perceives, and also strong, if it needs to fight when it catches something."

"There is certainly a need for all these things," he said.

"And to be courageous too, if it's going to fight well."

"How could it be otherwise?"

"But will a horse or a dog or any other animal whatever that's not spirited be likely to be courageous? Or haven't you noticed how indomitable and invincible spiritedness is,   b and how, when it's present, every soul is both fearless and unyielding against everything?"

"I've noticed."

"And surely it's obvious what the guardian needs to be like in the things that belong to his body."

"Yes."

"And particularly in what belongs to the soul, that he has to be spirited."

"That too."

"Then how, Glaucon," I said, "when they're that way in their natures, will they not be fierce toward each other and toward the other citizens?"

"By Zeus," he said, "not easily."

c   "But surely they need to be gentle toward their own people but rough on their enemies, and if they aren't, they won't wait for others to destroy them but do it first themselves."

"True," he said.

"So what will we do?" I said. "Where are we going to find a character that's gentle and high-spirited at the same time? For presumably a gentle nature is opposite to a spirited one."

"So it appears."

"But surely if someone lacks either one of these things, he won't become a good guardian. But these things seem like impossibilities, and so it follows that a good

d   guardian becomes an impossibility."

"It's liable to be that way," he said.

I too was stumped and was thinking over what had been said before, and I said, "Justly are we stumped, my friend, because we've gotten away from the image we were setting up."

"How do you mean that?"

"We didn't notice that there are natures, after all, of the sort we were imagining there aren't, that have these opposites in them."

"But where?"

"One might see it in other animals too, though not least in the one we set beside

e   the guardian for comparison. Because you know, no doubt, about pure bred dogs, that this is their character by nature, to be as gentle as possible with those they're accustomed to and know, but the opposite with those they don't know."

"Certainly I know it."

"Therefore," I said, "this is possible, and it's not against nature for the guardian to be of the sort we're looking for."

"It doesn't seem like it."

"Well then, does it seem to you that there's still a further need for this in the one who'll be fit for guarding, that in addition to being spirited he also needs to be a philosopher by nature?"

376   "How's that?" he said. "I don't get it."

"You'll notice this too in dogs," I said, "which is also worth wondering at in the beast."

"What sort of thing?"

"That when it sees someone it doesn't know, it gets angry, even when it hasn't been treated badly by that person before, while anyone familiar it welcomes eagerly, even when nothing good has ever been done to it by that one. Or haven't you ever wondered at this?"

"Till this moment," he said, "I haven't paid it any mind at all. That they do this, though, is certainly obvious."

"But surely it shows an appealing attribute of its nature and one that's philosophic   b
in a true sense."

"In what way?"

"In that it distinguishes a face as friend or enemy," I said, "by nothing other than
the fact that it has learned the one and is ignorant of the other. And indeed, how could it
not be a lover of learning when it determines what's its own and what's alien to it by
means of understanding and ignorance?"

"There's no way it couldn't," he said.

"But surely," I said, "the love of learning and the love of wisdom are the same
thing?"

"They're the same," he said.

"Then shall we have the confidence to posit for a human being too, that if he's
going to be at all gentle to his own people and those known to him, he needs to be by   c
nature a lover of wisdom and of learning?"

"Let's posit it."

"So someone who's going to be a beautiful and good guardian of our city will be
philosophic, spirited, quick, and strong by nature."

"Absolutely so," he said.

"So he'd start out that way. But now in what manner will they be brought up and
educated by us? And if we examine it, is there anything that gets us forward toward
catching sight of the thing for the sake of which we're examining all this, the manner in   d
which justice and injustice come into being in a city? The point is that we might not
allow enough discussion, or we might go through a long one."

And Glaucon's brother said, "For my part, I expect this examination to be one that
gets us very far along into that."

"By Zeus, Adeimantus my friend," I said, "it's not to be given up then, even if it
happens to be overlong."

"Not at all."

"Come then, and just as if they were in a story and we were telling the story and
remaining at leisure, let's educate the men in our speech."

"We should do just that."

*   *   *

BOOK III

*   *   *

"As far as gods are concerned, then," I said, "those are some of the things, it   386
seems, that need to be heard and not heard straight from childhood by people who are
going to respect both the gods and their parents and not treat their friendship with one
another as a small thing."

"And for my part," he said, "I too assume that the way it appears to us is right."

"And what if they're going to be courageous? Don't they need to be told those
things that are of the sort to make them least afraid of death? Or do you think anyone at
all could become courageous if he had this terror in him?"   b

"By Zeus," he said, "I don't."

"What next? Do you imagine that anyone who thinks there's a realm of Hades and terrible things there is going to be unafraid of death and prefer death in battle over defeat and slavery?"

"Not at all."

c
"So it seems that for these stories too, it's necessary for us to take charge of those who attempt to tell them, and require them not simply to slander the things in Hades's realm the way they do but instead to praise them, on the grounds that they're neither telling the truth nor saying things of benefit to people who'll be warriors."

"It's certainly necessary," he said.

"Then," I said, "we'll delete everything of that sort, starting with this verse,*

> I'd rather be a bond-servant to another, tilling the soil
> For a man without land of his own and not much to live on
> Than be lord over all those wasted away among the dead,

and this,

> And the dwelling of the dead would be seen by mortals and immortals,
> Gruesome, rotting things that the very gods abominate. . . .

387ᵇ
And we'll beg Homer and the other poets not to take it hard if we cross out these things and everything of the sort, not because they aren't poetic and pleasant for most people to hear, but the more poetic they are, that much less should they be heard by children and men who need to be free and be more in fear of slavery than of death."

"Absolutely so."

c
"Then too, don't all the terrible and frightening names for these things need to be thrown out, Cocytus and Styx, beneath the earth, withered, and all the other things of this type that are supposed to make everyone who hears them shudder when they're named? Maybe they're okay for some other purpose, but we're afraid on behalf of our guardians, that they don't get warmer and softer from that sort of shudder than we need them to be."

"And we're right to be afraid," he said.

"Then they're to be taken away?"

"Yes."

"And a general outline opposite to these is to be followed in speaking and writing?"

"That's clear."

d
"And therefore we'll take out the complaints and laments of celebrated men?"

"That's necessary," he said, "if the earlier things were too."

"Consider then," I said, "whether we'll be taking them out rightly or not. And surely we claim that a decent man will hold that dying is not a terrible thing for a decent man whose comrade he is."

"We do claim that."

"Then he wouldn't wail over him as having suffered something terrible."

"Certainly not."

"But surely we also say this, that such a person is the most self-sufficient, himself for himself, for living well, and to a degree that surpasses others, is least in need of anyone else."

e

---

*These quotations, and several more (excluded here), are all from Homer's *Odyssey*.

"That's true," he said.

"Therefore it's least terrible for him to be deprived of a son or brother, or of money or anything else of the sort."

"Least indeed."

"Then he's also least the sort to wail but bears it in the mildest way when any such misfortune overtakes him."

"Very much so."

"Then we would rightly take away the lamentations of noteworthy men and give them over to women, and not to women of serious stature, and among the men all those   388
of the bad sort would make them, in order that those we claim to be raising for guarding the land for us wouldn't be able to stand acting like those people."

"That would be right to do," he said.

*   *   *

"Okay," I said, "what would be the next thing after that for us to distinguish? Wouldn't it be which of these same people will rule and which will be ruled?"   412ᶜ

"Sure."

"And it's clear that the older ones should be the rulers and the younger should be ruled?"

"That's clear."

"And that it should be the best among them?"

"That too."

"And aren't the best farmers the ones most adept at farming?"

"Yes."

"But since in this case they need to be the best among the guardians, don't they need to be the most adept at safeguarding the city?"

"Yes."

"So don't they need, to start with, to be intelligent at that as well as capable, and also protective of the city?"

"That's so."   d

"But someone would be most protective of that which he happened to love."

"Necessarily."

"And surely someone would love that thing most which he regarded as having the same things advantageous to it as to himself, and believed that when it fared well it followed that he himself fared well, and the other way around when it didn't."

"That's the way it is," he said.

"Therefore the men who need to be selected from among the rest of the guardians are those who appear to us, when we examine the whole course of their lives, as if they   e
most of all would do wholeheartedly whatever they'd regard as advantageous to the city, and who wouldn't be willing in any way to do what was not."

"They'd be suited to it," he said.

"It seems to me, then, that they need to be observed in all stages of life to see if they're adept guardians of this way of thinking, and don't drop it when they're bewitched or subjected to force, forgetting their opinion that they ought to do what's best for the city."

"What do you mean by dropping?" he said.

"I'll tell you," I said. "It appears to me that an opinion goes away from one's thinking either willingly or unwillingly. A false one goes away willingly from someone   413
who learns differently, but every true one unwillingly."

"The case of the willing dropping I understand," he said, "but I need to learn about the unwilling case."

"What?" I said. "Don't you too believe human beings are deprived of good things unwillingly but of bad ones willingly? Isn't it a bad thing to think falsely about the truth and a good thing to think truly? Or doesn't believing things that are seem to you to be thinking truly?"

"You're certainly speaking rightly," he said, "and it does seem to me that people are unwilling to be deprived of the truth."

b   "And don't they suffer this by being robbed, bewitched, or overpowered?"

"Now I'm not understanding again," he said.

"I guess I'm speaking like a tragedy," I said. "By those who are robbed, I mean people who are persuaded to change their minds and people who forget, because from the latter, time, and from the former, speech takes opinions away without their noticing it. Now presumably you understand?"

"Yes."

"And by those who are overpowered I mean people that some grief or pain causes to change their opinions."

"I understand that too," he said, "and you're speaking rightly."

c   "And I imagine that you too would claim that people are bewitched who change their opinions when they're either entranced by pleasure or in dread of something frightening."

"Yes," he said, "it's likely that everything that fools people is bewitching."

"Then as I was just saying, one needs to find out which of them are the best guardians of the way of thinking they have at their sides, that the thing they always need to do is to do what seems to them to be best for the city. So they need to be observed right from childhood by people who set tasks for them in which someone would be most likely to forget such a thing or be fooled out of it; anyone who remembers it and is

d   hard to fool is to be chosen and anyone who doesn't is to be rejected. Isn't that so?"

"Yes."

"And laborious jobs, painful sufferings, and competitions also need to be set up for them in which these same things are to be observed."

"That's right," he said.

"Thus a contest needs to be made," I said, "for the third form as well, that of bewitchment, and it needs to be watched. The same way people check out whether colts are frightened when they lead them into noisy commotions, the guardians, when young,

e   need to be taken into some terrifying situations and then quickly shifted into pleasant ones, so as to test them much more than gold is tested in a fire. If someone shows himself hard to bewitch and composed in everything, a good guardian of himself and of the musical style that he learned, keeping himself to a rhythm and harmony well-suited to all these situations, then he's just the sort of person who'd be most valuable both to himself

414   and to a city. And that one among the children and the youths and the men who is tested and always comes through unscathed is to be appointed as ruler of the city as well as guardian, and honors are to be given to him while he's living and upon his death, when he's allotted the most prized of tombs and other memorials. Anyone not of that sort is to be rejected. It seems to me, Glaucon," I said, "that the selection and appointment of rulers and guardians is something like that, described in outline, not with precision."

"It looks to me too like it would be done some such way," he said.

b   "Isn't it most correct, then, to call these the guardians in the true sense, complete guardians for outside enemies and also for friends inside, so that the latter won't want to do any harm and the former won't have the power to? The young ones that we've been calling guardians up to now, isn't it most correct to call auxiliaries and reinforcements for the decrees of the rulers?"

"It seems that way to me," he said.

"Then could we come up with some contrivance," I said, "from among the lies that come along in case of need, the ones we were talking about just now, some one noble lie   c
told to persuade at best even the rulers themselves, but if not, the rest of the city?"

"What sort of thing?" he said.

"Nothing new," I said, "but something Phoenician* that has come into currency in many places before now, since the poets assert it and have made people believe; but it hasn't come into currency in our time and I don't know if it could—it would take a lot of persuading."

"You seem a lot like someone who's reluctant to speak," he said.

"And I'll seem to you very appropriately reluctant," I said, "when I do speak."

"Speak," he said. "Don't be shy."

"I'll speak, then. And yet I don't know how I'll get up the nerve or find the words   d
to tell it. First I'll try my hand at persuading the rulers themselves and the soldiers, and then also the rest of the city, that, after all, the things we nurtured and educated them on were like dreams; they seemed to be experiencing all those things that seemed to be happening around them, but in truth they themselves were at the time under the soil inside the earth being molded and cultivated, and their weapons and other gear were   e
being crafted, and when they were completely formed, the earth, that was their mother, made them spring up. So now, as if the land they dwell in were a mother and nurse, it's up to them to deliberate over it, to defend it if anyone were to attack, and to take thought on behalf of the rest of the citizens as their earthborn siblings."

"It's not without reason," he said, "that you were ashamed for so long to tell the lie."

"It was entirely reasonable," I said. "But all the same, listen to the rest of the story   415
as well. What we'll say in telling them the story is: 'All of you in the city are brothers, but the god, when he molded those of you who are competent to be rulers, mixed gold into them at their formation—that's why they're the most honorable—but all the auxiliaries have silver in them, and there's iron and bronze in the farmers and other skilled workers. So since you're all kin, for the most part you'll produce children like yourselves, but it's   b
possible for a silver offspring sometimes to be born from a gold parent, and a gold from a silver, and all the others likewise from one another. So the god exhorts the rulers first and foremost to be good guardians of their children, of nothing more diligently than that, and to keep watch for nothing so diligently as for what they have intermixed in their souls. And if a child of theirs is born with bronze or iron mixed in it, they'll by no means   c
give way to pity, but paying it the honor appropriate to its nature, they'll drive it out among the craftsmen or farmers, and if in turn any children are born from those parents with gold or silver mixed in them, they'll honor them and take them up, some to the guardian group, the others to the auxiliary, because there's an oracle foretelling that the city will be destroyed when an iron or bronze guardian has guardianship over it.' So do you have any contrivance to get them to believe this story?"

---

*Cadmus, the legendary founder of the Greek city Thebes, came from Phoenicia (the region roughly the same as modern Lebanon). To found the city he had to kill a dragon. A god told him to plant the dragon's teeth, and the first inhabitants of the city sprang up from those seeds. When Socrates says the story was current in many places, he means there were other local legends of races sprung from the ground they now live on, all originally brothers and sisters whose first mother is the land that feeds them and that they defend and love.

"There's no way," he said, "at least for these people themselves. There might be
d   one, though, for their sons and the next generation and the rest of humanity after that."

"But even that," I said, "would get things going well toward their being more protective of the city and of one another, because I understand pretty well what you mean.
And that's that it will carry on the way an oral tradition leads it. But once we've armed
these offspring of the earth, let's bring them forth with their rulers in the lead. And when
they've come, let them look for the most beautifully situated spot in the city to set up a
e   military camp, from which they could most effectively restrain the people in the city if
any of them were unwilling to obey the laws, and defend against those outside it if any
enemy, like a wolf, were to attack the flock. And when they've set up the camp and
offered sacrifices to those whom they ought, let them make places to sleep. Or how
should it be?"

"That way," he said.

"The sort of places that would be adequate to give shelter in both winter and
summer?"

"Of course," he said, "because you seem to be talking about dwellings."

"Yes," I said, "dwellings for soldiers anyway, but not for moneymakers."

416   "How do you mean the one differs from the other?" he said.

"I'll try to tell you," I said. "Because it's surely the most dreadful and shameful of
all things for a shepherd to raise dogs as auxiliaries for the flock that are of the sort and
brought up in such a way that, from intemperance or hunger or some bad habit of another
kind, the dogs themselves try to do harm to the sheep, acting like wolves instead of dogs."

"It is dreadful," he said; "how could it be anything else?"

b   "Then isn't there a need to be on guard in every way so that our auxiliaries won't
do that sort of thing to the citizens, since they're the stronger, becoming like savage
masters instead of benevolent allies?"

"There's a need to be on guard," he said.

"And wouldn't they have been provided with the most effective safeguard if
they've been beautifully educated in their very being?"

"But surely they have been," he said.

And I said, "That's not something that deserves to be asserted with certainty,
c   Glaucon my friend. What we were saying just now does deserve to be, though, that they
need to get the right education, whatever it is, if they're going to what's most important
for being tame, both toward themselves and toward those who are guarded by them."

"That's certainly right," he said.

"Now in addition to this education, any sensible person would claim that they
need to be provided with dwellings and other property of that sort, whatever it takes for
d   them not to be stopped from being the best possible guardians and not to be tempted to
do harm to the citizens."

"And he'll be claiming something true."

"Then see whether they need to live and be housed in some such way as this," I
said, "if they're going to be that sort of people. First, no private property that's not
completely necessary is to be possessed by any of them. Next, there's to be no house or
treasure room belonging to any of them except one that everyone who wants to will
enter. Provisions, of all things men need who are moderate and courageous fighters in
e   war, they're to receive at fixed times from the other citizens as recompense for guarding them, of such an amount that they have nothing over and nothing lacking each
year. Going regularly to public dining halls, they're to live in common like soldiers in
a camp. About gold and silver, it's to be said to them that they have the divine sort from

gods always in their souls, and have no further need of the human sort, and that it's not pious to defile their possession of the former by mixing with it the possession of mortal gold, because many impious deeds have occurred over the currency most people use, while the sort they have with them is uncorrupted. And for them alone of those in the city, it's not lawful to handle or touch gold and silver, or even to go under the same roof with them, or wear them as ornaments, or drink out of silver or gold cups.

417

"And in this way they'd keep themselves and the city safe. But whenever they possess private land and houses and currency, they'll be heads of households and farm owners instead of guardians, and they'll become hostile masters instead of allies of the other citizens, and spend their whole lives hating and being hated, and plotting and being plotted against, fearing those inside the city instead of and much more than the enemies outside it, as they and the rest of the city race onward, already very close to destruction.

b

"For all these reasons, then," I said, "we'll declare that's the way the guardians need to be provided for in the matter of housing and the rest, and we'll set these things down as laws, won't we?"

"Very much so," said Glaucon.

BOOK IV

* * *

"Your city, son of Ariston," I said, "[has] now be founded. So after that, take a look around in it yourself, once you've provided a light from somewhere, and call in your brother and Polemarchus and the others, if in any way we might see wherever its justice might be, and its injustice, and what differentiates the pair from each other, and which of the two someone who's going to be happy ought to get hold of, whether he goes unnoticed or not by all gods and human beings."

427^d

"You're talking nonsense," said Glaucon. "You took it on yourself to search for it because it's irreverent for you not to come to the aid of justice in every way to the limit of your power."

e

"It's true," I said, "as you remind me, and so it must be done, but you folks need to do your part too."

"Well that's what we'll do," he said.

"Then I hope to find it this way," I said. "I imagine our city, if in fact it's been correctly founded, is completely good."

"Necessarily," he said.

"So it's clear that it's wise and courageous and moderate and just."

"That's clear."

"Then whatever we find in it from among them, the leftover part will be what hasn't been found?"

428

"Of course."

"Then just as with any other four things, if we were looking for a particular one of them in whatever it was, whenever we recognized that one first that would be good enough for us, but if we recognized the three first, by that very means we would have recognized the thing we're looking for, because it's obvious that it couldn't any longer be anything else than the thing left over."

"You're saying it correctly," he said.

"So for these things too, since they happen to be four, they need to be looked for in the same way?"

"Obviously."

b   "Well then, the first thing that seems to me to be clearly visible in it is wisdom. And there seems to be something strange about it."

"What?" he said.

"The city that we went over seems to me to be wise in its very being. Because it is well-counseled, isn't it?"

"Yes."

"And surely it's clear that this very thing, good counsel, is a certain kind of knowledge, since it's presumably not by ignorance but by knowledge that people counsel well."

"That's clear."

"But many kinds of knowledge of all varieties are surely present in the city."

"How could there not be?"

"Then is it on account of the carpenters' knowledge that the city is called wise and well-counseled?"

c   "Not at all," he said, "on account of that it's called skilled in carpentry."

"Then it's not on account of the knowledge that counsels about how wooden equipment would be best that a city is called wise."

"No indeed."

"Well then, is it the knowledge about things made of bronze or anything else of that sort?"

"None whatever of those," he said.

"And it's not the knowledge about growing the fruits of the earth; that makes it skilled in farming."

"It seems that way to me."

"What about it, then?" I said. "Is there any knowledge in the city just now

d founded by us, on the part of any of its citizens, by which it counsels not about things in the city pertaining to someone in particular, but about itself as a whole, and in what way it would interact best within itself and with other cities?"

"There certainly is."

"What is it," I said, "and in which of them?"

"It's guardianship," he said, "and it's in those rulers whom we were just now naming complete guardians."

"So on account of this sort of knowledge, what do you call the city?"

"Well-counseled," he said, "and wise in its very being."

"Now do you imagine," I said, "that there will be more metalworkers present in

e our city than these true guardians?"

"A lot more metalworkers," he said.

"And compared also to all the rest who are given names for having any particular kinds of knowledge, wouldn't these guardians be the fewest of them all?"

"By a lot."

"Therefore it's by means of the smallest group and part of itself, the part that directs and rules, and by the knowledge in it, that a whole city founded in accord with

429 nature would be wise. And it seems likely that this turns out by nature to be the smallest class, the one that's appropriately allotted a share of that knowledge which, alone among the other kinds of knowledge, ought to be called wisdom."

"Very true, just as you say," he said.

"So we've discovered this one of the four—how we did it I don't know—both it and where in the city it's lodged."

"It seems to me at any rate," he said, "to have been discovered well enough."

"But as for courage, it and the part of the city it lies in, and through which the city is called courageous, are surely not very hard to see."

"How so?"

"Who," I said, "would say a city was cowardly or courageous by looking to anything other than that part of it which defends it and takes the field on its behalf?"   b

"No one," he said, "would look to anything else."

"Because I don't imagine," I said, "that whether the other people in it are cowards or courageous would be what determines it to be the one sort or the other."

"No."

"Then a city is also courageous by means of a certain part of itself, by its having in it a power such that it will safeguard through everything its opinion about what's to be feared, that it's the same things or the sorts of things that the lawgiver passed on to   c
them in their education. Or isn't that what you call courage?"

"I haven't quite understood what you're saying," he said; "just say it again."

"I mean," I said, "that courage is a certain kind of preservation."

"What kind of preservation exactly?"

"Of the opinion instilled by law through education about what things and what sorts of things are to be feared. By preserving it through everything I meant keeping it intact when one is in the midst of pains and pleasures and desires and terrors and not   d
dropping it. I'm willing to make an image of what it seems to me to be like if you want me to."

"I want you to."

"You know, don't you," I said, "that dyers, when they want to dye wool so it will be purple, first select, from among the many colors, wool of the single nature belonging to white things, and then prepare it in advance, taking care with no little preparation that it will accept the pigment as much as possible, and only so dip it in the dye? And what   e
is dyed in this way becomes impervious to fading, and washing it, whether without soaps or with them, has no power to remove the color from it, but what is not done that way—well, you know what it comes out like, whether one dyes it with other colors or this one without having taken care in advance."

"I know," he said, "that it's washed out and laughable."

"Then understand," I said, "that we too were doing something like that to the extent of our power when we were selecting the soldiers and educating them with music   430
and gymnastic training. Don't imagine that we devised that for any reason other than so they, persuaded by us, would take the laws into themselves like a dye in the most beautiful way possible, so that their opinion about what's to be feared, and about everything else, would become impervious to fading, because they'd had the appropriate nature and upbringing, and the dye couldn't be washed out of them by those soaps that are so formidable at scouring, either pleasure, which is more powerful at doing that than every   b
sort of lye and alkaline ash, or pain, terror, and desire, more powerful than any other soaps. This sort of power and preservation through everything of a right and lawful opinion about what is and isn't to be feared, I for my part call courage, and I set it down as such unless you say otherwise."

"No," he said, "I don't say anything different, because it seems to me that you're considering the right opinion about these same things that comes about without education, as animal-like or slavish, and not entirely reliable, and that you'd call it something other than courage."

c   "Entirely true," I said, "as you say."

"Then I accept this as being courage," he said.

"Yes, do accept it," I said, "but as a citizen's courage, and you'll be accepting it the right way. We'll go over something still more beautiful in connection with it later if you want, because what we've been looking for now is not that but justice. For the inquiry about that, I imagine this is sufficient."

"Yes," he said, "beautifully said."

"So two things are still left," I said, "that it's necessary to catch sight of in the city,

d   moderation, and the one for the sake of which we're looking for them all, justice."

"Quite so."

"How, then, might we discover justice so that we won't have to bother any more about moderation?"

"Well," he said, "I don't know and I wouldn't want it to come to light first anyway if we're no longer going to examine moderation. So if you want to gratify me, consider this before that."

"I certainly do want to," I said; "unless I'd be doing an injustice."

"Consider it, then," he said.

e   "It's got to be considered," I said, "and as seen from where we are, it looks more like a sort of consonance and harmony than the ones before."

"How?"

"Presumably," I said, "moderation is a certain well-orderedness, and a mastery over certain pleasures and desires, as people say—being stronger than oneself—though in what way they mean that I don't know. And some other things of that sort are said that are like clues to it, aren't they?"

"They most of all," he said.

"But then isn't being stronger than oneself absurd? Because the one who's stronger than himself would presumably also be weaker than himself, and the weaker

431   stronger, since the same person is referred to in all these terms."

"How could it not be the same one?"

"But it appears to me," I said, "that this phrase intends to say that there's something to do with the soul within a human being himself that has something better and something worse in it, and whenever what's better by nature is master over what's worse, calling this 'being stronger than oneself' at least praises it. But whenever, from a bad upbringing or some sort of bad company, the better part that's smaller is mastered

b   by the larger multitude of the worse part, this as a reproach is blamed and called 'being weaker than oneself,' and the person so disposed is called intemperate."

"That's likely it," he said.

"Then look over toward our new city," I said, "and you'll find one of these things present in it. Because you'll claim that it's justly referred to as stronger than itself, if in fact something in which the better rules over the worse ought to be called moderate and stronger than itself."

"I am looking over at it," he said, "and you're telling the truth."

c   "And surely one would find a multitude and variety of desires as well as pleasures and pains, in children especially, and in women and menial servants, and also in most of the lower sorts of people among those who are called free."

"Very much so."

"But you'll meet with simple and measured desires and pleasures, which are guided by reasoning with intelligence and right opinion, in few people, who are both best in nature and best educated."

"True," he said.

"Then don't you see that these too are present in your city, and that the desires in most people and those of the lower sorts are mastered there by the desires and intelligence of the lesser number of more decent people?" d

"I do," he said.

"So if one ought to refer to any city as stronger than pleasures and desires, and than itself, that needs to be applied to this one."

"Absolutely so," he said.

"So then isn't it moderate too in all these respects?"

"Very much so," he said.

"And also, if in any city the same opinion is present in both the rulers and the ruled about who ought to rule, it would be present in this one. Doesn't that seem so?" e

"Emphatically so," he said.

"Then as for being moderate, in which group of citizens will you say it's present when they're in this condition, in the rulers or in the ruled?"

"In both, presumably," he said.

"So do you see," I said, "that we had an appropriate premonition just now that moderation is like a certain harmony?"

"Why's that?"

"Because it's not like courage and wisdom, each of which by its presence in a certain part showed the city to be either wise or courageous. It doesn't act that way, but is 432 in fact stretched through the whole across the scale, showing the weakest, the strongest, and those in between to be singing the same song together, whether you want to rank them in intelligence, or, if you want, in strength, or even by their number or their money or by anything whatever of that sort. So we'd be most correct in claiming that this like-mindedness is moderation, a concord of the naturally worse and better about which ought to rule, both in the city and in each one." b

"The way it seems to me is completely in accord with that," he said.

"Well then," I said, "three of them have been spotted in our city—at least it seems that way. So what would be the remaining form by which the city would further partake in virtue? For it's clear that this is justice."

"That's clear."

"So now, Glaucon, don't we need to take up positions like hunters in a circle around a patch of woods and concentrate our attention, so that justice doesn't escape anywhere, disappear from our sight, and become obscure? Because it's evident that it's c in there somewhere. So look and make a spirited effort to catch sight of it, in case you spot it in any way before I do, and you'll show it to me."

"If only I were able to," he said. "Instead, if you treat me as a follower who's capable of seeing what's pointed out to him, you'll be handling me in an entirely sensible way."

"Follow then," I said, "after offering up prayers along with me."

"I'll do that," he said; "just you lead."

"The place sure does look like an inaccessible and shadowy one," I said; "at any rate it's dark and hard to scout through. But still, one needs to go on."

"Yes, one does need to go on," he said. d

And spotting something, I called, "Got it! Got it, Glaucon! We've probably got its trail, and I don't think it's going to get away from us at all."

"You bring good tidings," he said.

"But oh what a slug-like condition we were in," I said.

"In what sort of way?"

"All this time, you blessed fellow, and it seems it's been rolling around in front of our feet from the beginning, and we didn't see it for all that, but were utterly ridiculous; the way people holding something in their hands sometimes look for the things they're holding, we too weren't looking at the thing itself but were gazing off into the distance somewhere, which is probably the very reason it escaped our notice."

"How do you mean?" he said.

"Like this," I said: "it seems to me that although we've been saying it and hearing it all along, we haven't learned from our own selves that we were in a certain way saying it."

"That's a long prologue for someone who's eager to hear," he said.

"Well then, hear whether I mean anything after all," I said.

"Because from the beginning the thing we've set down as what we needed to do all through everything when we were founding the city, this, it seems to me, or else some form of this, is justice. Surely we set down, and said often, if you remember, that each one person needed to pursue one of the tasks that are involved in the city, the one to which his nature would be naturally best adapted."

"We did say that."

"And surely we've heard it said by many others that doing what's properly one's own and not meddling in other people's business is justice, and we've said it often ourselves."

"We have said that."

"This, then, my friend," I said, "when it comes about in a certain way, is liable to be justice, this doing what's properly one's own. Do you know where I find an indication of this?"

"No, tell me," he said.

"It seems to me," I said, "that the thing that's left over in the city from the ones we've considered—moderation, courage, and wisdom—is what provided all of them with the power to come into being in it and provides their preservation once they've come into being, for as long as it's in it. And in fact we were claiming that justice would be what was left over from them if we were to find the three."

"And that is necessary," he said.

"And certainly," I said, "if one had to judge which of these would do our city the most good by coming to be present in it, it would be hard to decide whether it's the agreement of opinion of the rulers and ruled, or the preservation of a lawful opinion that arises in the soldiers about what things are and aren't to be feared, or the judgment and guardianship present in the rulers, or whether it's this that does it the most good by being in it, in a child and a woman and a slave and a free person and a craftsman and a ruler and one who's ruled, the fact that each of them, being one person, did what was properly his own and didn't meddle in other people's business."

"It's hard to decide," he said; "how could it not be?"

"Therefore, it seems that, with a view to a city's virtue, the power that comes from each person's doing what's properly his own in it is a match for its wisdom and moderation and courage."

"Very much so," he said.

"And wouldn't you place justice as a match for these as to a city's virtue?"

"Absolutely so."

"Then consider whether it will seem that way in this respect too: will you assign   e
the judging of lawsuits in the city to the rulers?"

"Certainly."

"And will they judge them with their sights on anything else besides this, that
each party not have another's property or be deprived of his own?"

"No, only on that."

"Because it's the just thing?"

"Yes."

"Then in this respect too, having and doing what's properly one's own would be   434
agreed to be justice."

"That's so."

"Now see if the same thing seems so to you that does to me. If a carpenter tries to
work at the job of a leatherworker, or a leatherworker at that of a carpenter, or if they
trade their tools and honors with each other, or even if the same person tries to do both
jobs, and everything else gets traded around, would it seem to you to do the city any
great harm?"

"Not very great," he said.

"But I imagine when someone who's a craftsman by nature, or some other sort of
moneymaker, but proud of his wealth or the multitude of his household or his strength   b
or anything else of the sort, tries to get in among the warrior kind, or one of the warriors
into the deliberative and guardian kind when he doesn't merit it, and they trade their
tools and honors with each other, or when the same person tries to do all these jobs at
the same time, then I imagine it would seem to you too that this change and meddling
among them would be the ruin of the city."

"Absolutely so."

"Therefore among the three classes there are, any meddling or changing into one
another is of the greatest harm to the city, and would most correctly be referred to as the   c
greatest wrongdoing."

"Precisely so."

"And wouldn't you say the greatest wrongdoing toward one's own city is injustice?"

"How could it not be?"

"So this is injustice. And let's say this the other way around; the minding of their
own business by the moneymaking, auxiliary, and guardian classes, when each of them
does what properly belongs to it in a city, is the opposite of that and would be justice
and would show the city to be just?"

"It doesn't seem to be any other way than that to me," he said.

"Let's not say it in quite so rigid a way yet, but if this form is agreed by us to be   d
present in each one of the people as well and to be justice there, then we'll join in going
along with it. What more would there be to say? And if not, then we'll consider something else. But for now let's complete the examination by which we imagined it would be
easier to catch sight of what sort of thing justice is in one human being if we tried to see
it first in some bigger thing that has justice in it. And it seemed to us that a city is just   e
that, and so we founded the best one in our power, knowing well that it would be present
in a good one at least. So let's carry over what came to light for us there to one person,
and if they're in accord, it will turn out beautifully; but if something different shows up   435
in the single person, we'll go back to the city again and test it. And maybe, by examining
them side by side and rubbing them together like sticks, we could make justice flame
forth from them, and once it's become evident we could substantiate it for ourselves."

"Then it's down the road you indicate," he said, "and it behooves us to go there too."

"Well then," I said, "does the bigger or smaller thing that someone refers to by the same name happen to be unlike the other one in the respect in which it's called the same, or like it?"

"Like it," he said.

b   "Therefore a just man will not differ at all from a just city with respect to the form of justice, but he'll be like it."

"He'll be like it," he said.

"But the city seemed to be just because each of the three classes of natures present in it did what properly belonged to it, while it seemed also to be moderate, courageous, and wise on account of certain other attributes and characteristic activities of these same classes."

"True," he said.

c   "Therefore, my friend, we'll regard a single person in this way too, as having these same forms in his soul, and as rightly deserving to have the same names applied to them as in the city as a result of the same attributes."

"There's every need to," he said.

"It's certainly a light question about the soul we've landed ourselves into now, you strange fellow," I said, "whether it has these three forms in it or not."

"It's not quite such a light one we seem to me to be in," he said. "It's probably because the saying is true, Socrates, that beautiful things are difficult."

"So it appears," I said. "And know for sure, Glaucon, that it's my opinion we'll
d   never get hold of this in a precise way along the sorts of paths we're now taking in our arguments, because there's another, longer and more rigorous road that leads to it. Maybe, though, we can get hold of it in a way worthy, at least, of the things that have already been said and considered."

"Isn't that something to be content with?" he said. "For me, at present anyway, it would be good enough."

"Yes, certainly," I said, "that will be quite sufficient for me too."

"Don't get tired, then," he said; "just examine it."

"Well then," I said, "isn't there a great necessity for us to agree that the same
e   forms and states of character are present in each of us as are in the city? Because presumably they didn't get there from anywhere else. It would be ridiculous if anyone imagined the spirited character didn't come to be in the cities from particular people who also have this attribute, like those in Thrace and Scythia, and pretty generally in the
436   northern region, or similarly with the love of learning, which one might attribute especially to the region round about us, or the love of money that one might claim to be not least round about the Phoenicians and those in Egypt."

"Very much so," he said.

"That's just the way it is," I said, "and it's not difficult to recognize."

"Certainly not."

"But this now is difficult: whether we act each way by means of the same thing, or in the different ways by means of different things, of which there are three—whether we learn by means of one of the things in us, become spirited by means of another, and
b   feel desires in turn by means of a third for the pleasures having to do with nourishment and procreation and as many things as are closely related to these, or whether we act by means of the whole soul in each of them, once we're aroused. These are the things that will be difficult to determine in a manner worthy of the discussion."

"It seems that way to me too," he said.

"Then let's try to mark out whether they're the same as one another or different, in this way."

"How?"

"It's obvious that the same thing isn't going to put up with doing or undergoing opposite things in the same respect and in relation to the same thing at the same time, so presumably if we find that happening in the things in question, we'll know that they're not the same but more than one thing."

"Okay."

"Then consider what I say."

"Say it," he said.

"Does the same thing have the power to stand still and move," I said, "at the same time in the same respect?"

"Not at all."

"Then let's agree about it in a still more precise way, so that we won't be quibbling as we go on. Because if anyone were to say of a person who was standing still but moving his hands and his head, that the same person was standing still and moving at the same time, I imagine we wouldn't consider that he ought to say it that way, but that some one thing about the person stands still while another moves. Isn't that so?"

"It's so."

"So if the one who said that were to get still more cute, making the subtle point that tops stand still as a whole and move at the same time, when they spin around with the point fixed in the same place, or that anything else going around in a circle on the same spot does that, we wouldn't accept it, since it's not with respect to the same things about themselves that such things are in that case staying in place and being carried around, but we'd claim that they have in them something straight and something surrounding it, and stand still with respect to the straight part, since they don't tilt in any direction, but move in a circle with respect to the surrounding part; and when the straight axis is leaning to the right or the left, or forward or back, at the same time it's spinning around, then it's not standing still in any way."

"You've got that right," he said.

"Therefore, when such things are said they won't knock us off course at all, any more than they'll persuade us that in any way, the same thing, at the same time, in the same respect, in relation to the same thing, could ever undergo, be, or do opposite things."

"Not me at any rate," he said.

"Be that as it may," I said, "in order that we won't be forced to waste time going through all the objections of that sort and establishing that they aren't true, let's go forward on the assumption that this is how it is, having agreed that, if these things should ever appear otherwise than that, all our conclusions from it will have been refuted."

"That's what one ought to do," he said.

"Well then, would you place nodding 'yes' as compared to shaking one's head 'no' among things that are opposite to each other, and having a craving to get something as compared to rejecting it, and drawing something to oneself as compared to pushing it away, and everything of that sort? Whether they're things one does actively or experiences passively, there won't be any difference on that account."

"Sure," he said, "they're opposites."

"And what about thirst and hunger and the desires in general," I said, "as well as wishing and wanting? Wouldn't you place all these things somewhere in those forms just mentioned? For example, wouldn't you claim that the soul of someone who desires either has a craving for what it desires, or draws to itself what it wants to become its own, or, in turn, to the extent it wishes something to be provided to it, nods its assent to this to itself as though it had asked some question, stretching out toward its source?"

"I would indeed."

"And what about this? Won't we place not wanting and not wishing and not desiring in with pushing away and banishing from itself and in with all the opposites of the former things?"

"How could we not?"

d   "Now these things being so, are we going to claim that there's a form consisting of desires, and that among these themselves, the most conspicuous ones are what we call thirst and what we call hunger?"

"We're going to claim that," he said.

"And the one is for drink, the other for food?"

"Yes."

"Now to the extent that it's thirst, would it be a desire in the soul for anything beyond that of which we say it's a desire? For instance, is thirst a thirst for a hot drink or a cold one, or a big or a little one, or in a word, for any particular sort of drink? Or, if

e   there's any heat present in addition to the thirst, wouldn't that produce an additional desire for cold, or if cold is present, a desire for heat? And if by the presence of magnitude the thirst is a big one, that will add a desire for a big drink, or of smallness, for a little one? But being thirsty itself will never turn into a desire for anything other than the very thing it's naturally for, for drink, or being hungry in turn for food?"

"It's like that," he said; "each desire itself is only for the very thing it's naturally for, while the things attached to it are for this or that sort."

438   "Then let's not be unprepared, and let someone get us confused, on the grounds that no one desires drink, but decent quality drink, and not food but decent quality food, since everyone, after all, desires good things. So if thirst is a desire, it would be for a decent quality of drink, or of whatever else it's a desire for, and the same way with the other desires."

"Well, maybe there could seem to be something in what he's saying," he said, "when he says that."

"But surely," I said, "with all such things that are related to something, the ones

b   that are of particular kinds are related to something of a particular kind, as it seems to me, while the sorts that are just themselves are related only to something that's just itself."

"I don't understand," he said.

"Don't you understand," I said, "that what's greater is of such a sort as to be greater than something?"

"Certainly."

"Than a lesser thing?"

"Yes."

"And a much greater thing than one that's much less, right?"

"Yes."

"And also a thing that was greater than one that was less, and a thing that's going to be greater than one that's going to be less?"

"Yes, of course," he said.

"And something more numerous is related to something that's fewer, and some-

c   thing twice as many to something that's half as many, and all that sort of thing, and also something heavier to something lighter and faster to slower, and in addition, hot things are related to cold things, and isn't everything like that the same way?"

"Very much so."

"And what about the kinds of knowledge? Aren't they the same way? Knowledge just by itself is knowledge of what's learnable just by itself, or of whatever one ought to set down knowledge as being of, while a particular knowledge or a particular sort is of a particular thing or a particular sort of thing. I mean this sort of thing: when a knowledge of constructing houses came into being, didn't it differ from the other kinds of knowledge so that it got called housebuilding?"   d

"Certainly."

"And wasn't that because it's a particular kind of knowledge, and any of the others is a different sort?"

"Yes."

"And wasn't it because it was about a particular sort of thing that it too came to be of a particular sort, and the same way for the other arts and kinds of knowledge?"

"That's the way it is."

"Well then," I said, "if you've understood it now, call that what I meant to say then, that with all the things that are such as to be about something, the ones that are only themselves are about things that are only themselves, while the ones that are of particular kinds are about things of particular kinds. And I'm not saying at all that the sorts of things they're about are the same sorts they themselves are, as a result of which the knowledge of what's healthy and sick would be healthy and sickly, and the knowledge of bad and good things would be bad and good; instead, I'm saying that when a knowledge came into being that was not just about the very thing knowledge is about, but about a particular thing, and that was what's healthy and sick, it too as a result came to be of a particular sort. And this made it no longer be called simply knowledge, but, with the particular sort included, medicine."   e

"I've understood it," he said, "and it does seem that way to me."

"So wouldn't you place thirst," I said, "among those things in which to be for something is exactly what they are? Thirst is, of course, for something."   439

"I would, yes," he said; "it's for drink anyway."

"And isn't a particular sort of thirst for a particular sort of drink, while thirst itself is not for a lot or a little, or for a good or a bad one, or, in a word, for any particular sort, but thirst itself is naturally just for drink itself?"

"Absolutely so."

"Therefore the soul of someone who's thirsty, to the extent he's thirsty, wants nothing other than to drink, and stretches out to this, and sets itself in motion toward it."   b

"Clearly so."

"So if anything ever pulls it back when it's thirsty, it would be some different thing in it from the very thing that's thirsty, and that tows it like an animal toward drinking? Because we claim that the same thing couldn't be doing opposite things in the same part of itself in relation to the same thing at the same time."

"No, it couldn't."

"In the same way, I imagine, one doesn't do well to say about an archer that his hands push and pull the bow at the same time, but rather that one hand is the one pushing it and the other the one pulling it."   c

"Absolutely so," he said.

"Now do we claim that there are some people who sometimes, while they're thirsty, aren't willing to drink?"

"Very much so," he said, "many people and often."

"Well what should one say about them?" I said. "Isn't there something in their soul telling them to drink and something preventing them from it that's different from and mastering what's telling them to?"

"It seems that way to me," he said.

d   "And doesn't the thing that prevents such things come about in it, when it does come about, from reasoning? But the things that tug and pull come to it from passions and disorders?"

"It looks that way."

"So not unreasonably will we regard them as being two things and different from each other, referring to that in the soul by which it reasons as its reasoning part, and that by which it feels erotic love, hunger, and thirst, and is stirred with the other desires, as its irrational and desiring part, associated with certain satisfactions and pleasures."

"No, we'd regard them that way quite reasonably," he said.

e   "So let these two forms be marked off in the soul," I said. "But is the part that has to do with spiritedness, and by which we're spirited, a third thing, or would it be of the same nature as one of these two?"

"Maybe the same as one of them," he said, "the desiring part."

"But I once heard something that I believe," I said, "about how Leontius, Aglaion's son, was going up from Piraeus along the outside of the north wall, and noticed dead bodies lying beside the executioner. He desired to see them, but at the

440   same time felt disgust and turned himself away; for a while he struggled and covered his eyes, but then he was overcome by his desire, and running toward the bodies holding his eyes wide open, he said, 'See for yourselves, since you're possessed! Take your fill of the lovely sight.'"

"I've heard that myself," he said.

"This story certainly indicates," I said, "that anger sometimes makes war against the desires as though it were one thing acting against another."

"It does indicate that," he said.

"And don't we often observe it in many other ways as well," I said, "when desires

b   overpower someone contrary to his reasoning part, that he scolds himself and is aroused against the part in him that's overpowering him, and just as if there were a pair of warring factions, the spiritedness of such a person becomes allied with his reason? But as for its making a partnership with the desires to act in defiance when reason has decided what ought not to be done, I don't suppose you'd claim you'd ever noticed such a thing happening in yourself, or, I imagine, in anyone else."

"No, by Zeus!" he said.

"Then what about when someone thinks he's being unjust?" I said. "The more

c   noble he is, won't he be that much less capable of getting angry at being hungry or cold or suffering anything else at all of the sort from the person he thinks is doing those things to him justly, and won't he be unwilling, as I'm saying, for his spirit to be aroused against that person?"

"That's true," he said.

"But what about when he regards himself as being treated unjustly? Doesn't the spirit in him seethe and harden and ally itself with what seems just, and submitting to

d   suffering through hunger and cold and all such things, it prevails and doesn't stint its noble struggles until it gains its end or meets its death, or else, called back, like a dog by a herdsman, by the reason that stands by it, it becomes calm?"

"It is very much like what you describe," he said. "And certainly in our city we set up the auxiliaries like dogs obedient to the rulers, who were like shepherds of the city."

"You conceive what I want to say beautifully," I said, "especially if you've taken it to heart in this respect in addition to that one."

"In what sort of respect?"

"That it's looking the opposite of the way it did to us just now with the spirited part, because then we imagined it was something having to do with desire, but now we're claiming that far from that, it's much more inclined in the faction within the soul to take arms on the side of the reasoning part."

"Absolutely," he said.

"Then is it different from that too, or some form of the reasoning part, so that there aren't three but two forms in the soul, a reasoning one and a desiring one? Or just as, in the city, there were three classes that held it together, moneymaking, auxiliary, and deliberative, so too in the soul is there this third, spirited part, which is by nature an auxiliary to the reasoning part, unless it's corrupted by a bad upbringing?"

"It's necessarily a third part," he said.

"Yes," I said, "as long as it comes to light as something differing from the reasoning part, the same way it manifested itself as different from the desiring part."

"But it's not hard to make that evident," he said, "since one could see this even in small children, that they're full of spiritedness right from birth, while some of them seem to me never to get any share of reasoning, and most get one at a late time of life."

"Yes, by Zeus," I said, "you put it beautifully. And also in animals one could see that what you're describing is that way. And in addition to these things, what we cited from Homer in some earlier place in the conversation will bear witness to it:

Striking his chest, he scolded his heart with words.

Here Homer has clearly depicted that which reflects on the better and the worse as one thing rebuking another, that which is irrationally spirited."

"You've said it exactly right," he said.

"Well, with a lot of effort we've managed to swim through these waters, and we're tolerably well agreed that the same classes in the city are present in the soul of each one person, and are equal in number."

"They are."

"Isn't it already a necessary consequence, then, that a private person is wise in the same manner and by the same means that a city was wise?"

"How else?"

"And the means by which and manner in which a private person is courageous is that by which and in which a city was courageous, and everything else related to virtue is the same way for both?"

"Necessarily."

"So, Glaucon, I imagine we'll claim also that a man is just in the very same manner in which a city too was just."

"This too is entirely necessary."

"But surely we haven't forgotten somewhere along the way that the city was just because each of the three classes that are in it do what properly belongs to them."

"We don't seem to me to have forgotten that," he said.

"Therefore we need to remember also that for each of us, that whoever has each of the things within him doing what properly belongs to it will be just himself and be someone who does what properly belongs to him."

"It needs to be remembered very well indeed," he said.

"Then isn't it appropriate for the reasoning part to rule, since it's wise and has forethought on behalf of the whole soul, and for the spirited part to be obedient to it and allied with it?"

"Very much so."

"Then as we were saying, won't a blending of music with gymnastic exercise make them concordant, tightening up the one part and nourishing it with beautiful speeches and things to learn while relaxing the other with soothing stories, taming it with harmony and rhythm?"

"Exactly so," he said.

"So once this pair have been nurtured in this way, and have learned and been educated in the things that truly belong to them, they need to be put in charge of the desiring part, which is certainly the largest part of the soul in each person and by nature the most insatiable for money. This part needs to be watched over so that it doesn't get filled with the so-called pleasures of the body and, when it becomes big and strong, not do the things that properly belong to it, but try to enslave and rule over things that are not of a kind suited to it, so that it turns the whole life of all the parts upside-down."

"Very much so," he said.

"And wouldn't this pair also stand guard on behalf of the whole soul and body against their external enemies in the most beautiful way," I said, "one part deliberating while the other goes to war, following its ruler and accomplishing with its courage the things that have been decided?"

"That's the way it is."

"And I imagine we call each one person courageous on account of this part, when the spirited part of him preserves through pains and pleasures what's been passed on to it by speeches as something to be feared or not."

"Rightly so," he said.

"And wise by that little part, the one that ruled in him and passed those things on, and it in turn has knowledge in it of what's advantageous for each part and for the whole consisting of the three of them in common."

"Very much so."

"And what next? Isn't each person moderate by the friendship and concord among these same things, when the ruling part and the pair that are ruled are of the same opinion that the reasoning part ought to rule and aren't in revolt against it?"

"Moderation is certainly nothing other than that," he said, "in a city or a private person."

"But each person will be just on account of the thing we repeat so often, and in that manner."

"That's a big necessity."

"Then what about this?" I said. "Surely it hasn't gotten fuzzy around the edges for us in any way, has it, so it would seem to be some other sort of justice than the one that came to light in the city?"

"It doesn't seem to me it has," he said.

"Well," I said, "we could establish this beyond all doubt, if anything in our soul still stands unconvinced, by applying the commonplace standards to it."

"What sort of standards exactly?"

"For example, if we were asked to come to an agreement about that city and the man who's like that by nature and upbringing, as to whether it seemed such a man would steal a deposit of gold or silver he'd accepted in trust, do you think anyone would imagine he'd be more likely to do that than all those not of his sort?"

"No one would," he said.

"And wouldn't temple robberies, frauds, and betrayals, either of friends in private or cities in public capacities, be out of the question for this person?"

"Out of the question."

"And in no way whatever would he be unfaithful to oaths or other agreements."

"How could he?"

"And surely adultery, neglect of parents, and lack of attentiveness to the gods belong more to any other sort of person than to this one."

"Any other sort for sure," he said.

"And isn't the thing responsible for all that the fact that each of the parts within him does what properly belongs to it in connection with ruling and being ruled?"

"That and nothing else."

"So are you still looking for justice to be anything other than the power that produces men and cities of that sort?"

"By Zeus," he said, "not I."

"So our dream has come to complete fulfillment; we said we suspected, right from when we started founding the city, that by the favor of some god we were liable to have gotten to an origin and outline of justice."

"Absolutely so."

"And what it was in fact, Glaucon—and this is why it was so helpful—was an image of justice, that it was right for the natural leatherworker to do leatherwork and not do anything else, and for the carpenter to do carpentry, and the same way for the rest."

"So it appears."

"And the truth is, justice was something like that, as it seems, but not anything connected with doing what properly belongs to oneself externally, but with what's on the inside, that truly concerns oneself and properly belongs to oneself, not allowing each thing in him to do what's alien to it, or the classes of things in his soul to meddle with one another, but setting his own house in order in his very being, he himself ruling over and bringing order to himself and becoming his own friend and harmonizing three things, exactly like the three notes marking a musical scale at the low end, the high end, and the middle; and if any other things happen to be between them, he binds all of them together and becomes entirely one out of many, moderate and harmonized. Only when he's in this condition does he act, if he performs any action having to do with acquiring money, or taking care of the body, as well as anything of a civic kind or having to do with private transactions; in all these cases he regards an action that preserves that condition and helps to complete it as a just and beautiful act, and gives it that name, and regards as wisdom the knowledge that directs that action. Anything that always breaks down that condition, he regards as an unjust action, and the opinion that directs that, he regards as ignorance."

"You're absolutely telling the truth, Socrates," he said.

"Okay," I said, "if we were to claim that we've discovered the just man and the just city, and exactly what justice is in them, I imagine we wouldn't seem to be telling a total lie."

"By Zeus, certainly not," he said.

"Shall we claim that, then?"

"Let's claim it."

"So be it," I said. "What needs to be examined after this, I imagine, is injustice."

"Clearly."

"Doesn't it in turn have to be some sort of faction among these three things, a meddling and butting in and an uprising of a certain part of the soul against the whole, in order to rule in it when that's not appropriate, because it's of such a kind by nature that it's only fitting for it to be a slave? I imagine we'll claim something like that, and that the disorder and going off course of these parts is injustice as well as intemperance, cowardice, foolishness, and all vice put together."

c   "Those are the very things it is," he said.

"Then as for doing unjust things and being unjust," I said, "and in turn doing just things, isn't it by now patently obvious exactly what all these are, if indeed that's so for both injustice and justice?"

"How so?"

"Because," I said, "they don't happen to be any different from what's healthy or diseased; what those are in a body, these are in a soul."

"In what way?" he said.

"Presumably, healthful things produce health and diseased things produce disease."

"Yes."

"Then is it also the case that doing just things produces justice, while doing unjust
d   things produces injustice?"

"Necessarily."

"And producing health is settling the things in the body into a condition of mastering and being mastered by one another in accord with nature, while producing disease is settling them into ruling and being ruled one by another contrary to nature."

"That's it."

"Then in turn, as for producing justice," I said, "isn't that settling the things in the soul into a condition of mastering and being mastered by one another in accord with nature, while producing injustice is settling them into ruling and being ruled one by another contrary to nature?"

"Exactly," he said.

"Therefore, it seems likely that virtue would be a certain health, beauty, and good
e   condition of the soul, while vice would be a disease, deformity, and weakness."

"That's what they are."

"And don't beautiful practices lead to the acquisition of virtue, and shameful ones to vice?"

"Necessarily."

"So what remains at this point, it seems, is for us to consider next whether it's
445   profitable to perform just actions, pursue beautiful practices, and be just, whether or not it goes unnoticed that one is of that sort, or to do injustice and be unjust, so long as one doesn't pay the penalty or become better by being corrected."

"But Socrates," he said, "the question already appears to me to have become laughable, whether, when life doesn't seem worth living with the body's nature corrupted, even with all the foods and drinks and every sort of wealth and political rule, it
b   will then be worth living with the nature of that very thing by which we live disordered and corrupted, even if someone does whatever he wants, but not the thing by which he'll get rid of vice and injustice and acquire justice and virtue, seeing as how it's become obvious that each of them is of the sort we've gone over."

"It is laughable," I said. "Nevertheless, since we've come this far, far enough to be able to see clearly that this is the way it is, it wouldn't be right to get tired out."

"By Zeus," he said, "getting tired out is the last thing we ought to do."

c   "Come up to the mark now," I said, "so you too can see how many forms vice has, the way it seems to me, at least the ones that are even worth looking at."

"I'm following," he said; "just speak."

"Well," I said, "as though from a lookout spot, since we've climbed up to this point in the discussion, there appears to me to be one look that belongs to virtue and infinitely many to vice, but some four among them that are even worth mentioning."

"How do you mean?" he said.

"There are liable to be as many dispositions of a soul," I said, "as there are dispositions among polities that have looks to them."

"How many, exactly?"

"Five for polities," I said, "and five for a soul."   d

"Say which ones," he said.

"I say that one," I said, "would be this type of polity we've been going over, but it could be named in two ways, since if one exceptional man arose among the rulers it would be called kingship, but aristocracy if there were more than one."

"True," he said.

"This, then," I said, "is one form that I'm talking about, since whether one or more than one man arose, it wouldn't change any of the laws of the city worthy of mention,   e since the upbringing and education they got would be the way we went over."

"Likely not," he said.

BOOK V

"Well, I call that kind of city and polity, and that kind of man, good and right, and if this   449 sort are right, the rest are bad and wrong, in the ways the cities are managed and the way the soul's disposition is constituted in private persons, and the badness takes four forms."

"What sorts are they?" he said.

And I was going on to describe them in order, the way it appeared to me they change out of one another in each case, but Polemarchus, who was sitting a little way   b from Adeimantus, reached out his hand and grabbed him from above by his cloak at the shoulder, drew him near, stretching himself forward, and was saying something while stooping toward him, of which we heard nothing but this: "Shall we let it go, then," he said, "or what shall we do?"

"Not in the least," said Adeimantus, now speaking loudly.

And I said, "What in particular won't you let go?"

"You," he said.

"Because of what in particular?" I said.   c

"You seem to us to be taking the lazy way out," he said, "and to be cheating us out of a whole form that belongs to the argument, and not the least important one, to avoid going over it, and you seem to have imagined you'd get away with speaking of it dismissively, saying it's obvious, about women and children, that what belongs to friends will be shared in common."

"And wasn't I right, Adeimantus?" I said.

"Yes," he said, "but this 'right' needs explanation, like the rest of it, about what the manner of the sharing would be, since there could be many. So don't pass over which of them you're talking about, since we've been waiting all this time imagining   d you'd make some mention somewhere about the procreation of children, how they'll be produced and once they're born how they'll be raised, and of this whole sharing of women and children you're talking about. Because we think it has a big bearing, in fact a total impact, on whether the polity comes into being in the right way or not. But now, since you're taking on another polity before you've determined these things sufficiently, it seemed right to us to do what you've heard, to refuse to let you go until you've gone   450 over all these things just like the rest."

"Me too," said Glaucon; "put me down as a partner in this vote."

"Don't worry," said Thrasymachus, "consider these things as having seemed good to all of us, Socrates."

"Oh what you folks have done by ambushing me," I said. "So much discussion about the polity you're setting in motion again, as though from the beginning, when I was rejoicing at having already gotten to the end of it, feeling content if anyone would leave these things alone and accept them the way they were stated then. You have no idea
b   what a big swarm of arguments you've stirred up with the things you're now demanding; since I saw that at the time I passed it by, fearing it would cause a lot of trouble."

"What!" said Thrasymachus. "Do you imagine these people have come this far now to fritter away their time looking for gold rather than to listen to arguments?"

"All well and good," I said, "but within measure."

"The measure in hearing such arguments, Socrates," said Glaucon, "for anyone who has any sense, is a whole life. So give up on that as far as we're concerned; just see
c   that you don't get tired in any way of going all through the way it seems to you about the things we're asking, what the sharing of children and women will be among our guardians, and about the rearing of those who are still young that takes place in the time between birth and education, which seems to be the most troublesome time. So try to say in what way it needs to happen."

"It's not easy to go through, you happy fellow," I said, "because it has a lot of doubtful points, even more than the things we went through before. It could even be doubted that what's spoken of is possible, and even if it came about as much as it possibly could, there will also be doubts even in that case that this would be the best thing.
d   That's why there was a certain reluctance to touch on these things, for fear, dear comrade, the argument would seem to be only a prayer."

"Don't be reluctant at all," he said, "since your listeners won't be unfair or disbelieving or ill-disposed."

And I said, "Most excellent fellow, I take it you're saying that to give me courage?"

"I am," he said.

"Well you're doing exactly the opposite," I said. "If I believed I knew what I was
e   talking about, your pep talk would have been a beautiful one; to speak when one knows the truth, among people who are intelligent and friendly, about things that are of greatest importance and dear to us, is secure and encouraging, but to make one's arguments at the
451   same time one is doubtful and searching, which is exactly what I'm doing, is a frightening and perilous thing. It's not because I'm liable to be laughed at—that's childish—but from fear that I'll not only tumble away myself from the truth, about things one least ought to fall down on, but that I'll also be lying in ruins with the friends I've dragged down with me. So instead I'll fall on my face in obeisance to Adrasteia, Glaucon, for her favor for what I'm about to say. I hope it's a lesser sin to become an unwilling murderer of someone than a deceiver about what's beautiful and good and just and lawful. That's a risk it's better to run among enemies rather than friends, so it's a good thing you gave me encouragement."
b   And Glaucon, with a laugh, said, "Okay, Socrates, if we experience anything discordant from what you say, we'll release you like someone purified from being a murderer and cleared as no deceiver of us. Just speak up boldly."

"Well, certainly someone who's released even in that situation is purified," I said, "as the law says, so it's likely that if it's that way there, it is here too."

"Speak, then," he said, "with that assurance."

"It's necessary to go back again now," I said, "and say what probably should have been said then in the proper place. And maybe this would be the right way, after the   c
male drama has been completely finished, to finish the female drama in turn, especially since you're calling for it this way. To my way of thinking, for human beings born and educated in the way we went over, there is no other right way for them to get and treat children and women than to hasten down that road on which we first started them. We tried, I presume, in the argument, to set the men up like guardians of a herd."

"Yes."

"Then let's follow that up by giving them the sort of birth and rearing that closely   d
resemble that, and consider whether it suits us or not."

"How?" he said.

"This way. Do we imagine that the females among the guard dogs ought to join in guarding the things the males guard, and hunt with them and do everything else in common, or should they stay inside the house as though they were disabled by bearing and nursing the puppies, while the males do the work and have all the tending of the flock?"

"Everything in common," he said, "except that we'd treat the females as weaker and the males as stronger."

"Is it possible, then," I said, "to use any animal for the same things if you don't   e
give it the same rearing and training?"

"It's not possible."

"So if you're going to make use of women at the same tasks as men, they'll also have to be taught the same things."

"Yes."   452

"Music and gymnastic exercise were given to the men."

"Yes."

"Therefore this pair of arts needs to be made available to the women too, as well as the things connected with war, and they need to be applied in the same manner."

"It's likely, based on what you're saying," he said.

"Probably," I said, "many of the things being talked about now would look absurd if they're done the way they're being described, just because they're contrary to custom."

"Very much so indeed," he said.

"Do you see which of them would be most absurd?" I said. "Isn't it obvious that it would be for the women to be exercising naked in the wrestling schools alongside the   b
men, and not just the young ones but also those who're already on the older side, like the old men who're still devoted to exercising in the gyms when they're wrinkled and not a pleasant sight?"

"By Zeus," he said, "that would look absurd, at least the way things are at present."

"But as long as we've got ourselves started talking about it, we shouldn't be afraid, should we, of all the jokes of whatever sort from witty people at the advent such a change in both gymnastic exercise and music, and not least about having war 'tools'   c
and 'mounting' horses?"

"You've got that right," he said.

"Instead, since we have started to talk about it, we need to pass right to the tough part of the law, asking these guys not to do what properly belongs to them but to be serious, and to recall that it's not much time since it seemed to the Greeks the way it does now to many of the barbarians, that it's shameful and absurd to look at a naked man, and when the people of Crete first introduced gymnasiums, and then the Spartans, the fashionable people of the time took the opportunity to ridicule all that. Don't you imagine   d
they did?"

"I do."

"But since it appeared to those who adopted the practice, I imagine, that it was better to uncover all such things than to hide them, what had been absurd in their eyes was stripped away by what was exposed as best in their reasoning. And this reveals that one who considers anything absurd other than what's bad is empty-headed, as is one who tries to get a laugh by looking at any other sight as laughable than one that's sense-less and bad, or who takes seriously any mark of what's beautiful that he's set up other than what's good."

"Absolutely so," he said.

"Well then, isn't this the first thing that needs to be agreed about these things: whether they're possible or not? And shouldn't a chance for disputes be given to anyone who wants to dispute it, whether it's someone fun-loving or the serious type, as to whether female human nature is capable of sharing in all the work that belongs to the nature of the male kind, or not in any at all, or in some sorts and not others, and whether in particular this last applies to things connected with war? Wouldn't someone be likely to get to the end of the subject most beautifully by starting off the most beautifully in this way?"

"By far," he said.

"Then do you want us to carry on the dispute ourselves against ourselves, on behalf of the others," I said, "so that the opposing argument won't be under siege unde-fended?"

"There's no reason not to," he said.

"So let's say, on their behalf, 'Socrates and Glaucon, there's no need for anyone else to dispute with you, because you yourselves, at the beginning of the process of set-tling the city that you founded, agreed that each one person had to do the one thing that properly belonged to him by nature.'"

"Suppose we did agree to that; how could we not?"

"'Well is there any way that a woman isn't completely different from a man in her nature?'"

"How could she not be different?"

"Then isn't it also appropriate to assign each of them different work that's in accord with their nature?"

"Of course."

"So why aren't you mistaken now and contradicting yourselves, when you also declare that men and women ought to do the same things, despite having the most diverse natures? Will you be able to make any defense against this, you amazing fellow?"

"Not very easily, just on the spur of the moment," he said; "but I'll ask you, in fact I am asking you, to be the interpreter of the argument on our side too, whatever it is."

"This is what I was afraid of a long time ago, Glaucon," I said, "as well as many other things I foresaw, and I was reluctant to touch on the law about the way of having and bringing up women and children."

"No, by Zeus," he said, "it seems like it's no easy matter to digest."

"No, it's not," I said. "But it's like this: whether one falls into a little swimming tank or into the middle of the biggest sea, all the same one just swims none the less."

"Quite so."

"Well then, don't we too have to swim and try to save ourselves from the argu-ment, and just hope for some dolphin to pick us up on his back or for some other sort of rescue that's hard to count on?"

"It looks that way," he said.

"Come on then," I said, "let's find a way out somewhere if we can. Because we're e agreed that a different nature needs to follow a different pursuit, and that a woman and a man are different in nature; but we're claiming now that these different natures need to follow the same pursuits. Are these the things we're accused of?"

"Precisely."

"Oh Glaucon," I said, "what a noble power the debater's art has." 454

"Why in particular?"

"Because many people even seem to me to fall into it unwillingly," I said, "and imagine they're not being contentious but having a conversation, because they're not able to examine something that's being said by making distinctions according to forms, but pounce on the contradiction in what's been said according to a mere word, subjecting one another to contention and not conversation."

"That is exactly the experience of many people," he said, "but that surely doesn't apply to us in the present circumstance, does it?"

"It does absolutely," I said. "At any rate, we're running the risk of engaging in b debate unintentionally."

"How?"

"We're pouncing, in an altogether bold and contentious manner, on 'the nature that's not the same' as a result of a word, because that's what's required not to have the same pursuits, but we didn't give any consideration whatever to what form of different or same nature we were marking off, and how far it extended, at the time when we delivered up different pursuits to a different nature and the same ones to the same nature."

"No, we didn't consider that," he said.

"Well, according to that, then," I said, "it seems like we're entitled to ask ourselves c whether it's the same nature that belongs to bald people as to longhaired ones, and not the opposite one, and whenever we agree that it's opposite, if bald people do leatherwork, not allow longhaired people to, or if the longhaired ones do, not allow the others."

"That would certainly be ridiculous," he said.

"Well is it ridiculous for any other reason," I said, "than because we weren't reckoning on every sort of same and different nature at the time, but only watching out for that form of otherness and likeness that was relevant to the pursuits themselves? For d example, with a male doctor and a female doctor, we meant that it's the soul that has the same nature. Don't you think so?"

"I do."

"But with a male doctor and a male carpenter, it's different?"

"Completely different, I presume."

"So," I said, "if the men's or women's kind is manifestly superior in relation to any art or other pursuit, won't we claim that this needs to be given over to that one of the two? But if they apparently differ only in that the female bears the young and the male e mounts the female, we'll claim instead that it hasn't yet been demonstrated in any way that a woman differs from a man in respect to what we're talking about, and we'll still believe that our guardians and the women with them ought to pursue the same activities."

"Rightly so," he said.

"Now after this, don't we invite the one who says the opposite to teach us this 455 very thing, what art or what pursuit it is, among those involved in the setup of the city, for which the nature of a woman is not the same as but different from that of a man?"

"That's the just thing to do, anyway."

"And perhaps someone else as well might say the very thing you were saying a little while ago, that it's not easy to say anything adequate on the spot, but not hard if someone has been considering it."

"He would say that."

b "Then do you want us to ask the person who contradicts this sort of thing to follow us, if we somehow show him that no pursuit related to the running of a city is uniquely for a woman?"

"Certainly."

"'Come on then,' we'll say to him, 'answer: is this the way you meant that one person is naturally fitted for something and another isn't, that in it the one learns something easily, the other with difficulty? And that the one, on the basis of a brief study, would be apt to discover a lot about what he'd learned, while the other, even when he's gotten a lot of study and practice, couldn't even hang on to what he'd learned? And for c the one, the aptitudes of his body would adequately serve the purposes of his thinking, while for the other it would be the opposite? Are there any other things than these by which you marked off the one naturally suited for each thing from the one who's not?'"

"No one's going to claim there're any others," he said.

"Then do you know of anything practiced by human beings in which the man's kind isn't of a condition that surpasses the woman's in all these respects? Or shall we make a long story out of it, talking about the art of weaving, and tending to things that

Steps in Cloth-Making. Black-figure lekythos (oil jug) attributed to the potter Amasis (sixth century B.C.). The women on the left are hand spinning thread; those in the center are weaving wool. Given that Greek women generally remained at home fulfilling such domestic occupations, Plato's suggestions in the *Republic* were quite revolutionary. Though he claims that in all pursuits "a woman is weaker than a man," Plato's character, Socrates, concludes, " . . . there isn't any pursuit of the people who run a city that belongs to a woman because she's a woman or to a man because he's a man, but the kinds of natures are spread around among both. . . . " (*The Metropolitan Museum of Art, Fletcher Fund, 1931*)

are baked or boiled, the activities in which the female kind is held in high repute and for   d
which it's most absurd of all for it to be outdone?"

"You're telling the truth," he said, "that the one kind is dominated by the other by
far in everything, as one might put it. But many women are certainly better than many
men at many things, though on the whole it's the way you say."

"Therefore, my friend, there isn't any pursuit of the people who run a city that
belongs to a woman because she's a woman or to a man because he's a man, but the
kinds of natures are spread around among both kinds of animal alike, and by nature a
woman takes part in all pursuits and a man in them all, but in all of them a woman is   e
weaker than a man."

"Quite so."

"So are we going to assign all of them to men and none to women?"

"Really, how could we?"

"But we'll claim, I imagine, that there's a woman with an aptitude for the medical
art and another without it, and a woman with an aptitude for music and another who's
unmusical by nature."

"Of course."

"Then isn't there a woman with an aptitude for gymnastic training and warfare,   456
and one who's unwarlike and not fond of gymnastic exercise?"

"I imagine so."

"What else? Is one woman philosophic and another antiphilosophic? Is one spirited and another lacking in spirit?"

"These things are possible too."

"Then it's also possible for there to be a woman with an aptitude as a guardian,
and another without one. Wasn't it that sort of nature we also selected as belonging to
the men with an aptitude for being guardians?"

"That very sort."

"And therefore the same nature for guardianship of a city belongs to a woman as
to a man, except to the extent that one is weaker or stronger."

"So it appears."

"And so women of that sort need to be selected to live together and guard together   b
with men of that sort, since they're competent and are akin to them in their nature."

"Entirely so."

"And don't the same pursuits need to be assigned to the same natures?"

"The same ones."

"Then we've come back around to what we said before, and we're agreed that it's
not contrary to nature for the women among the guardians to be assigned to music and
gymnastic training."

"Absolutely so."

"So we weren't legislating things that are impossible or like prayers, since we set   c
down the law in accord with nature. But it seems instead that it's the things that are done
now, contrary to these, that are done contrary to nature."

"So it seems."

"Wasn't our question whether the things we'd be talking about are possible and
best?"

"It was indeed."

"And it's been agreed that they're possible?"

"Yes."

"And that they're best is the thing that needs to be agreed to next?"

"Clearly."

"Now as for turning out a woman skilled at guardianship, one education won't produce men for us and another one women, will it, especially since it gets the same nature to work with?"

"No other one."

"Then what's the state of your opinion about this in particular?"

"About what exactly?"

"About assuming in your own estimation that one man is better and another worse. Or do you regard them as all alike?"

"Not at all."

"Then in the city we've been founding, which do you imagine would turn out as better men, the guardians, when they've gotten the education we went over, or the leatherworkers, educated in leathercraft?"

"You're asking a ridiculous question," he said.

"I understand," I said. "What about it then? Compared to the rest of the citizens, aren't these the best men?"

"By far."

"And what about the women? Won't these be the best among the women?"

"They too, by far," he said.

"And is there anything better for a city than for the best possible women and men to arise in it?"

"There isn't."

"And music and gymnastic training, when they come to their aid in the way we've gone over, bring this about?"

"How could they not?"

"Therefore the ordinance we set down for the city is not only something possible but also the best thing."

"So it is."

"Then the women among the guardians need to take off their clothes, since they're going to be clothed in virtue instead of a cloak, and they need to share in war and the rest of the guardianship connected with the city, and not engage in other activities, but less arduous parts of these same activities need to be given to the women than to the men because of the weakness of their kind. And a man who laughs at naked women engaged in gymnastic exercise for the sake of what's best 'plucks a laugh from his wisdom while it's still an unripe fruit,' having no idea, it seems, what he's laughing at or what he's doing. For the most beautiful thing that's being said or will have been said is this: that what's beneficial is beautiful and what's harmful is ugly."

"Absolutely so."

"Then shall we claim that we're escaping from one wave, so to speak, by saying this about the law pertaining to women, so that we don't get completely swamped when we set it down that our male and female guardians must pursue all things in common, but that in a way the argument that says that's possible and beneficial is in agreement with itself?"

"And it's certainly no small wave you're escaping," he said.

"But you'll claim it's no big one either," I said, "when you see what comes after this."

"Speak, then, and I'll see," he said.

"A law that goes along with this one," I said, "and with the others that preceded it, is, as I imagine, the following."

"What?"

"That all these women are to be shared among all these men, and none of the   d
women is to live together privately with any of the men, and their children are to be
shared too; a parent is not to know the offspring that are its own, or a child its parent."

"This is much bigger than the former one," he said, "in respect to doubtfulness
about both what's possible and what's beneficial."

"About what's beneficial, anyway," I said, "I don't imagine there'd be any arguing
that it's not the greatest good for the women to be shared or for the children to be
shared, if possible; but about whether it's possible or not, I imagine there'd be a very
great dispute."

"There could very well be dispute about both," he said.   e

"You're talking about a unified front among arguments," I said, "and here I was
imagining I could run away from one of them, if it seemed to you to be beneficial, and
I'd have the one about whether it's possible or not left."

"But you didn't get away with running away," he said, "so give an account of
yourself on both counts."

"I'll have to stand trial," I said. "Do me this much of a favor though; let me go
about it holiday-style, like dawdlers who're in the habit of feasting on their own   458
thoughts when they're walking by themselves. People like that, you know, before finding out how there can be some thing they desire, put that aside so they won't wear themselves out pondering about what's possible or not, and taking it for granted that the
thing they want is already there, they're already arranging the rest and enjoying going
through the sorts of things they'll do when it happens, and otherwise making a lazy soul   b
even lazier. I've gotten soft myself by now, and on those questions I desire to put them
off and consider later how they're possible, but now, taking it for granted that they're
possible, if you let me, I'll consider how the rulers will organize them when they happen, and what would be the most advantageous way, for both the city and the guardians,
for them to be done. I'll try together with you to consider these things first, and those
later, if you give permission."

"I do give permission," he said; "go ahead and consider."

"I imagine, then," I said, "if in fact the rulers are going to be worthy of that
name, and their auxiliaries by the same token worthy of theirs, the ones will wish to   c
follow orders and the others to give them, while the latter themselves obey the laws on
some matters, but imitate the laws on all the other matters that we'll leave up to their
judgment."

"That sounds right," he said.

"Then you," I said, "as their lawgiver, once you've selected the women in the
same way you also selected the men, will distribute them as far as possible to those with
similar natures; and they, since they have their houses and meals in common, and none
of them possesses any property of that sort privately, will be together, and while they're   d
mingled together in the gyms and in the rest of their upbringing, they'll be led, I imagine, by an inborn necessity, toward mingling with each other sexually. Or do the things
I'm talking about not seem necessary to you?"

"Not in the geometrical sense anyway," he said, "but they seem to be necessities
of an erotic sort, which are liable to be sharper than the former at persuading and attract-
ing most of the populace."

"Very much so," I said. "But the next thing to consider, Glaucon, is that unregu-
lated sexual contact with one another, or doing anything else at all of that sort, isn't
pious in a city of people favored by destiny, and the rulers aren't going to allow it."   e

"No, it wouldn't be just," he said.

"So it's clear that the next thing we'll do is make marriages sacred to the greatest extent possible, and it's the most beneficial ones that would be sacred."

"Absolutely so."

459   "So in what way will they be the most beneficial? Tell me this, Glaucon, because I see in your household both hunting dogs and true-bred birds in great numbers. Well, by Zeus, have you paid any attention to their matings and breeding?"

"To what sort of thing?" he said.

"First, among those of the same kind, even though they're true bred, aren't there some that also turn out best?"

"There are."

"Then do you breed from all of them alike, or are you eager to breed as much as possible from the best ones?"

"From the best ones."

b   "And then what? From the youngest, or from the oldest, or as much as possible from those in their prime?"

"From those in their prime."

"And if they weren't bred that way, do you expect the race of birds or of dogs would be much worse?"

"I do," he said.

"And what do you suppose about horses," I said, "and the rest of the animals? That it would be any different?"

"That would certainly be strange," he said.

"Ayayay, dear comrade," I said, "how greatly in need we are, then, of top-notch c   rulers if it's also the same way with the human race."

"Well it is the same way," he said, "but what does that have to do with the rulers?"

"There'll be a necessity," I said, "for them to use a lot of medicines. Presumably we believe that for bodies that don't need medicines, those of people willing to follow a prescribed way of life, even a rather ordinary doctor is sufficient; but when there's a need to use medicine, we know that a more courageous doctor is needed."

"True, but what point are you making?"

d   "This one," I said: "our rulers are liable to need to use falsehood and deception in abundance for the benefit of those they rule. And we claimed, of course, that all that sort of thing is useful in the form of medicine."

"And rightly so," he said.

"Well, it seems like it's not least in the marriages and procreation that this rightness comes into play."

"How so?"

"It follows from the things that have been agreed to," I said, "that as often as possible the best men ought to have sex with the best women, and the worst on the contrary e   with the worst, and the offspring of the former ought to be reared, but not those of the latter, if the flock is going to be of top quality to the highest degree possible. And all these things ought to happen without the notice of anyone except the rulers themselves, if the guardians' herd is also going to be as free as possible of internal conflict."

"With the utmost rightness," he said.

"Then don't some sort of festivals and sacrifices need to be set up by law, in 460   which we'll bring together the brides and grooms, and suitable hymns need to be made by our poets for the marriages that take place? We'll make the number of marriages be up to the rulers, in order that they might preserve the same number of men as much as they can, having regard to wars, diseases, and everything of the sort, and in order that, as far as possible, our city might not become either big or little."

"Rightly," he said.

"I imagine some ingenious lotteries need to be made up, so that the ordinary man mentioned before will blame chance and not the rulers for each marriage pairing."

"Very much so," he said.

"And presumably those among the young men who are good in war or any-   b
where else need to be given special honors and prizes, and among other things a more unrestricted privilege to sleep with the women, so that on this pretext, as great a number of children as possible would also at the same time be begotten by such people."

"Rightly so."

"And won't the officials set up for this purpose take over the offspring born on each occasion, male or female officials or both, since, of course, the ruling offices are shared among the women and men?"

"Yes."

"So I expect they'll take those born to the good ones into the fold and turn them   c
over to some sort of nurses who live separately in a certain part of the city; but the off-spring of the worse sort of people, and any of the others that might have been born with defects, they'll hide away in a place not spoken of and not seen, as is fitting."

"If indeed the race of the guardians is going to be pure," he said.

"Won't these officials also be in charge of the feeding, bringing the mothers to the fold when they're swollen with milk, contriving every sort of means so that none of   d
them will recognize her own child, and providing other women who have milk if they don't have enough, and see to it that the mothers themselves suckle for a moderate time, but turn over the watchfulness and other work to wet nurses and nurses?"

"You're describing a great ease of childbearing," he said, "for the women among the guardians."

"And it's appropriate," I said. "Let's go on to the next thing we proposed, since we claimed that the offspring ought to be born particularly from those in their prime."

"True."

"Then do you share my opinion that twenty years is the average time of the prime   e
of life for a woman, and thirty for a man?"

"Which of the years?" he said.

"Starting from her twentieth and up to her fortieth, for a woman to bear children for the city," I said, "and for a man, once he passes his swiftest peak at running, to beget children for the city from then until his fifty-fifth."

"For them both," he said, "that's certainly their prime both in body and in   461
intelligence."

"Then if someone older or younger than that engages in generating offspring into the community, we'll claim it's a transgression that's not pious or just, since it produces for the city a child that, if it escapes notice, will have been brought forth without being born with the sacrifices and prayers that would be offered at every marriage by priest-esses, priests, and the whole city together, that from good and beneficial people better and more beneficial offspring might always come forth; instead, it will have been born   b
under cover of darkness in the presence of terrible unrestraint."

"We'll rightly make that claim," he said.

"And the same law applies," I said, "if any of the men still propagating has sexual contact with any of the women who are of childbearing age when a ruler hasn't joined him with her; we'll charge him with bringing a bastard child into the city, unsanctioned and unconsecrated."

"Quite rightly," he said.

"But, I imagine, when both the women and the men get beyond the age to repro-
c   duce, we'll no doubt leave them free to have sex with anyone they want, except with a
daughter, a mother, a daughter's children, a mother's parent, or the women with a son or
his children or with a father or his parent, and all that only after it's been insisted that
they take the most zealous care not to bring forth even a single fetus into the light of
day, if one is conceived, and if any is forced on them, to handle it on the understanding
that there's to be no raising of such a child."

"These things too are reasonably said," he said; "but how are they going to distinguish their fathers and daughters, and the others you just mentioned, one from
another?"

d   "There's no way," I said. "But from that day on which any of them becomes a
bridegroom, whatever offspring are born in the tenth month after that, or even the seventh, to all of these he'll apply the name sons to the males and daughters to the females,
and they'll call him father, and in the same way he'll call their offspring his grandchildren, and they in turn will call people like him grandfathers and grandmothers, and
they'll call those who were born at the same time their mothers and fathers were pro-
e   ducing children sisters and brothers, so that, as we were just saying, they won't have
sexual contact with one another. But the law will grant brothers and sisters permission
to be joined together if the lottery falls out that way and the Pythia* confirms it."

"Quite rightly," he said.

"So, Glaucon, this or something like it is the way of sharing women and children
among the guardians of your city. The next thing after this ought to be to have it established out of the argument that this goes along with the rest of the polity and is by far the
best way. Or how should we proceed?"

462   "That way, by Zeus," he said.

"Well then, wouldn't this be a source from which an agreement might come, that
we ask ourselves what's the greatest good we can state in the organization of a city, at
which the lawgiver ought to aim in setting down the laws, and what's the greatest evil,
and then consider on that basis whether the things we were just now going over fit into
the footprint of the good while they don't fit into that of the evil?"

"That most of all would be the way," he said.

"Then can we have any greater evil in a city than that which tears it apart and
b   makes it many instead of one? Or a greater good than that which binds it together and
makes it one?"

"No we can't."

"And doesn't the sharing of pleasure and pain bind it together, when as much as
possible all the citizens feel joy and pain in almost the same way at the coming into
being and passing away of the same things?"

"Absolutely so," he said.

"But the private appropriation of such things dissolves it, when some people
become overwhelmed with pain and others overcome with joy at the same experiences
of the city and of the people in the city?"

c   "How could it not?"

"And doesn't that sort of thing come from this, that people in the city don't utter
such words as mine and not mine at the same time, and the same with somebody else's?"

---

*The priestess of Apollo at Delphi. Presumably the rulers would know which cases involved actual
incest and avoid them, and would take her into their confidence.

"Exactly so."

"So isn't that city governed best in which the most people say this mine and not mine on the same occasion about the same things?"

"Much the best."

"And this is precisely whichever city is in a condition closest to that of a single human being? For instance, whenever a finger of any of us is wounded, presumably the whole community extending from the body to the soul in a single ordering under the   d ruler within it would be aware of it, and it all would suffer pain as a whole together with the part that's afflicted, and is that the sense in which we mean that a human being has a pain in his finger? And is it the same story for any other part of a human being what-ever, both for a part afflicted with pain and for one that's eased by pleasure?"

"It's the same," he said, "and as for what you're asking, the best constituted city is the one situated closest to such a condition."

"So I imagine that when one of its citizens undergoes anything at all, good or bad, such a city most of all will claim the thing that happened to him as its own, and all of it   e will share the pleasure or share the pain."

"Necessarily," he said, "if it's one with good laws, anyway."

"This would be the time," I said, "for us to go back to our own city, and examine in it the things agreed in the discussion, to see whether it has them the most or some other city has them more."

"We need to, don't we?" he said.

"What about it, then? There are certainly both rulers and people in other cities as   463 well as in this one, aren't there?"

"There are."

"And won't all of these call one another citizens?"

"How could they not?"

"And in addition to 'citizens,' what name do the people in other cities call their rulers by?"

"In most of them, despots, but in those that are democratically ruled, this very name, rulers."

"And what about the people in our city? In addition to citizens, what will they say their rulers are?"

"Protectors and auxiliaries," he said.

"And what will they call the people?"   b

"Givers of compensation and sustenance."

"And what do the rulers in other cities call the people?"

"Slaves," he said

"What do the rulers call one another?"

"Fellow rulers," he said.

"And what about ours?"

"Fellow guardians."

"And can you say whether any of the rulers in the other cities could refer to one of his fellow rulers as his kinsman and another as an outsider?"

"In fact many do."

"And does he consider his kinsman as one of his own people and speak of him that way, and of the outsider as not one of his own?"

"In that way."

"But what about the guardians there with you? Is there anyone at all among them   c who could regard or speak of any of his fellow guardians as an outsider?"

"Not at all," he said; "any time he bumps into anyone, he'll regard himself as meeting up with a brother, a sister, a father, a mother, a son, a daughter, or descendants or ancestors of these."

d   "You put it most beautifully," I said, "but also tell me this. Are you legislating only the names of kinship for them, or also the performing of all the actions that follow from the names, all the things custom calls for about respect for fathers and about taking care of parents and needing to be obedient to them, to avoid being on bad terms with gods and human beings because anyone who'd act otherwise would be doing things that aren't pious or just? Will you have these things or other ones singing around their ears straight from childhood as the common sayings coming from all the citizens about fathers,

e   whomever anyone points out to them as fathers, and about their other relatives?"

"These," he said; "it would be ridiculous if they only uttered the names of kinship with their mouths, without the deeds."

"Therefore, when any one person is doing well or badly, people will sound out in harmony the word we were just speaking, that what's mine is going well or what's mine is going badly."

"Most true," he said.

464   "And weren't we claiming that a sharing of pleasures and pains followed along with this opinion and this word?"

"And we were right in claiming it," he said.

"Then won't our citizens most of all share the same thing in common, the very thing they name mine? And by sharing that in that way, won't they most of all have a sharing of pain and pleasure?"

"By far."

"And isn't the cause of this, in addition to the rest of the set-up, the sharing of women and children among the guardians?"

"Most of all by a long way," he said.

b   "But surely we agreed that was the greatest good for a city, likening a well-governed city to the way a body stands in relation to the pain and pleasure of a part of it."

"And we were right in agreeing to that," he said.

"So the cause of the greatest good for the city has been revealed to us as the sharing of children and women among the auxiliaries."

"Very much so," he said.

"And so we're also agreeing to the things prior to that, because we claimed, no

c   doubt, that there had to be no private houses for them, or land, or any possession, but they were to get their sustenance from the other people as recompense for guardianship, and all consume it in common, if they were going to be guardians in their very being."

"Rightly," he said.

"Well then, what I mean is, don't the things said before as well as the things being said now fashion them still more into true guardians and make them not tear apart the city by giving the name mine not to the same thing but each to something different, with one of them dragging into his own house whatever he has the power to

d   acquire apart from the others, and another into his own house, which is a different one, and having different women and children, bringing in private pleasures and griefs for things that are private? But with one opinion about what's their own as they all strain toward the same goal to the limit of their power, won't they be affected alike by pain and pleasure?"

"Exactly so," he said.

"And what about this? Won't lawsuits and accusations against one another virtually vanish from among them because they possess nothing private but the body and everything else in common? And that's why it belongs to them from the start to be free of divisions, all the ones human beings divide over on account of having money, children, and relatives."   e

"It's a big necessity," he said, "that they'll be freed from that."

"And there couldn't justly be any lawsuits among them even for battery or assaults, since presumably we'll claim it's a beautiful and just thing for anyone to defend himself against someone his own age, which will make it necessary for them to keep their bodies in shape."

"That's right," he said.

"And this custom is also right in this respect," I said: "presumably if anyone gets his spiritedness aroused against someone, he'd be less likely to come to greater divisions if he gives his angry spirit its fill in such a way."   465

"Quite so."

"And surely an older person will be assigned to rule over all the younger ones and correct them."

"Obviously."

"And certainly it's likely a younger person will never raise his hand to hit or do any other violence to an older one, unless the rulers order him to, and I don't imagine he'll even do any other sort of dishonor to someone older, since a pair of sufficient safeguards prevent it, fear and respect, respect on the grounds that it bars him from laying a hand on parents, and fear that others would come to the defense of the one who suffered it, some as sons, some as brothers, and some as fathers."   b

"It does turn out that way," he said.

"So will the men keep peace with one another in every way as a result of the laws?"

"Very much so."

"And if these guardians are not at faction among themselves, there'll be no dire peril that the rest of the city will ever split into factions against them or against one another."

"No there won't."

"I'm reluctant even to mention, on account of their tackiness, the most petty of the evils they'd be freed from, the flatteries of the rich by the poor, the strained circumstances and all the grief they have in raising children and getting money for the necessary subsistence of the household, making debts and repudiating them, making all sorts of shifts to save money for the women and domestic slaves, to turn over to them to manage, and all the things, dear friend, they go through over these things and those like them, obvious and degrading and not worthy of talking about."   c

d

"They are obvious," he said, "even to a blind person."

"So they'll be free of all these things, and they'll live a more blessedly happy life than the most blessedly happy one the Olympic champions live."

"How so?"

"Presumably the latter are considered happy on account of a small part of what belongs to these people, because the victory these people win is a more beautiful one and the provision made for them by the public is more complete.* For the victory they win is the preservation of the whole city, and they're crowned with the provision of food

*Athletes at the Olympic games represented their cities, and the winners were given meals at public expense all their lives.

e   and of everything else needed for life for themselves and their children, and they receive
honors from their city while they live and share in a worthy burial when they die."

"And those are beautiful things," he said.

"And do you remember," I said, "that in the earlier discussion an argument—I
466   don't know whose—reprimanded us because we weren't making the guardians happy,
who, though they'd be capable of having everything that belonged to the citizens,
wouldn't have anything? I believe we said that if this fell in our way anywhere, we'd
consider it at a later time, but for now we were making the guardians guardians and
making the city as happy as we could, but we weren't looking to one group in it and
fashioning that to be happy."

"I remember," he said.

"What about it, then? If indeed the life of our auxiliaries appears as much more
beautiful and better than that of Olympic champions, is there any fear of how it appears
b   next to the life of leatherworkers or any other craftsmen or the life of farmers?"

"It doesn't seem so to me," he said.

"However, the just thing is to say here what I also said there, that if the guardian
is going to try to become happy in such a way that he won't even be a guardian, and a
life so measured and steady, that's also, as we're claiming, best, won't satisfy him, but
he falls into a senseless and juvenile opinion about happiness that will drive him to tak-
c   ing everything in the city for his own by means of his power, he'll know that Hesiod
was wise in his being when he said that there's a way in which 'the half is more than
the whole.' "

"If he asks my advice," he said, "he'll stay in this life."

"Do you go along, then," I said, "with the partnership of the women with the men,
which we've gone over, in their education, with their children, and in guarding the other
citizens, and agree that, both when they're staying in the city and when they're going to
war, they need to guard and hunt together the way dogs do, and share everything in
d   common in every way as far as is in their power, and that in so doing they'll be acting in
the best way and not contrary to the nature of the female in relation to the male, in the
way the pair is naturally fitted to share things in common with each other?"

"I go along with that," he said.

"Then doesn't this remain to be determined," I said, "whether after all it's possible among human beings too, the way it is among other animals, for this partnership to
come about, and in what way it's possible?"

"You beat me to it," he said, "by saying what I was just about to bring up."

e   "As for what's involved in war," I said, "I imagine the manner in which they'll go
to war is obvious."

"How's that?" he said.

"They'll take the field in common, and besides, they'll bring as many of the children to the war as are tough, so that, just like the children of the other craftsmen, they'll
467   see the things they'll need to do to work at the craft when they're grown up. And in
addition to watching, they'll help out and take subordinate roles in all the things that
have to do with war, and tend to the needs of their fathers and mothers. Or haven't you
noticed what happens with the arts, for instance with the children of potters, how long a
time they spend watching as helpers before taking a hand at making pots?"

"Very much so."

"Is it necessary for them to educate their children more carefully than the
guardians do theirs by experience and observation of the things that concern them?"

"That would be totally ridiculous," he said.

"And certainly every animal fights in an exceptional way in the presence of its   b
young."

"That is so, but Socrates, there's no small risk, for those who've been defeated,
and that sort of thing is apt to happen in war, that they'll have lost the children in addition to themselves and make it impossible for the rest of the city to recover."

"What you say is true," I said; "but first of all, do you think one ought to arrange
things so as never to run any risks?"

"By no means."

"Well what about it then? If it's necessary to take a risk, shouldn't it be one in
which they'll be better off when they succeed?"

"Obviously."

"Well do you imagine it makes little difference, and isn't worth a risk, whether   c
or not children who're going to be competent men at warfare watch the things
involved in war?"

"No, it makes a difference for what you're talking about."

"Then this is the way one needs to start out, by making the children observers of
war, and if some additional means of safety is devised for them, things will go well,
won't they?"

"Yes."

"And first of all," I said, "their fathers won't be ignorant, will they, but knowledgeable in every way human beings can be about all the things on campaigns that are
dangerous or not?"

"Likely so," he said.

"So they'll take them to the latter and be wary of the former."   d

"That's right."

"And presumably as rulers," I said, "they'll set over them people who are no
slouches but are qualified by experience and age to be leaders and tutors."

"That's fitting."

"But, we'll claim, many things also turn out for many people contrary to
expectation."

"Very much so."

"So with a view to such things, my friend, it behooves us to give them wings right
away while they're little children, so that if there's any need they'll escape by flying
away."

"How do you mean?" he said.

"They need to be mounted on horseback," I said, "as young as possible, and once   e
they've been taught to ride they need to be brought to the sight on horses, not on spirited
or aggressive ones, but on horses as swift of foot and docile as possible. Thus, in the
most beautiful way, they'll get a look at the work that belongs to them, and in the safest
way, if there's any need, they'll save themselves by following after older leaders."

"You seem to me to be getting it right," he said.   468

"And what about what's involved in war?" I said. "How should your soldiers bear
themselves toward one another and toward enemies? Is the way that seems evident to
me the right one or not?"

"Say what it's like," he said.

"If one of them leaves his post," I said, "or throws down his weapons or does anything of the sort out of cowardice, doesn't he need to be reassigned as some sort of
craftsman or farmer?"

"Very much so."

"And if one of them is taken alive by the enemy, shouldn't he be given as a gift to
b   his captors, to use their catch however they want?"

"Exactly."

"But if someone shows the highest distinction and gains a good reputation, doesn't
it seem to you that first, on the campaign, he should be crowned with wreaths by his
fellow soldiers, and by each of the youths and children in turn? Or not?"

"That seems good to me."

"And what about shaking his hand?"

"That too."

"But I don't imagine this too would seem good to you," I said.

"What's that?"

"That he kiss and be kissed by each."

"That most of all," he said. "And I have an addendum to the law, that as long as
c   they're on that campaign, no one he wants to kiss be allowed to refuse him, so that if
someone happens to be in love with anyone, male or female, he'd be more zealous to
carry off the highest honors."

"Beautiful," I said. "Because it's already been said that marriages will be more
readily arranged for someone good than for others, and selections of such people will be
more frequent, beyond the others, in order that the most children possible will be born
of such a person."

"We did say that," he said.

"And surely even according to Homer, it's just to do honor in such ways to all
d   those among the young who are good. For Homer also said that, when he gained a good
reputation in war, 'Ajax was rewarded with the whole back of the ox,' as if the appropriate honor for someone bursting with youth and courage was that by which he'd be
honored and at the same time grow in strength."

"Most rightly," he said.

"So we'll be persuaded by Homer," I said, "at least about these things. For we'll
honor good people at the sacrifices and at all such occasions, to the extent they've
e   shown themselves good, both with hymns and with the things we were just now speaking of, and on top of that 'with choice seats and meats and full wine cups,' so that along
with honoring them we'll be forming good men and women."

"You're speaking most beautifully," he said.

"Okay. Now if any of those who die on the campaign meets his death in a way
that gains him a good reputation, won't we first declare him to be of the golden race?"

"Most of all."

469   "And won't we be persuaded by Hesiod that when any people of such a race die,

They become consecrated as holy divinities on earth,
Good guardians, warding off evil from humans endowed with speech?"

"We'll be persuaded."

"Therefore, after finding out from the god how one ought to bury divinities and
godlike people and with what mark of distinction, won't we also bury them in whatever
way that he prescribes?"

"Why wouldn't we?"

b   "And for the rest of time, won't we care for their tombs and worship at them as at
those of divinities? And won't we follow these same observances when any of those judged
to have been surpassingly good in their lives die, of old age or in any other manner?"

"It would be just, at any rate," he said.

"And what about this? How will our soldiers deal with their enemies?"

"In what respect in particular?"

"In the first place, in respect to taking slaves, does it seem just for Greek cities to take Greeks as slaves, or as far as possible not even to leave them for another city to take, but to get them in the habit of sparing the Greek race as a precaution against   c
enslavement by the barbarians?"

"Sparing them is wholly and totally better," he said.

"Therefore they won't possess a Greek slave themselves, and they'll give that advice to the other Greeks?"

"Very much so," he said; "at least that way they'd turn against the barbarians instead, and hold off from their own kind."

"And what about stripping the dead of anything except weapons?"

I said. "When they win a victory, is that a desirable practice? Or doesn't it offer a pretext for cowards not to go up against someone who's fighting, on the grounds that they're performing one of their duties when they keep stooping down around a dead   d
body, though many an army has been destroyed before now by such rapacity?"

"Quite so."

"Doesn't it seem unbefitting a free person and a moneygrubbing thing to strip a corpse, and a sign of a womanish and petty way of thinking to consider as the enemy the body of a dead opponent who has fluttered away, leaving behind that with which he made war? Or do you suppose those who do this are behaving any differently from dogs   e
that take out their anger on the rocks thrown at them but don't touch the one throwing them?"

"Not even a little differently," he said.

"Therefore one should give up stripping corpses and preventing their recovery?"

"One should certainly give it up, by Zeus," he said.

"And no doubt we won't bring the captured weapons, and especially not those of Greeks, to the temples as offerings, if we have any consideration for the good will of the rest of the Greeks. Instead, we'd be afraid it would be a pollution to bring such things to   470
the temple from our own people, unless the god particularly says something different."

"Quite rightly," he said.

"And what about ravaging Greek land and setting fire to the houses? Will your soldiers do anything of that sort to their enemies?"

"I'd listen with pleasure," he said, "if you revealed your opinion."

"Well, it seems good to me," I said, "for them to do neither of these things, but to take away the year's crops. Do you want me to tell you why?"   b

"Very much indeed."

"It appears to me that war and civil war are two different things, just like these two names they're called by, which apply to two kinds of division in two respective things. The two things I mean are, on the one hand, one's own kind and kin, and on the other, what's foreign and alien. Civil war is the name applied to hostility within one's own kind, and war applies to hostility between foreigners."

"And there's certainly nothing off course about what you're saying," he said.

"Then see if I'm also on course when I say this: I claim that the Greek race is   c
itself with itself its own kind and kin, but alien and foreign to a barbarian race."

"Beautifully on course," he said.

"Therefore when Greeks fight with barbarians and barbarians with Greeks we'll claim they're at war and are natural enemies, and that this hostility of theirs should be d   called war, but whenever Greeks do anything of the sort to Greeks we'll claim they're natural friends, but in such circumstances Greece is sick and divided, and that this sort of hostility should be called civil war."

"I go along with regarding it that way," he said.

"Consider, then," I said, "that in the sort of civil war now acknowledged as such, wherever any such thing happens and a city is split apart, if each of the two sides ravages the land and burns the houses of the other, civil war is held to be an abomination and neither of the sides is considered loyal to the city, or they would never have dared to

e   devastate their nurse and mother. But it seems to be within measure for those who prevail to take away the crops from those they defeat, and to think of themselves as people who are going to be reconciled and not always be at war."

"This way of thinking is far more civilized than that other," he said.

"What about it, then?" I said. "Won't the city you're founding be Greek?"

"It's bound to be," he said.

"And won't the people be good and civilized?"

"Emphatically so."

"But won't they be loyal to all things Greek? Won't they regard Greece as their own place and participate in religious observances in common with the rest of the Greeks?"

"Emphatically so on that point too."

471   "Then won't they regard a division with Greeks, since it's with their own people, as civil war and not even name it merely war?"

"That's right."

"So they'll have their divisions in the spirit of people who're going to be reconciled?"

"Very much so."

"So they'll bring their opponents back to their senses and not punish them with slavery or destruction, not being enemies but people intent on inducing moderation."

"That's the way," he said.

"Therefore, being Greeks, they won't devastate Greece, or set fire to houses, and they won't agree with anyone who says that everyone in any city is their enemy—the

b   men, women, and children—but hold that a few enemies are always the ones responsible for the division. For all these reasons they won't be willing to devastate their land, since most of them are friendly, or to knock down their houses, but they'll maintain the conflict up to that point at which the responsible parties are forced to pay the penalty by the guiltless people who're suffering from it."

"I agree," he said, "that this is how our citizens ought to conduct themselves toward their opponents, but toward the barbarians they should act the way Greeks do now toward one another."

c   "So shall we also impose this as a law on the guardians, not to ravage land or burn houses?"

"Let's impose it," he said, "and certainly these things and the ones that preceded them are all well and good, but it seems to me, Socrates, that if anyone left it to you to discuss this sort of thing you'd never remember what was pushed aside before you'd mentioned all this, the question of whether it's possible for this type of polity to come into being and in what way it would ever be possible. Because I certainly grant that if it were to come into being, everything in the city in which it came into being would be

d   good, even things you're leaving out; I mean that they'd also fight their enemies best because they'd desert each other least, since they recognize their own troops as brothers, fathers, and sons and call to them by these names. And also if the female group were in combat along with them, either in the ranks themselves or drawn up in the rear, both to frighten the enemy and in case any need for assistance should arise, I know that with all this they'd be people no one could fight. And I see all the good things at home that would be to their benefit. But since I agree that there would be all these things and tens of thousands of others if this polity were to come into being, don't keep saying more about that, but let's try from this point on to persuade ourselves of this very thing, that it's possible and in what way, and let the rest go with our blessings."

"This is so sudden," I said. "It's as though you've launched an attack on my argument, and have no tolerance for me to squeeze out its last drops. Maybe you don't realize that when I've hardly escaped a pair of waves you're now bringing on the biggest and most crushing third wave; when you see and hear it, you'll have complete sympathy, understanding that it was fitting after all that I was hesitant and fearful to state and undertake the examination of an argument so contrary to general opinion."

"The more you say that sort of thing," he said, "the less you'll be let off by us from saying how it's possible for this polity to come into being. Just speak and don't waste any more time."

"Well then," I said, "isn't this the first thing that should be recalled, that it's because we were seeking what sorts of things justice and injustice are that we got to this point?"

"It should, but what about it?" he said.

"Nothing; except, if we find out what sort of thing justice is, will we also hold that the just man needs to be no different from that very thing, but be in every respect of the same sort that justice is? Or will we be satisfied if he's as close to it as possible and participates in it the most in comparison with other people?"

"The latter," he said. "We'll be satisfied."

"Then it was for the sake of a pattern," I said, "that we were seeking both what sort of thing justice itself is, and the completely just man, in case one could come into being, and what he'd be like if he were to come into being, as well as injustice and the most unjust man, so that by looking off toward them to see what they appear to us to be like in relation to happiness and its opposite, we'd be constrained to agree about our own selves as well, that whoever was most similar to them would have a lot in life most similar to theirs. But it wasn't for the sake of our demonstrating that it was possible for these things to come into being."

"That's true, as you say," he said.

"Do you imagine someone would be any less good a painter, who had painted a pattern of what the most beautiful human being would be like, and had rendered everything in the picture well enough, because he wasn't able to show that it was also possible for such a man to come into being?"

"Not I, by Zeus," he said.

"Well then, don't we claim that we too were making a pattern in speech of a good city?"

"Certainly."

"Then do you imagine we're describing it any less well on that account if we're not able to demonstrate that it's possible to found a city that's the way we were describing it?"

"Surely not," he said.

"So that's the way the truth of it is," I said; "but if it's also necessary for this effort to be made for your pleasure, to demonstrate in what way most of all and as a result of what it would be most possible, then you, the same as me, should make some concessions in return for such a demonstration."

"What sort of concessions?"

473   "Is it possible for anything to be done in practice the way it's described in speech, or does action have a nature to attain to truth less than speaking does, even if it doesn't seem that way to somebody? But do you agree or not that it's that way?"

"I agree," he said.

"Then don't require this of me, to be obliged to represent the sorts of things we went through in speech as coming into being in every respect in deed as well, but if we turn out to be able to discover that a city could be founded that's closest to the things described,

b   then declare that we've found out that it's possible for these things to come into being the way you ordered us to. Or will you not be satisfied if that happens? I'd be satisfied."

"I would too," he said.

"Then it looks like the next thing for us to do is try to search out and demonstrate whatever is now done badly in cities, on account of which they aren't managed this way, and what would be the smallest change by which a city could come into this mode of political association—preferably a change of one thing, or if not that, of two, and if not that, of as few things as possible in number and the smallest in strength."

c   "Absolutely so," he said.

"Well with one change," I said, "it seems to me we can show that it could be transformed, though it's not a small or easy one, but it is possible."

"What's that?" he said.

"I'm in for it now," I said, "up against what we likened to the biggest wave. But it's got to be said, even if, literally just like an uproarious wave, it's going to drown me in laughter and humiliation. Consider what I'm about to say."

"Say it," he said.

d   "Unless philosophers rule as kings in their cities," I said, "or those now called kings and supreme rulers genuinely and adequately engage in philosophy, and this combination of political power and philosophy joins together in the same position, while the many natures that are now carried away to one of the two in isolation are forcibly blocked off from that, there is no rest from evils for the cities, dear Glaucon, or, I think, for the human race, and this polity that we've now gone over in speech will never before

e   that sprout as far as it can and see the light of the sun. This is what's been putting a reluctance to speak in me all this time, my seeing that it would be proclaimed to be far beyond belief, because it's hard to see that in no other way would anyone be happy in private, or any city in public."

And he said, "Oh, Socrates, what a thing you've blurted out, both the words and

474   the meaning! Now that you've said it, you can expect a great many people after you this very instant, and no slouches, flinging off their cloaks, stripped down, grabbing up whatever weapon happens to be near each one, running full speed, ready to do amazing things. If you don't fend them off with arguments and get away, you'll pay the penalty by being well and truly ridiculed."

"And don't I have you to thank for this?" I said.

"And I'm doing a beautiful job of it," he said. "But I won't give you up for lost; I'll defend you with the means in my power. And I have the power to help out with good will and by cheering you on, and maybe I'd give you replies in a more harmonious spirit

b   than someone else would. So since you have such help, try to show the doubters that things are the way you say."

"The attempt has to be made," I said, "especially since you offer so formidable an alliance. Now it seems necessary to me, if we're somehow going to dodge the people you speak of, to define for them what we mean by philosophers when we have the audacity to claim they ought to rule, so that once it becomes thoroughly clear, one will have the power to defend oneself by showing that it's fitting by nature for them both to   c engage in philosophy and to take the lead in a city, and for everyone else not to engage in it and to follow a leader."

"This would be the time to define them," he said.

"Come then, and follow me here, if we're somehow or other going to explain it fittingly."

"Lead on," he said.

"Then will it be necessary to remind you," I said, "or do you remember that when we claim someone loves something, if it's being said correctly, it has to be clear that he doesn't love part of it and part not, but is devoted to it all?"

"It's necessary to remind me, it seems," he said, "since I have no recollection of it at all."

"It would be fitting for someone else to say what you're saying, Glaucon," I said,   d "but it's not fitting for an erotic man to be unmindful of the fact that all those in their first flowering in one way or another sting and arouse an erotic lover of boys, and seem to be worth paying attention to and giving a warm welcome. Don't you people behave that way toward the beautiful? One, because he's snub-nosed, is praised by you by being called adorable, and the hooked nose of another you folks claim is kingly, while you claim the one in the middle compared to them has proportion; you claim the dark   e ones look manly and the pale ones are children of the gods, and do you imagine the name 'honeychild' is anything but a product of a baby-talking lover who finds a yellow- ish complexion easy to take if it's in the flowering of youth? And in a word, you folks   475 make every excuse and come out with any utterance so as not to reject anyone blossom- ing in the first prime of life."

"If you want to pin it on me," he said, "to talk about the way erotic people behave, I go along with it for the sake of the argument."

"And what about wine-lovers," I said; "don't you see them doing these same things and welcoming every sort of wine on any excuse?"

"Very much so."

"And surely you notice, I assume, that lovers of honor, if they can't become gen- erals, are lieutenants, and if they can't be honored by grander and more prestigious people, are content with being honored by lesser and more ordinary ones, since they're   b desirous of honor as a whole."

"Exactly."

"Then affirm this or deny it: when we speak of someone as desiring something, will we claim he desires all of that form, or part of it and part not?"

"All of it," he said.

"Then won't we claim the philosopher too is a desirer of wisdom, not of part of it and part not, but of all of it?"

"That's true."

"Therefore if someone's picky about the things he learns, especially when he's young and doesn't yet have a rational account of what is or isn't useful, we'll claim that   c he's no lover of learning and not philosophic, just as we'd claim that someone who's picky about his food isn't hungry, doesn't desire food, and isn't a food-lover but a bad eater."

"And we'll be right in claiming it."

"But in justice, we'll claim that person who's readily willing to taste everything learnable and goes toward learning gladly and in an insatiable spirit is a philosopher, won't we?"

d   And Glaucon said, "Then many strange people will be like that according to you. Because all those who love sights seem to me to be that way, since they take delight in studying them, and those who love listening are some of the strangest people to include among philosophers; they wouldn't be willing to go voluntarily to discussions or any such way of passing the time, but just as if they'd hired out their ears for listening, they run around to all the choruses at the festivals of Dionysus, not missing any of those in the cities or in the villages. Are we going to claim that all these and everyone else

e   devoted to learning such things and to the superficial arts are philosophers?"

"Not at all," I said, "just that they're like philosophers."

"And who do you say are the true ones?" he said.

"The lovers of the sight of the truth," I said.

"And that would be right," he said, "but how do you mean it?"

"Not in any way that's easy to explain to someone else," I said; "but I imagine you'll grant me something like this."

"Like what?"

476   "That since beautiful is the opposite of ugly, the pair of them are two."

"How could that not be so?"

"And since they're two, each of them is also one?"

"That too."

"And it's the same story with just and unjust, and good and bad, and with all the forms: each of them itself is one, but since they make their appearance everywhere in common with actions and bodies and one another, each appears to be many."

"You're putting it correctly," he said.

"That's the way I make the distinction, then," I said: "on one side the lovers of sights, the lovers of the arts, and the practical people you were just speaking of, and on

b   the other side the people our discussion is about, the only ones anybody could rightly call philosophers."

"How do you mean?" he said.

"Presumably," I said, "the lovers of listening and of sights devote themselves to beautiful sounds and colors and shapes and everything crafted out of such things, but their thinking is incapable of seeing and devoting itself to the nature of the beautiful itself."

"That's exactly how it is," he said.

"But wouldn't those who are capable of getting to and seeing the beautiful itself, by itself, be rare?"

"Very much so."

c   "But if someone believes there are beautiful things, but doesn't believe in beauty itself, and isn't capable of following if anyone leads him up to the knowledge of it, does he seem to you to be living in a dream or awake? Just consider; isn't it dreaming when anyone, whether in sleep or waking, believes a likeness to something isn't a likeness but is the thing itself that it seems like?"

"I at least would claim that such a person is dreaming," he said.

"And what about the opposite of that, when someone believes there is a beautiful itself and is capable of catching sight of it as well as of the things that participate in it,

d   and doesn't think it is the things that participate or that the things that participate are it—does he seem to you to be living a waking life or a dream?"

"Very much a waking life," he said.

"Then since he's discerning something, wouldn't we be right in claiming that this person's thinking is knowledge, while that of the other person is opinion, since he's accepting the seeming?"

"Very much so."

"Then what if the latter, who we claim is accepting a seeming but not discerning anything, gets rough with us, and contends that we're not telling the truth? Will we be able to calm him down in any way and persuade him gently, concealing the fact that he's not in a healthy condition?"

"We'll certainly have to do exactly that," he said.

"Come on then, and consider what we're going to say to him. Or do you want us to do it this way, to ask him questions, telling him that no one will begrudge it if he does know anything, but we'd be glad to see that he knows something? But tell us this: does someone who does discern discern something or nothing? Let's have you answer me on his behalf."

"I'll answer that he discerns something," he said.

"Something that is or is not?"

"Something that is. For how could anything that is not be discerned?"

"Then even if we might consider it in more ways, have we got this sufficiently, that what completely is is completely knowable, while what is not is unknowable in any way at all?"

"Quite sufficiently."

"Okay; now if there is a way for something both to be and not be, wouldn't it lie between what is purely and simply and what in no way is?"

"Between."

"Then since knowledge applied to what is, and what applied to what is not was by necessity ignorance, doesn't one need to look for something in between ignorance and knowledge, if there happens to be any such thing, to apply to this in-between kind?"

"Very much so."

"Don't we say opinion is something?"

"How could it not be?"

"A capacity different from knowledge, or the same?"

"Different."

"Therefore opinion is directed at one thing and knowledge at another, each in accord with its own capacity."

"That's the way it is."

"And doesn't knowledge naturally apply to what is, to discern the way what is is? But it seems to me to be necessary instead to make a distinction in this way first."

"How so?"

"We'll assert that capacities are a certain class of beings by which we, and everything else that might have any power, have the power to do what we're capable of; I'm speaking of sight and hearing, for example, as being among the capacities, if that lets you understand what the form is that I mean to describe."

"I do understand," he said.

"Then hear what appears to me about them. In a capacity I don't see any color or shape or any of the many other things of that sort that I look to when I distinguish for myself that some are one thing and others another. In a capacity I look only at what it's directed to and what it accomplishes, and by that I call each of them a capacity, and that which is directed at the same thing and accomplishes the same thing I call the same capacity, while I call that which is directed at something different and accomplishes something different a different capacity. What about you? What do you do?"

"The same," he said.

"Then direct yourself here again, most excellent fellow," I said.

e

"Do you claim that knowledge is some sort of capacity, or what class do you put it in?"

"In this one," he said, "as, in fact, the most potent of all capacities."

"And what about opinion? Is it in with capacities or shall we carry it over to another form?"

"Not at all," he said, "since opinion is nothing other than that by which we're capable of accepting a seeming."

"But just a little while ago you agreed that knowledge and opinion aren't the same."

"How could anyone with any sense," he said, "ever posit that something infallible is the same as something not infallible?"

478

"A beautiful point," I said, "and it's clear that it's agreed by us that opinion is something different from knowledge."

"It's a different thing."

"Therefore, since each of them is a different capacity, each is of such a nature as to be directed at something different?"

"Necessarily."

"And knowledge is presumably directed at what is, to discern the way what is is?"

"Yes."

"And we claim opinion accepts a seeming"

"Yes."

"Is that the same thing that knowledge discerns? And will the same thing be both knowable and a matter of opinion? Or is that impossible?"

"It's impossible," he said, "based on the things that have been agreed; if indeed a different capacity is of such a nature as to be directed at something different, and the

b pair of them together are capacities, opinion and knowledge, and each of them a different capacity, as we claim, then based on these things, there's no room for what's knowable and what's a matter of opinion to be the same."

"Then if what's knowable is what is, what's a matter of opinion would be something other than what is?"

"Something other."

"Then does one accept a seeming of what is not? Or is it impossible at any rate for what is not even to have a seeming? Think about it. Doesn't someone who accepts a seeming refer his opinion to something? Or is it possible to accept a seeming when there's nothing to accept a seeming of?"

"It's impossible."

"But someone who accepts a seeming accepts a seeming of some one thing?"

"Yes."

"But surely what is not would not be spoken of in the most correct way as some

c one thing but as nothing?"

"Certainly."

"And by necessity, we assigned ignorance to what is not, and knowledge to what is?"

"Rightly," he said.

"Therefore one doesn't accept a seeming of what is or of what is not?"

"No."

"And therefore opinion would be neither ignorance nor knowledge?"

"It seems not."

"So then is it outside these, surpassing either knowledge in clarity or ignorance in absence of clarity?"

"Neither."

"But then," I said, "does it appear to you that opinion is something darker than knowledge but brighter than ignorance?"

"Very much indeed," he said.

"And it lies inside the pair of them?"   d

"Yes."

"Therefore opinion would be in between this pair?"

"Exactly so."

"Well, weren't we claiming in the earlier discussion that if anything would come to light as a sort of thing that is and is not at the same time, such a thing would lie between what is purely and simply and what in every way is not, and that neither knowledge nor ignorance would be directed at it, but instead something that came to light as between ignorance and knowledge?"

"Rightly so."

"And now the very thing we call opinion has come to light in between this pair?"

"It has come to light."

"So what would be left, it seems, is for us to find that thing that participates in   e
both being and not being, and isn't rightly referred to in either way purely and simply, so that if it comes to light, we could in justice refer to it as being what opinion is about, assigning the extremes to the extremes and the in-betweens to the in-betweens. Isn't that the way it is?"

"That's the way."

"So with these things as a foundation, let him tell me, I'll say, and let him give an answer, that good fellow who believes there isn't any beautiful itself or any sort of form   479
of beauty itself that's always the same in the same respects, but does believe in the many beautiful things, that lover of sights who doesn't stand for it in any way when anyone claims that the beautiful is a single thing, or the just, or the other things like that. 'Now, most excellent fellow,' we'll say, 'is there any of these many beautiful things that won't also show itself to be ugly? Or any of the just things that's not unjust? Or any of the pious things that's not impious?'"

"No," he said, "it's necessary for them to show themselves as both beautiful and ugly in some way, and for all the other things you're asking about as well."   b

"And what about the many double-sized things? Do they show themselves any the less as halves than as doubles?"

"Not that either."

"And things that we'll claim are big or little, and light or heavy—will these names be applied to them any more than their opposites will?"

"No," he said, "but each of them will always have a share of both."

"So is each of the many things that which anyone claims it is more than it isn't that?"

"It's like the plays on words at dinner parties," he said, "and the children's riddle,   c
the one about the eunuch, about throwing something at a bat, and they make a riddle out of what he threw and what it was on.* Because these many things too have double meanings, and it's not possible to think of any of them in a fixed way as being or not being, or as both or neither."

---

*[The riddle goes: "A man and not a man saw and didn't see a bird and not a bird on a stick and not a stick and threw and didn't throw at it a rock and not a rock." The solution is that it was a eunuch with bad eyesight who saw a bat on a reed and missed when he threw a piece of pumice.]

"Do you have any way you can handle them then," I said, "or any more beautiful place where you could put them than in between being, proper, and not being? Because presumably nothing will show itself to be darker than what is not in order to not-be more than it, or brighter than being in order to be more."

d   "Most true," he said.

"Then it seems we've made the discovery that the many things most people customarily believe about what's beautiful and the other things are rolling around between what is not and what is purely and simply."

"We've made that discovery."

"And we agreed beforehand that if any such thing would come to light, it would need to be said that it's what opinion is about but isn't knowable, a wandering, in-between thing captured by the in-between capacity."

"We are in agreement."

"Then as for those who gaze upon many beautiful things but don't see the beautiful
e   itself, and aren't even capable of following someone else who leads them to it, and upon many just things but not the just itself, and all the things like that, we'll claim that they accept the seeming of everything but discern nothing of what they have opinions about."

"Necessarily," he said.

"And what in turn about those who gaze upon each of the things themselves, that are always the same in the same respects? Won't we claim that they discern them and don't have opinion about them?"

"That too is necessary."

"And won't we also claim that these people devote themselves to and love those
480   things at which knowledge is directed, while the former devote themselves to and love those things at which opinion is directed? Or do we not recall that we claimed they love and gaze upon beautiful sounds and colors and that sort of thing, but can't stand for the beautiful itself to be anything?"

"We remember."

"So we won't be hitting any false note in calling them lovers of opinion rather than lovers of wisdom? And will they get violently angry with us if we speak of them that way?"

"Not if they're persuaded by me," he said, "since no one has a right to be angry with the truth."

"Therefore those who devote themselves to each thing itself that is ought to be called philosophers and not lovers of opinion?"

"Beyond a shadow of a doubt."

Book VI

*   *   *

"Then since, by effort our discussion of lamgiving has reached an end, don't the things that remain after it need to be spoken about: in what manner, by what kinds of
502^d   things learned and pursued, the saviors of the polity will be present among us, and at what ages each group of them will take up each activity?"

"That surely needs to be spoken about," he said.

"It didn't turn out to be a wise thing in the earlier discussion," I said, "for me to have left out the objectionable matter of possessing women, the propagation of children, and the instituting of the rulers, even though I knew that the complete truth would be offensive and a hard thing to bring about, because as it is, the need to go through these things came along nonetheless. And while the particular things about women and children are finished, it's necessary to go into the ones about the rulers as if from the beginning. And we were saying, if you recall, that they must be seen to be passionately devoted to the city, standing the test amid pleasures and pains, and being seen not to drop this conviction through drudgery or terrors or any other vicissitude, or else the person who's incapable is to be rejected, while the one who comes through untarnished in every way, like gold tested in the fire, is to be established as a ruler and given honors and prizes both while living and at his death. Some such things as that were being said when the discussion slipped past them with its face covered, in fear of setting in motion what's now at hand."

"You're telling the exact truth," he said; "I do recall."

"I was reluctant, dear friend," I said, "to state what has now been daringly exposed, but now let it be boldly stated: it's imperative to put philosophers in place as guardians in the most precise sense."

"Let it be so stated," he said.

"Then consider it likely that you'll have few of them, since the nature we went through needs to belong to them, but its parts are rarely inclined to grow together in the same place, but in most cases grow as something severed."

"How do you mean?" he said.

"With natures that are good learners, have memories, are intellectually flexible, are quick, and have everything else that goes with these things, and are youthfully spirited and lofty in their thinking as well, you know that they aren't willing at the same time to grow up being the sort of natures that want to live with calmness and stability in an orderly way, but instead are the kind that are carried off wherever their quickness happens to take them, and everything stable goes right out of them."

"You're telling the truth," he said.

"But with those natures with stable characters, on the other hand, that are not easily changeable, those one would treat as more trustworthy and that would be unmoved confronting terrors in war, wouldn't they be the same way confronting things to be learned also? They're hard to move and slow to learn as though they'd been numbed, and they're full of sleepiness and yawning whenever anything of the sort needs to be worked at."

"That's how they are," he said.

"But we claimed it was necessary to have a good-sized and high-quality share of both, or else not be allowed to take part in the most precise sort of education or in honor or in ruling."

"Rightly," he said.

"And don't you imagine that will be rare?"

"How could it not be?"

"So not only does it need to be tested in the labors, terrors, and pleasures we spoke of then but also, something we passed over then and speak of now, one needs to give it exercise in many kinds of studies to examine whether it will be capable of holding up under the greatest studies, or whether it will shy away like people who show cowardice in other areas."

"It's certainly appropriate to examine it that way," he said, "but what sort of studies in particular are you saying are the greatest?"

"No doubt you remember," I said, "that we pieced together what justice, moderation, courage, and wisdom each would be by distinguishing three forms that belong to the soul."

e

503

b

c

d

e

504

"If I didn't remember that," he said, "it would be just for me not to hear the rest."

"And what about what was said by way of preface to that?"

"What was it?"

b   "We were saying something to the effect that getting the most beautiful possible look at these things would take another, longer way around, which would make them become evident to someone who traveled that road, though it would be possible to provide illustrations approximating to the things that had already been said earlier, and you folks declared that would be sufficient. And so the things said at that time, as far as precision goes, as it appeared to me, were deficient; as for whether they were satisfactory to you people, that's something you could say."

"To me? In a measured way," he said; "and it looked like they were to the others as well."

c   "My friend," I said, "measuredness in such matters that stops short in any respect whatever of what *is* turns out not to measure anything at all, because nothing incomplete is a measure of anything.

"But sometimes it seems to some people that they're well enough off already and don't need to search any further."

"A great many people feel that way a lot," he said, "because of laziness."

"That feeling, anyway," I said, "is one there's the least need for in a guardian of a city and its laws."

"Likely so," he said.

"So, my comrade," I said, "it's necessary for such a person to go around by the

d   longer road, and he needs to work as a learner no less hard than at gymnastic training, or else, as we were just saying, he'll never get to the end of the greatest and most relevant study."

"So these aren't the greatest ones," he said, "but there's something still greater than justice and the things we've gone over?"

"Not only is there something greater," I said, "but even for those things themselves, it's necessary not just to look at a sketch, the way we've been doing now, but not to stop short of working them out to their utmost completion. Wouldn't it be ridiculous to make a concentrated effort in every way over other things of little worth, to have

e   them be as precise and pure as possible, while not considering the greatest things to be worthy of the greatest precision?"

"Very much so," he said, "and a creditable thought it is, but what you mean by the greatest study, and what it's about—do you imagine," he said, "that anyone's going to let you off without asking you what it is?"

"Not at all," I said. "Just you ask. For all that, you've heard it no few times, but

505   now you're either not thinking of it or else, by latching onto me, you think you'll cause me trouble. But I imagine it's more the latter, since you've often heard that the greatest learnable thing is the look of the good, which just things and everything else need in addition in order to become useful and beneficial. So now you know pretty well that I'm going to say that, and in addition to it that we don't know it well enough. But if we don't know it, and we do know everything else as much as possible without it, you can be sure

b   that nothing is any benefit to us, just as there would be none if we possessed something without the good. Or do you imagine it's any use to acquire any possession that's not good? Or to be intelligent about everything else without the good, and have no intelligence where anything beautiful and good is concerned?"

"By Zeus, I don't!" he said.

"And surely you know this too, that to most people, the good seems to be pleasure, and to the more sophisticated ones, intelligence."

"How could I not?"

"And, my friend, that the ones who believe the latter can't specify what sort of intelligence, but are forced to end up claiming it's about the good."

"It's very ridiculous," he said.

"How could it be otherwise," I said, "if after reproaching us because we don't know what's good they turn around and speak to us as though we do know? Because they claim that it's intelligence about the good as though we for our part understand what they mean when they pronounce the name of the good."

"That's very true," he said.

"And what about the people who define the good as pleasure? Are they any less full of inconsistency than the others? Aren't they also forced to admit that there are bad pleasures?"

"Emphatically so."

"So I guess they turn out to be conceding that the same things that are good are also bad. Isn't that so?"

"Certainly."

"Then isn't it clear that the disagreements about it are vast and many?"

"How could it not be clear?"

"And what about this? Isn't it clear that many people would choose the things that seem to be just and beautiful, and even when they aren't, would still do them, possess them, and have the seeming, though no one is content to possess what seems good, but people seek the things that are good, and in that case everyone has contempt for the seeming?"

"Very much so," he said.

"So this is exactly what every soul pursues, for the sake of which it does everything, having a sense that it's something but at a loss and unable to get an adequate grasp of what it is, or even have the reliable sort of trust it has about other things; because of this it misses out even on any benefit there may have been in the other things. On such a matter, of such great importance, are we claiming that even the best people in the city, the ones in whose hands we're going to put everything, have to be in the dark in this way?"

"Not in the least," he said.

"I imagine anyway," I said, "that when there's ignorance of the way in which just and beautiful things are good, they won't have gotten a guardian for themselves who's worth much of anything, in someone who's ignorant of that, and I have a premonition that no one's going to discern them adequately before that."

"You're very good at premonitions," he said.

"Then won't our polity be perfectly ordered if that sort of guardian does watch over it, one who knows these things?"

"Necessarily," he said. "But you in particular, Socrates, do you claim the good is knowledge or pleasure or some other thing besides these?"

"That's a man for you," I said; "you've done a beautiful job of making it plain all along that the way things seem to others about these things won't be good enough for you."

"But it doesn't seem just to me either, Socrates," he said, "to be able to state the opinions of others but not one's own, when one has been concerned about these things for such a long time."

"Well does it seem to you to be just," I said, "to talk about things one doesn't know as though one knew them?"

"Not by any means as though one knew them," he said, "but certainly it's just to be willing to say what one thinks as something one thinks."

"What?" I said, "Haven't you noticed about opinions without knowledge that they're all ugly? The best of them are blind. Or do people who hold any true opinion without insight seem to you to be any different from blind people who travel along the right road?"

"No different," he said.

"Then do you want to gaze on ugly things, blind and crooked, when you'll be able to hear bright and beautiful ones from others?"

d   "Before Zeus, Socrates," said Glaucon, "you're not going to stand down as if you were at the end. It'll be good enough for us if, the same way you went over what has to do with justice and moderation and the other things, you also go over what has to do with the good."

"For me too, comrade," I said, "and more than good enough. But I'm afraid I won't be capable of it, but I'll make a fool of myself in my eagerness and pay for it in ridicule. But, you blessed fellows, let's leave aside for the time being what the good

e   itself is, since it appears to me to be beyond the trajectory of the impulse we've got at present to reach the things that now seem to me to be the case. But I'm willing to speak about what appears to be an offspring of the good and most like it, if that's also congenial to you folks, or if not, to let it go."

"Just speak," he said, "and some other time you'll pay off the balance with a description of the father."

507   "I'd like to have the power to pay it in full and for you folks to receive it, and not just the interest on it as you will now. Give a reception, then, to this dividend and offspring of the good itself. Be on your guard, though, in case I unintentionally deceive you by paying my account with counterfeit interest."

"We'll be on guard according to our power," he said, "so just speak."

"After I've gotten your agreement," I said, "and reminded you of things mentioned in the previous discussion and often spoken of before now elsewhere."

"What sort of things?" he said.

b   "We claim that there are many beautiful things," I said, "and many good things, and the same way for each kind, and we distinguish them in speech."

"We do."

"But also a beautiful itself, and a good itself, and the same way with everything we were then taking as many, we go back the other way and take according to a single look of each kind, as though there is only one, and we refer to it as what each kind is."

"That's it."

"And we claim that the former are seen but not thought, while the 'looks' in turn are thought but not seen."

"Completely and totally so."

c   "And by which of the things within ourselves do we see the ones that are seen?"

"By sight," he said.

"And perceive the things heard by hearing, and all the perceptible things by the other senses?" I said.

"Of course."

"Well," I said, "have you reflected about the craftsman of the senses, how he was by far the most bountiful in crafting the power of seeing and being seen?"

"Not at all," he said.

"Then look at it this way: for one thing to hear and another to be heard, is there any need for another kind of thing in addition to the sense of hearing and a sound, such

d   that, if that third thing isn't present, the first won't hear and the second won't be heard?"

"There's nothing like that," he said.

"And I don't imagine," I said, "that there are many others either, not to say none, that have any additional need for such a thing, or can you name any?"

"Not for my part," he said.

"But don't you realize that the power of sight and being seen does have an additional need?"

"How's that?"

"Presumably you're aware that when sight is present in eyes and the one who has it attempts to use it, and color is present there in things, unless there's also a third kind of thing present, of a nature specifically for this very purpose, sight will see nothing and colors will be invisible."   e

"What's this thing you're speaking of?" he said.

"The one you call light," I said.

"It's true, as you say," he said.

"Then the sense of sight and the power of being seen have been bound together by a bond more precious, by no small look, than that uniting other pairs, unless light is something to be despised."   508

"Surely it's far from being despised," he said.

"And which of the divine beings in the heavens can you point out as the ruling power responsible for this, whose light makes our sight see and visible things be seen as beautifully as possible?"

"The same one you and everyone else would," he said, "since it's obvious you're asking about the sun."

"And is it this way that sight is by its nature related to this god?"

"How?"

"The sun is not sight itself, nor is it that in which sight is present, what we call an eye."   b

"No indeed."

"But I imagine that's the most sunlike of the sense organs."

"By far."

"And doesn't it acquire the power that it has as an overflow from that which is bestowed by the sun?"

"Very much so."

"So while the sun isn't sight, but is the thing responsible for it, isn't it seen by that very thing?"

"That's how it is," he said.

"Now then," I said, "say that this is what I'm calling the offspring of the good, which the good generated as something analogous to itself; the very thing the good itself is in the intelligible realm in relation to insight and the intelligible things, this is in the visible realm in relation to sight and the visible things."   c

"How so?" he said. "Go into it more for me."

"With eyes," I said, "do you know that when one no longer turns them on those things to whose colors the light of day extends, but on those on which nocturnal lights fall, they grow dim, and appear nearly blind, just as though no pure sight was present in them?"

"Very much so," he said.

"But I imagine that whenever one turns them to the things the sun illumines, they see them clearly, and pure sight is manifestly present in these very same eyes."   d

"Certainly."

"In this manner, think of the power of the soul too as being the same way. Whenever it becomes fixed on that which truth and being illumine, it has insight, discerns, and shows itself to have an intellect, but whenever it becomes fixed on something mixed with darkness, something that comes into and passes out of being, it deals in seeming and grows dim, changing its opinions up and down, and is like something that has no intellect."

"It does seem like that."

e   "Then say that what endows the things known with truth, and gives that which knows them its power, is the look of the good. Since it's the cause of knowledge and truth, think of it as something known, but though both of these, knowing and truth, are so beautiful, by regarding it as something else, still more beautiful than they are, you'll

509   regard it rightly. And as far as knowledge and truth are concerned, just as it's right over there to consider light and sight sunlike, but isn't right to consider them to be the sun, so too here it's right to consider both of these as like the good, but not right to regard either of them as being the good; the condition of the good requires that it be held in still greater honor."

"You're talking about a beauty hard to conceive," he said, "if it endows things with knowledge and truth but is itself beyond these in beauty, because it's sure not pleasure you mean."

"Watch your mouth," I said; "but look into the image of it still more closely."

"In what way?"

b   "I imagine you'd claim that the sun not only endows the visible things with their power of being seen, but also with their coming into being, their growth, and their nurture, though it's not itself coming-into-being."

"How could it be?"

"Then claim as well that the things that are known not only get their being-known furnished by the good, but they're also endowed by that source with their very being and their being what they are, even though the good is not being, but something over and above being, beyond it in seniority and surpassing it in power."

c   And Glaucon, in a very comical manner, said "By Apollo, that's a stupendous stretcher."

"You're to blame for it," I said, "for forcing me to tell the way things seem to me about it."

"And don't by any means stop," he said, "not if there are any other things for you to go over in the likeness to the sun, in case you're leaving something out anywhere."

"That's for sure," I said; "I'm leaving out scads of things."

"Well don't skip over any little bit," he said.

"I suspect I'll skip over a lot," I said, "but be that as it may, as far as it's possible at present, I won't willingly leave anything out."

"See that you don't," he said.

d   "Well then, as we're saying," I said, "think of them as being a pair, one ruling as king over the intelligible race and realm, and the other, for its part, over the visible—note that I'm not saying 'over the heavens,' so I won't seem to you to be playing verbal tricks with the name. But do you grasp these two forms, visible, intelligible?"

"I've got them."

"Then take them as being like a line divided into two unequal segments, one for the visible class and the other for the intelligible, and cut each segment again in the same ratio, and you'll get the parts to one another in their relation of clarity and obscu-

510   rity; in the visible section, one segment [A] will be for images, and by images I mean

first of all shadows, then semblances formed in water and on all dense, smooth, bright surfaces, and everything of that sort, if you get the idea."

"I get it."

"Then in the other part [B], put what this one is likened to, the animals around us, and every plant, and the whole class of artificial things."

"I'm putting them," he said.

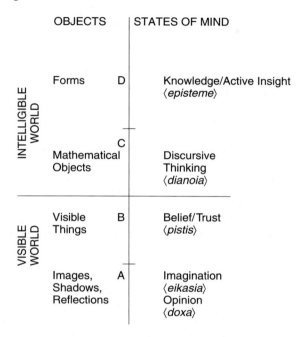

OBJECTS	STATES OF MIND

INTELLIGIBLE WORLD

Forms   D — Knowledge/Active Insight ⟨*episteme*⟩

C
Mathematical Objects — Discursive Thinking ⟨*dianoia*⟩

VISIBLE WORLD

Visible Things   B — Belief/Trust ⟨*pistis*⟩

Images, Shadows, Reflections   A — Imagination ⟨*eikasia*⟩ Opinion ⟨*doxa*⟩

"And would you also be willing to claim," I said, "that it's divided with respect to truth and its lack, such that the copy is to the thing it's copied from as a seeming is to something known?"

"I would," he said, "very much so."

"Then consider next the way the division of the intelligible part needs to be made."

"What way is that?"

"Such that in one part of it [C] a soul takes as images the things that were imitated before, and is forced to inquire based on presuppositions, proceeding not to a beginning but to an end, while in the other part [D] it goes from a presupposition to a beginning free of presuppositions, without the images involved in the other part, making its investigation into forms themselves and by means of them."

"I didn't sufficiently understand what you mean by these things," he said.

"Once more, then," I said; "since you'll understand more easily after the following preface. [C] Now I imagine you know that people who concern themselves with matters of geometry and calculation and such things presuppose in accord with each investigation the odd and the even, the geometrical shapes, the three kinds of angles, and other things related to these; treating these as known and making them presuppositions, they don't think it's worth giving any further account of them either to themselves or to anyone else, as though they were obvious to everyone, but starting from these things and going through the subsequent things from that point, they arrive at a conclusion in agreement with that from which they set their inquiry in motion."

"I do know that very well," he said.

"Then you also know that they make additional use of visible forms, and make their arguments about them, even though they're thinking not about these but about those things these are images of, since it's in regard to the square itself, and its diagonal

e   itself, that they're making those arguments, and not in regard to the one that they draw, and likewise in the other cases; these very things that they model and draw, which also

511   have their own shadows and images in water, they are now using as images in their turn, in an attempt to see those things themselves that one could not see* in any other way than by the power of thinking."

"What you're saying is true," he said.

"The latter, then, is what I meant by the intelligible form, and it's for the inquiry about it that the soul is forced to make use of presuppositions, not going to the source, because it doesn't have the power to step off above its presuppositions, but using as images those things that are themselves imaged down below, in comparison with which these images are reputed to be of preeminent clarity and are treated with honor."

"I understand," he said; "you're talking about the things dealt with by geometrical

b   studies and the arts akin to that."

"Then understand me to mean the following by the other segment of the intelligible part [D]: what rational speech itself gets hold of by its power of dialectical motion, making its presuppositions not sources but genuinely standing places, like stepping-stones and springboards, in order that, by going up to what is presuppositionless at the source of everything and coming into contact with this, by following back again the things that follow from it, rational speech may descend in that way to a conclusion,

c   making no more use in any way whatever of anything perceptible, but dealing with forms themselves, arriving at them by going through them, it ends at forms as well."

"I understand," he said, "though not sufficiently, because you seem to me to be talking about a tremendous amount of work; however, I understand that you want to mark off that part of what is and is intelligible that's contemplated by the knowledge that comes from dialectical thinking as being clearer than what's contemplated by what are called arts, which have presuppositions as their starting points. Those who contemplate things by means of the arts are forced to contemplate them by thinking and not by

d   sense perception, but since they examine things not by going up to the source but on the basis of presuppositions, they seem to you to have no insight into them, even though, by means of their starting point, they're dealing with things that are intelligible. And you seem to me to be calling the activity of geometers and such people thinking but not insight, on the grounds that thinking is something in between opinion and insight."

"You took it in utterly sufficiently," I said. "Along with me, take it too that for the four segments of the line there are these four kinds of experiences that arise in the soul,

e   active insight for the highest and thinking for the second, and assign the names trust to the third and imagination to the last, drawing them up as a proportion and holding that, in the same manner these experiences have their shares of clarity, the things they're directed to have corresponding shares of truth."

"I understand," he said, "and I go along with it and rank them as you say."

---

*A geometrical line is understood as having no breadth, and a plane figure as having no depth. A drawing in the sand, a shape cut out of some flat material, or even any appearance in our pictorial imaginations must falsify what it images if it is to image it at all.

Book VII

"Next," I said, "make an image of our nature as it involves education and the lack   514
of it, by likening it to a condition such as the following: picture human beings in a cave-
like dwelling underground, having a long pathway open to the light all across the cave.
They're in it from childhood on with their legs and necks in restraints, so that they're   b
held in place and look only to the front, restricted by the neck-restraint from twisting
their heads around. For them, the light is from a fire burning up above and a long way
behind them, and between the fire and the prisoners there's an upper road. Picture a little wall built along this road, like the low partitions puppeteers use to screen the humans
who display the puppets above them."

"I see it," he said.

"Then see the humans going along this little wall carrying all sorts of articles that   c
jut out over the wall, figurines of men and other animals fashioned out of stone and   515
wood and materials of all kinds, with some of the people carrying them past making
appropriate sounds and others silent."

"You're describing a bizarre image and bizarre prisoners," he said.

"Like us," I said. "First of all, do you imagine such people would have seen anything of themselves or one another other than the shadows cast by the fire onto the part
of the cave right across from them?"

"How could they," he said, "if they were forced to keep their heads immobile   b
throughout life?"

"And what would they have seen of the things carried past? Wouldn't that be the
same thing?"

"What else?"

"So if they were able to converse with one another, don't you think they'd speak
of these very things they see as the beings?"

"Necessarily."

"And what if their prison also had an echo from the side across from them? Any
time any of the people carrying things past uttered a sound, do you imagine they'd
believe anything other than the passing shadow had made the sound?"

"By Zeus, I don't," he said.

"So in every way," I said, "such people wouldn't consider anything to be the truth   c
other than the shadows of artificial things."

"That's a great necessity," he said.

"Then consider," I said, "what their release would be like, and their recovery
from their restraints and their delusion, if things like that were to happen to them by
nature. Whenever one of them would be released, and suddenly required to stand up,
and turn his neck around, and walk, and look up toward the light, he'd suffer pain
from doing all these things, and because of the blazes of light, he wouldn't have the   d
power to get a clear sight of the things whose shadows he'd seen before. What do you
imagine he'd say if someone were to tell him that he'd been seeing rubbish then, but
now, somewhat nearer to what is and turned toward the things that have more being,
he was seeing more accurately? And especially if, pointing to each of the things passing by, one forced him to answer as he asked what they are, don't you imagine he'd be
at a loss and believe the things he'd seen before were truer than the ones pointed out
to him now?"

"Very much so," he said.

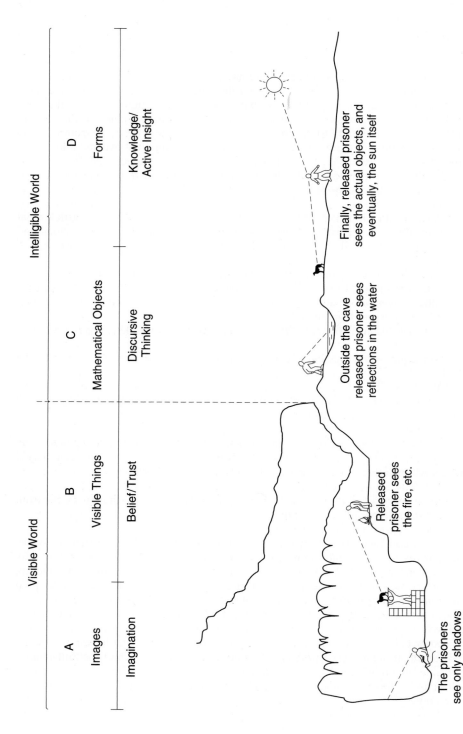

"And if one forced him to look at the light itself, wouldn't he have pain in his eyes   e
and escape by turning back toward those things he was able to make out, and consider
them clearer in their very being than the ones pointed out to him?"

"That's how it would be," he said.

"And if one were to drag him away from there by force," I said, "along the rough,
steep road up, and didn't let go until he'd dragged him out into the light of the sun,
wouldn't he be feeling pain and anger from being dragged, and when he came into the   516
light and had his eyes filled with its dazzle, wouldn't he be unable to see even one of the
things now said to be the true ones?"

"That's right," he said, "at least not right away."

"So I imagine he'd need to get accustomed to it, if he were going to have sight of
the things above. At first, he'd most easily make out the shadows, and after that the
images of human beings and other things in water, and only later the things themselves;
and turning from those things, he'd gaze on the things in the heavens, and at the heavens themselves, more easily by night, looking at the starlight and moonlight, than by   b
day, at the sun and its light."

"How could it be otherwise?"

"Then at last, I imagine, he'd gain sight of the sun, not its appearances in water or
in any setting foreign to it, but he'd have the power to see it itself, by itself, in its own
realm, and contemplate it the way it is."

"Necessarily," he said.

"And after that, he could now draw the conclusion about it that this is what provides the seasons and the years, and has the governance of all things in the visible   c
realm, and is in a certain manner the cause of all those things they'd seen."

"It's clear that he'd come to these conclusions after those experiences," he said.

"And then what? When he recalled his first home and the wisdom there and the
people he was imprisoned with then, don't you imagine he'd consider himself happy
because of the change and pity the others?"

"Greatly so."

"And if there had been any honors and commendations and prizes for them then
from one another for the person who had the sharpest sight of the things passing by and
remembered best all the things that usually passed by before and after them and at the   d
same time, and based on those things had greatest ability to predict what was going to
come, do you think he'd be longing for those rewards and feel jealousy toward the ones
honored by those people and in power among them, or would he feel what Homer
depicts, and wish powerfully

> To be a bond-servant to another, tilling the soil
> For a man without land of his own,

and submit to anything whatever rather than hold those opinions and live that way?"

"The latter, I imagine," he said; "he'd submit to enduring everything rather than   e
live in that way."

"Then give this some thought too," I said. "If such a person were to go back down
and sit in the same spot, wouldn't he get his eyes filled with darkness by coming suddenly out of the sun?"

"Indeed he would," he said.

"And if he had to compete with those who'd always been imprisoned, at passing
judgments on those shadows, at a time when his sight was dim before his eyes settled   517

back in, and if this period of adjustment was not very short, wouldn't he make a laughingstock of himself, and wouldn't it be said about him that after having gone up above he returned with his eyes ruined, and that it's not worth it even to make the effort to go up? And as for anyone who attempted to release them and lead them up, if they had the power in any way to get him into their hands and kill him, wouldn't they kill him?"

"Ferociously," he said.

b   "Now this image, dear Glaucon," I said, "needs to be connected as a whole with what was said before, by likening the realm disclosed by sight to the prison dwelling, and the light of the fire within it to the power of the sun; and if you take the upward journey and sight of the things above as the soul's road up into the intelligible region, you won't miss my intended meaning, since you have a desire to hear about that. No doubt a god knows whether it happens to be true. What appears true to me appears this way: in the knowable region, the last thing to be seen, with great effort, is the look of the

c   good, but once it's been seen, it has to be concluded that it's the very cause, for all things, of all things right and beautiful, that it generates light and its source in the visible realm, and is itself the source that bestows truth and insight in the intelligible realm. Anyone who's going to act intelligently in private or in public needs to have sight of it."

"I too join in assuming that," he said, "at least in whatever way I'm able to."

"Come, then," I said, "and join in assuming the following as well, and don't be surprised that those who've come to this point aren't willing to do what belongs to

d   human beings, but their souls are eager to spend all their time up above; presumably it's likely to be that way, if this also stands in accord with the image already described."

"It's certainly likely," he said.

"And what about this? Do you imagine it's anything surprising," I said, "if someone coming from contemplation of divine things to things of a human sort is awkward and looks extremely ridiculous while his sight is still dim and if, before he's become sufficiently accustomed to the darkness around him, he's forced, in law courts or anywhere else, to contend over the shadows of the just or the images they're the shadows

e   of, and to compete about that in whatever way these things are understood by people who've never looked upon justice itself?"

"It's not surprising in any way whatsoever," he said.

518   "But if someone had any sense," I said, "he'd remember that two sorts of disturbances occur in the eyes from two causes, when they're removed from light into darkness as well as from darkness into light. If he regarded these same things as occurring also with the soul, when he saw one that was confused and unable to make anything out, he wouldn't react with irrational laughter but would consider whether it had come from

b   a brighter life and was darkened by its unaccustomed condition, or was coming out of a greater ignorance into a brighter place and was overwhelmed by the dazzle of a greater radiance. That way, he'd congratulate the one soul on the happiness of its experience and life and pity the other, and if he did want to laugh at that one, he'd be less laughable for laughing at it than someone who laughed at the one coming out of the light above."

"You're speaking in a very balanced way," he said.

"So," I said, "if those things are true, we ought to regard them in the following way: education is not the sort of thing certain people who claim to be professors of it

c   claim that it is. Surely they claim they put knowledge into a soul it wasn't present in, as though they were putting sight into blind eyes."

"Indeed they do claim that," he said.

"But the current discussion indicates," I said, "that this power is present in the soul of each person, and the instrument by which each one learns, as if it were an eye that's not able to turn away from darkness toward the light in any other way than along

with the whole body, needs to be turned around along with the whole soul, away from
what's fleeting, until it becomes able to endure gazing at what is and at the brightest of   d
what is, and this, we're claiming, is the good. Isn't that right?"

"Yes."

"Then there would be an art to this very thing," I said, "this turning around, having to do with the way the soul would be most easily and effectively redirected, not an
art of implanting sight in it, but of how to contrive that for someone who has sight, but
doesn't have it turned the right way or looking at what it needs to."

"That seems likely," he said.

"Then the other virtues said to belong to a soul probably tend to be near the things
belonging to the body, since they're not present in the being of the soul before they've
been inculcated by habits and practice, but the virtue involving understanding, more   e
than all, attains to being something more divine, as it seems, which never loses its
power, but by the way it's turned becomes either useful and beneficial or useless and   519
harmful. Or haven't you ever reflected about the people said to be depraved but wise,
how penetrating a gaze their little souls have and how sharply they discern the things
they're turned toward, since they don't have poor sight but force it to serve vice, so that
the more sharply it sees, that much more evil it accomplishes?"

"Very much so," he said.

"But surely," I said, "if, straight from childhood, this tendency of such a nature
had been curtailed by having the edges knocked off that have an affinity with becoming,
like lead weights that, through eating and the pleasures and greediness involved in such   b
things, get to be growths on the soul that turn its sight excessively downward, and if,
freed from them, it was turned toward things that are true, this same power of these
same people would have seen them too most sharply, just as it sees the ones it's now
turned toward."

"Very likely," he said.

"And what about this?" I said. "Isn't it likely, even necessary from what's been
said before, that those who are uneducated and lacking experience with truth could   c
never adequately manage a city, and neither could those who've been allowed to devote
all their time to education—the former because they don't have any one goal in life that
they need to aim at in doing all the things they do in private and in public, and the latter
because they wouldn't willingly engage in action, believing they'd taken up residence
in the Isles of the Blessed while still living?"

"True," he said.

"So our job as founders," I said, "is to require the best natures to get to the study
we were claiming earlier is the greatest thing, to see the good as well as to climb the   d
path up to it, and when, having climbed up, they've seen it sufficiently, not to allow
what they're now permitted to do."

"What in particular?"

"To stay there," I said, "and not be willing to come back down among those prisoners or take part beside them in their labors and honors, the more frivolous ones or
even the more serious."

"What?" he said. "Are we going to do them an injustice and make them live worse
when it's possible for them to live better?"

"My friend," I said, "you let it slip back out of your memory that this is no concern   e
of the law, for some one class of people in a city to be exceptionally well off, but that it
contrive things so that this arises in the city as a whole, by harmonizing the citizens
through persuasion and compulsion and making them contribute to one another a share of   520
the benefit with which each sort is capable of improving the community; the law doesn't

produce men of this sort in the city to allow them to turn whichever way each one wants but so that it may make full use of them for the binding together of the city."

"That's true," he said; "that did slip my mind."

"Then consider, Glaucon," I said, "that we won't be doing any injustice anyway to the philosophers who arise among us, but we'll be asking just things of them in requiring

b   them also to care for the other people and watch over them. We'll tell them that when people of their sort come along in other cities, it's reasonable for them not to share the burdens in those cities, since they spring up spontaneously in each of them against the will of the polity, and something that grows up on its own, not owing its upbringing to anyone, has just cause not to be too keen on paying for its support. 'But we've bred you both for yourselves and for the rest of the city like the rulers and kings in beehives, to be

c   educated in a better and more complete way than the others and more capable of taking part in both ways of life. So it's necessary for each of you in turn to go down into the communal dwelling and to get used to gazing at dark objects with the others, because when you're used to it you'll see thousands of times better than the people there, and recognize each sort of image for what it is and what it's an image of, from having seen the truth about beautiful and just and good things. And so the city will be governed by you and by us wide awake, and not in a dream the way most are governed now by people who

d   fight with each other over shadows and form factions over ruling, as though that were some great good. But the truth is surely this: that city in which those who are going to rule are least eager to rule is necessarily governed best and with the least divisiveness, while the one that gets the opposite sort of rulers is governed in the opposite way.'"

"Quite so," he said.

"Then do you imagine those who've been brought up will be unpersuaded by us when they hear these things, and be unwilling to share, each in turn, in the labors of the city while dwelling among themselves a lot of the time in the pure region?"

e   "It's not possible," he said, "because we'll be giving just obligations to people who are just. More than anything, each of them will go into ruling as something unavoidable, which is opposite to what those who rule in each city now do."

"That's how it is, my comrade," I said; "if you find a way of life better than ruling

521   for those who are going to rule, there's a possibility for a well-governed city to come into being for you, because only in it will the rulers be those who are rich in their very being, not in gold but in that in which someone who's happy needs to be rich: a good and intelligent life. But if beggars and people hungry for private goods go into public life imagining that's where they need to go to steal off with the good, there's no possibility, because when ruling becomes something that's fought over, since that sort of war, being domestic and internal, destroys them and the rest of the city."

"Very true," he said.

b   "Well," I said, "do you know of any way of life other than that of true philosophy that looks down on political offices?"

"No, by Zeus," he said.

"It's necessary, though, for people who aren't in love with ruling to go after it; if they don't, the rival lovers will do battle."

"Certainly."

"And who else are you going to require to go into guarding the city than the people who are most thoughtful about those things by which a city is governed best, and who have other honors and a better life than the political sort?"

"None other than they," he said.

*   *   *

BOOK VIII

*   *   *

"Come on then, dear comrade; what's the turn by which tyranny comes into   562
being? Because it's pretty evident it changes out of democracy."

"It's evident."

"Well, doesn't tyranny come from democracy in something of the same manner
that democracy comes from oligarchy?"

"How so?"

"The good set before it," I said, "on account of which oligarchy was established,   b
was riches, isn't that right?"

"Yes."

"Then the insatiable desire for riches, and the neglect of everything else for the
sake of moneymaking destroyed it."

"True," he said.

"And isn't the insatiable desire for that which democracy defines as good also its
undoing?"

"What are you saying it defines it as?"

"Freedom," I said. "Because doubtless in a democratic city you'd hear that this   c
is the most beautiful thing it has, and is the reason it's the only place worth living for
anyone who's free by nature."

"That's exactly the wording that's used," he said, "and it's said a lot."

"Then isn't it exactly as I was headed for saying just now?" I said. "Doesn't the
insatiable desire for that sort of thing and the neglect of everything else alter this polity
too, and prepare the way for it to need a tyranny?"

"How?" he said.

"I imagine that when a democratic city that has a thirst for freedom happens to get
bad wine stewards as the people in charge of it, and it gets more deeply drunk than it   d
ought by drinking it unmixed, then if the rulers aren't completely lenient and don't provide loads of freedom, it punishes them, charging that they're tainted with oligarchic
leanings."

"That they do," he said.

"But the people who obey the rulers get smeared with mud as willing slaves and
nobodies, while the rulers who act like they're ruled and the ruled who act like rulers get
praised and honored in private and in public. Isn't it a necessity in such a city for freedom to extend to everything?"

"How could it not?"   e

"And for it to insinuate itself, my friend," I said, "into private households, with
anarchy finally taking root all the way down to the animals."

"What sort of thing are we talking about?" he said.

"The sort that happens," I said, "when a father gets used to being like a child and
is afraid of his sons, and a son gets used to being like a father, and has no respect for or   563
fear of his parents, so he can be free; and resident aliens are treated like townspeople
and townspeople like resident aliens, and there's the same equality for foreigners."

"It does get to be that way," he said.

"It gets to be that way with these things," I said, "and also with other little things
of just that kind. A teacher in such a situation is afraid of his students and fawns on
them, and students have contempt for their teachers and tutors alike, and in general the

b   young ape their elders and try to rival them in words and deeds, while the old stoop to the level of the young, filled with sprightliness and jokes as they imitate the young so they won't seem to be disagreeable or bossy."

"Very much so," he said.

"But the extreme limit of the freedom of the masses, my friend," I said, "is the extent it reaches in such a city when men and women bought as slaves are no less free than those who've paid for them. And how far equal rights and freedom go in the behavior of women toward men and men toward women, we've almost forgotten to mention."

c   "Aren't we going to mention, like Aeschylus," he said, "the thing that did 'just pop into your mouth'?"

"By all means," I said; "I'll speak of that, because anyone who had no experience of it wouldn't believe how much more freedom there is in the animals belonging to people there than anyplace else. Bitches literally take after the women who own them, as the proverb has it, and horses and asses get used to making their way quite freely and majestically down the roads, bumping into anyone who gets in their way if he doesn't step aside, and all the other things they do get filled with that sort of freedom."

d   "It's my own nightmare you're telling me about," he said, "because I experience it often myself on my way out to the country."

"So do you get the point about all these things put together," I said, "how touchy they make the souls of the citizens, so that when anyone brings in anything with the slightest hint of slavery about it, they get upset and can't stand it? Because, as you no doubt know, they end up paying no attention to the laws, written or unwritten, so that no

e   one can be their boss in any way."

"I know it very well," he said.

"So that, my friend," I said, "so beautiful and brash, is the origin out of which tyranny grows, as it seems to me."

PARMENIDES (in part)

Characters

Socrates ("quite young")
Parmenides
Zeno of Elea
Scene—Athens

127   And so Antiphon said that Pythodorus used to say that both Zeno and Parmenides
b   once came to the Great Panathenea. Now, Parmenides was already quite old—his hair all white—but the vision of a gentleman. He was sixty-five at most. Zeno was then nearly forty, tall and pleasing to look at. (He was said to have been Parmenides' young
c   beloved.) They were staying, he said, with Pythodorus outside the city-wall in the Potter's Quarter.

Plato, *Plato's Parmenides* (127a–135d), translated by Albert Keith Whitaker (Newburyport, MA: Focus Philosophical Library, 1996). Reprinted by permission of Focus Publishing/R. Pullins Company.

So Socrates and many others with him went there, since they desired to hear Zeno's writings—after all, that was the first time they had brought them there. Socrates was then very young. Zeno himself read to them, but Parmenides chanced to be out. And there was, all-in-all, only a short part of the speeches left to be read, Pythodorus said, when he and Parmenides with him came in from outside—and Aristotle too (who became one of the Thirty).* So they heard only a little of the writings. However, Pythodorus, in fact, had heard them before on his own from Zeno.

After listening, Socrates asked him to re-read the first hypothesis of the first speech. Once it was read he said, "Zeno, how do you mean that? If the things that *are,* are many, then, according to you, they must be both like and unlike. But this is clearly impossible, since the unlike cannot be like nor the like unlike. Isn't that what you mean?"

"That's so," replied Zeno.

"And so if it is impossible for the unlike to be like and the like unlike, it's also impossible for there to be many things? For if there should be many, they would suffer these impossibilities. Is this, then, what your speeches seek—nothing else than to battle against everything that is commonly said by maintaining that there *is* no many? And do you think that each of your speeches is a proof of this very thing—so that the supposed proofs that 'There is no many' are as many as the speeches you have written? Is that what you mean, or don't I understand you right?" 128

"No," said Zeno, "on the contrary, you have beautifully grasped the whole of what my writing seeks."

"I'm coming to understand, Parmenides," Socrates said, "that Zeno here seeks to be your partner not only in friendship but in writing! For he has written, in a certain way, the very same thing as you, but by changing it around he tries to trick us into thinking that he is saying some other thing. In your poems you say that All is one, and you do both a beautiful and a good job of proving that; but this fellow, in turn, says that it's not b many, and he offers proofs that are very many and very great. One says 'The One' and one says 'Not Many,' and so each speaks so as to seem to say nothing the same, while you are saying nearly the same thing. That's why what you say appears to be over the heads of the rest of us."

"Yes, Socrates," said Zeno. "But you have not perceived the entire truth of my writing. To be sure, you both chase and hunt down what I said like a Laconian hound! c But this much has escaped you from the first: that in no way whatsoever is my writing so pretentious as to have been written for the reason you offer, namely, to conceal from men that it's furthering some great plot. What you mentioned is just an accidental result. The truth is that it's a sort of aid to Parmenides' speech against those who attack him by joking that if one is, then he and his speech suffer many laughable and contradictory results. d So this writing refutes the asserters of the Many and pays back the same and more. It seeks to make this point clear: that if sufficiently prosecuted, their hypothesis—'If many is'—would suffer even more laughable results than that of the One's *being.* I wrote it, in fact, when I was young, because I loved to fight. But someone stole a copy, so I couldn't decide whether it should be brought to light or not. That's what escapes you, Socrates: e you don't think it was written because of a youth's love for fighting, but because of an older man's love of honor. Though, as I said, your description is not a bad likeness."

---

*The Thirty Tyrants (led by Plato's uncle Critias) took control of Athens in July 404 B.C. after her defeat by the Spartans in the Peloponnesian War. Their short but bloody reign of terror was ended in January 403 B.C. by the moderate oligarchs. The Thirty were all executed at that time or in the years following. One must remember that this Aristotle is not the same as the great fourth-century philosopher, the student of Plato.

129

b

c

d

e

130

b

c

"I accept that," replied Socrates, "and I believe it is as you say. But tell me this: don't you think that there exists, in itself, some form of Likeness, to which is opposed a different one, which is unlike, and that both you and I and the different things which we do in fact call 'many' come to partake of these two things which *are*? And that the things that come to partake of Likeness become like in both the manner and extent that they partake, but those of Unlikeness unlike, and those of both, both? And even if all things come to partake of both these opposing things and are, by partaking in both, both like and unlike in themselves—why wonder? For if someone were to show that the like things themselves become unlike or the unlike like, I'd think that a marvel. But if he shows that whatever partakes of both of these has experienced both, then, Zeno, it doesn't seem at all out of place to me. No, not even if he were to show that all things are one by partaking of the One and that these same things are many, in turn, by partaking in Multitude! But if he demonstrates that whatever one is, this very thing, is many and that the Many, in turn, are one—of course I'll wonder at that. Likewise for all the different things: if he should reveal that both the kinds and forms themselves experience these opposite experiences in themselves, it's right to wonder. But if someone demonstrates that I am one and many, why wonder? For when he seeks to show that I am many, he just mentions that my right is one thing and my left another, my front's one thing and my back's another, and likewise for upper and lower—for I do, I believe, partake of Multitude. But when he wants to show that I am one, he'll say that out of the seven of us who are here, I myself am one man and partake of the One. So he can show that both are true.

"If, then, someone shall try to show that for things such as stones and wood and the like, the same things are many and one, then we will say that he's demonstrated that some thing is many and one, not that the One is many or the Many's one. He's not even said anything wondrous, but only what in fact all of us should readily agree upon. But if someone, as I just said, shall first distinguish the forms as separate in themselves, such as Likeness and Unlikeness and Multitude and the One and Rest and Motion and all the like, and then will show that in themselves these things can be mixed together and separated, I'd admire that with wonder, Zeno!" he said. "Now I do believe that you've worked over these things quite bravely; but, as I've said, I would admire this much more: if someone could demonstrate that even in the forms themselves—in the things grasped by reasoning—there is everywhere tangled up that same impasse which you proved is present in the things we see."

While Socrates was speaking, Pythodorus said, he himself thought that at each word both Parmenides and Zeno were going to get angry. But they kept their mind on Socrates and, with frequent glances to one another, they smiled as if admiring him. Which is, in fact, what Parmenides told him, once he was done.

"Socrates," he said, "you ought to be admired for your zeal for speeches! And tell me, did you, on your own, come up with this division that you speak of between these forms, separate unto themselves, and, separated from them, the things that partake of them? And does it seem to you that Likeness itself is separate from the likeness that we possess? And so on with one and many and everything that you heard of just now from Zeno?"

"It certainly does," answered Socrates.

"Well how about these sorts of things," said Parmenides, "such as a form of Justice in itself and of Beauty and of Good and so on?"

"Yes," he said.

"But what about this: a form of Man separate from us and all those like us—some very form of Man, or of Fire or Water?"

"I've hit a dead end many times, Parmenides," he replied, "over these, over whether it's necessary to speak much the same about them or differently."

"Well then, Socrates, what about those things that would seem to be laughable, such as Hair and Mud and Dirt or any different thing that's very worthless and lowly? Are you at an impasse over whether it is or is not necessary to say that there is a separate form of each of these, something different than what we can lay our hands on?"   d

"No, not at all!" answered Socrates. "For these things are as we see them right here, and it would be grossly out of place to think that there is some form of them. To be sure, it has troubled me that the same case does not apply to all, but whenever I come to this, I run off, fearing to fall and perish in some abyss of foolishness. In the end, then, I return to these things that just now we were saying are forms and I spend my time working over them."

"Well, you are still young, Socrates," said Parmenides, "and philosophy has not   e yet grabbed you as it will, in my opinion. Then you will dishonor none of these things; but as for now, you still look to the opinions of men, because of your age. But tell me this, then: does it seem to you that, as you say, there are these forms from which the different things here, by partaking in them, get their names? For example, the things that partake in Likeness become like, but those in Greatness great, and those in Beauty and   131 Justice both just and beautiful?"

"Of course," replied Socrates.

"And so each thing that partakes comes to partake either of the whole form or of a part? Or could there be some way of partaking separate from these?"

"How could there be?" he said.

"Then does it seem to you that the whole form is in each of the many things, while still being one, or how?"

"What prevents it, Parmenides," said Socrates, "from being one?"

"Although one and the same, then, its whole will be in many separate beings at   b the same time, and so it would be separated from itself."

"Not if it is like a day," he said, "which, although one and the same, is many places at once and is not at all separate from itself. In this way each of the forms could be one, the same and in all things at once."

"Socrates," he replied, "how nicely you make one and the same thing many places at once! It is as if after covering many men with a sail you would say that it is one whole over many. Or is this not what you mean to say?"

"That's fair," he answered.   c

"Well then would the whole sail be over each man, or a different part of it over each different man?"

"A part."

"Then, Socrates," he said, "the forms themselves can be partitioned and the things that partake of them would partake of a part. The whole would no longer be in each, but each would possess a part."

"So it appears."

"Well then Socrates, are you willing to say that one form can, in truth, be partitioned by us and still be one?"

"No way," he replied.

"Try to see then," he said, "if you'll partition Greatness itself, then each of the many great things will be great by means of a part that's smaller than Greatness itself—   d doesn't that appear illogical?"

"Of course," he answered.

"But what? If something possesses an individual small part of the Equal, will it possess something that, though less than the Equal itself, will make its possessor equal to anything else?"

"Impossible!"

"Then let one of us possess a part of the Small. Since it's just a part, the Small will be greater than it. Get it?—the Small itself will be greater! But whatever that subtracted piece is added to will be smaller, not greater, than before!"

"Well that certainly can't be," he said.

"Is there, then, some other way, Socrates," he asked, "that the different things will partake of your forms, since they're able to partake neither as parts nor as wholes?"

"No by Zeus!" he exclaimed. "It doesn't seem to me to be at all easy to determine that!"

"But what then? How do you feel about this—"

"What's that?"

"—I think that you think that each form is one because of this: whenever many things seem to you to be great, it seems probable to you, as you look over them all, that there is some one and the same idea. From this you conclude that the Great is one."

"That's the truth," he replied.

"But what about the Great itself and the different great things if, in the same way, you look over them all with your soul, will there not appear, in turn, some great thing that makes all of them, by necessity, appear great?"

"It looks that way."

"A different form of Greatness, then, will be revealed, in addition to what was Greatness itself and the things that partake of it. And above all of these, in turn, another, that makes them all great. And so each of your forms will no longer be one, but will be boundless in multitude."

"But Parmenides," Socrates said, "couldn't it be that each of these forms is a thought and properly comes to *be* nowhere but in souls? Then each could in fact be one and would not still suffer the things you just mentioned."

"What then?" he asked. "Each is one of our thoughts—but are there thoughts of nothing?"

"Impossible," he replied.

"So of something?"

"Yes."

"Of something that is or is not?"

"That is."

"So of one thing—which thing in fact the thought thinks is present in all cases as some one idea?"

"Yes."

"Then won't a form be this thing that is thought to be one, since it's always the same in all cases?"

"It appears necessary."

"But what now?" asked Parmenides. "For doesn't it seem to you that, since it is necessary, you say, for other things to partake of forms, either each thing consists of thoughts and everything thinks or, although thoughts, they're thought-less?"

"Well that too," he replied, "makes no sense. However, Parmenides, here's how it really appears to me to be: these forms stand in nature like patterns. The different things resemble them and are likenesses, and so the different things' participation in the forms turns out to be nothing else than to be made in their likeness!"

"If then," he asked, "something looks like a form, can the form not be like its likeness, insofar as that thing's been made like it? Or is there some trick that can make the like be like what's not like it?"

"No, there isn't."

"But doesn't a great necessity force the like, along with the thing like it, to partake of one and the same form?"   e

"Necessarily."

"But whatever the like things are like by participating in—isn't that the form itself?"

"Entirely so."

"Nothing, then, can be like the form nor can the form be like anything else. Otherwise there will always appear a different form beyond the form; and if that is like   133 anything, another still. And there will never be an end to the genesis of new forms as long as the form becomes like the thing that partakes of it."

"That's most true."

"It's not by likeness, then, that the different things come to partake of forms. Instead it's necessary to seek a different way of partaking."

"It looks that way."

"Do you see then, Socrates," he asked, "how great an impasse lies before anyone who tries to determine that there are forms in themselves?"

"Very much so!"

"And so know well," he said, "that you have, so to speak, not even touched upon how great an impasse there is if you try to posit each form as one, somehow distin-   b guishing them from the beings."

"How's that?" he replied.

"There are many different reasons," he answered, "but here's the greatest. If someone should argue that the forms themselves—should they be as we say they must be—cannot, properly speaking, be known, no one could prove to whomever argues this that he's mistaken, unless the one arguing chanced to be experienced in many things and not naturally dull. This person would have to be willing to follow the fellow working over the proof through many cases and over a long distance, otherwise he who   c forces them to be unknowable would be persuasive."

"Why's that Parmenides?" asked Socrates.

"Because, Socrates, I think that both you and anyone else who posits that there's a certain beinghood in itself for each thing would first agree that none of them *are* among us."

"How could it still be 'in itself' then?" replied Socrates.

"Beautiful," he said. "And so all those ideas that are what they are relative to one another have their beinghood relative to themselves and not in relation to the things among us—whether likenesses or, however one posits them, what we partake of and   d from which, then, we are called by certain names. The things among us, then, these things which take the forms' names, are themselves related only to themselves, but not to the forms, and they belong only to themselves and not to whatever things are named the same."

"How do you mean that?" asked Socrates.

"Here's an example," said Parmenides. "If one of us is a master or a slave of someone, he is not, of course, a slave to what Master itself is, nor is the master a master of what Slave itself is. Instead, since he's a man, he's both of these to another man. For   e Mastership itself is what it is of Slavery itself, and likewise Slavery itself is slavery to

Mastership itself. The things among us have no power in relation to those things, nor they to us; instead, like I said, things belong to themselves and are in relation to themselves and so too the things among us to themselves. Or do you not understand what I mean?"

"Oh, I understand well," replied Socrates.

"And so also knowledge. Would what Knowledge itself is," he asked, "be knowledge of what Truth itself is?"

"Of course."

"But then what each branch of knowledge is would be knowledge of what each of the beings is, or no?"

"Yes."

"But wouldn't the knowledge among us be of the truth among us; and, in turn, each branch of knowledge among us would have to be knowledge of each of the beings among us?"

"Necessarily."

"And yet the forms themselves, as you agree—neither do we possess them nor could they *be* among us."

"No, they couldn't."

"But surely what each of the kinds themselves is, is known by that very form, the form of Knowledge?"

"Yes."

"Which we certainly don't possess."

"No, we don't."

"None of the forms, then, is known by us, since we don't partake of Knowledge itself."

"It doesn't look that way."

"Then what the Beautiful itself is and the Good and all the things that we do suppose to be ideas are unknown to us."

"I'm afraid so."

"See then something still more terrible than this!"

"What's that?"

"You would probably say that if there *is* in fact a certain kind itself of Knowledge, it is far more precise than the knowledge among us, and the same for Beauty and all the rest."

"Yes."

"And so if anything else does partake of Knowledge itself, wouldn't you say that god, more than anyone else, possesses this most precise knowledge?"

"Necessarily."

"Then will the god, in turn, be able to know the things among us, since he possesses Knowledge itself?"

"Why not?"

"Because," said Parmenides, "we agreed, Socrates, that whatever power they do have, those forms have no power relative to the things among us, nor the things among us relative to them. Instead, each group relates only to themselves."

"Yes, this was agreed."

"And so if the god possesses this most precise Mastership and this most precise Knowledge, then their mastership could never master us, nor could their knowledge know us or anything else of the things among us. Likewise, we do not rule over them by the authority among us, nor, by our knowledge, do we know anything of the divine. According to this speech, in turn, they are not our masters nor do they know anything of human affairs—since they are gods!"

"But what an altogether wondrous speech, if it strips the god of knowing!"

"Nevertheless, Socrates," said Parmenides, "the forms must, by necessity, have these problems and many more still, if there are these ideas of the beings and if one distinguishes each form on its own. The result is that whoever hears this hits a dead end and argues that these things *are* not; and if, at most, they should *be,* well, then, great necessity keeps them unknown to human nature. And while he says these things this fellow will even seem to be talking sense and, as we said before, he will be wondrously hard to convince. Only a naturally gifted man could learn that there is a certain kind and beinghood, in itself, for each thing; and only a still more wondrous person will discover all these things and be able teach someone else to judge them clearly and sufficiently for himself."

"I agree with you, Parmenides," Socrates said. "To my mind, you speak well."

"And yet," said Parmenides, "if someone, in turn, Socrates, after focusing on all these problems and others still, shall deny that there are forms of the beings and will not distinguish a certain form of each single thing, wherever he turns he'll understand nothing, since he does not allow that there is an ever-same idea for each of the beings. And so he will entirely destroy the power of dialogue. But you seem to me only too aware of this."

"That's the truth," he replied.

"What then will you do about philosophy? Where will you turn if all this is unknown?"

"At present, at least, I can't seem to see."

"It's because, Socrates," he said, "you are trying too soon, before being trained, to define some Beautiful and Just and Good and each one of the forms. I noticed this even the day before yesterday when I overheard your conversation with this fellow Aristotle. Know well: that zeal which drives you towards speeches is beautiful and divine. But you must draw yourself back and train more, while you're still young, in a gymnastic that seems useless and which the many call 'idle talk.' If you don't, the truth will escape you."

135

b

c

d

THEAETETUS (Selections)

Characters

Socrates
Theaetetus
Theodorus of Cyrene
Scene—Athens

SOCRATES: But knowledge, as I was just now speaking of it, do you suppose that to be a small thing to find out and not something for those who are top-notch in every way?

THEAETETUS: By Zeus, not I; it's precisely something for top-notch people.

SOCRATES: Then be confident about yourself and believe there's something in what Theodorus says, and show eagerness in every way, both about everything else and about knowledge, to get hold of a statement saying just exactly what it is.

148ᶜ

d

Plato, *Plato's Theaetetus,* (selections from 148c–210d) translated by Joe Sachs (Newburyport, MA: Focus Philosophical Library, 2004). Reprinted by permission of Focus Publishing/R. Pullins Company.

THEAETETUS: As far as it depends on eagerness, Socrates, it will come to light.

SOCRATES: Come on then—you led the way beautifully just now—try to imitate your answer about potential squares, and just as you encompassed them all, many as they are, in one look, so too try to address the many sorts of knowledge in one statement.

e   THEAETETUS: But know well, Socrates, that I've tried my hand many times at examining this, hearing the questions that are carried off from you, but I don't have the power to persuade myself either that I say anything adequately or that I hear anyone else speaking in the way that you call for. But on the other hand, I don't have the power to get myself free from caring about it.

SOCRATES: Dear Theaetetus, it's not because you're empty that you're laboring; you're in labor because you're pregnant.

THEAETETUS: I don't know about that, Socrates. I'm just telling you what I've experienced.

149   SOCRATES: So then, silly fellow, you haven't heard that I am the son of a thoroughly pure-bred and stern midwife, Phaenarete?

THEAETETUS: That I have heard before.

SOCRATES: Then have you heard also that I practice the same art?

THEAETETUS: By no means.

SOCRATES: Then know well that I do; but don't expose me to the others, my companion, for it has escaped detection that I have this art. Other people, since they don't know it, don't say that about me, but they say that I'm a most unsettling person and that I make people be at a loss. Have you heard that too?

b   THEAETETUS: I have.

SOCRATES: Then shall I tell you the reason?

THEAETETUS: Very much so.

SOCRATES: Just keep in mind how the whole thing having to do with midwives goes, and you will easily understand what I mean. For you know, presumably, that none of them is midwife to others while she herself is still conceiving and bearing, but only those who no longer have the power to give birth.

THEAETETUS: Very much so.

SOCRATES: They say that Artemis is the reason for this, because, though she is
c   without a mate or child, she has childbirth allotted for her protection. Now she has not therefore granted it to barren women to be midwives, because human nature is too weak to grasp an art dealing with things it has no experience of; but she assigned it to those who are not giving birth on account of their age, honoring their likeness to herself.

THEAETETUS: That's likely.

SOCRATES: Then isn't this too not only likely but even necessary, that those who are pregnant and those who aren't are recognized more by the midwives than by anyone else?

THEAETETUS: Entirely so.

d   SOCRATES: And surely also the midwives, by giving drugs and singing incantations, have the power either to awaken labor pangs or, if they wish, to make them milder, and also either to make those having trouble bearing give birth or, if it seems good to them when it's newly conceived to cause an abortion, they cause an abortion.

THEAETETUS: That's the way it is.

SOCRATES: Well then, have you perceived this further thing about them, that they are the cleverest matchmakers, since they are all-around wise about discerning what sort of woman needs to have intercourse with what sort of man to give birth to the best possible children?

THEAETETUS: I don't know that at all.

SOCRATES: Well, know that they take more pride in this than in cutting the umbil- e
ical cord. Consider this: do you think caring for and gathering in the fruits of the earth
belongs to the same art or to a different one than recognizing what sort of plant and seed
ought to be put into what sort of soil?

THEAETETUS: No, it would be the same.

SOCRATES: But in women, dear fellow, you suppose there is one art for this sort of
thing but a different one for gathering the harvest?

THEAETETUS: It's not likely, then.

SOCRATES: No it isn't. But on account of the unjust and unartful bringing   150
together of a man and a woman, which has the name pimping, the midwives avoid even
matchmaking, because they are respectable women, out of fear that they might fall
under the accusation of the former by reason of the latter, even though it is proper to
genuine midwives alone to engage in matchmaking correctly.

THEAETETUS: That appears so.

SOCRATES: The part played by the midwives then is so great a thing, but it is a
lesser one than my role. For it is not a property of women sometimes to give birth to   b
images, while there are other times when what they give birth to is true, with this not
being easy to distinguish. For if this were a property of theirs, the greatest and most
beautiful work for the midwives would be to judge what is true and what is not. Don't
you think so?

THEAETETUS: I do.

SOCRATES: But while everything else that belongs to their art of midwifery
belongs to mine, mine differs by acting as midwife to men and not to women, and by
looking to their souls when they are giving birth, and not to their bodies. But the greatest thing in our art is this: to have the power to put to the test in every way whether the   c
thinking of the young man is giving birth to something that is an image and false, or to
something that is generated and true. And since this at least belongs to me just as it does
to the midwives, that I am barren of wisdom, and the very thing belongs to me that
many people have blamed me for before now, that I question others but answer nothing
myself about anything on account of having nothing wise in me, what they blame me
for is true. But the cause of this is the following: the god (continually) forces me to be a
midwife but (each time) prevents me from generating anything. I myself, then, am not   d
at all anybody wise, nor has any discovery of that sort been generated in me as the offspring of my soul. But those who associate with me, while some of them at first appear
to be entirely without understanding, all, as the association goes on, if the god permits
them, improve to a wonderful extent, as it seems to them, and also to everyone else. And
this is incandescently clear: that they do so despite learning nothing from me ever, but
by discovering and bringing forth many beautiful things themselves out of themselves.
The midwifing, however, the god and I are responsible for. This too is clear: many people before now, who didn't recognize this, and held themselves responsible while they   e
looked down on me, either went away themselves, or were persuaded to by others, earlier than they should have. And when they had gone away they made what was left abort
by bad company, and lost the things that had been midwifed by me by rearing them
badly, and made more of false things and images than of what was true; and when they
were finished they seemed to themselves and to everyone else to be without understanding. Aristeides, the son of Lysimachus, became one of these, as did very many   151
others, and whenever they come back, begging for my company and carrying on wonderfully, the supernatural guardian <*daimonion*> that comes to me prevents me from
associating with some but permits it with others, and the latter improve again. And those

who associate with me also have this experience that is the same as women giving birth have: they have labor pains and are filled night and day with things they can't get through, much more than are those women, and my art has the power to awaken this

b   sort of labor pain or to make it stop. Now that's the way it is for these people, but for some, Theaetetus, who in some way seem to me not to be pregnant, recognizing that they have no need of me, I very graciously make a match, and—with a god's help, let it be said—place them quite adequately with those from whose company they might benefit. Many of them I have given over to Prodicus, and many to other wise and divinely inspired men.

Now I lengthened this out for you, best of fellows, on account of this: I have my suspicions that you, as you yourself also suppose, are in labor with something inside

c   you that you are pregnant with. Offer yourself to me, then, as to the son of a midwife who is himself skilled at midwifery, and be eager to answer whatever I ask in whatever way you are able to. And therefore if, after I have examined any of the things you say, I deem it an image and not true and then quietly take it out and throw it away, don't go wild the way women who give birth for the first time do about their children. For many people already, you wonderful fellow, have gotten in such a state toward me that they were simply ready to bite me, whenever I would take away some nonsense of theirs, and

d   they didn't believe that I was doing this out of goodwill, since they are far from knowing that no god has bad will toward human beings or that I don't do any such thing out of bad will either, but for me to go along with something false and conceal something true is absolutely illegitimate. So again from the beginning, Theaetetus, try to say whatever knowledge is, and never say that you are not able to, for if a god is willing and makes you manly, you will be able.

THEAETETUS: Really, Socrates, when you are so encouraging, it would be a

e   shameful thing for anyone not to be eager in every way to say whatever he has it in him to say. So it seems to me that one who knows anything perceives that which he knows, and as it appears to me now at least, knowledge is nothing other than perception.

SOCRATES: That's well said and spoken in a well-born way, my boy, for if it seems that way one needs to say so. But come on, let's examine in common whether it happens to be something generated or a wind-egg.* Perception is what you say knowledge is?

THEAETETUS: Yes.

SOCRATES: It's surely no lowly statement you are running the risk of making about

152   knowledge, but what Protagoras also used to say. But he said these same things in a somewhat different way, for he says somewhere that a human being is "the measure of all things, of the things that are, that they are, and of the things that are not, that they are not." Presumably you have read it?

THEAETETUS: I have read it—many times.

SOCRATES: Then isn't this somehow what he means, that of whatever sort things appear to me each by each, that's the sort they are for me, and of whatever sort they appear to you, that in turn is the sort they are for you, and that you are a human being and so am I?

THEAETETUS: He does mean it that way.

b   SOCRATES: Surely it's likely that a wise man is not talking nonsense, so let's follow after him. Now aren't there times when, with the same wind blowing, one person shivers with cold and another doesn't? Or one does so slightly and another violently?

---

*An egg not impregnated—that does not contain the principles of life. The name is perhaps explained by the fact that such eggs float in water.

THEAETETUS: Very much so.

SOCRATES: Well shall we say that at such a time the wind itself in itself is cold or not cold? Or shall we be persuaded by Protagoras that it's cold for the one who's shivering but not for the one who isn't?

THEAETETUS: That's likely.

SOCRATES: And then also it appears that way to each of them?

THEAETETUS: Yes.

SOCRATES: And certainly the "it appears" is a perceiving.

THEAETETUS: It surely is.

SOCRATES: Therefore appearance and perception are the same in hot things too, as well as in all things of that sort. For whatever sort of things each person perceives them as, they also run a risk of being of that sort for each person.

THEAETETUS: That's likely.

SOCRATES: Therefore perception is always of what is, and, being knowledge, is without falsity.

THEAETETUS: So it appears.

*   *   *

SOCRATES: . . . Whenever we claim that I, being of such an age that I neither grow nor undergo anything in the opposite direction, am in the course of a year bigger than you, who are now young, and afterward smaller, when nothing has been taken away from my bulk but yours has grown. For then I am afterward what I was not before, not having come to be that way, since without going through becoming a thing has no power to have become anything, and not having lost any bulk, I was never becoming smaller. And there are thousands upon thousands of other things that are this way, if indeed we accept these. I presume you're following, Theaetetus; at any rate it seems to me that you are not inexperienced in such things.

THEAETETUS: Yes indeed, Socrates, by the gods, and it's beyond what's natural, so that I'm in a state of wonder at what in the world these things are. To tell you the truth, sometimes when I look into them I whirl around in the dark.

SOCRATES: So, dear fellow, Theodorus appears to have placed your nature not badly, for this experience, wondering, belongs very much to the philosopher, since there is no other source of philosophy than this. And it's likely that the one who said Iris is the offspring of Thaumas made his genealogy not badly. But do you understand by now why these things are this way on the basis of the things we claim that Protagoras says, or not yet?

THEAETETUS: I don't think I do yet.

SOCRATES: Then will you be grateful to me if I join you in searching out the truth hidden away in the thinking of a famous man, or rather men, from them?

THEAETETUS: How could I not be, and very much at that?

SOCRATES: Then look all around and see that none of the uninitiated is listening. These are the people who believe that there is nothing other than what they have the power to hold clenched in their hands, and do not accept actions or becomings or anything invisible as having any part in being.

THEAETETUS: Surely, Socrates, you're talking about rigid and repellent human beings.

*   *   *

161   SOCRATES: You are a lover of arguments, anyway, Theodorus, naively so, and a simple soul if you suppose that I am some bag of arguments, easily coming out with one to say "On the other hand, these things aren't that way." But you aren't aware of what's

b   happening, that none of the arguments comes out of me, but they always come out of the person conversing with me; I know nothing more than a trifling amount, enough to get an account out of someone else who's wise and to accept it in a measured way. And now I will try to get this one out of this fellow here, not saying anything myself.

THEODORUS: That's a more beautiful thing, Socrates, as you say. Do it that way.

* * *

163   SOCRATES: So let's look in the following way, to see, therefore, whether knowledge and perception are the same or different. For presumably all our talk was straining toward that, and for the sake of that we set in motion these many unsettling things. Isn't that so?

THEAETETUS: Absolutely.

b   SOCRATES: Then should we in fact agree that all those things that we perceive by seeing or by hearing are also known at the same time? For example, before we understand the language of foreigners, should we say either that we don't hear it when they utter it, or that we both hear and know what they say? Or if, in turn, we don't know the letters of the alphabet, but we're looking at them, should we strongly insist either that we don't see them, or that we know them if we do see them?

THEAETETUS: We should say, Socrates, that we know just that very thing that we

c   see and hear, in the one case that we see and know the shape and the color, and in the other case that we hear and at the same time know the high and low pitch; but what the reading teachers and language interpreters teach about them, we should say that we neither perceive by sight or hearing nor know.

SOCRATES: That's the very best, Theaetetus, and it's not worth it to dispute with you about that, so that you may still grow. But look at this other thing that's coming at us, and see how we'll repel it.

THEAETETUS: What sort of thing now?

SOCRATES: This sort: if someone were to ask, "Is it in one's power, with anything

d   one has ever become a knower of, and still has and keeps a memory of that very thing, that there could ever be a time when he remembers but does not know this very thing that he remembers?" I'm being wordy, it seems, but all I want to ask is whether one who's learned something doesn't know it if he remembers it.

THEAETETUS: How could that be, Socrates? What you say would be a monstrosity.

SOCRATES: So I'm talking nonsense, maybe? But look: don't you say that to see is to perceive and sight is perception?

THEAETETUS: I do.

e   SOCRATES: So then one who has seen something has become a knower of that which he has seen, according to what's been said right now?

THEAETETUS: Yes.

SOCRATES: Then what? Don't you speak of memory, of course, as something?

THEAETETUS: Yes.

SOCRATES: Memory of nothing or of something?

THEAETETUS: Certainly of something.

SOCRATES: Isn't it of things one has learned and things one has perceived, of some sorts of things like that?

THEAETETUS: What else?

SOCRATES: And what someone has seen, presumably he sometimes remembers?

THEAETETUS: He remembers.

SOCRATES: Even with his eyes shut? Or does he forget when he does that?

THEAETETUS: That would surely be a terrible thing to claim, Socrates.

SOCRATES: It's necessary, however, if we're going to keep what was said before. If   164
we don't make this claim, that's swept away.

THEAETETUS: I suspect so too, by Zeus, but I'm not getting it sufficiently; tell me how.

SOCRATES: In this way: one who sees, we are saying, has become a knower of that very thing which he sees, since sight and perception and knowledge are agreed to be the same thing.

THEAETETUS: Entirely so.

SOCRATES: But one who sees and has become a knower of what he has seen, if he shuts his eyes, remembers it but is not seeing it—right?

THEAETETUS: Yes.

SOCRATES: But "is not seeing" means "does not know" if in fact sees means   b
knows.

THEAETETUS: True.

SOCRATES: Therefore, it follows that what someone has become a knower of and still remembers, he does not know since he is not seeing it—the very thing we were saying would be a monstrosity if it were to come about.

THEAETETUS: What you say is most true.

SOCRATES: So something impossible appears to result if one claims that knowledge and perception are the same.

THEAETETUS: It seems so.

SOCRATES: Therefore one must say that the two are different.

THEAETETUS: They run that risk.

*   *   *

SOCRATES: . . . Now perhaps you might say "Well, what sort of speech will Protagoras   165e
call up as a relief force for his own side?" Shall we do anything other than try to state it?

THEAETETUS: Let's try by all means.

SOCRATES: Well, there are all these things that we're saying in defending him, and   166
also I suppose, with contempt for us, he'll close in on the same thing, saying "This simple Socrates, when he frightened some little boy by asking him whether it's possible for the same person at the same time to remember and not know the same thing, and the frightened boy denied it, because he didn't have the power to see ahead, made me look ridiculous in his speeches. But, you most lackadaisical Socrates, it's like this: whenever you examine anything of mine by questioning, if the one who's asked is tripped up after answering with just exactly the sort of things I would answer, then I am refuted, but if   b
he answers with other sorts of things, the one who was asked is himself refuted. To start with, do you think anyone would go along with you that a memory that's present to him of things he experienced, when he's no longer experiencing them, is an experience of the same sort as he underwent at the time? It's far short of it. Or, next, that anyone would shrink from agreeing that it's possible for the same person to know and not know the same thing? Or even if he was afraid of this, that he'll ever grant that one who's becoming unlike is the same person he was before becoming unlike? More than that, do you think he'll grant that this person is a 'him' and not a 'them,' with these becoming   c
infinite, if in fact a process of becoming unlike is going on—that's if he's really going

to need to be on guard against getting caught in the words going back and forth? But, you blessed one," he'll say, "go up against the very thing that I say in a way more suited to a well-born man, if you have the power to, and prove that perceptions do not come privately to each of us, or that even though they do come privately, what appears would nonetheless not come about for each person alone—or if it has to be called 'being,' that it would not 'be' for just the one to whom it appears. So when you talk about a pig or a dog-faced baboon, not only are you being pig-ignorant yourself, you also carry over the

d   people who hear you to act this way toward my writings, which is no beautiful thing to do. I declare that the truth holds as I have written it, since each of us is a measure of the things that are and are not, and yet we differ one from another in thousands of ways for this very reason, that to one person some things are and appear, to another person others do. And far from denying that there is wisdom and a wise man, I say that very person is wise who, for any one of us to whom bad things appear and are, makes them change over into appearing and being good things. So don't go hounding the discourse again

e   for my wording, but learn still more clearly what I mean, in this way: recall the sort of thing that was in what was said before, that to the one who's sick, what he eats appears and is bitter, while to the one who's healthy the opposite is and appears. Now there's no

167   need to make either of them wiser, and one doesn't even have the power to, nor should one accuse the sick person of being lacking in understanding because he has such an opinion, while the healthy one is wise because he has a different sort, but one should produce a change from one to the other, since that other is a better condition to be holding in. In this way in education too, one should produce a change from one condition that holds to a better one, but while a doctor produces a change with drugs, a sophist does so with speeches. One does not, however, make someone who's been having some false opinion afterward have some true opinion, for there is no power to have as opinions either things that are not, or other things besides those one experiences, and the lat-

b   ter are always true. But I suppose that when someone with a burdensome condition holding in his soul has opinions akin to his own condition, a serviceable condition would make him have different opinions, of that sort, which latter appearances some people, from inexperience, call true, but I call the one sort better than the other, but not at all truer. And far from calling wise people frogs, dear Socrates, when they have to do with bodies I call them doctors and when they have to do with plants I call them farm-

c   ers; for I claim that the latter induce in plants, in place of burdensome perceptions, whenever any of them are sickly, serviceable and healthy perceptions and truths, and that wise and good rhetoricians make serviceable things, instead of burdensome ones, seem to cities to be just. Seeing as how whatever sorts of things seem just and beautiful to a city are those things for it so long as it considers them so, it's the wise man who, in place of each sort of things that are burdensome for them, induces serviceable things to be and seem so. And by the same account, the sophist who has the power to train in this

d   way those who are being educated is both wise and deserving of a lot of money from those who get educated. Thus it's the case both that some people are wiser than others, and that no one has false opinions, and also that you, whether you like it or not, have to hold still for being a measure, for in these ways, this account is saved. Which, if you have it in you to dispute it from the beginning, dispute it then, by going all the way through an account to replace it. But if you want to dispute it by asking questions, dispute it by asking questions, for this account is not something one ought to run away

e   from, but for anyone who has any sense, it most of all things ought to be chased after. Just do it this way: don't be unjust in your questioning. For in fact it's a big-time irra- tionality for someone who claims to care about virtue to do nothing else but keep on being unjust in the things he says. And it is being unjust in such a situation whenever anyone doesn't keep it separate when he's spending his time being competitive, and separate when he's having a conversation, and in the former he may be playful and trip people up as much as he has the power to, but in having a conversation he should be serious and help the person he's conversing with back upright again, pointing out to him only those stumbles in which he himself has been knocked off his feet by himself and by his previous associations. Now if you do this, those who spend their time with you will hold themselves responsible for their own confusion and helplessness, and not you, and they'll pursue you and love you, but hate themselves and run away from themselves to philosophy, in order to become different people and be set free from what they were before. But if you do the opposite of these things, as most people do, the opposite result will follow for you, and you'll make your associates show themselves as haters of this business instead of philosophers when they become older. So if you're persuaded by me of what was also said before, then in no hostile or combative way, but having come down in your thinking to join with me as gracious men, you'll truly examine what we mean when we declare that all things are in motion and that whatever seems so also is that way, both for each private person and for each city. And from these things you'll go on to examine whether knowledge and perception are the same or different, but not as you did just now on the basis of customary phrases and words, which most people, when they drag them around any which way at random, hold out as all sorts of insoluble difficulties for one another." With these things, Theodorus, I have come to the aid of your companion as much as is in my power, small aid from small power, but if he himself were alive, he would have helped out the things that belong to him more mightily.

*   *   *

SOCRATES: Then first, let's get hold of this again just where we had it before, and see whether we were correctly or incorrectly disdainful of the account when we found fault with it because it made each person self-sufficient in intelligence. Even Protagoras went along with us that some people surpass others about what is better and worse, and that they are in fact wise, didn't he?

THEODORUS: Yes.

SOCRATES: Then if he himself were present and agreeing to it, instead of our going along with it on his behalf to help him out, there would be no need to take it back up again and establish it, but now perhaps someone might hold that we have no authority for an agreement on his behalf. For this reason it would be more beautiful to make our agreement about this very thing more clear, since it causes no small shift for it to be this way or some other.

THEODORUS: What you say is true.

SOCRATES: Then not by means of any others but out of his own statement, let's get the agreement by the briefest possible means.

THEODORUS: How?

SOCRATES: Like this: he says, presumably, that what seems so to each human being also is that way for the one to whom it seems that way?

THEODORUS: Indeed he does say that.

SOCRATES: Well then, Protagoras, we're also stating opinions of a human being, or rather of all human beings, and claiming that no one at all does not consider himself wiser than others in some respects and other people wiser than himself in other respects, and in the greatest dangers at least, when people are in distress in military campaigns or b   diseases or at sea, they have the same relation to those who rule them in each situation as to gods, expecting them to be their saviors, even though they are no different from themselves by any other thing than by knowing; and all human things are filled with people seeking teachers and rulers for themselves and for the other animals, as well as for their jobs, and in turn with people who suppose themselves to be competent to teach and competent to rule. And in all these situations, what else are we going to say but that human beings themselves consider there to be wisdom and lack of understanding among them?

THEODORUS: Nothing else.

SOCRATES: Then do they consider wisdom true thinking and lack of understanding false opinion?

c   THEODORUS: What else?

SOCRATES: Well, Protagoras, how are we going to treat the statement? Are we going to claim human beings always hold true opinions, or sometimes true ones and sometimes false? From both claims, surely it follows that they do not always hold true opinions but both sorts. So consider, Theodorus, whether any of the people surrounding Protagoras, or you yourself, would want to insist pugnaciously that there's no other person who considers anyone else to be lacking in understanding or to hold false opinions.

THEODORUS: It's just not a believable thing, Socrates.

d   SOCRATES: And yet by necessity the statement asserting that a human being is the measure of all things comes down to this.

THEODORUS: How's that?

SOCRATES: Whenever you, having judged anything on your own, declare an opinion about it to me, then according to his account, let this be true for you; but isn't it possible for us others to become judges of your judgment, or do we always judge that you hold true opinions? Or do thousands of people on each occasion who hold opposite opinions do battle with you, regarding you as judging and believing false things?

e   THEODORUS: By Zeus, Socrates, that's right, many thousands, as Homer says, and they're the ones who cause the troubles I have with human beings.

SOCRATES: Well then, do you want us to say that at that time you hold an opinion that's true for yourself but false for the thousands?

THEODORUS: It appears from the account anyway that that's necessary.

SOCRATES: And what about Protagoras himself? Isn't it necessary, if neither he himself, nor most people, were to believe that a human being is a measure, as in fact the

171   others don't, that what he wrote is the truth for no one? But if he himself did believe it, while the multitude do not share his belief, you know that first of all, however many more there are to whom it doesn't seem so than there are to whom it does, then it is not so by that much more than it is.

THEODORUS: Necessarily, if indeed it's going to be and not be so according to each opinion.

SOCRATES: This next point is the most exquisite subtlety it has in it: he goes along with the belief about his own belief of those who hold the opposite opinion, by which they consider him to be saying something false, since presumably he agrees that the things all people hold as opinions are true.

THEODORUS: Very much so.

b   SOCRATES: Then he'd be going along with calling his own belief false, if he's agreeing that the belief is true of those who consider him to be saying something false?

THEODORUS: Necessarily.

SOCRATES: But the others do not go along with saying that their own opinions are false?

THEODORUS: No indeed.

SOCRATES: And he agrees again that even that opinion is true, from what he has written.

THEODORUS: It appears so.

SOCRATES: Therefore, from everybody starting from Protagoras, there will be a dispute, but by him instead there will be an agreement, whenever he goes along with it that someone who says the opposite is holding a true opinion, and then Protagoras himself will be agreeing that neither a dog nor any random human being is a measure about any single thing that he doesn't understand. Isn't that so?

THEODORUS: It's so.

SOCRATES: Then since it is disputed by everyone, the Truth of Protagoras will be true for no one, not for anyone else and not even for him himself.

THEODORUS: We're running down my companion too much, Socrates.

SOCRATES: But really, my friend, it's unclear whether we're also running past what's correct. It seems likely, therefore, that he, being older, would be wiser than we are, and if suddenly, right here, he would pop out his head as far as the neck, once he'd refuted me in many ways for speaking nonsense, which is likely, and you for agreeing, having sunk back, he'd be swept off and running away. But for us, I suppose, it's necessary that we make use of ourselves, of whatever sort we are, and always say those things that seem so.

*　　*　　*

SOCRATES: Then as it seems, when it's asked what knowledge is, this account answers that it's a correct opinion along with a knowledge of differentness, since according to it, that would be the taking hold in addition of an articulation.

THEAETETUS: So it seems.

SOCRATES: And it's totally silly, when we're inquiring about knowledge, to claim that it's correct opinion along with knowledge, whether about differentness or about anything whatever. Therefore, Theaetetus, neither perception nor true opinion, nor even an articulation that's become attached to a true opinion would be knowledge.

THEAETETUS: It seems not.

SOCRATES: Then are we still pregnant and in labor with anything about knowledge, dear fellow, or have we given birth to everything?

THEAETETUS: Yes we have, by Zeus, and I at least have said more, on account of you, than what I used to have in myself.

SOCRATES: Then our art of midwifery declares that all these things came into being as wind-eggs and aren't worth rearing?

THEAETETUS: Absolutely.

SOCRATES: Then if you try to become pregnant with other things after these, Theaetetus, and you do come to be so, you'll be full of better things on account of the present examination, and if you're barren, you'll be less severe with those who are around you and gentler, being moderate and not supposing that you know things you don't know. For that and nothing more is the only sort of thing my art has the power to do, and I don't know any of the things all the others do who are and have been great and wondrous men, but I and my mother have been allotted this midwifery as our portion from a god, she among women and I among the young and well-born, all those, that is, that are beautiful. But now there's something I need to go and face in the courtyard of the king-archon, in response to the indictment which Meletus has drawn up against me; but at dawn, Theodorus, let's meet here again.

TIMAEUS (in part)

Characters
Socrates
Timaeus of Locres
Scene—Athens

27ᵈ   TIMAEUS: Now then, in my opinion, one must first distinguish the following. What is it that always is and has no becoming; and what is it that comes to be and never

28   *is*? Now the one is grasped by intellection accompanied by a rational account, since it's always in the same condition; but the other in its turn is opined by opinion accompanied by irrational sensation, since it comes to be and perishes and never genuinely is. Again, everything that comes to be, of necessity comes to be by some cause; for apart from a cause, it's impossible for anything to have a coming to be.

Now so long as the craftsman* keeps looking to what's in a selfsame condition, using some such thing as a model, and fashions its look and power, then of necessity

b   everything brought to a finish in this way is beautiful; but if he should look to what has come to be, using a begotten model, the thing isn't beautiful. Now as for all the heaven (or cosmos, or whatever else it might be most receptive to being called, let it be called that by us), the first thing about it one must investigate is the very thing set down at the beginning whenever one has to investigate anything: whether it always was, having no beginning of a coming to be, or whether it has come to be, having begun from some

c   beginning. It has come to be; for it is visible and touchable and has body, and all such things are sensed; and things that are sensed, since they're grasped by opinion accompanied by sensation, came to light as coming to be and begotten. And again, for what comes to be, we claim that it's necessary that it come to be by some cause. Now to discover the poet and father of this all is quite a task, and even if one discovered him, to speak of him to all men is impossible. So one must go back again and investigate the

29   following about the all: to which of the two models the builder looked when he fashioned it—to the one that's in a self-same condition and consistent, or to the one that has come to be. Now if this cosmos here is beautiful and its craftsman good, then it's plain that he was looking to the one that's everlasting, but if otherwise—which isn't even right for anyone to say—then to the one that has come to be. Now it's clear to everyone that it was to the everlasting; for the cosmos is the most beautiful of things born and its craftsman the best of causes. Since that's how it has come to be, then it has been crafted with reference to that which is grasped by reason and prudence and is in a self-same condition.

Again, starting from these things, there's every necessity that this cosmos here

b   be the likeness of something. Now what is most important is to begin everything at a

---

*This is the first appearance in the dialogue of the famous "demiurge" or craftsman. He is introduced without fanfare and almost in passing.

Plato, *Plato's Timaeus* (27d–34b), translated by Peter Kalkavage (Newburyport, MA: Focus Philosophical Library, 2001). Reprinted by permission of Focus Publishing/R. Pullins Company.

beginning that's in accordance with nature. So then, when it comes to a likeness and its model, one must determine how the accounts are also akin to those very things of which the accounts are interpreters. Now accounts of what's abiding and unshakable and manifest with the aid of intellect are themselves abiding and unchanging; and to the extent that it's possible and fitting for accounts to be irrefutable and invincible, they must not fall short of this. But as for accounts of something made as a likeness of something else—since it is a likeness—it is fitting that they, in proportion to their objects, be likenesses: just as Being is to Becoming, so is truth to trust. So then, Socrates, if, in saying many things on many topics concerning gods and the birth of the all, we become incapable of rendering speeches that are always and in all respects in agreement with themselves and drawn with precision, don't wonder. But if we provide likelihoods inferior to none, one should be well-pleased with them, remembering that I who speak as well as you my judges have a human nature, so that it is fitting for us to receive the likely story about these things and not to search further for anything beyond it.

SOCRATES: Excellent, Timaeus! And it must be received entirely as you urge; so now that we've received your prelude so wonderfully, do for us what comes next in order and perform the song itself.*

TIMAEUS: Now let us say through what cause the constructor constructed becoming and this all. Good was he, and in one who is good there never arises about anything whatsoever any grudge; and so, being free of this, he willed that all things should come to resemble himself as much as possible. That this above all is the lordliest principle of becoming and cosmos one must receive, and correctly so, from prudent men. For since he wanted all things to be good and, to the best of his power, nothing to be shoddy, the god thus took over all that was visible, and, since it did not keep its peace but moved unmusically and without order, he brought it into order from disorder, since he regarded the former to be in all ways better than the latter. And it was not right—nor is it right—for him who is best to do anything except that which is most beautiful; so, once he did some calculating, he discovered that of all things visible by nature, nothing unintelligent will ever be a more beautiful work, comparing wholes with wholes, than what has intellect; and again, that it's impossible for intellect apart from soul to become present in anything. Through this calculation, then, by constructing intellect within soul and soul within body, he joined together the all so that he had fashioned a work that would be most beautiful and best in accordance with nature. So then, in this way, in keeping with the likely account, it must be said that this cosmos here in truth was born an animal having soul and intellect through the forethought of the god.

Again, with this beginning, we must say what comes next in order to these things: in similarity to which of the animals the constructor constructed it. Now we shall not count as worthy any of those that by nature have the form of part—for nothing that's like the incomplete would ever become beautiful—but let us set down the following about the cosmos. Among all animals, it's the one most similar to that of which the

---

*Socrates' word for the upcoming speech of Timaeus is neither <logos> (account) nor <mythos> (story) but <nomos>. In this context, the word can mean either law or song, just as <prooimion> can mean either preamble or prelude. "Perform the song" thus also means "Carry out the law." No doubt both meanings are intended.

others, individually and according to kind, are parts. For that one, having embraced all
d   the intelligible Animals, holds them within itself, just as this cosmos holds and
embraces us and all the other nurslings constructed as visible. For since the god wanted
31   to make it as similar as possible to the most beautiful of things intellected and in all
ways complete, he constructed it as an animal visible and one, holding within itself all
those animals that are akin to it according to nature.

So have we spoken correctly in naming the heaven "one," or was it more correct
to say that it's many and indefinite in number? One, if indeed it's been crafted in
accordance with its model. For that which embraces all the intelligible Animals (however many they are) wouldn't ever be second in company with another one; for again
there would have to be another animal surrounding them both, of which both of them
would be a part, and then this cosmos would be more correctly spoken of as copied no
longer from those two but from that other one which embraced them. So then, in
b   order that this cosmos might be similar to the altogether perfect Animal in unique-
ness, for this reason the maker did not make two or indefinitely many cosmoses; but
rather this heaven here that's come to be, both is and will continue to be one—alone
of its kind.

Now what has come to be must be bodily in form and both visible and touchable,
but separated from fire nothing would ever become visible, nor would it become
touchable without something solid, or solid without earth; hence, in beginning to construct the body of the all, the god proceeded to make it out of fire and earth. But it's not
c   possible for two things alone to be beautifully combined apart from some third: some
bond must get in the middle and bring them both together. And the most beautiful of
these bonds is that which, as much as possible, makes itself and the things bound
together one, and proportion is suited by nature to accomplish this most beautifully.
32   For whenever, of three numbers, the middle term of any two of them, whether cubic or
square, is such that as the first is to it so is it to the last—and again, conversely, as the
last is to the middle so is this middle to the first—then the middle term becomes first
and last, while the last and first in turn both become middle terms, so that of necessity
it will turn out that all the terms will be the same; and once they've come to be the
same in relation to each other, all will be one.* Now if the body of the all had to
become a plane having no depth at all, then one mean would have been enough to bind
together its fellow terms and itself; but as the case now stands, since it was appropriate
b   that it be solid in form, and since solids are joined together never through one mean but
always through two, in this way, then, the god set water and air midway between both
fire and earth.**

And having fashioned among them the condition of same ratio as far as possible,
so that fire was to air as air to water, and air was to water as water to earth, he bound
together and constructed a heaven visible and touchable. For these reasons and out of
c   such terms as these, four in number, the body of this cosmos was begotten to agree with

*The numbers 2, 4 and 8, for example, can be used to form the mean proportion 2:4::4:8 (where 4 is a
square number and 8 a cubic number). When the two ratios that compose the proportion are inverted, the
resulting proportion becomes 4:2::8:4 or 4:8::2:4. What was formerly the mean term is now at the extremes,
and the terms that were formerly extremes are now in the middle.

**Empedocles had posited four elements or, as he called them, roots of all things (fragment 6). For
Timaeus, the elements start out as being rationally interrelated. Water and air are the two mediators between
the more fundamental elements of fire and earth.

itself through proportion, and from them came to have friendship, so that having come together with itself in self-sameness, it was born indissoluble by none other save him who bound it together.

At this point the construction of the cosmos has taken up the whole of each one of the four terms. For the constructor constructed it from all of fire and water and air and earth, having left over no part or power of any of them outside, since he intended the following: first that it be as much as possible an animal whole and perfect, made up   d
of perfect parts; and in addition to this, that it be one, inasmuch as there wasn't any-
thing left over, out of which another such animal might come to be; and further that it   33
be free of old age and disease, since he observed that when hot and cold (and all things that have mighty powers) surround a composite body from the outside and attack it, they dissolve it in an untimely way and make it wither by bringing on disease and old age. Through this very cause and calculation he built it to be this one whole of all wholes taken together, perfect and free of old age and disease. And he gave it a figure that was fitting and akin to it. But for that animal that is to embrace within itself all ani-   b
mals, the fitting figure would be the one that has embraced all figures within itself, however many there are; so for this reason too, he worked it in circular fashion, sculpt-ing it into the form of a sphere, the figure that keeps itself in all directions equidistant from its center to its extremities and which, of all figures, is the most perfect and most similar to itself, since he considered that *similar* is vastly more beautiful than   c
dissimilar. So he made it all smooth on the outside and gave it a rounded finish, and this for many reasons. For of eyes it had no need at all, since nothing to be seen was left over on the outside; nor of hearing, since there was nothing to be heard; nor was there any atmosphere surrounding it that needed breathing; nor again was there need of any organ by which it might take food into itself or send it back out after it was digested. For nothing either went out from it nor went toward it from anywhere—since   d
there was nothing—for the animal was artfully born so as to provide its own waste as food for itself and to suffer and do everything within itself and by itself, since he who put it together considered that the animal would be much better by being self-sufficient than in need of other things. And as for hands, which would be useless for either tak-ing hold of or again warding off anything, he thought he didn't need to attach these to the animal in vain, nor feet nor anything that on the whole served for standing on. The   34
motion he did assign to it was the one congenial to its body, that motion among the seven kinds which especially attends intellect and prudence; so for this reason, he spun it around uniformly in the same spot and within itself and made it move by revolving in a circle, and he took away from it all the other six motions and fashioned it free from their various wanderings; and since for this revolving motion the animal had no need of feet, he begat it legless and footless.

All this calculation of a god who always is concerning the god who was one day to be—once it had been calculated—made the animal smooth and even and equidistant   b
from its center in every direction, a whole and perfect body made of perfect bodies. And after he put soul at its center, he stretched her throughout the whole, even to the point of covering the body on the outside with her as with a veil; and so, as a circle turning in a circle, he established a heaven that was one, alone, solitary—able by itself, because of its excellence, to be company to itself and to stand in need of no other at all, and sufficient unto itself as acquaintance and friend. For all these very reasons, he begat it a happy god.

LAWS (selections)

Characters

Athenian stranger
Clinias
Megillus
Scene—Island of Crete

BOOK X

893ᵇ   ATHENIAN: Come, then, and if ever we are to call upon the gods, let us call upon them now in all seriousness to come to the demonstration of their own existence. And so holding fast to the rope we will venture upon the depths of the argument. When questions of this sort are asked of me, my safest answer would appear to be as follows:

Some one says to me, "O Stranger, are all things at rest and nothing in motion, or is the exact opposite of this true, or are some things in motion and others at rest?

To this I shall reply that some things are in motion and others at rest . . .

"And when are all things created and how?"

894   Clearly, they are created when the first principle receives increase and attains to the second dimension, and from this arrives at the one which is neighbor to this, and after reaching the third becomes perceptible to sense. Everything which is thus changing and moving is in process of generation; only when at rest has it real existence, but when passing into another state it is destroyed utterly. Have we not mentioned all motions that there are, and comprehended them under their kinds and numbered them

b   with the exception, my friends, of two?

CLINIAS: Which are they?

ATHENIAN: Just the two, with which our present enquiry is concerned.

CLINIAS: Speak plainer.

ATHENIAN: I suppose that our enquiry has reference to the soul?

CLINIAS: Very true.

ATHENIAN: Let us assume that there is a motion able to move other things, but not to move itself;—that is one kind; and there is another kind which can move itself as well as other things, working in composition and decomposition, by increase and diminution and generation and destruction—that is also one of the many kinds of motion.

c   CLINIAS: Granted.

ATHENIAN: And we will assume that which moves other, and is changed by other, to be [sceondary], and that which changes itself and others, and is co-incident with every action and every passion, and is the true principle of change and motion in all that is—that we shall be inclined to call [primary].

CLINIAS: Certainly.

d   ATHENIAN: And which of these . . . motions ought we to prefer as being the mightiest and most efficient?

Translated by Benjamin Jowett.

CLINIAS: I must say that the motion which is able to move itself is ten thousand times superior to all the others.

*   *   *

ATHENIAN: [Now] when one thing changes another, and that another, of such will there be any primary changing element? How can a thing which is moved by another ever be the beginning of change? Impossible. But when the self-moved changes other, and that again other, and thus thousands upon tens of thousands of bodies are set in motion, must not the beginning of all this motion be the change of the self-moving principle?

894^e

895

CLINIAS: Very true, and I quite agree.

ATHENIAN: Or, to put the question in another way, making answer to ourselves: If, as most of these philosophers have the audacity to affirm, all things were at rest in one mass, which of the above-mentioned principles of motion would first spring up among them?

CLINIAS: Clearly the self-moving; for there could be no change in them arising out of any external cause; the change must first take place in themselves.

b

ATHENIAN: Then we must say that self-motion being the origin of all motions, and the first which arises among things at rest as well as among things in motion, is the eldest and mightiest principle of change, and that which is changed by another and yet moves other is second.

CLINIAS: Quite true.

ATHENIAN: At this stage of the argument let us put a question.

c

CLINIAS: What question?

ATHENIAN: If we were to see this power existing in any earthy, watery, or fiery substance, simple or compound—how should we describe it?

CLINIAS: You mean to ask whether we should call such a self-moving power life?

ATHENIAN: I do.

CLINIAS: Certainly we should.

ATHENIAN: And when we see soul in anything, must we not do the same—must we not admit that this is life?

CLINIAS: We must.

*   *   *

ATHENIAN: And what is the definition of that which is named "soul"? Can we conceive of any other than that which has been already given: the motion which can move itself?

896

CLINIAS: You mean to say that the essence which is defined as the self-moved is the same with that which has the name soul?

ATHENIAN: Yes; and if this is true, do we still maintain that there is anything wanting in the proof that the soul is the first origin and moving power of all that is, or has become, or will be, and their contraries, when she has been clearly shown to be the source of change and motion in all things?

b

CLINIAS: Certainly not; the soul as being the source of motion, has been most satisfactorily shown to be the oldest of all things.

ATHENIAN: And is not that motion which is produced in another, by reason of another, but never has any self-moving power at all, being in truth the change of an inanimate body, to be reckoned second, or by any lower number which you may prefer?

CLINIAS: Exactly.

ATHENIAN: Then we are right, and speak the most perfect and absolute truth, when
c we say that the soul is prior to the body, and that the body is second and comes afterwards, and is born to obey the soul, which is the ruler?

CLINIAS: Nothing can be more true.

*   *   *

ATHENIAN: Yes, very true; the soul then directs all things in heaven, and earth, and
897 sea by her movements, and these are described by the terms will, consideration, attention, deliberation, opinion true and false, joy and sorrow, confidence, fear, hatred, love,
and other primary motions akin to these; which again receive the secondary motions of
corporeal substances, and guide all things to growth and decay, to composition and
decomposition, and to the qualities which accompany them, such as heat and cold,
heaviness and lightness, hardness and softness, blackness and whiteness, bitterness and
b sweetness, and all those other qualities which the soul uses, herself a goddess, when
truly receiving the divine mind she disciplines all things rightly to their happiness; but
when she is the companion of folly, she does the very contrary of all this. Shall we
assume so much, or do we still entertain doubts?

CLINIAS: There is no room at all for doubt.

ATHENIAN: Shall we say then that it is the soul which controls heaven and earth,
and the whole world?—that it is a principle of wisdom and virtue, or a principle which
has neither wisdom nor virtue?

*   *   *

899ᵇ   CLINIAS: Yes, by every man who has the least particle of sense.

ATHENIAN: And of the stars too, and of the moon, and of the years and months and
seasons, must we not say in like manner, that since a soul or souls having every sort of
excellence are the causes of all of them, those souls are gods, whether they are living
beings and reside in bodies, and in this way order the whole heaven, or whatever be the
place and mode of their existence;—and will any one who admits all this venture to
deny that all things are full of gods?

c   CLINIAS: No one, Stranger, would be such a madman.

ATHENIAN: And now, Megillus and Clinias, let us offer terms to him who has hitherto denied the existence of the gods, and leave him.

CLINIAS: What terms?

ATHENIAN: Either he shall teach us that we were wrong in saying that the soul is
the original of all things, and arguing accordingly; or, if he be not able to say anything
better, then he must yield to us and live for the remainder of his life in the belief that
d there are gods.

ARISTOTLE
384–322 B.C.

Aristotle was born in Stagira, on the border of Macedonia. His mother, Phaestis, was from a family of doctors, and his father, Nicomachus, was the court physician to the king of Macedonia. At seventeen, Aristotle was sent to Athens. There he studied in Plato's Academy for two decades, but, as he later wrote, he loved the truth more than he loved Plato, and so he had no mind to remain a mere disciple. In 347 B.C., after Plato's death, he left Athens and spent the next four years conducting zoological investigations on the islands of Assos and Lesbos.

About 343 B.C., he was called to Macedonia by King Philip to tutor the king's son—the future Alexander the Great. Upon Alexander's ascension to the throne seven years later, Aristotle returned to Athens to set up the Lyceum, a rival to the Academy. Aristotle did much of his teaching walking up and down the colonnades with advanced students. As a result, his school and philosophy came to be called by the Greek word for walking around: <peripatetikos>, from which we get our word "peripatetic." Tradition has it that as Alexander the Great moved east, conquering Persia and moving into India, he would send back biological specimens for Aristotle's school. Although most scholars doubt this popular story, it is nevertheless clear that under Alexander's patronage, the Lyceum flourished.

However, the connection to Alexander proved a liability in the end. On Alexander's death in 323 B.C., Athenians went on a rampage against any and all associated with him. Indicted on charges of impiety, Aristotle fled Athens, "lest," as he put it, "the Athenians sin twice against philosophy" (referring, of course, to the unjust trial and death of Socrates). Aristotle died a year later. A popular but again highly questionable story says he drowned investigating marine life.

There is no doubt that after Plato, Aristotle is the most influential philosopher of all time. In the early Middle Ages, his thought was preserved and commented upon by the great Arab philosophers. He dominated later medieval philosophy to such an extent that St. Thomas Aquinas referred to him simply as *philosophus*, the "philosopher." Logic, as taught until about the time of World War II, was essentially Aristotle's logic. His *Poetics* is still a classic of literary criticism, and his dicta on tragedy are widely accepted even today. Criticism of Aristotle's metaphysical and epistemological views has spread ever since Bacon and Descartes inaugurated modern philosophy; but for all that, the problems Aristotle saw, the distinctions he introduced, and the terms he defined are still central in many, if not most, philosophical discussions. His influence and prestige, like Plato's, are international and beyond all schools.

*   *   *

Aristotle found Plato's theory of Forms unacceptable. Like Plato, he wanted to discover universals, but he did not believe they existed apart from particulars. The form of a chair, for instance, can be thought of apart from the matter out of which the chair is made, but the form does not subsist as a separate invisible entity. The universal of "chairness" exists only in particular chairs—there is no other-worldly "Form of Chairness." Accordingly, Aristotle began his philosophy not with reflection on or dialogue about eternal Forms but with observations of particular objects.

In observing the world, Aristotle saw four "causes" responsible for making an object what it is: the material, formal, efficient, and final. In the case of a chair, for example, the chair's material cause is its wood and cloth, its formal cause is the structure or form given in its plan or blueprint, its efficient cause is the worker who made it, and its final cause is sitting. The material cause, then, is that *out of which* a thing is made, the formal cause is that *into which* a thing is made, the efficient cause is that *by which* a thing is made, and the final cause is that *for which* a thing is made. It is the last of these, the final cause, that Aristotle held to be most important, for it determined the other three. The "goal" or "end" (*telos* in Greek), the final cause, of any given substance is the key to its understanding. This means that all nature is to be understood in terms of final causes or purposes. This is known as a "teleological" explanation of reality.

As Aristotle applied these insights to human beings, he asked what the *telos* of a person could be. By observing what is unique to persons and what they, in fact, do seek, Aristotle came to the conclusion that the highest good or end for humans is *eudaimonia*. While this word is generally translated as "happiness," one must be careful to acknowledge that Aristotle's understanding of "happiness" is rather different from ours. *Eudaimonia* happiness is not a feeling of euphoria—in fact, it is not a feeling at all. It is rather "activity in accordance with virtue." Much of the material from the *Nicomachean Ethics* presented here is devoted both to clarifying the word and to discovering how this kind of "happiness" is to be achieved.

*   *   *

Aristotle's extant works lack the literary grace of Plato's. Like Plato, Aristotle is said to have written popular dialogues—the "exoteric" writings intended for those who were not students at the Lyceum—but they have not survived. What we have instead are the difficult "esoteric" works: lecture notes for classes at school. According to some scholars, these are not even Aristotle's notes, but the notes of students collected by editors. In any case, the writings as we have them contain much overlapping, repetition, and apparent contradiction.

The first five chapters of the *Categories*, with which we begin, help clear up a number of questions about Aristotle's conception of substance. Written as a treatise on language, the *Categories* explains how the subject–predicate relationship in a grammatical sentence is analogous to the substance–attribute relationship in the world. This work also makes clear why Aristotle rejected Plato's approach to knowledge of the Forms.

The brief selection from *On Interpretation (De Interpretatione)* presents Aristotle's philosophy of language. He analyzes the structure of sentences that express propositions and, in Chapter 9, presents a famous puzzle about the present truth-value of propositions concerning future events. This material has been the subject of much recent debate by such thinkers as Heidegger and Derrida. The selections from the *Categories* and *On Interpretation* are both given in H.P. Cook's translation.

The *Posterior Analytics*, which deals with the forms of argument and inquiry, is divided into two books. The selection from Book I included here deals with the nature of knowledge, demonstration, and truth and defines several key terms. The material from Book II considers the four possible forms of inquiry and explains how the individual mind comes to know the basic truths. The translation is by Jonathan Barnes.

Book II of the *Physics* deals with some of the main questions of physical science. After defining the term "nature," Aristotle discusses change and necessity. And making a distinction between physics and mathematics, he discusses the four causes. Throughout this text, Aristotle displays his teleological understanding of nature—that is, that natural processes operate for an end or purpose.

The *Metaphysics* probably consists of several independent treatises. Book I (*Alpha*) of this collection develops Aristotle's four causes and reviews the history of philosophy to his time. Book XII (*Lambda*) employs many of the concepts previously introduced, such as substance, actuality, and potency, and then moves to Aristotle's theology of the Unmoved Mover. The work concludes with Aristotle's rejection of Platonic Forms as separate, mathematical entities. Apparently Aristotle was responding to Plato's successors, who emphasized the mathematical nature of the Forms.

The first part of the selection presented from Aristotle's *On the Soul (De Anima)* gives a definition of the soul and distinguishes its faculties. The second part discusses the passive and the active mind. As this selection makes clear, Aristotle rejected Plato's view of a soul separate from the body. The selections from the *Physics*, the *Metaphysics*, and *On the Soul* are all translated by Joe Sachs.

The *Nicomachean Ethics* is still considered one of the greatest works in ethics. Named for Aristotle's son, Nicomachus, it discusses the nature of the good and of moral and intellectual virtues, as well as investigating specific virtues. The lengthy selection presented here (about one-half of the complete work) reflects this vast range of topics and includes discussions of the subject matter and nature of ethics; of the good for an individual; of moral virtue; of the mean; of the conditions of responsibility for an action; of pride, vanity, humility, and the great-souled man (Aristotle's ideal); of the superiority of loving over being loved; and finally, of human happiness. The translation is Martin Ostwald's.

The selection from various portions of the *Politics* (translated by Benjamin Jowett) gives a sense of Aristotle's political theory. In this work, the implications of his ethics are applied to the community. After dicussing the nature and purpose of the state, Aristotle presents several options for a good state: rule of one (monarchy), rule of a few (aristocracy), or rule of the many (constitutional government). Any of these would be acceptable if it is focused on the common good, for "political society exists for the sake of noble actions." Aristotle concludes that a strong middle class is the best guarantee of a good state.

Our final selection, from the *Poetics*, gives Aristotle's famous definition of tragedy. Again, the translation is by Joe Sachs.

The marginal page numbers, with their "a" and "b," are those of all scholarly editions—Greek, English, German, French, and others.

*   *   *

Timothy A. Robinson, *Aristotle in Outline* (Indianapolis, IN: Hackett, 1995) provides an excellent short introduction for the beginning student. W.K.C. Guthrie, *A History of Greek Philosophy, VI: Aristotle: An Encounter* (Cambridge: Cambridge University Press, 1981) and the classic W.D. Ross, *Aristotle* (1923; reprinted in New York: Meridian Books, 1959) are more advanced studies. John Herman Randall, Jr., *Aristotle* (New York: Columbia University Press, 1960); Marjorie Grene, *A Portrait of Aristotle* (Chicago: University of Chicago Press, 1963); J.L. Ackrill, *Aristotle the Philosopher* (Oxford: Oxford University Press, 1981); Jonathan Barnes, *Aristotle* (Oxford: Oxford University Press, 1982); Jonathan Lear, *Aristotle: The Desire to Understand* (Cambridge: Cambridge University Press, 1988); Terence Irwin, *Aristotle's First Principles* (Oxford: Oxford University Press, 1988); Jonathan Barnes, ed., *The Cambridge Companion to Aristotle* (Cambridge: Cambridge University Press, 1995); Kenneth McLeisch, *Aristotle* (London: Routledge, 1999); and Christopher Shields, *Aristotle* (London: Routledge, 2006) also provide helpful overviews of Aristotle's life and thought. For general collections of essays, see R. Bambrough, ed., *New Essays on Plato and Aristotle* (London: Routledge & Kegan Paul, 1965); J.M.E. Moravcsik, ed., *Aristotle: A Collection of Critical Essays* (New York: Anchor Doubleday, 1967); J. Barnes, M. Schofield, and R. Sorabji, eds., *Articles on Aristotle*, four volumes. (London: Duckworth, 1979); Terence Irwin, ed., *Aristotle's Ethics, Aristotle: Substance, Form, and Matter* and *Aristotle: Metaphysics, Epistemology, Natural Philosophy* (all three, Hamden, CT: Garland Publishing, 1995); Cynthia A. Freeland, ed., *Feminist Interpretations of Aristotle* (College Park, PA: Pennsylvania State University Press, 1998); Lloyd P. Gerson, ed., *Aristotle* (London: Routledge, 1999); and George Klosko, ed., *Aristotle* (Burlington, VT: Ashgate, 2007). For help with specific works (besides the *Nicomachean Ethics*), see Lindsay Judson, ed., *Aristotle's* Physics: *A Collection of Essays* (Oxford: Oxford University Press, 1991); Helen S. Lang, *Aristotle's* Physics *and Its Medieval Varieties* (Albany: SUNY Press, 1992); Martha C. Nussbaum and Amelie O. Rorty, eds., *Essays on Aristotle's* De Anima (Oxford: Oxford University Press, 1992); Michael Durrant, ed., *Aristotle's* De Anima *in Focus* (Oxford: Routledge, 1993); Michael Davis, *The Politics of Philosophy: A Commentary on Aristotle's* Politics, (Lanham, MD: Rowan & Littlefield, 1996); Helen S. Lang, *The Order of Nature in Aristotle's* Physics (Cambridge: Cambridge University Press, 1998); Wolfgang-Rainer Mann, *The Discovery of*

Things: Aristotle's Categories *and Their Context* (Princeton: Princeton University Press, 2000); C.D.C. Reeve, *Substantial Knowledge: Aristotle's* Metaphysics (Indianapolis, IN: Hackett, 2000); Vasilas Politis, *Routledge Philosophy Guidebook to Aristotle and the* Metaphysics (London: Routledge, 2004); Richard Kraut and Steven Skultety, eds., *Aristotle's* Politics (Lanham, MD: Rowman & Littlefield, 2005); Judith Swanson, *Aristotle's* Politics: *A Reader's Guide* (London: Continuum, 2006); and Ronald Polansky, *Aristotle's* De Anima: *A Critical Commentary* (Cambridge: Cambridge University Press, 2007). The *Nicomachean Ethics* has been such an influential book that many commentaries and essays have been written about it. Among these are H.H. Joachim, *Aristotle: The* Nicomachean Ethics, edited by D.A. Rees (Oxford: Clarendon Press, 1951); W.F.R. Hardie, *Aristotle's Ethical Theory*, 2nd edition (Oxford: Oxford University Press, 1980); Amelie O. Rorty, ed., *Essays on Aristotle's Ethics* (Berkeley: University of California Press, 1980); J.O. Urmson, *Aristotle's* Ethics (Oxford: Basil Blackwell, 1988); Sarah Brodie, *Ethics with Aristotle* (Oxford: Oxford University Press, 1991); Francis Sparshott, *Taking Life Seriously: A Study of the Argument of the* Nicomachean Ethics (Toronto: University of Toronto Press, 1994); Nancy Sherman, ed., *Aristotle's* Ethics: *Critical Essays* (Lanham, MD: Rowman and Littlefield, 1999); Gerard J. Hughes, *Routledge Philosophy Guidebook to Aristotle on Ethics* (New York: Routledge, 2001); Michael Pakaluk, *Aristotle's* Nichomachean Ethics: *An Introduction* (Cambridge: Cambridge University Press, 2005); Christopher Warne, *Arisototle's* Nicomachean Ethics: *A Reader's Guide* (London: Continuum, 2006); and Ronna Burger, *Aristotle's Dialogues with Socrates:* On The Nicomachean Ethics (Chicago: University of Chicago Press, 2009). Alasdair C. MacIntyre's pair of books, *After Virtue: A Study in Moral Theory* (Notre Dame, IN: University of Notre Dame Press, 1981) and *Whose Justice? Which Rationality?* (Notre Dame, IN: University of Notre Dame Press, 1988) are interesting examples of recent attempts to apply Aristotle's ethics to contemporary moral problems.

CATEGORIES (in part)

1. Things are equivocally named, when they have the name only in common, the definition (or statement of essence) corresponding with the name being different. For instance, while a man and a portrait can properly both be called "animals," these are equivocally named. For they have the name only in common, the definitions (or statements of essence) corresponding with the name being different. For if you are asked to define what being an animal means in the case of the man and the portrait, you give in either case a definition appropriate to that case alone.

Things are univocally named, when not only they bear the same name but the name means the same in each case—has the same definition corresponding. Thus a man and an ox are called "animals." The name is the same in both cases; so also the statement

1a

5

10

of essence. For if you are asked what is meant by their both of them being called "animals," you give that particular name in both cases the same definition.

Things are "derivatively" named that derive their own name from some other, that is given a new verbal form, as, for instance, "grammarian" from "grammar," from "heroism," 15   "hero," and so on.

2. We may or we may not combine what we call words, expressions and phrases. Combine them; you have propositions—for instance, "man runs" or "man wins"— 20   while examples of uncombined forms are "man," "ox," "runs," and "wins" and the like.

But as for the things that are *meant*, when we thus speak of uncombined words, you can predicate some of a subject, but they never are present in one. You can predicate "man," for example, of this or that man as the subject, but man is not found in a subject. By "in," "present," "found in a subject" I do not mean present or found as its parts are contained in a whole; I mean that it cannot exist as apart from the subject referred to. And then 25   there is that class of things which are present or found in a subject, although they cannot be asserted of any known subject whatever. A piece of grammatical knowledge is there in the mind as a subject but cannot be predicated of any known subject whatever. Again, a particular whiteness is present or found in a body (all color implies some such basis as what we intend by "a body") but cannot itself be asserted of any known subject whatever. 1^b We find there are some things, moreover, not only affirmed of a subject but present also in a subject. Thus knowledge, for instance, while present in this or that mind as a subject, is also asserted of grammar. There is, finally that class of things which can neither be found 5   in a subject nor yet asserted of one—this or that man or horse, for example. For nothing of that kind is in or is ever affirmed of a subject. More generally speaking, indeed, we can never affirm of a subject what is in its nature individual and also numerically one. Yet in some, cases nothing prevents its being *present* or *found in* a subject. Thus a piece of grammatical knowledge is present, as we said, in a mind.

10   3. A word upon predicates here. When you predicate this thing or that of another thing as of a subject, the predicates then of the predicate will also hold good of the subject. We predicate "man" of *a* man; so of "man" do we predicate "animal." Therefore, of 15   this or that man we can predicate "animal" too. For a man is both "animal" and "man."

When genera are co-ordinate and different, differentiae will differ in kind. Take the genera, animal and knowledge. "Footed," "two-footed," "winged," "aquatic" are among 20   the differentiae of animal. But none will be found to distinguish a particular species of knowledge. No species of knowledge will differ from another in being "two-footed."

Where the genera, however, are subordinate, nothing whatever prevents them from having the same differentiae. For we predicate the higher or larger of the smaller or subordinate class. The differentiae, then, of the predicate will also belong to the subject.

25   4. Each uncombined word or expression means one of the following things:—what (or Substance), how large (that is, Quantity), what sort of thing (that is, Place), when (or Time), in what attitude (Posture, Position), how circumstanced (State or Condition), how active, what doing (or Action), how passive, what suffering (Affection). Examples, to speak 2^a but in outline, of Substance are "man" and "a horse," of Quantity "two cubits long," "three cubits in length" and the like, of Quality "white" and "grammatical." Terms such as "half," "double," "greater" are held to denote a Relation. "In the market-place," "in the Lyceum" and similar phrases mean Place, while Time is intended by phrases like "yesterday," "last year" and so on. "Is lying" or "sitting" means Posture, "is shod" or "is armed" means a State. "Cuts" or "burns," again, indicates Action, "is cut" or "is burnt" an Affection.

Discus Thrower, by Myron.
A Roman copy after a bronze original
of ca. 450 B.C. Myron's athlete
epitomizes the ideal Olympian goals
of godlike perfection and rational
beauty. (*Marble, life-size. Museo delle
Terme, Rome. Ministero per i Beni e le
Attivita Culturali–Soprintendenza
Archeologica di Roma.*)

Not one of these terms in itself will involve any positive statement. Affirmations,   5
as also denials, can only arise when such terms are combined or united together. Each
positive or negative statement must either be true or be false—that, at least, is allowed on
all hands—but an uncombined word or expression (for instance, "man," "white," "runs"
or "conquers") can neither be true nor be false.   10

5. Substance in the truest and strictest, the primary sense of that term, is that which is
neither asserted of nor can be found in a subject. We take as examples of this a particular   15
man or a horse. But we *do* speak of secondary substances—those within which, being
species, the primary or first are included, and those within which, being genera, the species
themselves are contained. For instance, a particular man we include in the species called
"man" and the species itself in its turn is included in the genus called "animal." These, then,
are secondary substances, that is to say, man and animal—otherwise, species and genus.

From what we have said it is plain that the name and definition of the predicates   20
can both be affirmed of the subject. For instance, we predicate "man" of an individual
man as the subject. The name of the species called "man" is asserted of each individual;

25 you predicate "man" of *a* man, in like manner, for a man is both man and an animal. The name and definition of the species will thus both apply to the subject.

When we come, on the contrary, to things which are present or found in a subject, we find that their names and definitions we cannot, at least in most cases, affirm or predicate of that subject. Indeed, the definition itself will in no case whatever apply. But

30 in some cases nothing prevents us from using the *name* of the subject. Suppose we take "white" as an instance. Now "white" is, no doubt, in a body and thus is affirmed of a body, for a body, of course, is called "white." The definition, however, of "white"—of the color, that is, we call "white"—can never be predicated of any such body whatever.

35 Everything else but first substance is either affirmed of first substance or present in such as its subject. This is evident from particular instances taken by way of examples. We predicate "animal" of "man." So we predicate "animal" also of any particular man. Were there no individuals existing of whom it could thus be affirmed, it could not be

2ᵇ affirmed of the species. Color, again, is in body; so also in this or that body. For were there no bodies existing wherein it could also exist, it could not be in body at all. In fine, then, all things whatsoever save what we call primary substances, are predicates of

5 primary substances or present in such as their subjects. And were there no primary substance, naught else could so much as exist.

Of secondary substances species is better called substance than genus: it is nearer to primary substance, while genus is more removed from it. Suppose someone ask you "what is it?" regarding a primary substance. Your answer is both more instructive and

10 also more apt to the subject, provided you mention its species than if you should mention its genus. Take this or that man, for example. You would give a more instructive account, if you stated the species or "man," than you would, if you called him "an animal." The former belongs the more to him, the latter is somewhat too wide. Or, again, take an individual tree. By mentioning the species or "tree" you will give a more instructive account than by giving the genus or "plant."

15 Moreover, the primary substances most of all merit that name, since they underlie all other things, which in turn will be either their predicates or present in such as their subjects. But exactly as primary substances stand to all else that exits, so also stands species to genus. Species is related to genus as subject is related to predicate.

20 We predicate genus of species; but never, indeed, can we predicate species of genus conversely. On this further ground we may hold that of secondary substances species is more truly substance than genus.

If we turn to the species themselves, none, unless it is also a genus, is more of a substance than another. No apter description is "man" of a concrete or individual man than is

25 "horse" of a concrete horse. So also of primary substances—none is more a substance than others. For this or that man, for example, could not well be *more truly* substance than, let us say, this or that ox.

Apart, then, from primary substances, species and genus alone of the things that will

30 then remain over are rightly called secondary substance, for they of all possible predicates alone define primary substance. For only by species or genus can this or that man be defined in a fit or appropriate way; and we make our definition more precise by stating the species or "man" than by stating the genus or "animal." Anything else we might state, as,

35 for instance, "he runs" or "is white," would be foreign from the purpose in hand. So species and genera only are rightly designated as substance, first substances only excepted.

"Substance," again, strictly speaking, applies to first substances only, because they not only underlie but provide all things else with their subjects. Exactly as primary

3ᵃ substance is related to all else whatever, so also are genus and species, in which is included that substance, related to all attributes not included in genus and species. For these are the subjects of such. You may call a man "learned in grammar." And, therefore, his species and genus, that is to say, man and animal, you may also call "learned in grammar." And this will be so in all cases.

That it never is present in a subject holds good of all substance whatever. For what we call primary substance can neither be present in a subject nor yet predicated of one. And as for the secondary substance, the following points, among others, will prove it is not in a subject. We predicate "man" of a man; "man," however, is not *in* a subject. For manhood is not *in* a man. As the species, so also the genus. For "animal" is also asserted of this or that man in particular but cannot be found present in him. Again, we may notice this point. When a thing can be found in a subject, then nothing prevents us from using its name of the subject in question; not so the definition, however. And yet of a secondary substance both name and definition hold good in the case of the subject as well. The definition of the species (or man) and that of the genus (or animal) are used of an individual man. Therefore, substance is not in a subject.

That they cannot be present in subjects is true not of substances only but holds of differentiae, too. Thus we can of the species called "man" assert "going on foot" and "two-footed." But these are not found present in it. For neither of these is *in* man. Where, again, you affirm the differentia, you also affirm its definition. Suppose of the species called "man" you should predicate "going on foot." The definition also of that attribute then will apply to that species. For "man" does, indeed, go on foot.

That the parts of the substances are present or found in the wholes as in subjects is a fact that need hardly disturb us or render us fearful of having to brand all such parts as no substances. Did we not qualify "present in a subject" by "not as the parts in a whole"?

Differentia and substance alike have this characteristic in common, that, wherever we predicate them, we predicate them univocally. For such propositions have always individuals or species for subjects. The primary substance, no doubt, being never predicated of anything, never itself can be predicate of any proposition whatever. Not so with the secondary substance. The species is predicated of all individual examples, the genus of these and the species. And so with differentiae also. Of species and individuals we predicate these in like manner. Both definitions, moreover, or those of the genus and species, apply to the primary substance and that of the genus to the species. For all we affirm of the predicate will also be affirmed of the subject. The definition of each differentia applies in a similar manner to both individuals and species. But, as we have already noticed, univocal is used of such things as not only possess the same name but are also defined the same way. Hence it follows that in all propositions having substance or difference for predicate that predicate is quite unequivocal.

All substance appears individual. And this is indisputably true in the case of the primary substances. What each denotes is a unit. In that of the secondary substances language may make it appear so, as when we say "animal," "man." This, however, is not really so, for a quality rather is meant. Second substance is not one and single, as, no doubt, the primary is; not of one but of many, indeed, do we predicate "animal," "man." Species and genus, however, do not merely indicate quality, as "white" merely indicates quality. Accidents, that is, like "white," mean a quality simply and merely. But species and genus determine a quality in reference to substance. They tell you *what sort* of a substance. In the case of the genus, however, such determining qualification will cover a much wider field than it does in the case of the species. Say "animal"; you comprehend more than you would, if instead you said "man."

Substances never have contraries. How could first substances have them—this man, for example, that animal? Nothing is contrary to them. And species and genus have none. This particular characteristic belongs not to substance alone. For it holds of a good

many things and, among them, for instance, of quantity. "Two cubits long" has no con-
30   trary; neither has "three cubits long"; nor has "ten" nor yet anything like it, unless,
indeed, someone should say "large" and "small," "much" and "little" are contraries.
Definite quantities, however, can certainly never have contraries.

No substance, it seems, has degrees or admits of a more and a less. I do not mean
35   here that one substance may not be more truly called substance, less truly called substance, than others; indeed, we have said that it may. But I mean that no substance as
such can admit of degrees in itself. For example, the same substance, man, cannot really
be more or less man as compared with himself or another. This man is not *more* man than
4ᵃ   that, as one white thing is more or less white than another white object may be or, again,
as one beautiful object has more or less beauty than others. The same quality in the same
object may vary at times in degree. For example, a body, if white, is called whiter just
5   now than it was or if warm, is called more or less warm. But a substance is not more or
less of whatever, *qua* substance, it is. For a man is not more of a man than he was at some
time in the past. And so of all substances else. Therefore, substance can have no degrees.

10   But what is most characteristic of substance appears to be this: that, although it
remains, notwithstanding, numerically one and the same, it is capable of being the recipient
of contrary qualifications. Of things that are other than substance we could hardly adduce
an example possessed of this characteristic. For instance, a particular colour, numerically
15   one and the same, can in no wise be both black and white, and an action, if one and the
same, can in no wise be both good and bad. So of everything other than substance. But substance, remaining the same, yet admits of such contrary qualities. One and the same indi-
20   vidual at one time is white, warm or good, at another time black, cold or bad. This is not so
with anything else, though it might be maintained that assertions or opinions admitted of
contraries. That is to say, the same statement may appear to be both true and false. "He sits"
25   may, for instance, be true. If he rises, it then becomes false. And so with opinions as well.
One may be of opinion, and truly, that such or such person is sitting. And yet, when that person has risen, that opinion, if held still, is false. Even though we allow this exception, it
30   would differ, in fact, from the rest in its manner of coming about. For whenever a substance
admits of such contrary qualifications, it is by a change in itself. It is by a change in itself
that a thing that was hot becomes cold (having passed from one state to another) or a thing
that was white becomes black or a thing that was good becomes bad. And so, too, in all
35   other cases where substance admits of such qualities. The statement or opinion, however,
remains in itself quite unaltered in any and every respect. If it takes on the contrary quality,
being now true and now false, then the facts of the case will have changed. For the statement
4ᵇ   "he sits" is unchanged; but according to existing conditions we call it now true and now
false. As with statements, so, too, with opinions. In its manner, then, of coming about it is
really peculiar to substance to admit of the contrary qualities—to wit, by a change in itself.

If a man, then, should make an exception in favor of opinions and statements, main-
5   taining that these admit also of contrary qualifications, his view would, in truth, be
unsound. If opinions and statements are said to admit of such qualifications, the fact is that
not they themselves but that *something else* undergoes change. For it is by the facts of the
10   case, by their being or not being so, that a statement is called true or false. It is not that the
statement itself can admit of such contrary qualities. For nothing, in one word, can alter
the nature of opinions and statements, and, seeing no change occurs in them, they cannot
admit of such contraries. But substance admits of such contraries by having received them
15   itself: it alternately takes to itself health, disease, whiteness, blackness, the like. By receiving them into itself is it said to admit of such contraries. So, to conclude, we may call this
above all distinctive of substance, that, remaining still one and the same, it may yet through
a change in itself receive contrary qualifications. Let so much on substance suffice.

ON INTERPRETATION (in part)

1. Let us, first of all, define noun and verb, then explain what is meant by denial, affirmation, proposition and sentence. 16^a

Words spoken are symbols or signs of affections or impressions of the soul; written words are the signs of words spoken. As writing, so also is speech not the same for all races of men. But the mental affections themselves, of which these words are primarily signs, are the same for the whole of mankind, as are also the objects of which those affections are representations or likenesses, images, copies. Whit these points, however, I dealt in my treatise concerning the soul; they belong to a different inquiry from that which we now have in hand. 5

As at times there are thoughts in our minds unaccompanied by truth or by falsity, while there are others at times that have necessarily one or the other, so also it is in our speech, for combination and division are essential before you can have truth and falsity. A noun or a verb by itself much resembles a concept or thought which is neither combined nor disjoined. Such is "man," for example, or "white," if pronounced without any addition. As yet it is not true nor false. And a proof of this lies in the fact that <*tragelaphos*> [goat-stag], while it means something, has no truth nor falsity in it, unless in addition you predicate being or not-being of it, whether generally (that is to say, without definite time-connotation) or in a particular tense. 10

15

2. A noun is a sound having meaning established by convention alone but no reference whatever to time, while no part of it has any meaning, considered apart from the whole. Take the proper name "Good-steed," for instance. The "steed" has no meaning apart, as it has in the phrase "a good steed." It is necessary to notice, however, that simple nouns differ from composite. While in the case of the former the parts have no meaning at all, in the latter they have a certain meaning but not as apart from the whole. Let us take "pirate-vessel," for instance. The "vessel" has no sense whatever, except as a part of the whole. 20

25

We have already said that a noun signifies this or that *by convention*. No sound is by nature a noun: it becomes one, becoming a symbol. Inarticulate noises mean something— for instance, those made by brute beasts. But no noises of that kind are nouns.

"Not-man" and the like are not nouns, and I know of no recognized names we can give such expressions as these, which are neither denials nor sentences. Call them (for want of a better) by the name of indefinite nouns, since we use them of all kinds of things, non-existent as well as existing. 30

"Of Philo," "to Philo," and so on are cases of nouns and not nouns. Otherwise we define all these cases as the noun in itself is defined; but when "is," "was" or "will be" is added, they do not then form propositions, which either are true or are false, as the noun itself always does then. For "of Philo is" cannot by itself constitute a true or false proposition. Nor yet can "of Philo is not." 16^b

5

3. A verb is a sound which not only conveys a particular meaning but has a time-reference also. No part by itself has a meaning. It indicates always that something is

said or asserted *of* something. Let me explain what I mean by "it has a time-reference also." Now, "health" is a noun, for example, "is healthy" is a verb, not a noun. For the latter conveys its own meaning but also conveys that the state signified (namely, health) now exists. Then, a verb was an indication of something asserted *of* something; I mean,

10   of a something predicated of a subject or found present in it.

"Is not-ill," "is not-well" and so on I should not, for my own part, call verbs. Though they certainly have the time-reference and function at all times as predicates, I know of no recognized name. Let us call them (for want of a better) by the name of indefinite verbs, since we use them of all kinds of things, non-existent as well as existent.

15   "He was healthy" or "he will be healthy" I likewise should not call a verb. I should call it the tense of a verb. Verb and tenses in this respect differ: the verb indicates present time but the tenses all times save the present.

Verbs by themselves, then, are nouns, and they stand for or signify something, for

20   the speaker stops his process of thinking and the mind of the hearer acquiesces. However, they do not as yet express positive or negative judgments. For even the infinitives "to be," "not to be," and the participle "being" are indicative only of fact, if and when something further is added. They indicate nothing themselves but imply a copulation or synthesis,

25   which we can hardly conceive of apart from the things thus combined.

4. A sentence is significant speech, of which this or that part may have meaning—as something, that is, that is uttered but not as expressing a judgment of a positive or negative character. Let me explain this more fully. Take "mortal." This, doubtless, has meaning

30   but neither affirms nor denies; some addition or other is needed before it can affirm or deny. But the syllables of "mortal" are meaningless. So it is also with "mouse," of which "-ouse" has no meaning whatever and is but a meaningless sound. But we saw that in composite nouns the particular parts have a meaning, although not apart from the whole.

17ᵃ   But while every sentence has meaning, though not as an instrument of nature but, as we observed, by convention, not all can be called propositions. We call propositions those only that have truth or falsity in them. A prayer is, for instance, a sentence but neither has truth nor has falsity. Let us pass over all such, as their study more properly belongs to the province of rhetoric or poetry. We have in our present inquiry propositions

5   alone for our theme.

5. A simple affirmation is the first kind, a simple negation the second of those propositions called simple. The rest are but one by conjunction.

10   Of all propositions a verb or a tense of a verb must form part. The definition, for instance, of "man," unless "is," "was" or "will be" is added or something or other of that kind, does not constitute a proposition. But someone may ask how the phrase, "footed animal, having two feet," can be held to be one and not many. That the words are pronounced in succession does not constitute them a unity. However, that question

15   belongs to a different inquiry from the present.

Now, those propositions are single which indicate one single fact or are one, as we said, by conjunction. And those propositions are many which indicate not one but many or else have their parts unconjoined.

Nouns and verbs let us call mere expressions. For we cannot use mere nouns or verbs, when expressing or enunciating something, for the purpose of making a statement, and that is so whether we happen to express a spontaneous opinion or someone propounded a question to which we are giving an answer.

20   And so, to return, we repeat that one kind of propositions is simple, comprising all those that affirm or deny some one thing of another, while the other is composite,

that is, compounded of simple propositions. And a simple proposition, more fully, is a statement possessing a meaning, affirming or denying the presence of some other thing in a subject in time past or present or future.

6. We mean by affirmation a statement affirming one thing of another; we mean   25
by negation a statement denying one thing of another.

As men can affirm and deny both the presence of that which is present and the presence of that which is absent and this they can do with a reference to times that lie   30
outside the present, whatever a man may affirm, it is possible as well to deny, and whatever a man may deny, it is possible as well to affirm. Thus, it follows, each affirmative statement will have its own opposite negative, just as each negative statement will have its affirmative opposite. Every such pair of propositions we, therefore, shall call contradictories, always assuming the predicates and subjects are really the same and the terms   35
used without ambiguity. These and some other provisos are needed in view of the puzzles propounded by importunate sophists.

7. Of things there are some universal and some individual or singular, according, I mean, as their nature is such that they can or they cannot be predicates of numerous subjects, as "man," for example, and "Callias."   17[b]

Propositions, affirmative and negative, must sometimes have universal subjects, at others individual or singular. Suppose we state two propositions, one affirmative, one of them negative, both universal in form, having one universal for subject; then these propositions are contrary. By "both universal in form, having one universal for subject,"   5
I mean to say such propositions as "every man is white," on the one hand, and "no man is white," on the other. When, however, the two propositions, while having a universal subject, are not universal in character, we cannot describe them as contraries, though on occasions, it may be, the meaning intended is contrary. Take as examples of these "man   10
is white," "man is not white" and so on. The subject or "man" is universal, and yet the propositions themselves are not stated as though universal. For neither contains the word "every." The subject is not a universal in virtue of having an "every"; but "every," applied to the subject, confers on the whole proposition its absolute universality. And yet, if *both* subject and predicate are used in their fullest extension, the resulting proposition will be false. For, indeed, no affirmation at all could, in those circumstances, be   15
true. "Every man is every animal" will serve as a good illustration of this.

When their subject is one and the same but of two propositions the affirmative clearly indicates in its terms that the subject is taken universally, the negative, however, that the subject is not universally taken, I call them contradictorily opposed. Examples are "every man is white," "not every man is white" and the like, or, again, we have "some men   20
are white," to which "no man is white" is opposed in the manner of which I am speaking. Propositions are contrarily opposed when affirmative and negative alike are possessed of a universal character—the subject, that is, in both cases as being marked as universally taken. Thus, "every man is white" or "is just" is the contrary, not the contradictory, of "no man is white" or "is just."   25

In the case of such contraries we see that not both can be true at one time. Notwithstanding, their contradictories sometimes are both of them true, though their subject be one and the same. On the one hand, "not every man is white," on the other hand, "some men are white" will be both of them true propositions. But of those contradictory opposites having universals for subjects and being universal in character, one must be true, the other false. This also holds good of propositions with singular terms for their subjects, as "Socrates is white" and "not white." When, however, the two propositions are   30

not universal in character, albeit about universals, not always do we find it the case that of these one is true, the other false. For, indeed, we can state very truly that man is and man is not white, and that man is and man is not beautiful. If ugly, a man is not beautiful; neither as yet is he beautiful, if he but tends to become so. This view on a summary notice
35   may well seem repugnant to reason, since "man is not white" would appear the equivalent of "no man is white." But they do not, in fact, mean the same, nor, again, are they both of necessity true at the same time or false. It is evident that the denial corresponding to a
18ᵃ   single affirmation itself must be single as well. The denial that is, must deny just the thing the affirmation affirms of the selfsame, identical subject. We further require that the subjects be both universal or singular and also that both should be used or not used in their fullest extension. "Socrates is white" and "not white" constitute in this manner a pair. But if anything else is denied or the subject itself should be changed, though the predicate yet may remain, the denial will not correspond but be one that is simply distinct. To "every
5   man is white," for example, "not every man is white" corresponds, as "no man is white," "man is not white" to "some men are white," "man is white."

Now to sum up the foregoing statements, we showed that a single negation is opposed to a single affirmation in the manner we called contradictory and also explained which these were. From the class of contradictory propositions we further distinguished the contrary, explaining which these also were. We, moreover, have proved of two oppo-
10   sites that it is not the case always that one must be true and one false, and we set forth the reasons for this and explained the conditions in which one is false, if the other is true.

8. A statement is single or one, when it either affirms or denies some one thing and no more of another, be the subject universal or not and the statement universal or
15   not. We may take for examples the following, provided that "white" has one meaning:

Every man is white.	Not every man is white.
Man is white.	Man is not white.
No man is white.	Some men are white.

If, however, one word has two meanings, which do not combine to make one, the affirmation itself is not one. If, for instance, you gave the name "garment" alike to a horse
20   and a man, then it follows that "garment is white," would be not one but two affirmations, as also would "garment is not white" be not one denial but two. For the statement that "garment is white" really means "horse and man both are white." And this statement, in turn, is the same as to say "horse is white," "man is white." And if these have more meanings than one and do not, in effect, make one statement, it follows that "garment is white"
25   must itself have more meanings than one or, if not, it means nothing at all. For no particular man is a horse. And accordingly not even here is one necessarily true and one false of two statements opposed contradictorily.

9. In regard to things present or past, propositions, whether positive or negative, are true of necessity or false. And of those contradictorily opposed one, again, must be
30   true and one false, when they have a universal for subject and are in themselves universal or else, as we noticed above, have a singular term for their subject. This need not, however, be so in the case of two such propositions as have universals for subjects but are not themselves universal. That question also we discussed.

When, however, we come to propositions whose subjects are singular terms, while their predicates refer to the future and not to the present or past, then we find that the case is quite changed. Propositions, whether positive or negative, being themselves
35   true or false, every predicate that we affirm must belong to its subject or not. Hence it is

that, if someone declares that a certain event will take place, while another declares it will not, one will clearly be speaking the truth, while the other as clearly will not. Both predicates cannot belong to one subject with regard to the future. For, if it is true to pronounce some particular thing to be white, it must be of necessity white. The reverse of this also holds good. As, again, it is white or not white, it was true to affirm or deny it. And, if it is not, in fact, white, then to say that it is will be false; if to say that it is will be false, then it follows the thing is not white. We are driven, therefore, to concluding that all affirmations and denials must either be true or be false.   18^b

Now, if all this is so, there is nothing that happens by chance or fortuitously; nothing will ever so happen. Contingency there can be none; all events come about of necessity. Either the man who maintains that a certain event will take place or the man who maintains the reverse will be speaking the truth on that point. Things could just as well happen as no, if the one or the other assertion is not of necessity true. For as that term is used in regard to both present and future events, the contingent is that which could just as well happen in this way as that.   5

If, moreover, a thing is now white, then it would have been true in past time to affirm that that thing *would* be white, and thus at all times was it true of whatever has now taken place to affirm that "it is" or "will be." But if it at all times was true to affirm that "it is" or "will be," how impossible that it should not be or not be about to be so! When a thing cannot! If, again, its not coming to be is impossible, as we assume, come to be then it certainly must. And in consequence future events, as we said, come about of necessity. Nothing is casual, contingent. For if a thing happened by chance, it would not come about of necessity.   10
    15

We cannot contend, notwithstanding, that neither proposition is true. For example, we cannot contend that a certain event neither will nor will not come to pass in the future. For, first, although one affirmation or denial should prove to be false, yet the other would still not be true. Were it, secondly, true to affirm that the same thing is both white and large, it would have both these marks of necessity. If it will have them to-morrow, it will of necessity have them. But if some event neither will nor will not come to pass on the morrow, contingency there will be none. Let us take, for example, a sea-fight. It is requisite on our hypothesis that it should neither take place nor yet fail to take place on the morrow.   20
    25

These and other strange consequences follow, provided we assume in the case of a pair of contradictory opposites having universals for subjects and being themselves universal or having an individual subject, that one must be true, the other false, that contingency there can be none and that all things that are or take place come about in the world by necessity. No need would there be for mankind to deliberate or to take pains, could we make the assumption that if we adopt a particular line, then a certain result will ensue and that, if we do not, it will not. There is nothing to prevent any man from predicting some future event (say) some ten thousand years beforehand, while another predicts the reverse: the event that was truly predicted must needs come to pass at long last. And, indeed, it is quite immaterial whether contradictory predictions were actually made beforehand. For that someone affirmed or denied does not alter the course of events. And events are not caused or prevented by someone's affirming or denying that at some future time they would happen. Nor yet, let us add, does it matter how old the predictions may be. And, in consequence, if through the ages the nature of things has been such that a certain prediction was true, that prediction must needs be fulfilled; and the nature of all things was such that events came about of necessity. For any event anyone in the past has once truly predicted must needs in due course come about, and of that which has once come about it was true at all times to affirm that it would in due time come about.   30
    35
    19^a
    5

All this is, however, impossible. We know from our personal experience that future events may depend on the counsels and actions of men, and that, speaking more

10   broadly, those things that are not uninterruptedly actual exhibit a potentiality, that is a "may or may not be." If such things may be or may not be, events may take place or may not. There are many plain cases of this. Thus this coat may be cut in two halves; yet it may not be cut in two halves. It may wear out before that can happen: then it may not be

15   cut into two. For, unless that were really the case, then its wearing out first were not possible. The same with all other events which in any such sense are potential. Thus it is clear that not everything is or takes place of necessity. Cases there are of contingency;

20   no truer is then the affirmative, no falser, than the negative statement. Some cases, moreover, we find that, at least, for the most part and commonly, tend in a certain direction, and yet they may issue at times in the other or rarer direction.

What is must needs be when it is; what is not cannot be when it is not. However, not all that exists any more than all that which does not comes about or exists by necessity.

25   That what is must be when "it is" does not mean the same thing as to say that all things come about by necessity. And so, too, with that which is not. And with two contradictory statements the same thing is found to hold good. That is, all things must be or not be, or must come or not come into being, at this or that time in the future. But we cannot deter-

30   minately say *which* alternative *must* come to pass. For example, a sea-fight must either take place on the morrow or not. No necessity is there, however, that it should come to pass or should not. What is necessary is that it either should happen to-morrow or not. And so, as the truth of propositions consists in corresponding with facts, it is clear in the case

35   of events where contingency or potentiality in opposite directions is found that the two contradictory statements about them will have the same character.

With what is not always existent or not at all times non-existent we find this exactly the case. For one half of the said contradiction must be true and the other half false. But we cannot say which half is which. Though it may be that one is more probable, it cannot be

19^b   true yet or false. There is evidently, then, no necessity that one should be true, the other false, in the case of affirmations and denials. For the case of those things which as yet are potential, not actually existent, is different from that of things actual. It is as we stated above.

POSTERIOR ANALYTICS (in part)

BOOK I

71^a   1. All teaching and all intellectual learning come about from already existing knowledge. This is evident if we consider it in every case; for the mathematical sciences are acquired in this fashion, and so is each of the other arts. And similarly too with

5   arguments—both deductive and inductive arguments proceed in this way; for both produce their teaching through what we are already aware of, the former getting their premises as from men who grasp them, the latter proving the universal through the particular's being

10   clear. (And rhetorical arguments too persuade in the same way; for they do so either through examples, which is induction, or through enthymemes, which is deduction.)

Aristotle, *Posterior Analytics*, Book I, 1–2; II, 19, translated by Jonathan Barnes from *Complete Works of Aristotle*, edited by Jonathan Barnes (Princeton: Princeton University Press, 1984). Copyright © 1984 by PUP. Reprinted by permission.

It is necessary to be already aware of things in two ways: of some things it is necessary to believe already that they are, of some one must grasp what the thing said is, and of others both—e.g., of the fact that everything is either affirmed or denied truly, one must believe that it is; of the triangle, that it signifies this; and of the unit both (both what it signifies and that it is). For each of these is not equally clear to us.   15

But you can become familiar by being familiar earlier with some things but getting knowledge of the others at the very same time—i.e., of whatever happens to be under the universal of which you have knowledge. For that every triangle has angles equal to two right angles was already known; but that there is a triangle in the semicircle here became familiar at the same time as the induction. (For in some cases learning occurs in this way, and the last term does not become familiar through the middle—in cases dealing with what are in fact particulars and not said of any underlying subject.)   20

Before the induction, or before getting a deduction, you should perhaps be said to understand in a way—but in another way not. For if you did not know if it is *simpliciter* [without qualification], how did you know that it has two right angles *simpliciter?* But it is clear that you understand it in this sense—that you understand it universally—but you do not understand it *simpliciter.* (Otherwise the puzzle in the *Meno* [80d] will result; for you will learn either nothing or what you know.)   30

For one should not argue in the way in which some people attempt to solve it: Do you or don't you know of every pair that it is even? And when you said Yes, they brought forward some pair of which you did not think that it was, nor therefore that it was even. For they solve it by denying that people know of every pair that it is even, but only of anything of which they know that it is a pair. Yet they know it of that which they have the demonstration about and which they got their premises about; and they got them not about everything of which they know that it is a triangle or that it is a number, but of every number and triangle *simpliciter.* For no proposition of such a type is assumed (that *what you know to be a number . . .* or *what you know to be rectilineal . . .*), but they are assumed as holding of every case.   71^b

                                                                                    5

But nothing, I think, prevents one from in a sense understanding and in a sense being ignorant of what one is learning; for what is absurd is not that you should know in some sense what you are learning, but that you should know it in this sense, i.e., in the way and sense in which you are learning it.

2. We think we understand a thing *simpliciter* (and not in the sophistic fashion accidentally) whenever we think we are aware both that the explanation because of which the object is is its explanation, and that it is not possible for this to be otherwise. It is clear, then, that to understand is something of this sort; for both those who do not understand and those who do understand—the former think they are themselves in such a state, and those who do understand actually are. Hence that of which there is understanding *simpliciter* cannot be otherwise.   10

                                                                                    15

Now whether there is also another type of understanding we shall say later; but we say now that we do know through demonstration. By demonstration I mean a scientific deduction; and by scientific I mean one in virtue of which, by having it, we understand something.

If, then, understanding is as we posited, it is necessary for demonstrative understanding in particular to depend on things which are true and primitive and immediate and more familiar than and prior to and explanatory of the conclusion (for in this way the principles will also be appropriate to what is being proved). For there will be deduction even without these conditions, but there will not be demonstration; for it will not produce understanding.   20

25   Now they must be true because one cannot understand what is not the case—e.g., that the diagonal is commensurate. And they must depend on what is primitive and non-demonstrable because otherwise you will not understand if you do not have a demonstration of them; for to understand that of which there is a demonstration non-accidentally is to have a demonstration. They must be both explanatory and more

30   familiar and prior explanatory because we only understand when we know the explanation; and prior, if they are explanatory, and we are already aware of them not only in the sense of grasping them but also of knowing that they are.

Things are prior and more familiar in two ways; for it is not the same to be prior by nature and prior in relation to us, nor to be more familiar and more familiar to us. I call

72ª   prior and more familiar in relation to us what is nearer to perception, prior and more familiar *simpliciter* what is further away. What is most universal is furthest away, and the

5   particulars are nearest; and these are opposite to each other.

Depending on things that are primitive is depending on appropriate principles; for I call the same thing primitive and a principle. A principle of a demonstration is an immediate proposition, and an immediate proposition is one to which there is no other prior.

10   A proposition is the one part of a contradiction, one thing said of one; it is dialectical if it assumes indifferently either part, demonstrative if it determinately assumes the one that is true. [A statement is either part of a contradiction.] A contradiction is an opposition which of itself excludes any intermediate; and the part of a contradiction saying something *of* something is an affirmation, the one saying something *from* something is a denial.

15   An immediate deductive principle I call a posit if one cannot prove it but it is not necessary for anyone who is to learn anything to grasp it; and one which it is necessary for anyone who is going to learn anything whatever to grasp, I call an axiom (for there are some such things); for we are accustomed to use this name especially of such things.

20   A posit which assumes either of the parts of a contradiction—i.e., I mean, that something is or that something is not—I call a supposition; one without this, a definition. For a definition is a posit (for the arithmetician posits that a unit is what is quantitatively indivisible) but not a supposition (for what a unit is and that a unit is are not the same).

25   Since one should both be convinced of and know the object by having a deduction of the sort we call a demonstration, and since this is the case when these things on which the deduction depends are the case, it is necessary not only to be already aware of the primitives (either all or some of them) but actually to be better aware of them. For a

30   thing always belongs better to that thing because of which it belongs—e.g., that because of which we love is better loved. Hence if we know and are convinced because of the primitives, we both know and are convinced of them better, since it is because of them that we know and are convinced of what is posterior.

It is not possible to be better convinced than one is of what one knows, of what one in fact neither knows nor is more happily disposed toward than if one in fact knew. But this will result if someone who is convinced because of a demonstration is not

35   already aware of the primitives, for it is necessary to be better convinced of the principles (either all or some of them) than of the conclusion.

Anyone who is going to have understanding through demonstration must not only be familiar with the principles and better convinced of them than of what is being

72b   proved, but also there must be no other thing more convincing to him or more familiar among the opposites of the principles on which a deduction of the contrary error may depend—if anyone who understands *simpliciter* must be unpersuadable.

*   *   *

BOOK II

19. Now as for deduction and demonstration, it is evident both what each is and how it comes about—and at the same time this goes for demonstrative understanding too (for that is the same thing). But as for the principles—how they become familiar and what is the state that becomes familiar with them—that will be clear from what follows, when we have first set down the puzzles. 99^b15

Now, we have said earlier that it is not possible to understand through demonstration if we are not aware of the primitive, immediate, principles. But as to knowledge of the immediates, one might puzzle both whether it is the same or not the same—whether there is understanding of each, or rather understanding of the one and some other kind of thing of the other—and also whether the states are not present in us but come about in us, or whether they are present in us but escape notice. 20 25

Well, if we have them, it is absurd; for it results that we have pieces of knowledge more precise than demonstration and yet this escapes notice. But if we get them without having them earlier, how might we become familiar with them and learn them from no pre-existing knowledge? For that is impossible, as we said in the case of demonstration too. It is evidently impossible, then, both for us to have them and for them to come about in us when we are ignorant and have no such state at all. Necessarily, therefore, we have some capacity, but do not have one of a type which will be more valuable than these in respect of precision. 30

And *this* evidently belongs to all animals; for they have a connate discriminatory capacity, which is called perception. And if perception is present in them, in some animals retention of the percept comes about, but in others it does not come about. Now for those in which it does not come about, there is no knowledge outside perceiving (either none at all, or none with regard to that of which there is no retention); but for some perceivers, it is possible to grasp it in their minds. And when many such things come about, then a difference comes about, so that some come to have an account from the retention of such things, and others do not. 35 100^a

So from perception there comes memory, as we call it, and from memory (when it occurs often in connection with the same thing), experience; for memories that are many in number form a single experience. And from experience, or from the whole universal that has come to rest in the soul (the one apart from the many, whatever is one and the same in all those things), there comes a principle of skill and of understanding—of skill if it deals with how things come about, of understanding if it deals with what is the case. 5

Thus the states neither belong in us in a determinate form, nor come about from other states that are more cognitive; but they come about from perception—as in a battle when a rout occurs, if one man makes a stand another does and then another, until a position of strength is reached. And the soul is such as to be capable of undergoing this. 10

What we have just said but not said clearly, let us say again: when one of the undifferentiated things makes a stand, there is a primitive universal in the mind (for though one perceives the particular, perception is of the universal—e.g., of man but not of Callias the man); again a stand is made in these, until what has no parts and is universal stands—e.g., *such and such* an animal stands, until animal does, and in this a stand is made in the same way. Thus it is clear that it is necessary for us to become familiar with the primitives by induction; for perception too instils the universal in this way. 15 100^b 5

Since of the intellectual states by which we grasp truth some are always true and some admit falsehood (e.g., opinion and reasoning—whereas understanding and comprehension are always true), and no kind other than comprehension is more precise than understanding, and the principles of demonstrations are more familiar, and all understanding involves an account—there will not be understanding of the principles; and since it is not possible for anything to be truer than understanding, except comprehension, there will be comprehension of the principles—both if we inquire from these facts and because demonstration is not a principle of demonstration so that understanding is not a principle of understanding either—so if we have no other true kind apart from understanding, comprehension will be the principle of understanding. And the principle will be of the principle, and understanding as a whole will be similarly related to the whole object.

PHYSICS (in part)

BOOK II

192^b 1. Of the things that are, some are by nature, others through other causes: by nature are animals and their parts, plants, and the simple bodies, such as earth, fire, air, and water (for these things and such things we say to be by nature), and all of them obviously differ from the things not put together by nature. For each of these has in itself a source of motion and rest, either in place, or by growth and shrinkage, or by alteration; but a bed or a cloak, or any other such kind of thing there is, in the respect in which it has happened upon each designation and to the extent that it is from art, has no innate impulse of change at all. But in the respect in which they happen to be of stone or earth or a mixture of these, they do have such an impulse, and to that extent, since nature is a certain source and cause of being moved and of coming to rest in that to which it belongs primarily, in virtue of itself and not incidentally. (I say not incidentally because someone might himself become a certain cause of health in himself if he is a doctor. Still, it is not in the respect in which he is cured that he has the medical art, but it happens to the same person to be a doctor and be cured, on account of which they are also sometimes separated from each other.) And similarly with each of the other things produced: for none of them has in itself the source of its making, but some in other things and external, such as a house and each of the other products of manual labor, others in themselves but not from themselves, as many as incidentally become causes for themselves.

Nature then is what has been said, and as many things as have a nature as have such a source. And every thing that has a nature is an independent thing, since it is something that underlies [and persists through change], and nature is always in an underlying thing. According to nature are both these things and as many things as belong to these in virtue of themselves, as being carried up belongs to fire. For this is not a nature, nor does it have a nature, but it is something by nature and according to nature. What nature is, then, has been said, and what is something by nature and according to nature. *That* nature is, it would be ridiculous to try to show, for it is clear that among the things that

Joe Sachs, *Aristotle's* Physics: *A Guided Study*, Book II. Copyright © 1995 by Joe Sachs. Reprinted by permission of Rutgers University Press.

are, such things are many. But to show things that are clear by means of things that are unclear is the act of one who cannot distinguish what is known through itself from what is known not through itself. (That it is possible to suffer this is not unclear, for someone blind from birth might reason about colors.) So it is necessary that the speech of such people be about names, while they have insight into nothing.

Now to some it seems that nature or the thinghood* of things by nature is the first thing present in each which is unarranged as far as it itself is concerned; thus the nature of a bed would be wood, and of a statue, bronze. And Antiphon says that a sign of this is that, if someone were to bury a bed, and what rotted had the power to put up a sprout, it would not become a bed but wood, since what belongs to it by accident is the arrangement according to convention and art, while the thinghood of it is that which remains continuously even while it is undergoing these things. And if each of *these* things is in the same case in relation to something else (as bronze or gold to water, and bones or wood to earth, and similarly with anything else at all), *that* would be the nature and thinghood of them. On account of which, some say fire, some earth, some air, some water, some say some of these, and some all of these to be the nature of things that are. For whatever from among these anyone supposes to be such, whether one of them or more, this one or this many he declares to be all thinghood, while everything else is an attribute or condition or disposition of these; and whatever is among these he declares to be eternal (since for them there could be no change out of themselves), while the other things come into being and pass away an unlimited number of times.

In one way then, nature is spoken of thus, as the first material underlying each of the things that have in themselves a source of motion and change, but in another way as the form, or the look that is disclosed in speech. For just as art is said of what is according to art or artful, so also nature is said of what is according to nature and natural. We would not yet say anything to be according to art if it is only potentially a bed and does not yet have the look of a bed, nor that it is art, and similarly not in the case of things composed by nature. For what is potentially flesh or bone does not yet have its own nature, until it takes on the look that is disclosed in speech, that by means of which we define when we say what flesh or bone is, and not until then is it by nature. So in this other way, nature would be, of the things having in themselves a source of motion, the form or look, which is not separate other than in speech. (What comes from these, such as a human being, is not nature but by nature.)

And this form or look is nature more than the material is. For each thing is meant when it is fully at work, more than when it *is* potentially. Moreover, a human being comes about from a human being, but not a bed from a bed. On this account, they say that not the shape but the wood is the nature, since if it were to sprout, it would become not a bed but wood. But if, therefore, this is nature, then also the form is nature, for from a human being comes a human being. And still further, the nature spoken of as coming into being is a road into nature. For it is not like the process of medicine, which is meant to be a road not into the medical art but into health, for it is necessary that the medical process be from the medical art and not into it. But not thus is nature related to nature, but the growing thing, insofar as it grows, does proceed from something into something. What then is it that grows? Not the from-which, but the to-which. Therefore nature is the form.

But form and nature are meant in two ways, for deprivation is a sort of form. But whether in the case of a simple coming-into-being there is or is not a deprivation and an opposite, must be looked into later.

---

*<*ousia*>, often translated "substance," means (as our translator puts it) "the way of being that belongs to anything which has attributes but is not an attribute of anything, which is also separate and a *this*. Whatever has being in this way is an independent thing."

2. Now that nature has been marked off in a number of ways, after this one must see how the mathematician differs from one who studies nature (for natural bodies too have
25   surfaces and solids and lengths and points, about which the mathematician inquires), and whether astronomy is different from or part of the study of nature. For if it belongs to the one who studies nature to know what the sun and moon are, but none of the properties that belong to them in themselves, this would be absurd, both in other ways and because those concerned with nature obviously speak about the shape of the moon and sun and espe-
30   cially whether the earth and the cosmos are of spherical shape or not.

The mathematician does busy himself about the things mentioned, but not insofar as each is a limit of a natural body, nor does he examine their properties insofar as they belong to them because they pertain to natural bodies. On account of this also he separates them. For in his thinking they are separated from motion, and it makes no difference, nor
35   do they become false by being separated. Those who speak of the forms also do this, but without being aware of it, for they separate the natural things, which are less separable
194ª   than the mathematical ones. This would become clear if one should try to state the definitions of each of these things, both of themselves and of their properties. For the odd and even, and the straight and the curved, and further, number, line, and figure will be without motion, but no longer so with flesh, bone, or human being, but these are spoken of like a
5   snub-nose and not like the curved. The more natural of the mathematical studies, such as optics, harmonics, and astronomy, also show this, for they in a certain way stand contrariwise to geometry. For geometry inquires about a natural line, but not as natural, but optics
10   about a mathematical line, not as mathematical but as natural.

But since nature is twofold, and is both form and material, we must consider it as though we were inquiring about what snubness is. As a result, such things will be neither without material, nor determined by their material. And in fact, since there are two natures,
15   one might be at an impasse about which of them belongs to the study of nature. Or is it about that which comes from both? But if it is about that which comes from both, it is also about each of the two. Then does it belong to the same study or different ones to know each? If one looks to the ancients, it would seem to be about material (for only a little bit
20   did Empedocles and Democritus touch on form or the what-it-is-to-be of things). But if art imitates nature, and if it belongs to the same knowledge to know the form and the material to some extent (as it is the doctor's job to know health and also bile and phlegm, in which
25   health is, and the housebuilder's to know both the form of a house and its material, that it is bricks and lumber, and in like manner with the rest), it would also be part of the study of nature to pay attention to both natures.

Further, that for the sake of which, or the end, as well as whatever is for the sake of these, belong to the same study. But nature is an end and a that-for-the-sake-of-which. (For
30   of those things of which there is an end, if the motion is continuous, the end is both the last stage and that for the sake of which; which induced the poet to say, absurdly, "He has his death, for the sake of which he was born." For not every last thing professes itself to be an end, but only what is best.) And the arts make even their material, some simply and others
35   working it up, and we make use of everything there is as though it is for our sake (for we are also in some way an end, and "that for the sake of which" is double in meaning, but this is discussed in the writings on philosophy). But the arts which govern and understand the
194ᵇ   material are two, one of using and one of directing the making. The art of using is for that very reason somehow directive of the making, but they differ in that the one is attentive to the form, the other, as productive, to the material. For the steersman recognizes and gives orders about what sort of form belongs to the rudder, but someone else about what sort of
5   wood and processes it will come from. In things that come from art, then, we make the material for the sake of the work, but in natural things it is in being from the beginning. Further, material is among the relative things: for a different form, a different material.

To what extent is it necessary for the one who studies nature to know the form or   10
whatness? Is it just as the doctor knows connective tissue or the metal-worker knows
bronze, to the extent of knowing what each is for the sake of, even about those things
which, while separate in form, are present in material? For both a human being and the
sun beget a human being. But what manner of being the separate thing and the whatness   15
have, it is the work of first philosophy to define.

   3. These things having been marked out, it is necessary to examine the causes, both
what sort there are and how many in number. For since this work is for the sake of knowing, but we think we do not yet know each thing until we have taken hold of the why of   20
it (and to do this is to come upon the first cause), it is clear that we too must do this about
both coming into being and passing away and about every natural change, so that, once
we know them, we may try to lead back to them each of the things we inquire about.
   One way cause is meant, then, is that out of which something comes into being,   25
still being present in it, as bronze of a statue or silver of a bowl, or the kinds of these. In
another way it is the form or pattern, and this is the gathering in speech of the what-it-is-
for-it-to-be, or again the kinds of this (as of the octave, the two-to-one ratio, or generally
number), and the parts that are in its articulation. In yet another it is that from which the
first beginning of change or of rest is, as the legislator is a cause, or the father of a child,   30
or generally the maker of what is made, or whatever makes a changing thing change. And
in still another way it is meant as the end. This is that for the sake of which, as health is
of walking around. Why is he walking around? We say "in order to be healthy," and in so
saying think we have completely given the cause. Causes also are as many things as   35
come between the mover of something else and the end, as, of health, fasting or purging
or drugs or instruments. For all these are for the sake of the end, but they differ from one
another in that some are deeds and others tools.   195^a
   The causes then are meant in just about this many ways, and it happens, since they
are meant in more than one way, that the non-accidental causes of the same thing are also   5
many, as of the statue both the art of sculpture and bronze, not as a consequence of anything
else but just as a statue, though they are not causes in the same way, but the one as material
and the other as that from which the motion was. And there are also in a certain way causes
of one another, as hard work is a cause of good condition and this in turn is a cause of hard
work, though again not in the same way, but the one as end and the other as source of   10
motion. Further, the same thing is a cause of opposite things. For the present thing is
responsible for this result, and we sometimes blame it, when it is absent, for the opposite
result, as the absence of the pilot for the ship's overturning, whose presence was the cause
of its keeping safe. But all the causes now being spoken of fall into four most evident ways.   15
For the letters of syllables and the material of processed things and fire (and such things) of
bodies and parts of a whole and hypotheses of a conclusion are causes as that out of which,
and while the one member of each of these pairs is a cause as what underlies, such as parts,
the other is so as the what-it-is-for-it-to-be, a whole or composite or form. But the semen   20
and the doctor and the legislator, and generally the maker, are all causes as that from which
the source of change or rest is, but other things are causes as the end or the good of the
remaining ones. For that-for-the-sake-of-which means to be the best thing and the end of   25
the other things, and let it make no difference to say the good itself or the apparent good.
   The causes then are these and are so many in form, but the ways the causes work
are many in number, though even these are fewer if they are brought under headings.
For cause is meant in many ways, and of those of the same form, as preceding and fol-   30
lowing one another. For example, the cause of health is the doctor and also the skilled
knower, and of the octave the double and also number, and always comprehensive
things in relation to particular ones. Further, there is what is incidental, and the kinds of

these, as of the statue, in one way Polycleitus and in another the sculptor, because it is
35   incidental to the sculptor to be Polycleitus. And there are the things comprehensive of
the incidental cause, as if a human being were the cause of a statue, or generally, an ani-
195ᵇ   mal. And also among incidental things, some are more remote and others nearer, as if
the pale man or the one with a refined education were said to be the cause of a statue.
And all of them, both those meant properly and those incidentally, are meant some as
5   potential and others as at-work, as of building a house, either the builder or the builder
building. And similarly to the things that have been said, an account will be given for
those things of which the causes are causes, as of this statue or a statue or in general an
image, and of this bronze or of bronze or in general of material, and likewise with the
10   incidental things. Further, things tangling these and those together will be said, such as
not Polycleitus nor a sculptor but the sculptor Polycleitus.

Nevertheless, all these are six in multitude, but spoken of in a twofold way: there
is the particular or the kind, the incidental or the kind of the incidental thing, and these
15   entangled or spoken of simply, and all as either at-work or in potency. And they differ to
this extent, that what is at-work and particular is and is not at the same time as that of
which it is the cause, as this one healing with this one being cured or this one building
20   with this thing being built, but not always so with what is potential. The house and the
housebuilder are not finished off simultaneously.

And it is necessary always to seek out the ultimate cause of each thing, and in just the
same way as with the others. (For example, a man builds because he is a builder, but is a
25   builder as a result of the housebuilder's art; this, then, is the prior cause, and thus with
everything.) Further, the kinds belong to the kinds and the particulars to the particulars (as
a sculptor to a statue, but this sculptor to this statue). Also the potencies belong to the poten-
30   cies, but what is at work corresponds to what is being worked upon. How many then are the
causes and in what way they are causes, let it have been marked out sufficiently for us.

4. Fortune and chance are spoken of among the causes, and many things are said to
35   be and to come about through fortune or through chance. In what way, then, fortune and
chance are among these causes, and whether fortune and chance are the same or different,
and in general what fortune and chance are, must be examined. For some people are at an
196ᵃ   impasse even about whether they exist or not. For they say nothing comes about from fortune, but that, for everything whatever that we say comes from chance or fortune, there is
some definite cause; for example, of coming by fortune into the marketplace and catching
up with someone whom one wanted, but did not expect, to find, the cause is wanting to go
to use the marketplace. And similarly with the rest of the things said to be from fortune,
5   there is always something to take as the cause, but not fortune, since if fortune were anything it would seem strange, and truly so; and one might find it impossible to understand
why in the world none of the ancient wise men, speaking about the causes of coming-to-
10   be and passing away, demarcated anything about fortune, but as it seems, they too
regarded nothing as being from fortune. But this too is to be wondered at. For many things
both come about and are from fortune and from chance, which everyone, though not ignorant that it is possible to refer each of them back to some cause of its coming about, which
15   the earlier argument declared to be the abolition of fortune, nevertheless says are from fortune, some of them, though some are not. For this reason they were obliged to make some
mention of it in some way. But surely they did not regard fortune to be any of those things
such as friendship and strife, or intellect, or fire, or anything else of that sort. It is strange,
then, either if they did not acknowledge it to be, or if, supposing it, they left it aside,
20   despite even sometimes making use of it, as Empedocles says that the air is not always
separated in the highest place, but however it falls out. Certainly he says in his cosmogony

that "it fell out thus as it was flowing at one time, but often otherwise." And most of them say that the parts of animals have come into being from fortune.

There are some who make chance responsible for this cosmos and all worlds. 25 For they say that by chance there came about a vortex and a motion of separating out and settling into this arrangement of the whole. And this itself is in fact mightily worth wondering at. For they are saying that animals and plants neither are nor come to be by fortune, but that either nature or intellect or some other such thing is the cause (for 30 what comes into being from each seed is not whatever falls out, but from this one an olive tree, from that one a human being), but that the heavens and the most divine of visible things have come from chance, and there is in no way such a cause as there is of the animals and plants. But if this is the way things are, this itself is worth bringing 35 one to a stop, and it would have been good for something to have been said about it. In this respect as well as others, what is said is strange, and it is stranger still to say these 196ᵇ things when one sees nothing in the heavens happening by chance, but many things falling out by fortune among the things not assigned to fortune, though it would surely seem that the opposite would happen.

There are others to whom it seems that fortune is a cause, but one not disclosed to 5 human understanding, as though it were something divine and more appropriate to mirac-ulous agency. So it is necessary to examine what each is, and whether chance and fortune are the same or different, and how they fall in with the causes that have been marked out.

5. First, then, since we see some things always happening in a certain way, and oth- 10 ers for the most part, it is clear that of neither of these is fortune or what comes from for-tune said to be the cause, neither of what is out of necessity and always, nor of what is for the most part. But since there are other things besides these that happen, and everyone says that they are from fortune, it is clear that fortune or chance is in some way. For we 15 know that things of this kind are from fortune and that things from fortune are of this kind.

Now of things that happen, some happen for the sake of something and some not (and of the former, some in accordance with choice, some not in accordance with choice, but both are among things for the sake of something), so that it is clear that even among things apart from what is necessary or for the most part, there are some to 20 which it is possible that being for the sake of something belongs. And for the sake of something are as many things as are brought about from thinking or from nature. But whenever such things come about incidentally, we say that they are from fortune. (For just as a thing is something either in virtue of itself or incidentally, so also is it possi- 25 ble to be a cause, as of a house, the cause in virtue of itself is the builder's art, but an incidental one is the pale or educated man; the cause in virtue of itself, then, is definite, but the incidental one indefinite, for to one thing, infinitely many things incidentally belong.) Just as was said, then, whenever this happens among things happening for 30 the sake of something, in that case it is said to be from chance or from fortune. (The difference between these in relation to one another is something that must be distin-guished later; for now let this be clearly seen, that both are among the things for the sake of something.) For example, someone gathering contributions would have come 35 for the sake of collecting money, if he had known; but he came not for the sake of this, but it happened to him incidentally to go and to do this. And this was not through fre-quenting the place for the most part or out of necessity, but the end, the collection, 197ᵃ though not belonging to the causes in him, is among choices and things that result from thinking. And in this case he is said to have come by fortune, but if he had chosen to, and for the sake of this, or if he frequented the place always or for the most part, not 5 by fortune. It is clear then that fortune is an incidental cause among things proceeding from choice, which in turn are among those for the sake of something. Whence thinking and fortune concern the same thing, for there is no choice without thinking.

It is necessary, then, that the causes be indefinite from which what arises from fortune comes about. Whence fortune too seems to be indefinite, and obscure to humans, and it is possible for it to seem that nothing comes about from fortune. For all these things are said correctly, reasonably. That is, there are things that come about from fortune: they come about incidentally, and fortune is an incidental cause, but of nothing is it the cause simply. As of a house, the cause is the builder's art, but incidentally a flute-player, also of coming to collect money when one has not come for the sake of this, the multitude of causes is unlimited. One wanted either to see someone, or look for someone, or get away from someone, or see a show. It is even correct to say that fortune is something non-rational, for a reasoned account belongs to what happens either always or for the most part, and fortune is among things that come about outside of these ways. Thus, since causes of this kind are indefinite, fortune too is indefinite. Still, in some situations, one might be at a loss whether the things that happen to occur would become causes of fortune, as of health, the wind or the sun's warmth, but not having had a haircut. For among incidental causes, some are nearer than others.

Whenever something good turns out, fortune is called good, or indifferent when it is something indifferent, but good fortune or ill fortune are only spoken of when these outcomes are of some magnitude. For this reason too, to come within a hairsbreadth of obtaining some great evil or good is to be fortunate or unfortunate, because our thinking picks out what comes out, but seems to hold off what was within a hairsbreadth as nothing. Further, good fortune is unstable, and reasonably, for fortune is unstable, since it is not possible for any of the things from fortune to be always or for the most part. Both, then, are causes, incidental ones as was said, both fortune and chance, among those things which admit of coming into being neither simply nor for the most part, belonging in turn to those which could come about for the sake of something.

6. They differ because chance is more extensive, for everything from fortune is from chance, but not everything from it is from fortune. For fortune and what comes from fortune are present to beings to whom being fortunate, or generally, action, might belong. For this reason also, fortune is necessarily concerned with actions. (A sign is that good fortune seems to be either the same thing as happiness or nearly so, while happiness is a kind of action, namely doing well.) So whatever cannot act cannot do anything as a result of fortune either. And for this reason no inanimate thing nor any animal or small child can do anything as a result of fortune, because they do not have the power to choose in advance. Neither good fortune nor misfortune belongs to them, except metaphorically, as Protarchus says the stones out of which altars are made are fortunate, because they are honored, while their quarry-mates are trampled on. But it belongs even to these things to be affected by fortune, whenever an active being acts on them in some way that results from fortune, but in no other way. Chance, though, belongs to the other animals and to many inanimate things, as we say a horse came along by chance, because he was saved by his coming, though he did not come for the sake of the being saved. Or a tripod fell down by chance, for it stood there in order to be sat upon, but did not fall down in order to be sat upon. So it is clear, among things happening for the sake of something simply, whenever they happen not for the sake of what turned out, of which the cause was external, we then say that they are from chance. And as many of these things that happen by chance are choices, and happen to those having the power of choice, as are from fortune.

A sign of this is the phrase "in vain," which is said whenever what is for the sake of another thing does not come to pass for the sake of that, as, if taking a walk were for

the sake of evacuation, but when one had walked this did not happen, we would say that
having walked was vain and taking a walk futile, as though this was the "in vain": for   25
something by nature for the sake of another thing, the not being brought to accomplish-
ment of that for the sake of which it was and to which it was naturally disposed, since if
someone said he had bathed in vain because the sun was not eclipsed, it would be
ridiculous, for this was not for the sake of that. Thus, even from its name, chance [*to
automaton*] is that which itself happens in vain [*to auto maten*]. For the stone fell not for
the sake of knocking someone out; therefore the stone fell by chance, because it could   30
have fallen by some agency and for the sake of the knocking out.

Chance is separated most of all from what comes from fortune in things that
happen by nature. For whenever something happens contrary to nature, we say that it
happened not by fortune but by chance. But it is also possible that this is for a differ-   35
ent reason, since of the one the cause is outside, of the other inside.

What, then, chance and fortune are has been said, and how they differ from each   198ᵃ
other. And of the ways of being a cause, both of them are among things from which the
source of motion is; for they are always among either things in some way by nature, or
causes that come from thinking, but the multitude of them is infinite. But since chance
and fortune are causes of things for which either intelligence or nature might have been   5
responsible, whenever something incidentally becomes responsible for these same
things, but nothing incidental is prior to things in virtue of themselves, it is clear that   10
neither is the incidental cause prior to what is in virtue of itself. Therefore chance and
fortune are subordinate to intelligence and nature, so that if chance is responsible for the
heavens as much as possible, it is necessary that intelligence and nature have a prior
responsibility, not only for many other things, but also for this whole.

7. That there are causes, and that they are as many in number as we said, is clear,   15
for the why includes so many in number. For the why ultimately leads back either to the
what-it-is, among motionless things (as in mathematics, for it ultimately leads back to
the definition of straight or commensurable or something else), or to the first source of
motion (as, Why did they go to war? Because they were plundered), or something for   20
the sake of which (in order to rule), or, among things that come into being, the material.

That the causes, then, are these and this many, is clear; and since there are four causes,
it belongs to the one who studies nature to know about all of them, and he will supply what
is due in the way of natural inquiry by tracing back the why to them all: the material, the
form, the mover, and that for the sake of which. But often three of them turn back into one,   25
for the what-it-is and that for the sake of which are one, and that whence the motion first is,
is the same in form with these; for a human being brings forth a human being, and in general, as many things as, being moved themselves, cause motion, are the same in form with
the things moved. (Whatever is not like this does not belong to the study of nature. For it
causes motion not by having motion or a source of motion in itself, but being motionless. On
which account there are three studies, one about motionless things, one about things moved   30
but indestructible, and one about destructible things.) So they supply what is due by tracing
back the why to the material, and to the what-it-is, and to the first mover. About coming into
being, they examine the cause mostly in this way: what comes about after what, and what   35
did it do first, or how was it acted upon, and so on always in succession.

The sources which bring about motion naturally are twofold, of which one kind is not
natural, for sources of that kind do not have in themselves a source of motion. And of this   198ᵇ
kind is whatever causes motion without being moved, as does not only what is completely
motionless and the first of all beings, but also the what-it-is or form, for it is an end and that
for the sake of which. So, since nature is for the sake of something, it is also necessary to

5   know this, and one must supply the why completely: for example, that from this necessarily comes that (from this either simply or for the most part), *and* that if it is going to be, this will be (as from the premises, the conclusion), and that this is what it is for it to be, and because it is better thus, not simply, but in relation to the thinghood of each thing.

10   8. One must say, first, why nature is among the causes for the sake of something, then, about the necessary, how it holds a place among natural things. For everybody traces things back to this cause, inasmuch as, since the hot and the cold and each thing of this kind are by nature a certain way, these things are and come into being out of necessity. For even if they also speak of another cause, they send it on its way after only

15   so much as touching on it, one on friendship and strife, another on intellect.

Here is an impasse: what prevents nature from doing things not for the sake of anything, nor because they are best, but just as Zeus rains, not in order that the grain might grow, but out of necessity? (For it is necessary that what is taken up be cooled, and that

20   what is cooled, becoming water, come down; when this happens, growing incidentally happens to the grain.) Likewise, if the grain is ruined on the threshing-floor, not for the sake of this did it rain, to spoil it, but this was incidental. So what prevents the parts in something that is by nature from being the same way, say the teeth growing with the

25   front ones sharp out of necessity, suitable for tearing, but the molars flat and useful for grinding the food, although not happening for the sake of this, but just falling together? Likewise with the other parts, to however many being for the sake of something seems to belong, wherever everything happened to come together just as if it had been for the sake of something, these were preserved, having been put together advantageously by chance.

30   Anything that is not like that has perished and still perishes, just as Empedocles says of man-headed offspring of cattle.

The account, then, by means of which one might come to an impasse, is this one or any other that might be of this kind; but it is impossible for things to be this way. For these

35   things and all things that are by nature come about as they do either always or for the most part, but none of the things from fortune or chance do. For it does not seem to be from fortune or by coincidence that it rains often in winter, but it does if this happens in the dog

199ª   days, nor scorching heat in the dog days, but in winter. If, then, it seems that something is either by coincidence or for the sake of something, and if things by nature cannot be by either coincidence or chance, they would be for the sake of something. But surely such

5   things are all by nature, as even those making these arguments would say. Therefore, there is being-for-the-sake-of-something among things that happen and are by nature.

Further, among all things that are for some end, it is for the sake of this that what precedes it in succession is done. Accordingly, in the way that one performs an action, so

10   also are things by nature, and as things are by nature, so does one perform each action unless something interferes. But one acts for the sake of something, and therefore what is by nature is for the sake of something. For example, if a house were something that came into being by nature, it would come about in just the way that it now does by art, and if the things by nature were to come about not only by nature but also by art, they too would

15   come about in exactly the same way as they do by nature. Therefore each is for the sake of another. And in general, art in some cases completes what nature is unable to finish off, but in others imitates nature. If then, what comes from art is for the sake of something, it is clear that what comes from nature is too, for the series of things from art and from nature are alike, each to each, in the way that the later things are related to the earlier.

20   This is clear most of all in the other animals, which do nothing by art, inquiry, or deliberation; for which reason some people are completely at a loss whether it is by intelligence or in some other way that spiders, ants, and such things work. But if we

move forward little by little in this way, it becomes apparent that even in plants what is brought together comes about in relation to the end, as the leaves for the sake of protec- 25 tion for the fruit. So if both by nature and for the sake of something the swallow makes a nest and the spider a web, and the plants make their leaves for the sake of their fruit, and their roots not upward but downward for the sake of nourishment, it is clear that there is such a cause in things that come into being and are by nature. And since nature 30 is twofold, both material and form, and the latter is an end but the former is for the sake of an end, the form would be the cause for the sake of which.

Now missing the mark happens even among things done according to art (for the grammarian on occasion writes, or the doctor gives out a drug, incorrectly), so it is clear 199^b that this is possible also among things done by nature. But if there are some things according to art in which what is done correctly is for the sake of something, but in the ones that miss the mark what is done is for the sake of something that is attempted but missed, it is the same among natural things, and monsters are failures of that for the 5 sake of which they are. Therefore even the cattle-offspring, in their original constitu- tion, if they were not able to come to some limit and end, would have come into being when some originating cause in them was disabled, as might happen now with the seed. Still it is necessary that a seed come into being first, and not straightaway the animals; "first the mixed-natured" was the seed. That for the sake of which is also present in plants, though less articulated. So then did there come about among the plants, like the 10 man-headed offspring of cattle, also olive-headed offspring of grapevines, or not? It would be strange, but it would be necessary, if it also happened among animals.

In general, it would be necessary, among seeds, that whatever chanced come into being, but the one speaking this way abolishes nature and what is by nature. For by nature are as many things as, moved continuously by some source in themselves, reach some 15 end; from each beginning does not come the same end for them all, nor just what chances, but each always reaches the same end unless something interferes. That for the sake of which, and that which is for the sake of this, might also happen by fortune, as we say that 20 a stranger came by fortune and, having paid the ransom, went away, when he acted as though having come for the sake of this, but did not come for the sake of this. And this is incidental (for fortune is among the incidental causes, just as we said before), but when- ever this happens always or for the most part, it is neither incidental nor by fortune. But 25 among natural things, things happen always in the same way, unless something interferes.

It is absurd to think that a thing does not happen for the sake of something if we do not see what sets it in motion deliberating. Surely even art does not deliberate. If shipbuilding were present in wood, it would act in the same way as nature does, so 30 if being for the sake of something is present in art, it is also present in nature. This is most clear when someone practices medicine himself on himself; for nature is like that. That, then, nature is a cause, and in this way, for the sake of something, is clear.

9. Does what is by necessity belong to things conditionally or simply? For now 35 people suppose that what is by necessity is in the coming into being of things, as if some- one were to think that the wall of a house came into being by necessity, because the 200^a heavy things are of a nature to be carried downward and the light ones on top, so that the stones and foundations are at the bottom, the earth above on account of its lightness, and at the very top the wood, since it is lightest. But even though it did not come into being without these things, it surely did not do so as a result of them, except as by means of 5 material, but rather for the sake of enclosing and sheltering certain things. And similarly with everything else, in whatever being-for-the-sake-of something is present, each thing is neither without things having necessity in their nature, nor as a result of them other

than as material, but for the sake of something. For example, why is a saw thus? In order
to do this and for the sake of this. But this which it is for the sake of would be incapable
of coming about if it were not made of iron. It is necessary, therefore, that it be of iron if
the saw and its work are to be. So the necessary is conditional, unlike the end. For the
necessary is in the material, but that for the sake of which is in what is grasped in speech.

The necessary is present both in mathematics and in things that come about by
nature, in ways closely resembling one another. For since the straight is a certain way,
it is necessary that the triangle be equal to two right angles, but not the former because
of the latter, despite the fact that were this not so, neither would the straight be as it is.
But in things that come to be for the sake of something, contrariwise, if the end is to be
or is, then what precedes it will be or is; and if not, just as there [in mathematics] the
first principle will not be so when the conclusion is not, so also here [in nature] with
the end and that for the sake of which. For this too is a starting point, not of action but
of reasoning (and of reasoning there; for there are no actions). So that if a house is to
be, it is necessary that there come into being or be present or in general be these things
as material for the sake of something, such as bricks and stones if it is a house.
Nevertheless, the end is not present as a result of these, other than as material, nor will
it be, just because of them. In general, however, neither the house nor the saw will be
if the bricks, in the former case, and the iron in the latter, are not; for neither will the
starting points be the case there if the triangle is not two right angles.

It is clear that the necessary in natural things is the so-called material and its motions.
And both must be stated as causes by the one who studies nature, but more so that for the
sake of which. For this is responsible for the material, but the material is not responsible for
the end. And the end is that for the sake of which, and the beginning comes from the definition and that which is grasped in speech; just as in things that come from art, since the
house is such, these things must come into being or be present necessarily, and since health
is such, *these* things must come into being or be present necessarily—so also if a human
being is such, these things, but if these, these others in turn. Perhaps the necessary is even in
the definition. For the work of sawing having been defined as a certain kind of dividing, this
will not be unless it has teeth of a certain kind, and these will not be of that kind unless they
are of iron. For even in the definition there are certain parts, as material of the definition.

METAPHYSICS (in part)

BOOK I

1. All human beings by nature stretch themselves out toward knowing. A sign of
this is our love of the senses; for even apart from their use, they are loved on their own
account, and above all the rest, the one through the eyes. For not only in order that we
might act, but even when we are not going to act at all, we prefer seeing, one might say,
as against everything else. And the cause is that, among the senses, this one most of all

makes us discover things, and makes evident many differences. By nature, then, the animals come into being having sense perception, though in some of them memory does not emerge out of this, while in others it does. And for this reason, these latter are more intelligent and more able to learn than those that are unable to remember, while as many of them as are not able to hear sounds are intelligent without learning (such as a bee, or any other kind of animal that might be of this sort), but as many do learn as have this sense in addition to memory. So the other animals live by images and memories, but have a small share of experience, but the human race lives also by art and reasoning. And for human beings, experience arises from memory, since many memories of the same thing bring to completion a capacity for one experience.

980^b

25

981^a

Now experience seems to be almost the same thing as knowledge or art, but for human beings, knowledge and art result from experience, for experience makes art, as Polus says and says rightly, but inexperience makes chance. And art comes into being whenever, out of many conceptions from experience, one universal judgment arises about those that are similar. For to have a judgment that this thing was beneficial to Callias when he was sick with this disease, and to Socrates, and one by one in this way to many people, belongs to experience. But the judgment that it was beneficial to all such people, marked out as being of one kind, when they were sick with this disease, such as to sluggish or irritable people when they were feverish with heat, belongs to art. For the purpose of acting, experience doesn't seem to differ from art at all, and we even see people with experience being more successful than those who have a rational account without experience. (The cause of this is that experience is familiarity with things that are particular, but art with those that are universal, while actions and all becoming are concerned with what is particular. For the doctor does not cure a human being, except incidentally, but Callias or Socrates or any of the others called by such a name, who happens to be a human being. So if someone without experience has the reasoned account and is familiar with the universal, but is ignorant of what is particular within it, he will often go astray in his treatment, since what is treated is particular.)

5

10

15

20

Nevertheless, we think that knowing and understanding are present in art more than is experience and we take the possessors of arts to be wiser than people with experience, as though in every instance wisdom is more something resulting from and following along with knowing; and this is because the ones know the cause while the others do not. For people with experience know the what, but do not know the why, but the others are acquainted with the why and the cause. For this reason we also think the master craftsmen in each kind of work are more honorable and know more than the manual laborers, and are also wiser, because they know the causes of the things they do, as though people are wiser not as a result of being skilled at action, but as a result of themselves having the reasoned account and knowing the causes. And in general, a sign of the one who knows and the one who does not is being able to teach, and for this reason we regard the art, more than the experience, to be knowledge, since the ones can, but the others cannot, teach.

25

30

981^b

5

Further, we consider none of the senses to be wisdom, even though they are the most authoritative ways of knowing particulars; but they do not pick out the why of anything, such as why fire is hot, but only that it is hot. So it is likely that the one who first discovered any art whatever that was beyond the common perceptions was wondered at by people, not only on account of there being something useful in his discoveries, but as someone wise and distinguished from other people. But once more arts had been discovered, and some of them were directed toward necessities but others toward a way of living, it is likely that such people as were discoverers of the latter kind were always considered wiser, because their knowledge was not directed toward use. Hence when all such arts had been built up, those among the kinds of knowledge directed at neither

10

15

20

pleasure nor necessity were discovered, and first in those places where there was
leisure. It is for this reason that the mathematical arts were first constructed in the
25   neighborhood of Egypt, for there the tribe of priests was allowed to live in leisure.

Now it has been said in the writings on ethics what the difference is among art,
demonstrative knowledge, and the other things of a similar kind, but the purpose for
which we are now making this argument is that all people assume that what is called
30   wisdom is concerned with first causes and origins. Therefore, as was said above, the
person with experience seems wiser than those who have any perception whatever, the
artisan wiser than those with experience, the master craftsman wiser than the manual
982ᵃ   laborer, and the contemplative arts more so than the productive ones. It is apparent,
then, that wisdom is a knowledge concerned with certain sources and causes.

2. Since we are seeking this knowledge, this should be examined: about what sort of
5   causes and what sort of sources wisdom is the knowledge. Now if one takes the accepted
opinions we have about the wise man, perhaps from this it will become more clear. We
assume first that the wise man knows all things, in the way that it is possible, though he
10   does not have knowledge of them as particulars. Next, we assume that the one who is able
to know things that are difficult, and not easy for a human being to know, is wise; for perceiving is common to everyone, for which reason it is an easy thing and nothing wise.
Further, we assume the one who has more precision and is more able to teach the causes
is wiser concerning each kind of knowledge. And among the kinds of knowledge, we
15   assume the one that is for its own sake and chosen for the sake of knowing more to be wisdom than the one chosen for the sake of results, and that the more ruling one is wisdom
more so than the more subordinate one; for the wise man ought not to be commanded but
to give orders, and ought not to obey someone else, but the less wise ought to obey him.

20   We have, then, such and so many accepted opinions about wisdom and those who
are wise. Now of these, the knowing of all things must belong to the one who has most of
all the universal knowledge, since he knows in a certain way all the things that come under
it; and these are just about the most difficult things for human beings to know, those that
are most universal, since they are farthest away from the senses. And the most precise of
25   the kinds of knowledge are the ones that are most directed at first things, since those that
reason from fewer things are more precise than those that reason from extra ones, as arithmetic is more precise than geometry. But surely the skill that is suited to teach is the one
that has more insight into causes, for those people teach who give an account of the causes
about each thing. And knowing and understanding for their own sakes belong most to the
30   knowledge of what is most knowable. For the one who chooses what is known through
982ᵇ   itself would most of all be choosing that which is knowledge most of all, and of this sort
is the knowledge of what is most knowable. But what are most knowable are the first
things and the causes, for through these and from these the other things are known, but
these are not known through what comes under them. And the most ruling of the kinds of
5   knowledge, or the one more ruling than what is subordinate to it, is the one that knows for
what purpose each thing must be done; and this is the good of each thing, and in general
the best thing in the whole of nature. So from all the things that have been said, the name
sought falls to the same kind of knowledge, for it must be a contemplation of the first
10   sources and causes, since also the good, or that for the sake of which, is one of the causes.

That it is not a productive knowledge is clear too from those who first engaged in
philosophy. For by way of wondering, people both now and at first began to philosophize, wondering first about the strange things near at hand, then going forward little by
15   little in this way and coming to impasses about greater things, such as about the attributes
of the moon and things pertaining to the sun and the stars and the coming into being of

the whole. But someone who wonders and is at an impasse considers himself to be ignorant (for which reason the lover of myth is in a certain way philosophic, since a myth is composed of wonders). So if it was by fleeing ignorance that they philosophized, it is clear that by means of knowing they were in pursuit of knowing, and not for the sake of any kind of use. And the following testifies to the same thing: for it was when just about all the necessities were present, as well as things directed toward the greatest ease and recreation, that this kind of understanding began to be sought. It is clear then that we seek it for no other use at all, but just as that human being is free, we say, who has his being for his own sake and not for the sake of someone else, so also do we seek it as being the only one of the kinds of knowledge that is free, since it alone is for its own sake.

For this reason one might justly regard the possession of it as not appropriate to humans. For in many ways human nature is slavish, so that, according to Simonides, "only a god should have this honor," but a man is not worthy of seeking anything but the kind of knowledge that fits him. If indeed the poets have a point and it is the nature of the divine power to be jealous, it would be likely to happen most of all in this case, and all extraordinary people would be ill-fated. But it is not even possible for the divine power to be jealous, but according to the common saying "many lyrics are lies," and one ought not to regard anything else as more honorable than this knowledge. For the most divine is also the most honorable, and this knowledge by itself would be most divine in two ways. For what most of all a god would have is that among the kinds of knowledge that is divine, if in fact any of them were about divine things. But this one alone happens to have both these characteristics; for the divine seems to be among the causes for all things, and to be a certain source, and such knowledge a god alone, or most of all, would have. All kinds of knowledge, then, are more necessary than this one, but none is better.

It is necessary, however, for the possession of it to settle for us in a certain way into the opposite of the strivings with which it began. For everyone begins, as we are saying, from wondering whether things are as they seem, such as the self-moving marvels, or about the reversals of the sun or the incommensurability of the diagonal (for it seems amazing to all those who have not yet seen the cause if anything is not measured by the smallest part). But it is necessary to end in what is opposite and better, as the saying goes, just as in these cases when people understand them; for nothing would be so surprising to a geometer as if the diagonal were to become commensurable. What, then, is the nature of the knowledge being sought, has been said, and what the object is on which the inquiry and the whole pursuit must alight.

3. Since it is clear that one must take hold of a knowledge of the causes that originate things (since that is when we say we know each thing, when we think we know its first cause), while the causes are meant in four ways, of which one is thinghood,* or what it is for something to be (since the why leads back to the ultimate reasoned account, and the first why is a cause and source), another is the material or underlying thing, a third is that from which the source of motion is, and the fourth is the cause opposite to that one, that for the sake of which or the good (since it is the completion of every coming-into-being and motion), which have been sufficiently looked into by us in the writings about nature, still, let us take up also those who came before us into the inquiry about beings and philosophized about truth. For it is clear that they too speak of certain sources and causes. So for those who go back over these things, there will be some profit for the

20

25

30

983ᵃ

5

10

15

20

25

30

983ᵇ

---

*<ousia>, often translated "substance," means (as our translator puts it) "the way of being that belongs to anything which has attributes but is not an attribute of anything, which is also separate and a *this*. Whatever has being in this way is an independent thing."

Bust of Aristotle, First century copy of Greek sculpture, Louvre. Using Aristotle's Four Causes, we would say the *material cause* of this bust is marble (that *out of which* it was made), the *formal cause* is a bust of Aristotle (that *into which* it was made), the *efficient cause* is the sculptor who carved it (that *by which* it was made), and the *final cause* is to honor or memorialize Aristotle (that *for the sake of which* it was made). (*Forrest E. Baird/Musee du Louvre/RMN Reunion des Musees Nationaux, France. SCALA/Art Resource, N.Y.*)

5   present pursuit; for we will either find out some other kind of cause or be more persuaded about the ones we are now speaking of. Of those who first engaged in philosophy,
most thought that the only sources of all things were of the species of material; that of
which all things are made, out of which they first come into being and into which they
10   are at last destroyed, its thinghood abiding but changing in its attributes, this they claim
is the element and origin of things, for which reason nothing ever comes into being or
perishes, since this sort of nature is always preserved, just as we would not say either that
Socrates simply comes into being when he becomes beautiful or educated in refined pur-
15   suits, or that he perishes when he sheds these conditions, since the underlying thing,
Socrates himself, persists, so neither does anything else. For there must be some nature,
either one or multiple, out of which the other things come into being while that one is
preserved. About the number and kind of such sources, however, they do not all say the
20   same thing, but Thales, the founder of this sort of philosophy, says it is water (for which
reason too he declared that the earth is on water), getting hold of this opinion perhaps
from seeing that the nourishment of all things is fluid, and that heat itself comes about
from it and lives by means of it (and that out of which things come into being is the
25   source of them all). So he got hold of this opinion by this means, and because the seeds
of all things have a fluid nature, while water is in turn the source of the nature of fluid
things.

There are some who think that very ancient thinkers, long before the present age,
who gave the first accounts of the gods, had an opinion of this sort about nature. For they
30   made Ocean and Tethys the parents of what comes into being, and made the oath of the

gods be by water, called Styx by them; for what is oldest is most honored, and that by which one swears is the most honored thing. But whether this opinion about nature is something archaic and ancient might perhaps be unclear, but Thales at least is said to have spoken in this way about the first cause. (One would not consider Hippo worthy to place among these, on account of his cut-rate thinking.) Anaximenes and Diogenes set down air as more primary than water and as the most originative of the simple bodies, while Hippasus of Metapontium and Heraclitus of Ephesus set down fire, and Empedocles, adding earth as a fourth to those mentioned, sets down the four (for he says these always remain and do not come into being except in abundance or fewness, being combined and separated into or out of one). Anaxagoras of Clazomenae, who was before Empedocles in age but after him in his works, said the sources were infinite; for he said that almost all homogeneous things are just like water or fire in coming into being or perishing only by combination and separation, but otherwise neither come into being nor perish but remain everlasting.

984ᵃ

5

10

15

From these things, then, one might suppose that the only cause is the one accounted for in the species of material; but as people went forward in this way, their object of concern itself opened a road for them, and contributed to forcing them to inquire along it. For no matter how much every coming-into-being and destruction is out of some one or more kinds of material, why does this happen and what is its cause? For surely the underlying material itself does not make itself change. I mean, for example, neither wood nor bronze is responsible, respectively, for its own changing, nor does the wood make a bed or the bronze a statue, but something else is responsible for the change. But to inquire after this is to seek that other kind of source, which we would call that from which the origin of motion is. Now some of these who from the very beginning applied themselves to this sort of pursuit and said that the underlying material was one thing, were not at all displeased with their own accounts, but some of those who said it was one, as though defeated by this inquiry, said that the one and the whole of nature were motionless, not only with respect to coming into being and destruction (for this is present from the beginning and everyone agrees to it), but also with respect to every other kind of change, and this is peculiar to them. So of those who said that the whole is one, none happened to catch sight of this sort of cause unless in fact Parmenides did, and he only to the extent that he set down the causes as being not only one but in some way two. But it is possible to say so about those who made things more than one, such as hot and cold, or fire and earth; for they use the nature of fire as having the power to set things in motion, but water and earth and such things as the opposite.

20

25

30

984ᵇ

5

But after these people and sources of this kind, since they were not sufficient to generate the nature of things, again by the truth itself, as we say, people were forced to look for the next kind of source. For that some beings are in a good or beautiful condition, or come into being well or beautifully, it is perhaps not likely that fire or earth or any other such thing is responsible, nor that they would have thought so. Nor, in turn, would it be a good idea to turn over so great a concern to chance or luck. So when someone said an intellect was present, just as in animals, also in nature as the cause of the cosmos and of all order, he looked like a sober man next to people who had been speaking incoherently beforehand. Obviously we know that Anaxagoras reached as far as saying these things, but Hermotimus of Clazomenae is given credit for saying them earlier. Those, then, who took things up in this way set down a source which is at the same time the cause of the beautiful among things and the sort of cause from which motion belongs to things.

10

15

20

4. One might suspect that Hesiod was the first one to seek out such a thing, or someone else who had set down love or desire among the beings as a source, as Parmenides

also did; for he, in getting things ready for the coming into being of the whole, says that
25   first "of all the gods, [the all-governing divinity] devised love," while Hesiod says

> Chaos came into being as the very first of all things, but then
> Broad-breasted earth . . . and also
> Love, who shines out from among all the immortals,

30   as though there needed to be present among beings some sort of cause that would move
things and draw them together. Now how I ought to distribute their portions to them
about who was first, permit me to postpone judging. But since the opposites of the good
985ᵃ   things are obviously also present in nature, and there is not only order and beauty but
also disorder and ugliness, and more bad and ordinary things than good and beautiful
ones, in this way someone else brought in friendship and strife, each as the cause of one
of these kinds of thing. For if one were to pursue and get hold of Empedocles' thinking,
5   rather than what he said inarticulately, one would find that friendship was the cause of
the good things and strife of the bad. So if one were to claim that Empedocles both says
and is the first to say that bad and good are sources, one would perhaps speak rightly, if
10   in fact the cause of all good things is the good itself.
     So these people, as we are saying, evidently got this far with two causes out of those
we distinguished in the writings about nature, the material and that from which the motion
is, but did so dimly and with no clarity, rather in the way non-athletes do in fights; for
15   while dancing around they often land good punches, but they do not do so out of knowledge, nor do these people seem to know what they are saying. For it is obvious that they
use these causes scarcely ever, and only to a tiny extent. For Anaxagoras uses the intellect
as a makeshift contrivance for cosmos production, and whenever he comes to an impasse
20   about why something is necessarily a certain way, he drags it in, but in the other cases he
assigns as the causes of what happens everything but the intellect; and Empedocles,
though he uses his causes more than that, surely does not either use them sufficiently or
come up with any consistency with them. Certainly in many places friendship separates
25   things for him, and strife combines things. For whenever the whole is divided by strife
into its elements, fire is combined into one, as is each of the other elements; but whenever
they come back together into one, the parts must be separated back out of each element.
Empedocles was the first who, beyond those before him, brought in this sort of cause by
30   dividing it, making the source of motion not one thing but different and opposite ones, and
furthermore, he first spoke of the so-called four elements as the causes in the species of
985ᵇ   material. (In fact, though, he didn't use them as four, but as though they were only two:
fire on one side by itself, and its opposites, earth, air, and water, as one nature on the other
side. One may get this by looking carefully at what is in the verses.)
     So as we are saying, he claimed that the sources were of this sort and this many.
5   But Leucippus and his colleague Democritus say the elements are the full and the void,
of which the one, as what is, is full and solid, while the other, what is not, is void (for
which reason they say that being in no sense *is* more than nonbeing, nor body more so
10   than void), and that these are responsible for things as material. And just as those who
make the underlying being one, and generate the other things by means of modifications of it, set down the rare and the dense as the sources of the modifications, in the
same way these people too say that the differences in the material are responsible for
15   the other things. They, however, say these differences are three: shape, order, and position. For they say that what is differs only by means of "design, grouping, and twist,"
but of these, design is shape, grouping is order, and twist is position. For A differs from
N in shape, AN from NA in order, and Z from N in position. As for motion, from what

source or in what way it belongs to things, these people, much like the others, lazily let   20
it go. So about the two causes, as we are saying, the inquiry seems to have gone this far
on the part of our predecessors.

5. But among these people and before them, those who are called Pythagoreans, taking up mathematical things, were the first to promote these, and having been reared on   25
them, they supposed that the sources of them were the sources of all things. And since
numbers are by nature primary among these, and in them they thought they saw many similarities to the things that are and come to be, more so than in fire or earth or water—that
such-and-such an attribute of numbers was justice, so-and-so is soul or intellect, another   30
one due measure, and likewise with, one might say, everything—and what's more, saw in
numbers the properties and explanations of musical harmonies, since then the entire nature
of the other things seemed to be after the likeness of numbers, and the numbers seemed to
be the primary things in all nature, they assumed that the elements of numbers were the ele-   986^a
ments of all things, and that the whole heaven was a harmony and a number. And as many
things among numbers and harmonies as had analogies to the attributes and parts of the
heavens and to the whole cosmic array, they collected and fit together. And if anything was
left out anywhere, they were persistent, so that everything would be strung together for   5
them as a system. I mean, for example, since the number ten seemed to be complete and to
include the whole nature of numbers, they said that the things that move through the heavens are also ten, but since there are only nine visible, for this reason they made the tenth the   10
counter-earth. But this is set out more precisely by us in other writings.*
But the purpose for which we are recounting these things is this: that we might
understand from these people both what they set down as causes, and how they fall in   15
with the kinds of causes described. Now it is obvious that they consider number to be a
cause both as material for things and as responsible for their attributes and states; that
they consider the elements of number to be the even and the odd, of which the latter is
limited but the former unlimited; that they consider the number one to be composed of   20
both of these (for it is both even and odd); and that they consider number to arise from
the one, and the whole heaven, as was said, to be numbers.
Various ones of these same people say that there are ten causes, gathered into a
series of corresponding pairs: 25

limit	unlimited
odd	even
one	many
right	left
male	female
still	moving
straight	crooked
light	dark
good	bad
square	oblong.

In this way too Alcmaeon of Croton seems to have taken it up, and he either got it from
them or they got this account from him, since Alcmaeon expressed himself in much the   30

*See *On the Heavens*, Bk. II, Ch. 13. The Pythagoreans, among other ancients, put the sun at the center
and the earth in motion. The counter-earth was conceived as a dark planet, moving at the same rate as the earth,
always concealed by the sun. (The number of nine celestial bodies counts the sphere of the fixed stars as one
thing, along with the five visible planets and the earth, moon, and sun.)

way they did. For he says that many human things are twofold, referring not just to the oppositions as they distinguished them, but to any there might happen to be, such as

986^b white/black, sweet/bitter, good/bad, big/little. So he spread out indiscriminate statements about the rest of them, but the Pythagoreans declared how many and what the oppositions were. From both Alcmaeon and the Pythagoreans there is this much that one may gather, that the sources of things are contraries, and from the latter, how many

5 and what these are. But in what way it is possible to bring them into line with the kinds of causes described was not clearly articulated by these people, though they seem to rank them as in the species of material, since they say that being is put together and molded out of these contraries as constituents.

10 So of the ancients who said that the elements of nature are more than one, it is also sufficient from the preceding to see their thinking. But there are some who declared about the whole that it is one nature, though not all in the same way, either in how good their thinking was or with respect to the nature. An account about them in no way fits

15 into the present examination of the causes (for they do not speak in the same way as some writers about nature, who set down being as one but generate things out of the one as from material, but in a different way, since those others add in motion when they generate the whole, but these people say that it is motionless). Nonetheless, it can find a home in this inquiry to this extent: Parmenides seems to take hold of what is one

20 according to reason, Melissus of what is one in material (on account of which one says that it is finite, the other infinite). But Xenophanes, the first of these who made things one (for Parmenides is said to have become a student of his), made nothing clear, nor does he seem to have made contact with nature in either of these two ways, but gazing

25 off into the whole heaven, he said that divinity was one. So these, as we say, must be dismissed from the present inquiry, two of them completely as being a little too crude, Xenophanes and Melissus, though Parmenides to some degree seems to speak with more insight; for since he thought it fit that besides being, nonbeing could not be in any

30 way, he necessarily supposed that being is one and that there is nothing else (about which we have spoken more clearly in the writings about nature), but being forced to follow appearances, and assuming that what is one from the standpoint of reason is more than one from the standpoint of perception, he set down in turn two causes and two sources, a hot one and a cold one, as though speaking of something like fire and

987^a earth, and of these he ranks the hot one under being and the other under nonbeing.

So from what has been said, and from the wise men who have so far sat in council in our account, we have ascertained these things: from the first ones that the origin of

5 things is corporeal (since water and fire and things of that sort are bodies), and from some of them that the corporeal source is one, from others more than one, both kinds, however, placing them as in the species of material; and from others that there is this sort of cause and in addition to it one from which the motion is, while from some of them that

10 this cause is one, from others that it is twofold. So up to the time of the Italians [i.e., the Pythagoreans], and apart from them, the others have spoken about these things in ways that made them murkier, except, as we say, they happened to use two kinds of cause, and one of these, that from which the motion is, some made one and others twofold. Now the

15 Pythagoreans have said in the same way that the sources are two, but they added on top of that this much that is peculiar to them, that they did not consider the limited and the unlimited to be natures belonging to any other things, such as fire or earth or anything else of that sort, but that the unlimited itself and the one itself are the thinghood of the

20 things to which they are attributed, for which reason also, number is the thinghood of all things. About these things, then, they spoke in this way, and they were the first to speak about and define the what-it-is of things, though they handled it in too simple a way. For

they defined superficially, and the primary thing to which the stated definition belonged, they considered to be the thinghood of the thing, just as if one were to suppose that the number two and double were the same thing, because doubleness belongs first of all to the number two. But still it is not the same thing to be double and to be two; otherwise what is one would be many, which in fact is the way it turned out for these people. So from those who came before us, there is this much to grasp.

6. After the philosophic speculations that have been mentioned came the careful work of Plato, which in many ways followed the lead of these people, but also had separate features that went beyond the philosophy of the Italians. For having become acquainted from youth at first with Cratylus and the Heracleitean teachings that all sensible things are always in flux and that there is no knowledge of them, he also conceived these things that way later on. And since Socrates exerted himself about ethical matters and not at all about the whole of nature, but in the former sought the universal and was the first to be skilled at thinking about definitions, Plato, when he adopted this, took it up as applying to other things and not to sensible ones, because of this: it was impossible that there be any common definition of any of the perceptible things since they were always changing. So he called this other sort of beings forms, and said the perceptible things were apart from these and all spoken of derivatively from these, for the many things with the same names as the forms were results of participation. He changed only the name participation, for the Pythagoreans said that beings *are* by way of imitation of the numbers, but Plato by way of participation, having changed the name. What this participation or imitation of the forms might be, however, they were in unison in leaving behind to be sought.

What's more, apart from the sensible things and the forms, he said there were among things mathematical ones, in between, differing from the sensible ones in being everlasting and motionless, and from the forms in that there are any multitude of them alike, while each form itself is only one. And since the forms are the causes of the others, he thought that the elements of the forms were the elements of all beings. As material, then, the great and the small were the sources, and as thinghood, the one, for out of the former, by participation in the one, the forms are composed as numbers. So in saying that the one was an independent thing, and not any other thing said to be one, he spoke in much the same way as the Pythagoreans, and in saying that numbers were the causes of thinghood for other things he spoke exactly as they did; but to have made a dyad in place of the infinite as one thing, and to have made the infinite out of the great and the small, was peculiar to him. It was also peculiar to him to set the numbers apart from the perceptible things, while they had said that the things themselves were numbers, and they did not set the mathematical things between them. Now his having made the one and the numbers be apart from the things we handle, and not the same way the Pythagoreans had said, and his introduction of the forms came about because of his investigation in the realm of definitions (for the earlier thinkers had no part in dialectic), but his having made the other nature a dyad was so that the numbers, outside of the primes, might be generated out of it in a natural way, as though from some sort of modeling clay.

But surely things happen in the opposite way, for this way is not reasonable. For they make many things out of this material, while the form generates only once, but it is apparent that from one material comes one table, while the person who brings the form to bear, though he is one, makes many tables. And it is similar with the male in relation to the female; for she becomes pregnant by one act of intercourse, while the male is the cause of many pregnancies, and surely these things are images of the origins of things. But Plato made distinctions in this way about the things that are being sought, and it is clear from what has been said that he used only two causes, the one that is responsible

for the what-it-is and the one that results from material (for the forms are causes for the other things of what they are, and the one is such a cause for the forms). And it is clear what the underlying material is said to be, over against which the forms are, in the case of perceptible things, and the one, among the forms, that it is the dyad of the great and
15   the small. And further, he referred the cause of what is good and bad respectively to each of the two elements, just as we say certain of the earlier philosophers, such as Empedocles and Anaxagoras, were trying to find a way to do.

7. In a curtailed way, then, and hitting the high spots, we have gotten hold of who happens to have spoken about origins and truth, and in what way. Still, we get this much
20   from them: that of those who have spoken about origin and cause, not one has said anything that went outside those that were distinguished by us in the writings on nature, but all of them, though murkily, have obviously touched on them in some way. For some speak of
25   the source as material, whether they set it down as one or more than one, and whether they set it up as a body or as bodiless. (For example, Plato speaks of the great and the small, the Italians of the unlimited, Empedocles of fire, earth, water, and air, and Anaxagoras of the infinity of homogeneous things; now all of these have gotten hold of this sort of cause, as
30   also have all those who speak of air or fire or water or something denser than fire but less dense than air, since some people have said that the primary element is of this sort.)
So these people have grasped only this sort of cause, but some others have grasped the sort from which the source of motion is (as have all those who make friendship and strife, or intellect, or love a source). But about what it is for something to be,
988ᵇ   and thinghood, no one has delivered up a clear account, but those who posit the forms speak of it most. (For they do not take up the forms as material of perceptible things or the one as material of the forms, nor either the forms or the one as anything from which the source of motion comes—for they say rather that they are responsible for motionlessness and being at rest—but they offer the forms as what it is for each of the other
5   things to be, and the one as what it is for the forms to be.)
That for the sake of which actions and changes and motions are, they speak of as a cause in a certain way, but they do not say it that way, nor speak of what is so by its very nature. For those who speak of intellect or friendship as good set these up as causes, but
10   do not speak as though anything that is either has its being or comes into being for the sake of these, but as though motions arose from these. And in the same way too, those who speak of the one or being as such a nature do say that it is the cause of thinghood, but not that it either is or comes about for the sake of this; so it turns out that they in a certain way both say and do not say that the good is a cause, since they say it is so not simply but
15   incidentally. So all these people seem also to bear witness that the right distinctions have been made by us about the causes, as to both how many and of what sort they are, since they have not been able to touch on another kind of cause; and it is clear in addition that the sources of things must be sought either all in this way or in some particular way from
20   among them. After this, then, let us go through the possible impasses that concern the way each of these people spoke and how each one stands toward the sources.

8. Now it is clear that all those who set down the whole as one, and some one nature as material, and this as bodily and having magnitude, erred in many ways. For
25   they set down elements of bodies only, but not of bodiless things, though there are also bodiless ones. And when they turn their hands to giving an account of the causes of coming-into-being and destruction, in fact when they give accounts of the natures of all things, they abolish the cause of motion. What's more, they err by not setting down

thinghood as a cause at all, nor the what-it-is of things, and on top of this by casually   30
calling any one whatever of the simple bodies, except earth, a source, without examining the way they are made by coming into being out of one another; I am speaking of
fire, water, earth, and air. For some of them do come into being out of others by combination, and others by separation, but this makes the greatest difference toward being
more primary and more derivative. For in one sense the most elementary thing of all
would seem to be that out of which things first come into being by combination, and it   989ª
is the most finely divided and lightest of bodies that would be of this sort. (For this reason, all those who set up fire as a source would be speaking most in conformity to this
argument, but each of the others also agrees that the element of bodies is of this sort. At   5
any rate, none of those who said there was one element thought it fitting for it to be
earth, obviously because of its coarse texture, while each of the three elements has won
over some judge, for some say this to be fire, some water, and some air. So why in the
world don't they also name earth, as most people do? For these do say everything is   10
earth, and Hesiod says that the earth was the first of bodies to come into being—so
ancient and popular has this judgment happened to be.) So according to this argument,
one could not speak rightly if he were to name any of these except fire, nor if he set up
something denser than air but less dense than water. On the other hand, if what is later   15
in its coming into being is more primary in its nature, and what is ripened and compounded is later in its coming into being, the contrary of these things would be the case,
and water would be more primary than air, and earth more primary than water.

Now about those people who set up one cause of the sort we are speaking of, let   20
these things we have said be sufficient; but the same thing may also be said if someone
sets these up as more than one, as Empedocles says the material consists of four bodies.
For in some ways the same things must turn out for him too, as well as others peculiar
to him. For we see them come into being out of one another, as though the same body
does not always remain fire or earth (but these things were spoken of in the writings   25
about nature), and as for the cause of moving things, whether one ought to set it down
as one or two, one ought not to suppose that he spoke either correctly or even completely reasonably. And it is necessary that those who speak this way abolish qualitative
change altogether, for cold will not come from hot nor hot from cold. For then something would undergo the opposite conditions themselves, and there would be some one   30
nature which became fire and water, which he denies.

And if one assumes that Anaxagoras spoke of two elements, one's assumption would
be very much in accord with reason, though he himself did not articulate this; nevertheless
it follows necessarily for those who track him down. Now while it is absurd to say that at
their source all things are mixed together, not only for other reasons, but also because they
would have to turn out to have been present all along as unmixed, and because it is not in   989ᵇ
accord with nature for any chance thing to be mixed with any other, and on top of these
things, because properties and incidental attributes could be separated from the things they
belong to (for of the same things of which there is mixing, there is also separating); nevertheless, it one were to follow it up, articulating thoroughly what he wanted to say, he would
perhaps appear to be speaking in something more like the latest fashion. For when nothing   5
was separated, it is clear that there was nothing true to say about the thinghood of that mixture; I mean, for example, that it was neither white nor black nor gray nor any other color,
but necessarily colorless, since it would otherwise have had a certain one of these colors.
Likewise, by this same argument, it was without flavor or any other similar attribute, for it   10
would not be possible for it to be of any sort or of any amount. For then some one in
particular of the forms spoken of would have belonged to it, but this is impossible since all

are mixed together; for it would already have been separated out, while he says that all
things are mixed together except the intellect, which is the only thing unmixed and pure. So
from these things it turns out that he is saying that the sources are the one (for this is simple
and unmixed), and another which is just like what we set down as the indeterminate prior
to its being made definite and participating in some form; so while he speaks neither
correctly nor wisely, nevertheless he means something very similar to those who spoke
later and who are more manifest now.

But it is the lot of these people to be at home only with talk about becoming,
perishing, and motion, for this is just about the only sort of thing for which they seek the
sources and causes. On the other hand, all those who pay attention to all beings, of
which some are perceptible and others are not accessible to the senses, obviously make
an investigation about both kinds. For this reason one might well spend more time on
them, dwelling on what they said well or badly that goes to the inquiry that now lies in
front of us.

Now those who are called Pythagoreans make use of more remote sources and
elements than do those who write about nature. (The reason is that they do not take
them from perceptible things, since the mathematical things, apart from the ones
involved in astronomy, are without motion.) Nonetheless, they do discourse about and
concern themselves with nature in all their work. For they generate the heavens, and
observe what becomes of its parts and attributes and doings, and they lavish their
sources and causes on these, as though they agreed with the other writers on nature that
what *is* is all this that is perceptible by the senses and surrounded by what is called
heaven. But the causes and sources they speak of are, as we say, sufficient to step up
also to the higher kinds of beings, and better fitted to this than to their accounts about
nature. By what means, however, there will be motion when the limit and the unlimited,
or the odd and the even are the only things presupposed, they do not say at all, nor how
without motion and change there can be becoming and perishing, or the things done by
the things that are carried along through the heavens. What's more, even if one were to
grant them that magnitude is made out of these things, or this were demonstrated, still,
by what means will there be some bodies that have lightness and some that have heaviness? From the things they assume and say, they are speaking about mathematical
things no more than about perceptible ones; for which reason they have not said anything at all about fire or earth or the other bodies of this sort, since, I suppose, nothing
that they say about perceptible things is about them in particular.

Again, how ought one to understand number and the attributes of number to be
causes of what is and what happens in the heavens, both in the beginning and now, *and*
that there is no other kind of number besides this very number out of which the cosmos
is composed? For when, say, in some part of the cosmos there is, according to them,
opinion and due measure, and a little above or below there is injustice and either separating or mixing, and they claim as a demonstration of this that each of these is a number, but it turns out that in the same place there are already several magnitudes
combined since these attributes go along with each of the various places, ought one to
understand that this is the same number, this one that is in the heavens, that every one of
these is, or another one beside this? For Plato says that it is a different one, even though
he too assumes both these things and their causes to be numbers, but the causes to be
intelligible numbers, while these other things are sensible numbers.

9. As far as the Pythagoreans are concerned, then, let the things now said be
left alone (for it is enough to touch on them this much). But as for those who set up

the forms, first of all, in seeking to understand the causes of the things around us, they brought in other things, equal to these in number, as though someone who wanted to count a smaller number of things thought he couldn't do it, but could count them if he made them more. For the forms are just about equal to, or not fewer than, those things in search of the causes of which they went on from the latter to the former. For over against each particular thing there is something with the same name, and also for the other things besides the beings, to which there belongs a one-over-many, both among the things around us and among the everlasting things. What's more, of those ways by which we show that there are forms, it is not evident by any of them. For from some of them no necessary conclusion results, while from others there turn out to be forms of those things which we believe do not have them. For as a result of the arguments from the kinds of knowledge, there will be forms of all those things of which there is knowledge, and as a result of the one-over-many there will even be forms of negations, while as a result of the thinking of something that has been destroyed, there will be forms of things that have passed away, since there is an image of these things. On top of this, some of the most precise of the arguments produce forms of relations, which we claim is not a kind in its own right, while other ones imply the third man.

And in general, the arguments about the forms abolish things which we want there to be, more than we want there to be forms. For it turns out that not the dyad, but number, is primary, and that what is relative is more primary than what *is* in its own right, as well as all those things which certain people who took the opinions about the forms to their logical conclusions showed to be opposed to the original sources of things. What's more, by the assumption by which we say there are forms, there will be forms not only of beings but also of many other things. (For the object of the intellect is one thing not only as concerns beings but also as applied to other things, and there is demonstrative knowledge not only about thinghood but also about other sorts of being, and vast numbers of other such conclusions follow.) But both necessarily and as a result of the opinions about them, if the forms are shared in, there must be forms only of independent things. For things do not share in them incidentally, but must share in each by virtue of that by which it is not attributed to an underlying subject. (I mean, for example, if something partakes of the double, then this also partakes of the everlasting, but incidentally, since it is incidental to the double to be everlasting.) Therefore, the forms will be the thinghood of things, and the same things will signify thinghood there as here. Otherwise, what would the something be that is said to be apart from the things around us, the one-over-many? And if the forms and the things that participate in them have the same form, there would be something common. (For why is *two* one and the same thing as applied both to destructible pairs and to those that are many but everlasting, more so than as applied both to itself and to something?) But if the form is not the same, there would be ambiguity, and it would be just as if someone were to call both Callias and a block of wood "human being" while observing nothing at all common to them.

But most of all, one might be completely at a loss about what in the world the forms contribute to the perceptible things, either to the everlasting ones or to the ones that come into being and perish. For they are not responsible for any motion or change that belongs to them. But they don't assist in any way toward the knowledge of the other things either (for they are not the thinghood of them, since in that case they would be in them), nor toward their being, inasmuch as they are not present in the things that partake of them. In that manner they might perhaps seem to be causes, after the fashion of the white that is mingled in white things, but this argument, which Anaxagoras first, Eudoxus later, and some others

5

10

15

20

25

30

991[a]

5

10

15

20   made, is truly a pushover (for it is easy to collect many impossibilities related to this opinion). But surely it is not true either that the other things are made out of the forms in any of the usual ways that is meant. And to say that they are patterns and the other things participate in them is to speak without content and in poetic metaphors. For what is the thing that is at work, looking off toward the forms? And it is possible for anything whatever

25   to be or become like something without being an image of it, so that whether Socrates is or is not, one might become like Socrates, and it is obvious that it would be the same even if Socrates were everlasting. And there would be more than one pattern for the same thing, and so too with the forms; for example, of a human being, there would be animal and at the

30   same time two footed, as well as human being itself. What's more, the forms will be patterns not only of the perceptible things but also of themselves, such as the form *genus*, since

991ᵇ   it is a genus of forms, and so the same thing would be a pattern and an image.

Further, one would think it was impossible for the thinghood and that of which it is the thinghood to be separate: so how could the forms be the thinghood of things if they are separate? In the *Phaedo* it is put this way: that the forms are responsible for both being and becoming. Yet even if there are forms, still the things that partake of

5   them do not come into being if there is not something that causes motion, and many other things do come into being, such as a house or a ring, of which we say there are no forms. So it is clear that the other things too admit of being and becoming by means of the sort of causes which produce the ones just mentioned.

10   Again, if the forms are numbers, how would they be causes? Is it because the beings are various numbers, this number human being, that one Socrates, this other one Callias? Why then are those the causes of these? And it will make no difference if the ones are everlasting and the others not. But if it is because the things here are ratios of numbers, as harmony is, it is clear that there is some one thing of which they

15   are ratios. So if this is something, as material, it is apparent that the numbers themselves will also be particular ratios of one thing to another. I mean, for example, if Callias is a ratio among numbers consisting of fire, earth, water, and air, then the form too will be a number consisting of certain other underlying things, and human being

20   itself, whether or not it is a sort of number, will still be a ratio among numbers *of something,* and not a number, nor would it be on this account a certain number. What's more, from many numbers comes one number, but in what way is one form made of forms? But if it is not made of them but of the things that are in a number, as in ten thousand, how does it stand with the units? For if they are homogeneous, many absurdities will follow, and also if they are not homogeneous, either one the same as

25   another or a whole group the same as a whole group; for in what respect will they differ if they are without attributes? For these things are neither reasonable nor in agreement with a thoughtful viewing of the matter.

And on top of this, it is necessary to construct a different kind of number, with which the art of arithmetic is concerned, and all those things that are said by some to be

30   in-between; in what way *are* they and from what sources? Or by what cause are they between the things here and those things? Again, each of the units in the number two

992ᵃ   comes from some more primary dyad, yet this is impossible. Again, by what cause is a number one thing when it is taken all together? Again, on top of the things that have been said, if the units are to differ, it would behoove one to speak in the same way as those

5   who say there are four, or two, elements. For each of these people speaks of as an element not what is common, such as body, but fire or earth, whether body is something common or not. But as it is, one speaks as though the one were homogeneous, just like fire or water; and if this is so, the numbers will not be independent things. But it is clear that, if there is something that is the one itself, and this is a source, *one* is meant in more

10   than one way, for otherwise it is impossible.

Now when we want to lead things back to their sources, we set down length as being composed of the short and the long, a certain kind of small and large, and surface of the wide and the narrow, and solid of the deep and the shallow. In what way, though, will the surface have a line in it, or the solid have a line or a surface? For the wide and the narrow are different kinds of thing from the deep and the shallow; so just as number is not present in them either, because the many and the few differ from these, it is clear that neither will any other of the higher things be present in the lower. But surely neither is the wide a class of the deep, for then a solid would be a certain kind of surface. And from what source will the points come to be present in them? Plato used to fight against this class of things as a geometrical dogma, but he called the source of the line—and he set this down often—indivisible lines. And yet there must necessarily be some limit of these; so from the argument from which the line is deduced, the point too is deduced.

In general, though we are seeking wisdom about what is responsible for the appearances, we have ignored this (for we say nothing about the cause from which the source of change is), but supposing that we are speaking about the thinghood of them, we say that there are other independent things, but as for how those are the thinghood of these we speak in vain. For "participating," as we said before, is no help. But on that which we see to be a cause in the various kinds of knowledge, for the sake of which every intellect and every nature produces things, and on that sort of cause which we say is one of the sources of things, the forms do not even touch, but philosophy has turned into mathematical things for people now, though they claim that it is for the sake of other things that one ought to study them. But still, one might assume that the underlying being which serves as material is too mathematical, and is something to be attributed to or be a distinction within the being or material, rather than being material; for instance, the great and the small are just the same as what the writers on nature call the rare and the dense, claiming that these are the first distinctions within the underlying material, since they are a certain kind of the more and less. And as for motion, if these are a process of moving, it is clear that the forms would be moved; but if they are not, where does it come from? For then the whole investigation about nature would be abolished.

And what seems to be easy, to show that all things are one, does not happen; for from the premises set out, even if one grants them all, it does not come out that all things are one, but that something is the one itself; and not even this comes out if one will not grant that the universal is a genus, which in some cases is impossible. And there is no explanation of the lengths, surfaces, and solids that are present with the numbers, not of how they are or could be nor of what capacity they have; for it is not possible for them to be forms (since they are not numbers), nor the in-between things (since those are the mathematical ones), nor perishable things, but this seems in turn to be some other fourth kind.

In general, to search for the elements of whatever *is* without distinguishing the many ways this is meant, is to seek what is impossible to find, both for those inquiring in other ways and those inquiring in this way about what sort of elements things are made of. For out of what elements acting is made, or being acted upon, or the straight, is just not there to be grasped, but if of anything, it is of independent things alone that it can possibly be. Therefore to suppose that one is seeking or has the elements of *all* beings is not true. And how could anyone learn the elements of all things? For it is clear that it is not possible for someone to begin by knowing it beforehand. For just as it is possible for the one who is learning to do geometry to know other things in advance, though he does not already know any of the things of which geometry is the knowledge and about which he is going to learn, so it is also with other things, so if there is any knowledge of all things, of the sort that some people say there is, he could not start out already knowing anything.

And yet all learning is by means of things all or some of which are already known, whether it is by means of demonstration or by way of definitions (for it is necessary that

993ª one already know and be familiar with those things out of which the definition is made), and likewise with learning through examples. But if it happens to be innate, it is surely a wonder how we fail to notice that we have the most powerful kind of knowledge. Furthermore, in what way will one know what something is made of, and how will it be evident? For this too contains an impasse: for one might dispute in the same way as about

5 some syllables. For some people say that *za* is made of *s, d,* and *a,* while some others say that it is a distinct sound and not made of any familiar ones. What's more, how could someone know those things of which sense perception consists if he did not have the sense capacity? And yet he must, if indeed the elements out of which all things are made are the

10 same, in just the way that composite sounds are made of the elements that belong to them.

10. That, then, everybody seems to be looking for the causes spoken of in our writings on nature [*Physics*], and that outside of these there is none that we could speak

15 of, is evident even from what has been said above. But they inquired murkily into these, and while in a certain way all the causes have been spoken of before, in another way they have not been spoken of at all. For the earliest philosophy about everything is like someone who lisps, since it is young and just starting out. Even Empedocles said that bone *is* by means of a ratio, and this is what it is for it to be and the thinghood of the

20 thing. But surely also flesh and each of the other things would have to be through a ratio in the same way, or not even one thing. Therefore it is through this that flesh and bone and each of the other things would have being, and not, as *he* says, through the material, the fire, earth, water, and air. But while he would necessarily concede these things if someone else said them, he did not say them clearly. Now what concerns these things

25 has also been made clear above; but let us go back again over all those things that any-one might find to be impasses about these same topics, for perhaps out of them we might provision ourselves in some way for the impasses that will come later.

*   *   *

BOOK XII

1. Our study concerns thinghood, for it is the sources and causes of independent

1069ª things that are being sought. For if the sum of things is some kind of whole, thinghood is its primary part, but also if the sum of things is just one thing next to another, even so the thing-hood of anything is primary, of-what-sort it is comes next, and then how much it is. And at the same time, these latter are not even beings, if one speaks strictly, but qualities and motions, or else even the not-white or not-straight would be beings; certainly we say that

25 even these things have being, for example that the not-white *is.* What's more, none of the others is separate. And the ancient thinkers bear witness to this by what they *do,* since they are looking for the sources and elements and causes of thinghood. Accordingly, while peo-ple now assume that it is rather universals that are independent things (for general classes are universal, and it is these that they say are more so sources and independent things, because they inquire from a logical standpoint), those in early times assumed that the inde-

30 pendent things were particulars, such as fire and earth, and not the common class, body.
And there are three kinds of thinghood: One kind is perceptible, of which one sort is everlasting and the other sort, which everyone acknowledges, is destructible, as with plants and animals, and it is necessary to grasp the elements of this kind of thinghood,

whether there is one or many. Another kind is motionless, and some people say that this is separate, some of them dividing it into two kinds, others making the forms and the mathematical things into one nature, and still others assume only the mathematical things among these. And the former kinds belong to the study of nature (since they include motion), but this kind belongs to a different study, if there is no source common to them.

Now perceptible thinghood is changeable, and if change is from opposites, or from things between opposites, but not from all kinds of opposites (since a sound is not-white), but only from a contrary, it is necessary that there be something underlying the thing that changes into the contrary condition, since the contraries themselves do not change.

2. Further, there is something that persists, while the contrary state does not persist; therefore there is a third thing besides the contraries, the material. So if there are four kinds of changes, with respect to what something is, of-what-sort it is, how much it is, or where it is, and simple coming-into-being or passing-away is change of the *this,* increase or decrease is change of the how-much, alteration is change of an attribute, and local motion is change of place, changes are into contrary states of these particular kinds. So the material has to be capable of changing into both, and since being is of two kinds, everything changes from something that has being in potency to something that has being at-work (as from potentially white to something actively white, and similarly too in the case of increase and decrease), so that things are able not only to come into being from what, in an incidental sense, is not, but also everything comes into being from what is, though from what is potentially but is not at work. And this is Anaxagoras's "one," since it is better than "everything together," and it is also the "mixture" spoken of by Empedocles and Anaximander, and what Democritus is talking about, but for us it is "all things were in potency, but not atwork." Therefore, these thinkers did get some grasp of material, but all things have material, all those that change, but different sorts of material; and material belongs to those everlasting things that are not generated but moved by change of place, though it is not material for coming into being but for from-somewhere-to-somewhere. (And one might in fact be at an impasse about what sort of not-being generation comes out of, since not-being is of three kinds.)

Now if something has being in potency, still this is not a potency to be any random thing, but a different thing comes to be from a different potency, and it is not sufficient to say that [even as potencies] all things are there together, for they differ in their material; why did they come to be an infinity of things and not just one? For intellect is one, so that if material also were one, that which the material was in potency would have come to be actively. So the causes are three, as are the sources, two of them being the pair of contraries of which one is the articulation or form and the other its deprivation, while the third is the material.

3. Next after that is the fact that neither material nor form comes into being—I am speaking of the ultimate ones. For with everything, something changes, by the action of something, and into something: that by the action of which it changes is the first thing that sets it in motion, that which changes is the material, and that into which it changes is the form. So this is an infinite process if it is not only the bronze that comes to be round, but the roundness or bronze too comes into being; and so it necessarily comes to a stop. And next after this is the fact that each independent thing comes into being from something that has the same name (for this is true both of natural independent things and of the rest). For it comes into being either by art or by nature, or else by fortune or chance. Now art is a source that is in something else, but nature is a source that is in the thing itself (since a human being begets a human being), while the rest of the causes are deprivations of these.

10   The kinds of thinghood are three, since the material is a *this* by coming forth into appearance (for whatever has being by way of contact, and not by having grown together, is material and underlies something else), while the nature of a thing is a *this* and an active condition into which it comes; and then the third kind is the particular thing that consists of these, such as Socrates or Callias. Now in some cases the *this* is

15 not present apart from the composite independent thing, as the form of a house does not have being apart, unless the art does (though there is no coming-into-being or destruction of these forms, but it is in a different way that a house without material, and health, and everything that results from art is and is not), and if it is present apart, it is in the case of things that are by nature; and so for this reason Plato said not badly that the

20 forms are as many things as there are by nature, if there are forms, though there are none of things like fire, flesh, or a head, since all these are material, and the final sort of material belongs to what is an independent thing most of all.

    Now things that cause motion are causes as being previously present, but things that are causes in the sense of rational patterns are simultaneous with what they produce. For at the time when a human being is healthy, then too the health is present, and

25 the shape of a bronze sphere is present at the same time as the bronze sphere. But one must examine whether any of these also remain afterward; for nothing prevents it in some cases, for instance if the soul is of this sort, not all of it but the intellect, since presumably this is impossible for the whole soul. So it is clear that there is no need on account of *these* reasons for there to be forms, since a human being begets a human being, a particular one begetting a particular one, and similarly too with the arts, since

30 the medical art is the reasoned account of health.

    4. Now there is a sense in which the causes and sources of different things are different, but there is a sense in which, if one speaks universally by way of analogy, they are the same for all things. For one might be at an impasse whether different sources

35 and elements, or the same ones, belong to independent things and to relations, and similarly with each of the different ways of attributing being. But it is absurd that they

1070^b should be the same for everything, for then relations and thinghood would come from the same things. What would these sources be? For aside from thinghood and the other ways of attributing being, there is no one thing common to them, but an element precedes those things of which it is an element. But surely thinghood is not an element of relations, nor is any relation an element of thinghood. What's more, in what way could

5 the same elements belong to all things? For none of the elements could be the same as that which is composed of elements, as B or A is not the same as BA (and so none of the intelligible things, such as being or oneness, is an element, since they belong also to each one of the composite things). Therefore none of the elements could be either an independent thing or a relative thing, but they would have to be of one sort or the other.

10 Therefore, the same elements cannot belong to all things. Or else, as we are saying, in one sense they do, but in another sense they do not; for example, of perceptible bodies, perhaps the source in the sense of form is the hot, and in another way the cold, as its lack, while the material is the first thing that is in virtue of itself potentially these, and these are the thinghood of perceptible bodies, as is also what consists of them, of which

15 they are the sources, or anything consisting of the hot and the cold that might come to be one, such as flesh or bone, since what comes from different things is different.

    Accordingly, these perceptible things have the same elements and sources (though different things have different ones of them), but it is not possible to say in this way that *all* things have the same elements and sources, except by analogy, just as if one were to say that there are three kinds of sources: form, deprivation, and material. But each of

these is different as it concerns each class of things; for instance, among colors they are 20
white, black, and a surface, or light, darkness, and air, out of which come day and night.
But since it is not only the constituents of things that are their causes, but these may also
be found among external things, such as that which sets them in motion, it is clear that a
source and an element are different, though both are causes, and sources are divided into
these kinds, the source that sets something in motion or brings it to a stop being one of 25
them, so that there are by analogy three kinds of elements, but the causes and sources are
of four kinds; but the elements are different in different things, and the first cause that
sets them in motion is also different in different things. With health, disease, and a body,
the mover is the medical art. With form, a certain particular kind of disorder, and bricks,
the mover is the house-building art. And since among natural things the mover is, say, for 30
a human being a human being, while among things that are produced by thinking it is the
form or its contrary, the causes would again in a certain way be three, though by this
means four. For health is in a certain way the medical art, and the form of a house is the
builder's art, and a human being begets a human being; but still, over and above these, is 35
the cause which, as the first of all things, sets all things in motion.

5. Now since some things are separate while others are not separate, the former are
independent things. And it is on account of this that all things have the same causes, 1071ᵃ
because without independent things, attributes and motions are not possible. So then these
causes will be, presumably, soul and body, or intellect, desire, and body. And in yet
another way, the sources of things are the same by analogy, namely being-at-work* and
potency, though these are both different and present in different ways in different things. 5
For with some things, the same thing is present at a certain time actively which was at
another time in potency, such as wine or flesh or a human being. (And these also fall into
the kinds of causes mentioned, since the form is at work if it is separate, as is the composite of both form and material, and even a deprivation such as darkness or [a composite of 10
a deprivation and material] such as a sick person, while the material has being as potency,
since it is what is capable of becoming both the form and its deprivation.) But being-at-
work and being in potency differ in different ways in things in which there is not the same
material, for which there is not the same form but a different one, just as the causes of a
human that by which the material is moved from lacking to having the form that will make 15
the thing what it is. The final cause is either identical to, or included in, that form. being
are elements, fire and earth as material and the proper form, and in addition something
else outside, such as a father, and besides these the sun and its slanted orbit, which are not
material or form or deprivation or of the same kind, but causes of motion.

Further, it is necessary to see that some things are possible to state universally, but
others not. Now the primary sources of all things are the *this* that is first at work and
something else which is in potency. So these are not the universal causes, since the 20
source of particular things is particular; for a human being is the source of a human being
universally, but no one is this universal, but rather Peleus is the source of Achilles and
your father of you, and this particular B is the source of this particular BA, but B in general is the source of BA simply. And then, if the causes and elements of independent
things are the sources of all things (but different ones of different ones), then as was said, 25
of things not in the same class (colors and sounds, or independent things and quantity)

*<energeia>, often translated "actuality." As our translator puts it, "Aristotle's central thought is that
all being is being-at-work, and that anything inert would cease to be. The primary sense of the word belongs
to activities that are not motions; examples of these are seeing, knowing, and happiness, each understood as
an ongoing state that is complete at every instant. . . ."

they are different except by analogy; of things that are in the same kind they are also different, but not in kind, but because they are different for particular things, your material and form and mover from mine, though they are the same in their universal statement.

30   So as for seeking out what are the sources or elements of independent things and of relations and the of-what-sorts of things, and whether they are the same or different, it is clear that, since they are meant in more than one way, they do belong to everything, but when they have been distinguished they are not the same but different, except in one sense. And the causes of all things are the same in this sense—by analogy—because they are material, form, deprivation, and a mover, and the causes of independent things are the causes of all things in this sense—because when they are taken away everything

35   is taken away; and further, the primary thing that is completely at work is the cause of all things. But the causes are different in this sense—they are as many as there are primary contraries, described neither generically nor ambiguously, and as there are kinds of material as well. So what the sources are of perceptible things, and how many there

1071ᵇ   are, and in what way they are the same and in what way different, have been said.

6. Now since there are three kinds of thinghood, two of them natural and one motionless, about the latter one must explain that it is necessary for there to be some

5   everlasting motionless independent thing. For independent things are primary among beings, and if they were all destructible, everything would be destructible; but it is impossible for motion either to come into being or to be destroyed (since it always is), and impossible too for time. For if there were no time, there could be no before and

10   after; and motion is continuous in just the way that time is, since time is either the same as or some attribute of motion. But there is no continuous motion other than in place, and among these, other than in a circle.

But surely if there is something capable of moving and producing things, but not at work in any way, there will not be motion; for what has a potency admits of not being at work. Therefore, there is no benefit even if we adopt everlasting independent

15   things, as do those who bring in the forms, unless there is in them some source capable of producing change; moreover, even this is not enough, not even if there is another independent thing besides the forms, since if it is not going to be at work, there will not be motion. What's more, it is not enough even if it will be at work, if the thinghood of it is potency, for there would not be everlasting motion, since what has being in

20   potency admits of not being. Therefore it is necessary that there be a source of such a kind that the thinghood of it is being-at-work. On top of that, it is necessary that these independent things be without material, for they must be everlasting, if indeed anything else is everlasting. Therefore they are being-at-work.

And yet there is an impasse: for it seems that, while everything that is at work is capable of it, not everything that is capable of it is at work, so that the potency would

25   take precedence. But surely if this were so, there would be no beings at all, since it is possible to be capable of being and not yet be. Nevertheless, there is the same impossibility if things are the way those who write about the gods say, who generate all things out of night, or the way of those who write about nature, who say "all things were together." For how will things have been set in motion, if there were not some

30   responsible thing at work? For material itself, at any rate, will not set itself in motion, but a craftsman will cause it to, nor will the menstrual fluid or the earth set themselves in motion, but semen or seeds will cause them to. And this is why some people, such as Leucippus and Plato, bring in an everlasting activity, for they say that there is always motion. But why there is this motion, and what it is, they do not say, nor the

35   cause of its being a certain way or some other way. For nothing moves at random, but

always something must be present to it, just as now something moves in a certain way by nature, but in some other way by force or by the action of intelligence or something else. And then, what sort of motion is primary? For this makes so much difference one can hardly conceive it. But surely it is not even possible for Plato to say 1072ᵃ what he sometimes thinks the source of motion is, which itself sets itself in motion; for the soul is derivative, and on the same level as the heavens, as he says.

Now to suppose that potency takes precedence over being-at-work is in a sense right but in a sense not right (and in what sense has been said); and Anaxagoras testifies that being-at-work takes precedence (since intellect is a being-at-work), as does Empedocles with love and strife, and so do those who say there is always motion, such as Leucippus; therefore there was not chaos or night for an infinite time, but the same things have always been so, either in a cycle or in some other way, if being-at-work takes precedence over potency. So if the same thing is always so in a cycle, it is necessary for something to persist always at work in the same way. But if there is going to be generation and destruction, there must be something else that is always at work in different ways. Therefore it must necessarily be at work in a certain way in virtue of itself, and in another way in virtue of something else, in virtue, that is, of either a different thing or the first one. And it is necessarily in virtue of the first one, since it would in turn be responsible for both itself and that different one. Accordingly it is better that it be the first one, for it was responsible for what is always the same way, while another thing was responsible for what happens in different ways, and obviously both together are responsible for what happens in different ways always. And without doubt motions are this way. Why then must one look for other sources?

7. But since it is possible for it to be this way, and if it is not this way things will come from night and from "all things together" and from not-being, these questions could be resolved; and there is a certain ceaseless motion that is always moving, and it is in a circle (and this is evident not only to reason but in fact), so that the first heaven would be everlasting. Accordingly, there is also something that moves it. And since what is in motion and causes motion is something intermediate, there is also something that causes motion without being in motion, which is everlasting, an independent thing, and a being-at-work. But what is desired and what is thought cause motion in that way: not being in motion, they cause motion. But the primary instances of these are the same things, for what is yearned for is what seems beautiful, while what is wished for primarily is what is beautiful; but we desire something because of the way it seems, rather than its seeming so because we desire it, for the act of thinking is the beginning. But the power of thinking is set in motion by the action of the thing thought, and what is thought in its own right belongs to an array of affirmative objects of which thinghood is primary, and of this the primary kind is that which is simple and at work. (But what is one and what is simple are not the same, for oneness indicates a measure, but what is simple is itself a certain way.) But surely the beautiful and what is chosen in virtue of itself are also in that same array, and what is primary is always best, or analogous to it. 1072ᵇ And that-for-the-sake-of-which is possible among motionless things, as the [following] distinction makes evident; for that-for-the-sake-of-which is either *for* something or *belonging to* something, of which the former is and the latter is not present among motionless things. And it causes motion in the manner of something loved, and by means of what is moved moves other things.

Now if something is moved, it admits of being otherwise than it is; and so, even if the primary kind of change of place is a being-at-work, insofar as something is moved, it is in that respect at least capable of being otherwise, with respect to place even if not with respect to thinghood. But since there is something that causes motion while being itself motionless, this does not admit of being otherwise than it is in any respect at all.

10   For among changes, the primary one is change of place, and of this the primary kind is in a circle, but this is what this mover causes. Therefore it is something that has being necessarily, and inasmuch as it is by necessity it is beautiful and in that way a source. For the necessary has this many senses: what is by force because it is contrary to a thing's impulse, that without which something will not be in a good condition, and that which does not admit of being any way other than in a simple condition. On such a source, therefore, the cosmos and nature depend.

15   And the course of its life is of such a kind as the best we have for a short time. This is because it is always the same way (which for us is impossible), and because its being-at-work is also pleasure (which is what makes being awake, perceiving, and thinking the most pleasant things, while hopes and memories are pleasant on account of these). And the thinking that is just thinking by itself is a thinking of what is best just as

20   itself, and especially so with what is so most of all. But by partaking in what it thinks, the intellect thinks itself, for it becomes what it thinks by touching and contemplating it, so that the intellect and what it thinks are the same thing. For what is receptive of the intelligible and of thinghood is the intellect, and it is at work when it has them; therefore it is the being-at-work rather than the receptivity the intellect has that seems godlike,

25   and its contemplation is pleasantest and best. So if the divine being is always in this good condition that we are sometimes in, that is to be wondered at; and if it is in it to a greater degree than we are, that is to be wondered at still more. And that is the way it is. But life belongs to it too, for the being-at-work of intellect is life, and that being *is* being-at-work, and its being-at-work is in itself the best life and is everlasting. And we

30   say that it is a god who everlastingly lives the best life, so that life and continuous and everlasting duration belong to a god; for this being is god.

    And those who assume, as do the Pythagoreans and Speusippus, that what is most beautiful and best is not present in the source of anything, since, while the sources of plants and or animals are responsible for them, what is beautiful and complete is in the effects that come from them, do not think rightly. For the seed comes from other, earlier,

1073ª   complete beings, and what is first is not the seed but the complete being, just as one would say that a human being precedes the germinal fluid, not the one who comes into being from it, but another one from whom the germinal fluid came.

    That, then, there is an independent thing that is everlasting, motionless, and separate

5   from perceptible things, is clear from what has been said. And it has also been demonstrated that this independent thing can have no magnitude, but is without parts and indivisible (for it causes motion for an infinite time, while no finite thing has an infinite power,

10   and since every magnitude must be either infinite or finite, it cannot have magnitude, either finite, for the reason given, or infinite, because there is no infinite magnitude at all). But surely it has also been demonstrated that it cannot be affected or altered, since all other motions are derivative from change of place. So it is clear why these things are this way.

    8. But whether one must set down one or more than one such independent thing, and how many, must not go unnoticed; but one has to mention, as far as the pronounce-

15   ments of others are concerned, that about the number of them they have said nothing which can even be stated clearly. For the assumption about the forms contains no particular speculation about it (for those who speak of the forms say the forms are numbers,

20   and about the numbers, sometimes they speak as though about infinitely many, but sometimes as though they had a limit at the number ten, but why the multitude of the numbers

is just so much, nothing is said with a serious effort at demonstrative reasoning). But it is necessary for us to argue from the things that have been laid down and distinguished. For the source and the first of beings is not movable either in its own right or incidentally, but sets in motion the primary motion, that is one and everlasting. But since what is in motion must be moved by something, and the first mover must be itself motionless, and an everlasting motion must be caused by an everlasting source of motion and one motion by one mover, while we see in addition to the simple motion of the whole heaven, which we claim the first motionless independent thing causes, other everlasting motions which belong to the planets (for the body that goes in a circle does so everlastingly and without stopping, which is demonstrated in the writings on nature), it is necessary that each of these motions also be caused by something that is itself motionless and an everlasting independent thing. For the nature of the stars is for each to be an everlasting independent thing, while the mover is everlasting and takes precedence over the thing moved, and what takes precedence over an independent thing must be an independent thing. Accordingly, it is clear that there must be that many independent things and that they must have a nature such that they are everlasting and motionless in virtue of themselves, and, for the reason stated above, without magnitude.

That, then, there are independent things, and of these a first one and a second, following the same order as the motions of the stars, is evident; but the number of motions is already something one must examine from that kind of mathematical knowledge that is the nearest kin to philosophy, namely from astronomy. For this kind makes its study about perceptible, everlasting thinghood, while the others, such as those concerned with numbers and with geometry, are not about thinghood at all. Now the fact that the motions are greater in number than the things moved is clear to those who have touched on the subject even moderately (since each of the wandering stars is carried along more than one motion); but as for how many these happen to be, we now state what some of the mathematicians say, for the sake of a conception of it, in order that some definite number be grasped in our thinking, and as for what remains, it is necessary to inquire into some things ourselves, while listening to what other inquirers say about others. If something should seem to those who busy themselves with these matters to be contrary to what has just now been said, it is necessary to welcome both accounts, but trust the more precise one.

Eudoxus, then, set it down that the motion of both the sun and the moon is in three spheres, of which the first is that of the fixed stars, the second rotates along a path through the midst of the zodiac, and the third along a path inclined along the width of the zodiac (but with that along which the moon is carried inclined to a greater width than that along which the sun is carried); but he set it down that the motion of each of the wandering stars is in four spheres, of which the first and second are the same as the former ones (for the sphere of the fixed stars is that which moves them all, and the sphere assigned to the place under this and having its motion along a path through the midst of the zodiac is common to them all), while the poles of the third sphere for all of them are in the path through the midst of the zodiac, and the motion of the fourth is along a path inclined to the equator of the third. And he set it down that the poles of the third sphere are peculiar to the different planets, but those for Venus and Mercury are the same. Callippus set down the same arrangement of spheres as did Eudoxus, and gave the same number as he did for Jupiter and Saturn, but for the sun and the moon he thought there were two spheres still to be added if one were going to account for the appearances, and one for each of the remaining planets.

But it is necessary, in order to account for the appearances, if all the spheres are going to be fit together, that there be for each of the planets (less one) other spheres, turning backwards and continuously restoring to the same position the first sphere of the star situated next below; for only in that way is it possible for them all to produce the motion of the planets. Since, then, the spheres in which they themselves are carried are eight [for Jupiter and Saturn] and twenty-five [for the sun and moon, Mars, Venus, and Mercury], and of these one, that in which the star situated lowest is carried, does not need to be counter-turned, the spheres to counter-turn those of the first two planets will be six, while the ones to counter-turn those of the four lower ones will be sixteen; so the number of all the carrying spheres plus those that turn backward against them will be fifty-five. But if one were not to add to the moon and the sun the motions which we mentioned, all the spheres will be forty-seven. So let the number of the spheres be so many, so that it is reasonable to assume that the number of independent things which are motionless sources is also that many (for let the number that is necessary be left for more relentless people to say).

But if it is impossible for there to be any motion that is not directed into the motion of a star, and if in addition every nature and every independent thing that is unaffected and has, by virtue of itself, attained its best condition, must be regarded as an end, there could be no other nature besides these, but this is necessarily the number of independent things. For if there were others, they would be movers as final causes of motion; but it is impossible for there to be other motions besides those mentioned. And this is reasonable to assume from the things that are moved. For if what carries something is naturally for the sake of what is carried, and every motion belongs to something that is carried, no motion could be for the sake of itself or for the sake of another motion, but they are for the sake of the stars. For if there were to be a motion for the sake of a motion, the latter too would have to be for the sake of another one; so since this cannot go to infinity, there will be as an end for every motion one of the divine bodies carried through the heaven. And it is clear that there is one heaven. For if there were a plurality of heavens, as there is of human beings, there would be one *kind* of source for each one, but many of them in number. But those things that are many in number contain material (for one and the same articulation belongs to many things, as does the articulation of a human being, but Socrates is one). But what it primarily is for something to be does not contain material, for it is a being-at-work-staying-itself.* Therefore the first motionless being that causes motion is one both in articulation and in number; and therefore what is moved always and continuously is also one. Therefore there is only one heaven.

There has been handed down from people of ancient and earliest times a heritage, in the form of myth, to those of later times, that these original beings are gods, and that the divine embraces the whole of nature. The rest of it was presently introduced in mythical guise for the persuasion of the masses and into the laws for use and benefit; for the myths say the gods are of human form or like some of the other animals, and other things that follow along with and approximate these that have been mentioned. If one were to take only the first of these things, separating it out, that they thought the primary independent things were gods, one would regard this as having been said by divine inspiration, and, since it is likely that every kind of art and philosophy has been discovered to the limit of its potential many times, and passed away in turn, one would consider these opinions of those people to have been saved like holy relics up to now. So the opinion of our forefathers that comes from the first ages is clear to us but only to this extent.

---

*<*entelecheia*>, often translated "actuality," means (as our translator puts it), "a fusion of the idea of completeness with that of continuity or persistence. Aristotle invents the word by combining <*enteles*> (complete, full-grown) with <*echein*> (to be a certain way by the continuing effort of holding on in that condition. . . ."

9. Now concerning the intellect there are certain impasses, for it seems to be the   15
most divine of the things that are manifest to us, but the way it is if it is to be of that sort
contains some things that are hard to digest. For if it thinks nothing, what would be
solemn about that? Rather, it would be just like someone sleeping. But if it does think,   20
but something else has power over it, then, since it is not thinking but potency that is the
thinghood of it, it could not be the best independent thing, for it is on account of its act
of thinking that its place of honor belongs to it. And still, whether the thinghood of it is
a power of thinking or an activity of thinking, what does it think? For this is either itself
or something else, and if it is something else, either always the same one or different
ones. And then does it make any difference, or none, whether its thinking is of what is
beautiful or of some random thing? Isn't it even absurd for its thinking to be about some   25
things? Surely it is obvious that it thinks the most divine and honorable things, and does
not change, since its change would be for the worse, and such a thing would already be
a motion. First, then, if it is not an activity of thinking but a potency, it is reasonable to
suppose that the continuation of its thinking would be wearisome; and next, it is clear   30
that something else would then be more honorable than the intellect, namely what it
thinks. For thinking and the activity of thinking would belong even to something that
thinks the worst thing, and if this is to be avoided (for it can even be more advantageous
not to see some things than to see them), then the activity of thinking would not be the
best thing. Therefore what it thinks is itself, if it is the most excellent thing, and its
thinking is a thinking of thinking.

But knowledge and perception and opinion and step-by-step thinking seem   35
always to be about something else, and about themselves only as something secondary.
What's more, if the thinking and the being thought are different, then in virtue of
which of them does what is good belong to it? For to be an act of thinking and to be
something thought are not the same. Or is it rather that in some cases the knowledge is   1075ᵃ
the thing it is concerned with, so that in the case of the kinds of knowing that make
something, the thinghood without material and what it is for something to be, or in
the case of the contemplative kinds of knowing, the articulation, is both the thing the
knowledge is concerned with and the activity of thinking it? So since what is thought
and what is thinking are not different with as many things as have no material, they
will be the same, and the act of thinking will be one with what is thought.

But there is still an impasse left as to whether what is thought is composite, for   5
then the thinking would be changing among the parts of the whole. Or is it the case that
everything that has no material is indivisible? So the condition the human intellect, or
that of any composite being, is in at some period of time (for it does not have hold of
what is good at this or that time, but in some whole stretch of time it has hold of what is
best, since that is something other than itself), is the condition the thinking that thinks   10
itself is in over the whole of time.

10. One must also consider in which of two ways the nature of the whole contains
what is good and what is best, whether as something separate, itself by itself, or as the
order of the whole of things. Or is it present in both ways, just as in an army? For its
good condition resides in its ordering but also is its general, and is more the latter; for he   15
does not depend on the order but it on him. And all things are in some way ordered
together, though not all similarly, the things that swim and fly and grow in the ground;
yet they are not such that nothing that pertains to one kind is related to another, but there
is some relation. For they are all organized toward one thing, but in the same way as in
a household, in which the free members of it are least of all allowed to do any random   20

thing, but all or most of what they do is prescribed, while for the slaves and livestock little that they do is for the common good and much is just at random, since the nature of each of them is that kind of source. I mean, for example, that it necessarily comes to
25   everything at least to be decomposed, and there are other things of this sort that all things take part in together that contribute to the whole.

But how many impossible or absurd consequences follow for those who speak of these things in other ways, and what sort of things those who speak of them most gracefully say, and what sort of opinions have the fewest impasses, must not be ignored. For everyone makes all things come from contraries, but neither the "all things" nor the "from contraries" is right, and even with those things in which contraries are present, they do not
30   say how they come from those contraries, for contraries are unaffected by one another. Now for us, this is resolved reasonably by there being a certain third thing. But other people make one of the contraries be material, as for instance, the unequal as material for the equal, or the many as material for the one. But this too is refuted in the same way, since for us the material has no contrary. What's more, all things outside of the one would
35   have a share in what is vile, since the bad is itself one of the two elements of things. Other people don't even make good and bad the sources of things, and yet in everything what is
1075ᵇ   good is a source most of all. Others say rightly that this is a source, but in what way the good is a source they do not say, whether as an end or as a mover or as a form.

And Empedocles too speaks absurdly; for he makes love the good, but this is a source both as causing motion (since it brings things together) and as material (since it is part of the mixture). Now even if it turns out that the same thing is a source in the role of
5   both material and mover, still being each of them is not the same thing. In which sense then is love a source? And it is also absurd that strife should be indestructible, but this is for him the nature of the bad. But Anaxagoras makes the good a source in the sense of a mover, for the intellect sets things in motion. But it moves them for the sake of something,
10   and so that is some other thing, unless, as we say, the medical art is in a certain respect health. And it is absurd not to make anything be contrary to the good or the intellect.

In fact all those who speak of contraries make no use of the contraries, unless one brings what they say into an orderly interpretation. And why some things are destructible and others indestructible, no one says, since they make all beings come from the same
15   sources. What's more, some of them make the beings come from not-being; others, to keep this from being necessary, make all things one. And further, why there will always be generation, and what the cause of generation is, no one says. And for those who make two sources, there has to be another more ruling source. And also those who speak of the forms need still another more ruling source, for why do things begin to participate or
20   continue to participate in them? Also, for the others there has to be something that is contrary to wisdom and to the most honorable kind of knowledge, but not so for us. For there is no contrary to what is primary, since all contraries have material, and such things have being by way of potency; but the ignorance that is contrary to wisdom would be directed to a contrary being, while to the primary being nothing is contrary.

25   Further, if there were not other things besides perceptible ones, there would be no source, no order, no generation, and no heavenly orbits, but a source would always have a source, just as with all the writers on the gods and on nature. But if there are forms or numbers, they will be responsible for nothing, or if so, certainly not for motion. What's more, how will continuous magnitude come from things without magnitude? For a num-
30   ber will not produce anything continuous, either as a mover or as a form. But surely there could be nothing among contraries which is the very thing that is productive or responsible for motion, since it would admit of not being. So its producing would be derivative from its potency, and therefore there could be no everlasting beings. But there are.

Therefore something in this argument must be annulled. But the way this stands has been said. On top of this, no one says anything about what it is by means of which numbers, or the soul and the body, or generally the form and the thing, are one; nor is it possible to say this, except in the way we say it—that the cause of motion makes them one. But those who say that mathematical number is primary, and in that way there is always another successive kind of thinghood, with different sources for each kind, make the thinghood of the sum of things arbitrarily episodic (since one kind contributes nothing to another by being or not being), and make there be many sources; but beings do not present the aspect of being badly governed. "A divided sovereignty is not good; let there be one lord."*

35

1076ᵃ

ON THE SOUL (in part)

BOOK II

1. Let this be our discussion of the things handed on about the soul by those who came before us. But let us go back again and, as though from the beginning, try to distinguish what the soul is and what articulation of it would be most common to all its instances. One of the most general ways of being we call thinghood**; of this, one sort has being as material, which in its own right is not a *this*, but another sort is the form or look of a thing, directly as a result of which something is called a *this*, and the third sort is what is made out of these. Now the material is a potency, but the form is a being-at-work-staying-itself***, and this in two senses, one in the manner of knowledge, the other in the manner of the act of contemplating.

The things that seem most of all to be independent things are bodies, and of these, the natural ones, for these are the sources of the others. And of natural bodies, some have life while others do not. By life we mean self-nourishing as well as growth and wasting away. So every natural body having a share in life would be an independent thing having thinghood as a composite [of material and form]. And since this is a body, and one of a certain sort, namely having life, the soul could not be a body, since it is not the body that is in an underlying thing, but rather the body has being as an underlying thing and material [for something else]. Therefore it is necessary that the soul have its thinghood as the form of a natural body having life as a potency. But this

412ᵃ

5

10

15

20

*With these words at *Iliad* II, 204, Odysseus turns the Achaean multitude back from a chaotic rout and into an orderly army. Similarly, the divine intellect described by Aristotle does not create things or the world but confers upon them their worldhood and thinghood.

**<*ousia*>, often translated "substance," means (as our translator puts it) "the way of being that belongs to anything which has attributes but is not an attribute of anything, which is also separate and a *this*. Whatever has being in this way is an independent thing."

***<*entelecheia*>, often translated "actuality," means (as our translator puts it), "a fusion of the idea of completeness with that of continuity or persistence. Aristotle invents the word by combining <*enteles*> (complete, full-grown) with <*echein*> (to be a certain way by the continuing effort of holding on in that condition). . . ."

Aristotle, *On the Soul* (Book II, 1–3 and III, 4–5), translated by Joe Sachs. Copyright © 2001 by Green Lion Press. Reprinted by permission of Green Lion Press.

Artemision Jockey, ca. 140 B.C. According to Aristotle, both a human jockey and the horse he rides have a "soul" while the bronze of this statue does not. The "soul" is what animates a plant, animal, or human body, i.e., what makes it alive. (*Forrest E. Baird; National Archeological Museum, Athens, Greece*)

sort of thinghood is a being-at-work-staying-itself; therefore the soul is the being-at-work-staying-itself of such a body. But this is meant in two ways, the one in the sense that knowledge is a being-at-work-staying-itself, the other in the sense that the act of contemplating is. It is clear, then, that the soul is a being-at-work-staying-itself in the way that knowledge is, for both sleep and waking are in what belongs to the soul, and waking is analogous to the act of contemplating but sleep to holding the capacity for contemplating while not putting it to work. But in the same person it is knowledge that is first in coming into being; for this reason the soul is a being-at-work-staying-itself of the first kind of a natural body having life as a potency. But such a body is organized [i.e., has parts subordinated to the whole as instruments of it]. (And even the parts of plants are organs, though utterly simple ones, as the leaf is a covering for the peel and the peel for the fruit, while the roots are analogous to the mouth, since both take in food.) So if one needs to say what is common to every soul, it would be that it is a being-at-work-staying-itself of the first kind of a natural, organized body. And for this reason it is not necessary to seek out whether the soul and body are one, any more than with wax and the shape molded in it, or generally with the material of each thing and that of which it is the material; for even though *one* and *are* are meant in more than one way, the governing sense of each of them is being-at-work-staying-itself.

So what soul is has been said in general, for it is thinghood as it is unfolded in   10
speech, and this is what such-and-such a body keeps on being in order to be at all. It would
be as though some tool, such as an axe, were a natural body, since its being-an-axe would
be the thinghood of it, and that would be its soul; for if this were separated from it, it would
no longer be an axe, other than ambiguously. But in fact it is an axe, since it is not of this   15
sort of body that the soul is the meaning and the what-it-is-for-it-to-be, but of a certain sort
of natural body, one that has a source of motion and rest in itself. But one ought to consider
what has been said as applying even to the parts of such a body. For if the eye were an animal, the soul of it would be its sight, since this is the thinghood of an eye as it is disclosed   20
in speech (and the eye is the material of sight); if its sight were left out it would no longer
be an eye, except ambiguously, in the same way as a stone eye or a painted one.

Now one should take what applies to the part up to the whole living body, for there
is an analogy: as part [of perceiving] is to part [of the body], so is perceiving as a whole to
the whole perceptive body as such. And it is not the body that has lost its soul that is in   25
potency to be alive, but the one that has it, and the seed and fruit are in potency to be
certain sorts of bodies. So just as the act of cutting is for the axe and the act of seeing for
the eye, so too is the waking condition a being-at-work-staying-itself, but as the power of   413ᵃ
sight is to the eye and the capacity of the tool to the axe, so is the soul a being-at-work-
staying-itself, while the body is what has being in potency. But just as the eyeball and the
power of sight are the eye, so here the soul and the body are the living thing. So it is not
difficult to see why the soul, or at least certain parts of it, is not separate from the body, if
the soul is of such a nature as to be divided, since for some parts of the body, the soul is the   5
being-at-work-staying-itself of those parts themselves. Nevertheless, nothing prevents
some parts from being separate, so long as they are not the being-at-work* of any part of
the body. But it would be difficult to see [why the soul is not separate from the body] if
the soul were the being-at-work of the body in the way that the sailor is of the boat. But let
this stand as marking off and sketching out in an outline what concerns the soul.   10

2. Now since what is clear and more knowable by reason arises out of what is
unclear but more obvious, it is necessary to try again to go on in this way about the soul.
For the defining statement not only needs to make clear what something is, as most definitions do, but also needs to include and display the cause. As it is, the statements of   15
definitions are like conclusions. For example, what is squaring? The equality of an equi-
lateral rectangle to an oblong rectangle. But this sort of definition is a statement of the
conclusion, while one who says that squaring is the finding of a mean proportional
states the cause of the thing.   20

So we say, taking this as a starting point for the inquiry, that what is ensouled is
distinguished from what is soulless by living. But living is meant in more than one way,
and if any one alone of the following is present in something, we say it is alive: intellect,
perception, moving and stopping with respect to place, and the motion that results from
nourishment, that is, wasting away as well as growing. And for this reason all plants
seem to be alive, since they evidently have in themselves this sort of power and source,   25
through which they have growth and decay in opposite directions, for they do not just
grow upward but not downward, but in both directions alike, and in every direction, all

---

*<energeia>, often translated "actuality." As our translator puts it, "Aristotle's central thought is that
all being is being-at-work, and that anything inert would cease to be. The primary sense of the word belongs
to activities that are not motions; examples of these are seeing, knowing, and happiness, each understood as
an ongoing state that is complete at every instant. . . ."

30   of them that are continually nourished and live for the sake of their ends, so long as they are able to get food. The latter capacity can be present in separation from the others, but the others cannot be present in separation from it in mortal beings. This is obvious in the case of plants, since no other potency of soul belongs to them.

413ᵇ   Life belongs to living things, then, through this source, but to an animal, first of all, through sense perception; for even those that do not move or change their places, if they have perception, we call animals and do not merely say they are alive. Now of perception, the kind that first belongs to them all is touch, and just as the nutritive power is able to be

5   present separately from touch and all sense perception, so is touch able to be present separately from the other senses. (By the nutritive power, we mean the part of the soul of which the plants have a share; and it is obvious that animals all have the sense of touch.) Through

10   what cause each of these things happens, we will say later. For now, let us say this much only, that the soul is the source of these things that have been mentioned and is defined by them: by nutrition, by sense perception, by thinking things through, and by motion.

    Whether each of these is a soul or part of a soul, and if a part, whether in such a

15   way as to be separated only in speech or also in place, is for some of these not difficult to see, but some present an impasse. For just as in the case of plants, some parts obviously live when divided and separated from each other, as though the soul in them is one in each plant in the sense of being-at-work-staying-itself but is in potency more

20   than one, so too we see it happen with other capacities of the soul in the case of insects that have been cut in half; for each of the two parts even has both perception and motion with respect to place, and if it has perception, also imagination and appetite, since where there is perception there is also pain and pleasure, and where these are there is

25   necessarily also desire. But about the intellect, that is, the contemplative faculty, nothing is yet clear, but it seems that it is a distinct class of soul and that it alone admits of being separated from body, as the everlasting from the destructible. As for the remaining parts of the soul, it is clear from what has been said that they cannot be separate, as some people say, though it is obvious that they are distinct in speech. For being percep-

30   tive is different from being capable of having opinion, if perceiving is also different from having opinion, and similarly with each of the other parts mentioned. Further, some animals have all these capacities, others some of them, and still others only one

414ᵃ   (and this makes the difference among animals); why this is so must be considered later. And it turns out much the same with the senses, since some animals have them all, others some of them, and still others the one that is most necessary, touch.

    And seeing that the means by which we live and perceive is meant two ways, as is the

5   means by which we know (by which is meant in one sense knowledge but in another the soul, since by means of each of these we say we know something), likewise also we are healthy in one sense by means of health, but in another by means of either some part of the body or the whole of it. Now of these, the knowledge or the health is a form, and a certain

10   look, and an articulation in speech, and a kind of being-at-work of what is receptive, in the one case a being-at-work of what is capable of knowing, in the other a being-at-work of what is capable of being healthy (for it seems that the being-at-work of what is active is present in what is acted on and placed in a certain condition). So since the soul is that by which in the primary sense we live and perceive and think things through, it would be a certain sort of articulation and form, and not an underlying material. For thinghood is meant in

15   three ways, as we said, of which one way is as form, one as material, and one as what is made of both, while of these the material is potency and the form is being-at-work-staying-itself, so since what is ensouled is made of both, it is not the body that is the being-at-work-staying-itself of the soul, but the soul is the being-at-work-staying-itself of some body.

For this reason, those who think the soul neither has being without a body, nor is   20
any sort of body, get hold of it well, for it is not a body but something that belongs to a
body, and this is why it is present in a body and in a body of a certain kind, and those
earlier thinkers did not think well who stuck it into a body without also distinguishing
which bodies and of what sort, even though there is no evidence that any random thing   25
admits just any random thing within it. And this happens in accord with reason, since
the being-at-work-staying-itself of each thing naturally comes to be present in something that *is* it in potency and in the material appropriate to it. That, then, the soul is a
certain being-at-work-staying-itself and articulation of that which has the potency to be
in that way, is clear from these things.

3. Now of the potencies of the soul, all of those that have been mentioned belong   30
to some living things, as we said, while to others some of them belong, and to still others only one. The potencies we are speaking of are those for nutrition, perception,
motion with respect to place, and thinking things through. And in plants the nutritive
potency alone is present, while in other living things this is present along with the per-   414ᵇ
ceptive. But if the perceptive potency is present, then so is that of appetite, for appetite
consists of desire and spiritedness and wishing, while all animals have at least one of
the senses, that of touch, and in that in which sense perception is present there are also
pleasure and pain, as well as pleasant and painful sensations, and where these are pre-   5
sent so is desire, since this is an appetite for the pleasant. Besides, they have a perception of food, for touch is the sense that perceives food since all animals are nourished by
what is dry or moist and warm or cold, of which the sense is touch, though incidentally
it is perceptive of other things. For neither sound nor color nor smell contributes any-   10
thing to nourishment, but the flavor that comes from food is one of the things perceived
by touch. Hunger and thirst are desires for, in the former case, what is dry and warm,
and in the latter, what is moist and cold, while the flavor is a way of making these pleasant. One must get clear about these things later, but for now let this much be said, that   15
those living things that have touch also have appetite; it is unclear whether they must
also have imagination, but this needs to be examined later. And in some living things, in
addition to these potencies, there is present also that for motion with respect to place,
and in others also the potency for thinking things through as well as intellect, as in
human beings and any other living things there might be that are of that sort or more
honorable.

So it is clear that there could be a single account of soul in the same way as of   20
geometrical figure; for neither in that case is there any figure aside from the triangle and
those that follow in succession, nor in this is there any soul aside from the ones discussed. But even in the case of the figures, there could be a common account which
would fit them all, but would be appropriate to none of them in particular, and similarly
in the case of the souls that were discussed. Hence it would be ridiculous to inquire after   25
the common account, both in the one case and in the other, which would not be the particular account of any thing there is, nor apply to any proper and indivisible kind, while
neglecting an account that is of that sort. (For what applies to the soul is just about the
same as what concerns geometrical figures, for always in the one next in succession
there is present in potency the previous one, both in figures and in things with souls, as   30
the triangle is in the quadrilateral and the nutritive potency in the perceptive one.)
Therefore, for each kind, one needs to inquire what the soul of each is, as for a plant, a
human, and a wild animal. And why they are in this sort of succession must be consid-   415ᵃ
ered. For without the nutritive potency there is no perceptive potency, while the nutritive

is present in separation from the perceptive in plants. Again, without the sense of touch
5   none of the other senses is present, but touch is present without the others, for many
animals have neither sight nor hearing nor a sense of smell. And among animals with
the perceptive potency, some have the potency for motion with respect to place while
others do not. Last and most rare are reasoning and thinking things through; for in those
10   destructible beings in which reasoning is present, all the other potencies are also present, while reasoning is not present in all animals, but some do not even have imagination, though others live by this alone. But about the contemplative intellect there is a
different account. It is clear, then, that the account that deals with each of these potencies is also the most appropriate account of the soul.

*   *   *

BOOK III

429ᵃ   4. About the part of the soul by which the soul knows and understands, whether it
is a separate part, or not separate the way a magnitude is but in its meaning, one must
consider what distinguishing characteristic it has, and how thinking ever comes about.
If thinking works the same way perceiving does, it would either be some way of being
15   acted upon by the intelligible thing, or something else of that sort. Therefore it must be
without attributes but receptive of the form and in potency not to be the form but to be
such as it is; and it must be similar so that as the power of perception is to the perceptible things, so is the intellect to the intelligible things. Therefore necessarily, since it
thinks all things, it is unmixed, just as Anaxagoras says, in order to master them, that is,
20   in order to know them (since anything alien that appeared in it besides what it thinks
would hinder it and block its activity); and so intellect has no nature at all other than
this, that it is a potency. Therefore the aspect of the soul that is called intellect (and
I mean by intellect that by which the soul thinks things through and conceives that
something is the case) is not actively any of the things that *are* until it thinks. This is
25   why it is not reasonable that it be mixed with the body, since it would come to be of a
certain sort, either cold or warm, and there would be an organ for it, as there is for the
perceptive potency, though in fact there is none. And it is well said that the soul is a
place of forms, except that this is not the whole soul but the thinking soul, and it is not
the forms in its being-at-work-staying-itself, but in potency.
30   The absence of attributes is not alike in the perceptive and thinking potencies; this
is clear in its application to the sense organs and perception. For the sense is unable to
429ᵇ   perceive anything from an excessive perceptible thing, neither any sound from loud
sounds, nor to see or smell anything from strong colors and odors, but when the intellect
thinks something exceedingly intelligible it is not less able to think the lesser things but
even more able, since the perceptive potency is not present without a body, but the
5   potency to think is separate from body. And when the intellect has come to be each
intelligible thing, as the knower is said to do when he is a knower in the active sense
(and this happens when he is able to put his knowing to work on his own), the intellect
is even then in a sense those objects in potency, but not in the same way it was before it
learned and discovered them, and it is then able to think itself.

Now since a magnitude is different from being a magnitude, and water is different   10
from being water (and so too in many other cases, though not in all, since in some cases
the two are the same), being flesh is distinguished either by a different potency from the
one that distinguishes flesh, or by the same one in a different relation. For flesh is not
present without material, but like a snub nose, it is this in that. So it is by the perceptive
potency that one distinguishes hot and cold, and the other things of which flesh is a   15
certain ratio, but it is by a different potency that one distinguishes the being-flesh, either
separate from the first or else with the two having the relation a bent line has to itself
straightened out. Among the things that have being in abstraction, straightness is in its
way just like snubness, since it is combined with continuity; but what it is for it to be, if
being straight is different from what is straight, is something else—let it be twoness.   20
Therefore one distinguishes it by a different potency, or by one in a different relation.
So in general, in whatever way things are separate from their material, so too are the
potencies that have to do with intellect separate from one another.

But one might find it an impasse, if the intellect is simple and without attributes
and has nothing in common with anything, as Anaxagoras says, how it could think, if   25
thinking is a way of being acted upon (for it seems to be by virtue of something common
that is present in both that one thing acts and another is acted upon), and also whether the
intellect is itself an intelligible thing. For either there would be intellect in everything
else, if it is not by virtue of something else that it is itself intelligible, but what is intelligible is something one in kind, or else there would be something mixed in it, which
makes it intelligible like other things. As for a thing's being acted upon in virtue of some-   30
thing common, the distinction was made earlier, that the intellect *is* in a certain way the
intelligible things in potency, but is actively none of them before it thinks them; it is in
potency in the same way a tablet is, when nothing written is present in it actively—this is   430ᵃ
exactly what happens with the intellect. And it is itself intelligible in the same way its
intelligible objects are, for in the case of things without material what thinks and what is
thought are the same thing, for contemplative knowing and what is known in that way are
the same thing (and one must consider the reason why this sort of thinking is not always   5
happening); but among things having material, each of them is potentially something
intelligible, so that there is no intellect present in them (since intellect is a potency to be
such things without their material), but there is present in them something intelligible.

5. But since in all nature one thing is the material for each kind (this is what is in   10
potency all the particular things of that kind), but it is something else that is the causal
and productive thing by which all of them are formed, as is the case with an art in relation to its material, it is necessary in the soul too that these distinct aspects be present;
the one sort is intellect by becoming all things, the other sort by forming all things, in   15
the way an active condition such as light does, for in a certain way light too makes the
colors that are in potency be at work as colors. This sort of intellect is separate, as well
as being without attributes and unmixed, since it is by its thinghood a being-at-work, for
what acts is always distinguished in stature above what is acted upon, as a governing
source is above the material it works on. Knowledge, in its being-at-work, is the same as   20
the thing it knows, and while knowledge in potency comes first in time in any one
knower, in the whole of things it does not take precedence even in time. This does not
mean that at one time it thinks but at another time it does not think, but when separated
it is just exactly what it is, and this alone is deathless and everlasting (though we have
no memory, because this sort of intellect is not acted upon, while the sort that is acted   25
upon is destructible), and without this nothing thinks.

NICOMACHEAN ETHICS (in part)

BOOK I

1094ª   *1. The Good as the Aim of Action:* Every art or applied science and every systematic investigation, and similarly every action and choice, seem to aim at some good;
the good, therefore, has been well defined as that at which all things aim.* But it is clear
that there is a difference in the ends at which they aim: in some cases the activity is the
5   end, in others the end is some product beyond the activity. In cases where the end lies
beyond the action the product is naturally superior to the activity.

Since there are many activities, arts, and sciences, the number of ends is correspondingly large: of medicine the end is health, of shipbuilding a vessel, of strategy,
victory, and of household management, wealth. In many instances several such pursuits
10   are grouped together under a single capacity: the art of bridle-making, for example, and
everything else pertaining to the equipment of a horse are grouped together under
horsemanship; horsemanship in turn, along with every other military action, is grouped
together under strategy; and other pursuits are grouped together under other capacities.
In all these cases the ends of the master sciences are preferable to the ends of the subor-
15   dinate sciences, since the latter are pursued for the sake of the former. This is true
whether the ends of the actions lie in the activities themselves or, as is the case in the
disciplines just mentioned, in something beyond the activities.

2. Politics as the Master Science of the Good: Now, if there exists an end in the
realm of action which we desire for its own sake, an end which determines all our other
desires; if, in other words, we do not make all our choices for the sake of something
20   else—for in this way the process will go on infinitely so that our desire would be futile
and pointless—then obviously this end will be the good, that is, the highest good. Will
not the knowledge of this good, consequently, be very important to our lives? Would it
not better equip us, like archers who have a target to aim at, to hit the proper mark? If
so, we must try to comprehend in outline at least what this good is and to which branch
25   of knowledge or to which capacity it belongs.

This good, one should think, belongs to the most sovereign and most comprehensive master science, and politics** clearly fits this description. For it determines which
sciences ought to exist in states, what kind of sciences each group of citizens must learn,
1094ᵇ   and what degree of proficiency each must attain. We observe further that the most honored capacities, such as strategy, household management, and oratory, are contained in
politics. Since this science uses the rest of the sciences, and since, moreover, it legislates

---

*We do not know who first gave this definition of the good. It is certainly implied in the Platonic dia-
logues, especially in *Republic,* Book VI; but the most likely candidate for the formulation here is Eudoxus.

**Politike* is the science of the city-state, the *polis,* and its members, not merely in our narrow "political"
sense of the word but also in the sense that a civilized human existence is, according to Plato and Aristotle, only
possible in the *polis.* Thus *politike* involves not only the science of the state, "politics," but of our concept of
"society" as well.

Aristotle, *The Nichomachean Ethics,* Books I–II; Book IV, 3; Books VI–VII; Book X, 6–8, translated by
Martin Ostwald (New York: Macmillan/Library of the Liberal Arts, 1962).

what people are to do and what they are not to do, its end seems to embrace the ends of   5
the other sciences. Thus it follows that the end of politics is the good for man. For even if
the good is the same for the individual and the state, the good of the state clearly is the
greater and more perfect thing to attain and to safeguard. The attainment of the good for   10
one man alone is, to be sure, a source of satisfaction; yet to secure it for a nation and for
states is nobler and more divine. In short, these are the aims of our investigation, which
is in a sense an investigation of social and political matters.

    3. The Limitations of Ethics and Politics: Our discussion will be adequate if it
achieves clarity within the limits of the subject matter. For precision cannot be expected in
the treatment of all subjects alike, any more than it can be expected in all manufactured articles. Problems of what is noble and just, which politics examines, present so much variety
and irregularity that some people believe that they exist only by convention and not by   15
nature. The problem of the good, too, presents a similar kind of irregularity, because in
many cases good things bring harmful results. There are instances of men ruined by wealth,
and others by courage. Therefore, in a discussion of such subjects, which has to start from
a basis of this kind, we must be satisfied to indicate the truth with a rough and general   20
sketch: when the subject and the basis of a discussion consist of matters that hold good only
as a general rule, but not always, the conclusions reached must be of the same order. The
various points that are made must be received in the same spirit. For a well-schooled man
is one who searches for that degree of precision in each kind of study which the nature of
the subject at hand admits: it is obviously just as foolish to accept arguments of probability   25
from a mathematician as to demand strict demonstrations from an orator.

    Each man can judge competently the things he knows, and of these he is a good
judge. Accordingly, a good judge in each particular field is one who has been trained in   1095^a
it, and a good judge in general, a man who has received an all-round schooling. For that
reason, a young man is not equipped to be a student of politics; for he has no experience
in the actions which life demands of him, and these actions form the basis and subject
matter of the discussion. Moreover, since he follows his emotions, his study will be
pointless and unprofitable, for the end of this kind of study is not knowledge but action.   5
Whether he is young in years or immature in character makes no difference; for his deficiency is not a matter of time but of living and of pursuing all his interests under the
influence of his emotions. Knowledge brings no benefit to this kind of person, just as it
brings none to the morally weak. But those who regulate their desires and actions by a   10
rational principle* will greatly benefit from a knowledge of this subject. So much by
way of a preface about the student, the limitations which have to be accepted, and the
objective before us.

    4. Happiness Is the Good, But Many Views Are Held About It: To resume the
discussion: since all knowledge and every choice is directed toward some good, let us dis-   15
cuss what is in our view the aim of politics, i.e., the highest good attainable by action. As
far as its name is concerned, most people would probably agree: for both the common run
of people and cultivated men call it happiness, and understand by "being happy" the same
as "living well" and "doing well." But when it comes to defining what happiness is, they

---

*The fundamental meaning of *Logos* is "speech," "statement," in the sense of a coherent and rational
arrangement of words; but it can apply to a rational principle underlying many things, and may be translated in
different contexts by "rational account," "explanation," "argument," "treatise," or "discussion." In Chapters 7
and 13 below, *Logos* is used in a normative sense, describing the human faculty which comprehends and
formulates rational principles and thus guides the conduct of a good and reasonable man.

20   disagree, and the account given by the common run differs from that of the philosophers. The former say it is some clear and obvious good, such as pleasure, wealth, or honor; some say it is one thing and others another, and often the very same person identifies it with different things at different times: when he is sick he thinks it is health, and when he is poor he says it is wealth; and when people are conscious of their own ignorance, they

25   admire those who talk above their heads in accents of greatness. Some thinkers used to believe that there exists over and above these many goods another good, good in itself and by itself, which also is the cause of good in all these things. An examination of all the different opinions would perhaps be a little pointless, and it is sufficient to concentrate on

30   those which are most in evidence or which seem to make some sort of sense.

Nor must we overlook the fact that arguments which proceed from fundamental principles are different from arguments that lead up to them. Plato, too, rightly recognized this as a problem and used to ask whether the discussion was proceeding from or leading up to fundamental principles, just as in a race course there is a difference

1095ᵇ   between running from the judges to the far end of the track and running back again.* Now, we must start with the known. But this term has two connotations: "what is known to us" and "what is known" pure and simple. Therefore, we should start perhaps from

5   what is known to us. For that reason, to be a competent student of what is right and just, and of politics generally, one must first have received a proper upbringing in moral conduct. The acceptance of a fact as a fact is the starting point, and if this is sufficiently clear, there will be no further need to ask why it is so. A man with this kind of background has or can easily acquire the foundations from which he must start. But if he neither has nor can acquire them, let him lend an ear to Hesiod's words:

10   That man is all-best who himself works out every problem. . . .
That man, too, is admirable who follows one who speaks well.
He who cannot see the truth for himself, nor, hearing it from others, store it away in his
    mind, that man is utterly useless.

5. Various Views on the Highest Good: But to return to the point from which we

15   digressed. It is not unreasonable that men should derive their concept of the good and of happiness from the lives which they lead. The common run of people and the most vulgar identify it with pleasure, and for that reason are satisfied with a life of enjoyment. For the most notable kinds of life are three: the life just mentioned, the political life, and the contemplative life.

The common run of people, as we saw, betray their utter slavishness in their pref-

20   erence for a life suitable to cattle; but their views seem plausible because many people in high places share the feelings of Sardanapallus.** Cultivated and active men, on the other hand, believe the good to be honor, for honor, one might say, is the end of the political life. But this is clearly too superficial an answer: for honor seems to depend on

25   those who confer it rather than on him who receives it, whereas our guess is that the good is a man's own possession which cannot easily be taken away from him. Furthermore, men seem to pursue honor to assure themselves of their own worth; at any

---

*A Greek race course was U-shaped with the starting line at the open end, which is also where the judges would have their place. The race was run around a marker set up toward the opposite end of the U, and back again to the starting line.

**Sardanapallus is the Hellenized name of the Assyrian king Ashurbanipal (669–626 B.C.). Many stories about his sensual excesses were current in antiquity.

rate, they seek to be honored by sensible men and by those who know them, and they want to be honored on the basis of their virtue or excellence [<aretē>].* Obviously, then, excellence, as far as they are concerned, is better than honor. One might perhaps   30
even go so far as to consider excellence rather than honor as the end of political life. However, even excellence proves to be imperfect as an end: for a man might possibly possess it while asleep or while being inactive all his life, and while, in addition, under-   1096ᵃ
going the greatest suffering and misfortune. Nobody would call the life of such a man happy, except for the sake of maintaining an argument. But enough of this: the sub-ject has been sufficiently treated in our publications addressed to a wider audience. In the third place there is the contemplative life, which we shall examine later on. As for   5
the money-maker, his life is led under some kind of constraint: clearly, wealth is not the good which we are trying to find, for it is only useful, i.e., it is a means to something else. Hence one might rather regard the aforementioned objects as ends, since they are valued for their own sake. But even they prove not to be the good, though many words have been wasted to show that they are. Accordingly, we may dismiss them.   10

6. *Plato's View of the Good:* But perhaps we had better examine the universal good and face the problem of its meaning, although such an inquiry is repugnant, since those who have introduced the doctrine of Forms** are dear to us. But in the interest of truth, one should perhaps think a man, especially if he is a philosopher, had better give up even [theories that once were] his own and in fact must do so. Both are dear to us, but   15
it is our sacred duty to honor truth more highly [than friends].

The proponents of this theory did not make Forms out of those classes within which they recognized an order involving priority and posteriority; for that reason they made no provision, either, for a Form comprising all numbers.*** However, the term "good" is used in the categories of substance, of quality, and of relatedness alike; but a thing-as-such, i.e., a substance, is by nature prior to a relation into which it can enter: 20
relatedness is, as it were, an offshoot or logical accident of substance. Consequently, there cannot be a Form common to the good-as-such and the good as a relation.

Secondly, the term "good" has as many meanings as the word "is": it is used to describe substances, e.g., divinity and intelligence are good; qualities, e.g., the virtues   25
are good; quantities, e.g., the proper amount is good; relatedness, e.g., the useful is good; time, e.g., the right moment is good; place, e.g., a place to live is good; and so forth. It is clear, therefore, that the good cannot be something universal, common to all cases, and single; for if it were, it would not be applicable in all categories but only in one.

Thirdly, since the things which are included under one Form are the subject matter of a single science, there should be a single science dealing with all good things. But in   30

Aretē denotes the functional excellence of any person, animal, or thing—that quality which enables the possessor to perform his own particular function well. Thus the *aretai* (plural) of man in relation to other men are his qualities which enable him to function well in society. The translation "virtue" often seems too narrow, and accordingly "excellence" and "goodness," or a combination of these, will also be used.

**The reference is of course to Plato's theory of *eide* or *ideai* and especially the Form of the Good, which is Aristotle's chief target here.

***Since for Plato and his followers the Forms are absolute being, in which there is no room for becoming or any kind of development, they do not recognize a Form of a developing series, in which each suc-cessive member implies the preceding members of the same series. But, as Aristotle proceeds to show, the term "good" belongs to such a developing series: if we call a certain quality, e.g., blueness, "good," we have to assume first that there is such a thing as blueness; i.e., we have to predicate it in the category of substance before we can predicate it in the category of quality.

actual fact there are many sciences dealing even with the goods that fall into a single category. To take, for example, the right moment: in war it is the proper concern of strategy, whereas in treating a disease it is part of the study of medicine. Or to take the proper amount: in food it is the subject of medicine; in physical training, of gymnastics.

35
1096ᵇ
One might even [go further and] raise the question what exactly they mean by a "thing-as-such"; for the selfsame definition of "man" applies to both "man-as-such" and a particular man. For inasmuch as they refer to "man," there will be no difference between the two; and if this is true, there will be no difference, either, between "good-as-such" and "good," since both are good. Nor indeed will the "good-as-such" be more of a good because it is everlasting: after all, whiteness which lasts for a long time is no whiter than whiteness which lasts only for a day.

5
The argument of the Pythagoreans on this point seems to be more convincing. They give unity a place in the column of goods; and indeed even Speusippus* seems to follow them. But more about this elsewhere.

An objection might be raised against what we have said on the ground that the [Platonic] doctrine does not refer to every kind of good, and that only things which are

10
pursued and loved for their own sake are called "good" by reference to one single Form. That which produces good or somehow guarantees its permanence, [the Platonists argue,] or that which prevents the opposite of a good from asserting itself is called "good" because it is conducive to the intrinsically good and in a different sense. Now, the term "good" has obviously two different meanings: (1) things which are intrinsically good, and (2) things which are good as being conducive to the intrinsically good. Let us,

15
therefore, separate the intrinsically good things from the useful things and examine whether they are called "good" by reference to a single Form.

What sort of things could be called intrinsically good? Are they the goods that are pursued without regard to additional benefits, such as thought, sight, certain pleasures and honors? For even if we pursue these also for the sake of something else, one would still classify them among things intrinsically good. Or is nothing good except the Form of Good? If

20
that is the case, the Form will be pointless. But if, on the contrary, thought, sight, etc. also belong to the group of intrinsically good things, the same definition of "good" will have to be manifested in all of them, just as, for example, the definition of whiteness is the same in snow and in white paint. But in actual fact, the definitions of "good" as manifested in honor, thought, and pleasure are different and distinct. The good, therefore, is not some element

25
common to all these things as derived from one Form.

What, then, is the meaning of "good" [in these different things]? Surely, it is not that they merely happen to have the same name. Do we call them "good" because they are derived from a single good, or because they all aim at a single good? Or do we rather call them "good" by analogy, e.g., as sight is good in the body, so intelligence is good in the soul, and so other things are good within their respective fields?

30
But perhaps this subject should be dismissed for the present, because a detailed discussion of it belongs more properly to a different branch of philosophy, [namely, first philosophy]. The same applies to the Form [of the Good]: for, assuming that there is some single good which different things possess in common, or that there exists a good absolutely in itself and by itself, it evidently is something which cannot be realized in action or attained by man. But the good which we are now seeking must be attainable.

35
1097ᵃ
Perhaps one may think that the recognition of an absolute good will be advantageous for the purpose of attaining and realizing in action the goods which can be attained and

*Speusippus was Plato's nephew and disciple who succeeded him a head of the Academy from 347–339 B.C.

realized. By treating the absolute good as a pattern, [they might argue,] we shall gain a better knowledge of what things are good for us, and once we know that, we can achieve them. This argument has, no doubt, some plausibility; however, it does not tally with the procedure of the sciences. For while all the sciences aim at some good and seek to fulfill it, they leave the knowledge of the absolute good out of consideration. Yet if this knowledge were such a great help, it would make no sense that all the craftsmen are ignorant of it and do not even attempt to seek it. One might also wonder what benefit a weaver or a carpenter might derive in the practice of his own art from a knowledge of the absolute Good, or in what way a physician who has contemplated the Form of the Good will become more of a physician or a general more of a general. For actually, a physician does not even examine health in this fashion; he examines the health of man, or perhaps better, the health of a particular man, for he practices his medicine on particular cases. So much for this.

7. The Good Is Final and Self-Sufficient; Happiness Is Defined: Let us return again to our investigation into the nature of the good which we are seeking. It is evidently something different in different actions and in each art: it is one thing in medicine, another in strategy, and another again in each of the other arts. What, then, is the good of each? Is it not that for the sake of which everything else is done? That means it is health in the case of medicine, victory in the case of strategy, a house in the case of building, a different thing in the case of different arts, and in all actions and choices it is the end. For it is for the sake of the end that all else is done. Thus, if there is some one end for all that we do, this would be the good attainable by action; if there are several ends, they will be the goods attainable by action.

Our argument has gradually progressed to the same point at which we were before, and we must try to clarify it still further. Since there are evidently several ends, and since we choose some of these—e.g., wealth, flutes, and instruments generally—as a means to something else, it is obvious that not all ends are final. The highest good, on the other hand, must be something final. Thus, if there is only one final end, this will be the good we are seeking; if there are several, it will be the most final and perfect of them. We call that which is pursued as an end in itself more final than an end which is pursued for the sake of something else; and what is never chosen as a means to something else we call more final than that which is chosen both as an end in itself and as a means to something else. What is always chosen as an end in itself and never as a means to something else is called final in an unqualified sense. This description seems to apply to happiness above all else: for we always choose happiness as an end in itself and never for the sake of something else. Honor, pleasure, intelligence, and all virtue we choose partly for themselves—for we would choose each of them even if no further advantage would accrue from them—but we also choose them partly for the sake of happiness, because we assume that it is through them that we will be happy. On the other hand, no one chooses happiness for the sake of honor, pleasure, and the like, nor as a means to anything at all.

We arrive at the same conclusion if we approach the question from the standpoint of self-sufficiency. For the final and perfect good seems to be self-sufficient. However, we define something as self-sufficient not by reference to the "self" alone. We do not mean a man who lives his life in isolation, but a man who also lives with parents, children, a wife, and friends and fellow citizens generally, since man is by nature a social and political being. But some limit must be set to these relationships; for if they are extended to include ancestors, descendants, and friends of friends, they will go on to infinity. However, this point must be reserved for investigation later. For the present we define as "self-sufficient" that which taken by itself makes life something desirable and deficient in nothing. It is happiness, in our opinion, which fits this description. Moreover, happiness is of all things the one most desirable, and it is not counted as one good thing among many others. But if it

were counted as one among many others, it is obvious that the addition of even the least of
the goods would make it more desirable; for the addition would produce an extra amount of
good, and the greater amount of good is always more desirable than the lesser. We see then
20   that happiness is something final and self-sufficient and the end of our actions.

To call happiness the highest good is perhaps a little trite, and a clearer account of
what it is, is still required. Perhaps this is best done by first ascertaining the proper function
of man. For just as the goodness and performance of a flute player, a sculptor, or any kind
25   of expert, and generally of anyone who fulfills some function or performs some action, are
thought to reside in his proper function, so the goodness and performance of man would
seem to reside in whatever is his proper function. Is it then possible that while a carpenter
and a shoemaker have their own proper functions and spheres of action, man as man has
30   none, but was left by nature a good-for-nothing without a function? Should we not assume
that just as the eye, the hand, the foot, and in general each part of the body clearly has its
own proper function, so man too has some function over and above the functions of his
parts? What can this function possibly be? Simply living? He shares that even with plants,
1098ª   but we are now looking for something peculiar to man. Accordingly, the life of nutrition
and growth must be excluded. Next in line there is a life of sense perception. But this, too,
man has in common with the horse, the ox, and every animal. There remains then an active
life of the rational element. The rational element has two parts: one is rational in that it
obeys the rule of reason, the other in that it possesses and conceives rational rules. Since the
5   expression "life of the rational element" also can be used in two senses, we must make it
clear that we mean a life determined by the activity, as opposed to the mere possession, of
the rational element. For the activity, it seems, has a greater claim to be the function of man.

The proper function of man, then, consists in an activity of the soul in conformity
with a rational principle or, at least, not without it. In speaking of the proper function of
a given individual we mean that it is the same in kind as the function of an individual
who sets high standards for himself: the proper function of a harpist, for example, is
the same as the function of a harpist who has set high standards for himself. The same
applies to any and every group of individuals: the full attainment of excellence must
10   be added to the mere function. In other words, the function of the harpist is to play the
harp; the function of the harpist who has high standards is to play it well. On these
assumptions, if we take the proper function of man to be a certain kind of life, and if this
kind of life is an activity of the soul and consists in actions performed in conjunction
with the rational element, and if a man of high standards is he who performs these
actions well and properly, and if a function is well performed when it is performed in
accordance with the excellence appropriate to it; we reach the conclusion that the good
15   of man is an activity of the soul in conformity with excellence or virtue, and if there are
several virtues, in conformity with the best and most complete.

But we must add "in a complete life." For one swallow does not make a spring,
nor does one sunny day; similarly, one day or a short time does not make a man
blessed* and happy.

This will suffice as an outline of the good: for perhaps one ought to make a general
20   sketch first and fill in the details afterwards. Once a good outline has been made, anyone,
it seems, is capable of developing and completing it in detail, and time is a good inventor
or collaborator in such an effort. Advances in the arts, too, have come about in this way,
for anyone can fill in gaps. We must also bear in mind what has been said above, namely

---

*The distinction Aristotle seems to observe between *makarios,* "blessed" or "supremely happy," and
eudaimon, "happy," is that the former describes happiness insofar as it is god-given, while the latter describes
happiness as attained by man through his own efforts.

that one should not require precision in all pursuits alike, but in each field precision varies   25
with the matter under discussion and should be required only to the extent to which it is
appropriate to the investigation. A carpenter and a geometrician both want to find a right
angle, but they do not want to find it in the same sense: the former wants to find it to the   30
extent to which it is useful for his work, the latter, wanting to see truth, tries to ascertain
what it is and what sort of thing it is. We must, likewise, approach other subjects in the
same spirit, in order to prevent minor points from assuming a greater importance than the   1098^b
major tasks. Nor should we demand to know a causal explanation in all matters alike; in
some instances, e.g., when dealing with fundamental principles, it is sufficient to point out
convincingly that such-and-such is in fact the case. The fact here is the primary thing and
the fundamental principle. Some fundamental principles can be apprehended by induction, others by sense perception, others again by some sort of habituation,* and others by
still other means. We must try to get at each of them in a way naturally appropriate to it,   5
and must be scrupulous in defining it correctly, because it is of great importance for the
subsequent course of the discussion. Surely, a good beginning is more than half the whole,
and as it comes to light, it sheds light on many problems.

 8. *Popular Views About Happiness Confirm Our Position:* We must examine the
fundamental principle with which we are concerned, [happiness,] not only on the basis
of the logical conclusion we have reached and on the basis of the elements which make
up its definition, but also on the basis of the views commonly expressed about it. For in   10
a true statement, all the facts are in harmony; in a false statement, truth soon introduces
a discordant note.
 Good things are commonly divided into three classes: (1) external goods, (2) goods
of the soul, and (3) goods of the body. Of these, we call the goods pertaining to the soul
goods in the highest and fullest sense. But in speaking of "soul," we refer to our soul's
actions and activities. Thus, our definition tallies with this opinion which has been current   15
for a long time and to which philosophers subscribe. We are also right in defining the end
as consisting of actions and activities; for in this way the end is included among the goods
of the soul and not among external goods.
 Also the view that a happy man lives well and fares well fits in with our definition: 20
for we have all but defined happiness as a kind of good life and well-being.
 Moreover, the characteristics which one looks for in happiness are all included in
our definition. For some people think that happiness is virtue, others that it is practical
wisdom, others that it is some kind of theoretical wisdom; others again believe it to be
all or some of these accompanied by, or not devoid of, pleasure; and some people also   25
include external prosperity in its definition.** Some of these views are expressed by
many people and have come down from antiquity, some by a few men of high prestige,
and it is not reasonable to assume that both groups are altogether wrong; the presumption is rather that they are right in at least one or even in most respects.

---

 *This, according to Aristotle, is the way in which the fundamental principles of ethics are learned, and for
that reason a person must be mature in order to be able to study ethics properly. Aristotle is not trying to persuade
his listener of the truth of these principles, but takes it for granted that the listener has learned them at home.
 **The view that virtue alone constitutes happiness was espoused by Antisthenes and the Cynics (and
later by the Stoics); the doctrine that all virtues are forms of *phronesis* or "practical wisdom" is attributed to
Socrates; theoretical wisdom as virtue may perhaps be attributed to Anaxagoras and his doctrine of *Nous;* the
view that pleasure must be added to virtue and wisdom is that of Plato; and the ancient commentators on this
passage identify Xenocrates, Plato's pupil and later head of the Academy, as regarding external goods as essential for the good life.

Now, in our definition we are in agreement with those who describe happiness as
virtue or as some particular virtue, for our term "activity in conformity with virtue"
implies virtue. But it does doubtless make a considerable difference whether we think
of the highest good as consisting in the possession or in the practice of virtue, viz., as
being a characteristic or an activity. For a characteristic may exist without producing
any good result, as for example, in a man who is asleep or incapacitated in some other
respect. An activity, on the other hand, must produce a result: [an active person] will
necessarily act and act well. Just as the crown at the Olympic Games is not awarded to
the most beautiful and the strongest but to the participants in the contests—for it is
among them that the victors are found—so the good and noble things in life are won by
those who act rightly.

The life of men active in this sense is also pleasant in itself. For the sensation of
pleasure belongs to the soul, and each man derives pleasure from what he is said to love:
a lover of horses from horses, a lover of the theater from plays, and in the same way a
lover of justice from just acts, and a lover of virtue in general from virtuous acts. In most
men, pleasant acts conflict with one another because they are not pleasant by nature, but
men who love what is noble derive pleasure from what is naturally pleasant. Actions
which conform to virtue are naturally pleasant, and, as a result, such actions are not only
pleasant for those who love the noble but also pleasant in themselves. The life of such
men has no further need of pleasure as an added attraction, but it contains pleasure within
itself. We may even go so far as to state that the man who does not enjoy performing
noble actions is not a good man at all. Nobody would call a man just who does not enjoy
acting justly, nor generous who does not enjoy generous actions, and so on. If this is true,
actions performed in conformity with virtue are in themselves pleasant.

Of course it goes without saying that such actions are good as well as noble, and
they are both in the highest degree, if the man of high moral standards displays any right
judgment about them at all; and his judgment corresponds to our description. So we see
that happiness is at once the best, noblest, and most pleasant thing, and these qualities
are not separate, as the inscription at Delos makes out:

> The most just is most noble, but health is the best, and to win what one loves is
> pleasantest.

For the best activities encompass all these attributes, and it is in these, or in the best one
of them, that we maintain happiness consists.

Still, happiness, as we have said, needs external goods as well. For it is impossible or at least not easy to perform noble actions if one lacks the wherewithal. Many
actions can only be performed with the help of instruments, as it were: friends, wealth,
and political power. And there are some external goods the absence of which spoils
supreme happiness, e.g., good birth, good children, and beauty: for a man who is very
ugly in appearance or ill-born or who lives all by himself and has no children cannot be
classified as altogether happy; even less happy perhaps is a man whose children and
friends are worthless, or one who has lost good children and friends through death.
Thus, as we have said, happiness also requires well-being of this kind, and that is the
reason why some classify good fortune with happiness, while others link it to virtue.

9. How Happiness Is Acquired: This also explains why there is a problem whether
happiness is acquired by learning, by discipline, or by some other kind of training, or
whether we attain it by reason of some divine dispensation or even by chance. Now, if there
is anything at all which comes to men as a gift from the gods, it is reasonable to suppose

that happiness above all else is god-given; and of all things human it is the most likely to be god-given, inasmuch as it is the best. But although this subject is perhaps more appropriate to a different field of study, it is clear that happiness is one of the most divine things, even if it is not god-sent but attained through virtue and some kind of learning or training. For the prize and end of excellence and virtue is the best thing of all, and it is something divine and blessed. Moreover, if happiness depends on excellence, it will be shared by many people; for study and effort will make it accessible to anyone whose capacity for virtue is unimpaired. And if it is better that happiness is acquired in this way rather than by chance, it is reasonable to assume that this is the way in which it is acquired. For, in the realm of nature, things are naturally arranged in the best way possible—and the same is also true of the products of art and of any kind of causation, especially the highest. To leave the greatest and noblest of things to chance would hardly be right.

A solution of this question is also suggested by our earlier definition, according to which the good of man, happiness, is some kind of activity of the soul in conformity with virtue. All the other goods are either necessary prerequisites for happiness, or are by nature co-workers with it and useful instruments for attaining it. Our results also tally with what we said at the outset: for we stated that the end of politics is the best of ends; and the main concern of politics is to engender a certain character in the citizens and to make them good and disposed to perform noble actions.

We are right, then, when we call neither a horse nor an ox nor any other animal happy, for none of them is capable of participating in an activity of this kind. For the same reason, a child is not happy, either; for, because of his age, he cannot yet perform such actions. When we do call a child happy, we do so by reason of the hopes we have for his future. Happiness, as we have said, requires completeness in virtue as well as a complete lifetime. Many changes and all kinds of contingencies befall a man in the course of his life, and it is possible that the most prosperous man will encounter great misfortune in his old age, as the Trojan legends tell about Priam. When a man has met a fate such as his and has come to a wretched end, no one calls him happy.

10. Can a Man Be Called "Happy" During His Lifetime?: Must we, then, apply the term "happy" to no man at all as long as he is alive? Must we, as Solon would have us do, wait to see his end?* And, on this assumption, is it also true that a man is actually happy after he is dead? Is this not simply absurd, especially for us who define happiness as a kind of activity? Suppose we do not call a dead man happy, and interpret Solon's words to mean that only when a man is dead can we safely say that he has been happy, since he is now beyond the reach of evil and misfortune—this view, too, is open to objection. For it seems that to some extent good and evil really exist for a dead man, just as they may exist for a man who lives without being conscious of them, for example, honors and disgraces, and generally the successes and failures of his children and descendants. This presents a further problem. A man who has lived happily to his old age and has died as happily as he lived may have many vicissitudes befall his descendants: some of them may be good and may be granted the kind of life which they deserve, and others may not. It is, further, obvious that the descendants may conceivably be removed from their ancestors by various degrees. Under such circumstances, it would be odd if the dead man would share in the vicissitudes of his descendants and be happy at one time and wretched at another. But it would also be odd if the fortunes of their descendants did not affect the ancestors at all, not even for a short time.

---

*This is one of the main points made by Solon, Athenian statesman and poet of the early sixth century B.C., in his conversation with the Lydian king, Croesus.

But we must return to the problem raised earlier, for through it our present problem perhaps may be solved. If one must look to the end and praise a man not as being happy but as having been happy in the past, is it not paradoxical that at a time when a man actually is happy this attribute, though true, cannot be applied to him? We are unwilling to call the living happy because changes may befall them and because we believe that happiness has permanence and is not amenable to changes under any circumstances, whereas fortunes revolve many times in one person's lifetime. For obviously, if we are to keep pace with a man's fortune, we shall frequently have to call the same man happy at one time and wretched at another and demonstrate that the happy man is a kind of chameleon, and that the foundations [of his life] are unsure. Or is it quite wrong to make our judgment depend on fortune? Yes, it is wrong, for fortune does not determine whether we fare well or ill, but is, as we said, merely an accessory to human life; activities in conformity with virtue constitute happiness, and the opposite activities constitute its opposite.

The question which we have just discussed further confirms our definition. For no function of man possesses as much stability as do activities in conformity with virtue: these seem to be even more durable than scientific knowledge. And the higher the virtuous activities, the more durable they are, because men who are supremely happy spend their lives in these activities most intensely and most continuously, and this seems to be the reason why such activities cannot be forgotten.

The happy man will have the attribute of permanence which we are discussing, and he will remain happy throughout his life. For he will always or to the highest degree both do and contemplate what is in conformity with virtue; he will bear the vicissitudes of fortune most nobly and with perfect decorum under all circumstances, inasmuch as he is truly good and "four-square beyond reproach."

But fortune brings many things to pass, some great and some small. Minor instances of good and likewise of bad luck obviously do not decisively tip the scales of life, but a number of major successes will make life more perfectly happy; for, in the first place, by their very nature they help to make life attractive, and secondly, they afford the opportunity for noble and good actions. On the other hand, frequent reverses can crush and mar supreme happiness in that they inflict pain and thwart many activities. Still, nobility shines through even in such circumstances, when a man bears many great misfortunes with good grace not because he is insensitive to pain but because he is noble and high-minded.

If, as we said, the activities determine a man's life, no supremely happy man can ever become miserable, for he will never do what is hateful and base. For in our opinion, the man who is truly good and wise will bear with dignity whatever fortune may bring, and will always act as nobly as circumstances permit, just as a good general makes the most strategic use of the troops at his disposal, and a good shoemaker makes the best shoe he can from the leather available, and so on with experts in all other fields. If this is true, a happy man will never become miserable; but even so, supreme happiness will not be his if a fate such as Priam's befalls him. And yet, he will not be fickle and changeable; he will not be dislodged from his happiness easily by any misfortune that comes along, but only by great and numerous disasters such as will make it impossible for him to become happy again in a short time; if he recovers his happiness at all, it will be only after a long period of time, in which he has won great distinctions.

Is there anything to prevent us, then, from defining the happy man as one whose activities are an expression of complete virtue, and who is sufficiently equipped with external goods, not simply at a given moment but to the end of his life? Or should we add that he must die as well as live in the manner which we have defined? For we cannot foresee the future, and happiness, we maintain, is an end which is absolutely final and complete in every respect. If this be granted, we shall define as "supremely happy" those living men who fulfill and continue to fulfill these requirements, but blissful only as human beings. So much for this question.   20

11. Do the Fortunes of the Living Affect the Dead?: That the fortunes of his descendants and of all those near and dear to him do not affect the happiness of a dead man at all, seems too unfeeling a view and contrary to the prevailing opinions. Many and different in kind are the accidents that can befall us, and some hit home more closely than others. It would, therefore, seem to be a long and endless task to make   25
detailed distinctions, and perhaps a general outline will be sufficient. Just as one's own misfortunes are sometimes momentous and decisive for one's life and sometimes seem comparatively less important, so the misfortunes of our various friends affect us to vary-   30
ing degrees. In each case it makes a considerable difference whether those who are affected by an event are living or dead; much more so than it matters in a tragedy whether the crimes and horrors have been perpetrated before the opening of the play or are part of the plot. This difference, too, must be taken into account and perhaps still more the problem whether the dead participate in any good or evil. These considera-   35
tions suggest that even if any good or evil reaches them at all, it must be something   1101[b]
weak and negligible (either intrinsically or in relation to them), or at least something too small and insignificant to make the unhappy happy or to deprive the happy of their bliss. The good as well as the bad fortunes of their friends seem, then, to have some effect   5
upon the dead, but the nature and magnitude of the effect is such as not to make the happy unhappy or to produce any similar changes.

12. The Praise Accorded to Happiness: Now that we have settled these ques-   10
tions, let us consider whether happiness is to be classified among the things which we praise or rather among those which we honor; for it is clear that it is not a potential [but an actual good].
      The grounds on which we bestow praise on anything evidently are its quality and the relation in which it stands to other things. In other words, we praise a just man, a courageous man, and in general any good man, and also his virtue or excellence, on the   15
basis of his actions and achievements; moreover, we praise a strong man, a swift runner, and so forth, because he possesses a certain natural quality and stands in a certain relation to something good and worth while. Our feelings about praising the gods provide a further illustration of this point. For it is ridiculous to refer the gods to our standards; but this is precisely what praising them amounts to, since praise, as we said, entails a   20
reference to something else. But if praise is appropriate only for relative things, it is clear that the best things do not call for praise but for something greater and better, as indeed is generally recognized: for we call the gods "blessed" and "happy" and use these terms also for the most godlike man. The same is true of good things: no one   25
praises happiness in the same sense in which he praises justice, but he exalts its bliss as something better and more nearly divine.
      Eudoxus, too, seems to have used the right method for advocating that pleasure is the most excellent, for he took the fact that pleasure, though a good, is not praised as an indication of its superiority to the things that are praised, as god and the good are, for   30
they are the standards to which we refer everything else.
      Praise is proper to virtue or excellence, because it is excellence that makes men capable of performing noble deeds. Eulogies, on the other hand, are appropriate for achievements of the body as well as of the mind. However, a detailed analysis of this

subject is perhaps rather the business of those who have made a study of eulogies. For our present purposes, we may draw the conclusion from the preceding argument that happiness is one of the goods that are worthy of honor and are final. This again seems to be due to the fact that it is a starting point or fundamental principle, since for its sake all of us do everything else. And the source and cause of all good things we consider as something worthy of honor and as divine.

13. The Psychological Foundations of the Virtues: Since happiness is a certain activity of the soul in conformity with perfect virtue, we must now examine what virtue or excellence is. For such an inquiry will perhaps better enable us to discover the nature of happiness. Moreover, the man who is truly concerned about politics seems to devote special attention to excellence, since it is his aim to make the citizens good and law-abiding. We have an example of this in the lawgivers of Crete and Sparta and in other great legislators. If an examination of virtue is part of politics, this question clearly fits into the pattern of our original plan.

There can be no doubt that the virtue which we have to study is human virtue. For the good which we have been seeking is a human good and the happiness a human happiness. By human virtue we do not mean the excellence of the body, but that of the soul, and we define happiness as an activity of the soul. If this is true, the student of politics must obviously have some knowledge of the workings of the soul, just as the man who is to heal eyes must know something about the whole body. In fact, knowledge is all the more important for the former, inasmuch as politics is better and more valuable than medicine, and cultivated physicians devote much time and trouble to gain knowledge about the body. Thus, the student of politics must study the soul, but he must do so with his own aim in view, and only to the extent that the objects of his inquiry demand: to go into it in greater detail would perhaps be more laborious than his purposes require.

Some things that are said about the soul in our less technical discussions are adequate enough to be used here, for instance, that the soul consists of two elements, one irrational and one rational. Whether these two elements are separate, like the parts of the body or any other divisible thing, or whether they are only logically separable though in reality indivisible, as convex and concave are in the circumference of a circle, is irrelevant for our present purposes.

Of the irrational element, again, one part seems to be common to all living things and vegetative in nature: I mean that part which is responsible for nurture and growth. We must assume that some such capacity of the soul exists in everything that takes nourishment, in the embryonic stage as well as when the organism is fully developed; for this makes more sense than to assume the existence of some different capacity at the latter stage. The excellence of this part of the soul is, therefore, shown to be common to all living things and is not exclusively human. This very part and this capacity seem to be most active in sleep. For in sleep the difference between a good man and a bad is least apparent—whence the saying that for half their lives the happy are no better off than the wretched. This is just what we would expect, for sleep is an inactivity of the soul in that it ceases to do things which cause it to be called good or bad. However, to a small extent some bodily movements do penetrate to the soul in sleep, and in this sense the dreams of honest men are better than those of average people. But enough of this subject: we may pass by the nutritive part, since it has no natural share in human excellence or virtue.

In addition to this, there seems to be another integral element of the soul which, though irrational, still does partake of reason in some way. In morally strong and morally weak men we praise the reason that guides them and the rational element of the soul, because it exhorts them to follow the right path and to do what is best. Yet we see in them also another natural strain different from the rational, which fights and resists the guidance of reason. The soul behaves in precisely the same manner as do the paralyzed limbs of the body. When we intend to move the limbs to the right, they turn to the 20 left, and similarly, the impulses of morally weak persons turn in the direction opposite to that in which reason leads them. However, while the aberration of the body is visible, that of the soul is not. But perhaps we must accept it as a fact, nevertheless, that there is something in the soul besides the rational element, which opposes and reacts against it. In what way the two are distinct need not concern us here. But, as we have stated, it too 25 seems to partake of reason; at any rate, in a morally strong man it accepts the leadership of reason, and is perhaps more obedient still in a self-controlled and courageous man, since in him everything is in harmony with the voice of reason.

Thus we see that the irrational element of the soul has two parts: the one is vegetative and has no share in reason at all, the other is the seat of the appetites and of 30 desire in general and partakes of reason insofar as it complies with reason and accepts its leadership; it possesses reason in the sense that we say it is "reasonable" to accept the advice of a father and of friends, not in the sense that we have a "rational" understanding of mathematical propositions. That the irrational element can be persuaded by the rational is shown by the fact that admonition and all manner of rebuke and exhortation are possible. If it is correct to say that the appetitive part, too, has reason, 1103[a] it follows that the rational element of the soul has two subdivisions: the one possesses reason in the strict sense, contained within itself, and the other possesses reason in the sense that it listens to reason as one would listen to a father.

Virtue, too, is differentiated in line with this division of the soul. We call some virtues "intellectual" and others "moral": theoretical wisdom, understanding, and 5 practical wisdom are intellectual virtues, generosity and self-control moral virtues. In speaking of a man's character, we do not describe him as wise or understanding, but as gentle or self-controlled; but we praise the wise man, too, for his characteristic, and 10 praiseworthy characteristics are what we call virtues.

BOOK II

1. Moral Virtue as the Result of Habits: Virtue, as we have seen, consists of two-kinds, intellectual virtue and moral virtue. Intellectual virtue or excellence owes its origin 15 and development chiefly to teaching, and for that reason requires experience and time. Moral virtue, on the other hand, is formed by habit, *ethos,* and its name, *ethike,* is therefore derived, by a slight variation, from *ethos.* This shows, too, that none of the moral virtues is implanted in us by nature, for nothing which exists by nature can be changed by habit. For 20 example, it is impossible for a stone, which has a natural downward movement, to become habituated to moving upward, even if one should try ten thousand times to inculcate the habit by throwing it in the air; nor can fire be made to move downward, nor can the direction of any nature-given tendency be changed by habituation. Thus, the virtues are implanted in us neither by nature nor contrary to nature: we are by nature equipped with the 25 ability to receive them, and habit brings this ability to completion and fulfillment.

Furthermore, of all the qualities with which we are endowed by nature, we are provided with the capacity first, and display the activity afterward. That this is true is shown by the senses: it is not by frequent seeing or frequent hearing that we acquired our senses, but on the contrary we first possess and then use them; we do not acquire them by use.

30   The virtues, on the other hand, we acquire by first having put them into action, and the same is also true of the arts. For the things which we have to learn before we can do them we learn by doing: men become builders by building houses, and harpists by playing the
1103^b   harp. Similarly, we become just by the practice of just actions, self-controlled by exercising self-control, and courageous by performing acts of courage.

This is corroborated by what happens in states. Lawgivers make the citizens good by inculcating [good] habits in them, and this is the aim of every lawgiver; if he does
5   not succeed in doing that, his legislation is a failure. It is in this that a good constitution differs from a bad one.

Moreover, the same causes and the same means that produce any excellence or virtue can also destroy it, and this is also true of every art. It is by playing the harp that men become both good and bad harpists, and correspondingly with builders and all the
10   other craftsmen: a man who builds well will be a good builder, one who builds badly a bad one. For if this were not so, there would be no need for an instructor, but everybody would be born as a good or a bad craftsman. The same holds true of the virtues: in our
15   transactions with other men it is by action that some become just and others unjust, and it is by acting in the face of danger and by developing the habit of feeling fear or confidence that some become brave men and others cowards. The same applies to the appetites and feelings of anger: by reacting in one way or in another to given circumstances some people become self-controlled and gentle, and others self-indulgent and
20   short-tempered. In a word, characteristics develop from corresponding activities. For that reason, we must see to it that our activities are of a certain kind, since any variations in them will be reflected in our characteristics. Hence it is no small matter whether one habit or another is inculcated in us from early childhood; on the contrary, it makes a
25   considerable difference, or, rather, all the difference.

2. *Method in the Practical Sciences:* The purpose of the present study is not, as it is in other inquiries, the attainment of theoretical knowledge: we are not conducting this inquiry in order to know what virtue is, but in order to become good, else there would be no advantage in studying it. For that reason, it becomes necessary to examine the
30   problem of actions, and to ask how they are to be performed. For, as we have said, the actions determine what kind of characteristics are developed.

That we must act according to right reason is generally conceded and may be assumed as the basis of our discussion. We shall speak about it later and discuss what right reason is and examine its relation to the other virtues. But let us first agree that any
1104^a   discussion on matters of action cannot be more than an outline and is bound to lack precision; for as we stated at the outset, one can demand of a discussion only what the subject matter permits, and there are no fixed data in matters concerning action and questions of what is beneficial, any more than there are in matters of health. And if this
5   is true of our general discussion, our treatment of particular problems will be even less precise, since these do not come under the head of any art which can be transmitted by precept, but the agent must consider on each different occasion what the situation
10   demands, just as in medicine and in navigation. But although such is the kind of discussion in which we are engaged, we must do our best.

First of all, it must be observed that the nature of moral qualities is such that they are destroyed by defect and by excess. We see the same thing happen in the case of strength and of health, to illustrate, as we must, the invisible by means of visible
15   examples: excess as well as deficiency of physical exercise destroys our strength, and similarly, too much and too little food and drink destroys our health; the proportionate amount, however, produces, increases, and preserves it. The same applies to self-control,

courage, and the other virtues: the man who shuns and fears everything and never stands   20
his ground becomes a coward, whereas a man who knows no fear at all and goes to meet
every danger becomes reckless. Similarly, a man who revels in every pleasure and
abstains from none becomes self-indulgent, while he who avoids every pleasure like a
boor becomes what might be called insensitive. Thus we see that self-control and   25
courage are destroyed by excess and by deficiency and are preserved by the mean.

Not only are the same actions which are responsible for and instrumental in the
origin and development of the virtues also the causes and means of their destruction, but
they will also be manifested in the active exercise of the virtues. We can see the truth of
this in the case of other more visible qualities, e.g., strength. Strength is produced by   30
consuming plenty of food and by enduring much hard work, and it is the strong man
who is best able to do these things. The same is also true of the virtues: by abstaining
from pleasures we become self-controlled, and once we are self-controlled we are best   35
able to abstain from pleasures. So also with courage: by becoming habituated to despise   1104^b
and to endure terrors we become courageous, and once we have become courageous we
will best be able to endure terror.

3. *Pleasure and Pain as the Test of Virtue:* An index to our characteristics is
provided by the pleasure or pain which follows upon the tasks we have achieved. A man   5
who abstains from bodily pleasures and enjoys doing so is self-controlled; if he finds
abstinence troublesome, he is self-indulgent; a man who endures danger with joy, or at
least without pain, is courageous; if he endures it with pain, he is a coward. For moral
excellence is concerned with pleasure and pain; it is pleasure that makes us do base   10
actions and pain that prevents us from doing noble actions. For that reason, as Plato
says, men must be brought up from childhood to feel pleasure and pain at the proper
things; for this is correct education.

Furthermore, since the virtues have to do with actions and emotions, and since
pleasure and pain are a consequence of every emotion and of every action, it follows   15
from this point of view, too, that virtue has to do with pleasure and pain. This is further
indicated by the fact that punishment is inflicted by means of pain. For punishment is a
kind of medical treatment and it is the nature of medical treatments to take effect
through the introduction of the opposite of the disease.* Again, as we said just now,
every characteristic of the soul shows its true nature in its relation to and its concern   20
with those factors which naturally make it better or worse. But it is through pleasures
and pains that men are corrupted, i.e., through pursuing and avoiding pleasures and
pains either of the wrong kind or at the wrong time or in the wrong manner, or by going
wrong in some other definable respect. For that reason some people define the virtues as
states of freedom from emotion and of quietude. However, they make the mistake of
using these terms absolutely and without adding such qualifications as "in the right   25
manner," "at the right or wrong time," and so forth. We may, therefore, assume as the
basis of our discussion that virtue, being concerned with pleasure and pain in the way
we have described, makes us act in the best way in matters revolving pleasure and pain,
and that vice does the opposite.

The following considerations may further illustrate that virtue is concerned with
pleasure and pain. There are three factors that determine choice and three that determine   30
avoidance: the noble, the beneficial, and the pleasurable, on the one hand, and on the other
their opposites: the base, the harmful, and the painful. Now a good man will go right and

*The idea here evidently is that the pleasure of wrongdoing must be cured by applying its opposite,
i.e., pain.

a bad man will go wrong when any of these, and especially when pleasure is involved. For pleasure is not only common to man and the animals, but also accompanies all objects of choice: in fact, the noble and the beneficial seem pleasant to us. Moreover, a love of pleasure has grown up with all of us from infancy. Therefore, this emotion has come to be ingrained in our lives and is difficult to erase. Even in our actions we use, to a greater or smaller extent, pleasure and pain as a criterion. For this reason, this entire study is necessarily concerned with pleasure and pain; for it is not unimportant for our actions whether we feel joy and pain in the right or the wrong way. Again, it is harder to fight against pleasure than against anger, as Heraclitus says; and both virtue and art are always concerned with what is harder, for success is better when it is hard to achieve. Thus, for this reason also, every study both of virtue and of politics must deal with pleasures and pains, for if a man has the right attitude to them, he will be good; if the wrong attitude, he will be bad.

We have now established that virtue or excellence is concerned with pleasures and pains; that the actions which produce it also develop it and, if differently performed, destroy it; and that it actualizes itself fully in those activities to which it owes its origin.

4. Virtuous Action and Virtue: However, the question may be raised what we mean by saying that men become just by performing just actions and self-controlled by practicing self-control. For if they perform just actions and exercise self-control, they are already just and self-controlled, in the same way as they are literate and musical if they write correctly and practice music.

But is this objection really valid, even as regards the arts? No, for it is possible for a man to write a piece correctly by chance or at the prompting of another: but he will be literate only if he produces a piece of writing in a literate way, and that means doing it in accordance with the skill of literate composition which he has in himself.

Moreover, the factors involved in the arts and in the virtues are not the same. In the arts, excellence lies in the result itself, so that it is sufficient if it is of a certain kind. But in the case of the virtues an act is not performed justly or with self-control if the act itself is of a certain kind, but only if in addition the agent has certain characteristics as he performs it: first of all, he must know what he is doing; secondly, he must choose to act the way he does, and he must choose it for its own sake; and in the third place, the act must spring from a firm and unchangeable character. With the exception of knowing what one is about, these considerations do not enter into the mastery of the arts; for the mastery of the virtues, however, knowledge is of little or no importance, whereas the other two conditions count not for a little but are all-decisive, since repeated acts of justice and self-control result in the possession of these virtues. In other words, acts are called just and self-controlled when they are the kind of acts which a just or self-controlled man would perform; but the just and self-controlled man is not he who performs these acts, but he who also performs them in the way just and self-controlled men do.

Thus our assertion that a man becomes just by performing just acts and self-controlled by performing acts of self-control is correct; without performing them, nobody could even be on the way to becoming good. Yet most men do not perform such acts, but by taking refuge in argument they think that they are engaged in philosophy and that they will become good in this way. In so doing, they act like sick men who listen attentively to what the doctor says, but fail to do any of the things he prescribes. That kind of philosophical activity will not bring health to the soul any more than this sort of treatment will produce a healthy body.

5. Virtue Defined: The Genus: The next point to consider is the definition of virtue or excellence. As there are three kinds of things found in the soul: (1) emotions, (2) capacities, and (3) characteristics, virtue must be one of these. By "emotions" I mean appetite, anger, fear, confidence, envy, joy, affection, hatred, longing, emulation, pity, and in general anything that is followed by pleasure or pain; by "capacities" I mean that by virtue of which we are said to be affected by these emotions, for example, the capacity which enables us to feel anger, pain, or pity; and by "characteristics" I mean the condition, either good or bad, in which we are, in relation to the emotions: for example, our condition in relation to anger is bad, if our anger is too violent or not violent enough, but if it is moderate, our condition is good; and similarly with our condition in relation to the other emotions. Now the virtues and vices cannot be emotions, because we are not called good or bad on the basis of our emotions, but on the basis of our virtues and vices. Also, we are neither praised nor blamed for our emotions: a man does not receive praise for being frightened or angry, nor blame for being angry pure and simple, but for being angry in a certain way. Yet we are praised or blamed for our virtues and vices. Furthermore, no choice is involved when we experience anger or fear, while the virtues are some kind of choice or at least involve choice. Moreover, with regard to our emotions we are said to be "moved," but with regard to our virtues and vices we are not said to be "moved" but to be "disposed" in a certain way.

For the same reason, the virtues cannot be capacities, either, for we are neither called good or bad nor praised or blamed simply because we are capable of being affected. Further, our capacities have been given to us by nature, but we do not by nature develop into good or bad men. We have discussed this subject before. Thus, if the virtues are neither emotions nor capacities, the only remaining alternative is that they are characteristics. So much for the genus of virtue.

6. Virtue Defined: The Differentia: It is not sufficient, however, merely to define virtue in general terms as a characteristic: we must also specify what kind of characteristic it is. It must, then, be remarked that every virtue or excellence (1) renders good the thing itself of which it is the excellence, and (2) causes it to perform its function well. For example, the excellence of the eye makes both the eye and its function good, for good sight is due to the excellence of the eye. Likewise, the excellence of a horse makes it both good as a horse and good at running, at carrying its rider, and at facing the enemy. Now, if this is true of all things, the virtue or excellence of man, too, will be a characteristic which makes him a good man, and which causes him to perform his own function well. To some extent we have already stated how this will be true; the rest will become clear if we study what the nature of virtue is.

Of every continuous entity that is divisible into parts it is possible to take the larger, the smaller, or an equal part, and these parts may be larger, smaller, or equal either in relation to the entity itself, or in relation to us. The "equal" part is something median between excess and deficiency. By the median of an entity I understand a point equidistant from both extremes, and this point is one and the same for everybody. By the median relative to us I understand an amount neither too large nor too small, and this is neither one nor the same for everybody. To take an example: if ten is many and two is few, six is taken as the median in relation to the entity, for it exceeds and is exceeded by the same amount, and is thus the median in terms of arithmetical proportion. But the median relative to us cannot be determined in this manner: if ten pounds of food is much for a man to eat and two pounds little, it does not follow that the trainer will prescribe six pounds, for this may in turn be much or little for him to eat; it may be little for Milo* and much for someone who has just begun to take up athletics. The same applies to running and wrestling. Thus we see that an expert in any field avoids excess and deficiency, but seeks the median and chooses it—not the median of the object but the median relative to us.

---

*Milo of Croton, said to have lived in the second half of the sixth century B.C., was a wrestler famous for his remarkable strength.

If this, then, is the way in which every science perfects its work, by looking to the median and by bringing its work up to that point—and this is the reason why it is usually said of a successful piece of work that it is impossible to detract from it or to add to it, the implication being that excess and deficiency destroy success while the mean safeguards it (good craftsmen, we say, look toward this standard in the performance of their work)— and if virtue, like nature, is more precise and better than any art, we must conclude that virtue aims at the median. I am referring to moral virtue: for it is moral virtue that is concerned with emotions and actions, and it is in emotions and actions that excess, deficiency, and the median are found. Thus we can experience fear, confidence, desire, anger, pity, and generally any kind of pleasure and pain either too much or too little, and in either case not properly. But to experience all this at the right time, toward the right objects, toward the right people, for the right reason, and in the right manner—that is the median and the best course, the course that is a mark of virtue.

Similarly, excess, deficiency, and the median can also be found in actions. Now virtue is concerned with emotions and actions; and in emotions and actions excess and deficiency miss the mark, whereas the median is praised and constitutes success. But both praise and success are signs of virtue or excellence. Consequently, virtue is a mean in the sense that it aims at the median. This is corroborated by the fact that there are many ways of going wrong, but only one way which is right—for evil belongs to the indeterminate, as the Pythagoreans imagined, but good to the determinate. This, by the way, is also the reason why the one is easy and the other hard: it is easy to miss the target but hard to hit it. Here, then, is an additional proof that excess and deficiency characterize vice, while the mean characterizes virtue: for "bad men have many ways, good men but one."

We may thus conclude that virtue or excellence is a characteristic involving choice, and that it consists in observing the mean relative to us, a mean which is defined

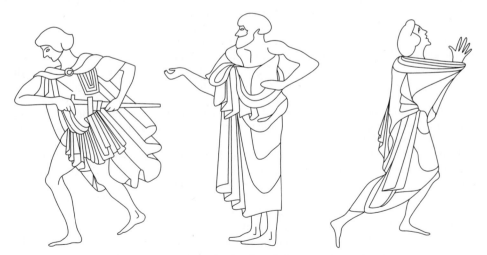

According to Aristotle, virtue or excellence "is the mean by reference to two vices: the one of excess and the other of deficiency." For example, in this drawing the person on the left has an excess of confidence and hence is reckless. The person on the right is deficient in confidence and so is cowardly. In terms of fear, the person on the left has a defect and the person on the right has an excess. In both these cases we should seek to rationally choose the "Golden Mean" of the person in the middle: courage.

by a rational principle, such as a man of practical wisdom would use to determine it. It   1107ᵃ
is the mean by reference to two vices: the one of excess and the other of deficiency. It is,
moreover, a mean because some vices exceed and others fall short of what is required in   5
emotion and in action, whereas virtue finds and chooses the median. Hence, in respect
of its essence and the definition of its essential nature virtue is a mean, but in regard to
goodness and excellence it is an extreme.

   Not every action nor every emotion admits of a mean. There are some actions and
emotions whose very names connote baseness, e.g., spite, shamelessness, envy; and   10
among actions, adultery, theft, and murder. These and similar emotions and actions
imply by their very names that they are bad; it is not their excess nor their deficiency
which is called bad. It is, therefore, impossible ever to do right in performing them: to   15
perform them is always to do wrong. In cases of this sort, let us say adultery, rightness
and wrongness do not depend on committing it with the right woman at the right time
and in the right manner, but the mere fact of committing such action at all is to do
wrong. It would be just as absurd to suppose that there is a mean, an excess, and a deficiency in an unjust or a cowardly or a self-indulgent act. For if there were, we would
have a mean of excess and a mean of deficiency, and an excess of excess and a defi-   20
ciency of deficiency. Just as there cannot be an excess and a deficiency of self-control
and courage—because the intermediate is, in a sense, an extreme—so there cannot be a
mean, excess, and deficiency in their respective opposites: their opposites are wrong
regardless of how they are performed; for, in general, there is no such thing as the mean   25
of an excess or a deficiency, or the excess and deficiency of a mean.

   7. Examples of the Mean in Particular Virtues: However, this general statement is
not enough; we must also show that it fits particular instances. For in a discussion of   30
moral actions, although general statements have a wider range of application, statements
on particular points have more truth in them: actions are concerned with particulars and
our statements must harmonize with them. Let us now take particular virtues and vices
from the following table.

   In feelings of fear and confidence courage is the mean. As for the excesses, there
is no name that describes a man who exceeds in fearlessness—many virtues and vices   1107ᵇ
have no name; but a man who exceeds in confidence is reckless, and a man who exceeds
in fear and is deficient in confidence is cowardly.

   In regard to pleasures and pains—not all of them and to a lesser degree in the case
of pains—the mean is self-control and the excess self-indulgence. Men deficient in   5
regard to pleasure are not often found, and there is therefore no name for them, but let
us call them "insensitive."

   In giving and taking money, the mean is generosity, the excess and deficiency are
extravagance and stinginess. In these vices excess and deficiency work in opposite   10
ways: an extravagant man exceeds in spending and is deficient in taking, while a stingy
man exceeds in taking and is deficient in spending. For our present purposes, we may
rest content with an outline and a summary, but we shall later define these qualities   15
more precisely.

   There are also some other dispositions in regard to money: magnificence is a mean
(for there is a difference between a magnificent and a generous man in that the former
operates on a large scale, the latter on a small); gaudiness and vulgarity are excesses, and
niggardliness a deficiency. These vices differ from the vices opposed to generosity. But   20
we shall postpone until later a discussion of the way in which they differ.

   As regards honor and dishonor, the mean is high-mindedness, the excess is what
we might call vanity, and the deficiency small-mindedness. The same relation which, as

we said, exists between magnificence and generosity, the one being distinguished from
the other in that it operates on a small scale, exists also between high-mindedness and
another virtue: as the former deals with great, so the latter deals with small honors. For
it is possible to desire honor as one should or more than one should or less than one
should: a man who exceeds in his desires is called ambitious, a man who is deficient
unambitious, but there is no name to describe the man in the middle. There are likewise
no names for the corresponding dispositions except for the disposition of an ambitious
man which is called ambition. As a result, the men who occupy the extremes lay claim
to the middle position. We ourselves, in fact, sometimes call the middle person ambitious and sometimes unambitious; sometimes we praise an ambitious and at other times
an unambitious man. The reason why we do that will be discussed in the sequel; for the
present, let us discuss the rest of the virtues and vices along the lines we have indicated.

In regard to anger also there exists an excess, a deficiency, and a mean. Although
there really are no names for them, we might call the mean gentleness, since we call a
man who occupies the middle position gentle. Of the extremes, let the man who exceeds
be called short-tempered and his vice a short temper, and the deficient man apathetic
and his vice apathy.

There are, further, three other means which have a certain similarity with one
another, but differ nonetheless one from the other. They are all concerned with human
relations in speech and action, but they differ in that one of them is concerned with truth
in speech and action and the other two with pleasantness: (a) pleasantness in amusement
and (b) pleasantness in all our daily life. We must include these, too, in our discussion, in
order to see more clearly that the mean is to be praised in all things and that the extremes
are neither praiseworthy nor right, but worthy of blame. Here, too, most of the virtues
and vices have no name, but for the sake of clarity and easier comprehension we must try
to coin names for them, as we did in earlier instances.

To come to the point; in regard to truth, let us call the man in the middle position
truthful and the mean truthfulness. Pretense in the form of exaggeration is boastfulness
and its possessor boastful, while pretense in the form of understatement is self-depreciation
and its possessor a self-depreciator.

Concerning pleasantness in amusement, the man in the middle position is witty
and his disposition wittiness; the excess is called buffoonery and its possessor a buffoon;
and the deficient man a kind of boor and the corresponding characteristic boorishness.

As far as the other kind of pleasantness is concerned, pleasantness in our daily life,
a man who is as pleasant as he should be is friendly and the mean is friendliness.
A man who exceeds is called obsequious if he has no particular purpose in being pleasant, but if he is acting for his own material advantage, he is a flatterer. And a man who is
deficient and unpleasant in every respect is a quarrelsome and grouchy kind of person.

A mean can also be found in our emotional experiences and in our emotions. Thus,
while a sense of shame is not a virtue, a bashful or modest man is praised. For even in
these matters we speak of one kind of person as intermediate and of another as exceeding if he is terror-stricken and abashed at everything. On the other hand, a man who is
deficient in shame or has none at all is called shameless, whereas the intermediate man is
bashful or modest.

Righteous indignation is the mean between envy and spite, all of these being concerned with the pain and pleasure which we feel in regard to the fortunes of our neighbors.
The righteously indignant man feels pain when someone prospers undeservedly; an envi-
ous man exceeds him in that he is pained when he sees anyone prosper; and a spiteful man
is so deficient in feeling pain that he even rejoices [when someone suffers undeservedly].

But we shall have an opportunity to deal with these matters again elsewhere. After that, we shall discuss justice; since it has more than one meaning, we shall distinguish the two kinds of justice and show in what way each is a mean.   10

8. The Relation between the Mean and Its Extremes: There are, then, three kinds of disposition: two are vices (one marked by excess and one by deficiency), and one, virtue, the mean. Now, each of these dispositions is, in a sense, opposed to both the others: the extremes are opposites to the middle as well as to one another, and the middle is opposed to the extremes. Just as an equal amount is larger in relation to a smaller and smaller in relation to a larger amount, so, in the case both of emotions and of actions,   15
the middle characteristics exceed in relation to the deficiencies and are deficient in relation to the excesses. For example, a brave man seems reckless in relation to a coward, but in relation to a reckless man he seems cowardly. Similarly, a self-controlled man   20
seems self-indulgent in relation to an insensitive man and insensitive in relation to a self-indulgent man, and a generous man extravagant in relation to a stingy man and stingy in relation to an extravagant man. This is the reason why people at the extremes each push the man in the middle over to the other extreme: a coward calls a brave man reckless and a reckless man calls a brave man a coward, and similarly with the   25
other qualities.

However, while these three dispositions are thus opposed to one another, the extremes are more opposed to one another than each is to the median; for they are further apart from one another than each is from the median, just as the large is further removed from the small and the small from the large than either one is from the equal.   30
Moreover, there appears to be a certain similarity between some extremes and their median, e.g., recklessness resembles courage and extravagance generosity; but there is a very great dissimilarity between the extremes. But things that are furthest removed from one another are defined as opposites, and that means that the further things are   35
removed from one another the more opposite they are.

In some cases it is the deficiency and in others the excess that is more opposed to   1109ª
the median. For example, it is not the excess, recklessness, which is more opposed to courage, but the deficiency, cowardice; while in the case of self-control it is not the defect, insensitivity, but the excess, self-indulgence which is more opposite. There are two causes for this. One arises from the nature of the thing itself: when one of   5
the extremes is closer and more similar to the median, we do not treat it but rather the other extreme as the opposite of the median. For instance, since recklessness is believed to be more similar and closer to courage, and cowardice less similar, it is cowardice rather than recklessness which we treat as the opposite of courage. For what is   10
further removed from the middle is regarded as being more opposite. So much for the first cause which arises from the thing itself. The second reason is found in ourselves: the more we are naturally attracted to anything, the more opposed to the median does this thing appear to be. For example, since we are naturally more attracted to pleasure   15
we incline more easily to self-indulgence than to a disciplined kind of life. We describe as more opposed to the mean those things toward which our tendency is stronger; and for that reason the excess, self-indulgence, is more opposed to self-control than is its corresponding deficiency.

9. How to Attain the Mean: Our discussion has sufficiently established (1) that moral virtue is a mean and in what sense it is a mean; (2) that it is a mean between two   20
vices, one of which is marked by excess and the other by deficiency; and (3) that it is a

mean in the sense that it aims at the median in the emotions and in actions. That is why
25   it is a hard task to be good; in every case it is a task to find the median: for instance, not
everyone can find the middle of a circle, but only a man who has the proper knowledge.
Similarly, anyone can get angry—that is easy—or can give away money or spend it; but
to do all this to the right person, to the right extent, at the right time, for the right reason,
and in the right way is no longer something easy that anyone can do. It is for this reason
that good conduct is rare, praiseworthy, and noble.

30   The first concern of a man who aims at the median should, therefore, be to avoid
the extreme which is more opposed to it, as Calypso advises: "Keep clear your ship of
yonder spray and surf." For one of the two extremes is more in error than the other, and
35   since it is extremely difficult to hit the mean, we must, as the saying has it, sail in the
1109^b second best way and take the lesser evil; and we can best do that in the manner we have
described.

Moreover, we must watch the errors which have the greatest attraction for us
personally. For the natural inclination of one man differs from that of another, and we
each come to recognize our own by observing the pleasure and pain produced in us [by
the different extremes]. We must then draw ourselves away in the opposite direction, for
5   by pulling away from error we shall reach the middle, as men do when they straighten
warped timber. In every case we must be especially on our guard against pleasure and
10   what is pleasant, for when it comes to pleasure we cannot act as unbiased judges. Our
attitude toward pleasure should be the same as that of the Trojan elders was toward
Helen, and we should repeat on every occasion the words they addressed to her. For if
we dismiss pleasure as they dismissed her, we shall make fewer mistakes.

In summary, then, it is by acting in this way that we shall best be able to hit the
median. But this is no doubt difficult, especially when particular cases are concerned.
15   For it is not easy to determine in what manner, with what person, on what occasion, and
for how long a time one ought to be angry. There are times when we praise those who are
deficient in anger and call them gentle, and other times when we praise violently angry
persons and call them manly. However, we do not blame a man for slightly deviating
20   from the course of goodness, whether he strays toward excess or toward deficiency, but
we do blame him if his deviation is great and cannot pass unnoticed. It is not easy to
determine by a formula at what point and for how great a divergence a man deserves
blame; but this difficulty is, after all, true of all objects of sense perception: determina-
tions of this kind depend upon particular circumstances, and the decision rests with our
[moral] sense.

This much, at any rate, is clear: that the median characteristic is in all fields the
25   one that deserves praise, and that it is sometimes necessary to incline toward the excess
and sometimes toward the deficiency. For it is in this way that we will most easily hit
upon the median, which is the point of excellence.

Book III

30   *1. Actions Voluntary and Involuntary:* Virtue or excellence is, as we have seen,
concerned with emotions and actions. When these are voluntary we receive praise and
blame; when involuntary, we are pardoned and sometimes even pitied. Therefore, it is,
I dare say, indispensable for a student of virtue to differentiate between voluntary and

involuntary actions, and useful also for lawgivers, to help them in meting out honors and punishments.

It is of course generally recognized that actions done under constraint or due to ignorance are involuntary. An act is done under constraint when the initiative or source of motion comes from without. It is the kind of act in which the agent or the person acted upon contributes nothing. For example, a wind might carry a person somewhere he did not want to go, or men may do so who have him in their power. But a problem arises in regard to actions that are done through fear of a greater evil or for some noble purpose, for instance, if a tyrant were to use a man's parents or children as hostages in ordering him to commit a base deed, making their survival or death depend on his compliance or refusal. Are actions of this kind voluntary or involuntary? A similar problem also arises when a cargo is jettisoned in a storm. Considering the action itself, nobody would voluntarily throw away property; but when it is a matter of saving one's own life and that of his fellow passengers, any sensible man would do so. Actions of this kind are, then, of a mixed nature, although they come closer to being voluntary than to being involuntary actions. For they are desirable at the moment of action; and the end for which an action is performed depends on the time at which it is done. Thus the terms "voluntary" and "involuntary" are to be used with reference to the moment of action. In the cases just mentioned, the agent acts voluntarily, because the initiative in moving the parts of the body which act as instruments rests with the agent himself; and where the source of motion is within oneself, it is in one's power to act or not to act. Such actions, then, are voluntary, although in themselves they are perhaps involuntary, since nobody would choose to do any one of them for its own sake.

[That actions of this kind are considered as voluntary is also shown by the fact that] sometimes people are even praised for doing them, for example, if they endure shameful or painful treatment in return for great and noble objectives. If the opposite is the case, reproach is heaped upon them, for only a worthless man would endure utter disgrace for no good or reasonable purpose. There are some instances in which such actions elicit forgiveness rather than praise, for example, when a man acts improperly under a strain greater than human nature can bear and which no one could endure. Yet there are perhaps also acts which no man can possibly be compelled to do, but rather than do them he should accept the most terrible sufferings and death. Thus, the circumstances that compel Alcmaeon in Euripides' play to kill his own mother are patently absurd.* In making a choice, it is sometimes hard to decide what advantages and disadvantages should be weighed against one another, and what losses we should endure to gain what we want; but it is even harder to abide by a decision once it is made. For as a rule, what we look forward to is painful and what we are forced to do is base. It is because of this difficulty that praise or blame depends on whether or not a man successfully resists compulsion.

What kind of actions can we say, then, are done under constraint? To state the matter without qualification, are all actions done under constraint of which the cause is external and to which the agent contributes nothing? On the other hand, actions which are in themselves involuntary, yet chosen under given circumstances in return for certain benefits and

35
1110ᵃ

5

10

15

20

25

30

1110ᵇ

*Euripides' play has not come down to us. According to the myth, Alcmaeon killed his mother, Eriphyle, to avenge the death of his father, Amphiaraus. Amphiaraus, foreknowing through his gift of prophecy that he would be doomed if he joined the expedition of the Seven against Thebes, refused to join it until compelled to do so by his wife, who had been bribed by the gift of a necklace to make him join. An ancient commentator on this passage tells us that Alcmaeon's motive for killing his mother in Euripides' play was to escape the curse of his father.

performed on the initiative of the agent—although such actions are involuntary considered
in themselves, they are nonetheless voluntary under the circumstances, and because benefits are expected in return. In fact, they have a greater resemblance to voluntary actions. For
actions belong among particulars, and the particular act is here performed voluntarily. But
it is not easy to lay down rules how, in making a choice, two alternatives are to be balanced
against one another; there are many differences in the case of particulars.

[There is a conceivable objection to this definition of "voluntary."] Suppose
someone were to assert that pleasant and noble acts are performed under constraint
because the pleasant and the noble are external to us and have a compelling power. But
on this view, all actions would be done under constraint: for every man is motivated by
what is pleasant and noble in everything he does. Furthermore, it is painful to act under
constraint and involuntarily, but the performance of pleasant and noble acts brings
pleasure. Finally, it is absurd to blame external circumstances rather than oneself for
falling an easy prey to such attractions, and to hold oneself responsible for noble deeds,
while pleasure is held responsible for one's base deeds.

It appears, thus, that an act done under constraint is one in which the initiative or
source of motion comes from without, and to which the person compelled contributes
nothing.

Turning now to acts due to ignorance, we may say that all of them are nonvolun-
tary, but they are involuntary only when they bring sorrow and regret in their train: a
man who has acted due to ignorance and feels no compunction whatsoever for what he
has done was not a voluntary agent, since he did not know what he was doing, nor yet
was he involuntary, inasmuch as he feels no sorrow. There are, therefore, two distinct
types of acts due to ignorance: a man who regrets what he has done is considered an
involuntary agent, and a man who does not may be called a non-voluntary agent; for as
the two cases are different, it is better to give each its own name.

There also seems to be a difference between actions *due to* ignorance and acting
in ignorance. A man's action is not considered to be due to ignorance when he is drunk
or angry, but due to intoxication and anger, although he does not know what he is doing
and is in fact acting in ignorance.

Now every wicked man is in a state of ignorance as to what he ought to do and what
he should refrain from doing, and it is due to this kind of error that men become unjust
and, in general, immoral. But an act can hardly be called involuntary if the agent is ignorant of what is beneficial. Ignorance in moral choice does not make an act involuntary—it
makes it wicked; nor does ignorance of the universal, for that invites reproach; rather, it is
ignorance of the particulars* which constitute the circumstances and the issues involved
in the action. It is on these that pity and pardon depend, for a person who acts in ignorance
of a particular circumstance acts involuntarily.

It might, therefore, not be a bad idea to distinguish and enumerate these circumstances. They are: ignorance of (1) who the agent is, (2) what he is doing, (3) what thing
or person is affected, and sometimes also (4) the means he is using, e.g., some tool,

---

*A few remarks ought to be made about the practical syllogism involved in this passage. Reasoning on
matters of conduct involves two premises, one major and one minor. The major premise is always universal,
e.g., "to remove by stealth another person's property is stealing," and the minor premise particular, e.g., "this
horse is another person's property," so that the conclusion would be: "To remove this horse by stealth is stealing." What Aristotle says here is that ignorance of the major premise produces an immoral act, while ignorance
of the minor premise produces an involuntary act that may be pitied or pardoned. Thus it is a moral defect for a
man not to know that to remove by stealth another person's property is stealing. In an involuntary act, on the
other hand, the agent does know the universal premise, but is ignorant of the particular, i.e., that this horse is the
property of another. We shall hear more about the practical syllogism later, especially in VII, 3.

(5) the result intended by his action, e.g., saving a life, and (6) the manner in which he   5
acts, e.g., gently or violently.

Now no one except a madman would be ignorant of all these factors, nor can he
obviously be ignorant of (1) the agent; for how could a man not know his own identity?
But a person might be ignorant of (2) what he is doing. For example, he might plead that
something slipped out of his mouth, or that he did not know that he was divulging a
secret, as Aeschylus said when he was accused of divulging the Mysteries;* or again, as   10
a man might do who discharges a catapult, he might allege that it went off accidentally
while he only wanted to show it. Moreover, (3) someone might, like Merope, mistake a
son for an enemy;** or (4) he might mistake a pointed spear for a foil, or a heavy stone
for a pumice stone. Again, (5) someone might, in trying to save a man by giving him
something to drink, in fact kill him; or, (6) as in sparring, a man might intend merely to   15
touch, and actually strike a blow.

As ignorance is possible with regard to all these factors which constitute an action,
a man who acts in ignorance of any one of them is considered as acting involuntarily,
especially if he is ignorant of the most important factors. The most important factors are
the thing or person affected by the action and the result. An action upon this kind of ignorance is called involuntary, provided that it brings also sorrow and regret in its train.   20

Since an action is involuntary when it is performed under constraint or through
ignorance, a voluntary action would seem to be one in which the initiative lies with the
agent who knows the particular circumstances in which the action is performed.

[This implies that acts due to passion and appetite are voluntary.] For it is perhaps
wrong to call involuntary those acts which are due to passion and appetite. For on that   25
assumption we would, in the first place, deny that animals or even children are capable of
acting voluntarily. In the second place, do we perform none of the actions that are motivated by appetite and passion voluntarily? Or do we perform noble acts voluntarily and
base acts involuntarily? The latter alternative is ridiculous, since the cause in both cases is
one and the same. But it is no doubt also absurd to call those things which we ought to
desire "involuntary." For in some cases we should be angry and there are some things for   30
which we should have an appetite, as for example, health and learning. Moreover, we
think of involuntary actions as painful, while actions that satisfy our appetite are pleasant.
And finally, what difference is there, as far as involuntariness is concerned, between a
wrong committed after calculation and a wrong committed in a fit of passion? Both are to   1111ᵇ
be avoided; but the irrational emotions are considered no less a part of human beings than
reasoning is, and hence, the actions of a man which spring from passion and appetite [are
equally a part of him]. It would be absurd, then, to count them as involuntary.

2. Choice: After this definition of voluntary and involuntary actions, our next
task is to discuss choice. For choice seems to be very closely related to virtue and to be   5
a more reliable criterion for judging character than actions are.

Choice clearly seems to be something voluntary, but it is not the same as voluntariness; voluntariness is a wider term. For even children and animals have a share in the
voluntary, but not in choice. Also, we can describe an act done on the spur of the
moment as a voluntary act, but not the result of choice.   10

---

*The Mysteries were a secret form of religious worship whose doctrines and rites were revealed only
to the initiated; Aeschylus was accused before the Areopagus of having divulged some of the secrets of the
Eleusinian Mysteries. Aeschylus pleaded that he had not known the matter was secret and was acquitted.

**In a lost play of Euripides, Merope was about to slay her son Cresphontes, believing him to be an
enemy.

It seems to be a mistake to identify choice, as some people do, with appetite, passion, wish, or some form of opinion. For choice is not shared by irrational creatures, whereas appetite and passion are. Moreover, the acts of a morally weak person are accompanied by appetite, but not by choice, while a morally strong person acts from 15   choice, but not from appetite. Also, appetite can be opposed to choice, but not appetite to appetite. Again, appetite deals with what is pleasant and painful, while choice deals neither with the pleasant nor with the painful. The resemblance between choice and passion is even slighter. For an act due to passion hardly seems to be based on choice.

Choice is not even the same as wish, although the two seem to be close to one 20   another. For choice does not have the impossible as its object, and if anyone were to assert that he was *choosing* the impossible, he would be considered a fool. But wish can be for the impossible, e.g., immortality.* Wish has as its objects also those things which 25   cannot possibly be attained through our own agency. We might, for instance, wish for the victory of a particular actor or a particular athlete. But no one chooses such things, for we choose only what we believe might be attained through our own agency. Furthermore, wish is directed at the end rather than the means, but choice at the means which are conducive to a given end. For example, we *wish* to be healthy and *choose* the things that will give us health. Similarly, we say that we *wish* to be happy and describe 30   this as our wish, but it would not be fitting to say that we *choose* to be happy. In general, choice seems to be concerned with the things that lie within our power.

Again, choice cannot be identified with opinion. For opinion may refer to any matter, the eternal and the impossible no less than things within our power. Also, opinions are characterized by their truth or falsity, not by their moral goodness or badness, as choices are.

Now, perhaps no one identifies choice with opinion in general; but it would not 1112ª   even be correct to identify it with some particular opinion. For our character is determined by our choosing good or evil, not by the opinions we hold. We choose to take or avoid a 5   good or an evil, but we hold opinions as to what a thing is, whom it will benefit, or how: but [the decision] to take or avoid is by no means an opinion. Also, a choice is praised for being directed to the proper object or for being correctly made, but opinions are praised for being true. Moreover, we make a choice of things which we definitely know to be good, whereas we form opinions about what we do not quite know. Nor does it seem that 10   the same people make the best choices and also hold the best opinions: some hold rather good opinions, but because of a moral depravity they do not make the right choice. Whether opinion precedes or follows choice is immaterial; for we are not concerned with this problem, but only whether choice is to be identified with some form of opinion.

Since choice, then, is none of the things mentioned, what is it or what kind of thing? As we have said, it clearly seems to be something voluntary, but not everything voluntary is the object of choice. Could it be the result of preceding deliberation? [This 15   is probably correct,] for choice involves reason and thought. The very name "choice" seems to suggest that it is something "chosen before" other things.

3. Deliberation: [To turn to deliberation:] do people deliberate about everything? And is everything an object of deliberation? Or are there some things about which one cannot deliberate? Perhaps we ought to say that an object of deliberation is what a sensi- 20   ble man would deliberate about, but not a fool or madman. Now, nobody deliberates

---

*This statement should not be regarded as a rejection on Aristotle's part of a doctrine of immortality. What he is asserting here is merely a reflection of the common Greek distinction between "mortal" men and "immortal" gods: it is impossible to choose to live forever, but it is possible to wish it.

about the eternal, such as the order of the universe or the incommensurability of the diagonal and the side of the square. Nor, on the other hand, do we deliberate about things that are in motion if they always occur in the same way, whether by sheer necessity, by nature, or by some other cause: for example, we do not deliberate about solstices and sunrises. Neither do we deliberate about irregular occurrences, such as drought or rain, nor about chance events, such as the discovery of a treasure. We do not even deliberate about anything and everything that concerns man: no Spartan deliberates about what form of government would be best for the Scythians. For none of these things can happen through our agency.

But what we do deliberate about are things that are in our power and can be realized in action; in fact, these are the only things that remain to be considered. For in addition to nature, necessity, and chance, we regard as causal principles intelligence and anything done through human agency. But of course different groups of people deliberate only about what is attainable by their own actions. Also, there can be no deliberation in any science that is exact and self-contained, such as writing the letters of the alphabet: we have no differences of opinion as to how they are to be written. Rather, we deliberate about matters which are done through our own agency, though not always in the same manner, e.g., about questions of medicine or of acquiring wealth. We deliberate more about navigation than about physical training, because navigation is less exact as a discipline. The same principle can also be applied to the other branches of knowledge. But we deliberate more about the arts than about the sciences, since we have more differences of opinion about them. Deliberation, then, operates in matters that hold good as a general rule, but whose outcome is unpredictable, and in cases in which an indeterminate element is involved. When great issues are at stake, we distrust our own abilities as insufficient to decide the matter and call in others to join us in our deliberations.

We deliberate not about ends but about the means to attain ends: no physician deliberates whether he should cure, no orator whether he should be convincing, no statesman whether he should establish law and order, nor does any expert deliberate about the end of his profession. We take the end for granted, and then consider in what manner and by what means it can be realized. If it becomes apparent that there is more than one means by which it can be attained, we look for the easiest and best; if it can be realized by one means only, we consider in what manner it can be realized by that means, and how that means can be achieved in its turn. We continue that process until we come to the first link in the chain of causation, which is the last step in order of discovery. For when a man deliberates, he seems to be seeking something and to be analyzing his problem in the manner described, as he would a geometrical figure: the last step in the analysis is at once the first in constructing the figure. (By the way, it seems that not all investigation is deliberation—mathematical investigation is not— though every deliberation is an investigation.) Moreover, if in the process of investigation we encounter an insurmountable obstacle, for example, if we need money and none can be procured, we abandon our investigation; but if it turns out to be possible, we begin to act. By "possible" I mean those things which can be realized through our own agency: for even what our friends do for us is, in a way, done through our own agency, since the initiative is our own. Sometimes the object of our investigation is to find the instruments we need and sometimes to discover how to use them. The same is true of other matters, too: sometimes we have to find what the means are, and sometimes how they are to be used or through whom they can be acquired. To sum up our conclusions: (1) man is the source of his actions; (2) deliberation is concerned with things attainable by human action; and (3) actions aim at ends other than themselves. For we cannot

1113ᵃ deliberate about ends but about the means by which ends can be attained. Nor can we deliberate about particular facts, e.g., whether this is a loaf of bread or whether this loaf of bread has been properly baked: such facts are the object of sense perception. And if we continue deliberating each point in turn, we shall have to go on to infinity.

The object of deliberation and the object of choice are identical, except that the object of choice has already been determined, since it has been decided upon on the basis

5 of deliberation. For every man stops inquiring how he is to act when he has traced the initiative of action back to himself and to the dominant part of himself: it is this part that exercises choice. This may be illustrated by the ancient political systems represented in Homer, where the kings would make a choice and then proclaim it to the people.

Since, then, the object of choice is something within our power which we desire

10 as a result of deliberation, we may define choice as a deliberate desire for things that are within our power: we arrive at a decision on the basis of deliberation, and then let the deliberation guide our desire. So much for an outline of choice, its objects, and the fact that it is concerned with means rather than ends.

15 *4. Wish:* That wish is concerned with the end has already been stated. Now, some people think that its object is the good, and others think that it is what seems good. Those who maintain that it is the good are faced with the conclusion that a man who makes a wrong choice does not really wish what he wishes: for if it is the object of his wish it must be good, while in the case in question it is actually bad. On the other

20 hand, those who assert that the object of wish is what seems good must conclude that nothing is by nature the object of wish, but only what seems good to a particular individual. Yet different, and in many instances opposite things seem good to different individuals.

If these consequences are unacceptable, must we not admit that in an unqualified sense and from the standpoint of truth the object of wish is the good, but that for each individual it is whatever seems good to him? [This distinction solves the problem.] Thus, what seems good to a man of high moral standards is truly the object of wish,

25 whereas a worthless man wishes anything that strikes his fancy. It is the same with the human body: people whose constitution is good find those things wholesome which really are so, while other things are wholesome for invalids, and similarly their opinions will vary as to what is bitter, sweet, hot, heavy, and so forth. [Just as a healthy man judges these matters correctly, so in moral questions] a man whose standards are high

30 judges correctly, and in each case what is truly good will appear to him to be so. Thus, what is good and pleasant differs with different characteristics or conditions, and perhaps the chief distinction of a man of high moral standards is his ability to see the truth in each particular moral question, since he is, as it were, the standard and measure for such questions. The common run of people, however, are misled by pleasure. For

1113ᵇ though it is not the good, it seems to be, so that they choose the pleasant in the belief that it is good and avoid pain thinking that it is evil.

5. Man as Responsible Agent: Now, since the end is the object of wish, and since the means to the end are the objects of deliberation and choice, it follows that actions

5 concerned with means are based on choice and are voluntary actions. And the activities in which the virtues find their expression deal with means. Consequently, virtue or excellence depends on ourselves, and so does vice. For where it is in our power to act, it is also in our power not to act, and where we can say "no," we can also say "yes." Therefore, if we have the power to act where it is noble to act, we also have the power

not to act where not to act is base; and conversely, if we have the power not to act where   10
inaction is noble, we also have the power to act where action is base. But if we have the
power to act nobly or basely, and likewise the power not to act, and if such action or
inaction constitutes our being good and evil, we must conclude that it depends on us
whether we are decent or worthless individuals. The saying, "No one is voluntarily   15
wicked nor involuntarily happy," seems to be partly false and partly true. That no one is
involuntarily happy is true, but wickedness is voluntary. If we do not accept that, we
must contradict the conclusions at which we have just arrived, and must deny that man
is the source and begetter of his actions as a father is of his children. But if our conclusions are accepted, and if we cannot trace back our actions to starting points other than   20
those within ourselves, then all actions in which the initiative lies in ourselves are in our
power and are voluntary actions.

These conclusions are corroborated by the judgment of private individuals and by
the practice of lawgivers. They chastise and punish evildoers, except those who have
acted under constraint or due to some ignorance for which they are not responsible, but
honor those who act nobly; their intention seems to be to encourage the latter and to   25
deter the former. Yet nobody encourages us to perform what is not within our power and
what is not voluntary: there would be no point in trying to stop by persuasion a man
from feeling hot, in pain, or hungry, and so forth, because we will go on feeling these
conditions no less for that.

Even ignorance is in itself no protection against punishment if a person is thought   30
to be responsible for his ignorance. For example, the penalty is twice as high if the
offender acted in a state of drunkenness, because the initiative is his own: he had the
power not to get drunk, and drunkenness was responsible for his ignorance. Moreover,
punishment is inflicted for offenses committed in ignorance of such provisions of the
law as the offender ought to have known or might easily have known. It is also inflicted   1114a
in other cases in which ignorance seems to be due to negligence: it was in the offender's
power not to be ignorant, it is argued, and he could have made sure had he wanted to.

But, it might be objected, carelessness may be part of a man's character. We
counter, however, by asserting that a man is himself responsible for becoming careless,
because he lives in a loose and carefree manner; he is likewise responsible for being   5
unjust or self-indulgent, if he keeps on doing mischief or spending his time in drinking
and the like. For a given kind of activity produces a corresponding character. This is
shown by the way in which people train themselves for any kind of contest or performance: they keep on practicing for it. Thus, only a man who is utterly insensitive can be
ignorant of the fact that moral characteristics are formed by actively engaging in partic-   10
ular actions.

Moreover, it is unreasonable to maintain that a man who acts unjustly or self-
indulgently does not wish to be unjust or self-indulgent. If a man is not ignorant of what
he is doing when he performs acts which will make him unjust, he will of course
become unjust voluntarily; nor again, can wishing any more make him stop being unjust
and become just than it can make a sick man healthy. Let us assume the case of a man
who becomes ill voluntarily through living a dissolute life and disobeying doctors'   15
orders. In the beginning, before he let his health slip away, he could have avoided
becoming ill: but once you have thrown a stone and let it go, you can no longer recall it,
even though the power to throw it was yours, for the initiative was within you.   20
Similarly, since an unjust or a self-indulgent man initially had the possibility not to
become unjust or self-indulgent, he has acquired these traits voluntarily; but once he has
acquired them it is no longer possible for him not to be what he is.

There are some cases in which not only the vices of the soul, but also those of the body are voluntary and are accordingly criticized. Nobody blames a man for being ugly by nature; but we do blame those who become ugly through lack of exercise and

25   through taking no care of their person. The same applies to infirmities and physical handicaps: every one would pity rather than reproach a man who was blind by nature or whose blindness is due to disease or accident, but all would blame him if it were caused by drunkenness or some other form of self-indulgence. In other words, those bodily vices which depend on ourselves are blamed and those which do not are not blamed.

30   This being so, we may conclude that other kinds of vice for which we are blamed also depend upon ourselves.

But someone might argue as follows: "All men seek what appears good to them,

1114ᵇ but they have no control over how things appear to them; the end appears different to different men." If, we reply, the individual is somehow responsible for his own characteristics, he is similarly responsible for what appears to him [to be good]. But if he is not so responsible, no one is responsible for his own wrongdoing, but everyone does wrong through ignorance of the proper end, since he believes that his actions will bring him the

5   greatest good. However, the aim we take for the end is not determined by the choice of the individual himself, but by a natural gift of vision, as it were, which enables him to make correct judgments and to choose what is truly good: to be well endowed by nature means to have this natural gift. For to be well and properly provided by nature with the

10   greatest and noblest of gifts, a gift which can be got or learned from no one else, but which is one's possession in the form in which nature has given it: that is the meaning of being well endowed by nature in the full and true sense of the word.

But if this theory is true, how will virtue be any more voluntary than vice? The end has been determined for, and appears to, a good man and a bad man alike by nature

15   or something of that sort; and both will use the end thus determined as the standard for any actions they may undertake. Thus, whether the end that appears [to be good] to a particular person, whatever it may be, is not simply given to him by nature but is to some extent due to himself; or whether, though the end is given by nature, virtue is voluntary in the sense that a man of high moral standards performs the actions that lead up to the end voluntarily: in either case vice, too, is bound to be no less voluntary than

20   virtue. For, like the good man, the bad man has the requisite ability to perform actions through his own agency, even if not to formulate his own ends. If, then, our assertion is correct, viz., that the virtues are voluntary because we share in some way the responsibility for our own characteristics and because the ends we set up for ourselves are deter-

25   mined by the kind of persons we are, it follows that the vices, too, are voluntary; for the same is true of them.

To sum up: we have described the virtues in general and have given an outline of the genus to which they belong, i.e., that they are means and that they are characteristics. We have stated that they spontaneously tend to produce the same kind of actions as those to which they owe their existence; that they are in our power and voluntary; and that they

30   follow the dictates of right reason. However, our actions and our characteristics are not voluntary in the same sense: we are in control of our actions from beginning to end, insofar as we know the particular circumstances surrounding them. But we control only the

1115ᵃ beginning of our characteristics: the particular steps in their development are imperceptible, just as they are in the spread of a disease; yet since the power to behave or not to behave in a given way was ours in the first place, our characteristics are voluntary.

*   *   *

BOOK IV

*   *   *

3. High-Mindedness, Pettiness, and Vanity: High-mindedness, as its very name   1123ᵃ
suggests, seems to be concerned with great and lofty matters. Let us take the nature of
these matters as the first point of our discussion. It makes no difference whether we   1123ᵇ
investigate the characteristic or the man who is characterized by it. A man is regarded as
high-minded when he thinks he deserves great things and actually deserves them; one
who thinks he deserves them but does not is a fool, and no man, insofar as he is virtuous, is either foolish or senseless. This then is the description of a high-minded man.
A person who deserves little and thinks he deserves little is not high-minded, but is a   5
man who knows his limitations. For high-mindedness implies greatness, just as beauty
implies stature in body: small people may have charm and proportion but not beauty.
A man who thinks he deserves great things but does not deserve them is vain, though
not everybody who overestimates himself is vain. One who underestimates himself is   10
small-minded regardless of whether his actual worth is great or moderate, or whether it
is small and he thinks that it is smaller still. A man of great deserts, it would seem, is
most [liable to be small-minded,] for what would he do if his deserts were not as great
as they are? Thus, measured by the standard of greatness, the high-minded man is an
extreme, but by the standard of what is right he occupies the median; for his claims
correspond to his deserts, whereas the others exceed or fall short.   15

Accordingly, if a high-minded man thinks he deserves and actually does deserve
great things, especially the greatest, there is one matter that will be his major concern.
"Deserts" is a relative term that refers to external goods; and as the greatest external good,
we may posit that which we pay as a tribute to the gods, for which eminent people strive
most, and which is the prize for the noblest achievements. Honor fits that description, for
it is the greatest of external goods. Consequently, it is in matters of honor and dishonor   20
that a high-minded man has the right attitude. It is an obvious fact, and need not be argued,
that the high-minded are concerned with honor. For they regard themselves as worthy of
honor above all else, but of an honor that they deserve. A small-minded man falls short
both in view of his own deserts and in relation to the claims of a high-minded person,
while a vain man exceeds his own deserts but does not exceed the high-minded.   25

This means that the high-minded man, inasmuch as he deserves what is greatest,
is the best. For the deserts of the better man are always greater, and those of the best
man the greatest. It follows that a truly high-minded man must be good. And what is
great in each virtue would seem to be the mark of a high-minded person. It would be   30
quite out of character for him to run away in battle with arms swinging or to do wrong
to anyone. For what motive does he have to act basely, he to whom nothing is great?
If we were to examine [his qualities] one by one, we should see the utter absurdity of
thinking of a high-minded man as being anything but good. If he were base, he would
not even deserve honor, for honor is the prize of excellence and virtue, and it is reserved   35
as a tribute to the good. High-mindedness thus is the crown, as it were, of the virtues: it   1124ᵃ
magnifies them and it cannot exist without them. Therefore, it is hard to be truly high-
minded and, in fact, impossible without goodness and nobility.

A high-minded man is, then, primarily concerned with honor and dishonor. From   5
great honors and those that good men confer upon him he will derive a moderate amount
of pleasure, convinced that he is only getting what is properly his or even less. For no
honor can be worthy of perfect virtue. Yet he will accept it, because they have no greater

tribute to pay to him. But he will utterly despise honors conferred by ordinary people and
10 on trivial grounds, for that is not what he deserves. Similarly, he will despise dishonor,
for no dishonor can be justified in his case. A high-minded man, as we have stated, is
concerned primarily with honors. But he will of course also have a moderate attitude
toward wealth, power, and every manner of good or bad luck that may befall him. He will
15 not be overjoyed when his luck is good, nor will bad luck be very painful to him. For
even toward honor, his attitude is that it is not of the greatest moment. Power and wealth
are desirable for the honor they bring; at any rate, those who have them wish to gain
honor through them. But a person who attaches little importance even to honor will also
attach little importance to power and wealth. As a result, he is regarded as haughty.
20   Gifts of fortune, it is believed, also contribute to high-mindedness. Men of noble
birth, of power, or of wealth are regarded as worthy of honor, since they occupy a superior
position, and whatever is superior in goodness is held in greater honor. That is why the
gifts of fortune make men more high-minded, for they are honored by some people [for
25 having them]. But in truth it is the good man alone that ought to be honored, though a man
who has both excellence and good fortune is regarded as still more worthy of honor.
Whoever possesses the goods of fortune without possessing excellence or virtue is not
justified in claiming great deserts for himself, nor is it correct to call him high-minded, for
neither is possible without perfect virtue. Their good fortune notwithstanding, such people
30 become haughty and arrogant, for without virtue it is not easy to bear the gifts of fortune

Alexander the Great, detail from Ancient Roman mosaic of the Battle of Issus. Aristotle tutored the young
Alexander and later benefitted from Alexander's patronage. (*Corbis/Bettmann*)

gracefully. Unable to bear them and considering themselves superior, they look down upon others, while they themselves do whatever they please. They imitate the high-minded man wherever they can, but they are not really like him. Thus, they look down upon others, but they do not act in conformity with excellence. A high-minded person is justified in looking down upon others for he has the right opinion of them, but the common run of people do so without rhyme or reason.

A high-minded man does not take small risks and, since there are only a few things which he honors, he is not even fond of risks. But he will face great risks, and in the midst of them he will not spare his life, aware that life at any cost is not worth having. He is the kind of man who will do good, but who is ashamed to accept a good turn, because the former marks a man as superior, the latter as inferior. Moreover, he will requite good with a greater good, for in this way he will not only repay the original benefactor but put him in his debt at the same time by making him the recipient of an added benefit. The high-minded also seem to remember the good turns they have done, but not those they have received. For the recipient is inferior to the benefactor, whereas a high-minded man wishes to be superior. They listen with pleasure to what good they have done, but with displeasure to what good they have received. That is apparently why Thetis does not mention the good turns she had done to Zeus,* and why the Spartans did not mention theirs to the Athenians, but only the good they had received. It is, further, typical of a high-minded man not to ask for any favors, or only reluctantly, but to offer aid readily. He will show his stature in his relations with men of eminence and fortune, but will be unassuming toward those of moderate means. For to be superior to the former is difficult and dignified, but superiority over the latter is easy. Furthermore, there is nothing ignoble in asserting one's dignity among the great, but to do so among the lower classes is just as crude as to assert one's strength against an invalid. He will not go in for pursuits that the common people value, nor for those in which the first place belongs to others. He is slow to act and procrastinates, except when some great honor or achievement is at stake. His actions are few, but they are great and distinguished. He must be open in hate and open in love, for to hide one's feelings and to care more for the opinion of others than for truth is a sign of timidity. He speaks and acts openly: since he looks down upon others his speech is free and truthful, except when he deliberately depreciates himself in addressing the common run of people. He cannot adjust his life to another, except a friend, for to do so is slavish. That is, [by the way,] why all flatterers are servile and people from the lower classes are flatterers. He is not given to admiration, for nothing is great to him. He bears no grudges, for it is not typical of a high-minded man to have a long memory, especially for wrongs, but rather to overlook them. He is not a gossip, for he will talk neither about himself nor about others, since he is not interested in hearing himself praised or others run down. Nor again is he given to praise; and for the same reason he does not speak evil of others, not even of his enemies, except to scorn them. When he encounters misfortunes that are unavoidable or insignificant, he will not lament and ask for help. That kind of attitude belongs to someone who takes such matters seriously. He is a person who will rather possess beautiful and profitless objects than objects which are profitable and useful, for they mark him more as self-sufficient.

Further, we think of a slow gait as characteristic of a high-minded man, a deep voice, and a deliberate way of speaking. For a man who takes few things seriously is unlikely to be in a hurry, and a person who regards nothing as great is not one to be excitable. But a shrill voice and a swift gait are due to hurry and excitement.

*The reference is to Thetis' intercession with Zeus to help avenge the wrong done her son Achilles by Agamemnon.

20   Such, then, is the high-minded man. A man who falls short is small-minded, and one who exceeds is vain. Now here, too, these people are not considered to be bad—for they are not evildoers—but only mistaken. For a small-minded man deprives himself of the good he deserves. What seems to be bad about him is due to the fact that he does not

25   think he deserves good things and that he does not know himself; if he did, he would desire what he deserves, especially since it is good. It is not that such people are regarded as foolish, but rather [that they are looked upon] as retiring. However, a reputation of this sort seems to make them even worse. For while any given kind of man strives to get what he deserves, these people keep aloof even from noble actions and pursuits and from external goods as well, because they consider themselves undeserving.

30   Vain people, on the other hand, are fools and do not know themselves, and they show it openly. They take in hand honorable enterprises of which they are not worthy, and then they are found out. They deck themselves out with clothes and showy gear and that sort of thing, and wish to publicize what fortune has given them. They talk about

35   their good fortune in the belief that that will bring them honor.

Small-mindedness is more opposed to high-mindedness than vanity is, for it occurs more frequently and is worse. Thus, as we have said, high-mindedness is concerned with high honors.

*   *   *

BOOK VI

1. Moral and Intellectual Excellence; the Psychological Foundations of

1138^b *Intellectual Excellence:* We stated earlier that we must choose the median, and not

20   excess or deficiency, and that the median is what right reason dictates. Let us now analyze this second point.

In all the characteristics we have discussed, as in all others, there is some target on which a rational man keeps his eye as he bends and relaxes his efforts to attain it. There is also a standard that determines the several means which, as we claim, lie between

25   excess and deficiency, and which are fixed by right reason. But this statement, true though it is, lacks clarity. In all other fields of endeavor in which scientific knowledge is possible, it is indeed true to say that we must exert ourselves or relax neither too much nor too little, but to an intermediate extent and as right reason demands. But if this is the only thing a person knows, he will be none the wiser: he will, for example, not know

30   what kind of medicines to apply to his body, if he is merely told to apply whatever medical science prescribes and in a manner in which a medical expert applies them. Accordingly, in discussing the characteristics of the soul, too, it is not enough that the statement we have made be true. We must also have a definition of what right reason is and what standard determines it.

35   In analyzing the virtues of the soul we said that some are virtues of character and

1139^a others excellence of thought or understanding. We have now discussed the moral virtues, [i.e., the virtues of character]. In what follows, we will deal with the others, [i.e., the intellectual virtues,] beginning with some prefatory remarks about the soul. We said in our earlier discussion that the soul consists of two parts, one rational and one

5   irrational. We must now make a similar distinction in regard to the rational part. Let it

be assumed that there are two rational elements: with one of these we apprehend the realities whose fundamental principles do not admit of being other than they are, and with the other we apprehend things which do admit of being other. For if we grant that knowledge presupposes a certain likeness and kinship of subject and object, there will   10 be a generically different part of the soul naturally corresponding to each of two different kinds of object. Let us call one the scientific and the other the calculative element. Deliberating and calculating are the same thing, and no one deliberates about objects that cannot be other than they are. This means that the calculative constitutes one element of the rational part of the soul. Accordingly, we must now take up the question   15 which is the best characteristic of each element, since that constitutes the excellence or virtue of each. But the virtue of a thing is relative to its proper function.

   2. The Two Kinds of Intellectual Excellence and Their Objects: Now, there are three elements in the soul which control action and truth: sense perception, intelligence, and desire. Of these sense perception does not initiate any action. We can see this from the fact that animals have sense perception but have no share in action.* What affirmation and   20 negation are in the realm of thought, pursuit and avoidance are in the realm of desire. Therefore, since moral virtue is a characteristic involving choice, and since choice is a deliberate desire, it follows that, if the choice is to be good, the reasoning must be true and   25 the desire correct; that is, reasoning must affirm what desire pursues. This then is the kind of thought and the kind of truth that is practical and concerned with action. On the other hand, in the kind of thought involved in theoretical knowledge and not in action or production, the good and the bad state are, respectively, truth and falsehood; in fact, the attainment of truth is the function of the intellectual faculty as a whole. But in intellectual activity concerned with action, the good state is truth in harmony with correct desire.   30

   Choice is the starting point of action: it is the source of motion but not the end for the sake of which we act, i.e., the final cause. The starting point of choice, however, is desire and reasoning directed toward some end. That is why there cannot be choice either without intelligence and thought or without some moral characteristic; for good and bad action in human conduct are not possible without thought and character. Now thought   35 alone moves nothing; only thought which is directed to some end and concerned with action can do so. And it is this kind of thought also which initiates production. For who-   1139^b ever produces something produces it for an end. The product he makes is not an end in an unqualified sense, but an end only in a particular relation and of a particular operation. Only the goal of action is an end in the unqualified sense: for the good life is an end, and desire is directed toward this. Therefore, choice is either intelligence motivated by desire or desire operating through thought, and it is as a combination of these two that man is a starting point of action.   5

   (No object of choice belongs to the past: no one chooses to have sacked Troy. For deliberation does not refer to the past but only to the future and to what is possible; and it is not possible that what is past should not have happened. Therefore, Agathon is right when he says: 10

   One thing alone is denied even to god:
   to make undone the deeds which have been done.**)

---

   *Throughout the *Ethics,* Aristotle uses *praxis* ("action") as equivalent to "moral action," "conduct," and assumes animals are not capable of this.

   **Agathon was a tragic poet who flourished in the last quarter of the fifth century B.C. Plato's *Symposium* is set in his house.

As we have seen, truth is the function of both intellectual parts [of the soul]. Therefore, those characteristics which permit each part to be as truthful as possible will be the virtues of the two parts.

3. The Qualities by Which Truth Is Attained: (a) Pure Science or Knowledge: So let us make a fresh beginning and discuss these characteristics once again. Let us take for granted that the faculties by which the soul expresses truth by way of affirmation or denial are five in number: art, science, practical wisdom, theoretical wisdom, and intelligence. Conviction and opinion do not belong here, for they may be false.

What pure science or scientific knowledge is—in the precise sense of the word and not in any of its wider uses based on mere similarity—will become clear in the following. We are all convinced that what we *know* scientifically cannot be otherwise than it is; but of facts which can possibly be other than they are we do not know whether or not they continue to be true when removed from our observation. Therefore, an object of scientific knowledge exists of necessity, and is, consequently, eternal. For everything that exists of necessity in an unqualified sense is eternal, and what is eternal is ungenerated and imperishable [and hence cannot be otherwise].

Moreover, all scientific knowledge is held to be teachable, and what is scientifically knowable is capable of being learned. All teaching is based on what is already known, as we have stated in the *Analytics;* some teaching proceeds by induction and some by syllogism. Now, induction is the starting point [for knowledge] of the universal as well [as the particular], while syllogism proceeds *from* universals. Consequently, there are starting points or principles from which a syllogism proceeds and which are themselves not arrived at by a syllogism. It is, therefore, induction that attains them. Accordingly, scientific knowledge is a capacity for demonstration and has, in addition, all the other qualities which we have specified in the *Analytics.* When a man believes something in the way there specified, and when the starting points or principles on which his beliefs rest are known to him, then he has scientific knowledge; unless he knows the starting points or principles better than the conclusion, he will have scientific knowledge only incidentally. So much for our definition of scientific knowledge or pure science.

1140ª   *4. (b) Art or Applied Science:* Things which admit of being other than they are include both things made and things done. Production is different from action—for that point we can rely even on our less technical discussions. Hence, the characteristic of acting rationally is different from the characteristic of producing rationally. It also follows that one does not include the other, for action is not production nor production action. Now, building is an art or applied science, and it is essentially a characteristic or trained ability of rationally producing. In fact, there is no art that is not a characteristic or trained ability of rationally producing, nor is there a characteristic of rationally producing that is not an art. It follows that art is identical with the characteristic of producing under the guidance of true reason. All art is concerned with the realm of coming-to-be, i.e., with contriving and studying how something which is capable both of being and of not being may come into existence, a thing whose starting point or source is in the producer and not in the thing produced. For art is concerned neither with things which exist or come into being by necessity, nor with things produced by nature: these have their source of motion within themselves.

Since production and action are different, it follows that art deals with production and not with action. In a certain sense, fortune and art are concerned with the same things, as Agathon says: "Fortune loves art and art fortune." So, as we have said, art is a characteristic of producing under the guidance of true reason, and lack of art, on the contrary, is a characteristic of producing under the guidance of false reason; and both of them deal with what admits of being other than it is.

5. *(c) Practical Wisdom:* We may approach the subject of practical wisdom by studying the persons to whom we attribute it. Now, the capacity of deliberating well about what is good and advantageous for oneself is regarded as typical of a man of practical wisdom—not deliberating well about what is good and advantageous in a partial sense, for example, what contributes to health or strength, but what sort of thing contributes to the good life in general. This is shown by the fact that we speak of men as having practical wisdom in a particular respect, i.e., not in an unqualified sense, when they calculate well with respect to some worthwhile end, one that cannot be attained by an applied science or art. It follows that, in general, a man of practical wisdom is he who has the ability to deliberate.

Now no one deliberates about things that cannot be other than they are or about actions that he cannot possibly perform. Since, as we saw, pure science involves demonstration, while things whose starting points or first causes can be other than they are do not admit of demonstration—for such things too and not merely their first causes can all be other than they are—and since it is impossible to deliberate about what exists by necessity, we may conclude that practical wisdom is neither a pure science nor an art. It is not a pure science, because matters of action admit of being other than they are, and it is not an applied science or art, because action and production are generically different.

What remains, then, is that it is a truthful characteristic of acting rationally in matters good and bad for man. For production has an end other than itself, but action does not: good action is itself an end. That is why we think that Pericles* and men like him have practical wisdom. They have the capacity of seeing what is good for themselves and for mankind, and these are, we believe, the qualities of men capable of managing households and states.

This also explains why we call "self-control" *sophrosyne:* it "preserves" our "practical wisdom." What it preserves is the kind of conviction we have described. For the pleasant and the painful do not destroy and pervert every conviction we hold—not, for example, our conviction that a triangle has or does not have the sum of its angles equal to two right angles—but only the convictions we hold concerning how we should act. In matters of action, the principles or initiating motives are the ends at which our actions are aimed. But as soon as a man becomes corrupted by pleasure or pain, the goal no longer appears to him as a motivating principle: he no longer sees that he should choose and act in every case for the sake of and because of this end. For vice tends to destroy the principle or initiating motive of action.

Necessarily, then, practical wisdom is a truthful rational characteristic of acting in matters involving what is good for man. Furthermore, whereas there exists such a thing as excellence in art, it does not exist in practical wisdom.** Also, in art a man who makes a mistake voluntarily is preferable to one who makes it involuntarily; but in practical wisdom, as in every virtue or excellence, such a man is less desirable. Thus it is clear that practical wisdom is an excellence or virtue and not an art. Since there are two parts of the soul that contain a rational element, it must be the virtue of one of them, namely of the part that forms opinions.*** For opinion as well as practical wisdom

25

30

35

1140^b

5

10

15

20

25

---

*The name of Pericles (ca. 495–429 B.C.) is almost synonymous with the Athenian democracy.

**Because practical wisdom is itself a complete virtue or excellence, while the excellence of art depends on the goodness or badness of its product.

***"Opinion" here corresponds to the "calculative element" in Chapter 1: both are defined by reference to contingent facts, those which may be otherwise than they are.

deals with things that can be other than they are. However, it is not merely a rational characteristic or trained ability. An indication that it is something more may be seen in the fact that a trained ability of that kind can be forgotten, whereas practical wisdom cannot.

6. (d) Intelligence: Since pure science or scientific knowledge is a basic conviction concerning universal and necessary truths, and since everything demonstrable and all pure science begins from fundamental principles (for science proceeds rationally), the fundamental principle or starting point for scientific knowledge cannot itself be the object either of science, of art, or of practical wisdom. For what is known scientifically is demonstrable, whereas art and practical wisdom are concerned with things that can be other than they are. Nor are these fundamental principles the objects of theoretical wisdom: for it is the task of a man of theoretical wisdom to have a demonstration for certain truths.* Now, if scientific knowledge, practical wisdom, theoretical wisdom, and intelligence are the faculties by which we attain truth and by which we are never deceived both in matters which can and in those matters which cannot be other than they are; and if three of these—I am referring to practical wisdom, scientific knowledge, and theoretical wisdom—cannot be the faculty in question, we are left with the conclusion that it is intelligence that apprehends fundamental principles.

7. (e) Theoretical Wisdom: We attribute "wisdom" in the arts to the most precise and perfect masters of their skills: we attribute it to Phidias as a sculptor in marble and to Polycletus as a sculptor in bronze. In this sense we signify by "wisdom" nothing but excellence of art or craftsmanship. However, we regard some men as being wise in general, not in any partial sense or in some other particular respect, as Homer says in the *Margites:*

> The gods let him not be a digger or a ploughman nor wise at anything.

It is, therefore, clear, that wisdom must be the most precise and perfect form of knowledge. Consequently, a wise man must not only know what follows from fundamental principles, but he must also have true knowledge of the fundamental principles themselves. Accordingly, theoretical wisdom must comprise both intelligence and scientific knowledge. It is science in its consummation, as it were, the science of the things that are valued most highly.

For it would be strange to regard politics or practical wisdom as the highest kind of knowledge, when in fact man is not the best thing in the universe. Surely, if "healthy" and "good" mean one thing for men and another for fishes, whereas "white" and "straight" always mean the same, "wise" must mean the same for everyone, but "practically wise" will be different. For each particular being ascribes practical wisdom in matters relating to itself to that thing which observes its interests well, and it will entrust itself to that thing. That is the reason why people attribute practical wisdom even to some animals—to all those which display a capacity of forethought in matters relating to their own life.

It is also evident that theoretical wisdom is not the same as politics. If we are to call "theoretical wisdom" the knowledge of what is helpful to us, there will be many kinds of

---

*In other words, the undemonstrable first or fundamental principles cannot be the proper and complete object of theoretical wisdom: as the next chapter shows, they are included within its sphere.

wisdom. There is no single science that deals with what is good for all living things any more than there is a single art of medicine dealing with everything that is, but a different science deals with each particular good. The argument that man is the best of living things makes no difference. There are other things whose nature is much more divine than man's: to take the most visible example only, the constituent parts of the universe.   1141^b

Our discussion has shown that theoretical wisdom comprises both scientific knowledge and [apprehension by the] intelligence of things which by their nature are valued most highly. That is why it is said that men like Anaxagoras and Thales have theoretical but not practical wisdom: when we see that they do not know what is advantageous to   5
them, we admit that they know extraordinary, wonderful, difficult, and superhuman things, but call their knowledge useless because the good they are seeking is not human.

Practical wisdom, on the other hand, is concerned with human affairs and with matters about which deliberation is possible. As we have said, the most characteristic function of a man of practical wisdom is to deliberate well: no one deliberates about   10
things that cannot be other than they are, nor about things that are not directed to some end, an end that is a good attainable by action. In an unqualified sense, that man is good at deliberating who, by reasoning, can aim at and hit the best thing attainable to man by action.

Nor does practical wisdom deal only with universals. It must also be familiar with particulars, since it is concerned with action and action has to do with particulars. This   15
explains why some men who have no scientific knowledge are more adept in practical matters, especially if they have experience, than those who do have scientific knowledge. For if a person were to know that light meat is easily digested, and hence wholesome, but did not know what sort of meat is light, he will not produce health, whereas someone who knows that poultry is light and wholesome is more likely to produce health.*   20

Now, practical wisdom is concerned with action. That means that a person should have both [knowledge of universals and knowledge of particulars] or knowledge of particulars rather [than knowledge of universals]. But here, too, it seems, there is a supreme and comprehensive science involved, [i.e., politics].

8. Practical Wisdom and Politics: Political wisdom and practical wisdom are both the same characteristic, but their essential aspect is not the same. There are two kinds of wisdom concerning the state: the one, which acts as practical wisdom supreme   25
and comprehensive, is the art of legislation; the other, which is practical wisdom as dealing with particular facts, bears the name which, [in everyday speech,] is common to both kinds, politics, and it is concerned with action and deliberation. For a decree, [unlike a law, which lays down general principles,] is a matter for action, inasmuch as it is the last step [in the deliberative process]. That is why only those who make decrees are said to engage in politics, for they alone, like workmen, "do" things.**

It is also commonly held that practical wisdom is primarily concerned with one's own person, i.e., with the individual, and it is this kind that bears the name "practical   30
wisdom," which properly belongs to others as well. The other kinds are called household

---

*The point here is that, in practical matters, a man who knows by experience that poultry is wholesome is likely to be more successful than a man who only has the scientific knowledge that light meat is digestible and therefore wholesome, without knowing the particular fact that poultry is light meat.

**I.e., lawgivers and other men who are concerned with political wisdom in the supreme and comprehensive sense are not generally regarded as being engaged in politics. The analogy to workmen represents of course not Aristotle's view, which vigorously distinguishes action from production, but rather reflects a widespread attitude toward politics.

management, legislation, and politics, the last of which is subdivided into deliberative and judicial.*

1142ᵃ
Now, knowing what is good for oneself is, to be sure, one kind of knowledge; but it is very different from the other kinds. A man who knows and concerns himself with his own interests is regarded as a man of practical wisdom, while men whose concern is politics are looked upon as busybodies. Euripides' words are in this vein:

5
> How can I be called "wise," who might have filled a common soldier's place, free from all care, sharing an equal lot . . .? For those who reach too high and are too active. . . .

For people seek their own good and think that this is what they should do. This opinion has given rise to the view that it is such men who have practical wisdom. And yet, surely one's own good cannot exist without household management nor without a political
10   system. Moreover, the problem of how to manage one's own affairs properly needs clarification and remains to be examined.

An indication that what we have said is correct is the following common observation. While young men do indeed become good geometricians and mathematicians and attain theoretical wisdom in such matters, they apparently do not attain practical wisdom. The reason is that practical wisdom is concerned with particulars as well [as with universals], and knowledge of particulars comes from experience. But a young
15   man has no experience, for experience is the product of a long time. In fact, one might also raise the question why it is that a boy may become a mathematician but not a philosopher or a natural scientist. The answer may be that the objects of mathematics are the result of abstraction, whereas the fundamental principles of philosophy and natural science come from experience. Young men can assert philosophical and scientific principles but can have no genuine convictions about them, whereas there is no
20   obscurity about the essential definitions in mathematics.

Moreover, in our deliberations error is possible as regards either the universal principle or the particular fact: we may be unaware either that all heavy water is bad, or that the particular water we are faced with is heavy.

That practical wisdom is not scientific knowledge is [therefore] evident. As we stated, it is concerned with ultimate particulars, since the actions to be performed are
25   ultimate particulars. This means that it is at the opposite pole from intelligence. For the intelligence grasps limiting terms and definitions that cannot be attained by reasoning, while practical wisdom has as its object the ultimate particular fact, of which there is perception but no scientific knowledge. This perception is not the kind with which [each of our five senses apprehends] its proper object, but the kind with which we perceive that in mathematics the triangle is the ultimate figure. For in this direction, too, we shall have to reach a stop. But this [type of mathematical cognition] is more truly
30   perception than practical wisdom, and it is different in kind from the other [type of perception which deals with the objects proper to the various senses].

9. Practical Wisdom and Excellence in Deliberation: There is a difference between investigating and deliberating: to deliberate is to investigate a particular kind of object. We must also try to grasp what excellence in deliberation is: whether it is some sort of scientific knowledge, opinion, shrewd guessing, or something generically different from any of these.

---

*In Athens, "deliberative" politics referred to matters debated in the Council and the Popular Assembly, and "judicial" politics to matters argued in the lawcourts.

Now, scientific knowledge it is certainly not:* people do not investigate matters they already know. But good deliberation is a kind of deliberation, and when a person deliberates he is engaged in investigating and calculating [things not yet decided]. Nor yet is it shrewd guessing. For shrewd guessing involves no reasoning and proceeds quickly, whereas deliberation takes a long time. As the saying goes, the action which follows deliberation should be quick, but deliberation itself should be slow. Furthermore, quickness of mind is not the same as excellence in deliberation: quickness of mind is a kind of shrewd guessing. Nor again is excellence in deliberation any form of opinion at all. But since a person who deliberates badly makes mistakes, while he who deliberates well deliberates correctly, it clearly follows that excellence in deliberation is some kind of correctness. But it is correctness neither of scientific knowledge nor of opinion. There cannot be correctness of scientific knowledge any more than there can be error of scientific knowledge; and correctness of opinion is truth. Moreover, anything that is an object of opinion is already fixed and determined, while deliberation deals with objects which remain to be determined. Still, excellence in deliberation does involve reasoning, and we are, consequently, left with the alternative that it is correctness of a process of thought; for thinking is not yet an affirmation. For while opinion is no longer a process of investigation but has reached the point of affirmation, a person who deliberates, whether he does so well or badly, is still engaged in investigating and calculating something [not yet determined].

1142^b

5

10

15

Good deliberation is a kind of correctness of deliberation. We must, therefore, first investigate what deliberation is and with what objects it is concerned. Since the term "correctness" is used in several different senses, it is clear that not every kind of correctness in deliberation [is excellence in deliberation]. For (1) a morally weak or a bad man will, as a result of calculation, attain the goal which he has proposed to himself as the right goal to attain. He will, therefore, have deliberated correctly, but what he will get out of it will be a very bad thing. But the result of good deliberation is generally regarded as a good thing. It is this kind of correctness of deliberation which is good deliberation, a correctness that attains what is good.

20

But (2) it is also possible to attain something good by a false syllogism, i.e., to arrive at the right action, but to arrive at it by the wrong means when the middle term is false. Accordingly, this process, which makes us attain the right goal but not by the right means, is still not good deliberation.

25

Moreover, (3) it is possible that one man attains his goal by deliberating for a long time, while another does so quickly. Now, long deliberation, too, is not as such good deliberation: excellence in deliberation is correctness in assessing what is beneficial, i.e., correctness in assessing the goal, the manner, and the time.

Again, (4) it is possible for a person to have deliberated well either in general, in an unqualified sense, or in relation to some particular end. Good deliberation in the unqualified sense of course brings success in relation to what is, in an unqualified sense, the end, [i.e., in relation to the good life]. Excellence in deliberation as directed toward some particular end, however, brings success in the attainment of some particular end.

30

Thus we may conclude that, since it is a mark of men of practical wisdom to have deliberated well, excellence in deliberation will be correctness in assessing what is conducive to the end, concerning which practical wisdom gives a true conviction.

10. Practical Wisdom and Understanding: Understanding, i.e., excellence in understanding, the quality which makes us call certain people "men of understanding"

1143^a

---

*Here, as in most of the following paragraph, Aristotle seems to be taking issue with Plato, who had identified the two, e.g., in *Republic,* Book IV, 428b.

and "men of good understanding," is in general not identical with scientific knowledge or with opinion. For [if it were opinion,] everyone would be a man of understanding, [since everyone forms opinions]. Nor is it one of the particular branches of science, in the sense in which medicine, for example, is the science of matters pertaining to health, or geometry the science which deals with magnitudes. For understanding is concerned neither with eternal and unchangeable truth nor with anything and everything that comes into being [and passes away again]. It deals with matters concerning which doubt and deliberation are possible. Accordingly, though its sphere is the same as that of practical wisdom, understanding and practical wisdom are not the same. Practical wisdom issues commands: its end is to tell us what we ought to do and what we ought not to do. Understanding, on the other hand, only passes judgment. [There is no difference between understanding and excellence in understanding:] for excellence in understanding is the same as understanding, and men of understanding are men of good understanding.

Thus understanding is neither possession nor acquisition of practical wisdom. Just as learning is called "understanding" when a man makes use of his faculty of knowledge, so [we speak of "understanding"] when it implies the use of one's faculty of opinion in judging statements made by another person about matters which belong to the realm of practical wisdom—and in judging such statements rightly, for *good* understanding means that the judgment is right. It is from this act of learning or understanding [what someone else says] that the term "understanding" as predicated of "men of good understanding" is derived. For we frequently use the words "learning" and "understanding" synonymously.

11. Practical Wisdom and Good Sense: As for what is called "good sense," the quality which makes us say of a person that he has the sense to forgive others, [i.e., sympathetic understanding], and that he has good sense, this is a correct judgment of what is fair or equitable. This is indicated by the fact that we attribute to an equitable man especially sympathetic understanding and that we say that it is fair, in certain cases, to have the sense to forgive. Sympathetic understanding is a correct critical sense or judgment of what is fair; and a correct judgment is a true one.

All these characteristics, as one would expect, tend toward the same goal. We attribute good sense, understanding, practical wisdom, and intelligence to the same persons, and in saying that they have good sense, we imply at the same time that they have a mature intelligence and that they are men of practical wisdom and understanding. For what these capacities [have in common is that they are] all concerned with ultimate particular facts. To say that a person has good judgment in matters of practical wisdom implies that he is understanding and has good sense or that he has sympathetic understanding; for equitable acts are common to all good men in their relation with someone else. Now, all matters of action are in the sphere of the particulars and ultimates. Not only must a man of practical wisdom take cognizance of particulars, but understanding and good sense, too, deal with matters of action, and matters of action are ultimates. As for intelligence, it deals with ultimates at both ends of the scale. It is intelligence, not reasoning, that has as its objects primary terms and definitions as well as ultimate particulars. Intelligence grasps, on the one hand, the unchangeable, primary terms and concepts for demonstrations; on the other hand, in questions of action, it grasps the ultimate, contingent fact and the minor premise. For it is particular facts that form the starting points or principles for [our knowledge of] the goal of action: universals arise out of particulars. Hence one must have perception of particular facts, and this perception is intelligence.* Intelligence is, therefore, both starting point and end; for demonstrations start with ultimate terms and have ultimate facts as their objects.

That is why these characteristics are regarded as natural endowments and, although no one is provided with theoretical wisdom by nature, we do think that men have good sense, understanding, and intelligence by nature. An indication of this is that we think of these characteristics as depending on different stages of life, and that at a given stage of life a person acquires intelligence and good sense: the implication is that [human] nature is the cause. Therefore, we ought to pay as much attention to the sayings and opinions, undemonstrated though they are, of wise and experienced older men as we do to demonstrated truths. For experience has given such men an eye with which they can see correctly.**   10

We have now completed our discussion of what practical and theoretical wisdom are; we have described the sphere in which each operates, and we have shown that each   15
is the excellence of a different part of the soul.

12. The Use of Theoretical and Practical Wisdom: One might raise some questions about the usefulness of these two virtues. Theoretical wisdom, [as we have described it,] will study none of the things that make a man happy, for it is not at all concerned with the sphere of coming-to-be [but only with unchanging realities].   20
Practical wisdom, on the other hand, *is* concerned with this sphere, but for what purpose do we need it? (1) It is true that practical wisdom deals with what is just, noble, and good for man; and it is doing such things that characterizes a man as good. But our ability to perform such actions is in no way enhanced by knowing them, since the virtues are characteristics, [that is to say, fixed capacities for action, acquired by habit]. The same also applies, after all, to matters of health and well-being (not in the sense of   25
"producing health and well-being" but in the sense of "being healthy and well" as the manifestation of a physical condition or a characteristic): our ability to perform actions [which show that we are healthy and well] is in no way enhanced by a mastery of the science of medicine or of physical training.

(2) But if we are to say that the purpose of practical wisdom is not to *know* what is just, noble, and good, but to *become* just, noble, and good, it would be of no use at all to a man who is already good. Moreover, it is of no use to those who do not have virtue, for it makes no difference whether they have practical wisdom themselves or listen to   30
others who have it. It is quite sufficient to take the same attitude as we take toward health: we want to be healthy, yet we do not study medicine.

(3) In addition, it would seem strange if practical wisdom, though [intrinsically] inferior to theoretical wisdom, should surpass it in authority, because that which produces a thing rules and directs it.   35

These, then, are the questions we must discuss: so far we have only stated them as problems.

First of all, then, we should insist that both theoretical and practical wisdom are   1144ª
necessarily desirable in themselves, even if neither of them produces anything. For each one of them is the virtue of a different part of the soul.

Secondly, they do in fact produce something: theoretical wisdom produces happiness, not as medicine produces health, but as health itself makes a person healthy. For since theoretical wisdom is one portion of virtue in its entirety, possessing and   5

---

*I.e., we can attain the end—happiness—only by discovering the general rules of moral conduct, and these, in turn, rest on the immediate apprehension by intelligence of particular moral facts.

**The "eye given by experience" is of course *nous,* "intelligence."

actualizing it makes a man happy. [For happiness, as we have seen (Book I, 7) consists in the activity of virtue.]

In the third place, a man fulfills his proper function only by way of practical wisdom and moral excellence or virtue: virtue makes us aim at the right target, and practical wisdom makes us use the right means. The fourth part of the soul, the nutri-
10   tive, does not have a virtue [which makes man fulfill his proper function,] since it does not play any role in the decision to act or not to act.

Finally, the argument has to be met that our ability to perform noble and just acts is in no way enhanced by practical wisdom. We have to begin a little further back and take the following as our starting point. It is our contention that people may perform just acts without actually being just men, as in the case of people who do what has been laid
15   down by the laws but do so either involuntarily or through ignorance or for an ulterior motive, and not for the sake of performing just acts. [Such persons are not just men] despite the fact that they act the way they should, and perform all the actions which a morally good man ought to perform. On the other hand, it seems that it is possible for a man to be of such a character that he performs each particular act in such a way as to
20   make him a good man—I mean that his acts are due to choice and are performed for the sake of the acts themselves. Now, it is virtue which makes our choice right. It is not virtue, however, but a different capacity, which determines the steps which, in the nature of the case, must be taken to implement this choice.

We must stop for a moment to make this point clearer. There exists a capacity
25   called "cleverness," which is the power to perform those steps which are conducive to a goal we have set for ourselves and to attain that goal. If the goal is noble, cleverness deserves praise; if the goal is base, cleverness is knavery. That is why men of practical wisdom are often described as "clever" and "knavish." But in fact this capacity [alone] is not practical wisdom, although practical wisdom does not exist without it. Without
30   virtue or excellence, this eye of the soul, [intelligence,] does not acquire the character- istic of practical wisdom: that is what we have just stated and it is obvious. For the syllogisms which express the principles initiating action run: "Since the end, or the highest good, is such-and-such . . ."—whatever it may be; what it really is does not mat- ter for our present argument. But whatever the true end may be, only a good man can
35   judge it correctly. For wickedness distorts and causes us to be completely mistaken about the fundamental principles of action. Hence it is clear that a man cannot have practical wisdom unless he is good.

114^b   *13. Practical Wisdom and Moral Virtue:* Accordingly, we must also re-examine virtue or excellence. Virtue offers a close analogy to the relation that exists between practical wisdom and cleverness. Just as these two qualities are not identical but similar, so we find the same relation between natural virtue and virtue in the full sense. It seems that the various kinds of character inhere in all of us, somehow or other, by nature. We
5   tend to be just, capable of self-control, and to show all our other character traits from the time of our birth. Yet we still seek something more, the good in a fuller sense, and the possession of these traits in another way. For it is true that children and beasts are endowed with natural qualities or characteristics, but it is evident that without intelli- gence these are harmful. This much, to be sure, we do seem to notice: as in the case of
10   a mighty body which, when it moves without vision, comes down with a mighty fall because it cannot see, so it is in the matter under discussion. If a man acts blindly, i.e., using his natural virtue alone, he will fail; but once he acquires intelligence, it makes a great difference in his action. At that point, the natural characteristic will become that virtue in the full sense which it previously resembled.

Consequently, just as there exist two kinds of quality, cleverness and practical wisdom, in that part of us which forms opinions, [i.e., in the calculative element,] so also there are two kinds of quality in the moral part of us, natural virtue and virtue in the full sense. Now virtue in the full sense cannot be attained without practical wisdom. That is why some people maintain that all the virtues are forms of practical wisdom, and why Socrates' approach to the subject was partly right and partly wrong. He was wrong in believing that all the virtues are forms of wisdom, but right in saying that there is no virtue without wisdom. This is indicated by the fact that all the current definitions of virtue,* after naming the characteristic and its objects, add that it is a characteristic "guided by right reason." Now right reason is that which is determined by practical wisdom. So we see that these thinkers all have some inkling that virtue is a characteristic of this kind, namely, a characteristic guided by practical wisdom.   15   20   25

But we must go a little beyond that. Virtue or excellence is not only a characteristic which is guided by right reason, but also a characteristic which is united with right reason; and right reason in moral matters is practical wisdom.** In other words, while Socrates believed that the virtues *are* rational principles—he said that all of them are forms of knowledge—we, on the other hand, think that they are *united with* a rational principle.   30

Our discussion, then, has made it clear that it is impossible to be good in the full sense of the word without practical wisdom or to be a man of practical wisdom without moral excellence or virtue. Moreover, in this way we can also refute the dialectical argument which might be used to prove that the virtues exist independently of one another. The same individual, it might be argued, is not equally well-endowed by nature for all the virtues, with the result that at a given point he will have acquired one virtue but not yet another. In the case of the natural virtues this may be true, but it cannot happen in the case of those virtues which entitle a man to be called good in an unqualified sense. For in the latter case, as soon as he possesses this single virtue of practical wisdom, he will also possess all the rest.   35   1145ᵃ

It is now clear that we should still need practical wisdom, even if it had no bearing on action, because it is the virtue of a part of our soul. But it is also clear that [it does have an important bearing on action, since] no choice will be right without practical wisdom and virtue. For virtue determines the end, and practical wisdom makes us do what is conducive to the end.   5

Still, practical wisdom has no authority over theoretical wisdom or the better part of our soul*** any more than the art of medicine has authority over health. [Just as medicine does not use health but makes the provisions to secure it, so] practical wisdom does not use theoretical wisdom but makes the provisions to secure it. It issues commands to attain it, but it does not issue them to wisdom itself. To say the contrary would be like asserting that politics governs the gods, because it issues commands about everything in the state, [including public worship].   10

BOOK VII

1. Moral Strength and Moral Weakness: Their Relation to Virtue and Vice and Current Beliefs about Them: We have to make a fresh start now by pointing out that the   15

---

*The reference is to the doctrines of Plato's successors in the Academy.

**I.e., right reason is not only an external standard of action, but it also lives in us and makes us virtuous.

***That is, the scientific or cognitive part in the soul, the rational element which grasps necessary and permanent truths.

qualities of character to be avoided are three in kind: vice, moral weakness, and brutishness. The opposites of two of these are obvious: one is called virtue or excellence and the other moral strength. The most fitting description of the opposite of brutishness would be to say that it is superhuman virtue, a kind of heroic and divine excellence; just as Homer has Priam say about Hector that he was of surpassing excellence:

20

for he did not seem like one who was child of a mortal man, but of god.

Therefore, if, as is said, an excess of virtue can change a man into a god, the characteristic opposed to brutishness must evidently be something of this sort. For just as vice and virtue do not exist in brute beasts, no more can they exist in a god. The quality of gods is something more worthy of honor than [human] virtue or excellence, and the quality of a brute is generically different from [human] vice.

25

If it is rare to find a man who is divine—as the Spartans, for example, customarily use the attribute "divine man" to express an exceptionally high degree of admiration for a person—it is just as rare that a brute is found among men. It does happen, particularly among barbarians, but in some cases disease and physical disability can make a man brutish. "Brutishness" is also used as a term of opprobrium for those who exceed all other men in vice.

30

But we must defer until later some mention of this kind of disposition, and vice has already been discussed. We must now discuss moral weakness, softness, and effeminacy, also moral strength and tenacity. We will do so on the assumption that each of these two sets of characteristics is neither identical with virtue or with wickedness nor generically different from it, but different species respectively of the covering genera, [namely, qualities to be sought and qualities to be avoided].

35

1145ᵇ

The proper procedure will be the one we have followed in our treatment of other subjects: we must present phenomena, [that is, the observed facts of moral life and the current beliefs about them,] and, after first stating the problems inherent in these, we must, if possible, demonstrate the validity of all the beliefs about these matters,* and, if not, the validity of most of them or of the most authoritative. For if the difficulties are resolved and current beliefs are left intact, we shall have proved their validity sufficiently.

5

Now the current beliefs are as follows: (1) Moral strength and tenacity are qualities of great moral value and deserve praise, while moral weakness and softness are base and deserve blame. (2) A man who is morally strong tends to abide by the results of his calculation, and a morally weak man tends to abandon them. (3) A morally weak man does, on the basis of emotion, what he knows to be base, whereas a morally strong man, knowing that certain appetites are base, refuses to follow them and accepts the guidance of reason. (4) Though a self-controlled man is called morally strong and tenacious, some people affirm and others deny [the converse, namely,] that a morally strong person is self-controlled in every respect; likewise, some people call a self-indulgent person "morally weak" and a morally weak person "self-indulgent" without discriminating between the two, while others say that they are different. (5) Sometimes it is said that a man of practical wisdom cannot possibly be morally weak, and sometimes people who have practical wisdom and who are clever are said to be morally weak. (6) Finally, it is said that moral weakness is shown even in anger and in the pursuit of honor and profit. These, then, are the opinions commonly heard.

10

15

20

---

*"Matters" here translates the Greek word *pathos,* which we usually render as "emotion" or "affect." Here, however, it is used in a loose and general sense to include the whole class of moral phenomena. In other words, Aristotle does not mean to deny here that the qualities enumerated above are lasting characteristics.

2. Problems in the Current Beliefs About Moral Strength and Moral Weakness: The problems we might raise are these. [As to (3):] how can a man be morally weak in his actions, when his basic assumption is correct [as to what he should do]? Some people claim that it is impossible for him to be morally weak if he has knowledge [of what he ought to do]. Socrates, for example, believed that it would be strange if, when a man possesses knowledge, something else should overpower it and drag it about like a slave. In fact, Socrates was completely opposed to the view [that a man may know what is right but do what is wrong], and did not believe that moral weakness exists. He claimed that no one acts contrary to what is best in the conviction [that what he is doing is bad], but through [ignorance of the fact that it is bad].

Now this theory is plainly at variance with the observed facts, and one ought to investigate the emotion [involved in the acts of a morally weak man]: if it comes about through ignorance, what manner of ignorance is it? For evidently a man who is morally weak in his actions does not think [that he ought to act the way he does] before he is in the grip of emotion.

There are some people* who accept only certain points of Socrates' theory, but reject others. They agree that nothing is better or more powerful than *knowledge,* but they do not agree that no one acts contrary to what he *thought* was the better thing to do. Therefore, they say, a [morally weak person] does not have knowledge but opinion when he is overpowered by pleasures.

However, if it really is opinion and not knowledge, if, in other words, the basic conviction which resists [the emotion] is not strong but weak, as it is when people are in doubt, we can forgive a man for not sticking to his opinions in the face of strong appetites. But we do not forgive wickedness or anything else that deserves blame [as moral weakness does. Hence it must be something stronger than opinion which is overpowered]. But does that mean that it is practical wisdom** which resists [the appetite]? This, after all, is the strongest [kind of conviction]. But that would be absurd: for it would mean that the same man will have practical wisdom and be morally weak at the same time, and there is no one who would assert that it is the mark of a man of practical wisdom to perform voluntarily the basest actions. In addition, it has been shown before that a man of practical wisdom is a man of action he is concerned with ultimate particulars that he possesses the other virtues.

Furthermore, [as regards (4)]: if being a morally strong person involves having strong and base appetites, a self-controlled man will not be morally strong nor a morally strong man self-controlled. It is out of character for a self-controlled person to have excessive or base appetites. Yet a morally strong man certainly must have such appetites: for if the appetites are good, the characteristic which prevents him from following them is bad, and that would mean that moral strength is not always morally good. If, on the other hand, our appetites are weak and not base, there is nothing extraordinary in resisting them, nor is it a great achievement if they are base and weak.

Again, [to take (1) and (2),] if moral strength makes a person abide by any and every opinion, it is a bad thing; for example, if it makes him persist in a false opinion. And if moral weakness makes a man abandon any and every opinion, moral weakness will occasionally be morally good, as, for example, in the case of Neoptolemus in Sophocles' *Philoctetes.* Neoptolemus deserves praise when he does not abide by the resolution which Odysseus had persuaded him to adopt, because it gives him pain to tell a lie.

---

*I.e., Plato's followers in the Academy.

**The point is this: if the kind of conviction a morally weak man has is neither knowledge nor a weak conviction, it must be a strong conviction, and practical wisdom is such a conviction.

Further, [concerning (1) and (3),] the sophistic argument presents a problem. The Sophists want to refute their opponents by leading them to conclusions which contradict generally accepted facts. Their purpose is to have success bring them the reputation of being clever, and the syllogism which results only becomes a problem or quandary [for their opponents]. For the mind is in chains when, because it is dissatisfied with the conclusion it has reached, it wishes not to stand still, while on the other hand its inability to resolve the argument makes forward movement impossible. Now, they have one argument which leads to the conclusion that folly combined with moral weakness is virtue. This is the way it runs: [if a man is both foolish and morally weak,] he acts contrary to his conviction because of his moral weakness; but [because of his folly,] his conviction is that good things are bad and that he ought not to do them. Therefore, [acting contrary to his conviction,] he will do what is good and not what is bad.

A further problem [arises from (2) and (4)]. A person who, in his actions, pursues, and prefers what is pleasant, convinced or persuaded [that it is good],* would seem to be better than one who acts the same way not on the basis of calculation, but because of moral weakness. For since he may be persuaded to change his mind, he can be cured more easily. To a morally weak man, on the other hand, applies the proverb, "When water chokes you, what can you wash it down with?" For if he had been persuaded to act the way he does, he would have stopped acting that way when persuaded to change his mind. But as it is, though persuaded that he ought to do one thing, he nevertheless does another.

Finally, if everything is the province of moral weakness and moral strength, who would be morally weak in the unqualified sense of the word? No one has every form of moral weakness, but we do say of some people that they are morally weak in an unqualified sense.

These are the sort of problems that arise. Some of the conflicting opinions must be removed and others must be left intact. For the solution of a problem is the discovery [of truth].

3. Some Problems Solved: Moral Weakness and Knowledge: Our first step is, then, to examine (1) whether morally weak people act knowingly or not, and, if knowingly, in what sense. Secondly, (2) we must establish the kind of questions with which a morally weak and a morally strong man are concerned. I mean, are they concerned with all pleasure and pain or only with certain distinct kinds of them? Is a morally strong person the same as a tenacious person or are they different? Similar questions must also be asked about all other matters germane to this study.

The starting point of our investigation is the question *(a)* whether the morally strong man and the morally weak man have their distinguishing features in the situations with which they are concerned or in their manner [of reacting to the situation]. What I mean is this: does a morally weak person owe his character to certain situations to [which he reacts], or to the manner [in which he reacts], or to both? Our second question *(b)* is whether or not moral weakness and moral strength are concerned with all [situations and feelings. The answer to both these questions is that] a man who is morally weak in the unqualified sense is not [so described because of his reaction] to every situation, but only to those situations in which also a self-indulgent man may get involved. Nor is he morally weak because of the mere fact of his relationship to these situations, [namely, that he yields to temptation]. In that case moral weakness would be the same as self-indulgence. Instead, his moral weakness is defined by the manner

*I.e., a self-indulgent person.

[in which he yields]. For a self-indulgent person is led on by his own choice, since he believes that he should always pursue the pleasure of the moment. A morally weak man, on the other hand, does not think he should, but pursues it, nonetheless.

(1) The contention that it is true opinion rather than knowledge which a morally weak man violates in his actions has no bearing on our argument. For some people have no doubts when they hold an opinion, and think they have exact knowledge. Accordingly, if we are going to say that the weakness of their belief is the reason why those who hold opinion will be more liable to act against their conviction than those who have knowledge, we shall find that there is no difference between knowledge and opinion. For some people are no less firmly convinced of what they believe than others are of what they know: Heraclitus is a case in point.* *(a)* But the verb "to know" has two meanings: a man is said to "know" both when he does not use the knowledge he has and when he does use it. Accordingly, when a man does wrong it will make a difference whether he is not exercising the knowledge he has, [viz., that it is wrong to do what he is doing,] or whether he is exercising it. In the latter case, we would be baffled, but not if he acted without exercising his knowledge.

Moreover, *(b)* since there are two kinds of premise,** [namely, universal and particular,] it may well happen that a man knows both [major and minor premise of a practical syllogism] and yet acts against his knowledge, because the [minor] premise which he uses is universal rather than particular. [In that case, he cannot apply his knowledge to his action,] for the actions to be performed are particulars. Also, there are two kinds of universal term to be distinguished: one applies to *(i)* the agent, and the other *(ii)* to the thing. For example, when a person knows that dry food is good for all men, [he may also know] *(i)* that he is a man, or *(ii)* that this kind of food is dry. But whether the particular food before him is of this kind is something of which a morally weak man either does not have the knowledge or does not exercise it. So we see that there will be a tremendous difference between these two ways of knowing. We do not regard it as at all strange that a morally weak person "knows" in the latter sense [with one term nonspecific], but it would be surprising if he "knew" in the other sense, [namely with both terms apprehended as concrete particulars].

There is *(c)* another way besides those we have so far described, in which it is possible for men to have knowledge. When a person has knowledge but does not use it, we see that "having" a characteristic has different meanings. There is a sense in which a person both has and does not have knowledge, for example, when he is asleep, mad, or drunk. But this is precisely the condition of people who are in the grip of the emotions. Fits of passion, sexual appetites, and some other such passions actually cause palpable changes in the body, and in some cases even produce madness. Now it is clear that we

---

*The reference is not to any specific utterance of Heraclitus, but to the tone of intense conviction with which he asserted all his doctrines, some of which Aristotle finds patently false, and hence examples of opinion rather than knowledge.

**What is involved in this paragraph is the practical syllogism. However, a refinement is added here, which requires further explanation. A major premise, Aristotle says, may contain two kinds of universal, e.g., the premise that "dry food is good for all men" makes a universal statement about *(i)* men and *(ii)* about dry food. Accordingly, two kinds of syllogism can be developed from this major premise. The first: "dry food is good for all men"; "I am a man"; therefore, "dry food is good for me" is here neglected by Aristotle, because the agent is obviously always aware of being a person. But the second possible syllogism: "dry food is good for all men"; "this kind of food is dry"; therefore, "this kind of food is good for me," leaves the agent only with the general knowledge that, for example, cereals are good, but the individual will not yet know whether this barley is a cereal. "Knowledge" of this sort will obviously not serve to check a healthy appetite faced with an attractive bowl of porridge.

must attribute to the morally weak a condition similar to that of men who are asleep, mad, or drunk. That the words they utter spring from knowledge [as to what is good] is no evidence to the contrary. People can repeat geometrical demonstrations and verses of
20   Empedocles even when affected by sleep, madness, and drink; and beginning students can reel off the words they have heard, but they do not yet know the subject. The subject must grow to be part of them, and that takes time. We must, therefore, assume that a man who displays moral weakness repeats the formulae [of moral knowledge] in the same way as an actor speaks his lines.

Further, *(d)* we may also look at the cause [of moral weakness] from the viewpoint of the science of human nature, in the following way. [In the practical syllogism,] one of
25   the premises, the universal, is a current belief, while the other involves particular facts which fall within the domain of sense perception. When two premises are combined into one, [i.e., when the universal rule is realized in a particular case,] the soul is thereupon bound to affirm the conclusion, and if the premises involve action, the soul is bound to perform this act at once. For example, if [the premises are]: "Everything sweet ought to
30   be tasted" and "This thing before me is sweet" ("this thing" perceived as an individual particular object), a man who is able [to taste] and is not prevented is bound to act accordingly at once.

Now, suppose that there is within us one universal opinion forbidding us to taste [things of this kind], and another [universal] opinion which tells us that everything sweet is pleasant, and also [a concrete perception], determining our activity, that the particular thing before us is sweet; and suppose further that the appetite [for pleasure] happens to be present. [The result is that] one opinion tells us to avoid that
35   thing, while appetite, capable as it is of setting in motion each part of our body, drives us to it. [This is the case we have been looking for, the defeat of reason in moral weakness.] Thus it turns out that a morally weak man acts under the influence of
1147ᵇ   some kind of reasoning and opinion, an opinion which is not intrinsically but only incidentally opposed to right reason; for it is not opinion but appetite that is opposed to right reason.* And this explains why animals cannot be morally weak: they do not
5   have conceptions of universals, but have only the power to form mental images and memory of particulars.

How is the [temporary] ignorance of a morally weak person dispelled and how does he regain his [active] knowledge [of what is good]? The explanation is the same as it is for drunkenness and sleep, and it is not peculiar to the affect of moral weakness. To get it we have to go to the students of natural science.
10   The final premise, consisting as it does in an opinion about an object perceived by the senses, determines our action. When in the grip of emotion, a morally weak man either does not have this premise, or he has it not in the sense of knowing it, but in the sense of uttering it as a drunken man may utter verses of Empedocles. [Because he is not in active possession of this premise,] and because the final [concrete] term of his reasoning is not a universal and does not seem to be an object of scientific knowledge in the same way that a universal is, [for both these reasons] we seem to be led to the

---

*The point is this: there is a kind of reasoning involved in the actions of a morally weak person: such a person starts out with the opinion that everything sweet is pleasant, finds a particular sweet thing, and knows that the thing is pleasant. But this person also has right reason, which warns not to taste everything sweet. However, the appetite for pleasure, taking hold of the opinion that everything sweet is pleasant, transforms this opinion into the action of tasting. What is contrary to right reason (i.e., contrary to the knowledge that not everything sweet should be tasted) is not the person's opinion (that sweet things are pleasant) but rather the person's appetite for pleasure.

conclusion which Socrates sought to establish. Moral weakness does not occur in the   15
presence of knowledge in the strict sense, and it is sensory knowledge, not science,
which is dragged about by emotion.

This completes our discussion of the question whether a morally weak person
acts with knowledge or without knowledge, and in what sense it is possible for him to
act knowingly.

4. More Problems Solved: The Sphere in Which Moral Weakness Operates:
(2) The next point we have to discuss is whether it is possible for a man to be morally   20
weak in the unqualified sense, or whether the moral weakness of all who have it is concerned with particular situations. If the former is the case, we shall have to see with
what kind of situations he is concerned.

Now, it is clearly in their attitude to pleasures and pains that men are morally
strong and tenacious and morally weak and soft. There are two sources of pleasure:
some are necessary, and others are desirable in themselves but admit of excess. The necessary kind are those concerned with the body: I mean sources of pleasure such as food   25
and drink and sexual intercourse, in short, the kind of bodily pleasures which we
assigned to the sphere of self-indulgence and self-control.* By sources of pleasure
which are not necessary but desirable in themselves, I mean, for example, victory,   30
honor, wealth, and similar good and pleasant things. Now, *(a)* those who violate the
right reason that they possess by excessive indulgence in the second type of pleasures,
are not called morally weak in the unqualified sense, but only with a qualification: we
call them "morally weak in regard to material goods," or profit, or honor, or anger,
but not "morally weak" pure and simple. They are different from the morally weak in
the unqualified sense and share the same name only by analogy, as in our example of   35
the man called Man, who won an Olympic victory. In his case there is not much differ-   1148ᵃ
ence between the general definition of man and the definition proper to him alone, and
yet there was a difference. [That there is similarly a difference between the two senses
of morally weak] is shown by the fact that we blame moral weakness—regardless of
whether it is moral weakness in the unqualified sense or moral weakness concerning
some particular bodily pleasure—not only as an error, but also as a kind of vice. But we   5
do not blame as vicious those [who are morally weak in matters of material goods,
profit, ambition, anger, and so forth].

(b) We now come to those bodily enjoyments which, we say, are the sphere of the
self-controlled and the self-indulgent. Here a man who pursues the excesses of things
pleasant and avoids excesses of things painful (of hunger, thirst, heat, cold, and of anything we feel by touch or taste), and does so not by choice but against his choice and
thinking, is called "morally weak" without the addition of "in regard to such-and-such,"   10
e.g., "in regard to feelings of anger," but simply morally weak without qualification.
The truth of this is proved by the fact that persons who indulge in bodily pleasures are
called "soft," but not persons who indulge in feelings of anger and so forth. For this
reason, we class the morally weak man with the self-indulgent, and the morally strong
with the self-controlled. But we do not include [in the same category] those who
indulge in feelings of anger, because moral weakness and self-indulgence are, in a way,
concerned with the same pleasures and pains. That is, they are concerned with the same   15
pleasures and pains but not in the same way. Self-indulgent men pursue the excess by
choice, but the morally weak do not exercise choice.

---

*I.e., the sensual pleasures of taste and touch.

That is why we are probably more justified in calling a person self-indulgent who shows little or no appetite in pursuing an excess of pleasures and in avoiding moderate pains, than a person who is driven by strong appetite [to pursue pleasure and to avoid pain]. For what would the former do, if, in addition, he had the vigorous appetite of youth and felt strong pain at lacking the objects necessary for his pleasure?

Some appetites and desires are generically noble and worth while—[let us remember] our earlier distinction of pleasant things into those which are by nature desirable, the opposite of these, and those which are intermediate between the two—for example, material goods, profit, victory, and honor. Now, people are not blamed for being affected by all these and similar objects of pleasure and by those of the intermediate kind, nor are they blamed for having an appetite or a liking for them; they are blamed only for the manner in which they do so, if they do so to excess. This, by the way, is why [we do not regard as wicked] all those who, contrary to right reason, are overpowered by something that is noble and good by nature, or who pursue it—those, for example, who devote themselves to the pursuit of honor or to their children and parents more than they should. All these things are good, and those who devote themselves to them are praised. And yet even here there is an element of excess, if, like Niobe, one were to fight against the gods [for the sake of one's children], or if one showed the same excessively foolish devotion to his father as did Satyros, nicknamed "the filial."* So we see that there cannot be any wickedness in this area, because, as we stated, each of these things is in itself naturally desirable. But excess in one's attachment to them is base and must be avoided.

Similarly, there cannot be moral weakness in this area [of things naturally desirable]. Moral weakness is not only something to be avoided, but it is also something that deserves blame. Still, because there is a similarity in the affect, people do call it "moral weakness," but they add "in regard to [such-and-such]," in the same way as they speak of a "bad" doctor or a "bad" actor without meaning to imply that the person is bad in the unqualified sense. So just as in the case of the doctor and the actor [we do not speak of "badness" in the unqualified sense], because their badness is not vice but only something similar to vice by analogy, so it is clear that, in the other case, we must understand by "moral weakness" and "moral strength" only that which operates in the same sphere as self-control and self-indulgence. When we use these terms of anger, we do so only in an analogous sense. Therefore, we add a qualification and say "morally weak in regard to anger," just as we say "morally weak in regard to honor or profit."

5. Moral Weakness and Brutishness: (1) Some things are pleasant by nature, partly *(a)* without qualification, and partly *(b)* pleasant for different classes of animals and humans. Then (2) there are things which are not pleasant by nature, but which come to be pleasant *(a)* through physical disability, *(b)* through habit, or *(c)* through an [innate] depravity of nature. We can observe characteristics corresponding to each of the latter group (2), just as [we did in discussing (1), things pleasant by nature]. I mean (2c) characteristics of brutishness, for instance, the female who is said to rip open pregnant women and devour the infants; or what is related about some of the savage tribes near the Black Sea, that they delight in eating raw meat or human flesh, and that

---

*Niobe boasted that, with her six (or in some versions, seven) sons and an equal number of daughters, she was at least equal to the goddess Leto, who only had two children, the twins Apollo and Artemis. Apollo and Artemis thereupon killed all her children, and Niobe was turned into stone. Who exactly Satyros was, we do not know. Ancient commentators tell us that he committed suicide when his father died, or that he called his father a god.

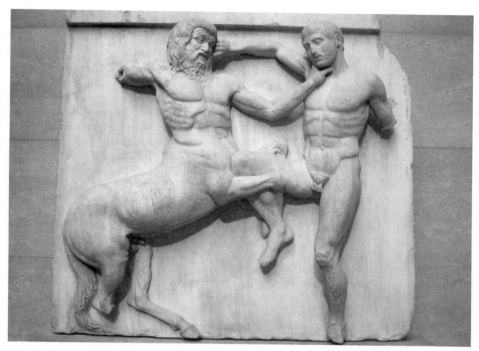

Lapith and Centaur, Metope from Parthenon 477–438 B.C. According to a Greek myth, the Lapiths invited the Centaurs to the wedding feast of their king. Peirthon, as a gesture of goodwill. Upon seeing the beauty of the Lapiety bride, the Centaurs succumbed to their animal instincts of lust and drunkenness and turned the feast into an abduction attempt and brawl. The Lapith warriors, under the cool wisdom of Apollo, brought a sense of calm to the chaos. The image is a symbolic lesson in its appeal for human reason and order over the lower animal instinct of passion and brutishness—a lesson also taught by Aristotle in the *Nicomachean Ethics.* (*Forrest E. Baird; British Museum, London, Great Britain/© The Trustees of the British Museum/Art Resource, NY*)

some of them lend each other their children for a feast; or the story told about Phalaris.*

    These are characteristics of brutishness. Another set of characteristics (*2a*) develops through disease and occasionally through insanity, as, for example, in the case of the man who offered his mother as a sacrifice to the gods and ate of her, or the case of the slave who ate the liver of his fellow slave. Other characteristics are the result of disease or (*2b*) of habit, e.g., plucking out one's hair, gnawing one's fingernails, or even chewing coal or earth, and also sexual relations between males. These practices are, in some cases, due to nature, but in other cases they are the result of habit, when, for example, someone has been sexually abused from childhood.

    When nature is responsible, no one would call the persons affected morally weak any more than one would call women morally weak, because they are passive and not

25

30

---

*Phalaris, tyrant of Acragas in the second quarter of the sixth century B.C., was said to have built a hollow brazen bull, in which he roasted his victims alive, presumably to eat them afterwards. There were several other stories current in antiquity about his brutality.

active in sexual intercourse. Nor would we apply the term to persons in a morbid condition as a result of habit. To have one of these characteristics means to be outside the limits of vice, just as brutishness, too, lies outside the limits of vice. To have such characteristics and to master them or be mastered by them does not constitute moral [strength or] weakness in an unqualified sense but only by analogy, just as a person is not to be called morally weak without qualification when he cannot master his anger, but only morally weak in regard to the emotion involved.

For all excessive folly, cowardice, self-indulgence, and ill-temper is either brutish or morbid. When someone is by nature the kind of person who fears everything, even the rustling of a mouse, his cowardice is brutish, while the man's fear of the weasel was due to disease. In the case of folly, those who are irrational by nature and live only by their senses, as do some distant barbarian tribes, are brutish, whereas those whose irrationality is due to a disease, such as epilepsy, or to insanity, are morbid.

Sometimes it happens that a person merely possesses one of these characteristics without being mastered by it—I mean, for example, if a Phalaris had restrained his appetite so as not to eat the flesh of a child or so as not to indulge in some perverse form of sexual pleasure. But it also happens that a man not only has the characteristic but is mastered by it. Thus, just as the term "wickedness" refers in its unqualified sense to man alone, while in another sense it is qualified by the addition of "brutish" or "morbid," in precisely the same way it is plain that there is a brutish and a morbid kind of moral weakness [i.e., being mastered by brutishness or disease], but in its unqualified sense the term "moral weakness" refers only to human self-indulgence.

It is, accordingly, clear that moral weakness and moral strength operate only in the same sphere as do self-indulgence and self-control, and that the moral weakness which operates in any other sphere is different in kind, and is called "moral weakness" only by extension, not in an unqualified sense.

6. Moral Weakness in Anger: At this point we may observe that moral weakness in anger is less base than moral weakness in regard to the appetites. For (1) in a way, anger seems to listen to reason, but to hear wrong, like hasty servants, who run off before they have heard everything their master tells them, and fail to do what they were ordered, or like dogs, which bark as soon as there is a knock without waiting to see if the visitor is a friend. In the same way, the heat and swiftness of its nature make anger hear but not listen to an order, before rushing off to take revenge. For reason and imagination indicate that an insult or a slight has been received, and anger, drawing the conclusion, as it were, that it must fight against this sort of thing, simply flares up at once. Appetite, on the other hand, is no sooner told by reason and perception that something is pleasant than it rushes off to enjoy it. Consequently, while anger somehow follows reason, appetite does not. Hence appetite is baser [than anger]. For when a person is morally weak in anger, he is in a sense overcome by reason, but the other is not overcome by reason but by appetite.

Further, (2) it is more excusable to follow one's natural desires, inasmuch as we are also more inclined to pardon such appetites as are common to all men and to the extent that they are common to all. Now anger and ill temper are more natural than are the appetites which make us strive for excess and for what is not necessary. Take the example of the man who was defending himself against the charge of beating his father with the words: "Yes, I did it: my father, too, used to beat his father, and he beat his, and"—pointing to his little boy—"he will beat me when he grows up to be a man. It runs in the family." And the story goes that the man who was being dragged out of the house by his son asked him to stop at the door, on the grounds that he himself had not dragged his father any further than that.

Moreover, (3) the more underhanded a person is, the more unjust he is. Now, a hot-tempered man is not underhanded; nor is anger: it is open. But appetite has the same attribute as Aphrodite, who is called "weaver of guile on Cyprus born," and as her "pattern-pierced zone," of which Homer says: "endearment that steals the heart away even from the thoughtful." Therefore, since moral weakness of this type [which involves the appetite] is more unjust and baser than moral weakness concerning anger, it is this type which constitutes moral weakness in the unqualified sense and is even a kind of vice.*

Again, (4) no one feels pain when insulting another without provocation, whereas everyone who acts in a fit of anger acts with pain. On the contrary, whoever unprovoked insults another, feels pleasure. If, then, acts which justify outbursts of anger are more unjust than others, it follows that moral weakness caused by appetite [is more unjust than moral weakness caused by anger], for anger does not involve unprovoked insult.

It is now clear that moral weakness in regard to the appetites is more disgraceful than moral weakness displayed in anger, and also that moral strength and weakness oper-ate in the sphere of the bodily appetites and pleasures. But we must still grasp the distinc-tions to be made within bodily appetites and pleasures. For, as we stated at the beginning, some pleasures are human, i.e., natural in kind as well as in degree, while others are brutish, and others again are due to physical disability and disease. It is only with the first group of these, [i.e., the human pleasures,] that self-control and self-indulgence are concerned. For that reason, we do not call beasts either self-controlled or self-indulgent; if we do so, we do it only metaphorically, in cases where a general distinction can be drawn between one class of animals and another on the basis of wantonness, destructiveness, and indiscriminate voracity. [This use is only metaphorical] because beasts are incapable of choice and calculation, but [animals of this type] stand outside the pale of their nature, just as madmen do among humans.

Brutishness is a lesser evil than vice, but it is more horrifying. For [in a beast] the better element cannot be perverted, as it can be in man, since it is lacking. [To compare a brute beast and a brutish man] is like comparing an inanimate with an animate being to see which is more evil. For the depravity of a being which does not possess the source that initiates its own motion is always less destructive [than the depravity of a being that possesses this source], and intelligence is such a source. A similar comparison can be made between injustice [as such] and an unjust man: each is in some sense worse than the other, for a bad man can do ten thousand times as much harm as a beast.

7. Moral Strength and Moral Weakness: Tenacity and Softness: As regards the pleasures, pains, appetites, and aversions that come to us through touch and taste, and which we defined earlier as the sphere of self-indulgence and self-control, it is possible to be the kind of person who is overcome even by those which most people master; but it is also possible to master those by which most people are overcome. Those who are overcome by pleasure or master it are, respectively, morally weak and morally strong; and in the case of pain, they are, respectively, soft and tenacious. The disposition which characterizes the majority of men lies between these two, although they tend more to the inferior characteristics.

Some pleasures are necessary, up to a certain point, and others are not, whereas neither excesses nor deficiencies of pleasure are necessary. The same is also true of appetites and pains. From all this it follows that a man is self-indulgent when he pursues excesses of pleasant things, or when he [pursues necessary pleasures] to excess, by

---

*But it is not vice in the unqualified sense, for that would involve choice.

choice, for their own sakes, and not for an ulterior result. A man of this kind inevitably feels no regret, and is as a result incorrigible. For a person who feels no regret is incorrigible. A person deficient [in his pursuit of the necessary pleasures] is the opposite [of self-indulgent], and the man who occupies the middle position is self-controlled. In the same way, a man who avoids bodily pain [is self-indulgent], provided he does so by choice and not because he is overcome by them.

25   A choice is not exercised either by a person who is driven by pleasure, or by a person who is avoiding the pain of [unsatisfied] appetite. There is, accordingly, a difference between indulging by choice and not by choice. Everyone would think worse of a man who would perform some disgraceful act actuated only slightly or not at all by appetite, than of a person who was actuated by a strong appetite. And we would regard as worse a man who feels no anger as he beats another man, than someone who does so in anger.

30   For what would he do, if he were in the grip of emotion when acting? Hence a self-indulgent man is worse than one who is morally weak.

So we see that one of the characteristics described, [viz., the deliberate avoidance of pain,] constitutes rather a kind of softness, while a person possessing the other, [viz., the deliberate pursuit of excessive pleasures,] is self-indulgent.

A morally strong is opposed to a morally weak man, and a tenacious to a soft man. For being tenacious consists in offering resistance, while moral strength consists

35   in mastering. Resistance and mastery are two different things, just as not being defeated differs from winning a victory. Hence, moral strength is more desirable than tenacity.

1150^b   A man who is deficient [in his resistance to pains] which most people withstand successfully is soft and effeminate. For effeminacy is a form of softness. A man of this kind lets his cloak trail, in order to save himself the pain of lifting it up, and plays the invalid

5   without believing himself to be involved in the misery which a true invalid suffers.

The situation is similar in the case of moral strength and moral weakness. If a person is overcome by powerful and excessive pleasures or pains, we are not surprised. In fact, we find it pardonable if he is overcome while offering resistance, as, for example, Theodectes' Philoctetes* does when bitten by the snake, or as Cercyon in Carcinus'

10   *Alope,*** or as people who try to restrain their laughter burst out in one great guffaw, as actually happened to Xenophantus.*** But we are surprised if a man is overcome by and unable to withstand those [pleasures and pains] which most people resist successfully, unless his disposition is congenital or caused by disease, as among the kings of

15   Scythia, for example, in whom softness is congenital,† and as softness distinguishes the female from the male.

A man who loves amusement is also commonly regarded as being self-indulgent, but he is actually soft. For amusement is relaxation, inasmuch as it is respite from work, and a lover of amusement is a person who goes in for relaxation to excess.

---

*Theodectes (ca. 375–334 B.C.) spent most of his life at Athens. He studied under Plato, Isocrates, and Aristotle, and in addition to writing tragedies, won a considerable reputation as an orator. An ancient note on this passage tells us that, in Theodectes' tragedy, Philoctetes, after repressing his pain for a long time, finally bursts out: "Cut off my hand!"

**Carcinus was a fourth-century B.C. Athenian tragic poet. According to an ancient commentator, "Cercyon had a daughter Alope. Upon learning that his daughter Alope had committed adultery, he asked her who had perpetrated the deed, and said: 'If you tell me, I will not be grieved at all.' When Alope told him who the adulterer was, Cercyon was so overcome with grief that he could no longer stand life and renounced living."

***The occasion is not known. Xenophantus is said to have been a musician at the court of Alexander the Great (356–323 B.C.). Seneca tells us that when Xenophantus sang, Alexander was so stirred that he seized his weapons in his hands.

†According to the Hippocratic treatise *On Airs, Waters, and Places* 22, horseback riding caused softness among the Scythian aristocracy.

One kind of moral weakness is impetuosity and another is a lack of strength. People of the latter kind deliberate but do not abide by the results of their deliberation, because they are overcome by emotion, while the impetuous are driven on by emotion, because they do not deliberate. [If they deliberated, they would not be driven on so easily,] for as those who have just been tickled are immune to being tickled again, so some people are not overcome by emotion, whether pleasant or painful, when they feel and see it coming and have roused themselves and their power of reasoning in good time. Keen and excitable persons are the most prone to the impetuous kind of moral weakness. Swiftness prevents the keen and vehemence the excitable from waiting for reason to guide them, since they tend to be led by their imagination.

8. Moral Weakness and Self-Indulgence: A self-indulgent man, as we stated, is one who feels no regret, since he abides by the choice he has made. A morally weak person, on the other hand, always feels regret. Therefore, the formulation of the problem, as we posed it above, does not correspond to the facts: it is a self-indulgent man who cannot be cured, but a morally weak man is curable. For wickedness is like a disease such as dropsy or consumption, while moral weakness resembles epilepsy: the former is chronic, the latter intermittent. All in all, moral weakness and vice are generically different from each other. A vicious man is not aware of his vice, but a morally weak man knows his weakness.

Among the morally weak, those who lose themselves in [emotion, i.e., the impetuous,] are better than those who have a rational principle but do not abide by it, [i.e., those who lack strength]. For they are overcome by a lesser emotion and do not yield without previous deliberation, as the impetuous do. A man who has this kind of moral weakness resembles those who get drunk quickly and on little wine, or on less wine than most people do.

That moral weakness is not a vice [in the strict sense] is now evident, though in a certain sense it is perhaps one. For moral weakness violates choice, whereas vice is in accordance with choice. Nevertheless, they are similar in the actions to which they lead, just as Demodocus said of the Milesians:

The Milesians are no stupid crew, except that they do what the stupid do.*

Similarly, the morally weak are not unjust, but they will act like unjust men.

A morally weak man is the kind of person who pursues bodily pleasures to excess and contrary to right reason, though he is not persuaded [that he ought to do so]; the self-indulgent, on the other hand, is persuaded to pursue them because he is the kind of man who does so. This means that it is the former who is easily persuaded to change his mind, but the latter is not. For virtue or excellence preserves and wickedness destroys the initiating motive or first cause [of action], and in actions the initiating motive or first cause is the end at which we aim, as the hypotheses are in mathematics. For neither in mathematics nor in moral matters does reasoning teach us the principles or starting points; it is virtue, whether natural or habitual, that inculcates right opinion about the principle or first premise. A man who has this right opinion is self-controlled, and his opposite is self-indulgent.

But there exists a kind of person who loses himself under the impact of emotion and violates right reason, a person whom emotion so overpowers that he does not act according to the dictates of right reason, but not sufficiently to make him the kind of

*Demodocus wrote lampooning epigrams in the sixth century B.C.

man who is persuaded that he must abandon himself completely to the pursuit of such
pleasures. This is the morally weak man: he is better than the self-indulgent, and he is
not bad in the unqualified sense of the word. For the best thing in him is saved: the principle or premise [as to how he should act]. Opposed to him is another kind of man, who
remains steadfast and does not lose himself, at least not under the impact of emotion.
These considerations make it clear that moral strength is a characteristic of great moral
worth, while moral weakness is bad.

9. Steadfastness in Moral Strength and Moral Weakness: Is a man morally strong
when he abides by any and every dictate of reason and choice, or only when he abides
by the right choice? And is a man morally weak when he does not abide by every choice
and dictate of reason, or only when he fails to abide by the rational dictate which is not
false and the choice which is right? This is the problem we stated earlier. Or is it true
reason and right choice as such, but any other kind of choice incidentally, to which the
one remains steadfast and the other does not? [This seems to be the correct answer,] for
if a person chooses and pursues the attainment of *a* by means of *b,* his pursuit and
choice are for *a* as such but for *b* incidentally. And by "as such" we mean "in the
unqualified sense." Therefore, there is a sense in which the one abides by and the other
abandons any and every kind of opinion, but in the unqualified sense, only true opinion.
There are those who remain steadfast to their opinion and are called "obstinate."
They are hard to convince and are not easily persuaded to change their mind. They bear
a certain resemblance to a morally strong person, just as an extravagant man resembles
one who is generous, and a reckless man resembles one who is confident. But they are,
in fact, different in many respects. The one, the morally strong, will be a person who
does not change under the influence of emotion and appetite, but on occasion he will be
persuaded [by argument]. Obstinate men, on the other hand, are not easily persuaded by
rational argument; but to appetites they are amenable, and in many cases are driven on
by pleasures. The various kinds of obstinate people are the opinionated, the ignorant,
and the boorish. The opinionated let themselves be influenced by pleasure and pain:
they feel the joy of victory, when someone fails to persuade them to change their mind,
and they feel pain when their views are overruled, like decrees that are declared null and
void. As a result, they bear a greater resemblance to the morally weak than to the
morally strong.
Then there are those who do not abide by their decisions for reasons other than
moral weakness, as, for example, Neoptolemus in Sophocles' *Philoctetes.* Granted it
was under the influence of pleasure that he did not remain steadfast, but it was a
noble pleasure: it was noble in his eyes to be truthful, but he was persuaded by
Odysseus to tell a lie. For not anybody who acts under the influence of pleasure is
self-indulgent, bad, or morally weak, but only those who do so under the influence
of a base pleasure.
There is also a type who feels less joy than he should at the things of the body
and, therefore, does not abide by the dictates of reason. The median between this type
and the morally weak man is the man of moral strength. For a morally weak person does
not abide by the dictates of reason, because he feels more joy than he should [in bodily
things], but the man under discussion feels less joy than he should. But a morally strong
man remains steadfast and does not change on either account. Since moral strength is
good, it follows that both characteristics opposed to it are bad, as they in fact turn out to
be. But since one of the two opposites is in evidence only in a few people and on few
occasions, moral strength is generally regarded as being the only opposite of moral
weakness, just as self-control is thought to be opposed only to self-indulgence.

Since many terms are used in an analogical sense, we have come to speak analogically of the "moral strength" of a self-controlled man. [There is a resemblance between the two] since a morally strong man is the kind of person who does nothing contrary to the dictates of reason under the influence of bodily pleasures, and the same is true of a self-controlled man. But while a morally strong man has base appetites, a self-controlled   35
man does not and is, moreover, a person who finds no pleasure in anything that violates   1152ª
the dictates of reason. A morally strong man, on the other hand, does find pleasure in such things, but he is not driven by them. There is also a similarity between the morally weak and the self-indulgent in that both pursue things pleasant to the body; but they are   5
different in that a self-indulgent man thinks he ought to pursue them, while the morally weak thinks he should not.

10. Moral Weakness and Practical Wisdom: It is not possible for the same person to have practical wisdom and be morally weak at the same time, for it has been shown that a man of practical wisdom is *ipso facto* a man of good character. Moreover, to be a man of practical wisdom, one must not only know [what one ought to do], but he must also be able to act accordingly. But a morally weak man is not able so to act. However, there is no reason why a clever man could not be morally weak. That is why occasion-   10
ally people are regarded as possessing practical wisdom, but as being morally weak at the same time; it is because cleverness differs from practical wisdom in the way we have described in our first discussion of the subject. They are closely related in that both follow the guidance of reason, but they differ in that [practical wisdom alone] involves moral choice.

Furthermore, a morally weak man does not act like a man who has knowledge and exercises it, but like a man asleep or drunk. Also, even though he acts voluntarily—   15
for he knows in a sense what he is doing and what end he is aiming at—he is not wicked, because his moral choice is good,* and that makes him only half-wicked. He is not unjust, either, for he is no underhanded plotter. [For plotting implies deliberation,] whereas one type of morally weak man does not abide by the results of his deliberation, while the other, the excitable type, does not even deliberate. So we see that a morally weak person is like a state which enacts all the right decrees and has laws of a high   20
moral standard, but does not apply them, a situation which Anaxandrides made fun of: "Thus wills the state, that cares not for its laws."** A wicked man, on the other hand, resembles a state which does apply its laws, but the laws are bad.

In relation to the characteristics possessed by most people, moral weakness and moral strength lie at the extremes. For a morally strong person remains more steadfast   25
and a morally weak person less steadfast than the capacity of most men permits.

The kind of moral weakness displayed by excitable people is more easily cured than the moral weakness of those who deliberate but do not abide by their decisions; and those who are morally weak through habituation are more curable than those who are morally weak by nature. For it is easier to change habit than to change nature. Even   30
habit is hard to change, precisely because it resembles nature, as Euenus says:

A habit, friend, is of long practice born,
and practice ends in fashioning man's nature.***

*I.e., his basic moral purpose is good, even though it is eventually vitiated by appetite.
**Anaxandrides (fl. 382–349 B.C.) migrated from his native Rhodes (or Colophon) to Athens, where he gained fame as a poet of the Middle Comedy.
***Euenus of Paros was a famous Sophist, who lived in the late fifth century B.C.

We have now completed our definitions of moral strength, moral weakness,
35   tenacity, and softness, and stated how these characteristics are related to one another.

1152^b   *11. Pleasure: Some Current Views:* It is the role of a political philosopher to
study pleasure and pain. For he is the supreme craftsman of the end to which we look
when we call one particular thing bad and another good in the unqualified sense.
5   Moreover, an examination of this subject is one of the tasks we must logically undertake, since we established that virtue and vice of character are concerned with pains and
pleasures, and most people claim that happiness involves pleasure. That is why the
word "blessed" is derived from the word "enjoy."

Now, (1) some people believe that no pleasure is good, either in itself or incidentally,
10   since the good and pleasure are not the same thing.* (2) Others hold that, though some
pleasures are good, most of them are bad.** (3) Then there is a third view, according to
which it is impossible for pleasure to be the highest good, even if all pleasures are good.***

[The following arguments are advanced to support (1) the contention that] pleasure is not a good at all: *(a)* All pleasure is a process or coming-to-be leading to the
natural state [of the subject] and perceived [by the subject]; but no process is of the
same order as its ends, e.g., the building process is not of the same order as a house.
15   Further, *(b)* a self-controlled man avoids pleasures. Again, *(c)* a man of practical wisdom does not pursue the pleasant, but what is free from pain.† Moreover, *(d)* pleasures
are an obstacle to good sense: the greater the joy one feels, e.g., in sexual intercourse,
the greater the obstacle; for no one is capable of rational insight while enjoying sexual relations.†† Also, *(e)* there is no art of pleasure; yet every good is the result of
an art. Finally, *(f)* children and beasts pursue pleasures, whereas they do not know
what is good.
20   [The arguments for the view (2) that] not all pleasures are good are: *(a)* Some
pleasures are disgraceful and cause for reproach; and *(b)* some pleasures are harmful,
for there are pleasant things that may cause disease.

[And the argument in favor of (3), the contention that] pleasure is not the highest
good, is that it is not an end but a process or coming-to-be. These are roughly the views
put forward.

12. The Views Discussed: (1) Is Pleasure a Good Thing?: But the following
25   considerations will show that the arguments we have enumerated do not lead us to the
conclusion that (1) pleasure is not a good, or (3) that it is not the highest good. In the
first place, [to answer argument (1*a*) and (3),] we use the word "good" in two senses: a
thing may be good in the unqualified sense, or "good" for a particular person. Hence the
term has also two meanings when applied to natural states and characteristics [of per-
sons], and consequently also when applied to their motions and processes. This means

---

*This view seems to have been propounded by Speusippus, Plato's nephew and disciple, who suc-
ceeded him as head of the Academy from 347–339 B.C. A similar view had been espoused by Antisthenes
(ca. 455–ca. 360 B.C.), the friend of Socrates and precursor of the Cynic School.
**This is probably a reference to the view stated by Plato in *Philebus* 13b.
***No particular proponents of this view can be identified, but they are also discussed in Plato's
Philebus 53c–55c.
†Arguments *(b)* and *(c)* had probably been used by Speusippus and before him perhaps by
Antisthenes.
††This argument may come from Archytas, a Pythagorean philosopher, mathematician, ruler of
Tarentum, and friend of Plato, in the first half of the fourth century B.C.

that motions and processes which are generally held to be bad are partly bad without qualification, but not bad for a particular person, and even desirable for him; and partly   30
not even desirable for a particular person except on occasion and for a short time, though they are not desirable in an unqualified sense. Others again are not even pleasures, but only appear to be, for example, all processes accompanied by pain and undergone for remedial purposes, such as the processes to which the sick are subjected.

Secondly, the good has two aspects: it is both an activity and a characteristic. Now, the processes which restore us to our natural characteristic condition are only incidentally pleasant; but the activity which is at work when our appetites [want to see us restored] is   35
the activity of that part of our characteristic condition and natural state which has been left unimpaired. For that matter, there are pleasures which do not involve pain and appetite (e.g., the activity of studying) and we experience them when there is nothing deficient in   1153ᵃ
our natural state. [That processes of restoration are only incidentally pleasant] is shown by the fact that the pleasant things which give us joy while our natural state is being replenished are not the same as those which give us joy once it has been restored. Once restored, we feel joy at what is pleasant in the unqualified sense, but while the replenishment goes on, we enjoy even its opposite: for instance, we enjoy sharp and bitter things, none of   5
which are pleasant either by nature or in the unqualified sense. Consequently, the pleasures [derived from them, too, are not pleasant either by nature or in the unqualified sense], for the difference that exists between various pleasant things is the same as that which is found between the pleasures derived from them.

In the third place, there is no need to believe that there exists something better than pleasure which is different from it, just as, according to some, the end is better than the process which leads to it. For pleasures are not processes, nor do all pleasures involve processes: they are activities and an end, and they result not from the process of   10
development we undergo, but from the use we make of the powers we have. Nor do all pleasures have an end other than themselves; that is only true of the pleasures of those who are being led to the perfection of their natural states. For that reason, it is not correct, either, to say that pleasure is a process perceived [by the subject]: one should rather call it an "activity of our characteristic condition as determined by our natural state," and instead of "perceived" we should call it "unobstructed." (There are some who   15
believe pleasure to be process on the ground that it is good in the true sense of the word, for they think that activity is process, but it is, as a matter of fact, different.)

The argument (2b) that pleasures [are bad, because] some pleasant things may cause disease, is like arguing that wholesome things are bad, because some of them are bad for making money. Both pleasant and wholesome things are bad in the relative senses mentioned, but that does not make them bad in themselves: even studying is occasionally harmful to health.   20

Also, (1d) neither practical wisdom nor any characteristic is obstructed by the pleasure arising from it, but only by alien pleasures extraneous to it. The pleasures arising from study and learning will only intensify study and learning, [but they will never obstruct it].

The argument (1e) that no pleasure is the result of an art makes good sense. For art never produces any activity at all: it produces the capacity for the activity.   25
Nevertheless, the arts of perfume-making as well as of cooking are generally regarded as arts of pleasure.

The arguments (1b) that a self-controlled person avoids pleasure, (1c) that a man of practical wisdom pursues a life free from pain, and (1f) that children and beasts pursue pleasure, are all refuted by the same consideration. We have stated in what sense

30   pleasures are good without qualification and in what sense not all pleasures are good. These last mentioned are the pleasures which beasts and children pursue, while a man of practical wisdom wants to be free from the pain which they imply. They are the pleasures that involve appetite and pain, i.e., the bodily pleasures—for they are of this

35   sort—and their excesses, in terms of which a self-indulgent man is self-indulgent. That is why a self-controlled man avoids these pleasures. But there are pleasures even for the self-controlled.

13. The Views Discussed: (3) Is Pleasure the Highest Good?: To continue: there

1153ᵇ   is general agreement that pain is bad and must be avoided. One kind of pain is bad in the unqualified sense, and another kind is bad, because in some way or other it obstructs us. Now, the opposite of a thing to be avoided—in the sense that it must be avoided and is bad—is good. It follows, therefore, necessarily that pleasure is a good.

5   Speusippus tried to solve the question by saying that, just as the greater is opposed both to the less and to the equal, [so pleasure is opposed both to pain and to the good]. But this solution does not come out correctly: surely, he would not say that pleasure is essentially a species of evil.

But (2a) even if some pleasures are bad, it does not mean that the highest good cannot be some sort of pleasure, just as the highest good may be some sort of knowledge, even though some kinds of knowledge are bad. Perhaps we must even draw the necessary conclusion that it is; for since each characteristic has its unobstructed activities, the activity

10   of all characteristics or of one of them—depending on whether the former or the latter constitutes happiness—if unobstructed, must be the most desirable of all. And this activity is pleasure. Therefore, the highest good is some sort of pleasure, despite the fact that most pleasures are bad and, if you like, bad in the unqualified sense of the word. It is for this

15   reason that everyone thinks that the happy life is a pleasant life, and links pleasure with happiness. And it makes good sense this way: for no activity is complete and perfect as long as it is obstructed, and happiness is a complete and perfect thing. This is why a happy man also needs the goods of the body, external goods, and the goods of fortune, in order not to be obstructed by their absence.

But those who assert* that a man is happy even on the rack and even when great

20   misfortunes befall him, provided that he is good, are talking nonsense, whether they know it or not. Since happiness also needs fortune, some people regard good fortune as identical with happiness. But that is not true, for even good fortune, if excessive, can be an obstruction; perhaps we are, in that case, no longer justified in calling it "good fortune," for its definition is determined by its relation to happiness.

25   Also, the fact that all beasts and all men pursue pleasure is some indication that it is, in a sense, the highest good:

> There is no talk that ever quite dies down,
> if spread by many men. . . .

But since no single nature and no single characteristic condition is, or is regarded, as the

30   best [for all], people do not all pursue the same pleasure, yet all pursue pleasure. Perhaps they do not even pursue the pleasure which they think or would say they pursue, but they all pursue the same [thing], pleasure. For everything has by nature something divine about it. But the bodily pleasures have arrogated the name "pleasure" unto themselves as their own private possession, because everyone tends to follow them and participates in

*The Cynics are probably meant.

them more frequently than in any others. Accordingly, since these are the only pleasures   35
with which they are familiar, people think they are the only ones that exist.

It is also evident that if pleasure, i.e., the activity [of our faculties], is not good, it   1154ª
will be impossible for a happy man to live pleasantly. For to what purpose would he
need pleasure, if it were not a good and if it is possible that a happy man's life is one of
pain? For if pain is neither good nor bad, pleasure is not, either: so why should he avoid   5
it? Surely, the life of a morally good man is no pleasanter [than that of anyone else], if
his activities are not more pleasant.

14. *The Views Discussed: (2) Are Most Pleasures Bad?:* The subject of the pleasures of the body demands the attention of the proponents of the view that, though some
pleasures—for instance, the noble pleasures—are highly desirable, the pleasures of the
body—that is, the pleasures which are the concern of the self-indulgent man—are not.   10
If that is true, why then are the pains opposed to them bad? For bad has good as its
opposite. Is it that the necessary pleasures are good in the sense in which anything not
bad is good? Or are they good up to a certain point? For all characteristics and motions
which cannot have an excess of good cannot have an excess of pleasure, either; but
those which can have an excess of good can also have an excess of pleasure. Now,   15
excess is possible in the case of the goods of the body, and it is the pursuit of excess, but
not the pursuit of necessary pleasures, that makes a man bad. For all men get some kind
of enjoyment from good food, wine, and sexual relations, but not everyone enjoys these
things in the proper way. The reverse is true of pain: a bad person does not avoid an
excess of it, but he avoids it altogether. For the opposite of an excess is pain only for the
man who pursues the excess.   20

It is our task not only to say what is true, but also to state what causes error, since
that helps carry conviction. For when we can give a reasoned explanation why something which appears to be true is, in fact, not true, it makes us give greater credence to
what is true. Accordingly, we must now explain why the pleasures of the body appear to   25
be more desirable.

The first reason, then, is that pleasure drives out pain. When men experience an
excess of pain, they pursue excessive pleasure and bodily pleasure in general, in the
belief that it will remedy the pain. These remedial [pleasures] become very intense—
and that is the very reason why they are pursued—because they are experienced in   30
contrast with their opposite.

As a matter of fact, these two reasons which we have stated also explain why
pleasure is not regarded as having any moral value: some pleasures are the actions that
spring from a bad natural state—either congenitally bad, as in the case of a beast, or bad
by habit, as in the case of a bad man—while other pleasures are remedial and indicate a
deficient natural state, and to be in one's natural state is better than to be moving toward
it. But since the remedial pleasures only arise in the process of reaching the perfected   1154ᵇ
state, they are morally good only incidentally.

The second reason is that the pleasures of the body are pursued because of their
intensity by those incapable of enjoying other pleasures. Take, for example, those who
induce themselves to be thirsty. There is no objection to this practice, if the pleasures
are harmless; but if they are harmful, it is bad. For many people have nothing else to
give them joy, and because of their nature, it is painful for them to feel neither [pleasure   5
nor pain]. Actually, animal nature is under a constant strain, as the students of natural
science attest when they say that seeing and hearing are painful, but [we do not feel the
pain because,] as they assert, we have become accustomed to it. Similarly, whereas   10
the growing process [we go through] in our youth puts us into the same [exhilarated]

state as that of a drunken man, and [makes] youth the age of pleasure, excitable natures, on the other hand, always need remedial action: as a result of [the excess of black bile in their] constitutional blend, their bodies are exposed to constant gnawing sensations, and they are always in a state of vehement desire. Now, since pain is driven out by the pleasure opposed to it or by any strong pleasure at all, excitable people become self-indulgent and bad.

Pleasures unattended by pain do not admit of excess. The objects of these pleasures are what is pleasant by nature and not what is incidentally pleasant. By "things incidentally pleasant" I mean those that act as remedies. For since it is through some action of that part of us which has remained sound that a cure is effected, the remedy is regarded as being pleasant. But [pleasant by nature it is not]: pleasant by nature are those things which produce the action of an unimpaired natural state.

There is no single object that continues to be pleasant forever, because our nature is not simple but contains another natural element, which makes us subject to decay. Consequently, whenever one element does something, it runs counter to the nature of the other; and whenever the two elements are in a state of equilibrium, the act performed seems neither painful nor pleasant. If there is a being with a simple nature, the same action will always be the most pleasant to him. That is why the divinity always enjoys one single and simple pleasure: for there is not only an activity of motion but also an activity of immobility, and pleasure consists in rest rather than in motion. But "change in all things is pleasant," as the poet has it, because of some evil in us. For just as a man who changes easily is bad, so also is a nature that needs to change. The reason is that such a nature is not simple and not [entirely] good.

This completes our discussion of moral strength and moral weakness, and of pleasure and pain. We have stated what each of them is and in what sense some of them are good and some bad. It now remains to talk about friendship.

*   *   *

BOOK X

*   *   *

6. Happiness and Activity: Now that we have completed our discussion of the virtues, and of the different kinds of friendship and pleasure, it remains to sketch an outline of happiness, since, as we assert, it is the end or goal of human [aspirations]. Our account will be more concise if we recapitulate what we have said so far.

We stated, then, that happiness is not a characteristic; if it were, a person who passes his whole life in sleep, vegetating like a plant, or someone who experiences the greatest misfortunes could possess it. If, then, such a conclusion is unacceptable, we must, in accordance with our earlier discussion, classify happiness as some sort of activity. Now, some activities are necessary and desirable only for the sake of something else, while others are desirable in themselves. Obviously, happiness must be classed as an activity desirable in itself and not for the sake of something else. For happiness lacks nothing and is self-sufficient. Activities desirable in themselves are those from which we seek to derive nothing beyond the actual exercise of the activity. Actions in conformity with virtue evidently constitute such activities; for to perform noble and good deeds is something desirable for its own sake.

Pleasant amusements, too, [are desirable for their own sake]. We do not choose them for the sake of something else, since they lead to harm rather than good when we become neglectful of our bodies and our property. But most of those who are considered happy find an escape in pastimes of this sort, and this is why people who are well versed in such pastimes find favor at the courts of tyrants; they make themselves pleasant by providing what the tyrants are after, and what they want is amusement. Accordingly, such amusements are regarded as being conducive to happiness, because men who are in positions of power devote their leisure to them. But perhaps such persons cannot be [regarded as] evidence. For virtue and intelligence, which are the sources of morally good activities, do not consist in wielding power. Also, if these men, who have never tasted pure and generous pleasure, find an escape in the pleasures of the body, this is no sufficient reason for thinking that such pleasures are in fact more desirable. For children, too, think that what they value is actually the best. It is, therefore, not surprising that as children apparently do not attach value to the same things as do adults, so bad men do not attach value to the same things as do good men. Accordingly, as we have stated repeatedly, what is valuable and pleasant to a morally good man actually is valuable and pleasant. Each individual considers that activity most desirable which corresponds to his own proper characteristic condition, and a morally good man, of course, so considers activity in conformity with virtue.

Consequently, happiness does not consist in amusement. In fact, it would be strange if our end were amusement, and if we were to labor and suffer hardships all our life long merely to amuse ourselves. For, one might say, we choose everything for the sake of something else—except happiness; for happiness is an end. Obviously, it is foolish and all too childish to exert serious efforts and toil for purposes of amusement. Anacharsis* seems to be right when he advises to play in order to be serious; for amusement is a form of rest, and since we cannot work continuously we need rest. Thus rest is not an end, for we take it for the sake of [further] activity. The happy life is regarded as a life in conformity with virtue. It is a life which involves effort and is not spent in amusement.

Moreover, we say that what is morally good is better than what is ridiculous and brings amusement, and the better the organ or man—whichever may be involved in a particular case—the greater the moral value of the activity. But the activity of the better organ or the better man is in itself superior and more conducive to happiness.

Furthermore, any person at all, even a slave, can enjoy bodily pleasures no less than the best of men. But no one would grant that a slave has a share in happiness any more than that he lives a life of his own. For happiness does not consist in pastimes of this sort, but in activities that conform with virtue, as we have stated earlier.

7. Happiness, Intelligence, and the Contemplative Life: Now, if happiness is activity in conformity with virtue, it is to be expected that it should conform with the highest virtue, and that is the virtue of the best part of us. Whether this is intelligence or something else which, it is thought, by its very nature rules and guides us and which gives us our notions of what is noble and divine; whether it is itself divine or the most divine thing in us; it is the activity of this part [when operating] in conformity with the excellence or virtue proper to it that will be complete happiness. That it is an activity concerned with theoretical knowledge or contemplation has already been stated.

This would seem to be consistent with our earlier statements as well as the truth. For this activity is not only the highest—for intelligence is the highest possession we have in us, and the objects which are the concern of intelligence are the highest objects

15

20

25

30

35
1177ᵃ

5

10

15

20

*Anacharsis, who is said to have lived early in the sixth century B.C., was a Scythian whose travels all over the Greek world brought him a reputation for wisdom. He allegedly met Solon at Athens and was numbered in some ancient traditions among the Seven Wise Men.

of knowledge—but also the most continuous: we are able to study continuously more easily than to perform any kind of action. Furthermore, we think of pleasure as a necessary ingredient in happiness. Now everyone agrees that of all the activities that conform with virtue activity in conformity with theoretical wisdom is the most pleasant. At any rate, it seems that [the pursuit of wisdom or] philosophy holds pleasures marvelous in purity and certainty, and it is not surprising that time spent in knowledge is more pleasant than time spent in research. Moreover, what is usually called "selfsufficiency" will be found in the highest degree in the activity which is concerned with theoretical knowledge. Like a just man and any other virtuous man, a wise man requires the necessities of life; once these have been adequately provided, a just man still needs people toward whom and in company with whom to act justly, and the same is true of a self-controlled man, a courageous man, and all the rest. But a wise man is able to study even by himself, and the wiser he is the more is he able to do it. Perhaps he could do it better if he had colleagues to work with him, but he still is the most self-sufficient of all. Again, study seems to be the only activity which is loved for its own sake. For while we derive a greater or a smaller advantage from practical pursuits beyond the action itself, from study we derive nothing beyond the activity of studying. Also, we regard happiness as depending on leisure; for our purpose in being busy is to have leisure, and we wage war in order to have peace. Now, the practical virtues are activated in political and military pursuits, but the actions involved in these pursuits seem to be unleisurely. This is completely true of military pursuits, since no one chooses to wage war or foments war for the sake of war; he would have to be utterly bloodthirsty if he were to make enemies of his friends simply in order to have battle and slaughter. But the activity of the statesman, too, has no leisure. It attempts to gain advantages beyond political action, advantages such as political power, prestige, or at least happiness for the statesman himself and his fellow citizens, and that is something other than political activity: after all, the very fact that we investigate politics shows that it is not the same [as happiness]. Therefore, if we take as established (1) that political and military actions surpass all other actions that conform with virtue in nobility and grandeur; (2) that they are unleisurely, aim at an end, and are not chosen for their own sake; (3) that the activity of our intelligence, inasmuch as it is an activity concerned with theoretical knowledge, is thought to be of greater value than the others, aims at no end beyond itself, and has a pleasure proper to itself—and pleasure increases activity; and (4) that the qualities of this activity evidently are self-sufficiency, leisure, as much freedom from fatigue as a human being can have, and whatever else falls to the lot of a supremely happy man; it follows that the activity of our intelligence constitutes the complete happiness of man, provided that it encompasses a complete span of life; for nothing connected with happiness must be incomplete.

However, such a life would be more than human. A man who would live it would do so not insofar as he is human, but because there is a divine element within him. This divine element is as far above our composite nature* as its activity is above the active exercise of the other, [i.e., practical,] kind of virtue. So if it is true that intelligence is divine in comparison with man, then a life guided by intelligence is divine in comparison with human life. We must not follow those who advise us to have human thoughts, since we are [only] men, and mortal thoughts, as mortals should; on the contrary, we should try to become immortal as far as that is possible and do our utmost to live in accordance with what is highest in us. For though this is a small portion [of our nature],

*Human beings, consisting of soul and body, i.e., of form and matter, are composite beings, whereas the divine, being all intelligence, is not.

it far surpasses everything else in power and value. One might even regard it as each man's true self, since it is the controlling and better part. It would, therefore, be strange if a man chose not to live his own life but someone else's.

Moreover, what we stated before will apply here, too: what is by nature proper to each thing will be at once the best and the most pleasant for it. In other words, a life guided by intelligence is the best and most pleasant for man, inasmuch as intelligence, above all else, is man. Consequently, this kind of life is the happiest.

8. The Advantages of the Contemplative Life: A life guided by the other kind of virtue, [the practical,] is happy in a secondary sense, since its active exercise is confined to man. It is in our dealings with one another that we perform just, courageous, and other virtuous acts, when we observe the proper kind of behavior toward each man in private transactions, in meeting his needs, in all manner of actions, and in our emotions, and all of these are, as we see, peculiarly human. Moreover, some moral acts seem to be determined by our bodily condition, and virtue or excellence of character seems in many ways closely related to the emotions. There is also a close mutual connection between practical wisdom and excellence of character, since the fundamental principles of practical wisdom are determined by the virtues of character, while practical wisdom determines the right standard for the moral virtues. The fact that these virtues are also bound up with the emotions indicates that they belong to our composite nature, and the virtues of our composite nature are human virtues; consequently, a life guided by these virtues and the happiness [that goes with it are likewise human]. The happiness of the intelligence, however, is quite separate [from that kind of happiness]. That is all we shall say about it here, for a more detailed treatment lies beyond the scope of our present task.

It also seems that such happiness has little need of external trimmings, or less need than moral virtue has. Even if we grant that both stand in equal need of the necessities of life, and even if the labors of a statesman are more concerned with the needs of our body and things of that sort—in that respect the difference between them may be small—yet, in what they need for the exercise of their activities, their difference will be great. A generous man will need money to perform generous acts, and a just man will need it to meet his obligations. For the mere wish to perform such acts is inscrutable, and even an unjust man can pretend that he wishes to act justly. And a courageous man will need strength if he is to accomplish an act that conforms with his virtue, and a man of self-control the possibility of indulgence. How else can he or any other virtuous man make manifest his excellence? Also, it is debatable whether the moral purpose or the action is the more decisive element in virtue, since virtue depends on both. It is clear of course that completeness depends on both. But many things are needed for the performance of actions, and the greater and nobler the actions the more is needed. But a man engaged in study has no need of any of these things, at least not for the active exercise of studying; in fact one might even go so far as to say that they are a hindrance to study. But insofar as he is human and lives in the society of his fellow men, he chooses to act as virtue demands, and accordingly, he will need externals for living as a human being.

A further indication that complete happiness consists in some kind of contemplative activity is this. We assume that the gods are in the highest degree blessed and happy. But what kind of actions are we to attribute to them? Acts of justice? Will they not look ridiculous making contracts with one another, returning deposits, and so forth? Perhaps acts of courage—withstanding terror and taking risks, because it is noble to do so? Or generous actions? But to whom will they give? It would be strange to think that they actually have currency or something of the sort. Acts of self-control? What would they be? Surely, it would be in poor taste to praise them for not having bad appetites. If we went through the whole list we would see that a concern with actions is petty and unworthy of the gods. Nevertheless, we all assume that the gods exist and, consequently, that they are active; for surely we do not assume them to be always asleep like Endymion.* Now, if we take away action from a living being, to say nothing of production, what is left except contemplation? Therefore, the activity of the divinity which surpasses all others in bliss must be a contemplative activity, and the human activity which is most closely akin to it is, therefore, most conducive to happiness.

This is further shown by the fact that no other living being has a share in happiness, since they all are completely denied this kind of activity. The gods enjoy a life blessed in its entirety; men enjoy it to the extent that they attain something resembling the divine activity; but none of the other living beings can be happy, because they have no share at all in contemplation or study. So happiness is coextensive with study, and the greater the opportunity for studying, the greater the happiness, not as an incidental effect but as inherent in study; for study is in itself worthy of honor. Consequently, happiness is some kind of study or contemplation.

But we shall also need external well-being, since we are only human. Our nature is not self-sufficient for engaging in study: our body must be healthy and we must have food and generally be cared for. Nevertheless, if it is not possible for a man to be supremely happy without external goods, we must not think that his needs will be great and many in order to be happy; for self-sufficiency and moral action do not consist in an excess [of possessions]. It is possible to perform noble actions even without being ruler of land and sea; a man's actions can be guided by virtue also if his means are moderate. That this is so can be clearly seen in the fact that private individuals evidently do not act less honorably but even more honorably than powerful rulers. It is enough to have moderate means at one's disposal, for the life of a man whose activity is guided by virtue will be happy.

Solon certainly gave a good description of a happy man, when he said that he is a man moderately supplied with external goods, who had performed what he, Solon, thought were the noblest actions, and who had lived with self-control. For it is possible to do what one should even with moderate possessions. Also Anaxagoras, it seems, did not assume that a happy man had to be rich and powerful. He said that he would not be surprised if a happy man would strike the common run of people as strange, since they judge by externals and perceive nothing but externals. So it seems that our account is in harmony with the opinion of the wise.

Now, though such considerations carry some conviction, in the field of moral action truth is judged by the actual facts of life, for it is in them that the decisive element lies. So we must examine the conclusions we have reached so far by applying them to the actual facts of life: if they are in harmony with the facts we must accept them, and if they clash we must assume that they are mere words.

A man whose activity is guided by intelligence, who cultivates his intelligence and keeps it in the best condition, seems to be most beloved by the gods. For if the gods have any concern for human affairs—and they seem to have—it is to be expected that they rejoice in what is best and most akin to them, and that is our intelligence; it is also to be expected that they requite with good those who most love and honor intelligence, as being men who care for what is dear to the gods and who act rightly and nobly. That a wise man, more than any other, has all these qualities is perfectly clear. Consequently,

*Supposedly the most beautiful of men, Endymion was loved by the Moon, who cast him into a perpetual sleep that she might descend and embrace him each night.

he is the most beloved by the gods, and as such he is, presumably, also the happiest. 30
Therefore, we have here a further indication that a wise man attains a higher degree of
happiness than anyone

9. Ethics and Politics: Now that we have given an adequate outline of these matters,
of the virtues, and also of friendship and pleasure, can we regard our project as having
reached its completion? Must we not rather abide by the maxim that in matters of action 35
the end is not to study and attain knowledge of the particular things to be done, but rather 1179ᵇ
to do them? Surely, knowing about excellence or virtue is not enough: we must try to possess it and use it, or find some other way in which we may become good.

Now, if words alone would suffice to make us good, they would rightly "harvest
many rewards and great," as Theognis says,* and we would have to provide them. But as 5
it is, while words evidently do have the power to encourage and stimulate young men of
generous mind, and while they can cause a character well-born and truly enamored of
what is noble to be possessed by virtue, they do not have the capacity to turn the common
run of people to goodness and nobility. For the natural tendency of most people is to be 10
swayed not by a sense of shame but by fear, and to refrain from acting basely not because
it is disgraceful, but because of the punishment it brings. Living under the sway of emotion, they pursue their own proper pleasures and the means by which they can obtain
them, and they avoid the pains that are opposed to them. But they do not even have a
notion of what is noble and truly pleasant, since they have never tasted it. What argument 15
indeed can transform people like that? To change by argument what has long been
ingrained in a character is impossible or, at least, not easy. Perhaps we must be satisfied if
we have whatever we think it takes to become good and attain a modicum of excellence.

Some people believe that it is nature that makes men good, others that it is habit, 20
and others again that it is teaching. Now, whatever goodness comes from nature is obviously not in our power, but is present in truly fortunate men as the result of some divine
cause. Argument and teaching, I am afraid, are not effective in all cases: the soul of the
listener must first have been conditioned by habits to the right kind of likes and dislikes, 25
just as land (must be cultivated before it is able) to foster the seed. For a man whose life
is guided by emotion will not listen to an argument that dissuades him, nor will he
understand it. How can we possibly persuade a man like that to change his ways? And
in general it seems that emotion does not yield to argument but only to force. Therefore
there must first be a character that somehow has an affinity for excellence or virtue, a 30
character that loves what is noble and feels disgust at what is base.

To obtain the right training for virtue from youth up is difficult, unless one has
been brought up under the right laws. To live a life of self-control and tenacity is not
pleasant for most people, especially for the young. Therefore, their upbringing and pursuits must be regulated by laws; for once they have become familiar, they will no longer 35
be painful. But it is perhaps not enough that they receive the right upbringing and atten- 1802
tion only in their youth. Since they must carry on these pursuits and cultivate them by
habit when they have grown up, we probably need laws for this, too, and for the whole
of life in general. For most people are swayed rather by compulsion than argument, and 5
by punishments rather than by (a sense of) what is noble. This is why some believe that
lawgivers ought to exhort and try to influence people toward (a life of) virtue because of
its inherent nobility, in the hope that those who have made good progress through their

*Theognis, lines 432–434, which are, incidentally, also quoted by Plato, *Meno* 95e, read in full: "If a
god had granted to the descendants of Asclepius to cure wickedness and the destruction-bent mind of men,
they would harvest many great rewards."

habits will listen to them. Chastisement and penalties, they think, should be imposed
10   upon those who do not obey and are of an inferior nature, while the incorrigible ought
to be banished abroad.* A good man, they think, who orients his life by what is noble
will accept the guidance of reason, while a bad man, whose desire is for pleasure, is corrected by pain like a beast of burden. For the same reason, they say that the pains
inflicted must be those that are most directly opposed to the pleasures he loves.

Accordingly, if, as we have said, a man must receive a good upbringing and disci-
15   pline in order to be good, and must subsequently lead the same kind of life, pursuing what
is good and never involuntarily or voluntarily doing anything base, this can be effected by
living under the guidance of a kind of intelligence and right order which can be enforced.
Now, a father's command does not have the power to enforce or to compel, nor does, in
general, the command of a single man, unless he is a king or someone in a similar position.
20   But law does have the power or capacity to compel, being the rule of reason derived from
some sort of practical wisdom and intelligence. While people hate any men who oppose,
however rightly, their impulses, the law is not invidious when it enjoins what is right.

25   But, with a few exceptions, Sparta is the only state in which the lawgiver seems to
have paid attention to upbringing and pursuits. In most states such matters are utterly
neglected, and each man lives as he pleases, "dealing out law to his children and his
wife" as the Cyclopes do.** Now, the best thing would be to make the correct care of

School of Athens, 1510–11, by Raphael
(1483–1520), Vatican Museums,
Rome, Italy. In this detail from the
larger fresco, Plato is holding a copy
of his *Timaeus* while pointing upward
to the world of the Forms, indicating
the importance of the universal.
Aristotle holds a copy of his *Ethics*
while motioning downward to
emphasize the reality of the physical
world and the importance of the
particular. (*Scala/Art Resource*)

*This is the view attributed by Plato to Protagoras in *Protagoras* 325a.
**Homer, *Odyssey* IX. 114–115. The Cyclopes, according to Homer, were savage one-eyed giants.

these matters a common concern. But if the community neglects them, it would seem to   30
be incumbent upon every man to help his children and friends attain virtue. This he will
be capable of doing, or at least intend to do.

It follows from our discussion that he will be better capable of doing it if he knows
something about legislation. For clearly matters of common concern are regulated by
laws, and good concerns by laws which set high moral standards. Whether the laws are   35
written or unwritten would seem to make no difference, nor whether they give education   1180[b]
to one person or many, just as it makes no difference in the case of mental or physical
training or any other pursuit. For just as legal traditions and (national) character prevail
in states, so paternal words and (ancestral) habits prevail in households—and the latter   5
have an even greater authority because of the tie of kinship and of benefits rendered, (for
members of a household) have the requisite natural affection and obedience (toward the
father) to start with. Furthermore, individual treatment is superior to group treatment in
education as it is in medicine. As a general rule, rest and abstaining from food are good
for a man with a fever, but perhaps they are not good in a particular case. And an expert   10
boxer perhaps does not make all his pupils adopt the same style of fighting. It seems that
each particular is worked out with greater precision if private attention is given, since
each person has more of an opportunity to get what he needs.

But a physician, a physical trainer, or any other such person can take the best
care in a particular case when he knows the general rules, that is, when he knows what
is good for everyone or what is good for a particular kind of person; for the sciences
are said to be, and actually are, concerned with what is common to particular cases.   15
Of course, there is probably nothing to prevent even a person with no scientific
knowledge from taking good care of a particular case, if he has accurately observed
by experience what happens in a particular case, just as there are some who seem to
be their own best physicians, even though they are incapable of giving aid to another.   20
Nevertheless, if a man wants to master a skill or art or some theoretical knowledge, he
ought, one would think, probably to go on to a universal principle, and to gain knowledge of it as best as possible. For, as we have stated, it is with this that the sciences are
concerned.

Moreover, a man who wants to make others better by devoting his care to them—
regardless of whether they are many or few—should try to learn something about legislation, if indeed laws can make us good. To inculcate a good disposition in any person,   25
that is, any person who presents himself, is not a job for just anyone; if anyone can do
it, it is the man who knows, just as it is in medicine and in all other matters that involve
some sort of care and practical wisdom.

Is it not, then, our next task to examine from whom and how we can learn to
become legislators? Is it not, as always, from the experts, in this case the masters of   30
politics? For, as we saw, legislation is a part of politics. Or does politics not appear to
be like the rest of the sciences and capacities? In the other sciences and faculties we
find that the people who transmit the capacity are at the same time actively engaged
in practicing what they know, as, for example, physicians and painters. The Sophists,   35
on the other hand, profess to teach social and political matters, but none of them practices them. That is done by the politicians, whose practice, it would seem, owes more   1181[a]
to some sort of native capacity and to experience than to thought. We find that they
neither discuss nor write about these matters—though that would certainly be nobler
than making speeches for the law courts and the assemblies—nor again that they have
succeeded in making masters of politics of their own sons or any of their friends. But   5
one would expect that they would have done so, had they been able; for they could not

have left a better bequest to their cities, nor is there anything they would rather choose to have for themselves, and thus also for those dearest to them, than a capacity of this
10   kind. Nonetheless, experience does seem to make no mean contribution; for they would not have become masters of politics simply through their familiarity with political matters. This is why those who aim at a knowledge of politics also seem to need experience.

But, as we can see, those Sophists who profess to teach politics are very far from teaching it.* By and large, they do not even know what sort of thing it is or with what kind of subjects it deals. For (if they did,) they would not have classified it as identical
15   with or even inferior to rhetoric; nor would they have believed that it is easy to legislate by collecting the most highly regarded laws. They think that it is possible to select the best laws, as if the very selection were not an act of understanding and as if correct judgment were not the most important thing here, as it is in matters of music. In every
20   field, it is those who are experienced that judge its products correctly, and are privy to the means and the manner in which they were accomplished and understand what combinations are harmonious. The inexperienced, on the other hand, must be satisfied if they do not fail to recognize whether the work has been produced well or badly. That is the case, for example, in painting. Laws are, as it were, the products of politics.
1181^b Accordingly, how can a man learn from them to become a legislator or to judge which are the best? We do not even find men becoming medical experts by reading textbooks. Yet medical writers try at least not only to describe the treatments, but also how particular patients, whom they distinguish by their various characteristics, can be cured and how the treatments are to be applied. Though their books seem useful for experienced
5   people, they are useless for those who do not have the requisite knowledge. So also collections of laws and constitutions** may perhaps be of good use to those who have the capacity to study them and judge what enactments are good and which are not, and what kind of measures are appropriate to what circumstances. But those who go through such collections without the trained ability as (to do so) do not have the requi-
10   site good judgment, unless they have it spontaneously, though they may perhaps gain a deeper understanding of these matters.

Accordingly, since previous writers have left the subject of legislation unexamined, it is perhaps best if we ourselves investigate it and the general problem of the
15   Constitution of a state, in order to complete, as best we can, our philosophy of human affairs. First of all, then, let us try to review any discussion of merit contributed by our predecessors on some particular aspect; and then, on the basis of our collection of constitutions, let us study what sort of thing preserves and what destroys states, what preserves and destroys each particular kind of constitution, and what the causes are that
20   make some states well administered and others not. Once we have studied this, we shall perhaps also gain a more comprehensive view of the best form of constitution, of the way in which each is organized, and what laws and customs are current in each. So let us begin our discussion.***

---

*The whole of this paragraph (1181a12–b12) is aimed at Isocrates (436–338 B.C.), who founded a school of rhetoric at Athens which competed with Plato's Academy. Aristotle's special target here seems to be Isocrates' *Antidosis,* written in 354–353 B.C., in which Isocrates states his views on education.

**Aristotle is referring to the collection of 158 constitutions of Greek and non-Greek states which was undertaken under his supervision.

***This final paragraph leads back to the point made at the opening of the work in Book I, 2 (page 000): the study of ethics is a part of politics. At the same time, this paragraph serves as a general introduction to the *Politics.*

POLITICS (in part)

BOOK I

1. Every state is a community of some kind, and every community is established with a view to some good; for everyone always acts in order to obtain that which they think good. But, if all communities aim at some good, the state or political community, which is the highest of all, and which embraces all the rest, aims at good in a greater degree than any other, and at the highest good.

Some people think that the qualifications of a statesman, king, householder, and master are the same, and that they differ, not in kind, but only in the number of their subjects. For example, the ruler over a few is called a master; over more, the manager of a household; over a still larger number, a statesman or king, as if there were no difference between a great household and a small state. The distinction which is made between the king and the statesman is as follows: When the government is personal, the ruler is a king; when, according to the rules of the political science, the citizens rule and are ruled in turn, then he is called a statesman.

But all this is a mistake, as will be evident to any one who considers the matter according to the method which has hitherto guided us. As in other departments of science, so in politics, the compound should always be resolved into the simple elements or least parts of the whole. We must therefore look at the elements of which the state is composed, in order that we may see in what the different kinds of rule differ from one another, and whether any scientific result can be attained about each one of them.

2. He who thus considers things in their first growth and origin, whether a state or anything else, will obtain the clearest view of them. In the first place there must be a union of those who cannot exist without each other; namely, of male and female, that the race may continue (and this is a union which is formed, not of choice, but because, in common with other animals and with plants, mankind have a natural desire to leave behind them an image of themselves), and of natural ruler and subject, that both may be preserved. For that which can foresee by the exercise of mind is by nature lord and master, and that which can with its body give effect to such foresight is a subject, and by nature a slave; hence master and slave have the same interest. Now nature has distinguished between the female and the slave. For she is not niggardly, like the smith who fashions the Delphian knife for many uses; she makes each thing for a single use, and every instrument is best made when intended for one and not for many uses. But among barbarians no distinction is made between women and slaves, because there is no natural ruler among them: they are a community of slaves, male and female. That is why the poets say,

It is meet that Hellenes should rule over barbarians;

as if they thought that the barbarian and the slave were by nature one.

Out of these two relationships the first thing to arise is the family, and Hesiod is right when he says,

First house and wife and an ox for the plough,

Aristotle, *Politics*, (I, 1–2; III, 6–9; IV, 11–12; VII, 3b–4, 9), translated by Benjamin Jowett.

1252ª

5

10

15

20

25

30

1252ᵇ

5

10

for the ox is the poor man's slave. The family is the association established by nature for the supply of men's everyday wants, and the members of it are called by Charondas, "companions of the cupboard," and by Epimenides the Cretan, "companions of the

15   manger." But when several families are united, and the association aims at something more than the supply of daily needs, the first society to be formed is the village. And the most natural form of the village appears to be that of a colony from the family composed of the children and grandchildren, who are said to be, "suckled with the same milk." And this is the reason why Hellenic states were originally governed by kings; because the

20   Hellenes were under royal rule before they came together, as the barbarians still are. Every family is ruled by the eldest, and therefore in the colonies of the family the kingly form of government prevailed because they were of the same blood. As Homer says:

> Each one gives law to his children and to his wives.

For they lived dispersedly, as was the manner in ancient times. That is why men say that

25   the Gods have a king, because they themselves either are or were in ancient times under the rule of a king. For they imagine not only the forms of the Gods but their ways of life to be like their own.

When several villages are united in a single complete community, large enough to be nearly or quite self-sufficing, the state comes into existence, originating in the bare

30   needs of life, and continuing in existence for the sake of a good life. And therefore, if the earlier forms of society are natural, so is the state, for it is the end of them, and the nature of a thing is its end. For what each thing is when fully developed, we call its

1253ᵃ   nature, whether we are speaking of a man, a horse, or a family. Besides, the final cause and end of a thing is the best, and to be self-sufficing is the end and the best.

Hence it is evident that the state is a creation of nature, and that man is by nature a political animal. And he who by nature and not by mere accident is without a state, is either a bad man or above humanity; he is like the

5   Tribeless, lawless, hearthless one,

whom Homer denounces—the natural outcast is forthwith a lover of war; he may be compared to an isolated piece at draughts.

Now, that man is more of a political animal than bees or any other gregarious animals is evident. Nature, as we often say, makes nothing in vain, and man is the only

10   animal who has the gift of speech. And whereas mere voice is but an indication of pleasure or pain, and is therefore found in other animals (for their nature attains to the perception of pleasure and pain and the intimation of them to one another, and no further), the power of speech is intended to set forth the expedient and inexpedient, and therefore likewise the just and the unjust. And it is a characteristic of man that he alone has any

15   sense of good and evil, of just and unjust, and the like, and the association of living beings who have this sense makes a family and a state.

Further, the state is by nature clearly prior to the family and to the individual,

20   since the whole is of necessity prior to the part; for example, if the whole body be destroyed, there will be no foot or hand, except in an equivocal sense, as we might speak of a stone hand; for when destroyed the hand will be no better than that. But things are defined by their function and power; and we ought not to say that they are the same when they no longer have their proper quality, but only that they have the same

25   name. The proof that the state is a creation of nature and prior to the individual is that the individual, when isolated, is not self-sufficing; and therefore he is like a part in relation to the whole. But he who is unable to live in society, or who has no need because he

is sufficient for himself, must be either a beast or a god: he is no part of a state. A social instinct is implanted in all men by nature, and yet he who first founded the state was the greatest of benefactors. For man, when perfected, is the best of animals, but, when separated from law and justice, he is the worst of all; since armed injustice is the more dangerous, and he is equipped at birth with arms, meant to be used by intelligence and excellence, which he may use for the worst ends. That is why, if he has not excellence, he is the most unholy and the most savage of animals, and the most full of lust and gluttony. But justice is the bond of men in states; for the administration of justice, which is the determination of what is just, is the principle of order in political society.

*   *   *

BOOK III

6. Having determined these questions, we have next to consider whether there is only one form of government or many, and if many, what they are, and how many, and what are the differences between them.

A constitution is the arrangement of magistracies in a state, especially of the highest of all. The government is everywhere sovereign in the state, and the constitution is in fact the government. For example, in democracies the people are supreme, but in oligarchies, the few; and, therefore, we say that these two constitutions also are different: and so in other cases.

First, let us consider what is the purpose of a state, and how many forms of rule there are by which human society is regulated. We have already said, in the first part of this treatise, when discussing household management and the rule of a master, that man is by nature a political animal. And therefore, men, even when they do not require one another's help, desire to live together; not but that they are also brought together by their common interests in so far as they each attain to any measure of well-being. This is certainly the chief end, both of individuals and of states. And mankind meet together and maintain the political community also for the sake of mere life (in which there is possibly some noble element so long as the evils of existence do not greatly overbalance the good). And we all see that men cling to life even at the cost of enduring great misfortune, seeming to find in life a natural sweetness and happiness.

There is no difficulty in distinguishing the various kinds of rule; they have been often defined already in our popular discussions. The rule of a master, although the slave by nature and the master by nature have in reality the same interests, is nevertheless exercised primarily with a view to the interest of the master, but accidentally considers the slave, since, if the slave perish, the rule of the master perishes with him. On the other hand, the government of a wife and children and of a household, which we have called household management, is exercised in the first instance for the good of the governed or for the common good of both parties, but essentially for the good of the governed, as we see to be the case in medicine, gymnastic, and the arts in general, which are only accidentally concerned with the good of the artists themselves. For there is no reason why the trainer may not sometimes practise gymnastics, and the helmsman is always one of the crew. The trainer or the helmsman considers the good of those committed to his care. But, when he is one of the persons taken care of, he accidentally participates in the advantage, for the helmsman is also a sailor, and the trainer becomes one of those in training. And so in politics: when the state is framed upon the principle of

equality and likeness, the citizens think that they ought to hold office by turns.
10 Formerly, as is natural, everyone would take his turn of service; and then again, somebody else would look after his interest, just as he, while in office, had looked after
theirs. But nowadays, for the sake of the advantage which is to be gained from the pub-
15 lic revenues and from office, men want to be always in office. One might imagine that
the rulers, being sickly, were only kept in health while they continued in office; in that
case we may be sure that they would be hunting after places. The conclusion is evident:
that governments which have a regard to the common interest are constituted in accor-
20 dance with strict principles of justice, and are therefore true forms; but those which
regard only the interest of the rulers are all defective and perverted forms, for they are
despotic, whereas a state is a community of freemen.

7. Having determined these points, we have next to consider how many forms of
25 government there are, and what they are; and in the first place what are the true forms, for
when they are determined the perversions of them will at once be apparent. The words
constitution and government have the same meaning, and the government, which is the
30 supreme authority in states, must be in the hands of one, or of a few, or of the many. The
true forms of government, therefore, are those in which the one, or the few, or the many,
govern with a view to the common interest; but governments which rule with a view to
the private interest, whether of the one, or of the few, or of the many, are perversions. For
the members of a state, if they are truly citizens, ought to participate in its advantages. Of
forms of government in which one rules, we call that which regards the common interest,
35 kingship; that in which more than one, but not many, rule, aristocracy; and it is so called,
either because the rulers are the best men, or because they have at heart the best interests
of the state and of the citizens. But when the many administer the state for the common
interest, the government is called by the generic name—a constitution. And there is a
40 reason for this use of language. One man or a few may excel in excellence; but as the
1279^b number increases it becomes more difficult for them to attain perfection in every kind of
excellence, though they may in military excellence, for this is found in the masses.
Hence in a constitutional government the fighting-men have the supreme power, and
those who possess arms are the citizens.
Of the above-mentioned forms, the perversions are as follows:—of kingship, tyranny;
5 of aristocracy, oligarchy; of constitutional government, democracy. For tyranny is a kind of
monarchy which has in view the interest of the monarch only; oligarchy has in view the
10 interest of the wealthy; democracy, of the needy: none of them the common good of all.

8. But there are difficulties about these forms of government, and it will therefore
be necessary to state a little more at length the nature of each of them. For he who
would make a philosophical study of the various sciences, and is not only concerned
15 with practice, ought not to overlook or omit anything, but to set forth the truth in every
particular. Tyranny, as I was saying, is monarchy exercising the rule of a master over the
political society; oligarchy is when men of property have the government in their hands;
democracy, the opposite, when the indigent, and not the men of property, are the rulers.
20 And here arises the first of our difficulties, and it relates to the distinction just drawn.
For democracy is said to be the government of the many. But what if the many are men
of property and have the power in their hands? In like manner oligarchy is said to be the
government of the few; but what if the poor are fewer than the rich, and have the power
25 in their hands because they are stronger? In these cases the distinction which we have
drawn between these different forms of government would no longer hold good.
Suppose, once more, that we add wealth to the few and poverty to the many, and
name the governments accordingly—an oligarchy is said to be that in which the few and

the wealthy, and a democracy that in which the many and the poor are the rulers—there   30
will still be a difficulty. For, if the only forms of government are the ones already mentioned, how shall we describe those other governments also just mentioned by us, in
which the rich are the more numerous and the poor are the fewer, and both govern in
their respective states?

The argument seems to show that, whether in oligarchies or in democracies,   35
the number of the governing body, whether the greater number, as in a democracy, or the
smaller number, as in an oligarchy, is an accident due to the fact that the rich everywhere
are few, and the poor numerous. But if so, there is a misapprehension of the causes of   40
the difference between them. For the real difference between democracy and oligarchy is
poverty and wealth. Wherever men rule by reason of their wealth, whether they be few or   1280ª
many, that is an oligarchy, and where the poor rule, that is a democracy. But in fact the rich
are few and the poor many; for few are well-to-do, whereas freedom is enjoyed by all, and
wealth and freedom are the grounds on which the two parties claim power in the state.   5

9. Let us begin by considering the common definitions of oligarchy and democracy,
and what is oligarchical and democratic justice. For all men cling to justice of some kind,
but their conceptions are imperfect and they do not express the whole idea. For example,   10
justice is thought by them to be, and is, equality—not, however, for all, but only for
equals. And inequality is thought to be, and is, justice; neither is this for all, but only for
unequals. When the persons are omitted, then men judge erroneously. The reason is that   15
they are passing judgement on themselves, and most people are bad judges in their own
case. And whereas justice implies a relation to persons as well as to things, and a just distribution, as I have already said in the *Ethics,* implies the same ratio between the persons
and between the things, they agree about the equality of the things, but dispute about the
equality of the persons, chiefly for the reason which I have just given—because they are   20
bad judges in their own affairs; and secondly, because both the parties to the argument are
speaking of a limited and partial justice, but imagine themselves to be speaking of
absolute justice. For the one party, if they are unequal in one respect, for example wealth,
consider themselves to be unequal in all; and the other party, if they are equal in one
respect, for example free birth, consider themselves to be equal in all. But they leave out   25
the capital point. For if men met and associated out of regard to wealth only, their share in
the state would be proportioned to their property, and the oligarchical doctrine would then
seem to carry the day. It would not be just that he who paid one mina should have the same
share of a hundred minae, whether of the principal or of the profits, as he who paid the   30
remaining ninety-nine. But a state exists for the sake of a good life, and not for the sake of
life only: if life only were the object, slaves and brute animals might form a state, but they
cannot, for they have no share in happiness or in a life based on choice. Nor does a state
exist for the sake of alliance and security from injustice, nor yet for the sake of exchange   35
and mutual intercourse; for then the Tyrrhenians and the Carthaginians, and all who have
commercial treaties with one another, would be the citizens of one state. True, they have
agreements about imports, and engagements that they will do no wrong to one another,   40
and written articles of alliance. But there are no magistracies common to the contracting   1280ᵇ
parties; different states have each their own magistracies. Nor does one state take care that
the citizens of the other are such as they ought to be, nor see that those who come under
the terms of the treaty do no wrong or wickedness at all, but only that they do no injustice
to one another. Whereas, those who care for good government take into consideration   5
political excellence and defect. Whence it may be further inferred that excellence must be
the care of a state which is truly so called, and not merely enjoys the name: for without
this end the community becomes a mere alliance which differs only in place from
alliances of which the members live apart; and law is only a convention, "a surety to one   10

another of justice," as the sophist Lycophron says, and has no real power to make the citizens good and just.

15 This is obvious; for suppose distinct places, such as Corinth and Megara, to be brought together so that their walls touched, still they would not be one city, not even if the citizens had the right to intermarry, which is one of the rights peculiarly characteristic of states. Again, if men dwelt at a distance from one another, but not so far off as to have no intercourse, and there were laws among them that they should not wrong each other in their exchanges, neither would this be a state. Let us suppose that one man is a carpenter, another 20 a farmer, another a shoemaker, and so on, and that their number is ten thousand: nevertheless, if they have nothing in common but exchange, alliance, and the like, that would not constitute a state. Why is this? Surely not because they are at a distance from one another; 25 for even supposing that such a community were to meet in one place, but that each man had a house of his own, which was in a manner his state, and that they made alliance with one another, but only against evil-doers; still an accurate thinker would not deem this to be a 30 state, if their intercourse with one another was of the same character after as before their union. It is clear then that a state is not a mere society, having a common place, established for the prevention of mutual crime and for the sake of exchange. These are conditions without which a state cannot exist; but all of them together do not constitute a state, which is a community of families and aggregations of families in well-being, for the sake of a perfect 35 and self–sufficing life. Such a community can only be established among those who live in the same place and intermarry. Hence there arise in cities family connexions, brotherhoods, common sacrifices, amusements which draw men together. But these are created by friend-40 ship, for to choose to live together is friendship. The end of the state is the good life, and 1281ᵃ these are the means towards it. And the state is the union of families and villages in a perfect and self-sufficing life, by which we mean a happy and honourable life.

Our conclusion, then, is that political society exists for the sake of noble actions, 5 and not of living together. Hence they who contribute most to such a society have a greater share in it than those who have the same or a greater freedom or nobility of birth but are inferior to them in political virtue; or than those who exceed them in wealth but are surpassed by them in virtue.

From what has been said it will be clearly seen that all the partisans of different 10 forms of government speak of a part of justice only.

*   *   *

Book IV

1295ᵃ   11. We have now to inquire what is the best constitution for most states, and the best life for most men, neither assuming a standard of virtue which is above ordinary persons, nor an education which is exceptionally favoured by nature and circumstances, 30 nor yet an ideal state which is an aspiration only, but having regard to the life in which the majority are able to share, and to the form of government which states in general can attain. As to those aristocracies, as they are called, of which we were just now speaking, they either lie beyond the possibilities of the greater number of states, or they approximate to the so-called constitutional government, and therefore need no separate discussion. And in fact the conclusion at which we arrive respecting all these forms rests upon 35 the same grounds. For if what was said in the *Ethics* is true, that the happy life is the life according to excellence lived without impediment, and that excellence is a mean, then

the life which is in a mean, and in a mean attainable by everyone, must be the best. And the same principles of excellence and badness are characteristic of cities and of constitutions; for the constitution is so to speak the life of the city.   40
1295^b

Now in all states there are three elements: one class is very rich, another very poor, and a third in a mean. It is admitted that moderation and the mean are best, and therefore it will clearly be best to possess the gifts of fortune in moderation; for in that condition of   5
life men are most ready to follow rational principle. But he who greatly excels in beauty, strength, birth, or wealth, or on the other hand who is very poor, or very weak, or of very low status, finds it difficult to follow rational principle. Of these two the one sort grow into violent and great criminals, the others into rogues and petty rascals. And two sorts of   10
offences correspond to them, the one committed from violence, the other from roguery [Again, the middle class is least likely to shrink from rule, or to be over-ambitious for it], both of which are injuries to the state. Again, those who have too much of the goods of fortune, strength, wealth, friends, and the like, are neither willing nor able to submit to   15
authority. The evil begins at home; for when they are boys, by reason of the luxury in which they are brought up, they never learn, even at school, the habit of obedience. On the other hand, the very poor, who are in the opposite extreme, are too degraded. So that the one class cannot obey, and can only rule despotically; the other knows not how to com-   20
mand and must be ruled like slaves. Thus arises a city, not of freemen, but of masters and slaves, the one despising, the other envying; and nothing can be more fatal to friendship and good fellowship in states than this: for good fellowship springs from friendship; when men are at enmity with one another, they would rather not even share the same path. But a   25
city ought to be composed, as far as possible, of equals and similars; and these are gener- ally the middle classes. Wherefore the city which is composed of middle-class citizens is necessarily best constituted in respect of the elements of which we say the fabric of the state naturally consists. And this is the class of citizens which is most secure in a state, for they do not, like the poor, covet other men's goods; nor do others covet theirs, as the poor   30
covet the goods of the rich; and as they neither plot against others, nor are themselves plotted against, they pass through life safely. Wisely then did Phocylides pray—"Many things are best in the mean; I desire to be of a middle condition in my city."

Thus it is manifest that the best political community is formed by citizens of the   35
middle class, and that those states are likely to be well-administered in which the mid- dle class is large, and stronger if possible than both the other classes, or at any rate than either singly; for the addition of the middle class turns the scale, and prevents either of the extremes from being dominant. Great then is the good fortune of a state in which the   40
citizens have a moderate and sufficient property; for where some possess much, and the   1296^a
others nothing, there may arise an extreme democracy, or a pure oligarchy; or a tyranny may grow out of either extreme—either out of the most rampant democracy, or out of an oligarchy; but it is not so likely to arise out of the middle constitutions and those akin to them. I will explain the reason for this hereafter, when I speak of the revolutions of   5
states. The mean condition of states is clearly best, for no other is free from faction; and where the middle class is large, there are least likely to be factions and dissensions. For a similar reason large states are less liable to faction than small ones, because in them   10
the middle class is large; whereas in small states it is easy to divide all the citizens into two classes who are either rich or poor, and to leave nothing in the middle. And democ- racies are safer and more permanent than oligarchies, because they have a middle class   15
which is more numerous and has a greater share in the government; for when there is no middle class, and the poor are excessive in number, troubles arise, and the state soon comes to an end. A proof of the superiority of the middle class is that the best legislators have been of a middle condition; for example, Solon, as his own verses testify; and   20
Lycurgus, for he was not a king; and Charondas, and almost all legislators.

These considerations will help us to understand why most governments are either democratic or oligarchical. The reason is that the middle class is seldom numerous in them, and whichever party, whether the rich or the common people, transgresses the mean and predominates, draws the constitution its own way, and thus arises either oligarchy or democracy. There is another reason—the poor and the rich quarrel with one another, and whichever side gets the better, instead of establishing a just or popular government, regards political supremacy as the prize of victory, and the one party sets up a democracy and the other an oligarchy. Further, both the parties which had the supremacy in Greece looked only to the interest of their own form of government, and established in states, the one, democracies, and the other, oligarchies; they thought of their own advantage, and of the advantage of the other states not at all. For these reasons the middle form of government has rarely, if ever, existed, and among a very few only. One man alone of all who ever ruled in Greece was induced to give this middle constitution to states. But it has now become a habit among the citizens of states not even to care about equality; all men are seeking for dominion, or, if conquered, are willing to submit.

What then is the best form of government, and what makes it the best, is evident; and of other constitutions, since we say that there are many kinds of democracy and many of oligarchy, it is not difficult to see which has the first and which the second or any other place in the order of excellence, now that we have determined which is the best. For that which is nearest to the best must of necessity be better, and that which is further from the mean worse, if we are judging absolutely and not relatively to given conditions: I say "relatively to given conditions," since a particular government may be preferable, but another form may be better for some people.

12. We have now to consider what and what kind of government is suitable to what and what kind of men. I may begin by assuming, as a general principle common to all governments, that the portion of the state which desires the permanence of the constitution ought to be stronger than that which desires the reverse. Now every city is composed of quality and quantity. By quality I mean freedom, wealth, education, good birth, and by quantity, superiority of numbers. Quality may exist in one of the classes which make up the state, and quantity in the other. For example, the meanly-born may be more in number than the well-born, or the poor than the rich, yet they may not so much exceed in quantity as they fall short in quality; and therefore there must be a comparison of quantity and quality. Where the number of the poor exceeds a given proportion, there will naturally be a democracy, varying in form with the sort of people who compose it in each case. If, for example, the farmers exceed in number, the first form of democracy will then arise; if the artisans and labouring class, the last; and so with the intermediate forms. But where the rich and the notables exceed in quality more than they fall short in quantity, there oligarchy arises, similarly assuming various forms according to the kind of superiority possessed by the oligarchs.

The legislator should always include the middle class in his government; if he makes his laws oligarchical, let him look to the middle class; if he makes them democratic, he should equally by his laws try to attach this class to the state. There only can the government ever be stable where the middle class exceeds one or both of the others, and in that case there will be no fear that the rich will unite with the poor against the rulers. For neither of them will ever be willing to serve the other, and if they look for some form of government more suitable to both, they will find none better than this, for the rich and the poor will never consent to rule in turn, because they mistrust one another. The arbiter is always the one most trusted, and he who is in the middle is an arbiter. The more perfect the admixture of the political elements, the more lasting will be the constitution. Many even of those who desire to form aristocratic governments make a mistake, not only in giving too much power to the rich, but in attempting to cheat the people. There comes a time when out of a false good there arises a true evil, since the encroachments of the rich are more destructive to the constitution than those of the people.   10

*   *   *

Book VII

3. . . . If we are right in our view, and happiness is assumed to be acting well, the active life will be the best, both for every city collectively, and for individuals. Not that a life of action must necessarily have relation to others, as some persons think, nor are those ideas only to be regarded as practical which are pursued for the sake of practical results, but much more the thoughts and contemplations which are independent and complete in themselves; since acting well, and therefore a certain kind of action, is an end, and even in the case of external actions the directing mind is most truly said to act. Neither, again, is it necessary that states which are cut off from others and choose to live alone should be inactive; for activity, as well as other things, may take place by sections; there are many ways in which the sections of a state act upon one another. The same thing is equally true of every individual. If this were otherwise, the gods and the universe, who have no external actions over and above their own energies, would be far enough from perfection. Hence it is evident that the same life is best for each individual, and for states and for mankind collectively.   1325^b   20   25   30

4. Thus far by way of introduction. In what has preceded I have discussed other forms of government; in what remains the first point to be considered is what should be the conditions of the ideal or perfect state; for the perfect state cannot exist without a due supply of the means of life. And therefore we must presuppose many purely imaginary conditions, but nothing impossible. There will be a certain number of citizens, a country in which to place them, and the like. As the weaver or shipbuilder or any other artisan must have the material proper for his work (and in proportion as this is better prepared, so will the result of his art be nobler), so the statesman or legislator must also have the materials suited to him.   35   40   1326^a

First among the materials required by the statesman is population: he will consider what should be the number and character of the citizens, and then what should be the size and character of the country. Most persons think that a state in order to be happy ought to be large; but even if they are right, they have no idea what is a large and what a small state. For they judge of the size of the city by the number of the inhabitants; whereas they ought to regard, not their number, but their power. A city too, like an individual, has a work to do; and that city which is best adapted to the fulfilment of its work is to be deemed greatest, in the same sense of the word great in which Hippocrates might be called greater, not as a man, but as a physician, than some one else who was taller. And even if we reckon greatness by numbers, we ought not to include everybody, for, there must always be in cities a multitude of slaves and resident aliens and foreigners; but we should include those only who are members of the state, and who form an essential part of it. The number of the latter is a proof of the greatness of a city; but a city which produces numerous artisans and comparatively few soldiers cannot be great, for a great city is not the same as a populous one. Moreover, experience shows that a   5   10   15   20   25 very populous city can rarely, if ever, be well governed; since all cities which have a reputation for good government have a limit of population. We may argue on grounds of reason, and the same result will follow. For law is order, and good law is good order; but

30   a very great multitude cannot be orderly: to introduce order into the unlimited is the work of a divine power—of such a power as holds together the universe. Beauty is realized in number and magnitude, and the state which combines magnitude with good

35   order must necessarily be the most beautiful. To the size of states there is a limit, as there is to other things, plants, animals, implements; for none of these retain their natural power when they are too large or too small, but they either wholly lose their nature,

40   or are spoiled. For example, a ship which is only a span long will not be a ship at all, nor a ship a quarter of a mile long; yet there may be a ship of a certain size, either too large or too small, which will still be a ship, but bad for sailing. In like manner a state when

1326ᵇ   composed of too few is not, as a state ought to be, self-sufficient; when of too many, though self-sufficient in all mere necessaries, as a nation may be, it is not a state, being almost incapable of constitutional government. For who can be the general of such a

5   vast multitude, or who the herald, unless he have the voice of a Stentor?

A state, then, only begins to exist when it has attained a population sufficient for a

10   good life in the political community: it may indeed, if it somewhat exceeds this number, be a greater state. But, as I was saying, there must be a limit. What the limit should be will be easily ascertained by experience. For both governors and governed have duties to per-

15   form; the special functions of a governor are to command and to judge. But if the citizens of a state are to judge and to distribute offices according to merit, then they must know each other's characters; where they do not possess this knowledge, both the election to offices arid the decision of lawsuits will go wrong. When the population is very large they are manifestly settled at haphazard, which clearly ought not to be. Besides, in an overpopulous state foreigners and resident aliens will readily acquire the rights of citizens, for who will find them out? Clearly then the best limit of the population of a state is the

25   largest number which suffices for the purposes of life, and can be taken in at a single view.

*   *   *

1328ᵇ   9. . . . Since we are here speaking of the best form of government, i.e. that under which the state will be most happy (and happiness, as has been already said, cannot exist without excellence), it clearly follows that in the state which is best governed and possesses men who are just absolutely, and not merely relatively to the principle of the

40   constitution, the citizens must not lead the life of artisans or tradesmen, for such a life is ignoble and inimical to excellence. Neither must they be farmers, since leisure is neces-

1329ᵃ   sary both for the development of excellence and the performance of political duties.

Again, there is in a state a class of warriors, and another of councillors, who

5   advise about the expedient and determine matters of law, and these seem in an especial manner parts of a state. Now, should these two classes be distinguished, or are both functions to be assigned to the same persons? Here again there is no difficulty in seeing that both functions will in one way belong to the same, in another, to different persons. To different persons in so far as these employments are suited to different primes of life, for the one requires wisdom and the other strength. But on the other hand, since it is an

10   impossible thing that those who are able to use or to resist force should be willing to remain always in subjection, from this point of view the persons are the same; for those who carry arms can always determine the fate of the constitution. It remains therefore that both functions should be entrusted by the ideal constitution to the same persons,

15   not, however, at the same time, but in the order prescribed by nature, who has given to

young men strength and to older men wisdom. Such a distribution of duties will be expedient and also just, and is founded upon a principle of conformity to merit. Besides, the ruling class should be the owners of property, for they are citizens, and the citizens of a state should be in good circumstances; whereas artisans or any other class which is   20
not a producer of excellence have no share in the state. This follows from our first principle, for happiness cannot exist without excellence, and a city is not to be termed happy in regard to a portion of the citizens, but in regard to them all. And clearly property should be in their hands, since the farmers will of necessity be slaves or barbarian   25
country people.

Of the classes enumerated there remain only the priests, and the manner in which their office is to be regulated is obvious. No farmer or artisan should be appointed to it; for the gods should receive honour from the citizens only. Now since the body of the   30
citizens is divided into two classes, the warriors and the councillors, and it is fitting that the worship of the gods should be duly performed, and also a rest provided in their service for those who from age have given up active life, to the old men of these two classes should be assigned the duties of the priesthood.

We have shown what are the necessary conditions, and what the parts of a state: 35
farmers, artisans, and labourers of all kinds are necessary to the existence of states, but the parts of the state are the warriors and councillors. And these are distinguished severally from one another, the distinction being in some cases permanent, in others not.

POETICS (in part)

CHAPTER SIX

Let us speak about tragedy, taking up again the definition of the kind of thing it is that   1449ᵇ
comes into being out of what has been said. Tragedy, then, is an imitation of an action of serious stature and complete, having magnitude, in language made pleasing in distinct   25
forms in its separate parts, imitating people acting and not using narration, accomplishing by means of pity and fear the cleansing <katharsis> of these states of feeling. By "language made pleasing" I mean that which has rhythm and harmony, and by "in distinct forms" I mean accomplishing this in some parts through meters alone and in others in turn through   30
song. And since people engaged in action produce the imitation, the adornment of the spectacle would necessarily be a first component of a tragedy; next would be song-making and wording, since they make the imitation in these. By "wording" I mean the composition itself of the verses; as for song-making, the meaning it has is completely evident. And since tragedy is an imitation of an action, and action is performed by particular people engaged   35
in action, who must necessarily be of some particular sort in both character and thinking, [and] it is natural for there to be two causes of actions, thinking and character (for it is on account of these that we say the actions too are of certain sorts, and as a result of these that   1450a
everyone succeeds or fails), and the imitation of the action is the story (since by "story"

Aristotle, *Poetics* (Book VI), translated by Joe Sachs (Newburyport, MA: Focus Philosophical Library, 2006). Reprinted by permission of Focus Publishing/R. Pullins Company.

I mean this—the composition of the things done—while by "states of character" I mean that as a result of which we say the people who act are of certain particular sorts, and by "thinking" all those things they say in which they demonstrate something or even declare an opinion), then it is necessary that there be six parts of every tragedy, as a result of which the tragedy is of a particular sort. These are story, states of character, wording, thinking, spectacle, and song-making.

Two parts are those in which they make the imitation, one the manner in which they imitate, and three are the things that they imitate, and there is none besides these. Not a few poets, so to speak, have used these as forms of tragedy, for even spectacle contains all of it, and character, story, wording, song, and thinking do so in the same way. But the greatest of these is the organization of the things done. For tragedy is an imitation not of people but of actions and life. Both happiness and wretchedness consist in action, and the end is a certain sort of action, not a quality; while people are of certain sorts as a result of their characters, it is as a result of their actions that they are happy or the opposite. Therefore, it is not that they act in order that they might imitate states of character; rather, they include states of character conjointly on account of the actions. So the actions performed and the story are the end of tragedy, and the end is the greatest of all things. Also, without action a tragedy could not come to be, but without states of character it could, for the tragedies of most of the new poets are characterless, and many poets generally are of that sort, the sort that Zeuxis also is inclined to be, among painters, as compared with Polygnotus. For while Polygnotus is good at depicting character, Zeuxis's painting has no character in it. Further, if one puts in a row phrases that show character, well made in both wording and thinking, he will not perform what was said to be the work of a tragedy, but the tragedy that uses these things in a more deficient way, but has a story and an organization of actions, will perform that work much more.

On top of these things, the greatest means by which tragedy draws the soul are parts of the story, namely reversals and discoveries. A further sign of this is that even those attempting to be poets have the capacity to be precise in wording and states of character earlier than in organizing the actions, as did just about all the first poets. The story, then, is the source and is like the soul of the tragedy, and states of character rank second. (It is pretty much the same in the art of painting as well, for if one were to dab on the most beautiful paints in a conglomeration, that would not give delight in the same way as if one had painted a white silhouette.) Tragedy is an imitation of action, and it is mostly on account of this that it is an image of the people acting.

Thinking ranks third; this is the ability to say the things that are involved in the situation and are fitting to it, which is exactly the task in the speeches that belong to the political and rhetorical arts, for the old poets made people speak in a political way, while those nowadays make them speak rhetorically. It is a particular sort of character that shows of what sort the choice is; hence character has nothing to do with speeches in which there is nothing of a general sort which the one speaking chooses or rejects. But thinking is present in speeches in which they demonstrate the way something is or is not or state some universal proposition. And wording ranks fourth. As was said before, I mean by wording the conveying by words of a meaning which has the same force whether it is in metrical verses or in speeches. Of the remaining components of tragedy, song-making is the greatest of the things by which it is made pleasing, and the spectacle, while it is able to draw the soul, is the component most foreign to the art and least inherent in poetry. For the power of tragedy is present even without a crowd of spectators and even without actors; what is more, the art of making masks and set decorations has more control over bringing off the spectacle than does the art of the poets.

HELLENISTIC AND ROMAN PHILOSOPHY

Following the death of Alexander the Great in 323 B.C., three of his generals, Ptolemy, Seleucus, and Antigonus, carved up the empire he had created. For the next three centuries the descendants of these three men ruled the eastern Mediterranean world. By 30 B.C., with the Roman Emperor Octavian's defeat of Anthony and Cleopatra and the annexation of Egypt, the period of Greek rule (known as the "Hellenistic" period from the word *<hellen>*, meaning "Greek") was over. Real power in the area had shifted westward to emerging Rome.

This shift from Greek to Roman authority did not happen without social and political turmoil, and the philosophies that developed during this period reflect that turmoil. The emphasis now was not on complete systems of thought, such as those proposed by Plato and Aristotle. In their place were theories focusing on the practical questions of the good life for individuals. In a world that seemed more and more chaotic and uncontrollable, philosophers began to seek personal salvation more than comprehensive theories. Even the Platonic Academy and the Aristotelian Lyceum, which continued for centuries, moved from the constructive doctrines of their founders to more narrowly defined critical issues.

Reprinted in this section are selections from the three major Hellenistic schools—the Epicurean, the Stoic, and the Skeptical. All three of these schools continued into the Roman period and were adapted and modified by their Roman adherents. In order to understand these Hellenistic schools, we must return to Socrates because all three schools had roots in his life and teaching.

The roots of the Epicurean school can be traced back to an early Socratic school, the Cyrenaics. The Cyrenaic school was founded by one of Socrates' associates and admirers, Aristippus of Cyrene, from Libya, in northern Africa. The Cyrenaics disparaged speculative philosophy and extolled the pleasure of the moment. But, following Aristippus, they maintained that the purest pleasure derives from self-mastery and the philosophic life. Only philosophy can protect human beings from passion, which inevitably brings suffering. While despising popular opinion, the Cyrenaics did believe that custom, law, and altruism contributed to long-range pleasure. The Cyrenaic philosophy, with its understanding of the good life as enjoyment of stable pleasures, led to the development of the Epicurean school as expressed by Epicurus and Lucretius.

The history of the Stoic school begins with the thought of Socrates' follower Antisthenes. Antisthenes, a rhetorician with an Athenian father and a Phrygian, non-Greek mother, had been a teacher before he met Socrates, who made a profound impression on him. It seems to have been Socrates' character—his self-control and self-sufficiency, his indifference to winter cold (see the *Symposium*), his serenely ironic superiority in every experience, and the opinions of others (see the *Apology*)—that struck Antisthenes with the force of revelation. What he learned from Socrates was neither a metaphysic nor even a philosophic method but, as he put it, "to live with myself." When he disposed of his possessions, keeping only a ragged old coat, Socrates is said to have taunted him: "I see your vanity through the holes of your coat." Antisthenes founded a school whose members acquired the nickname of "Cynics" <*kynikos*>, Greek for "doglike." The Cynics slept on the ground, neglected their clothes, let their beards grow to unusual

Laocoön, second century B.C., by Hagesandros, Polydoros, and Athenodoros, all of Rhodes. The Trojan priest Laocoön protested against bringing the Greeks' wooden horse into the city. According to one version of the legend, he was punished for his interference when Apollo sent two serpents to kill him and his sons. The Hellenistic philosophers sought relief from tortured emotions such as this work depicts. (*Hirmer Fotoarchiv*)

lengths, and despised the conventions of society, insisting that virtue and happiness consist of self-control and independence. They believed that human dignity was independent of human laws and customs.

Of Antisthenes' Cynic disciples, none was more famous than Diogenes, who went about carrying a lantern in daylight and, when asked why, would reply, "I am looking for an honest man." He made his home in a tub. His eccentric behavior attracted the attention of even Alexander the Great, who, on visiting him, asked whether there was anything at all that he could do to please him. Diogenes replied: "Yes, get out of my sunlight."

Emphasizing self-control and independence, and locating human dignity outside law and convention, the Cynicism of Antisthenes and Diogenes flowed like a tributary into Stoicism. Stoicism, in turn, became the dominant philosophy of the Roman Empire.

A third Hellenistic school of philosophy, Skepticism, also had its roots in Socrates' teachings: specifically, in Socrates' repeated claim that he did not know anything. Based on the work of Pyrrho of Elis (ca. 360–270 B.C.), this movement stressed the contradictory nature of knowledge and advocated suspending judgment and achieving an attitude of detachment.

Reviewing the development of Greek philosophy from the Pre-Socratics to the Stoics, Epicureans, and Skeptics, one is struck by the overwhelming concern in the later schools with peace of mind. There is, as a consequence, one quality that preclassical and classical Greeks possessed preeminently and that Stoics, Epicureans, and Skeptics preeminently lacked: enthusiasm. But there was another movement developing in the ancient world—one that abounded in enthusiasm and changed the course of Western philosophy: Christianity. Though the dates of this movement overlap the dates of the philosophers in this volume, the Christian story appears in Volume II as an introduction to medieval philosophy.

The last great movement of Greek philosophy was Neoplatonism. The leader of this return to Platonic concepts, Plotinus (A.D. 204–270), did not lack enthusiasm, but he was, nevertheless, more remote from classical Greek attitudes than were the Hellenistic philosophers. He extolled the spirit to the point of saying he was ashamed to have a body; his fervor was entirely mystical, and he longed, to cite his famous words, to attain "the flight of the Alone to the Alone." Thus he perfected the less classical tendencies of Plato's thought, merging those tendencies with Neopythagoreanism and with Oriental notions such as the emanations from the One.

In A.D. 529, Plato's Academy was closed by Emperor Justinian, bringing to an end a millennium of Greek philosophy.

*   *   *

For clear, concise introductions to the Hellenistic and Roman philosophers, see Frederick Copleston, "Post-Aristotelian Philosophy," in his *A History of Philosophy: Volume I, Greece & Rome, Part II* (Garden City, NY: Image Books, 1962), and D.W. Hamlyn, "Greek Philosophy after Aristotle," in D.J. O'Connor, ed., *A Critical History of Western Philosophy* (New York: The Free Press, 1964). Eduard Zeller, *The Stoics, Epicureans, and Sceptics,* translated by Oswald J. Reichel (New York: Russell & Russell, 1962); Émile Bréhier, *The Hellenistic and Roman Age,* translated by Wade Baskin (Chicago: University of Chicago Press, 1965); A.A. Long,

Hellenistic Philosophy: Stoics, Epicureans, Sceptics (New York: Scribners, 1974); R.W. *Sharples, Stoics, Epicureans and Sceptics* (Oxford: Routledge, 1996); John Dillon, *The Middle Platonists, 80 B.C. to A.D. 220* (Ithaca, NY: Cornell University Press, 1996); and Mark Morford, *Roman Philosophers* (London: Routledge, 2002) are all solid histories of the period. A.A. Long and D.N. Sedley, eds., *The Hellenistic Philosophers,* two volumes (Cambridge: Cambridge University Press, 1987) and Keimpe Algra et al., eds., *The Cambridge History of Hellenistic Philosophy* (Cambridge: Cambridge University Press, 1999) provide source material and discussions, while Jacques Brunschwig, *Papers in Hellenistic Philosophy,* translated by Janet Lloyd (Cambridge: Cambridge University Press, 1994); Terence Irwin, ed., *Hellenistic Philosophy* (Hamden, CT: Garland Publishing, 1995); and A.A. Long, *From Epicurus to Epictetus: Studies in Hellenistic and Roman Philosophy* (Oxford: Oxford University Press, 2006) give technical expositions of a number of important issues. For an interesting comparative approach to the Hellenistic thinkers, see Martha C. Nussbaum, *The Therapy of Desire: Theory and Practice in Hellenistic Ethics* (Princeton: Princeton University Press, 1994). For primary sources and helpful introductions, see Whitney J. Oates, ed., *The Stoic and Epicurean Philosophers: The Complete Extant Writings of Epicurus, Epictetus, Lucretius, Marcus Aurelius* (New York: Random House, 1940).

EPICURUS
341–270 B.C.

Like Pythagoras, Epicurus was born on the Greek island of Samos. At eighteen he went to Athens for a year, then joined his father in Colophon, the city where Xenophanes had been born. He studied the writings of Democritus and eventually set up his own school on the island of Lesbos. From there he moved to the Hellespont and, finally, to Athens in 307 B.C. As he moved from place to place, many of his students followed him. In Athens he established a community known as the "Garden," where he spent the rest of his life teaching and writing.

Epicurus's community welcomed people of all classes and of both sexes. The school required no fee from students, accepting what each individual was able and willing to pay. Epicurus himself was almost worshiped by his disciples, and members of his group had to swear an oath: "I will be faithful to Epicurus in accordance with whom I have made it my choice to live."* Among the later followers of Epicurus's thought, the Roman poet Lucretius (98–55 B.C.) considered him to be a god. Yet Epicurus was not overbearing or authoritarian. According to all accounts, he was kind and generous, treating his followers as friends, not subordinates. While dying in agony from a urinary obstruction, Epicurus wrote a letter that illustrates his gracious spirit. The extant portion includes these words to his friend Idomeneus: "I have a bulwark against all this pain from the joy in my soul at the memory of our conversations together."**

Epicurus wrote over three hundred volumes, but all that has survived are some fragments, three complete letters, and a short treatise summarizing his views.

---

*Reported in J.V. Luce, *Introduction to Greek Philosophy* (New York: Thames and Hudson, 1992), p. 140.
**Ibid.

These surviving works provide an understanding of Epicurus's physics and ethics and give some sense of his psychology and theory of knowledge. Epicurus's first letter, *To Herodotus,* explains his atomistic theory. Like Democritus, Epicurus asserts that reality is composed of atoms and the void. But unlike Democritus, whose atomism is deterministic, Epicurus broaches the notion that atoms sometimes inexplicably "swerve." As atoms "fell downward" through the void, some of them swerved from their paths and collided with other atoms, setting off a chain reaction that eventually led to the world as we know it. Epicurus goes on to explore the implications of this theory for perception and knowledge.

The second letter, *To Pythocles,* on astronomy and meteorology, is of questionable origin and adds little to our understanding of Epicurus's thought. But the third letter, *To Menoeceus,* together with the short work *Principle Doctrines* explains his central ethical theory. Epicurus declares that pleasure is the highest good, though some pleasures are unnatural and unnecessary. In contrast to the modern understanding of the word "epicurean," Epicurus opposed exotic meals and profuse consumption. Such indulgences never bring permanent pleasure and frequently lead to its opposite: pain. Instead Epicurus advocates enjoying only the "natural" pleasures—those most likely to lead to contentment and repose.

The surviving complete works were incorporated by Diogenes Laertius in his *Lives of Eminent Philosophers.* Using the Russel M. Geer translations, all but the second letter are given here.

*   *   *

The classic secondary work on Epicurus is Cyril Bailey, *The Greek Atomists and Epicurus* (Oxford: Clarendon Press, 1928). Norman Wentworth De Witt, *Epicurus and His Philosophy* (Minneapolis: University of Minnesota Press, 1954), provides an interesting interpretation—one which John M. Rist, *Epicurus: An Introduction* (Cambridge: Cambridge University Press, 1972), contests. A.E. Taylor, *Epicurus* (1911; reprinted New York: Books for Libraries Press, 1969); G.K. Stradach, *The Philosophy of Epicurus* (Evanston, IL: Northwestern University Press, 1963); and Diskin Clay, *Lucretius and Epicurus* (Ithaca, NY: Cornell University Press, 1983), give helpful overviews. A.J. Festugière, *Epicurus and His Gods,* translated by C.W. Chilton (1955; reprinted London: Russell, 1969), James H. Nichols, Jr., *Epicurean Political Philosophy* (Ithaca, NY: Cornell University Press; and Tim O'Keefe, *Epicurus on Freedom* (Cambridge: Cambridge University Press, 2005), 1976), deal with specific topics.

LETTER TO HERODOTUS

I. Introduction

A. Reasons for the Letter

This letter presents a brief compendium of the physics to refresh the memories of those already familiar with the theories.

Epicurus to Herodotus, greeting.

Some, Herodotus, are not able to study carefully all my works on natural science or to examine closely the longer treatises. For them I have already written an epitome of the whole system so that they may acquire a fair grasp of at least the general principles and thereby have confidence in themselves on the chief points whenever they take up the study of physics. Those, too, who have acquired a reasonably complete view of all the parts ought to keep in mind an outline of the principles of the whole; for such a comprehensive grasp is often required, the details not so often. You must continually return to these primary principles and memorize them thoroughly enough to secure a grasp of the essential parts of the system. Accurate knowledge of the details will follow if once you have understood and memorized the outline of the whole. Even for the thoroughly trained student this is the most important result of his accurate knowledge: he is able to make immediate use of the things he perceives and of the resulting concepts by assigning them to the simple classes and calling them by their own names; for it is not possible for anyone to hold in mind in condensed form the whole interrelated system unless he is able to comprehend by means of short formulas all that might be expressed in detail. Therefore, since such a course is useful to all who are engaged with natural science, I, who recommend continuous activity in this field and am myself gaining peaceful happiness from just this life, have composed for you such a brief compendium of the chief principles of my teaching as a whole.

B. Methods of Proof

Words must be used in their natural meanings. All natural science rests on the evidence of the senses.

First, Herodotus, we must understand the meanings of words in order that by expressing our opinions, investigations, and problems in exact terms, we may reach judgments and not use empty phrases, leaving matters undecided although we argue endlessly. We must accept without further explanation the first mental image brought up by each word if we are to have any standard to which to refer a particular inquiry, problem, or opinion.

Epicurus, *Letters, Principal Doctrines, and Vatican Sayings,* translated by Russel M. Geer (New York: Macmillan/Library of the Liberal Arts, 1964).

Next, we must use our sensations as the foundation of all our investigations; that is, we must base investigations on the mental apprehensions,* upon the purposeful use of the several senses that furnish us with knowledge, and upon our immediate feelings.** In these ways we can form judgments on those matters that can be confirmed by the senses and also on those beyond their reach.

II. THE UNIVERSE

A. BASIC PRINCIPLES

Matter can be neither created nor destroyed. The universe as a whole is unchanging.

Now that this has been established we must consider the phenomena that cannot be perceived by the senses. The first principle is that nothing can be created from the non-existent; for otherwise anything would be formed from any thing without the need of seed. If all that disappears were destroyed into the non-existent, all matter would be destroyed, since that into which it would be dissolved has no existence. Truly this universe has always been such as it now is, and so it shall always be; for there is nothing into which it can change, and there is nothing outside the universe that can enter into it and bring about a change.

B. ATOMS AND THE VOID

The universe consists of matter, recognized by the senses, and void, in which matter moves. Other conceivable things are "accidents" or "properties" of these. Sensible objects are composed of atoms, which themselves are indestructible.

Moreover, the universe consists of material bodies and void. That the bodies exist is made clear to all by sensation itself, on which reason must base its judgment in regard to what is imperceptible, as I have said above. If that which we call "void" and "space" and "the untouchable" did not exist, the particles of matter would have no place in which to exist or through which to move, as it is clear they do move.

In addition to these two, there is nothing that we can grasp in the mind, either through concepts or through analogy with concepts,*** that has real existence and is not referred to merely as a property or an accident of material things or of the void.

Of material things, some are compounds, others are the simple particles from which the compounds are formed. The particles are indivisible and unchangeable, as is necessary if all is not to be dissolved to nothing, but something strong is to remain after the dissolution of the compounds, something solid, which cannot be destroyed

---

*That is, upon the apprehension by the mind of the mental concepts that are themselves the result of repeated sensations.

**The feelings are concerned with ethical matters only.

***That is, either through mental images formed by emanations received by the senses or directly by the mind from material things, or through mental combinations of these images.

in any way. Therefore, it is necessary that the first beginnings be indivisible particles of matter.

C. The Infinity of the Universe

i. The universe is infinite, for there is nothing to bound it, and each of its elements is also infinite.

Moreover, the universe as a whole is infinite, for whatever is limited has an outermost edge to limit it, and such an edge is defined by something beyond. Since the universe does not have an edge, it has no limit; and since it lacks a limit, it is infinite and unbounded. Moreover, the universe is infinite both in the number of its atoms and in the extent of its void. If, on the one hand, the void were infinite and matter finite, the atoms would not remain anywhere but would be carried away and scattered through the infinite void, since there would be no atoms from without to support them and hold them together by striking them. If, on the other hand, the void were finite, there would not be room in it for an infinite number of atoms.

ii. To account for the differences in sensible objects, the atoms must exist in many forms, the number of different forms being inconceivably great but not infinite, while the number of atoms of each form is infinite.

In addition, the indivisible, solid particles of matter, from which composite bodies are formed and into which such bodies are dissolved, exist in so many different shapes that the mind cannot grasp their number; for it would not be possible for visible objects to exhibit such great variation in form and quality if they were made by repeated use of atoms of conceivable variety. The number of atoms of each shape is infinite; but the number of varieties cannot be infinite, only inconceivably great.

D. The Motion of the Atoms

The atoms move continuously, both freely in space, and with more limited motion forming gases, liquids, and solids. This motion had no beginning.

The atoms move without interruption through all time. Some of them fall in a straight line; some swerve from their courses; and others move back and forth as the result of collisions. These last make up the objects that our senses recognize. Some of those that move in this way after collisions separate far from each other; the others maintain a vibrating motion, either closely entangled with each other or confined by other atoms that have become entangled. There are two reasons for this continued vibration. The nature of the void that separates each of the atoms from the next permits it, for the void is not able to offer any resistance; and the elasticity that is characteristic of the atoms causes them to rebound after each collision. The degree of entanglement of the atoms determines the extent of the recoil from the collision. These motions had no beginning, for the atoms and the void have always existed.

If all these things are remembered, a statement as brief as this provides a sufficient outline for our understanding of the nature of that which exists.

E. The Infinite Number of Worlds

Because atoms and space are infinite, the number of worlds, like or unlike ours, is also infinite.

Finally, the number of worlds, some like ours and some unlike, is also infinite. For the atoms are infinite in number, as has been shown above, and they move through the greatest distances. The atoms suited for the creation and maintenance of a world have not been used up in the formation of a single world or of a limited number of them, whether like our world or different from it. There is nothing therefore that will stand in the way of there being an infinite number of worlds.

III. Sense Perception

A. Sight

i. Thin films, which we call "idols," are constantly given off by objects, retaining the form and color of the object.

Moreover, there are images of the same shape as the solid bodies from which they come but in thinness far surpassing anything that the senses can perceive. It is not impossible that emanations of this sort are formed in the air that surrounds a body, that there are opportunities for the creation of these thin, hollow films, and that the particles composing them retain as they flow from the solid object the same position and relative order* that they had while on its surface. Such images we call "idols."

ii. Because their unsurpassed fineness frees them from internal and external collisions, the idols move with almost atomic speed.

Nothing in nature as we see it prevents our believing that the idols are of a texture unsurpassed in fineness. For this reason, their velocity is also unsurpassed, since they always find a proper passage, and since moreover their course is retarded by few if any collisions, while a body made up of an inconceivably large number of atoms suffers many collisions as soon as it begins to move.

iii. These films, which are replaced by new matter as soon as they leave the surfaces of bodies, usually retain their forms; but sometimes a new idol is formed in midair.

Moreover, there is nothing to prevent our believing that the creation of idols is as swift as thought. They flow from the surfaces of a body in a constant stream, but this is not made evident by any decrease in the size of the body since other atoms are flooding in. For a long time the idols keep their atoms in the same relative position and order that they occupied on the surface of the solid, although sometimes the idols do become confused, and sometimes they combine in the air. This combination takes place quickly since there is no need of filling up their substance within. There are also some

---

*By keeping the same position (orientation), they retain the color of the object; by keeping the same relative order, its shape.

other ways in which idols come into being. No one of these statements is contradicted by sensation if we examine the ways in which sensation brings us clear visions of external objects and of the relations between them.

iv. Both thought and sight are due to idols coming from objects to us.

We must suppose that we see or think of the outer form of a thing when something comes to us from its surface. We could not as readily perceive the color and shape of external objects by means of impressions made on the air that lies between us and them, or by means of rays or beams of some sort sent from us to them, as we can when outlines of some kind, like the objects in color and shape and of the proper size to affect either our eyes or our minds, come to us from the objects. Since these move in rapid succession they present a single uninterrupted image; and they maintain a quality in harmony with their source because their energy, which has been imparted to them by the vibrations of the atoms in the depths of the solid object, is itself proportionate to the energy of that source.

v. The mental picture from the intent look or the concentrated thought is true. Error results when opinion adds something.

When, by the purposeful use of our mind or of our organs or sense, we receive a mental picture of the shape of an object or of its concomitant qualities, this picture is true, since it is created by the continuous impact of the idols or by an impression left by one of them. Whatever is false and erroneous is due to what opinion adds to an image that is waiting to be confirmed, or at least not to be contradicted, by further evidence of the senses, and which then fails to be so confirmed or is contradicted. The mental pictures that we receive in the images that either come to our minds in sleep or are formed by the purposeful use of the mind or of the other instruments of judgment would not have such similarity to those things that exist and that we call true if there were not some such material effluence actually coming to us from the objects; and the errors would not occur if we did not permit in ourselves some other activity similar to the purposeful apprehension of mental images but yet different. From this other activity error results if its conclusions are not confirmed by further evidence or are contradicted, but truth if they are so confirmed or are not contradicted. Therefore, we must do our best to hold opinion in check in order that we may neither destroy the criteria of judgment, which depend on the clear view, nor confuse everything by placing erroneous opinion on an equality with firmly established truth.

B. HEARING

An effluence from the source of sound, splitting up into particles each like the whole, which come in sequence to the ear, causes hearing.

Moreover, we hear when a kind of stream is carried to our ears from a person who speaks or from an object that makes a sound or noise or in any way whatever arouses in us the sense of hearing. This stream divides into particles, each of which is of the same nature as the whole, and these particles preserve a common relationship to each other and a peculiar continuity that extends back to the source of the sound and usually arouses comprehension in the hearer; or if it fails to do this, it at least makes clear that there is something outside. Without some common relationship extending out from the source, there would not be such awareness. We must not suppose that the air itself receives an impression from the spoken word or sound, for indeed the air is far from admitting any such thing. Rather, the force that is created in us when we speak causes such a displacement of particles, capable of forming a breathlike stream, that it produces in the person to whom we are speaking the sensation of hearing.

C. Smell

Effluences likewise rouse the sense of smell.

We must also suppose that, like sounds, smells could not produce any sensation if there were not carried from the object certain particles of a nature proper to stir the organ of this sense. Some of these are disorderly and unpleasant; some are gentle and agreeable.

IV. The Atoms

A. Properties of the Atoms

i. The unchanging atoms possess no qualities save size, mass, and shape. Other qualities result from atomic position or motion.

We must suppose that the atoms possess none of the qualities of visible things except shape, mass, and size, and whatever is a necessary concomitant of shape.* For every quality changes; but the atoms do not change in any way, since in the dissolution of composite things something hard and indestructible must survive that will make changes possible—not changes into nothingness and from nothingness, but changes brought about by alterations in the positions of some atoms and by the addition or removal of some. It is necessary that the particles that alter their positions and come and go be indestructible, not sharing in the nature of the visible things that are changed, but having their own peculiar shapes and masses; for this much must be unalterable. Even among sensible things, we see that those that are altered by the loss of matter on all sides still retain shape; but the other qualities do not survive in the changing object, as shape survives, but are removed from the whole body. These properties that remain are enough to cause the differences in composite things, since it is necessary that something survive and be not utterly destroyed.

ii. The atoms vary in size, but are not of every size, for if they were, some would be visible.

We must not think that there are atoms of every size lest the visible world prove us wrong; yet we must suppose that there are some differences in size. If there are some differences, it will be easier to explain our feelings and sensations. But the atoms need not be of every size in order to account for the differences in qualities; and if they were of every size, some would necessarily be large enough for us to see. It is clear that this is not the case, and it is impossible to think how an atom might become visible.

*For example, roughness or smoothness.

B. The Parts of the Atom

i. We cannot assume matter to be infinitely divisible. A thing containing infinite material parts, no matter how small they were, would itself be infinitely large.

Next, we cannot suppose that in a finite body the parts, no matter how small, are infinite in number. Therefore, not only must we exclude infinite division into smaller and smaller parts lest we make everything weak, and in our conception of the parts that compose a whole be compelled to make them less and less, finally reducing real things to nothingness; but also in dealing with finite things we must not accept as possible an infinite progression to parts each smaller than the last. For if once you say that in a finite thing there are parts infinite in number even if of the least possible size, you cannot think how this can be. For how can a thing containing infinite parts be finite in size? It is clear that the infinite parts are each of some size, and however small they may be, the whole must be infinite in magnitude.

ii. As in a visible thing there is a smallest part recognizable by the eye, which cannot be seen by itself and the total number of these smallest parts measures the whole, so in the atom there is also a least part recognizable by the mind, which cannot exist by itself, and the total number of these parts measures the atom.

Again, if in the finite body there is a part that can just be distinguished by the eye even if it is not visible by itself, we must believe that there is an adjacent part similar to this, and that if one went on in this way in his mind from one point to the next, he could not continue without end. We must suppose that the smallest perceptible part is not like those bodies that are large enough that we can move our eyes from one part to another, nor yet is it wholly unlike such bodies. Although it has some similarity to them,* it does not admit division into parts. But if because of this similarity we think to mark off mentally a separate portion of the part on this side or that, we find that we are looking at the similar part adjacent to it. If, starting out from the first of these parts and not dwelling on the same one, we inspect them one after another, we find that they do not touch each other part against part,** but by their own one special characteristic they measure magnitude, there being many of them in large bodies, few in small.*** We must suppose that the least part of the atom has the same relation to the whole as the least perceptible part has to the whole visible object. It is clear that the least part of the atom is smaller than the least perceptible part, but it has the same relationship to the whole of which it is a part. We have already stated from its relationship to sensible bodies that the atom has size, although far inferior to them in this respect. Furthermore, the uncompounded least parts of the atoms must be regarded as fixed units, which offer themselves to us in our mental survey of the invisible as a means for the measurement of the atoms, both greater and smaller.† The similarity between the least parts of atoms and the least perceptible parts of sensible things is

---

*That is, it is like them in that it has extension, which a geometrical point lacks.

**A peculiar but logical idea. Ordinarily, when two bodies are in contact, the left part of one, let us say, touches the right part of the other. But these smallest visible parts are so small that they themselves have no visible parts. They therefore appear to us to touch each other, not part against part, but whole against whole.

***Their special characteristic is that they have extension but lack parts. They are therefore suitable units of measurement, since every visible body will consist of a whole number of such parts with no fractions remaining.

†As each sensible body must consist of a given number of the least visible parts, so each atom must consist of a given whole number of these atomic least parts.

sufficient to justify our reasoning up to this point; but it is not possible that the least parts of atoms ever moved individually and came together.

C. THE MOTION OF THE ATOMS

i. Although there can be neither top nor bottom in infinite space, the terms up and down have meaning with respect to ourselves.

Next, we cannot predicate up or down of infinite space as if there were a highest or lowest. Yet if it were possible to draw a line from the point where we are standing upward to infinity in the space above our heads, neither this line nor one drawn downward from the observer to infinity would appear to be at the same time both up and down with reference to the same spot, for this would be nonsense. Thus it is possible to think of one motion extending to infinity in the direction that we call up and one extending down, even if what moves from us into the spaces above our heads comes a thousand times to the feet of those above us and what moves downward comes to the heads of those below; for one of the motions is nonetheless regarded as extending as a whole to infinity in one direction, and the other motion in the other direction.

ii. The atoms, always moving in the void, always possess equal velocity, whether their motion be caused by collision or by weight. If unchecked, an atom will cross any conceivable distance in an inconceivably short time.

Moreover, it is necessary that the atoms possess equal velocity whenever they are moving through the void and nothing collides with them. For heavy bodies will not be carried more quickly than small, light ones when nothing at all opposes them, nor do the small bodies, because they all find suitable passages, excel the large ones, provided the latter are not obstructed. This is equally true of the atoms' motions upwards or to the side because of collisions and of their downward motion because of their own weight. The atom will traverse space with the speed of thought as long as the motion caused in either of these ways maintains itself; that is, until the atom is deflected either by some external force, or by its own weight which counteracts the force of the earlier collision. Moreover, since the motion through the void takes place without any interference from colliding particles, any conceivable distance is completed in an inconceivably brief time. For it is the occurrence or nonoccurrence of collisions that gives the appearance of slow or rapid motion.

iii. At any point of time the atoms of a compound body are moving in all directions with atomic speed, but because of their constant collisions and changes of direction, the motion of the body as a whole in any appreciable time may be brought within the reach of our senses.

Although all atoms have the same velocity, it will be said that in the case of compounds some atoms move faster than others. Men will say this because even in the shortest continuous period of time the compound and the atoms in it do move in one direction. However, in points of time recognized only by the reason, the atoms are not in motion in one direction but are constantly colliding with each other until the motion as a continuous whole comes within the reach of our senses. For what opinion adds about what the senses cannot perceive, namely that in times perceptible only by the reason there will be a continuity of motion, is not true in the case of the atoms. What is grasped by the purposeful use of the senses or by the mental apprehension of concepts contains the whole truth. We must not suppose that in times perceptible by the reason the whole moving compound moves in various directions, for this is unthinkable; and if this were true, when the body arrived in a perceptible time from any quarter whatever, the direction from which we observe its motion would not be that from which it originally started. The visible motion of the body will be the result of the internal collisions, even if below the visible level we leave the velocity of the atoms unaffected by the collisions. An understanding of this principle will be useful.

V. THE SOUL

A. COMPOSITION OF THE SOUL

The soul is material, composed of finely divided particles, some like breath, some like fire, and some of a third, unnamed kind.

Next, referring to the sensations and the feelings as the most certain foundation for belief, we must see that, in general terms, the soul is a finely divided, material thing, scattered through the whole aggregation of atoms that make up the body, most similar to breath with a certain admixture of heat,* in some ways resembling the one, in some ways the other. But there is also a part of the soul that goes beyond even these two in fineness, and for this reason it is more ready to share in the feelings of the body. All this is made evident to us by the powers of the soul, that is, by its feelings, its rapidity of action, its rational faculties, and its possession of those things whose loss brings death to us.

B. THE SOUL AND THE BODY IN SENSATION

The soul experiences sensation only when enclosed in the body; and the body receives from the soul a share in this sensation. Sensation may survive the loss of parts of the body, but it ceases with the destruction of the soul or of the whole body.

Next, we must conclude that the primary cause of sensation is in the soul; yet it would not have acquired sensation if it had not been in some way enclosed by the rest of the body. But the rest of the body, having given the soul the proper setting for experiencing sensation, has itself also gained from the soul a certain share in this capacity. Yet it does not fully share with the soul, and for this reason when the soul departs, the body no longer experiences sensation; for the body did not have this capacity in itself but made sensation possible for that other that had come into existence along with it, namely the soul. The soul, thanks to the power perfected in it by the motions of the body, at once bringing to completion its own power to experience sensation, returned a share of this power to the body because of their close contact and common feelings, as I have said. For this reason, sensation is never lost while the soul remains, even though other parts of the body have been destroyed. Indeed, even if a portion of the soul is lost

*Epicurus believed heat was a material substance.

with the loss in whole or in part of that portion of the body that enclosed it, if any part at all of the soul survives, it will still experience sensation; but when the rest of the body survives both as a whole and part by part, it has no sensation if that collection of atoms, small though it be, that makes up the soul has been lost. However, if the whole body is destroyed, the soul is scattered and no longer enjoys the same powers and motions; and as a result, it no longer possesses sensation. Whenever that in which the soul has existed is no longer able to confine and hold it in, we cannot think of the soul as still enjoying sensation, since it would no longer be within its proper system and would no longer have the use of the appropriate motions.

C. MATERIAL NATURE OF THE SOUL

The term "incorporeal" is properly applied only to the void, which cannot act or be acted on. Since the soul can act and be acted upon, it is not incorporeal.

Moreover, we must clearly observe this also, that the word "incorporeal" in its common use is applied only to that which we can think of as existing by itself.* Now there is no incorporeal thing that we can think of as existing by itself except the void. The void can neither act nor be acted upon; it only gives to corporeal things a space through which to move. Therefore, those who say that the soul is incorporeal are talking nonsense; for in that case the soul would be unable to act or be acted upon, and we clearly see that the soul is capable of both.

D. CONCLUSION

If you refer all this discussion about the soul to your feelings and sensations, remembering what was said at the beginning of the discussion, you will find enough embraced in this outline to enable you, starting from it, to work out the details with certainty.

VI. PROPERTIES AND ACCIDENTS

A. PROPERTIES

Shape, mass, etc., are properties of things. They cannot exist by themselves; they are not separable parts of the things to which they belong; without them the things could not be perceived.

In the next place, shapes, colors, sizes, mass, and all other things that are spoken of as belonging to a body must be thought of as properties either of bodies in general or of bodies that are perceptible and are recognized by our perception of these properties.** These properties are not to be regarded as having existence by themselves, for we cannot think of them apart from things of which they are properties; nor are they wholly without existence. They are not some kind of immaterial thing attached to the body, nor are they

*That is, we do not apply the term to attributes or properties.
**Shape, size, and mass are properties of all bodies; color, of visible bodies only.

parts of the body; but from all of them together the body as a whole receives its permanent character. We do not mean that these properties come together and form the body as happens when a large body is formed from its separate parts, either from the primary parts or from large parts that are smaller than the whole, whatever it is; we merely mean, as I have said, that the whole body receives its own permanent character from the presence in it of these properties. Each of the properties of a body has its own appropriate way of being perceived and distinguished; and the body as a whole is perceived along with its properties, not separately from them, and is identified by this composite recognition.

B. ACCIDENTS

i. Like properties, accidents can be recognized only in connection with bodies; but they are not permanent attributes as are the properties.

It also often happens that there are qualities that do not permanently accompany bodies. They, too, do not exist by themselves, yet they are not wholly without being. They do not belong to the class that is below the level of perception, nor are they incorporeal. In applying to them the term "accidents" in its commonest meaning, we make it clear that they have neither the nature of the whole that we comprehend as a composite and call "body," nor the nature of the permanent properties without which a body cannot be thought of. By the appropriate senses each of them can be recognized in company with the composite body to which it belongs; but we see a particular accident only when it is present with the body, since accidents are not unchanging attendants. We must not deny the reality of this clear vision of the accidents on the ground that they neither possess the nature of the whole which they accompany and which we call body, nor share in its permanent properties; and we must not think that they exist by themselves, since this is not conceivable for the accidents or for the properties. They must all be accepted as what they appear to be, namely accidents belonging to bodies, not permanent properties nor things having any place by themselves in nature; but they are seen to have just the character that our senses ascribe to them.

ii. Time presents a special problem. We cannot visualize it, and we can recognize it only as an accident of an event, which is itself an accident.

Before turning from this subject, we must carefully consider one more matter. Time is not to be sought for like other things that we seek in an underlying object by comparing them with the mental images that we look for in our own minds,* but we must consider the clear data of experience by virtue of which we distinguish between a long time and a short one, regarding the empirical data as closely allied to the concept of time. We need not search for better descriptions of time, but we must use the very ones that are at hand; nor need we assert that something else is of the same nature as this unique entity, as some indeed do; but we should take into consideration as of chief importance only the things with which we associate time and the ways in which we measure it. This requires no elaborate demonstration, only a review of the facts. We associate time with days and nights and their parts, and in the same way with changes in our own feelings and with motion and rest, recognizing that the very thing that we call time is in its turn a special sort of accident of these accidents.

*One can visualize an object or even a property or an accident in connection with an object, but one cannot visualize time.

VII. THE WORLDS

A. THE CREATION OF WORLDS

Each world was formed by being separated from its own whirling mass, and will be dissolved again.

In addition to what we have said, it is necessary to believe that the worlds* and every limited complex that has a continuous similarity to the visible world have been formed from the infinite, each of them, greater and smaller, separating out from its own whirling mass. We must suppose also that these will all be dissolved again, some more quickly and some more slowly, some afflicted by one calamity and others by another.

One must not suppose that because of necessity worlds in a single pattern were created, or in every possible pattern. . . .

B. FORMS OF LIFE IN THE WORLDS

We may assume animal and vegetable life in the other worlds similar to that on ours.
. . . Moreover, we may believe that in all the worlds there are animals, plants, and the other things we see; for no one can show that the seeds from which grow animals, plants, and the other things we see might or might not have been included in one particular world and that in another kind of world this was impossible.

VIII. THE DEVELOPMENT OF CIVILIZATION

A. THE ARTS AND CRAFTS

Instinct led men to the first developments, which reason then improved upon.

Moreover, we may assume that by the conditions that surround them, men were taught or forced by instinct to do many things of many kinds, but reason later elaborated on what had been begun by instinct and introduced new inventions. In some fields, great progress was made, in others, less; and in some times and ages reason had more success in freeing men from their fears of the powers above than in others.

B. LANGUAGE

Language was a natural development, differing in different tribes. Later, speech was clarified by deliberate selection.

So too we may suppose that in the beginning words did not receive meaning by design. The natural characters of men who underwent different experiences and received

---

*Each world consists of an earth and the heavenly bodies associated with it. (Epicurus stated above that the number of worlds is infinite.)

different impressions according to their tribes, caused them to emit air from their lips formed in harmony with each of the experiences and impressions, the men of each tribe differing in their own separate ways as the tribes differed because of their differing environments. But later in each race, by common agreement, men assigned particular meanings to particular sounds so that what they said to each other might be less ambiguous and the meaning be more quickly made clear. When men who had known them introduced certain things not previously seen, they assigned names to them, sometimes being forced instinctively to utter the word, but sometimes making their meaning clear by logically selecting the sound in accordance with the general usage.*

IX. THE PHENOMENA OF THE HEAVENS

A. CAUSES OF CELESTIAL PHENOMENA

No divinity directs the heavenly bodies, for this is inconsistent with divine happiness; nor are they themselves divine.

Now as to celestial phenomena, we must believe that these motions, periods, eclipses, risings, settings, and the like do not take place because there is some divinity in charge of them, who so arranges them in order and will maintain them in that order, and who at the same time enjoys both perfect happiness and immortality; for activity and anxiety, anger and kindness are not in harmony with blessedness, but are found along with weakness, fear, and dependence on one's neighbors. We must also avoid the belief that masses of concentrated fire have attained a state of divine blessedness and undertaken these motions of their own free will. In all the terms with which we set forth our conceptions of such blessedness, we must preserve due reverence lest from irreverent words there grow opinions that deny this majesty. If we fail, this contradiction will cause the greatest confusion in our souls. Therefore we must believe that, at the time of the first formation of these bodies at the creation of the world, the law of their motions was fully ordained.

B. PURPOSES OF, AND LIMITATIONS ON, THE STUDY OF CELESTIAL PHENOMENA

i. While knowledge of the general principles governing these matters is essential to our happiness, the study of the details is vain. We must accept the possibility of multiple causes.

Now we must accept the following beliefs: that to acquire exact knowledge about basic causes is the task of natural philosophy; that, as far as the heavenly bodies are concerned, our happiness depends on this basic knowledge and upon knowing the general nature of the visible phenomena of the heavens and whatever is necessary for certainty up to this point; that in these first principles there is neither multiformity nor any possibility of variation; and that in the immortal and blessed nature there is

*That is, by giving a name suggested by the similarity of the new thing to something that had already been named.

absolutely nothing that causes doubt and confusion. That these statements are true without qualification we can ascertain by reason. But we must also know that whatever belongs to the investigations of settings and risings, periods and eclipses, and the like—that this is of no import for the happiness that comes from knowledge; and that those who have learned these things but are ignorant of the original nature and the basic causes are subject to fears as great as if they knew nothing, or perhaps to even greater fears because the amazement that follows the study of these phenomena is not able to solve the problem of their relation to the essential principles.* Therefore, if we find that there are many possible causes for periods, settings, risings, eclipses, and the like, just as we found many possible causes in our investigation of details, we need not think that our investigation of these matters has not reached a certainty sufficient to secure for us peace of mind and happiness. We must search for the causes of celestial phenomena and in general of that which cannot be clearly perceived by first finding in how many ways similar phenomena are produced within the range of our senses; and we must pay no heed to those who, in the case of phenomena that can only be seen from a distance, fail to distinguish between that which is and remains single and that which may happen in many different ways,** and who do not know under what conditions it is possible and under what conditions impossible to achieve peace of mind. If we know this, that phenomena may take place in many ways, we shall be as little disturbed if we merely think it possible that a particular phenomenon happens in some particular way as we would be if we knew this as an absolute fact.

> *ii. Men imagine that the celestial bodies are divine yet ascribe to them purposes inconsistent with divinity; and they anticipate eternal suffering after death. Peace of mind follows freedom from such fears, and will be gained if we trust to our immediate feelings and sensations.*

In addition to these general matters, we must observe this also, that there are three things that account for the major disturbances in men's minds. First, they assume that the celestial bodies are blessed and eternal yet have impulses, actions, and purposes quite inconsistent with divinity. Next, they anticipate and foresee eternal suffering as depicted in the myths, or even fear the very lack of consciousness that comes with death as if this could be of concern to them. Finally, they suffer all this, not as a result of reasonable conjecture, but through some sort of unreasoning imagination; and since in imagination they set no limit to suffering, they are beset by turmoil as great as if there were a reasonable basis for their dread, or even greater. But it is peace of mind to have been freed from all this and to have constantly in memory the essential principles of the whole system of belief. We must therefore turn our minds to immediate feelings and sensations***—in matters of general concern to the common feelings and sensations of mankind, in personal matters, to our own—and to every immediate evidence from each of the means of judgment. If we heed these, we shall rightly track down the sources of disturbance and fear, and when we have learned the causes of celestial phenomena and of the other occasional happenings, we shall be free from what other men most dread.

---

*Epicurus has in mind astrology and its effect upon its devotees.

**That is, between the basic principle (the atomic system), which is fixed and unalterable, and such observed phenomena as eclipses, which may be caused in different ways at different times and in different worlds.

***Our sensations lead to knowledge of what a thing is; our feelings, chiefly in terms of pleasure and pain, tell us what to seek and what to avoid, that is, what is good and what is evil.

X. CONCLUSION

This summary will be useful both for the beginner and also, as an easily remembered outline, for the more proficient.

Here then, Herodotus, you have the most important points in regard to natural science set down in such condensed form that this discourse may be accurately held in mind. I think that one who masters this, even if he does not progress to all the parts of a detailed study, will have very great strength compared with other men. He will also be able of himself to make clear many detailed points in regard to our system as a whole, and these general principles themselves will constantly aid him if he but hold them in memory. For these points are such that those who have made considerable progress and even those who are proficient in the detailed study, by solving their problems with reference to this survey, will make the greatest advances in the knowledge of the whole; and some of those who have made less progress toward perfect knowledge can, hastily and without oral instruction, run through the matters of most importance for peace of mind.

LETTER TO MENOECEUS

I. INTRODUCTION

Epicurus to Menoeceus, greeting.

Let no young man delay the study of philosophy, and let no old man become weary of it; for it is never too early nor too late to care for the well-being of the soul. The man who says that the season for this study has not yet come or is already past is like the man who says it is too early or too late for happiness. Therefore, both the young and the old should study philosophy, the former so that as he grows old he may still retain the happiness of youth in his pleasant memories of the past, the latter so that although he is old he may at the same time be young by virtue of his fearlessness of the future. We must therefore study the means of securing happiness, since if we have it we have everything, but if we lack it we do everything in order to gain it.

II. BASIC TEACHINGS

A. THE GODS

The gods exist; but it is impious to accept the common beliefs about them. They have no concern with men.

Epicurus, *Letters, Principal Doctrines, and Vatican Sayings,* translated by Russel M. Geer (New York: Macmillan/Library of the Liberal Arts, 1964).

Practice and study without ceasing that which I was always teaching you, being assured that these are the first principles of the good life. After accepting god as the immortal and blessed being depicted by popular opinion, do not ascribe to him anything in addition that is alien to immortality or foreign to blessedness, but rather believe about him whatever can uphold his blessed immortality. The gods do indeed exist, for our perception of them is clear; but they are not such as the crowd imagines them to be, for most men do not retain the picture of the gods that they first receive. It is not the man who destroys the gods of popular belief who is impious, but he who describes the gods in the terms accepted by the many. For the opinions of the many about the gods are not perceptions but false suppositions. According to these popular suppositions, the gods send great evils to the wicked, great blessings to the righteous, for they, being always well disposed to their own virtues, approve those who are like themselves, regarding as foreign all that is different.*

Temple of Olympian Zeus (Olympieion). Begun in the 6th century B.C., it was finished by the Roman Emperor Hadrian over 600 years later. The largest temple in Greece, it was made up of 104 columns (of which 15 remain). According to Epicurus, while there are gods such as Zeus, "they are not such as the crowd imagines them to be." So attacking the beliefs of the masses who worshiped here is not impious; the impious one is "he who describes the gods in the terms accepted by the many." *(Forrest E. Baird)*

---

*The ambiguous rendition of the last part of this sentence is intentional. "They" may be the gods, who approve men like themselves, or men, who approve gods.

B. DEATH

Philosophy, showing that death is the end of all consciousness, relieves us of all fear of death. A life that is happy is better than one that is merely long.

Accustom yourself to the belief that death is of no concern to us, since all good and evil lie in sensation and sensation ends with death. Therefore the true belief that death is nothing to us makes a mortal life happy, not by adding to it an infinite time, but by taking away the desire for immortality. For there is no reason why the man who is thoroughly assured that there is nothing to fear in death should find anything to fear in life. So, too, he is foolish who says that he fears death, not because it will be painful when it comes, but because the anticipation of it is painful; for that which is no burden when it is present gives pain to no purpose when it is anticipated. Death, the most dreaded of evils, is therefore of no concern to us; for while we exist death is not present, and when death is present we no longer exist. It is therefore nothing either to the living or to the dead since it is not present to the living, and the dead no longer are.

But men in general sometimes flee death as the greatest of evils, sometimes long for it as a relief from the evils of life.

The wise man neither renounces life nor fears its end; for living does not offend him, nor does he suppose that not to live is in any way an evil. As he does not choose the food that is most in quantity but that which is most pleasant, so he does not seek the enjoyment of the longest life but of the happiest.

He who advises the young man to live well, the old man to die well, is foolish, not only because life is desirable, but also because the art of living well and the art of dying well are one. Yet much worse is he who says that it is well not to have been born, but once born, be swift to pass through Hades' gates.

If a man says this and really believes it, why does he not depart from life? Certainly the means are at hand for doing so if this really be his firm conviction. If he says it in mockery, he is regarded as a fool among those who do not accept his teaching.

Remember that the future is neither ours nor wholly not ours, so that we may neither count on it as sure to come nor abandon hope of it as certain not to be.

III. THE MORAL THEORY

A. PLEASURE AS THE MOTIVE

The necessary desires are for health of body and peace of mind; if these are satisfied, that is enough for the happy life.

You must consider that of the desires some are natural, some are vain, and of those that are natural, some are necessary, others only natural. Of the necessary desires, some are necessary for happiness, some for the ease of the body, some for life itself. The man who has a perfect knowledge of this will know how to make his every choice or rejection tend toward gaining health of body and peace of mind, since this is the final end of the blessed life. For to gain this end, namely freedom from pain and fear, we do everything. When once this condition is reached, all the storm of the soul is stilled, since the creature need make no move in search of anything that is lacking, nor seek after anything else to make complete the welfare of the soul and the body. For we only feel the lack of pleasure when from its absence we suffer pain; but when we do not suffer pain, we no longer are in need of pleasure. For this reason we say that pleasure is the beginning and the end of the blessed life. We recognize pleasure as the first and natural good; starting from pleasure we accept or reject; and we return to this as we judge every good thing, trusting this feeling of pleasure as our guide.

B. PLEASURES AND PAINS

Pleasure is the greatest good; but some pleasures bring pain, and in choosing, we must consider this.

For the very reason that pleasure is the chief and the natural good, we do not choose every pleasure, but there are times when we pass by pleasures if they are outweighed by the hardships that follow; and many pains we think better than pleasures when a greater pleasure will come to us once we have undergone the long-continued pains. Every pleasure is a good since it has a nature akin to ours; nevertheless, not every pleasure is to be chosen. Just so, every pain is an evil, yet not every pain is of a nature to be avoided on all occasions. By measuring and by looking at advantages and disadvantages, it is proper to decide all these things; for under certain circumstances we treat the good as evil, and again, the evil as good.

C. SELF-SUFFICIENCY

The truly wise man is the one who can be happy with a little.

We regard self-sufficiency as a great good, not so that we may enjoy only a few things, but so that, if we do not have many, we may be satisfied with the few, being firmly persuaded that they take the greatest pleasure in luxury who regard it as least needed, and that everything that is natural is easily provided, while vain pleasures are hard to obtain. Indeed, simple sauces bring a pleasure equal to that of lavish banquets if once the pain due to need is removed; and bread and water give the greatest pleasure when one who is in need consumes them. To be accustomed to simple and plain living is conducive to health and makes a man ready for the necessary tasks of life. It also makes us more ready for the enjoyment of luxury if at intervals we chance to meet with it, and it renders us fearless against fortune.

D. TRUE PLEASURE

The truest happiness does not come from enjoyment of physical pleasures but from a simple life, free from anxiety, with the normal physical needs satisfied.

When we say that pleasure is the end, we do not mean the pleasure of the profligate or that which depends on physical enjoyment—as some think who do not understand our teachings, disagree with them, or give them an evil interpretation—but by pleasure we mean the state wherein the body is free from pain and the mind from anxiety. Neither continual drinking and dancing, nor sexual love, nor the enjoyment of fish and whatever else the luxurious table offers brings about the pleasant life; rather, it is produced by the reason which is sober, which examines the motive for every choice and rejection, and which drives away all those opinions through which the greatest tumult lays hold of the mind.

E. PRUDENCE

Prudence or practical wisdom should be our guide.
Of all this the beginning and the chief good is prudence. For this reason prudence is more precious than philosophy itself. All the other virtues spring from it. It teaches that it is not possible to live pleasantly without at the same time living prudently, nobly, and justly, nor to live prudently, nobly, and justly without living pleasantly; for the virtues have grown up in close union with the pleasant life, and the pleasant life cannot be separated from the virtues.

IV. CONCLUSION

A. PANEGYRIC* ON THE PRUDENT MAN

Whom then do you believe to be superior to the prudent man: he who has reverent opinions about the gods, who is wholly without fear of death, who has discovered what is the highest good in life and understands that the highest point in what is good is easy to reach and hold and that the extreme of evil is limited either in time or in suffering, and who laughs at that which some have set up as the ruler of all things, Necessity? He thinks that the chief power of decision lies within us, although some things come about by necessity, some by chance, and some by our own wills; for he sees that necessity is irresponsible and chance uncertain, but that our actions are subject to no power. It is for this reason that our actions merit praise or blame. It would be better to accept the myth about the gods than to be a slave to the determinism of the physicists; for the myth hints at a hope for grace through honors paid to the gods, but the necessity of determinism is inescapable. Since the prudent man does not, as do many, regard chance as a god for the gods do nothing in disorderly fashion or as an unstable cause of all things, he believes that chance does not give man good and evil to make his life happy or miserable, but that it does provide opportunities for great good or evil. Finally, he thinks it better to meet misfortune while acting with reason than to happen upon good fortune while acting senselessly; for it is better that what has been well-planned in our actions should fail than that what has been ill-planned should gain success by chance.

B. FINAL WORDS TO MENOECEUS

Meditate on these and like precepts, by day and by night, alone or with a like-minded friend. Then never, either awake or asleep, will you be dismayed; but you will live like a god among men; for life amid immortal blessings is in no way like the life of a mere mortal.

*[Formal praise for a festival]

PRINCIPAL DOCTRINES

I. That which is blessed and immortal is not troubled itself, nor does it cause trouble to another. As a result, it is not affected by anger or favor, for these belong to weakness.

II. Death is nothing to us; for what has been dissolved has no sensation, and what has no sensation is nothing to us.

III. The removal of all that causes pain marks the boundary of pleasure. Wherever pleasure is present and as long as it continues, there is neither suffering nor grieving nor both together.

IV. Continuous bodily suffering does not last long. Intense pain is very brief, and even pain that barely outweighs physical pleasure does not last many days. Long illnesses permit physical pleasures that are greater than the pain.

V. It is impossible to live pleasantly without living prudently, well, and justly, and to live prudently, well, and justly without living pleasantly. Even though a man live well and justly, it is not possible for him to live pleasantly if he lacks that from which stems the prudent life.

VI. Any device whatever by which one frees himself from the fear of others is a natural good.

VII. Some, thinking thus to make themselves safe from men, wished to become famous and renowned. They won a natural good if they made their lives secure; but if their lives were not secure, they did not have that for which, following the rule of nature, they first sought.

VIII. No pleasure is evil in itself; but the means by which certain pleasures are gained bring pains many times greater than the pleasures.

IX. If every pleasure were cumulative, and if this were the case both in time and in regard to the whole or the most important parts of our nature, then pleasures would not differ from each other.

X. If the things that produce the pleasures of the dissolute were able to drive away from their minds their fears about what is above them and about death and pain, and to teach them the limit of desires, we would have no reason to find fault with the dissolute; for they would fill themselves with pleasure from every source and would be free from pain and sorrow, which are evil.

XI. If our dread of the phenomena above us, our fear lest death concern us, and our inability to discern the limits of pains and desires were not vexatious to us, we would have no need of the natural sciences.

XII. It is not possible for one to rid himself of his fears about the most important things if he does not understand the nature of the universe but dreads some of the things he has learned in the myths. Therefore, it is not possible to gain unmixed happiness without natural science.

XIII. It is of no avail to prepare security against other men while things above us and beneath the earth and in the whole infinite universe in general are still dreaded.

XIV. When reasonable security from men has been attained, then the security that comes from peace of mind and withdrawal from the crowd is present, sufficient in strength and most unmixed in well-being.

Epicurus, *Letters, Principal Doctrines, and Vatican Sayings,* translated by Russel M. Geer (New York: Macmillan/Library of the Liberal Arts, 1964).

XV. Natural wealth is limited and easily obtained; the wealth defined by vain fancies is always beyond reach.

XVI. Fortune seldom troubles the wise man. Reason has controlled his greatest and most important affairs, controls them throughout his life, and will continue to control them.

XVII. The just man is least disturbed; the unjust man is filled with the greatest turmoil.

XVIII. When once the pain caused by need has been removed, bodily pleasure will not be increased in amount but only varied in quality. The mind attains its utmost pleasure in reflecting on the very things that used to cause the greatest mental fears and on things like them.

XIX. Time that is unlimited and time that is limited afford equal pleasure if one measures pleasure's extent by reason.

XX. The flesh believes that pleasure is limitless and that it requires unlimited time; but the mind, understanding the end and limit of the flesh and ridding itself of fears of the future, secures a complete life and has no longer any need for unlimited time. It does not, however, avoid pleasure; and when circumstances bring on the end of life, it does not depart as if it still lacked any portion of the good life.

XXI. The man who understands the limits of living knows that it is easy to obtain that which removes the pain caused by want and that which perfects the whole life. Therefore, he has no need of things that involve struggle.

XXII. It is necessary to take into account the real purpose of knowledge and all the evidence of that clear perception to which we refer our opinions. If we do not, all will be full of bad judgment and confusion.

XXIII. If you struggle against all your sensations, you will have no standard of comparison by which to measure even the sensations you judge false.

XXIV. If you reject any sensation, and if you fail to distinguish between conjecture based upon that which awaits confirmation and evidence given by the senses, by the feelings, and by the mental examinations of confirmed concepts, you will confuse the other sensations with unfounded conjecture and thus destroy the whole basis for judgment. If among all opinions you accept as equally valid both those that await confirmation and those that have been confirmed, you will not free yourself from error, since you will have preserved all the uncertainty about every judgment of what is true and what is not true.

XXV. If you do not at all times refer each of your actions to the natural end,* but fall short of this and turn aside to something else in choosing and avoiding, your deeds will not agree with your words.

XXVI. Those desires that do not bring pain if they are not satisfied are not necessary; and they are easily thrust aside whenever to satisfy them appears difficult or likely to cause injury.

XXVII. Of the things that wisdom prepares for insuring lifelong happiness, by far the greatest is the possession of friends.

XXVIII. The same wisdom that permits us to be confident that no evil is eternal or even of long duration also recognizes that in our limited state the security that can be most perfectly gained is that of friendship.

XXIX. Of the desires, some are natural and necessary; some are natural but not necessary; and others are neither natural nor necessary but arise from empty opinion.

*That is, to pleasure.

XXX. Among the bodily desires, those rest on empty opinion that are eagerly pursued although if unsatisfied they bring no pain. That they are not got rid of is because of man's empty opinion, not because of their own nature.

XXXI. Natural justice is a compact resulting from expediency by which men seek to prevent one man from injuring others and to protect him from being injured by them.

XXXII. There is no such thing as justice or injustice among those beasts that cannot make agreements not to injure or be injured. This is also true of those tribes that are unable or unwilling to make agreements not to injure or be injured.

XXXIII. There is no such thing as justice in the abstract; it is merely a compact between men in their various relations with each other, in whatever circumstances they may be, that they will neither injure nor be injured.

XXXIV. Injustice is not evil in itself, but only in the fear and apprehension that one will not escape those who have been set up to punish the offense.

XXXV. If a man has secretly violated any of the terms of the mutual compact not to injure or be injured, he cannot feel confident that he will be undetected in the future even if he has escaped ten thousand times in the past; for until his death it will remain uncertain whether he will escape.

XXXVI. In general, justice is the same for all, a thing found useful by men in their relations with each other; but it does not follow that it is the same for all in each individual place and circumstance.

XXXVII. Among the things commonly held just, that which has proved itself useful in men's mutual relationships has the stamp of justice whether or not it be the same for all; if anyone makes a law and it does not prove useful in men's relationships with each other, it is no longer just in its essence. If, however, the law's usefulness in the matter of justice should change and it should meet men's expectations only for a short time, nonetheless during that short time it was just in the eyes of those who look simply at facts and do not confuse themselves with empty words.

XXXVIII. If, although no new circumstances have arisen, those things that were commonly held just in these matters did not in their actual effects correspond with that conception, they were not just. Whenever, as a result of new circumstances, the same things that had been regarded as just were no longer useful, they were just at the time when they were useful for the relations of citizens to each other; but afterwards, when they were no longer useful, they were no longer just.

XXXIX. He who has best controlled his lack of confidence in the face of external forces has, as far as possible, treated these externals as akin to himself or, when that was impossible, at least as not alien. Where he was not able to do even this, he kept to himself and avoided whatever it was best to avoid.

XL. Those who were best able to prepare security for themselves in relation to their neighbors* lived most pleasantly with their neighbors since they had the most perfect assurance; and enjoying the most complete intimacy, they did not lament the death of one who died before his time as if it were an occasion for sorrow.

---

*That is, those who were most self-sufficient and least dependent upon others.

LUCRETIUS
ca. 99–55 B.C.

Virtually nothing is known of Titus Lucretius Carus except his famous poem, *On the Nature of the Universe* (*De Rerum Natura*). According to a secondhand report, he was driven insane by a love potion and eventually committed suicide. Apart from this story, our knowledge of his life can be gained only from his poem. From internal evidence, it seems he came from a wealthy Roman family and that he did some traveling. He also seems to have intentionally avoided the social and political upheavals of his day.

In his poem, Lucretius embraces and expounds the philosophy of Epicurus. In particular, he develops his master's atomistic materialism. Lucretius holds that in all nature there are only atoms moving in a void. As these atoms fall downward in empty space, some swerve from their course and collide with others. These collisions lead to the world as we experience it.

Lucretius uses this theory to explain human activity as well. The human soul is made up of very fine atoms, and free will is simply the result of a "swerve" of atoms. Sensation occurs when thin films or "idols" (i.e., images) are thrown off from objects and, entering through our sense organs, jostle the atoms of the mind. Consciousness is also explained atomistically as the motion of our soul atoms.

In our selection from Book Two of *On the Nature of the Universe,* reprinted here in Sir Ronald Melville's translation, Lucretius describes this atomic swerve. Book Three from the same work, excerpted here, presents Lucretius's claim that death is simply the cessation of sensation and consciousness. As he explains, ". . . death is nothing to us, nothing that matters at all, since mind we know is mortal." There is no afterlife to fear, no immortality to be sought: Death awaits everyone and is final.

* * *

On the Nature of the Universe is noted as much for its literary qualities as for its philosophy, and numerous books have been written about Lucretius's hexameter verse. George Santayana, *Three Philosophical Poets: Lucretius, Dante, and Goethe* (Cambridge, MA: Harvard University Press, 1910) and Henri Bergson, *The Philosophy of Poetry: The Genius of Lucretius,* translated by Wade Baskin (New York: Philosophical Library, 1959), consider Lucretius as both philosopher and poet. For a general explication of Lucretius's philosophy, see John Masson, *Lucretius, Epicurean and Poet* (London: Murray, 1907); George Depue Hadzsits, *Lucretius and His Influence* (New York: Cooper Square Publishers, 1963); E.J. Kenney, *Lucretius* (Oxford: Oxford University Press, 1977); Diskin Clay, *Lucretius and Epicurus* (Ithaca, NY: Cornell University Press, 1983); and Stuart Gillespie and Philip Hardie, eds., *The Cambridge Companion to Lucretius* (Cambridge: Cambridge University Press, 2007). David Konstan, *Some Aspects of Epicurean Psychology* (Leiden, Netherlands: Brill, 1973), and James H. Nichols, Jr., *Epicurean Political Philosophy: The De Rerum Natura of Lucretius* (Ithaca, NY: Cornell University Press, 1976) are specialized studies; while Cosmo Alexander Gordon, *A Bibliography of Lucretius* (London: Rupert Hart-Davis, 1962) provides a bibliography.

ON THE NATURE OF THINGS (in part)

BOOK TWO

*   *   *

       I want you to understand,
that when the first bodies are moving straight downward through the void
by their own weight, at times completely undetermined
and in undetermined places they swerve a little from their course,

220   but only so much as you could call a change of motion.
Because unless they were accustomed to swerving, all would fall
downwards like drops of rain through the deep void,
nor would a collision occur, nor would a blow be produced
by the first beginnings. Thus nature would never have created anything.

225   But if by chance anyone believes that heavier bodies,
because they are carried along more quickly straight through the void,
fall upon lighter ones from above and so produce
the blows which are able to supply generating motions,
he goes astray, far from true reasoning.

230   For whatever things fall through water and insubstantial air
must hasten their falls in proportion to their weight,
since the body of water and the thin nature of air

Lucretius, *On the Nature of Things* (Book Two, 216–284; Book Three, selections through 831), translated by Walter Englert (Newburyport, MA: Focus Philosophical Library, 2003). Reprinted by permission of Focus Publishing/R. Pullins Company.

are not at all able to delay each thing equally,
but yield more quickly when they are overcome by heavier things.
But on the other hand neither on any side nor at any   235
time can empty void hold up anything,
but must, as its nature requires, hasten to give way.
Therefore all must be borne on through the peaceful void
moved at equal rates, though not of equal weights.
Thus heavier bodies will never be able to fall on lighter   240
ones from above nor on their own to cause collisions which produce
the various motions through which nature accomplishes things.
Wherefore again and again it is necessary that bodies
swerve a little, but no more than a minimum, lest we seem
to be inventing oblique motions, and the true facts refute it.   245
For we see that this is clear and manifest, that weights,
in so far as in them lies, cannot travel obliquely,
when they fall from above, as far as you can perceive.
But that it does not make itself swerve at all
from the straight direction of its path, who is there who can perceive?   250

          And next if every motion is always linked,
and a new one always arises from an old one in sure succession,
and if by declining the primary bodies do not make
a certain beginning of motion to burst the laws of fate,
so that cause does not follow cause from infinity,   255
from where does there arise for living creatures throughout the world,
from where, I say, is this free will, torn from fate,
by which we go wherever pleasure leads each of us,
and likewise decline our motions at no fixed time
or fixed region of space, but where the mind itself carries us?   260
For doubtless one's own will provides for each a beginning
of these things, and from it motions stream through the limbs.

          For don't you also see that while the starting gates drop in an instant,
the desirous force of the horses is nevertheless not able
to burst forth as suddenly as the mind itself desires?   265
For the entire store of matter throughout the whole body has
to be stimulated to motion, so that once it is stimulated and has exerted itself
throughout every limb it can follow the mind's eagerness.
So you can see that a beginning of motion is created in the heart,
and comes forth first from the will of the mind,   270
and then is conveyed through the whole body and limbs.

          Nor is it similar to when we are struck by a blow and travel forward
by the great strength and great constraint of another.
For then it is clear that the whole matter of our entire
body moves and is seized against our will,   275
until the will reins it in throughout the limbs.
Now you see, don't you, that although an external force pushes many,
and often forces them to move forward and to be thrown headlong
against their will, there is nevertheless something in our breast
which is able to offer resistance and fight back?   280
And at its bidding too the store of matter
is sometimes forced to change direction through the limbs and joints,
and although it is pushed forward, it is checked and again comes to rest.

*   *   *

BOOK THREE

From shadows so sheer you [Epicurus] were the first who was able to cast
such clear light and illuminate all that makes life worthwhile:
it is you I follow, O glory of the Greek race, and now
in the tracks you have laid down I fix my firm footprints,
5   not so much eager to compete with you, but because from love
I desire to imitate you. For why would a swallow contend with
swans, or what can young goats with their shaky legs
accomplish in a race to match the powerful energy of a horse?
You are our father, the discover of how things are, you supply us
10   with a father's precepts, and from your pages, o illustrious one,
just as bees sample everything in the flower-strewn meadow,
so we too feed upon all of your golden words,
golden they are, and always worthy of eternal life.
For as soon as your philosophy, sprung from your divine mind,
15   begins to give voice to the nature of things,
the mind's terrors dissipate, the walls of the world
dissolve, I see things carried along through the whole void.
The divinity of the gods appears, and their quiet dwelling-places,
which neither winds buffet nor clouds soak with violent
20   rains, nor does snow formed from biting frost, falling
white, disturb them, but an always cloudless atmosphere
spreads over them and smiles with light diffused in all directions.*
Nature, moreover, supplies all their needs, nor does anything
nibble away at their peace of mind at any time.
25   But in contrast, never do the regions of Acheron [i.e., hell] appear,
nor does the earth prevent from being seen all the things
which are carried along through the void below beneath our feet.
Then, from these things a kind of divine rapture
and shivering awe seizes me, because in this way nature
30   by your power has been uncovered and laid open in all directions.

And since I have shown of what sort are the beginnings
of all things, and how, differing in their various shapes,
they fly around on their own, stirred up by eternal motion,
and how from them all things are able to be created,
35   next after these things it appears that the nature of the mind
and soul must now be made clear in my verses,
and the fear of Acheron must be thrown violently out the door.
This fear throws human life into deep and utter confusion,
staining everything with the black darkness of death,
40   and leaves no pleasure clear and pure.
For although people often assert that sickness and a bad reputation
are more to be feared than the infernal regions of death,
and that they know the nature of the mind is made up of blood,
or maybe of wind, if by chance they want it that way,
45   and further, that they have no need at all of our philosophy,
you can tell from the following that they proclaim all this to gain

---

*Lucretius' description of the residences of the gods is based on Homer, *Odyssey* 6.42–46.

praise rather than because the idea itself is thought to be true:
These same people, exiled from their country and banished far
from the sight of humans, befouled by some awful crime,
inflicted in short with every trouble, continue living,   50
and wherever these wretched people go they sacrifice to their ancestors,
and slaughter black cattle and send down offerings
to the shades below, and in intense situations turn
their minds much more intensely to religion.
Wherefore it is more effective to gauge a person in times   55
of doubt and danger, and to learn what they are like in adversity.
For then at last real voices are extracted from the bottom
of the heart and the mask is ripped off: reality remains.
So too, greed and blind burning after elected office,
which coerce wretched people to go beyond the boundaries   60
of what is right, and at times as allies in crime and accomplices
they exert themselves night and day with outstanding effort
to rise to the level of the greatest wealth—these lacerations of life
are nourished in no small way by the fear of death.
For low social standing and bitter poverty nearly always   65
seem to be far removed from a calm and pleasant life,
and to be a kind of loitering, so to speak, before the gates of death.
This is why people, attacked by false fears,
desiring to escape far away and to withdraw themselves far away,
amass wealth through civil bloodshed and in their greed double   70
their riches, piling up slaughter on slaughter.
Unmercifully they rejoice in the sad death of a brother
and they disdain and fear eating with their relatives.
In a similar way, often as a result of the same fear,
envy taunts them that before their very eyes he is powerful,   75
he is the center of attention, who parades in official glory,
while they whine that they themselves are mired in obscurity.
Some perish to acquire a statue or good name.
And often through fear of death such a great hatred of life
and of seeing the light grabs hold of human beings,   80
that they inflict death on themselves with a sad heart,
forgetting that this fear is the source of their cares.
It convinces one to abuse honor, another to burst
the ties of friendship, and in short to abandon responsible conduct.
For these days people often betray their country   85
and dear parents, trying to escape the regions of Acheron.
For just like children who tremble and fear everything
in the dark night, so we are afraid in the light sometimes
of things that ought to be no more feared than
the things that children tremble at and imagine will happen.   90
Therefore this fear and darkness of the mind must be shattered
apart not by the rays of the sun and the clear shafts
of the day but by the external appearance and inner law of nature.

       First, I say that the mind, which we often call the intellect,
in which the rational and guiding principle of life is located,   95
is part of a person no less than a hand and a foot
and eyes are parts of the whole living creature.
However certain philosophers have thought
that the mind's power of sensation is not located in a particular part,

but is a certain state of the body that produces life,
100 which the Greeks call a "harmony," something which gives us
life and sensation, although there is no intellect in any part—
as when often the body is said to possess good health,
and yet this health is no part of the healthy person.
They thus do not locate the mind's consciousness in a particular part;
105 in this they seem to me to wander seriously astray.
And so the body, which is plainly visible, is often sick,
although we still feel pleasure in another part unseen.
And on the contrary it happens that the opposite is often true in turn,
when one troubled in mind feels pleasure throughout the entire body.
110 This is no different than if, when a sick person's foot felt pain,
the head, meanwhile, happened to be in no pain.
Moreover when the limbs are given over to soft sleep
and the body lies sprawled out, heavy and senseless,
there is nevertheless something in us which during this time
115 is stirred in many ways and receives into itself all
the motions of joy and empty cares of the heart.

Now so that you can understand that the soul also is present
in the limbs and that it is not by harmony that the body secures sensation,
first it happens that when a large portion of the body is dragged
120 away, often life still remains in our limbs.
And again this same life, when a few particles of heat
have dispersed and air has been ejected out through the mouth,
it at once deserts the veins and leaves the bones.
Thus from this you can understand that not all particles
125 have the same functions nor do they equally sustain existence,
but rather that these, which are seeds of wind and hot
warmth, ensure that life remains in the limbs.
There are therefore heat and life-giving wind
present in the body which abandon our dying appendages.

130 Wherefore, since the nature of the mind and soul has been found
to be a part, so to speak, of a person, give up the name "harmony,"
conveyed to musicians from lofty Helicon—or maybe they
themselves in turn borrowed it from some other source and applied
it to a thing which then was lacking a name of its own—whatever
135 the case, let them have it: you pay attention to the rest of my words.

Now I maintain that the mind and soul are held joined together
with each other and make one nature from each other,
but that the rational principle which we call mind and intellect
is the head, as it were,* and lords it over the whole body.
140 It is situated and stays in the middle region of the breast.
For here leaps panic and fear, around this location
feelings of pleasure radiate; here then is the intellect and mind.
The other part of the soul, spread through the entire body,
obeys and is moved at the direction and impulse of the mind.
145 The mind thinks alone for itself by itself, it rejoices for itself,
when nothing moves the soul or body at the same time.

*Lucretius writes, "head, as it were" because as becomes clear, Epicurus taught that the mind was
located in the chest, not in the head. Many ancient philosophers, including Aristotle and the Stoics, believed
the same thing.

And just as, when the head or eye is assailed by pain
and is troubled for us, we are not co-tortured in our whole
body, so likewise the mind itself is sometimes troubled
or blooms in gladness, although the other part of the soul   150
is roused by no new sensation throughout the limbs and appendages.
But when the mind has been stirred by a more violent fear, we see
that the entire soul is equally affected throughout the limbs,
next sweat and pallor break out over the whole
body, the tongue stops working and the voice is aborted,   155
the eyes grow dark, the ears fill with noise, the limbs give way,
and indeed we often see people collapse because their minds are
so frightened. So from this anyone can easily recognize
that the soul is joined with the mind, and that when it is struck by the force
of the mind, it immediately strikes and pushes the body forward.   160
This same reasoning shows that the nature of the mind and soul
is corporeal. For when it is seen to push the limbs forward,
snatch the body from sleep, change facial expression,
and act as guide and turn the entire person—
and we see that none of these things can happen without touch, and again   165
that there is no touch without body—don't we have to admit
that mind and soul are made up of a corporeal nature?
Moreover you discern that our mind suffers commensurately
with the body and feels and is equally affected in the body.
If the shivering force of a spear does not smash out life   170
after it is driven within, separating the bones and sinews,
still faintness follows and a sweet swooning to the ground
and on the ground a churning of the mind which occurs,
and now and then a wavering wish to rise.
Therefore the nature of the mind must be corporeal,   175
since it suffers trouble from corporeal weapons and blows.

　　　What sort of body this soul has and from what things
it is composed I will now proceed to give an account with my words.
First, I assert that it is incredibly fine and is made up of
exceedingly small particles. That this is so you may,   180
if you pay attention, thoroughly grasp from the following.
Nothing is able to happen in such a rapid fashion
as what the mind proposes to itself to happen and itself commences.
Therefore the mind stirs itself more quickly than anything
whose nature is seen right in front of our eyes.   185
But that which is so highly mobile must be made up of
exceedingly round particles and exceedingly tiny ones,
so that they are able to be moved when struck by a small impulse.
And so water is moved and ripples at the slightest impulse,
since it is composed of shapes small and ready to roll.   190
In contrast, honey by nature is harder to move,
its fluid lazier and its action less hurried.
For the whole mass of its matter sticks more
to itself, no doubt since it is not made up
of particles so light, nor so fine and round.   195
For the merest breath of wind is able to cause a tall
pile of poppy seeds to lose its top before your eyes.
In contrast, in no way can it move a heap of rocks
or wheat spikes. Therefore the tinier and lighter

200   the particles are, the more mobility they enjoy.
In contrast, whatever things are found to have more
weight or are pricklier, the more stability they have.

Now then, since the nature of the mind has been discovered
to be incredibly mobile, it must consist
205   of exceedingly small, light, and round particles.
This thing, when known to you, dear reader,
in many things will be found useful and will be called opportune.
The following thing too shows the nature of the mind,
of what tenuous texture it is and in how small a place
210   it might be contained, if it could be gathered together:
that as soon as the untroubled quiet of death has taken hold
of a person and the nature of mind and soul has departed,
you cannot tell then that anything has been taken away
in appearance, anything in weight. Death preserves everything
215   except life-giving sensation and warm heat.
Therefore the whole soul must be made up of very small
particles and be interwoven through veins, flesh, and sinews.
Since, even when the whole soul has now left
the entire body, still the external configuration of the limbs
220   preserves itself unchanged and not a speck of weight is lost.
It is the same when the bouquet of Bacchus [i.e., wine] fades or when
the sweet scent of perfume dissipates in the air
or when the flavor has now left some substance,
yet the thing itself appears not at all diminished to our eyes
225   because of it, nor does anything seem subtracted from its weight,
no doubt because many minute particles produce flavors
and smells in the whole substance of these things.
Wherefore again and again one can know that the nature
of the intellect and soul has been created from exceedingly small
230   particles, since when it escapes it takes away no weight.

Nor nevertheless should we think that this nature is single.
For a kind of tenuous breath leaves the dying,
mixed with heat, and heat then draws air with it.
Nor is there any heat at all which does not
235   also have air mixed in with it. For because its nature is attenuated,
many first beginnings of air must move within it.
Now therefore the nature of the mind has been found to be triple.*
Yet all these things are not enough to produce sensation,
since the mind will not admit that any of these can produce
240   motions that cause sensation and the thoughts the mind ponders.
That is why a fourth kind of nature must also
be added to these. It is has no name at all.
Nothing exists which is more mobile or tenuous than it;
245   it is the first to distribute the motions that cause sensation throughout the limbs.
For it is the first to be roused, made up as it is of small shapes.
Next, heat and the invisible power of wind receive
the motions, and next air. Next everything is set in motion,
the blood is jostled, then the flesh begins to feel everything
250   throughout, last of all it is given over to the bones and marrow,

---

*That is, he has so far shown that there are three types of mind atoms: breath, heat, and air. He now
argues that there must be a fourth, unnamed type of mind atom.

whether it be pleasure or its opposite stinging passion [i.e., pain].
Neither can pain penetrate so far without effect, nor fierce
injury permeate, without everything being thrown into such great turmoil
that there is no place left for life and the soul's
parts disperse through every pore of the body.   255
But more often it is very near the surface of the body that a stop is put
to these motions. This is why we succeed in hanging on to life.

      Now while I yearn to give an account of how these things
are mixed with one another and in what ways they are arranged and function,
the poverty of our native speech holds me back unwillingly.   260
But nonetheless I will treat the matter as best I can in brief.
For the first bodies shoot back and forth among themselves
with the motions of first beginnings, so that none can be separated off
by itself, nor can its power be separated off by space,
but they are the many powers, so to speak, of a single body.   265
Just as in any flesh from living creatures commonly
there is a certain smell, temperature, and taste, and yet from these
taken altogether a single compilation of body is created,
so heat and air and the invisible power of wind
mixed together produce a single nature together with that mobile   270
force* which distributes from itself a beginning of motion to the others,
from which source the motion that brings sensation first arises in the flesh.
For deep down this nature lies hidden and concealed,*
nor is there anything further below this in our body,
and further it is itself the "soul" of the whole soul.   275
Just as in our limbs and whole body the force of the mind
and power of the soul lie mixed and hidden,
since it is composed of bodies small in size and number,
so, you should know, this force without a name, composed of minute
bodies, lies hidden and further is itself the soul, so to speak,   280
of the whole soul and lords it over the whole body.
In a similar way it is necessary that wind and air
and heat, mixed up together, function in the limbs,
and one is situated further below or above the others
so that some single thing is seen to have been made from all,   285
otherwise heat and wind separately and separately the power
of air should if divided destroy and dissolve sensation.
Also present in the mind is that heat which it adopts when in anger
it boils up and fire flashes from fierce eyes.
There is also much cold breath, the companion of fear,   290
which stirs up trembling in the limbs and rouses parts of the body.
There is also too that state of peaceful air,
which occurs when the breast is calm and the face serene.
But there is more heat in those whose fierce hearts
and anger-prone minds readily boil over into anger.   295
First in this class is the violent violence of lions,
who often rupture their ribs roaring and growling
and are unable to contain the waves of anger in their breast.
But the chilly mind of the deer is more windy
and more quickly stirs up icy breezes in its flesh   300
which set up a trembling motion in the limbs.

*The fourth unnamed type of mind atom.
*Lucretius here describes how the fourth unnamed element lies farthest from our senses.

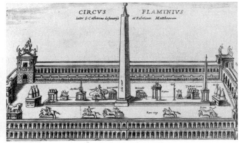

Roman Construction

The Romans were masters of practical construction. Many of their greatest architectural feats were devoted to transportation, commerce, and amusement (not unlike today).

a. The Roman Forum. Artist's Reconstruction. The Forum was the primary market and meeting place in Rome. (*Library of Congress/Instructional Resources Corp.*)

b. Appian Way. The Romans built excellent roads to places as far away as Britain. The roads were constructed of six inches of lava on top of twelve inches of gravel on top of nine inches of small stones on top of ten to twenty inches of large stones. The result was a solid thoroughfare that the army could use in all weather. (*Italian Tourist Office*)

c. Aqueduct. Aqueducts were used to bring water into the cities of the Empire. This one, in Segovia, Spain, is still in use. (*Forrest E. Baird*)

d. Circus Flaminius. Huge stadiums such as this one allowed for chariot races, horse races, and other spectacles. Admission was free and over 100,000 people would often attend. (*Pearson Eduction/PH College*)

> But the nature of the cow gets its life more from peaceful air,
> and the torch of anger never sparks and ignites it too much,
> smoking and spreading its darkness of blinding black,
> 305   nor is it transfixed and immobilized by icy shafts of fear:
> it is situated in between both deer and savage lions.
> So it is with the human race. Although a standard education may make
> some people fairly polished, it still leaves intact those
> original traces of the nature of each person's mind.
> 310   You must not think that such evils can be pulled out by the roots,
> so that one will not run off more quickly to sharp anger,

another be attacked a little more quickly by fear, or a
third put up with some things with more forbearance than is right.
And in many other respects too it is necessary that there be differences among
the various natures of people and their resulting behaviors.   315
I am unable now to explain the invisible causes of these
or to find enough names for all the shapes taken by
the first beginnings, from which this variety of affairs arises.
I see that I can assert this fact in these matters:
that the traces of our characters which reason cannot remove   320
from us are so small, that nothing prevents
us from living a life worthy of the gods.

      This nature [i.e., the soul] then is protected by the whole body
and is itself the guardian of the body and the source of its life.
For they cling to each other with common roots   325
and obviously cannot be pulled apart without destruction.
Just as it is not easy to separate the scent from bits
of frankincense without its very nature also being destroyed,
so it is not easy to extract the nature of the mind
and soul from the whole body without all of them disintegrating.   330
With their first beginnings thus intertwined from the very start
with each other they come into being, endowed with co-partners for life.
And neither the power of the body nor the soul is seen to be able
to feel sensations separately for itself without the energy of the other,
but sensation is kindled and ignited throughout our flesh   335
by shared and interdependent movements from both sides.
Moreover the body is never created by itself
nor does it grow on its own nor is it seen to endure after death.
For never, just as the moisture of water often releases heat
which it has acquired, and it is itself not ripped apart for this reason,   340
but remains intact, never, I say, in this way can
the limbs left behind endure the dissolution of the soul,
but they are ripped apart and deeply destroyed, rotting away.
So from the moment life begins, the reciprocal union
of body and soul learns life-giving motions,   345
even when preserved in a mother's body and womb,
so that dissolution cannot happen without death and destruction.
Thus you can see, since the source of their life is conjoined,
so too does their nature stand conjoined.
What is more, if anyone denies that it is the body that senses   350
and believes that it is the soul which when mixed with the whole body
experiences this motion which we call sensation,
he wages an uphill battle against facts which are quite obvious and true.
For who will ever convey what it is for the body to sense,
if it is not what experience itself has demonstrated and taught us.   355
"But when the soul is dissolved the body is completely without sensation."
Yes—it loses what was not its own in life,
and it loses many things besides when it is driven out from life.

      Further, to say that the eyes are unable to perceive anything,
but the mind gazes through them as if through open doors,   360
is difficult, since the feeling in the eyes leads us in the opposite direction.
For this feeling pulls and pushes us down to the eyes themselves,
especially since often we are unable to perceive shiny
things because our sight is hindered by bright sights.

365 This does not happen with doors. Nor indeed do doors, through which
     we ourselves perceive, experience any distress when open.
     In addition to that, if our eyes function as doors,
     then the mind clearly ought to perceive things better
     when the eyes are yanked out and the door posts completely removed.

370   In these matters you can in no way maintain
     what the holy opinion of the great man Democritus asserts,
     that the first beginnings of the body and mind, juxtaposed one
     to another, are varied in alternation and fasten the limbs together.
     For, as the particles of soul are much smaller
375 than those of which our body and flesh consist,
     so too they are fewer in number and are sparsely scattered
     throughout the limbs, so that at least you can assure this,
     that however small the bodies are which first, when placed on us,
     have the power to arouse sense-bearing motions in our body, so great
380 are the intervals which lie between the first beginnings of the soul.*
     For sometimes we do not feel dust clinging
     to the body, nor that chalk lies sprinkled on our limbs,
     nor do we feel fog at night nor a spider's slender filaments
     met straight on, when we are ennetted as we go,
385 nor that its shriveled shroud has fallen on top of our heads,
     nor birds' feathers or fibers floating from plants
     which because of their incredible lightness usually fall with difficulty,
     nor do we feel the movement of any and every crawling
     creature, nor each and every single footstep
390 which gnats and other bugs take on our body.
     So many particles must be stirred up in us
     before the soul seeds which are mixed within our bodies throughout the limbs
     begin to feel that the first beginnings have been struck,
     and before they pound away at such great distances and are able
395 to rush at each other, meet, and leap apart in turn.

          And the mind is better at keeping the doors of life locked
     and a better master over life than the power of the soul is.
     For without the intelligence and mind no part of the soul
     can reside in the limbs for even a tiny part of time,
400 but follows easily as its companion and departs into the breezes,
     and leaves the chilly limbs in the coolness of death.
     But a person remains in life whose intelligence and mind remains.
     However lacerated the trunk is, with its limbs cut off all around,
     although the soul has been snatched off and removed from the limbs,
405 the person lives on and takes in life-sustaining ethereal breezes.
     But if not the entire soul, but a great part of it, has been taken
     from a person, still he remains alive and hangs on.
     It is just as when the eye has been lacerated all over: if the pupil remains
     uninjured, the living power of sight stands firm,
410 provided only that you do not destroy the whole orb of the eye,
     cutting around the pupil and leaving it all alone:
     for this also could not occur without the destruction of both.*

*Lucretius means that we can tell how far apart the soul atoms are by noting how big the smallest
object is that we can feel when touched to our skin. In the examples that follow, Lucretius also includes cases
where we fail to feel things because of their lightness, not just their small size.
     *That is, the pupil and rest of the eye.

But if this tiny ▮
its light immedi▮
although the shi▮   415
In such an arrang▮   d forever.

Moreover i▮   rtal and is able
to have sensation when separa▮   dy,   625
we must assume, I suppose, that it is equi▮   th five senses.
For in no other way can we possibly imagine for ourselves
souls wandering below the earth in Acheron.
Painters therefore and earlier generations of writers
have thus introduced souls equipped with senses.   630
But neither the eyes nor nose nor hand itself is able
to exist for the soul when it is separated off, nor the tongue, nor ears.
Therefore not at all can souls have sensation and exist on their own.

                    *   *   *

Moreover, if the nature of the soul is immortal, and works   670
its way into our body as we are being born,
why are we unable to remember our past life as well?
Why do we not hold on to any traces of things we have done?
For if the power of the mind is changed to so great an extent
that all recollection of things done before is lost,   675
that, I think, does not stray very far from death.
Therefore it is necessary to admit that what existed before
has perished and what exists now was created now.

                    *   *   *

Next, why does fierce violence go with the stern breed
of lions, and craft with wolves, and why is fleeing passed on
to deer from their fathers and why does fatherly fear rouse their limbs,
and why now do all other things of this sort
come into being in limbs and character from the beginning of life,   745
if not because a power of the mind, fixed by seed and breed,
grows in tandem with each and every body?
But if the soul were immortal and had the habit of changing
bodies, living creatures would have mixed-up manners.
A dog from Hyrcanian* seed would often flee the charge   750
of a horn-sporting stag, and the hawk would flee in terror
through the currents of the air at the coming of the dove, humans would lack
reason, and the wild races of wild beasts would be wise.
For this is put forward by false reasoning, when they say
that the immortal soul is altered with a change of body.   755
For what is changed is dissolved, and therefore passes away.
Indeed, parts are transposed and move from their order.
Therefore they must also be able to be dissolved throughout the limbs,
so that in the end they might all perish as one with the body.

*The Hyrcani were people who lived by the Caspian Sea and were famous for raising fierce dogs.

760   But if they say that the[...]
into human bodies, still I will [...]

762   a stupid one can be produced, [...]

764   and no foal of a mare is as well [...]rse?

765   Naturally they will take refuge i[...]enilized
in a juvenile body. But if this we[...]to admit
that the soul is mortal, since if it [...]
to so great an extent, it loses its li[...]
Or in what way will the force of t[...]

770   together with each body and be al[...]
flowering of youth, unless it is its [...]
Or what does it mean by going out[...]
Can it be that it fears staying shut up[...]
lest its house, worn out by a long spac[...]

775   crash in ruin? But no dangers threaten [...]

          Next, that there are souls hangin[...]
of Venus and the births of wild beasts see[...]
immortal souls awaiting mortal members,[...]
innumerable in number, contesting in fierc[...]

780   over which will be first and foremost to wo[...]
Unless of course treaties have been drawn up[...]
so that whichever flies and arrives first will w[...]
first and so they do not compete and struggle wi[...] each other at all.

                *   *   *

          Moreover, whatever endures eternally must do so
either by having a solid body and repelling blows
and not allowing anything to penetrate it which might be able
to dissociate its tightly-fastened parts within, just as the bodies

810   of matter are whose nature we have made known above,
or by being able to endure for all time for this reason,
that they are not subject to impacts, just as the void is,
which endures untouched and does not suffer from blows at all,
or also by having no supply of space around it,

815   into which things might be able, as it were, to disperse and be dissolved,
just as the universal universe is eternal, for neither is there outside of it
any place into which things may scatter nor are there bodies that
are able to encounter it and dissolve it with a forceful impact.

          But if by chance the soul must be held to be immortal more because of this,

820   that it is held together and protected by vital principles,
either because things foreign to its well-being never attack,
or because the things which attack for some reason withdraw
beaten back before we can feel how much harm they do,
For besides the fact that it [i.e., the mind] grows ill with the diseases of the body,

825   there often comes to it that which torments it about things in the future
and vexes and terrifies it and wears it down with cares
and even when the misdeeds it has committed are past, its offenses gnaw at it.
Add the madness peculiar to the mind and forgetfulness of things,
add that it is submerged in the dark waves of a coma.

830   Therefore death is nothing to us nor does it concern us at all,
inasmuch as the nature of the mind has been shown to be mortal.

THE EARLY STOA

Zeno was born in the small town of Citium on the island of Cyprus. As a young man he moved to Athens, where, it is said, he discovered philosophy by reading Xenophon's description of Socrates, the *Memorabilia.* Socrates being long dead, Zeno attached himself for some time to the Cynics. Zeno agreed with the Cynics that self-control over emotions was essential to a virtuous life. Zeno was also attracted to the teachings of Heraclitus—particularly to the Heraclitean notion of an eternal fire or *Logos* that controls the universe. Sometime around 300 B.C., Zeno set up a school of philosophy in the Painted Porch *<stoa poikile>,* a school that came to be known as "Stoic." His Stoic school may have been established specifically to counter the philosophy of Epicurus. At any rate, he argued that virtue, not pleasure, was the only good, and that natural law, not the random swerving of atoms, was the key principle of the universe. While teaching at his school, Zeno read widely and was greatly respected for his learning, his character, and the simplicity of his life. A severe and austere man, he was, like some of the Pre-Socratics, a sage as well as a philosopher. Zeno believed strongly in divine signs. He is said to have committed suicide after breaking his toe on a rock, believing the incident to be a sign of God's will.

Like Epicurus before him, Zeno divided philosophy into logic (including the theory of knowledge), physics, and ethics. In their discussions of logic, Zeno and his followers examined at great length the relationships among words, their meanings, and the objects to which they refer. They developed several subtle distinctions that are still examined and discussed today (see the suggested readings). They also developed an understanding of sensory knowledge based on impressions that was similar to the theories of Epicurus.

In physics, Zeno developed an elaborate cosmology that includes both a passive and an active principle. The passive principle is matter, while the active principle is the "fiery breath" *<pneuma>,* known by such names as god, mind, fate, Zeus, and *Logos.* This active principle is not separate from the world, but permeates it, molding passive matter into an ordered universe. Permeating everything, god/mind directs the course of affairs and connects all parts into one whole, like a giant organism. The key to ethics for Zeno and his disciples is to live in harmony with this active principle. This requires both the wisdom to know what part we are to play and the "apathy" <*apatheia*>, or avoidance of strong emotions, to accept what we cannot change. Happiness, or more accurately, contentment, is possible in any condition. In fact, among prominent later Stoics, Epictetus was born a slave, whereas Marcus Aurelius was a Roman emperor.

The selection here is from Diogenes Laertius's *Lives of Eminent Philosophers,* in which Laertius summarizes Stoic ethics and physics. It should be noted that Laertius refers not only to Zeno and Cleanthes, but also to Chrysippus, Cleanthes' successor at the Stoa, and to the later Stoics Archedemus and Posidonius. The translation is that of R.D. Hicks.

Cleanthes was born in Assos and raised in Athens. He too studied first with the Cynics before becoming a disciple of Zeno at the Stoa. Following Zeno's death, Cleanthes became head of the Stoic school. Unlike his master, Cleanthes was known as a gentle man with great patience. He was like his master in another respect, however—he too is reported to have killed himself. Cleanthes is best known for his "Hymn to Zeus," a strong tribute to nature's orderliness and benevolence. The translation here is a paraphrase by Tom Trelogan.

*   *   *

For general introductions to the Stoics, see E. Vernon Arnold, *Roman Stoicism* (1911; reprinted New York: Humanities Press, 1958); L. Edelstein, *The Meaning of Stoicism* (Cambridge, MA: Harvard University Press, 1966); John M. Rist, *Stoic Philosophy* (Cambridge: Cambridge University Press, 1969); F.H. Sandbach, *The Stoics* (New York: Norton, 1975); Margaret E. Reeser, *The Nature of Man in Early Stoic Philosophy* (New York: St. Martin's Press, 1989); and Brad Inwood, ed., *The Cambridge Companion to the Stoics* (Cambridge: Cambridge University Press, 2003). For comparisons between Stoicism and other Hellenistic schools, see R.M. Wenley, *Stoicism and Its Influence* (1924; reprinted New York: Cooper Square, 1963); Edwin R. Bevan, *Stoics and Sceptics* (Oxford: Clarendon Press, 1913); and R.D. Hicks, *Stoic and Epicurean* (1910; reprinted New York: Russell and Russell, 1962). For collections of essays consult A.A. Long, ed., *Problems in Stoicism* (London: Athlone Press, 1971); J.M. Rist, ed., *The Stoics* (Berkeley: University of California Press, 1978); A.A. Long, ed., *Stoic Studies* (Cambridge: Cambridge University Press, 1996); and Steven K. Strange and Jack Zupko, eds., *Stoicism: Traditions and Transformations* (Cambridge: Cambridge University Press, 2004). For specialized studies, consult Benson Mates, *Stoic Logic* (Berkeley: University of California Press, 1953); Samuel Sambursky, *Physics of the Stoics* (London: Russell, 1959); Gerard Watson, *The Stoic Theory of Knowledge* (Belfast: Queen's University, 1966); and Ricardo Salles, *The Stoics on Determinism and Compatibilism* (Burlington, VT: Ashgate, 2005).

ZENO OF CITIUM (selections from Diogenes Laertius)

ETHICS

An animal's first impulse, say the Stoics, is to self-preservation, because nature from the outset endears it to itself, as Chrysippus affirms in the first book of his work *On Ends:* his words are, "The dearest thing to every animal is its own constitution and its consciousness thereof"; for it was not likely that nature should estrange the living thing from itself or that she should leave the creature she has made without either estrangement from or affection for its own constitution. We are forced then to conclude that nature in constituting the animal made it near and dear to itself; for so it comes to repel all that is injurious and give free access to all that is serviceable or akin to it.

As for the assertion made by some people that pleasure is the object to which the first impulse of animals is directed, it is shown by the Stoics to be false. For pleasure, if it is really felt, they declare to be a by-product, which never comes until nature by itself has sought and found the means suitable to the animal's existence or constitution; it is an aftermath comparable to the condition of animals thriving and plants in full bloom. And nature, they say, made no difference originally between plants and animals, for she regulates the life of plants too, in their case without impulse and sensation, just as also certain processes go on of a vegetative kind in us. But when in the case of animals impulse has been superadded, whereby they are enabled to go in quest of their proper aliment, for them, say the Stoics, Nature's rule is to follow the direction of impulse. But when reason by way of a more perfect leadership has been bestowed on the beings we call rational, for them life according to reason rightly becomes the natural life. For reason supervenes to shape impulse scientifically.

This is why Zeno was the first (in his treatise *On the Nature of Man*) to designate as the end "life in agreement with nature" (or living agreeably to nature), which is the same as a virtuous life, virtue being the goal towards which nature guides us. So too Cleanthes in his treatise *On Pleasure,* as also Posidonius, and Hecato in his work *On Ends.* Again, living virtuously is equivalent to living in accordance with experience of the actual course of nature, as Chrysippus says in the first book of his *De finibus;* for our individual natures are parts of the nature of the whole universe. And this is why the end may be defined as life in accordance with nature, or, in other words, in accordance with our own human nature as well as that of the universe, a life in which we refrain from every action forbidden by the law common to all things, that is to say, the right reason which pervades all things, and is identical with this Zeus, lord and ruler of all that is. And this very thing constitutes the virtue of the happy man and the smooth current of life, when all actions promote the harmony of the spirit dwelling in the individual man with the will of him who orders the universe. Diogenes then expressly declares the end to be to act with good reason in the selection of what is natural. Archedemus says the end is to live in the performance of all befitting actions.

Reprinted by permission of the publishers and the Loeb Classical Library from Diogenes Laertius, *Lives of Eminent Philosophers,* Volume II, translated by R.D. Hicks (Cambridge, MA: Harvard University Press, 1925). Copyright © 1925 by Harvard University Press.

The Stoa (or "Porch") of Attalos as reconstructed in Athens. Zeno of Citium first taught at a similar site, and his philosophy came to be called "Stoicism" (literally "porchism"). (*Forrest E. Baird*)

By the nature with which our life ought to be in accord, Chrysippus understands both universal nature and more particularly the nature of man, whereas Cleanthes takes the nature of the universe alone as that which should be followed, without adding the nature of the individual.

And virtue, he holds, is a harmonious disposition, choice-worthy for its own sake and not from hope or fear or any external motive. Moreover, it is in virtue that happiness consists; for virtue is the state of mind which tends to make the whole of life harmonious. When a rational being is perverted, this is due to the deceptiveness of external pursuits or sometimes to the influence of associates. For the starting-points of nature are never perverse.

*   *   *

They hold the emotions to be judgements, as is stated by Chrysippus in his treatise *On the Passions:* avarice being a supposition that money is a good, while the case is similar with drunkenness and profligacy and all the other emotions.

And grief or pain they hold to be an irrational mental contraction. Its species are pity, envy, jealousy, rivalry, heaviness, annoyance, distress, anguish, distraction. Pity is grief felt at undeserved suffering; envy, grief at others' prosperity; jealousy, grief at the possession by another of that which one desires for oneself; rivalry, pain at the possession by another of what one has oneself. Heaviness or vexation is grief which weighs us down, annoyance that which coops us up and straitens us for want of room, distress a pain brought on by anxious thought that lasts and increases, anguish painful grief, distraction irrational grief, rasping and hindering us from viewing the situation as a whole.

Fear is an expectation of evil. Under fear are ranged the following emotions: terror, nervous shrinking, shame, consternation, panic, mental agony. Terror is a fear which produces fright; shame is fear of disgrace; nervous shrinking is a fear that one will have to act; consternation is fear due to a presentation of some unusual occurrence; panic is fear with pressure exercised by sound; mental agony is fear felt when some issue is still in suspense.

Desire or craving is irrational appetency, and under it are ranged the following states: want, hatred, contentiousness, anger, love, wrath, resentment. Want, then, is a craving when it is baulked and, as it were, cut off from its object, but kept at full stretch and attracted towards it in vain. Hatred is a growing and lasting desire or craving that it should go ill with somebody. Contentiousness is a craving or desire connected with partisanship; anger a craving or desire to punish one who is thought to have done you an undeserved injury. The passion of love is a craving from which good men are free; for it is an effort to win affection due to the visible presence of beauty. Wrath is anger which has long rankled and has become malicious, waiting for its opportunity, as is illustrated by the lines:

> Even though for the one day he swallow his anger, yet doth he still keep his displeasure thereafter in his heart, till he accomplish it.*

Resentment is anger in an early stage.

Pleasure is an irrational elation at the accruing of what seems to be choiceworthy; and under it are ranged ravishment, malevolent joy, delight, transport. Ravishment is pleasure which charms the ear. Malevolent joy is pleasure at another's ills. Delight is the mind's propulsion to weakness, its name in Greek <terpsis> being akin to <trepsis> or turning. To be in transports of delight is the melting away of virtue.

And as there are said to be certain infirmities in the body, as for instance gout and arthritic disorders, so too there is in the soul love of fame, love of pleasure, and the like. By infirmity is meant disease accompanied by weakness; and by disease is meant a fond imagining of something that seems desirable. And as in the body there are tendencies to certain maladies such as colds and diarrhea, so it is with the soul, there are tendencies like enviousness, pitifulness, quarrelsomeness, and the like.

Also they say that there are three emotional states which are good, namely, joy, caution, and wishing. Joy, the counterpart of pleasure, is rational elation; caution, the counterpart of fear, rational avoidance; for though the wise man will never feel fear, he will yet use caution. And they make wishing the counterpart of desire (or craving), inasmuch as it is rational appetency. And accordingly, as under the primary passions are classed certain others subordinate to them, so too is it with the primary eupathies or good emotional states. Thus under wishing they bring well-wishing or benevolence, friendliness, respect, affection; under caution, reverence and modesty; under joy, delight, mirth, cheerfulness.

Now they say that the wise man is passionless, because he is not prone to fall into such infirmity. But they add that in another sense the term apathy is applied to the bad man, when, that is, it means that he is callous and relentless. Further, the wise man is said

*Iliad, I. 81, 82.

to be free from vanity; for he is indifferent to good or evil report. However, he is not alone in this, there being another who is also free from vanity, he who is ranged among the rash, and that is the bad man. Again, they tell us that all good men are austere or harsh, because they neither have dealings with pleasure themselves nor tolerate those who have. The term harsh is applied, however, to others as well, and in much the same sense as a wine is said to be harsh when it is employed medicinally and not for drinking at all.

Again, the good are genuinely in earnest and vigilant for their own improvement, using a manner of life which banishes evil out of sight and makes what good there is in things appear. At the same time they are free from pretence; for they have stripped off all pretence or "make-up" whether in voice or in look. Free too are they from all business cares, declining to do anything which conflicts with duty. They will take wine, but not get drunk. Nay more, they will not be liable to madness either; not but what there will at times occur to the good man strange impressions due to melancholy or delirium, ideas not determined by the principle of what is choice-worthy but contrary to nature. Nor indeed will the wise man ever feel grief; seeing that grief is irrational contraction of the soul, as Apollodorus says in his *Ethics*.

*   *   *

It is also their doctrine that amongst the wise there should be a community of wives with free choice of partners, as Zeno says in his Republic and Chrysippus in his treatise *On Government* [and not only they, but also Diogenes the Cynic and Plato]. Under such circumstances we shall feel paternal affection for all the children alike, and there will be an end of the jealousies arising from adultery. The best form of government they hold to be a mixture of democracy, kingship, and aristocracy (or the rule of the best).

Such, then, are the statements they make in their ethical doctrines, with much more besides, together with their proper proofs: let this, however, suffice for a statement of them in a summary and elementary form.

PHYSICS

Their physical doctrine they divide into sections (1) about bodies; (2) about principles; (3) about elements; (4) about the gods; (5) about bounding surfaces and space whether filled or empty. This is a division into species; but the generic division is into three parts, dealing with (i) the universe; (ii) the elements; (iii) the subject of causation.

The part dealing with the universe admits, they say, of division into two: for with one aspect of it the mathematicians also are concerned, in so far as they treat questions relating to the fixed stars and the planets, *e.g.* whether the sun is not just so large as it appears to be, and the same about the moon, the question of their revolutions, and other inquiries of the same sort. But there is another aspect or field of cosmological inquiry, which belongs to the physicists alone: this includes such questions as what the substance of the universe is, whether the sun and the stars are made up of forms and matter, whether the world has had a beginning in time or not, whether it is animate or inanimate, whether it is destructible or indestructible, whether it is governed by providence, and all the rest. The part concerned with causation, again, is itself subdivided into two. And in one of its aspects medical inquiries have a share in it, in so far as it involves investigation of the ruling principle of the soul and the phenomena of soul, seeds, and the like. Whereas the other part is claimed by the mathematicians also, *e.g.* how vision is to be explained, what causes the image on the mirror, what is the origin of clouds, thunder, rainbows, halos, comets, and the like.

They hold that there are two principles in the universe, the active principle and the passive. The passive principle, then, is a substance without quality, *i.e.* matter, whereas the active is the reason inherent in this substance, that is God. For he is everlasting and is the artificer of each several thing throughout the whole extent of matter. This doctrine is laid down by Zeno of Citium in his treatise *On Existence,* Cleanthes in his work *On Atoms,* Chrysippus in the first book of his *Physics* towards the end, Archedemus in his treatise *On Elements,* and Posidonius in the second book of his *Physical Exposition.* There is a difference, according to them, between principles and elements; the former being without generation or destruction, whereas the elements are destroyed when all things are resolved into fire. Moreover, the principles are incorporeal and destitute of form, while the elements have been endowed with form.

Body is defined by Apollodorus in his *Physics* as that which is extended in three dimensions, length, breadth, and depth. This is also called solid body. But surface is the extremity of a solid body, or that which has length and breadth only without depth. That surface exists not only in our thought but also in reality is maintained by Posidonius in the third book of his *Celestial Phenomena.* A line is the extremity of a surface or length without breadth, or that which has length alone. A point is the extremity of a line, the smallest possible mark or dot.

God is one and the same with Reason, Fate, and Zeus; he is also called by many other names. In the beginning he was by himself; he transformed the whole of substance through air into water, and just as in animal generation the seed has a moist vehicle, so in cosmic moisture God, who is the seminal reason of the universe, remains behind in the moisture as such an agent, adapting matter to himself with a view to the next stage of creation. Thereupon he created first of all the four elements, fire, water, air, earth. They are discussed by Zeno in his treatise *On the Whole,* by Chrysippus in the first book of his *Physics,* and by Archedemus in a work *On Elements.* An element is defined as that from which particular things first come to be at their birth and into which they are finally resolved. The four elements together constitute unqualified substance or matter. Fire is the hot element, water the moist, air the cold, earth the dry. Not but what the quality of dryness is also found in the air. Fire has the uppermost place; it is also called aether, and in it the sphere of the fixed stars is first created; then comes the sphere of the planets, next to that the air, then the water, and lowest of all the earth, which is at the centre of all things.

The term universe or cosmos is used by them in three senses: (1) of God himself, the individual being whose quality is derived from the whole of substance; he is indestructible and ingenerable, being the artificer of this orderly arrangement, who at stated periods of time absorbs into himself the whole of substance and again creates it from himself. (2) Again, they give the name of cosmos to the orderly arrangement of the heavenly bodies in itself as such; and (3) in the third place to that whole of which these two are parts. Again, the cosmos is defined as the individual being qualifying the whole of substance, or, in the words of Posidonius in his elementary treatise on *Celestial Phenomena,* a system made up of heaven and earth and the natures in them, or, again, as a system constituted by gods and men and all things created for their sake. By heaven is meant the extreme circumference or ring in which the deity has his seat.

The world, in their view, is ordered by reason and providence: so says Chrysippus in the fifth book of his treatise *On Providence* and Posidonius in his work *On the Gods,* book iii—inasmuch as reason pervades every part of it, just as does the soul in us. Only there is a difference of degree; in some parts there is more of it, in others less. For through some parts it passes as a "hold" or containing force, as is the case with our bones and sinews; while through others it passes as intelligence, as in the ruling part of the soul. Thus, then, the whole world is a living being, endowed with soul and reason, and having aether for its ruling principle: so says Antipater of Tyre in the eighth book of his treatise *On the Cosmos*. Chrysippus in the first book of his work *On Providence* and Posidonius in his book *On the Gods* say that the heaven, but Cleanthes that the sun, is the ruling power of the world. Chrysippus, however, in the course of the same work gives a somewhat different account, namely, that it is the purer part of the aether; the same which they declare to be preeminently God and always to have, as it were in sensible fashion, pervaded all that is in the air, all animals and plants, and also the earth itself, as a principle of cohesion.

The world, they say, is one and finite, having a spherical shape, such a shape being the most suitable for motion, as Posidonius says in the fifth book of his *Physical Discourse* and the disciples of Antipater in their works on the Cosmos. Outside of the world is diffused the infinite void, which is incorporeal. By incorporeal is meant that which, though capable of being occupied by body, is not so occupied. The world has no empty space within it, but forms one united whole. This is a necessary result of the sympathy and tension which binds together things in heaven and earth. Chrysippus discusses the void in his work *On Void* and in the first book of his *Physical Sciences;* so too Apollophanes in his *Physics,* Apollodorus, and Posidonius in his *Physical Discourse,* book ii. But these, it is added [*i.e.* sympathy and tension], are likewise bodies.

Time too is incorporeal, being the measure of the world's motion. And time past and time future are infinite, but time present is finite. They hold that the world must come to an end, inasmuch as it had a beginning, on the analogy of those things which are understood by the senses. And that of which the parts are perishable is perishable as a whole. Now the parts of the world are perishable, seeing that they are transformed one into the other. Therefore the world itself is doomed to perish. Moreover, anything is destructible if it admits of deterioration; therefore the world is so, for it is first evaporated and again dissolved into water.

The world, they hold, comes into being when its substance has first been converted from fire through air into moisture and then the coarser part of the moisture has condensed as earth, while that whose particles are fine has been turned into air, and this process of rarefaction goes on increasing till it generates fire. Thereupon out of these elements animals and plants and all other natural kinds are formed by their mixture. The generation and the destruction of the world are discussed by Zeno in his treatise *On the Whole*, by Chrysippus in the first book of his *Physics,* by Posidonius in the first book of his work *On the Cosmos,* by Cleanthes, and by Antipater in his tenth book *On the Cosmos.* Panaetius, however, maintained that the world is indestructible.

The doctrine that the world is a living being, rational, animate, and intelligent, is laid down by Chrysippus in the first book of his treatise *On Providence,* by Apollodorus in his *Physics,* and by Posidonius. It is a living thing in the sense of an animate substance endowed with sensation; for animal is better than non-animal, and nothing is better than the world, ergo the world is a living being. And it is endowed with soul, as is clear from our several souls being each a fragment of it. Boëthus, however, denies that the world is a living thing. The unity of the world is maintained by Zeno in his treatise *On the Whole,* by Chrysippus, by Apollodorus in his *Physics,* and by Posidonius in the first book of his *Physical Discourse.* By the totality of things, the All, is meant, according to Apollodorus, (1) the world, and in another sense (2) the system composed of the world and the void outside it. The world then is finite, the void infinite.

Of the stars some are fixed, and are carried round with the whole heaven; others, the wandering stars or planets, have their special motions. The sun travels in an oblique path through the zodiac. Similarly the moon travels in a spiral path. The sun is pure fire: so Posidonius in the seventh book of his *Celestial Phenomena.* And it is larger than the earth, as the same author says in the sixth book of his *Physical Discourse.* Moreover it is spherical in shape like the world itself according to this same author and his school. That it is fire is proved by its producing all the effects of fire; that it is larger than the earth by the fact that all the earth is illuminated by it; nay more, the heaven beside. The fact too that the earth casts a conical shadow proves that the sun is greater than it. And it is because of its great size that it is seen from every part of the earth.

The moon, however, is of a more earthy composition, since it is nearer to the earth. These fiery bodies and the stars generally derive their nutriment, the sun from the wide ocean, being a fiery kindling, though intelligent; the moon from fresh waters, with an admixture of air, close to the earth as it is: thus Posidonius in the sixth book of his *Physics;* the other heavenly bodies being nourished from the earth. They hold that the stars are spherical in shape and that the earth too is so and is at rest; and that the moon does not shine by her own light, but by the borrowed light of the sun when he shines upon her.

An eclipse of the sun takes place when the moon passes in front of it on the side towards us, as shown by Zeno with a diagram in his treatise *On the Whole.* For the moon is seen approaching at conjunctions and occulting it and then again receding from it. This can best be observed when they are mirrored in a basin of water. The moon is eclipsed when she falls into the earth's shadow: for which reason it is only at the full moon that an eclipse happens [and not always then], although she is in opposition to the sun every month; because the moon moves in an oblique orbit, diverging in latitude relatively to the orbit of the sun, and she accordingly goes farther to the north or to the south. When, however, the moon's motion in latitude has brought her into the sun's path through the zodiac, and she thus comes diametrically opposite to the sun, there is an eclipse. Now the moon is in latitude right on the zodiac, when she is in the constellations of Cancer, Scorpio, Aries and Taurus: so Posidonius and his followers tell us.

The deity, say they, is a living being, immortal, rational, perfect or intelligent in happiness, admitting nothing evil [into him], taking providential care of the world and all that therein is, but he is not of human shape. He is, however, the artificer of the universe and, as it were, the father of all, both in general and in that particular part of him which is all-pervading, and which is called many names according to its various powers. They give the name Dia <*Dia*> because all things are due to <*dia*> him; Zeus <*Zana*> in so far as he is the cause of life <*zan*> or pervades all life; the name Athena is given, because the ruling part of the divinity extends to the aether; the name Hera marks its extension to the air; he is called Hephaestus since it spreads to the creative fire; Poseidon, since it stretches to the sea; Demeter, since it reaches to the earth. Similarly men have given the deity his other titles, fastening, as best they can, on some one or other of his peculiar attributes.

The substance of God is declared by Zeno to be the whole world and the heaven, as well as by Chrysippus in his first book *Of the Gods,* and by Posidonius in his first book with the same title. Again, Antipater in the seventh book of his work *On the Cosmos* says that the substance of God is akin to air, while Boëthus in his work *On Nature* speaks of the sphere of the fixed stars as the substance of God. Now the term Nature is used by them to mean sometimes that which holds the world together, sometimes that which causes terrestrial things to spring up. Nature defined as a force moving of itself, producing and preserving in being its offspring in accordance with seminal principles within definite periods, and effecting results homogeneous with their sources. Nature, they hold, aims both at utility and at pleasure, as is clear from the analogy of human craftsmanship. That all things happen by fate or destiny is maintained by Chrysippus in his treatise *De fato,* by Posidonius in his *De fato,* book ii, by Zeno and by Boëthus in his *De fato,* book i. Fate is defined as an endless chain of causation, whereby things are, or as the reason or formula by which the world goes on. What is more, they say that divination in all its forms is a real and substantial fact, if there is really Providence. And they prove it to be actually a science on the evidence of certain results: so Zeno, Chrysippus in the second book of his *De divinatione,* Athenodorus, and Posidonius in the second book of his *Physical Discourse* and the fifth book of his *De divinatione.* But Panaetius denies that divination has any real existence.

The primary matter they make the substratum of all things: so Chrysippus in the first book of his *Physics,* and Zeno. By matter is meant that out of which anything whatsoever is produced. Both substance and matter are terms used in a twofold sense according as they signify (1) universal or (2) particular substance or matter. The former neither increases nor diminishes, while the matter of particular things both increases and diminishes. Body according to them is substance which is finite: so Antipater in his second book *On Substance,* and Apollodorus in his *Physics.* Matter can also be acted upon, as the same author says, for if it were immutable, the things which are produced would never have been produced out of it. Hence the further doctrine that matter is divisible *ad infinitum.* Chrysippus says that the division is not *ad infinitum,* but itself infinite; for there is nothing infinitely small to which the division can extend. But nevertheless the division goes on without ceasing.

Hence, again, their explanation of the mixture of two substances is, according to Chrysippus in the third book of his *Physics,* that they permeate each other through and through, and that the particles of the one do not merely surround those of the other or lie beside them. Thus, if a little drop of wine be thrown into the sea, it will be equally diffused over the whole sea for a while and then will be blended with it.

Also they hold that there are daemons *<daimones>* who are in sympathy with mankind and watch over human affairs. They believe too in heroes, that is, the souls of the righteous that have survived their bodies.

Of the changes which go on in the air, they describe winter as the cooling of the air above the earth due to the sun's departure to a distance from the earth; spring as the right temperature of the air consequent upon his approach to us; summer as the heating of the air above the earth when he travels to the north; while autumn they attribute to the receding of the sun from us. As for the winds, they are streams of air, differently named according to the localities from which they blow. And the cause of their production is the sun through the evaporation of the clouds. The rainbow is explained as the reflection of the sun's rays from watery clouds or, as Posidonius says in his *Meteorology,* an image of a segment of the sun or moon in a cloud suffused with dew, which is hollow and visible without intermission, the image showing itself as if in a mirror in the form of a circular arch. Comets, bearded stars, and meteors are fires which arise when dense air is carried up to the region of aether. A shooting star is the sudden kindling of a mass of fire in rapid motion through the air, which leaves a trail behind it presenting an appearance of length. Rain is the transformation of cloud into water, when moisture drawn up by the sun from land or sea has been only partially evaporated. If this is cooled down, it is called hoar-frost. Hail is frozen cloud, crumbled by a wind; while snow is moist matter from a cloud which has congealed: so Posidonius in the eighth book of his *Physical Discourse*. Lightning is a kindling of clouds from being rubbed together or being rent by wind, as Zeno says in his treatise *On the Whole;* thunder the noise these clouds make when they rub against each other or burst. Thunderbolt is the term used when the fire is violently kindled and hurled to the ground with great force as the clouds grind against each other or are torn by the wind. Others say that it is a compression of fiery air descending with great force. A typhoon is a great and violent thunderstorm whirlwind-like, or a whirlwind of smoke from a cloud that has burst. A "prester" is a cloud rent all round by the force of fire and wind. Earthquakes, say they, happen when the wind finds its way into, or is imprisoned in, the hollow parts of the earth: so Posidonius in his eighth book; and some of them are tremblings, others openings of the earth, others again lateral displacements, and yet others vertical displacements.

They maintain that the parts of the world are arranged thus. The earth is in the middle answering to a centre; next comes the water, which is shaped like a sphere all round it, concentric with the earth, so that the earth is in water. After the water comes a spherical layer of air. There are five celestial circles: first, the arctic circle, which is always visible; second, the summer tropic; third, the circle of the equinox; fourth, the winter tropic; and fifth, the antarctic, which is invisible to us. They are called parallel, because they do not incline towards one another; yet they are described round the same centre. The zodiac is an oblique circle, as it crosses the parallel circles. And there are five terrestrial zones: first, the northern zone which is beyond the arctic circle, uninhabitable because of the cold; second, a temperate zone; a third, uninhabitable because of great heats, called the torrid zone; fourth, a counter-temperate zone; fifth, the southern zone, uninhabitable because of its cold.

Nature in their view is an artistically working fire, going on its way to create; which is equivalent to a fiery, creative, or fashioning breath. And the soul is a nature capable of perception. And they regard it as the breath of life, congenital with us; from which they infer first that it is a body and secondly that it survives death. Yet it is perishable, though the soul of the universe, of which the individual souls of animals are parts, is indestructible. Zeno of Citium and Antipater, in their treatises *De anima,* and Posidonius define the soul as a warm breath; for by this we become animate and this enables us to move. Cleanthes indeed holds that all souls continue to exist until the general conflagration; but Chrysippus says that only the souls of the wise do so.

They count eight parts of the soul: the five senses, the generative power in us, our power of speech, and that of reasoning. They hold that we see when the light between the visual organ and the object stretches in the form of a cone: so Chrysippus in the second book of his *Physics* and Apollodorus. The apex of the cone in the air is at the eye, the base at the object seen. Thus the thing seen is reported to us by the medium of the air stretching out towards it, as if by a stick.

We hear when the air between the sonant body and the organ of hearing suffers concussion, a vibration which spreads spherically and then forms waves and strikes upon the ears, just as the water in a reservoir forms wavy circles when a stone is thrown into it. Sleep is caused, they say, by the slackening of the tension in our senses, which affects the ruling part of the soul. They consider that the passions are caused by the variations of the vital breath.

Semen is by them defined as that which is capable of generating offspring like the parent. And the human semen which is emitted by a human parent in a moist vehicle is mingled with parts of the soul, blended in the same ratio in which they are present in the parent. Chrysippus in the second book of his *Physics* declares it to be in substance identical with vital breath or spirit. This, he thinks, can be seen from the seeds cast into the earth, which, if kept till they are old, do not germinate, plainly because their fertility has evaporated. Sphaerus and his followers also maintain that semen derives its origin from the whole of the body; at all events every part of the body can be reproduced from it. That of the female is according to them sterile, being, as Sphaerus says, without tension, scanty, and watery. By ruling part of the soul is meant that which is most truly soul proper, in which arise presentations and impulses and from which issues rational speech. And it has its seat in the heart.

Such is the summary of their Physics which I have deemed adequate.

CLEANTHES—HYMN TO ZEUS

1   Most glorious of the deathless gods, called by many a name:
Great King of Nature, Changeless One, All-Powerful!
You are the just ruler of all that is.
We hail you as mortals hail you everywhere.
5   Hail, Zeus!

We are your children.
And because of all the things that live and move
on earth's broad ways, you gave the form of gods to us alone,
I shall always praise and celebrate your power.

10   Look! The heaven that whirls round the earth follows your command,
and still it pays glad homage to you. Your unconquerable hand
wields the two-edged sword of flaming lightning
whose immortal power pulsates through everything
that nature brings to light:
15   the lightning that carries the universal logos that flows through everything that is
and glows in the celestial light of every star, both large and small.

Through endless ages, God, you are a king of kings,
and it is your eternal purpose that is responsible for everything there is
on land and in the sea and in the vastness of the heavens—
20   except for what the bad man does in vain.

But you know how to make the crooked straight.
Chaos is order to you.
Even what no man loves is lovely in your eyes,
you who harmonize what is bad with what is good
so that one logos runs through everything forever.
25   One logos—which, alas! bad men do not heed.

Their spirits hunger for the good, yet even though they see and hear,
they do not hear and do not see your universal law:
the law revered by those who, guided by reason, win happiness.
The rest—the bad men quite devoid of reason—
pursue on their own the various forms of vice.   30
Some fight vainly on the battlefield of fame
to make themselves a name. Others lust for wealth.
Still others, utterly dissolute, pursue the pleasures of the flesh.
Achieving nothing, they wander here and there,
always seeking what is good but finding only what is bad.   35

All-bountiful Zeus, shrouded in darkness!
Your lightning flashes in the thundercloud!
Save your children from the deadly rule of ignorance.
Turn away the darkness from their souls and give them knowledge.
For by knowledge you are strengthened   40
and made able to rule justly over everything.

Honored by you, we honor you in turn,
praising your works continually with songs as mortals should.
Even the gods cannot lay claim to any higher good
than that of justly adoring the universal law forever.   45

EPICTETUS
ca. A.D. 50–ca. A.D. 130

Epictetus was born a slave in Hierapolis, a small town in Phrygia, Asia Minor (in present-day Turkey). His master was Epaphroditus, a member of Emperor Nero's personal staff in Rome. As was often done at that time, Epaphroditus saw to it that Epictetus had a good education, sending him to study with the Roman Stoic, Rufus. Epictetus gained his freedom sometime after the death of the emperor in A.D. 68 and began to teach philosophy in Rome. In A.D. 89 or 93 Emperor Domitian expelled all philosophers from Rome. Domitian seems to have been especially angry with the Stoics for teaching that sovereignty comes from God and is for the benefit of the people. (Epictetus's reported claim that he had the same regard for the emperor as for his water-pot could not have helped.) Epictetus moved to Nicropolis in Epirus (northwestern Greece), where he established a thriving Stoic school and lived a simple life with few material goods. As an old man, he married so that he could adopt a child who otherwise would have been "exposed," that is, left to die. Those whom he taught described him as a humble, charitable man of great moral and religious devotion.

Epictetus never wrote anything, but one of his admiring students, Arrian, composed eight *Discourses* based on Epictetus's lectures, along with a summary of the great man's thought, the *Handbook* (*Enchiridion*). The *Handbook,* given here complete in the outstanding new Keith Seddon translation, builds on the early Stoa's concept of *Logos*. Since the *Logos* or natural law permeates everything, it provides us with moral intuition, so all persons have the capacity for virtue. But in order to live the moral life, one must apply these intuitions to specific cases. Education is necessary if we are to learn how to properly connect moral insights with life. We must begin by recognizing the fact that we cannot change events that happen to us, but we can change our attitude toward those events. To accomplish this and achieve the good life, we must go through three stages. First, we must order our desires and overcome our fears. Next, we must perform our duties—in whatever role fate has given us. Finally, we must think clearly and judge accurately. Only then will we gain inner tranquility.

Despite Emperor Domitian's condemnation, Stoicism had a special appeal to the Roman mind. The Romans were not much interested in the speculative and theoretical content of Zeno's early Stoa. Instead, in the austere moral emphasis of Epictetus, with his concomitant stress on self-control and superiority to pain, the Romans found an ideal for the wise man, whereas the Stoic description of natural law provided a basis for Roman law. One might say that the pillars of republican Rome tended to be Stoical, even if some Romans had never heard of Stoicism.

*   *   *

For works on the Stoics in general, which include Epictetus, see the introductory material on the Early Stoa on page 506. For volumes specifically on Epictetus, see John Bonforte, *The Philosophy of Epictetus* (New York: Philosophical Library, 1955); and William O. Stephens, *Stoic Ethics: Epictetus and Happiness as Freedom* (London: Continuum, 2007). lason Xenakis, *Epictetus. Philosopher-Therapist* (The Hague, Netherlands: Martinus Nijhoff, 1969), makes an interesting application of Epictetus; while W.A. Oldfather, *Contributions Towards a Bibliography of Epictetus* (Urbana: University of Illinois Press, 1927; supplement, 1952), furnishes a bibliography. For a study of Epictetus's star pupil, see Philip A. Stadter, *Arrian of Nicomedia* (Chapel Hill: University of North Carolina Press, 1980).

HANDBOOK (ENCHIRIDION)

Chapter 1: [1] On the one hand, there are things that are in our power, whereas other things are not in our power. In our power are opinion, impulse, desire, aversion, and, in a word, whatever is our own doing. Things not in our power include our body, our possessions, our reputations, our status, and, in a word, whatever is not our own doing.

[2] Now, things that are in our power are by nature free, unhindered, unimpeded; but things not in our power are weak, slavish, hindered, and belong to others. [3] Remember, therefore, that whenever you suppose those things that are by nature slavish to be free, or those things that belong to others to be your own, you will be hindered, miserable and distressed, and you will find fault with both gods and men. If, however, you suppose to be yours only what is yours, and what belongs to another to belong to another (as indeed it does), no one will ever compel you, no one will hinder you; you will find fault with no one, reproach no one, nor act against your own will; you will have no enemies and no one will harm you, for no harm can touch you.

[4] Thus, when aiming at such great things remember that securing them requires more than a modest effort: some things you will have to give up altogether, and others

Translated by Keith Seddon © 2005. From Keith Seddon, *Epictetus' Handbook and the Tablet of Cebes*, Routledge 2005. Reprinted by permission of Routledge Press.

you will have to put aside for the time being. If you want such great things but at the same time strive for status and wealth, you may well not even obtain these latter things because you are seeking the former; at any rate, you will certainly fail to secure those former great things which alone bring freedom and happiness.

[5] Straightaway then, train yourself to say to every unpleasant impression, "You are an impression, and by no means what you appear to be." Then examine it and test it by the rules that you have, first (in this way especially) by asking whether it concerns things that are in our power or things that are not in our power: and if it concerns something not in our power, have ready to hand the answer, "This is nothing to me."

Chapter 2: [1] Remember that, on the one hand, desires command you to obtain what you long for and, on the other, aversions command you to avoid what you dislike. Those who fail to gain what they desire are unfortunate, whilst those who fall into what they seek to avoid are miserable. So if you seek to avoid only those things contrary to nature amongst the things that are in your power, you will accordingly fall into nothing to which you are averse; but if you seek to avoid sickness, or death, or poverty, you will be miserable. [2] Therefore, remove altogether your aversion for anything that is not in our power, and transfer it to those things contrary to nature that *are* in our power. For the time being, completely restrain your desires, for if you desire any of those things not in our power you are bound to suffer misfortune. For of those things in our power, which it would be proper to desire, none is yet within your grasp. Use only impulse and repulsion, but use even these lightly, with reservation, and without straining.

Chapter 3: With respect to any of those things you find attractive or useful or have a fondness for, recall to mind what kind of thing it is, beginning with the most trifling. So if you are fond of an earthenware pot, say, "I am fond of an earthenware pot." Then you will not be upset if it gets broken. When you kiss your child or wife, say that you are kissing a human being; then, should they die, you will not be distressed.

Chapter 4: When you are about to undertake some task, remind yourself what sort of business it is. If you are going out to bathe, bring to mind what happens at the baths: there will be those who splash you, those who will jostle you, some will be abusive to you, and others will steal from you. And thus you will undertake the affair more securely if you say to yourself from the start, "I wish to take a bath, but also to keep my moral character in accordance with nature." Do likewise with every undertaking. For thus, if anything should happen that interferes with your bathing, be ready to say, "Oh well, it was not only this that I wanted, but also to keep my moral character in accordance with nature, and I cannot do that if I am irritated by things that happen."

Chapter 5: It is not circumstances themselves that trouble people, but their judgments about those circumstances. For example, death is nothing terrible, for if it were, it would have appeared so to Socrates; but having the opinion that death is terrible, *this* is what is terrible. Therefore, whenever we are hindered or troubled or distressed, let us never blame others, but ourselves, that is, our own judgments. The uneducated person blames others for their failures; those who have just begun to be instructed blame themselves; those whose learning is complete blame neither others nor themselves.

Chapter 6: Do not take pride in any excellence that is not your own. If a horse were to say proudly, "I am beautiful," one could put up with that. But when you say proudly, "I have a beautiful horse," remember that you are boasting about something good that belongs to the horse. What, then, belongs to *you*? The use of impressions. Whenever you are in accordance with nature regarding the way you use impressions, then be proud, for then you will be proud of a good that is your own.

Chapter 7: Just as on a voyage, when the ship has anchored, if you go ashore to get water you may also pick up a shell-fish or a vegetable from the path, but you should keep your thoughts fixed on the ship, and you should look back frequently in case the captain calls, and, if he should call, you must give up all these other things to avoid being bound and thrown on board like a sheep; so in life also, if instead of a vegetable and a shell-fish you are given a wife and a child, nothing will prevent you from taking them—but if the captain calls, give up all these things and run to the ship without even turning to look back. And if you are old, do not even go far from the ship, lest you are missing when the call comes.

Chapter 8: Do not demand that things should happen just as you wish, but wish them to happen just as they do, and all will be well.

Chapter 9: Illness interferes with one's body, but not with one's moral character, unless one so wishes. Lameness interferes with one's leg, but not with one's moral character. Say this to yourself regarding everything that happens to you, for you will find that what happens interferes with something else, but not with you.

Chapter 10: On every occasion when something happens to you, remember to turn to yourself to see what capacity you have for dealing with it. If you are attracted to a beautiful boy or woman, you will find that self-control is the capacity to use for that. If hardship befalls you, you will find endurance; if abuse, you will find patience. Make this your habit and you will not be carried away by impressions.

Chapter 11: Never say of anything, "I have lost it," but rather "I have given it back." Has your child died? It has been given back. Has your wife died? She has been given back. Has your land been taken from you? Well, that too has been given back. "But the one who took it from me is a bad man!" What concern is it of yours by whose hand the Giver asks for its return? For the time that these things are given to you, take care of them as things that belong to another, just as travelers do an inn.

Chapter 12: [1] If you want to make progress, set aside all considerations like these: "If I neglect my affairs, I will have nothing to live on"; "If I do not punish my slave-boy, he will be bad." For it is better to die of hunger, free from distress and fear, than to live perturbed amidst plenty. It is better for your slave-boy to be bad than for you to be wretched. [2] Begin therefore with little things. The olive oil is spilled. The wine is stolen. Say to yourself, "This is the price for peace of mind, and this is the price for being free of troubles. Nothing can be had without paying the price." And when you call your slave-boy, bear in mind that it is quite possible he won't heed you, or even if he does heed you it is quite possible that he won't do the things you tell him to. But he is not in so fine a position that your peace of mind depends upon him.

Chapter 13: If you want to make progress, submit to appearing foolish and stupid with regard to external things. Do not wish to appear knowledgeable about anything and, if others think you amount to something, distrust yourself. For you should know that it is not easy both to keep your moral character in accordance with nature and to keep secure external things, for in attending to one, you will inevitably neglect the other.

Chapter 14: [1] It is foolish to wish that your children and your wife and your friends should live forever, for you are wishing for things to be in your power which are not, and wishing for what belongs to others to be your own. It is foolish in the same way, too, to wish that your slave-boy should never do wrong, for now you want badness not to be badness, but something else. However, if you wish not to fail in what you desire, this you are able to do. Exercise yourself, therefore, in what you *are* able to do. [2] A person's master is the one who has power over that which is wished for or not wished for, so as to secure it or take it away. Therefore, anyone who wishes to be free should neither wish for anything nor avoid anything that depends on others; those who do not observe this rule will of necessity be the slaves of others.

Chapter 15: Remember, you ought to behave in life as you would at a banquet. Something is carried round and comes to you: reach out and take a modest portion. It passes by? Do not stop it. It has not yet arrived? Do not stretch your desire towards it, but wait until it comes to you. So it should be concerning your children, your wife, your status, your wealth, and one day you will be worthy to share a banquet with the gods. If, however, you do not take these things even when they are put before you, but have no regard for them, not only will you share a banquet with the gods, but also rule with them. By acting in this way, Diogenes and Heraclitus, and people like them, were deservedly gods and were deservedly called so.

Chapter 16: When you see someone weeping in grief because their child has gone abroad or because they have lost their property, take care not to be carried away by the impression that these external things involve them in anything bad, but be ready to say immediately, "This person is not distressed by what has happened (for it does not distress anyone else), but by the judgement they make of it." Do not hesitate, however, to sympathise with words, or if it so happens, to weep with them; but take care not to weep inwardly.

Chapter 17: Remember that you are an actor in a play of such a kind as the playwright chooses: short, if he wants it short, long if he wants it long. If he wants you to play the part of a beggar, play even this part well; and so also for the parts of a disabled person, an administrator, or a private individual. For this is your business, to play well the part you are given; but choosing it belongs to another.

Chapter 18: When a raven croaks inauspiciously, do not be carried away by the impression, but straightaway draw a distinction and say to yourself, "This portent signifies nothing with respect to me, but only with regard to my body, my possessions, my reputation, my children or my wife. To me, however, all portents are auspicious, if I wish them so. For however the affair turns out, it is in my power to benefit from it."

Chapter 19: [1] You can be invincible if you never enter a contest in which it is not in your power to win. [2] Beware that, when you see someone honoured before others, enjoying great power, or otherwise highly esteemed, you do not get carried away by the impression and think them happy. For if the essence of good lies in what is in our power, it is wrong to feel envy or jealousy, and you yourself will not wish to be praetor, senator or consul, but someone who is free. There is only one way to attain this end, and this is to have no concern for the things that are not in our power.

Chapter 20: Remember that the insult does not come from the person who abuses you or hits you, but from your judgement that such people are insulting you. Therefore, whenever someone provokes you, be aware that it is your own opinion that provokes you. Try, therefore, in the first place, not to be carried away by your impressions, for if you can gain time and delay, you will more easily control yourself.

Chapter 21: Let death and exile, and all other things that seem terrible, appear daily before your eyes, but especially death—and you will never entertain any abject thought, nor long for anything excessively.

Chapter 22: If you set your heart on philosophy, be prepared from the very start to be ridiculed and jeered at by many people who will say, "Suddenly he's come back to us a philosopher!" and "Where do you suppose he got that supercilious look?" Now, for your part, do not show a supercilious look, but hold to the things that seem best to you, as someone who has been assigned to this post by God. And remember that if you persist in your principles, those who at first ridiculed you will later admire you. But if, on the other hand, you are defeated by such people, you will be doubly ridiculed.

Theater at Hieropolis, Phrygia, Asia Minor (present-day Turkey). Built during Epictetus's lifetime—in his hometown—this theater had a capacity for more than twelve thousand spectators. All-day festivals of drama on every phase of life from the tragic to the comic were presented here. It is not surprising that Epictetus uses the image of the play and the playwright to make his point. *(Forrest E. Baird)*

Chapter 23: If at any time it should happen that you turn to external things with the aim of pleasing someone, understand that you have ruined your life's plan. Be content, then, in everything, with being a philosopher; and if you wish also to be regarded as such, appear so to yourself, and that will be sufficient.

Chapter 24: [1] Do not be troubled by thoughts such as these: "I will be valued by no one my whole life long, a nobody everywhere!" For if lacking value is something bad (which it is), you cannot be involved in anything bad through other people any more than you can be involved in anything disgraceful. Is it any business of yours, then, to acquire status or to be invited to a banquet? Certainly not! How, then, can this be regarded as lacking value? And how will you be a nobody everywhere, when all you have to be is a somebody concerning those things that are in your power, with respect to which you can be someone of the greatest value?

[2] "But my friends," you say, "will lack support."

What do you mean, "lack support"? Certainly they won't get much cash from you, neither will you make them Roman citizens! Who told you, then, that these things are amongst those that are in our power, and not the business of other people? And who can give to others things they do not have themselves?

[3] "Get some money, then," someone says, "so that we can have some too!"

If I can get it whilst also preserving my self-respect, my trustworthiness, my magnanimity, show me how, and I will get it. But if you ask me to forsake those things that are good and my own, in order that you may acquire those things that are not good, see for yourself how unfair and thoughtless you are. Besides, what would you rather have, money, or a friend who is trustworthy and has self-respect? Therefore help me towards this end, and do not ask me to do anything by which I will lose those very qualities.

[4] "But my country," you say, "as far as it depends on me, will be without my help."

I ask again, what help do you mean? It will not have colonnades and bathhouses on your account. But what does that mean? For neither is it provided with shoes by a smith, nor weapons by a shoemaker: it is enough if everyone properly attends to their own business. But if you were to provide it with another trustworthy citizen who has self-respect, would that not be of use to your country?

"Yes."

Well, then, you also cannot be useless to it.

[5] "What place, then," you ask, "will I have in the community?"

That which you may have whilst also preserving your trustworthiness and self-respect. But if, by wishing to be useful, you throw away these qualities, of what use can you be to your community if you become shameless and untrustworthy?

Chapter 25: [1] Has someone been honoured above you at a banquet, or in a greeting, or in being called in to give advice? If these things are good, you should be pleased for the person who has received them. If, on the other hand, they are bad, do not be upset that you did not receive them yourself. Remember, with respect to acquiring things that are not in our power, you cannot expect an equal share if you do not behave in the same way as other people. [2] How is it possible, if you do not hang around someone's door, accompany them or praise them, to have an equal share with people who do these things? You will be unjust, therefore, and insatiable, if you refuse to pay the price for which these things are sold, but wish instead to obtain them for nothing. [3] For what price are lettuces sold? An obol, let's say. When someone else, then, pays an obol and takes the lettuce, whilst you, not paying it go without, do not imagine that this person has gained an advantage over you. Whereas they have the lettuce, you still have the obol that you did not pay.

[4] So, in the present case, if you have not been invited to someone's banquet, that is because you have not paid them the price for which a banquet is sold. They sell it for praise; they sell it for flattery. Pay the price, then, for which it is sold, if you think this will be to your advantage. But if at the same time you do not want to pay the one, yet wish to receive the other, you are insatiable and foolish.

[5] Do you have nothing, then, in place of the banquet? You have this—you have not had to praise the person you did not want to praise, and you have not had to bear the insolence of their doorkeepers.

Chapter 26: We can understand the will of nature from those things in which we do not differ from one another. For example, when our neighbour's slave has broken a cup, we are immediately ready to say, "Well, such things happen." Understand, then, that when your own cup gets broken you should react in just the same way as when someone else's cup gets broken. Apply the same principle to matters of greater importance. Has someone else's child or wife died? There is no one who would not say, "Such is the way of things." But when someone's own child dies they immediately cry, "Woe is me! How wretched I am!" But we should remember how we feel when we hear of the same thing happening to other people.

Chapter 27: Just as a target is not set up in order to be missed, so neither does the nature of evil exist in the world.

Chapter 28: How angry you would be if someone handed over your body to just any person who happened to meet you! Are you not ashamed, then, when you hand over your mind to just any person you happen to meet, such that when they abuse you, you are upset and troubled?

Chapter 29: [1] In every undertaking, consider what comes first and what comes after, then proceed to the action itself. Otherwise you will begin with a rush of enthusiasm having failed to think through the consequences, only to find that later, when difficulties appear, you will give up in disgrace. [2] Do you want to win at the Olympic Games? So do I, by the gods! For that is a fine achievement. But consider what comes first and what comes after, and only then begin the task. You must be well-disciplined, submit to a diet, abstain from sweet things, follow a training schedule at the set times, in the heat, in the cold—no longer having cold drinks or wine just when you like. In a word, you must hand yourself over to your trainer, just as you would to a doctor. And then, when the contest comes, you may strain your wrist, twist your ankle, swallow lots of sand, sometimes be whipped, and after all that, suffer defeat. [3] Think about all this, and if you still want to, then train for the games, otherwise you will behave like children, who first play at being wrestlers, then at being gladiators, then they blow trumpets, then act in a play. In the same way, you will first be an athlete, then a gladiator, then an orator, then a philosopher, but you will do none of these things wholeheartedly—but like a monkey, you will mimic whatever you see, as first one thing, then another, takes your fancy. All this because you do not undertake anything after properly considering it from all sides, but randomly and half-heartedly. [4] So it is when some people go to see a philosopher and hear someone speak such as Euphrates (and who can speak like him?)—they too want to be philosophers. [5] But first consider what sort of undertaking this is, then examine your own capacities to see if you can bear it. So you want to be a pentathlete or a wrestler? Look at your arms, your thighs, examine your back. Different people are naturally suited to different tasks. [6] Do you think that if you do these things you can still eat in the same way, drink in the same way, give way to anger and irritation, just as you do now? You must go without sleep, endure hardship, live away from home, be looked down on by a slave-boy, be laughed at by those whom you meet, and in everything get the worst of it: in honours, in status, in the law courts, and in every little affair. [7] Consider carefully whether you are willing to pay such a price for peace of mind, freedom and serenity, for if you are not, do not approach philosophy, and do not behave like children, being first a philosopher, next a tax-collector, then an orator, and later a procurator of the Emperor. These things are not compatible. You must be one person, either good or bad. You must cultivate either your ruling principle or external things, seek to improve things inside or things outside. That is, you must play the role either of a philosopher or an uneducated person.

Chapter 30: The actions that are appropriate for us can generally be determined by our relationships. He is your father. This tells you to take care of him, to yield to him in all things, to put up with him when he abuses you or beats you.

"But he is a bad father."

Nature did not provide for you a good father, but a father. Your brother wrongs you? Well then, maintain your relationship to him. Do not think about what he is doing, but about what you will have to do if you want to keep your moral character in accordance with nature. For no one can harm you unless you wish it. You will be harmed only when you think you are harmed. If you get into the habit of looking at the relationships implied by "neighbour," "citizen," "commander," you will discover what is proper to expect from each.

Chapter 31: [1] Know that the most important thing regarding devotion to the gods is to have the right opinions about them—that they exist and administer the universe well and justly—to stand ready to obey them, to submit to everything that happens, and to follow it willingly as something being accomplished by the most perfect intelligence. Do this and you will never blame the gods nor accuse them of neglecting you. [2] But you will not be able to do this unless you remove the notions of good and bad from things that are *not* in our power, and apply them only to those things that *are* in our power. For if you believe that anything not in our power is good or bad, then when you fail to get what you want or get what you do not want, it is inevitable that you will blame and hate those responsible. [3] For every living thing naturally flees and avoids things that appear harmful (and their causes), and pursues and admires things that are beneficial (and their causes). It is impossible, then, for someone who thinks they are being harmed to take delight in what they suppose is causing the harm, just as it is impossible for them to take delight in the harm itself. [4] This is why even a father is reproached by his son when he does not give him a share of those things the son regards as good. Thus, in thinking a king's throne to be something good, Eteocles and Polynices became enemies. This is why the farmer reproaches the gods, and so too the sailor, the merchant, and those who lose their wives and children. For people are devoted to what they find advantageous. Therefore, whoever takes proper care of their desires and aversions, at the same time also cares properly for their devotion. [5] But it is everyone's duty to offer libations, sacrifices and first-fruits according to tradition, with a pure disposition, not slovenly or carelessly, neither too meanly nor beyond our means.

Chapter 32: [1] When you make use of divination, remember that you do not know how events will turn out (this is what you have come to learn from the diviner), but if you really are a philosopher you know before you come what sort of thing it is. For if it is one of the things that are not in our power, then necessarily what will happen will be neither good nor bad. [2] Therefore do not bring desire and aversion to the diviner (for, if you do, you will be fearful of what you may hear), but go with the understanding that everything that happens will be indifferent and of no concern to you, for whatever it may be it is in your power to make good use of it, and in this no one can hinder you. Go with confidence to the gods as your counselors, and afterwards, when some advice has been given, remember from whom you have received it and whose counsel you will be disregarding if you disobey. [3] Approach the diviner in the way Socrates thought appropriate, that is, only in those cases when the whole question turns upon the outcome of events, and when there are no means afforded by reason or any other art for discovering what is going to happen. Therefore, when it is necessary to share a danger with a friend or with your country, do not ask the diviner whether you should share the danger. For even if the diviner should happen to tell you that the omens are unfavourable, that death is foretold, or mutilation to some part of the body, or exile—even at this risk, reason requires you to stand by your friend or share the danger with your country. Pay attention, therefore, to the greater diviner, Pythian Apollo, who threw from the temple the man who did not help his friend when he was being murdered.

Chapter 33: [1] From the outset, establish for yourself a certain character and disposition that you will maintain both when you are by yourself and with other people.

[2] For the most part, keep silent, or say only what is required in few words. On rare occasions, when circumstances call for it, we will speak, but not about ordinary things: not about gladiators, nor horse-racing, not about athletes, nor about food and drink (which are the usual topics); and especially do not talk about people, blaming or praising or comparing them. [3] If at all possible, turn the conversation of the company by what you say to more suitable topics; and if you happen to be alone amidst strangers, keep silent. [4] Do not laugh a great deal, nor at many things, nor without restraint. [5] Avoid swearing oaths altogether, if possible; otherwise refuse to do so as far as circumstances allow. [6] Avoid banquets given by strangers and uneducated people. But if there is ever an occasion to join

in them, take every care never to slip into the ways of the uneducated; be assured that if your companion is dirty it is inevitable that in their company you will become dirty yourself, even if you happen to start out clean. [7] As to things concerning the body, take only what bare necessity requires with respect to such things as food, drink, clothing, shelter and household slaves: exclude everything that is for outward show or luxury. [8] As for sex, you should stay pure before marriage as far as you can, but if you have to indulge, do only what is lawful. However, do not be angry with those who do indulge, or criticise them, and do not boast of the fact that you do not yourself indulge. [9] If you are told that someone is saying bad things about you, do not defend yourself against what is said, but answer, "Obviously this person is ignorant of my other faults, otherwise they would not have mentioned only these ones." [10] It is not necessary for the most part to go to public games; but if it is ever appropriate for you to go, show that your first concern is for no one other than yourself—that is, wish only to happen what does happen, and wish only those to win who do win, and in this way you will meet with no hindrance. Refrain entirely from shouting or laughing at anyone, or getting greatly excited. And after you have left, do not talk a great deal about what happened (except in so far as it contributes to your own improvement), for doing so would make it clear that you have been impressed by the spectacle. [11] Do not go randomly or thoughtlessly to public readings; but when you do go, maintain your own dignity and equanimity, and guard against offending anyone. [12] When you are about to meet someone, especially someone who enjoys high esteem, ask yourself what Socrates or Zeno would have done in such circumstances, and you will have no difficulty in making proper use of the occasion. [13] When you go to see someone who has great power, propose to yourself that you will not find them at home, that you will be shut out, that the doors will be slammed in your face, that this person will pay no attention to you. And if in spite of all this it is your duty to go, then go, and bear what happens, and never say to yourself, "It wasn't worth the trouble!" For that is the way of the uneducated person, someone who is bewildered by external things. [14] In conversations, avoid talking at great length or excessively about your own affairs and adventures; however pleasant it may be for you to talk about the risks you have run, it is not equally pleasant for other people to hear about your adventures. [15] Avoid also trying to excite laughter, for this is the sort of behaviour that slips easily into vulgarity and at the same time is liable to diminish the respect your neighbours have for you. [16] There is danger also in lapsing into foul language. So whenever anything like this happens, if the opportunity arises, go so far as to rebuke those who behave in this way; otherwise, by keeping silent and blushing and frowning, make it clear that you disapprove of such language.

Chapter 34: When you get an impression of some pleasure, as in the case of other impressions, guard against being carried away by it, but let the matter wait for you, and delay a little. Now consider these two periods of time, that during which you will enjoy the pleasure, and that when the pleasure has passed during which you will regret it and reproach yourself. Next set against these how pleased you will be if you refrain, and how you will commend yourself. When, however, the time comes to act, take care that the attraction, allure and seductiveness of the pleasure do not overcome you, but set against all this the thought of how much better it is to be conscious of having won this victory over it.

Chapter 35: When you do something from a clear judgement that it ought to be done, never try to avoid being seen doing it, even if you expect most people to disapprove. If, however, it would not be right to do it, avoid the deed itself. But if it *is* right, why be afraid of anyone who wrongly disapproves?

Chapter 36: Just as the propositions "It is day" and "It is night" can be used meaningfully in a disjunctive proposition, but make no sense in a conjunctive proposition, so at a banquet, to choose the largest share may make sense with respect to nourishing the body, but makes no sense for maintaining the proper kind of social feeling. Therefore, when you are eating with someone else, bear in mind not merely the value to your body of what is set before you, but also the value of maintaining the proper respect for your host.

Chapter 37: If you undertake a role that is beyond your capacities, you both disgrace yourself in that one and also fail in the role that you might have filled successfully.

Chapter 38: Just as in walking about you take care not to step on a nail or twist your ankle, so also you should take care not to harm your ruling principle. If we guard against this in every action, we will engage in affairs with greater security.

Chapter 39: Everyone's body is the measure for their possessions, as the foot is a measure for the shoe. If then you hold to this principle you will maintain the proper measure, but if you go beyond it, you will inevitably be carried over a cliff. Thus, in the case of the shoe, if you go beyond the foot, first you will get a gilded shoe, then a purple one, and then an embroidered one. For once you have gone beyond the measure, there is no limit.

Chapter 40: Once they reach the age of fourteen years, women are addressed by men as "madam." Accordingly, when they see that there is nothing else but pleasing men with sex, they begin to use cosmetics and dress up, and to place all their hopes in that. It is worth our while, then, to make sure they understand that they are valued for nothing other than their good behaviour and self-respect.

Chapter 41: It is a sign of foolishness to spend a lot of time on things that concern the body, such as exercising a great deal, eating and drinking a lot, defecating and having sex. These are things that should be done in passing. Instead, you should turn your whole attention to the care of your mind.

Chapter 42: When someone treats you badly or says bad things about you, remember that they do or say these things because they think it is appropriate. This is because it is not possible for someone to act on how things appear *to you*, but on how things appear *to them*. Accordingly, if someone holds a false opinion, because *this* is the person who has been deceived, it is *they* who suffer the harm. In the same way, if someone supposes that a true conjunction is false, it is not the conjunction that is harmed, but the person who has been deceived. If you proceed, then, from these principles, you will be gentle with the person who abuses you, saying on all such occasions, "To them, this is how it seemed."

Chapter 43: Every circumstance has two handles. Use one, and it may be carried; but use the other, and it cannot be carried. Therefore, whenever your brother treats you unjustly, do not take hold of the matter by the handle that he has wronged you (for this is the handle by which the matter cannot be carried), but rather by the other handle, that he is your brother, that you were raised up together, and you will take hold of it using the handle by which it may be carried.

Chapter 44: These inferences are invalid: "I am richer than you, therefore I am better than you"; "I am more eloquent than you, therefore I am better than you." But these are better argued: "I am richer than you, therefore my property is greater than yours;" "I am more eloquent than you, therefore my speech is superior to yours." For *you,* of course, are neither property nor speech.

Chapter 45: Does someone bathe hastily? Do not say that they do so badly, but hastily. Does someone drink a great deal of wine? Do not say that they do this badly, but that they drink a great deal. For until you understand their motives, how do you know that what they do is bad? Understand this and you will never receive convincing impressions but assent to quite different ones.

Chapter 46: [1] On no occasion call yourself a philosopher, and do not talk a great deal amongst uneducated people about philosophical principles, but do what follows from those principles. For example, at a banquet do not talk about how people ought to eat, but eat as someone should. Remember how Socrates had so completely eliminated ostentation that people would come to him wanting him to introduce them to philosophers, and he would take them off to other philosophers: so little did he care about being overlooked. [2] And if a discussion about philosophical principles should arise in uneducated people, keep silent for the most part, for there is great danger that you will immediately vomit up what you have not yet digested. And when someone says to you that you know nothing, and you are not offended, then know that you have begun your work. For sheep do not show the shepherd how much they have eaten by vomiting up their fodder, but they digest their food within to produce wool and milk on the outside. So do not display your philosophical principles to uneducated people, but show them the actions that result from the principles when you digest them.

Chapter 47: Once you have adapted your body to plain simple living, do not make a show of it. When you drink water, do not declare on every occasion that you are drinking water. If you want to train yourself to endure hardships, do it by yourself, away from other people. Do not embrace statues, but if you are ever thirsty, take a mouthful of cold water and spit it out without telling anyone.

Chapter 48: [1] The condition and character of the uneducated person is this: they never look for benefit or harm to come from themselves, but from external things. The condition and character of the philosopher is this: they look for every benefit and harm to come from themselves. [2] The signs that someone is making progress are these: they blame no one, they praise no one, they find fault with no one, they accuse no one, they never say anything of themselves as though they amount to something or know anything. When they are impeded or hindered, they blame themselves. If someone praises them, they laugh inwardly at the person who praises them, and if anyone censures them, they make no defence. They go about as if they were sick, cautious not to disturb what is healing before they are fully recovered. [3] They have rid themselves of all desires, and have transferred their aversion to only those things contrary to nature that are in our power. They have no strong preferences in regard to anything. If they appear foolish or ignorant, they do not care. In a word, they keep guard over themselves as though they are their own enemy lying in wait.

Chapter 49: When someone prides themselves on being able to understand and explain Chrysippus, say to yourself, "If Chrysippus had not written obscurely, this person would have nothing on which to pride themselves." But what do I want? To understand nature, and to follow her. Therefore I seek someone who can explain this to me, and when I hear that Chrysippus can do so, I go to him. But I do not understand his writings; so I seek someone who can explain them to me. Now, up to this point there is nothing to be proud of. When I find someone to explain them, what remains is my putting his principles into practice; this is the only thing to be proud of. But if I am impressed merely by the act of explaining, what else have I accomplished but become a philologist instead of a philosopher, except only that I can explain Chrysippus instead of Homer? No, when someone says to me, "Explain Chrysippus to me," rather than feel proud, I would blush when I am unable to manifest actions that agree and harmonise with Chrysippus' teaching.

Chapter 50: Hold fast to the things herein proposed as if they were laws, as if it would be sacrilegious to transgress them. Pay no attention to what people say about you, for this is no longer yours.

Chapter 51: [1] For how long will you put off demanding of yourself the best, and never to transgress the dictates of reason? You have received the philosophical principles to which you ought to agree, and you have accepted them. What sort of teacher are you waiting for, that you put off improving yourself until they come? You are no longer a child, but a grown adult. If you remain negligent and lazy, always piling up delay upon delay, fixing first one day then another after which you will attend to yourself, you will fail to make progress without even realising, but will continue to live as someone uneducated until you die. [2] From this moment commit yourself to living as an adult, as someone who is making progress, and let everything that appears best to you be a law that you cannot transgress. And if you are presented with anything laborious, or something pleasant, with anything reputable or disreputable, remember that the contest is *now*, that the Olympic Games are *now*, that it is no longer possible to put them off, and that progress is won or lost as the result of just once giving in. [3] This is how Socrates attained perfection, by paying attention to nothing but reason in everything that he encountered. But even if you are not yet Socrates, you should live as someone who wishes to be Socrates.

Chapter 52: [1] The first and most necessary topic in philosophy concerns putting principles to practical use, such as, "We ought not to lie." The second is concerned with demonstrations, such as, "Why is it that we ought not to lie?" And the third is concerned with confirming and articulating the first two: for example, "Why is this a demonstration?" For what is a demonstration, what is entailment, what is contradiction, what is truth, and what is falsehood? [2] Thus the third topic of study is necessary for the second, and the second is necessary for the first. But the most necessary, the one where we ought to rest, is the first. But we do the opposite—we spend our time on the third topic, upon this we expend all our efforts, whilst entirely neglecting the first topic. Thus, whilst at the same time as lying, we are more than ready to explain why it is wrong to lie.

Chapter 53: [1] We must always have these thoughts at hand:

> "Lead me, Zeus, and you too, Destiny,
> Wherever you have assigned me to go,
> and I'll follow without hesitating; but if I am not willing,
> because I am bad, I'll follow all the same."
> —Cleanthes

[2] "Whosoever properly with necessity complies
we say is wise, and understands things divine."
—Euripides

[3] "Well, Crito, if this pleases the gods, let it happen this way."
—Socrates [Crito, 43D]

[4] "Certainly, Anytus and Meletus may put me to death, but they cannot harm me."
—Socrates [Apology, 30C]

MARCUS AURELIUS
A.D. 121–180

Marcus Aurelius was born to a patrician family of Rome. Following the death of his parents, he was raised by his grandfather and eventually adopted by the future emperor, Aurelius Antonius. While still a boy, he became a Stoic, giving himself fully to the study and practice of Stoicism. Following the death of Aurelius Antonius in 161, Marcus Aurelius became emperor of Rome. By nature a gentle and peace-loving man, he nevertheless spent most of his reign fighting in campaigns against the barbarians on the borders of the empire. He was also forced to deal with an epidemic of the plague, a revolt by one of his generals, the death of four of his five sons, and a perceived threat from a new religion, Christianity. Yet as eighteenth-century historian Edward Gibbon explains in *The Decline and Fall of the Roman Empire:*

> His life was the noblest commentary on the precepts of Zeno [of Citium—founder of Stoicism]. He was severe to himself, indulgent to the imperfections of others, just and beneficent to all mankind. He regretted that Avidius Cassius, who excited a rebellion in Syria, had disappointed him, by a voluntary death, of the pleasure of converting an enemy into a friend; and he justified the sincerity of that sentiment, by moderating the zeal of the senate against the adherents of the traitor. War he detested, as the disgrace and calamity of human nature, but when the necessity of a just defence called upon him to take up arms, he readily exposed his person to eight winter campaigns on the frozen banks of the Danube, the severity of which was at last fatal [he died in A.D. 180] to the weakness of his constitution. His memory was revered by a grateful posterity, and above a century after his death, many persons preserved the image of Marcus [Aurelius], among those of their household gods.

While on his miliary campaigns, Marcus Aurelius wrote a book of disconnected reflections on life known as the *Meditations*. These *Meditations* reflect a

Stoic acceptance of nature and of the need for self-control in the face of adversity. As a practical Roman, Marcus Aurelius was not interested in the metaphysical materialism of the early Stoa. Instead, he stressed the need for active benevolence and the acceptance of divine providence, or fate. Touching on several topics, the passage here, translated by George Long, includes Marcus Aurelius's claim that apparent evil is actually a part of the overall good of the universe. As Alexander Pope (*Essay on Man*) said fifteen hundred years later:

> All Nature is but Art, unknown to thee;
> All Chance, Direction, which thou canst not see;
> All Discord, Harmony, not understood;
> All partial Evil, universal Good:
> And, spite of Pride, in erring Reason's spite,
> One truth is clear, "Whatever IS, is RIGHT."

*　　*　　*

A.S.L. Farquharson, *Marcus Aurelius: His Life and His World,* edited by D.A. Rees (Oxford: Basil Blackwell, 1951), provides a helpful general study of Marcus Aurelius. E.R. Dodds, *Pagan and Christian in an Age of Anxiety* (Cambridge: Cambridge University Press, 1965), examines the culture in which Marcus Aurelius lived and wrote; while Henry D. Sedgwick, *Marcus Aurelius* (New Haven, CT: Yale University Press, 1922), and Anthony Richard Birley, *Marcus Aurelius: A Biography* (New Haven, CT: Yale University Press, 1987), provide general biographies. For commentaries on the *Meditations,* see the classic, A.S.L. Farquharson, ed., *The Meditations of the Emperor Marcus Antonius* (Oxford: Clarendon Press, 1944); R.B. Rutherford, *The Meditations of Marcus Aurelius: A Study* (Oxford: Oxford University Press, 1989); and Pierre Hadot, *The Inner Citadel: The Meditations of Marcus Aurelius,* translated by Michael Chase (Cambridge, MA: Harvard University Press, 1998).

MEDITATIONS (in part)

BOOK IV

1. The attitude of that which rules within us towards outside events, if it is in accord with nature, is ever to adapt itself easily to what is possible in the given circumstances. It does not direct its affection upon any particular set of circumstances to work upon, but it starts out toward its objects with reservations, and converts any obstacle into material for its own action, as fire does when it overpowers what is thrown upon it.

Marcus Aurelius Antonius, *Meditations,* translated by G.M.A. Grube (New York: Macmillan. Library of the Liberal Arts, 1963).

Dying Gaul, a Roman copy after a bronze original of ca. 225 B.C. The original statue depicts a casualty inflicted by the troops of Attalus I of Pergamon (241–197 B.C.). Marcus Aurelius, despite his pacifist philosophy, also led his troops against the barbarian Gauls. *(Alinari-Scala/Art Resource)*

A small flame might be quenched by it, but a bright fire very rapidly appropriates to itself whatever is put upon it, consumes it and rises higher because of these obstacles.

2. Let no action be done at random, or in any other way than in accordance with the principle which perfects the art.

3. Men seek retreats for themselves in country places, on beaches and mountains, and you yourself are wont to long for such retreats, but that is altogether unenlightened when it is possible at any hour you please to find a retreat within yourself. For nowhere can a man withdraw to a more untroubled quietude than in his own soul, especially a man who has within him things of which the contemplation will at once put him perfectly at ease, and by ease I mean nothing other than orderly conduct. Grant yourself this withdrawal continually, and refresh yourself. Let these be brief and elemental doctrines which when present will suffice to overwhelm all sorrows and to send you back no longer resentful of the things to which you return.

For what is it you resent? The wickedness of men? Reflect on the conclusion that rational beings are born for the sake of each other, that tolerance is a part of righteousness, and that men do not sin on purpose. Consider how many men have been hostile and suspicious, have hated and waged war, and then been laid out for burial or reduced to ashes. Desist then. Do you resent the portions received from the whole? Consider the alternatives afresh, namely "Providence or atoms," and how many proofs there are that the universe is like a city community. Are you still affected by the things of the body? Reflect that the mind, once it has freed itself and come to know its own capacities, is no longer involved in the movements of animal life, whether these be smooth or tumultuous. For the rest, recall all you have heard about pain and pleasure, to which you have given assent.

Does paltry fame disturb you? Look how swift is the forgetting of all things in the chaos of infinite time before and after, how empty is noisy applause, how liable to change and uncritical are those who seem to speak well of us, how narrow the boundaries within which fame is confined. The whole earth is but a point in the universe, and how small a part of the earth is the corner in which you live. And how many are those who there will praise you, and what sort of men are they?

From now on keep in mind the retreat into this little territory within yourself. Avoid spasms and tensions above all: be free and look at your troubles like a man, a citizen and a mortal creature. Among the foremost things which you will look into are these two: first, that external matters do not affect the soul but stand quietly outside it, while true disturbances come from the inner judgment; second, that everything you see has all but changed already and is no more. Keep constantly in mind in how many things you yourself have witnessed changes already. The universe is change, life is understanding.

4. If we have intelligence in common, so we have reason which makes us reasoning beings, and that practical reason which orders what we must or must not do; then the law too is common to us and, if so, we are citizens; if so, we share a common government; if so, the universe is, as it were, a city—for what other common government could one say is shared by all mankind?

From this, the common city, we derive our intelligence, our reason and our law—from what else? Just as the dry earth-element in me has been portioned off from earth somewhere, and the water in me from the other element, the air or breath from some other source and the dry and fiery from a source of its own (for nothing comes from what does not exist or returns to it), so also then the intelligence comes from somewhere.

5. Death, like birth, is a mystery of nature. The one is a joining together of the same elements into which the other is a dissolving. In any case, it is nothing of which one should be ashamed, for it is not incompatible with the nature of a rational being or the logic of its composition.

6. Their nature inevitably required that they behave in this way. He who wants this not to be wants a fig tree not to produce its acrid juice. In any case remember this: within a very short time both you and he will have died, and soon not even your name will survive.

7. Discard the thought of injury, and the words "I have been injured" are gone; discard the words "I have been injured," and the injury is gone.

8. What does not make a man worse does not make his life worse, and does him no injury, external or internal.

9. The nature of the universally beneficial has inevitably brought this about.

10. "Everything which happens, is right." Examine this saying carefully and you will find it so. I do not mean right merely in the sense that it fits the pattern of events, but in the sense of just, as if someone were giving each his due. Examine this then as you have begun to do, and, whatever you do, do it as a good man should, as the word good is properly understood. Safeguard this goodness in your every action.

11. Do not think the thoughts of an insolent man or those he wishes you to think, but see things as they truly are.

12. You should always be ready for two things, first, to do only what reason, as embodied in the arts of kingship and legislation, perceives to be to the benefit of mankind; second, to change your course if one be present to put you right and make you abandon a certain opinion. Such change, however, should always result from being convinced of what is just and for the common good, and what you choose to do must be of that nature, not because pleasure or fame may result from it.

13. "You are endowed with reason." "I am." "Then why not use it, for, if it fulfills its proper function, what more do you want?"

14. You exist as a part of the Whole. You will disappear into the Whole which created you, or rather you will be taken up into the creative Reason when the change comes.

15. Many grains of incense on the same altar; one was cast earlier, the other later, but it makes no difference.

16. Within ten days you will seem a god to the same men who now think you a beast or an ape, if you go back to your principles and the worship of Reason.

17. Live not as if you had ten thousand years before you. Necessity is upon you. While you live, while you may, become good.

18. How much ease he gains who does not look at what his neighbor says or does or thinks, but only at what he himself is doing in order that his own action may be just, pious, and good. Do not glance aside at another's black character but run the straight course to the finishing line, without being diverted.

19. The man who thrills at the thought of later fame fails to realize that every one of those who remember him will very shortly die, as well as himself. So will their successors, until all memory of him is quenched as it travels through the minds of men, the flame of whose life is lit and then put out. But suppose those who will remember you to be immortal and the memory of you everlasting; even so, what is it to you? And I do not mean that praise is nothing to you when dead, but what is it to you while you live, except insofar as it affects your management of affairs? For now you inopportunely neglect nature's gift of virtue while you cling to some other concern.

20. All that has any beauty at all owes this to itself, and is complete in itself, but praise is no part of it. Nothing becomes either better or worse for being praised, and I mean this to apply also to things more commonly called beautiful, such as works of nature or works of art. As for the truly beautiful, it has no need of anything further, any more than does law, or truth, or kindness or reverence. Which of these things is made beautiful by praise or destroyed by censure? Does an emerald become less beautiful if it is not praised? What of gold, ivory, purple, a lyre, a dagger, a little flower or a bush?

21. If souls live on, how has the air of heaven made room for them through eternity? How has the earth made room for such a long time for the bodies of those who are buried in it? Just as on earth, after these bodies have persisted for a while, their change and decomposition makes room for other bodies, so with the souls which have migrated into the upper air. After they have remained there for a certain time, they change and are dissolved and turned to fire as they are absorbed into the creative Reason, and in this way make room for those additional souls who come to share their dwelling place. Thus might one answer on the assumption that souls live on.

One should not, however, consider only the multitude of bodies that are buried thus, but also take into account the multitude of animals eaten every day by us and by other animals, how great is the number thus consumed and in a manner buried in the bodies of those who eat them. Yet there is room for them nevertheless because they are transformed into blood and changed into air and fire.

Where lies the investigation of the truth in this matter? In distinguishing between the matter and the cause.

22. Do not wander aimlessly, but give every impulse its just due, and in every sensation preserve the power of comprehension.

23. Everything which is in tune with you, O Universe, is in tune with me. Nothing which happens at the right time for you is early or late for me. Everything, O Nature, which your seasons produce is fruit to me. All things come from you, exist in you, and

will return to you. If he could say: "Beloved city of Cecrops," will you not say: "Beloved city of Zeus"?

24. "Do but little, if you would have contentment." Surely it is better to do what is necessary, as much as the reason of one who is by nature a social creature demands, and in the manner reason requires it to be done. This will not only bring the contentment derived from right conduct, but also that of doing little, since most of our words and actions are unnecessary and whoever eliminates these will have more leisure and be less disturbed. Hence one should on each occasion remind oneself: "Surely this is not one of the necessary actions?" One should eliminate not only unnecessary actions but also unnecessary imaginings, for then no irrelevant actions will follow.

25. Make trial of how the life of the good man turns out for you, of the man who is glad of the share he receives from the Whole and satisfied if his own action be just and his own disposition kindly.

26. You have seen those things; look also at these: do not disturb yourself, achieve simplicity in yourself. Someone does wrong? The wrong is to himself. Something has happened to you? It is well. From the beginning all that happens has been ordained and fated for you as your part of the Whole. In a word, life is short; we must therefore derive benefit from the present circumstances with prudence and with justice. Be sober and relaxed.

27. Either a universe with order and purpose or a medley thrown together by chance, but that too has order. Or can there be order of a kind in your inner world, but no order in the Whole, especially as all things are distinguished from one another, yet intermingle, and respond to each other?

28. A character that is black, effeminate, obstinate, beast-like, subhuman, childish, stupid, repulsive, vulgar, money-grubbing, tyrannical.

29. If the man who does not understand the truths embodied in the universe is a stranger in it, no less a stranger is he who does not understand what happens in the world of sense. An exile is he who flees from social principle; blind, who keeps the eye of his mind closed; a beggar, who has need of another and does not possess within himself all that is of use in life. A tumor on the universe is he who cuts himself off in rebellion against the logic of our common nature because he is dissatisfied with his lot, for it is that nature which brought it about, as it also brought you about. He is but a splinter off the community who separates his own soul from that of all rational beings, which is one.

30. One man practices philosophy though he has no tunic, another, though he has no book. Yet another man is half naked: "I have no bread," says he, "but I stay on the path of Reason." I have the nurture provided by learning, but I do not stay on that path.

31. Treasure what little you have learnt and find refreshment in it. Go through what remains of your life as one who has wholeheartedly entrusted all that is his to the gods and has not made himself either despot or slave to any man.

32. Consider, for the sake of argument, the times of Vespasian; you will see all the same things: men marrying, begetting children, being ill, dying, fighting wars, feasting, trading, farming, flattering, asserting themselves, suspecting, plotting, praying for the death of others, grumbling at their present lot, falling in love, hoarding, longing for con-sulships and kingships. But the life of those men no longer exists, anywhere. Then turn to the times of Trajan; again, everything is the same; and that life too is dead. Contemplate and observe in the same way the records of the other periods of time, indeed of whole nations: how many men have struggled eagerly and then, after a little

while, fell and were resolved into their elements. But above all call to mind those whom you yourself have witnessed vainly struggling because they would not act in accord with their own nature and cling to it, and be satisfied with it. It is necessary thus to remind ourselves that every action requires the attention we give it to be measured according to its value, for if you do not dwell more than is fitting upon things of lesser importance, you will not impatiently give up the struggle.

33. Words of old in common usage now sound strange; so the names of men much sung of old are strange today. Camilius, Caeso, Volesus, Dentatus, a little later Scipio and Cato, too, then even Augustus, then even Hadrian and Antoninus. For all things fade and quickly become legend, soon to be lost in total forgetting. This I say of those who shone in wondrous glory; as for other men, they are no sooner dead than "unknown, unheard of." But in any case, what is eternal remembrance? It is altogether vain.

What is it which should earnestly concern us? This only: a just mind, actions for the common good, speech which never lies, and a disposition which welcomes all that happens as necessary and comprehensible, as flowing from a like origin and source.

34. Surrender yourself willingly to Clotho to help her spin whatever fate she will.

35. All is ephemeral, the one remembering and the one remembered.

36. Observe continually all that is born through change, and accustom yourself to reflect that the nature of the Whole loves nothing so much as to change existing things and to make similar new things. All that exists is in a sense the seed of what will be born from it, but you regard as seeds only those which are cast into the earth or the womb. But that is too unenlightened.

37. You will now soon be dead, but you are not yet simple, nor undisturbed, nor free of the suspicion that harm may come to you from outside, nor gracious to all, nor convinced that the only wisdom lies in righteous action.

38. Look to their directing minds, observe the wise: what they avoid and what they pursue.

39. Whether a thing is bad for you does not depend upon another man's directing mind, nor upon any turn or change in your environment. Upon what then? Upon that part of you which judges what is bad. Let it make no such judgment and all is well. Even when that which is closest to it, your body, is cut, burnt, suppurating or festering, let the judging part of you keep calm. That is, let it judge that anything which happens equally to a bad and a good man cannot be either bad or good; for that which happens both to the man who lives in disaccord with nature and to the man who lives in accord with it cannot itself be either in accord with nature or contrary to it.

40. One should continually think of the universe as one living being, with one substance and one soul—how all it contains falls under its one unitary perception, how all its actions derive from one impulse, how all things together cause all that happens, and the nature of the resulting web and pattern of events.

41. You are a little soul carrying a corpse, as Epictetus says.

42. There is no evil in things in process of change, nor any good in things resulting from change.

43. Time is a river of things that become, with a strong current. No sooner is a thing seen than it has been swept away, and something else is being carried past, and still another thing will follow.

44. Everything that happens is as customary and understandable as the rose in springtime or the fruit in summer. The same is true of disease, death, slander and conspiracy, and all the things which delight or pain foolish men.

45. What happens next is always intimately related to what went before. It is not a question of merely adding up disparate things connected by inevitable succession, but events are logically interdependent. Just as the realities are established in tune with one another, so, in the world of sense, phenomena do not occur merely in succession, but they display an amazing affinity with one another.

46. Always remember the words of Heraclitus that "the death of earth becomes water and the death of water becomes air, and that of air, fire, and so back again." Remember also what he says about the man who has forgotten whither the road leads. And "men are at odds with that with which they are in most constant touch, namely the Reason" which governs all; and again, "those things seem strange to them which they meet every day"; and "we must not act and speak as if asleep," for even then we seem to act and speak. And that one should not accept things "like children from parents" simply because they have been handed down to us.

47. If a god were to tell you that you will die tomorrow, or at any rate the day after, you would not make much of the difference between the day after and tomorrow—not unless you were altogether ignoble, for how short is the time between!

So now consider that the difference between the last possible year and tomorrow is no great matter.

48. Think continually how many doctors have died who often knit their brows over their dying patients, how many astrologers who had foretold the deaths of others as a matter of importance, how many philosophers who had discoursed at great length on death and immortality, how many heroic warriors who had killed many men, how many tyrants who had used their power over men's lives with terrible brutality, as if immortal themselves. How often have not whole cities died, if I may use the phrase, Helike, Pompeii, Herculaneum, and innumerable others. Go over in your mind the dead whom you have known, one after the other: one paid the last rites to a friend and was himself laid out for burial by a third, who also died; and all in a short time. Altogether, human affairs must be regarded as ephemeral, and of little worth: yesterday sperm, tomorrow a mummy or ashes.

Journey then through this moment of time in accord with nature, and graciously depart, as a ripened olive might fall, praising the earth which produced it, grateful to the tree that made it grow.

49. Be like a rock against which the waves of the sea break unceasingly. It stands unmoved, and the feverish waters around it are stilled.

"I am unfortunate because this has happened to me." No indeed, but I am fortunate because I endure what has happened without grief, neither shaken by the present nor afraid of the future. Something of this sort could happen to any man, but not every man can endure it without grieving. Why then is this more unfortunate than that is fortunate? Would you call anything a misfortune which is not incompatible with man's nature, or call incompatible with the nature of man that which is not contrary to his nature's purpose? You have learned to know that purpose. What has happened can then in no way prevent you from being just, great-hearted, chaste, wise, steadfast, truthful, self-respecting and free, or prevent you from possessing those other qualities in the presence of which man's nature finds its own fulfillment. Remember in the future, when something happens which tends to make you grieve, to cling to this doctrine: this is no misfortune, but to endure it nobly is good fortune.

50. It is simple but effective in helping you despise death to go over the list of those who clung to life a long time. What advantage have they over those who died prematurely? Anyway, wherever are they? Caedicianus, Fabius, Julianus, Lepidus, and any

other there may be. They assisted at the burial of many and then were buried themselves. In any case, the difference in time is short; among what great troubles we endure it to the end, in what poor company, in how puny a body! Is it not rather a burden? See the abyss of past time behind you and another infinity of time in front. In that context, what difference is there between one who lives three days and a Nestor who lives for three generations?

51. Hasten always along the short road—the road in accord with nature is short—so that you always say and do what is most wholesome. To keep this aim before one frees a man from the wearisome troubles of military service, management of all kinds of affairs, and affectation.

PYRRHO
ca. 360–ca. 270 B.C.

SEXTUS EMPIRICUS
A.D. third century

Pyrrho was born in the town of Elis on the Greek Peloponnesus. He joined the expedition of Alexander the Great to India and there met several of the learned magi of the East. Following Alexander's death in 323 B.C., Pyrrho returned to Elis and spent the rest of his life teaching there.

Pyrrho was greatly influenced by the Democritean notion that the world is not as our sense perceptions would lead us to believe. According to Pyrrho, we can know only appearances relative to each person—there is no way we can know things as they really are. This means that any statement we might make about reality can be opposed by an equally valid statement that contradicts it. Given this inability to know which assertion is true, Pyrrho said we should develop an attitude of "suspended judgment" <epoche> and thus gradually attain "unperturbedness" or "quietude" <ataraxia>. This claimed inability to know came to be called "Skepticism."

Pyrrho left no writings, but his philosophy is well represented by the works of the third-century A.D. author Sextus Empiricus. Little is known about this writer other than that he was apparently a Greek physician, that he was the head of a Skeptical school in some major city, and that he wrote the Outlines of Pyrrhonism. The selection reprinted here, in the R.G. Bury translation, begins by dividing philosophers into three categories: "Dogmatists," who claim to know the truth; those inheritors of Plato's Academy, such as Carneades, who made the opposite dogmatic claim that no truth is possible; and the Pyrrhoist skeptics, who suspend judgment while looking for the truth. Sextus Empiricus goes on to explain the nature of such a suspension of judgment and concludes with a discussion of how this suspension leads to "quietude." In the process of his explication, Sextus avoids self-refutation by explaining that he is not describing what is really true (which would be dogmatism), but only how things *appear* to him to be.

As for its impact, elements of Pyrrhoist skepticism are echoed in Hegel's concept of the dialectic (with the claim that every statement can be contradicted by its opposite) and in Husserl's use of <*epochē*>. Thinkers such as Montaigne, Hume, and Santayana have used skepticism to attack the dogmatic philosophies of their day. While it has rarely been an established school of thought, skepticism has raised questions for all systematic philosophers since the time of Pyrrho.

*   *   *

For general accounts of Greek skepticism, see Mary Mills Patrick, *The Greek Skeptics* (New York: Columbia University Press, 1929); Charlotte L. Stough, *Greek Skepticism: A Study in Epistemology* (Berkeley: University of California Press, 1969); Leo Groarke, *Greek Scepticism: Anti-Realist Trends in Ancient Thought* (Montreal: McGill-Queen's University Press, 1990); R.J. Hankinson, *The Skeptics* (Oxford: Routledge, 1995); Myles Burnyest and Michael Frede, *The Original Sceptics* (Indianapolis, IN: Hackett, 1996); and a collection of essays, Malcolm Schofield, Myles Burnyeat, and Jonathan Barnes, eds., *Doubt and Dogmatism: Studies in Hellenistic Epistemology* (Oxford: Clarendon Press, 1979). For a study of Pyrrho, see Richard Bett, *Pyrrho, His Antecedents, and His Legacy* (Oxford: Oxford University Press, 2000). For works on Sextus Empiricus, see Mary Mills Patrick, *Sextus Empiricus and Greek Scepticism* (Cambridge: D. Bell, 1899) and Benson Mates, *The Skeptic Way: Sextus Empiricus's Outlines of Pyrrhonism* (Oxford: Oxford University Press, 1995). Edwyn Robert Bevan, *Stoics and Skeptics* (Oxford: Clarendon Press, 1913); Benson Mates, *Stoic Logic* (Berkeley: University of California Press, 1953); and Adrian Kuzminski, *Pyrronism: How the Ancient Greeks Reinvented Buddhism* (Lanham, MD: Lexington Books, 2008) provide more specialized studies.

OUTLINES OF PYRRHONISM (in part)

BOOK I

1. *Of the Main Difference Between Philosophic Systems.* The natural result of any investigation is that the investigators either discover the object of their search or deny that it is discoverable and confess it to be inapprehensible or persist in their search. So, too, with regard to the objects investigated by philosophy, this is probably why some have claimed to have discovered the truth, others have asserted that it cannot be apprehended, while others again go on inquiring. Those who believe they have discovered it are the "Dogmatists," specially so called—Aristotle, for example, and Epicurus and the Stoics and certain others; Cleitomachus and Carneades and other Academics

Reprinted by permission of the publishers and the Loeb Classical Library from Sextus Empiricus, *Outlines of Pyrrhonism,* Book I, Chapters 1–13, translated by Rev. R.G. Bury (Cambridge, MA: Harvard University Press, 1933). Copyright © 1993 by Harvard University Press.

treat it as inapprehensible; the Sceptics keep on searching. Hence it seems reasonable to hold that the main types of philosophy are three—the Dogmatic, the Academic, and the Sceptic. Of the other systems it will best become others to speak: our task at present is to describe in outline the Sceptic doctrine, first premising that of none of our future statements do we positively affirm that the fact is exactly as we state it, but we simply record each fact, like a chronicler, as it appears to us at the moment.

2. *Of the Arguments of Scepticism.* Of the Sceptic philosophy one argument (or branch of exposition) is called "general," the other "special." In the general argument we set forth the distinctive features of Scepticism, stating its purport and principles, its logical methods, criterion, and end or aim; the "Tropes," also, or "Modes," which lead to suspension of judgment, and in what sense we adopt the Sceptic formulae, and the distinction between Scepticism and the philosophies which stand next to it. In the special argument we state our objections regarding the several divisions of so-called philosophy. Let us, then, deal first with the general argument, beginning our description with the names given to the Sceptic School.

3. *Of the Nomenclature of Scepticism.* The Sceptic School, then, is also called "Zetetic" from its activity in investigation and inquiry, and "Ephectic" or Suspensive from the state of mind produced in the inquirer after his search, and "Aporetic" or Dubitative either from its habit of doubting and seeking, as some say, or from its indecision as regards assent and denial, and "Pyrrhonean" from the fact that Pyrrho appears to us to have applied himself to Scepticism more thoroughly and more conspicuously than his predecessors.

4. *What Scepticism Is.* Scepticism is an ability, or mental attitude, which opposes appearances to judgements in any way whatsoever, with the result that, owing to the equipollence of the objects and reasons thus opposed, we are brought firstly to a state of mental suspense and next to a state of "unperturbedness" or quietude. Now we call it an "ability" not in any subtle sense, but simply in respect of its "being able." By "appearances" we now mean the objects of sense-perception, whence we contrast them with the objects of thought or "judgements." The phrase "in any way whatsoever" can be connected either with the word "ability," to make us take the word "ability," as we said, in its simple sense, or with the phrase "opposing appearances to judgements"; for inasmuch as we oppose these in a variety of ways—appearances to appearances, or judgements to judgements, or *alternando* appearances to judgements,—in order to ensure the inclusion of all these antitheses we employ the phrase "in any way whatsoever." Or, again, we join "in any way whatsoever" to "appearances and judgements" in order that we may not have to inquire how the appearances appear or how the thought-objects are judged, but may take these terms in the simple sense. The phrase "opposed judgements" we do not employ in the sense of negations and affirmations only but simply as equivalent to "conflicting judgements." "Equipollence" we use of equality in respect of probability and improbability, to indicate that no one of the conflicting judgements takes precedence of any other as being more probable. "Suspense" is a state of mental rest owing to which we neither deny nor affirm anything. "Quietude" is an untroubled and tranquil condition of soul. And how quietude enters the soul along with suspension of judgement we shall explain in our chapter [12] "What Is the End of Scepticism."

5. *Of the Sceptic.* In the definition of the Sceptic system there is also implicitly included that of the Pyrrhonean philosopher: he is the man who participates in this "ability."

6. *Of the Principles of Scepticism.* The originating cause of Scepticism is, we say, the hope of attaining quietude. Men of talent, who were perturbed by the contradictions

in things and in doubt as to which of the alternatives they ought to accept, were led on to inquire what is true in things and what false, hoping by the settlement of the question to attain quietude. The main basic principle of the Sceptic system is that of opposing to every proposition an equal proposition; for we believe that as a consequence of this we end by ceasing to dogmatize.

7. *Does the Sceptic Dogmatize?* When we say that the Sceptic refrains from dogmatizing we do not use the term "dogma," as some do, in the broader sense of "approval of a thing" (for the Sceptic gives assent to the feelings which are the necessary results of sense-impressions, and he would not, for example, say when feeling hot or cold "I believe that I am not hot or cold"); but we say that "he does not dogmatize" using "dogma" in the sense, which some give it, of "assent to one of the non-evident objects of scientific inquiry"; for the Pyrrhonean philosopher assents to nothing that is non-evident. Moreover, even in the act of enunciating the Sceptic formulae concerning things non-evident—such as the formula "No more (one thing than another)," or the formula "I determine nothing," or any of the others which we shall presently mention,—he does not dogmatize. For whereas the dogmatizer posits the things about which he is said to be dogmatizing as really existent, the Sceptic does not posit these formulae in any absolute sense; for he conceives that, just as the formula "All things are false" asserts the falsity of itself as well as of everything else, as does the formula "Nothing is true," so also the formula "No more" asserts that itself like all the rest, is "No more this than that," and thus cancels itself along with the rest. And of the other formulae we say the same. If then, while the dogmatizer posits the matter of his dogma as substantial truth, the Sceptic enunciates his formulae so that they are virtually canceled by themselves, he should not be said to dogmatize in his enunciation of them. And, most important of all, in his enunciation of these formulae he states what appears to himself and announces his own impression in an undogmatic way, without making any positive assertion regarding the external realities.

8. *Has the Sceptic a Doctrinal Rule?* We follow the same lines in replying to the question "Has the Sceptic a doctrinal rule?" For if one defines a "doctrinal rule" as "adherence to a number of dogmas which are dependent both on one another and on appearances," and defines "dogma" as "assent to a non-evident proposition," then we shall say that he has not a doctrinal rule. But if one defines "doctrinal rule" as "procedure which, in accordance with appearance, follows a certain line of reasoning, that reasoning indicating how it is possible to seem to live rightly (the word 'rightly' being taken, not as referring to virtue only, but in a wider sense) and tending to enable one to suspend judgement," then we say that he has a doctrinal rule. For we follow a line of reasoning which, in accordance with appearances, points us to a life conformable to the customs of our country and its laws and institutions, and to our own instinctive feelings.

9. *Does the Sceptic Deal with Physics?* We make a similar reply also to the question "Should the Sceptic deal with physical problems?" For while, on the one hand, so far as regards making firm and positive assertions about any of the matters dogmatically treated in physical theory, we do not deal with physics; yet, on the other hand, in respect of our mode of opposing to every proposition an equal proposition and of our theory of quietude we do treat of physics. This, too, is the way in which we approach the logical and ethical branches of so-called "philosophy."

10. *Do the Sceptics Abolish Appearances?* Those who say that "the Sceptics abolish appearances," or phenomena, seem to me to be unacquainted with the statements of our School. For, as we said above, we do not overthrow the affective sense-impressions which induce our assent involuntarily; and these impressions are "the appearances." And when we

question whether the underlying object is such as it appears, we grant the fact that it appears, and our doubt does not concern the appearance itself but the account given of the appearance,—and that is a different thing from questioning the appearance itself. For example, honey appears to us to be sweet (and this we grant, for we perceive sweetness through the senses), but whether it is also sweet in its essence is for us a matter of doubt, since this is not an appearance but a judgement regarding the appearance. And even if we do actually argue against the appearances, we do not propound such arguments with the intention of abolishing appearances, but by way of pointing out the rashness of the Dogmatists; for if reason is such a trickster as to all but snatch away the appearances from under our very eyes, surely we should view it with suspicion in the case of things non-evident so as not to display rashness by following it.

11. *Of the Criterion of Scepticism.* That we adhere to appearances is plain from what we say about the Criterion of the Sceptic School. The word "Criterion" is used in two senses: in the one it means "the standard regulating belief in reality or unreality," (and this we shall discuss in our refutation); in the other it denotes the standard of action by conforming to which in the conduct of life we perform some actions and abstain from others; and it is of the latter that we are now speaking. The criterion, then, of the Sceptic School is, we say, the appearance, giving this name to what is virtually the sense-presentation. For since this lies in feeling and involuntary affection, it is not open to question. Consequently, no one, I suppose, disputes that the underlying object has this or that appearance; the point in dispute is whether the object is in reality such as it appears to be.

Adhering, then, to appearances we live in accordance with the normal rules of life, undogmatically, seeing that we cannot remain wholly inactive. And it would seem that this regulation of life is fourfold, and that one part of it lies in the guidance of Nature, another in the constraint of the passions, another in the tradition of laws and customs, another in the instruction of the arts. Nature's guidance is that by which we are naturally capable of sensation and thought; constraint of the passions is that whereby hunger drives us to food and thirst to drink; tradition of customs and laws, that whereby we regard piety in the conduct of life as good, but impiety as evil; instruction of the arts, that whereby we are not inactive in such arts as we adopt. But we make all these statements undogmatically.

12. *What Is the End of Scepticism?* Our next subject will be the End of the Sceptic system. Now an "End" is "that for which all actions or reasonings are undertaken, while it exists for the sake of none"; or, otherwise, "the ultimate object of appetency." We assert still that the Sceptic's End is quietude in respect of matters of opinion and moderate feeling in respect of things unavoidable. For the Sceptic, having set out to philosophize with the object of passing judgement on the sense-impressions and ascertaining which of them are true and which false, so as to attain quietude thereby, found himself involved in contradictions of equal weight, and being unable to decide between them suspended judgement; and as he was thus in suspense there followed, as it happened, the state of quietude in respect of matters of opinion. For the man who opines that anything is by nature good or bad is forever being disquieted: when he is without the things which he deems good he believes himself to be tormented by things naturally bad and he pursues after the things which are, as he thinks, good; which when he has obtained he keeps falling into still more perturbations because of his irrational and immoderate elation, and in his dread of a change of fortune he uses every endeavour to avoid losing the things which he deems good. On the other hand, the man who determines nothing as to what is

naturally good or bad neither shuns nor pursues anything eagerly; and, in consequence, he is unperturbed.

The Sceptic, in fact, had the same experience which is said to have befallen the painter Apelles. Once, they say, when he was painting a horse and wished to represent in the painting the horse's foam, he was so unsuccessful that he gave up the attempt and flung at the picture the sponge on which he used to wipe the paints off his brush, and the mark of the sponge produced the effect of a horse's foam. So, too, the Sceptics were in hopes of gaining quietude by means of a decision regarding the disparity of the objects of sense and of thought, and being unable to effect this they suspended judgement; and they found that quietude, as if by chance, followed upon their suspense, even as a shadow follows its substance. We do not, however, suppose that the Sceptic is wholly untroubled; but we say that he is troubled by things unavoidable; for we grant that he is old at times and thirsty, and suffers various affections of that kind. But even in these cases, whereas ordinary people are afflicted by two circumstances,— namely, by the affections themselves and in no less a degree, by the belief that these conditions are evil by nature,—the Sceptic, by his rejection of the added belief in the natural badness of all these conditions, escapes here too with less discomfort. Hence we say that, while in regard to matters of opinion the Sceptic's End is quietude, in regard to things unavoidable it is "moderate affection." But some notable Sceptics have added the further definition "suspension of judgement in investigations."

13. *Of the General Modes Leading to Suspension of Judgement.* Now that we have been saying that tranquility follows on suspension of judgement, it will be our next task to explain how we arrive at this suspension. Speaking generally, one may say that it is the result of setting things in opposition. We oppose either appearances to appearances or objects of thought to objects of thought or *alternando.* For instance, we oppose appearances when we say "The same tower appears round from a distance, but square from close at hand"; and thoughts to thoughts, when in answer to him who argues the existence of Providence from the order of the heavenly bodies we oppose the fact that often the good fare ill and the bad fare well, and draw from this the inference that Providence does not exist. And thoughts we oppose to appearances, as when Anaxagoras countered the notion that snow is white with the argument, "Snow is frozen water, and water is black; therefore snow also is black." With a different idea we oppose things present sometimes to things present, as in the foregoing examples, and sometimes to things past or future, as, for instance, when someone propounds to us a theory which we are unable to refute, we say to him in reply, "Just as, before the birth of the founder of the School to which you belong, the theory it holds was not as yet apparent as a sound theory, although it was really in existence, so likewise it is possible that the opposite theory to that which you now propound is already really existent, though not yet apparent to us, so that we ought not as yet to yield assent to this theory which at the moment seems to be valid."

PLOTINUS
ca. A.D. 204–270

The last great school of Greek philosophy was Neoplatonism, and its most famous representative was Plotinus, born in Lykopolis, Egypt, in A.D. 204. In his late-twenties, Plotinus began to study in Alexandria with Ammonius Saccas, a shadowy figure who was also the teacher of the theologian Origen. After eleven years with Ammonius, Plotinus joined an expedition to Persia to learn Persian and Indian wisdom. The trek proved unsuccessful and Plotinus moved to Rome. There he established a school of philosophy and a friendship with the emperor Gallenius. At one point, he sought permission to found a city based on Plato's *Republic,* but the plan came to naught. He stayed in Rome, teaching and writing, until the death of the emperor in 268. He then moved to the home of a friend where he died in 270, apparently from leprosy.

Developing Plato's dualistic understanding of reality, Plotinus taught that true reality lies "beyond" the physical world. This "reality beyond reality" has no limits and so cannot be described by words, since words invariably have limits. Plotinus, again borrowing from Plato, calls this ultra-reality the "Good" or the "One." The One/Good has no limits and is so supremely rich that it overflows or "emanates" to produce "Intellectual-Principle" or "Divine Mind" <*nous*>. This Intellectual-Principle, in turn, overflows and "Divine-Soul" emanates from it. This process continues as Divine-Soul generates the material world. The lowest level of emanation, at the furthest extreme from the One/Good, is the utter formlessness and unreality of matter.

The goal of philosophy is to awaken individuals to the reality beyond the material world. But philosophy alone cannot take a person to the highest reality of the One. Only mystical experience can unite an individual with the One. Plotinus himself claimed to have achieved such a union four times during his life.

Plotinus's writings were edited by one of his pupils, Porphyry, in the form of six groups of nine "Tractates" (treatises), published as the so-called *Enneads* (from the Greek word for "nine"). The selections given here, in the A.H. Armstrong translation, begin with the Treatise on Beauty. This Tractate explains how the ascent of the soul to the One/Good is dependent on the beauty of soul, a god-like disposition. Plotinus' description parallels the ascending dialectic in Plato's *Symposium* (210a). The second selection discusses the three "hypostases," or stages—the One/Good, the Intellectual-Principle, and the World-Soul—explaining how each is generated from the one above. The final selection is thought to have been written late in Plotinus's life and gives a detailed description of the soul's ascent to ecstatic union. At the end of this tractate, Plotinus, in order to represent the One/Good, borrows Plato's image of the sun from the Myth of the Cave.

Neoplatonism, with its emphasis on the otherworldly and the need for escape from the physical world, was the perfect philosophy for the chaotic final days of the Roman Empire. Plotinus' thought had a profound influence on Christian thought, especially on St. Augustine. Indeed, if St. Thomas is considered an Aristotelian, St. Augustine may be called a Neoplatonist. Many later thinkers, such as Eckhart, Nicolas of Cusa, Comenius, Boehme, Hegel, and Schelling, also had their philosophy molded by Neoplatonist doctrines.

* * *

Joseph Katz, *Plotinus' Search for the Good* (New York: King's Crown Press, 1950); Émile Bréhier, *The Philosophy of Plotinus,* translated by Joseph Thomas (Chicago: University of Chicago Press, 1958); and Lloyd P. Gerson, *Plotinus* (Oxford: Routledge, 1994) are good introductions to the study of Plotinus. For more advanced studies, see A.H. Armstrong, *The Architecture of the Intelligible Universe in the Philosophy of Plotinus* (Cambridge: Cambridge University Press, 1940); J.M. Rist, *Plotinus: The Road to Reality* (Cambridge: Cambridge University Press, 1967); Lloyd P. Gerson, ed., *The Cambridge Companion to Plotinus* (Cambridge: Cambridge University Press, 1996); and Margaret R. Miles, *Plotinus on Body and Beauty* (Oxford: Basil Blackwell, 1999). E.R. Dodds, *Select Passages Illustrating Neoplatonism,* translated by E.R. Dodds (New York: Macmillan, 1923), and Dominic J. O'Meara, *Plotinus: An Introduction to the Enneads* (Oxford: Oxford University Press, 1993), provide anthologies of the *Enneads* with discussions of important passages. For discussions of Neoplatonism as a school, see Thomas Whittaker, *The Neo-Platonists* (Cambridge: Cambridge University Press, 1918); Arthur O. Lovejoy's influential book, *The Great Chain of Being* (Cambridge, MA: Harvard University Press, 1936); R.T. Wallis, *Neoplatonism* (London: Duckworth, 1972); and the collection of essays, R. Baine Harris, ed., *The Structure of Being: A Neoplatonic Approach* (Norfolk, VA: International Society for Neoplatonic Studies, 1982). John Dillon, *The Middle Platonists* (Ithaca, NY: Cornell University press, 1996) provides an overview of Platonism in the period leading up to Plotinus.

ENNEADS (in part)

ENNEAD I, TRACTATE 6: BEAUTY

1. Beauty is mostly in sight, but it is to be found too in things we hear, in combinations of words and also in music, and in all music [not only in songs]; for tunes and rhythms are certainly beautiful: and for those who are advancing upwards from sense-perception

The School of Plato, Pompeiian mosaic. 1st century. The Platonism of late antiquity (and the Middle Ages) was strongly influenced by Plotinus's development and modification of Plato's thought. (*Museo Archeologico Nazionale, Naples, Italy.* © *Scala/Art Resource, N.Y.*)

ways of life and actions and characters and intellectual activities are beautiful, and there is the beauty of virtue. If there is any beauty prior to these, this discussion will reveal it.

Very well then, what is it which makes us imagine that bodies are beautiful and attracts our hearing to sounds because of their beauty? And how are all the things which depend on soul beautiful? Are they all made beautiful by one and the same beauty or is there one beautifulness in bodies and a different one in other things? And what are they, or what is it? Some things, bodies for instance, are not beautiful from the nature of the objects themselves, but by participation, others are beauties themselves, like the nature of virtue. The same bodies appear sometimes beautiful, sometimes not beautiful, so that their being bodies is one thing, their being beautiful another. What is this principle, then, which is present in bodies? We ought to consider this first. What is it that attracts the gaze of those who look at something, and turns and draws them to it and makes them enjoy the sight? If we find this perhaps we can use it as a stepping-stone and get a sight of the rest. Nearly everyone says that it is good proportion of the parts to each other and to the whole, with the addition of good colour, which produces visible beauty, and that with the objects of sight and generally with everything else, being beautiful is being well-proportioned and measured. On this theory nothing single and simple but only a composite thing will have any beauty. It will be the whole which is beautiful, and the parts will not have the property of beauty by themselves, but will contribute to the beauty of the whole. But if the whole is beautiful the parts must be beautiful too; a beautiful whole can certainly not be composed of ugly parts; all the parts must have beauty. For these people, too, beautiful colours, and the light of the sun as well, since they are simple and do not derive their beautifulness from good proportion, will be excluded from beauty. And how do they think gold manages to be beautiful? And what makes lightning in the night and stars beautiful to see? And in sounds in the same way the simple will be banished, though often in a composition which is beautiful as a whole each separate sound is beautiful. And when, though the same good proportion is there all the time, the same face sometimes appears beautiful and sometimes does not, surely we must say that being beautiful is something else over and above good proportion, and good proportion is beautiful because of something else? But if when these people pass on to ways of life and beautiful expressions of thought they allege good proportion as the cause of beauty in these too, what can be meant by good proportion in beautiful ways of life or laws or studies or branches of knowledge? How can speculations be well-proportioned in relation to each other? If it is because they agree, there can be concord and agreement between bad ideas. The statement that "righteousness is a fine sort of silliness" agrees with and is in tune with the saying that "morality is stupidity;" the two fit perfectly. Again, every sort of virtue is a beauty of the soul, a truer beauty than those mentioned before; but how is virtue well-proportioned? Not like magnitudes or a number. We grant that the soul has several parts, but what is the formula for the composition or mixture in the soul of parts or speculations? And what [on this theory], will the beauty of the intellect alone by itself be?

2. So let us go back to the beginning and state what the primary beauty in bodies really is. It is something which we become aware of even at the first glance; the soul speaks of it as if it understood it, recognises and welcomes it and as it were adapts itself to it. But when it encounters the ugly it shrinks back and rejects it and turns away from it and is out of tune and alienated from it. Our explanation of this is that the soul, since it is by nature what it is and is related to the higher kind of reality in the realm of being, when it sees something akin to it or a trace of its kindred reality, is delighted and thrilled and returns to itself and remembers itself and its own possessions. What likeness, then, is there between beautiful things here and There? If there is a likeness, let us agree that

they are alike. But how are both the things in that world and the things in this beautiful? We maintain that the things in this world are beautiful by participating in form; for every shapeless thing which is naturally capable of receiving shape and form is ugly and outside the divine formative power as long as it has no share in formative power and form. This is absolute ugliness. But a thing is also ugly when it is not completely dominated by shape and formative power, since its matter has not submitted to be completely shaped according to the form. The form, then, approaches and composes that which is to come into being from many parts into a single ordered whole; it brings it into a completed unity and makes it one by agreement of its parts; for since it is one itself, that which is shaped by it must also be one as far as a thing can be which is composed of many parts. So beauty rests upon the material thing when it has been brought into unity, and gives itself to parts and wholes alike. When it comes upon something that is one and composed of like parts it gives the same gift to the whole; as sometimes art gives beauty to a whole house with its parts, and sometimes nature gives beauty to a single stone. So then the beautiful body comes into being by sharing in a formative power which comes from the divine forms.

3. The power ordained for the purpose recognises this, and there is nothing more effective for judging its own subject-matter, when the rest of the soul judges along with it; or perhaps the rest of the soul too pronounces the judgment by fitting the beautiful body to the form in itself and using this for judging beauty as we use a ruler for judging straightness. But how does the bodily agree with that which is before body? How does the architect declare the house outside beautiful by fitting it to the form of house within him? The reason is that the house outside, apart from the stones, is the inner form divided by the external mass of matter, without parts but appearing in many parts. When sense-perception, then, sees the form in bodies binding and mastering the nature opposed to it, which is shapeless, and shape riding gloriously upon other shapes, it gathers into one that which appears dispersed and brings it back and takes it in, now without parts, to the soul's interior and presents it to that which is within as something in tune with it and fitting it and dear to it; just as when a good man sees a trace of virtue in the young, which is in tune with his own inner truth, the sight delights him. And the simple beauty of colour comes about by shape and the mastery of the darkness in matter by the presence of light which is incorporeal and formative power and form. This is why fire itself is more beautiful than all other bodies, because it has the rank of form in relation to the other elements; it is above them in place and is the finest and subtlest of all bodies, being close to the incorporeal. It alone does not admit the others; but the others admit it for it warms them but is not cooled itself; it has colour primarily and all other things take the form of colour from it. So it shines and glitters as if it was a form. The inferior thing which becomes faint and dull by the fire's light, is not beautiful any more, as not participating in the whole form of colour. The melodies in sounds, too, the imperceptible ones which make the perceptible ones, make the soul conscious of beauty in the same way, showing the same thing in another medium. It is proper to sensible melodies to be measured by numbers, not according to any and every sort of formula but one which serves for the production of form so that it may dominate. So much, then, for the beauties in the realm of sense, images and shadows which, so to speak, sally out and come into matter and adorn it and excite us when they appear.

4. But about the beauties beyond, which it is no more the part of sense to see, but the soul sees them and speaks of them without instruments—we must go up to them and contemplate them and leave sense to stay down below. Just as in the case of the beauties of sense it is impossible for those who have not seen them or grasped their beauty— those born blind, for instance,—to speak about them, in the same way only those can

speak about the beauty of ways of life who have accepted the beauty of ways of life and kinds of knowledge and everything else of the sort; and people cannot speak about the splendour of virtue who have never even imagined how fair is the face of justice and moral order; "neither the evening nor the morning star are as fair." But there must be those who see this beauty by that with which the soul sees things of this sort, and when they see it they must be delighted and overwhelmed and excited much more than by those beauties we spoke of before, since now it is true beauty they are grasping. These experiences must occur whenever there is contact with any sort of beautiful thing, wonder and a shock of delight and longing and passion and a happy excitement. One can have these experiences by contact with invisible beauties, and souls do have them, practically all, but particularly those who are more passionately in love with the invisible, just as with bodies all see them, but all are not stung as sharply, but some, who are called lovers, are most of all.

5. Then we must ask the lovers of that which is outside sense "What do you feel about beautiful ways of life, as we call them, and beautiful habits and well-ordered characters and in general about virtuous activities and dispositions and the beauty of souls? What do you feel when you see your own inward beauty? How are you stirred to wild exultation, and long to be with yourselves, gathering your selves together away from your bodies?" For this is what true lovers feel. But what is it which makes them feel like this? Not shape or colour or any size, but soul, without colour itself and possessing a moral order without colour and possessing all the other light of the virtues; you feel like this when you see, in yourself or in someone else, greatness of soul, a righteous life, a pure morality, courage with its noble look, and dignity and modesty advancing in a fearless, calm and unperturbed disposition, and the godlike light of intellect shining upon all this. We love and delight in these qualities, but why do we call them beautiful? They exist and appear to us and he who sees them cannot possibly say anything else except that they are what really exists. What does "really exists" mean? That they exist as beauties. But the argument still requires us to explain why real beings make the soul lovable. What is this kind of glorifying light on all the virtues? Would you like to take the opposites, the uglinesses in soul, and contrast them with the beauties? Perhaps a consideration of what ugliness is and why it appears so will help us to find what we are looking for. Suppose, then, an ugly soul, dissolute and unjust, full of all lusts, and all disturbance, sunk in fears by its cowardice and jealousies by its pettiness, thinking mean and mortal thoughts as far as it thinks at all, altogether distorted, loving impure pleasures, living a life which consists of bodily sensations and finding delight in its ugliness. Shall we not say that its ugliness came to it as a "beauty" brought in from outside, injuring it and making it impure and "mixed with a great deal of evil," with its life and perceptions no longer pure, but by the admixture of evil living a dim life and diluted with a great deal of death, no longer seeing what a soul ought to see, no longer left in peace in itself because it keeps on being dragged out, and down, and to the dark? Impure, I think, and dragged in every direction towards the objects of sense, with a great deal of bodily stuff mixed into it, consorting much with matter and receiving a form other than its own it has changed by a mixture which makes it worse; just as if anyone gets into mud or filth he does not show any more the beauty which he had, what is seen is what he wiped off on himself from the mud and filth; his ugliness has come from an addition of alien matter, and his business, if he is to be beautiful again, is to wash and clean himself and so be again what he was before. So we shall be right in saying that the soul becomes ugly by mixture and dilution and inclination towards the body and matter. This is the soul's ugliness, not being pure and unmixed, like gold, but full of earthiness; if anyone takes the earthy stuff away the gold is left, and is beautiful, when it is singled

out from other things and is alone by itself. In the same way the soul too, when it is separated from the lusts which it has through the body with which it consorted too much, and freed from its other affections, purged of what it gets from being embodied, when it abides alone has put away all the ugliness which came from the other nature.

6. For, as was said in old times, self-control, and courage and every virtue, is a purification, and so is even wisdom itself. This is why the mysteries are right when they say riddlingly that the man who has not been purified will lie in mud when he goes to Hades, because the impure is fond of mud by reason of its badness; just as pigs, with their unclean bodies, like that sort of thing. For what can true self-control be except not keeping company with bodily pleasures, but avoiding them as impure and belonging to something impure? Courage, too, is not being afraid of death. And death is the separation of body and soul; and a man does not fear this if he welcomes the prospect of being alone. Again, greatness of soul is despising the things here and wisdom is an intellectual activity which turns away from the things below and leads the soul to those above. So the soul when it is purified becomes form and formative power, altogether bodiless and intellectual and entirely belonging to the divine, whence beauty springs and all that is akin to it. Soul, then, when it is raised to the level of intellect increases in beauty. Intellect and the things of intellect are its beauty, its own beauty and not another's, since only then [when it is perfectly conformed to intellect] is it truly soul. For this reason it is right to say that the soul's becoming something good and beautiful is its being made like to God, because from Him comes beauty and all else which falls to the lot of real beings. Or rather, beautifulness is reality, and the other kind of thing is the ugly, and this same is the primary evil; so for God the qualities of goodness and beauty are the same, or the realities, the good and the beautiful. So we must follow the same line of enquiry to discover beauty and goodness, and ugliness and evil. And first we must posit beauty which is also the good; from this immediately comes intellect, which is beauty; and soul is given beauty by intellect. Everything else is beautiful by the shaping of soul, the beauties in actions and in ways of life. And soul makes beautiful the bodies which are spoken of as beautiful; for since it is a divine thing and a kind of part of beauty, it makes everything it grasps and masters beautiful, as far as they are capable of participation.

7. So we must ascend again to the good, which every soul desires. Anyone who has seen it knows what I mean when I say that it is beautiful. It is desired as good, and the desire for it is directed to good, and the attainment of it is for those who go up to the higher world and are converted and strip off what we put on in our descent; (just as for those who go up to the celebrations of sacred rites there are purifications, and strippings off of the clothes they wore before, and going up naked) until, passing in the ascent all that is alien to the God, one sees with one's self alone That alone, simple, single and pure, from which all depends and to which all look and are and live and think for it is the cause of life and mind and being. If anyone sees it, what passion will he feel, what longing in his desire to be united with it, what a shock of delight! The man who has not seen it may desire it as good, but he who has seen it glories in its beauty and is full of wonder and delight, enduring a shock which causes no hurt, loving with true passion and piercing longing; he laughs at all other loves and despises what he thought beautiful before; it is like the experience of those who have met appearances of gods or spirits and do not any more appreciate as they did the beauty of other bodies. "What then are we to think, if anyone contemplates the absolute beauty which exists pure by itself, uncontaminated by flesh or body, not in earth or heaven, that it may keep its purity?" All these other things are external additions and mixtures and not primary, but derived from it. If then one sees That which provides for all and remains by itself and gives to all but receives

nothing into itself, if he abides in the contemplation of this kind of beauty and rejoices in being made like it, how can he need any other beauty? For this, since it is beauty most of all, and primary beauty, makes its lovers beautiful and lovable. Here the greatest, the ultimate contest is set before our souls; all our toil and trouble is for this, not to be left without a share in the best of visions. The man who attains this is blessed in seeing that "blessed sight," and he who fails to attain it has failed utterly. A man has not failed if he fails to win beauty of colours or bodies, or power or office or kingship even, but if he fails to win this and only this. For this he should give up the attainment of kingship and of rule over all earth and sea and sky, if only by leaving and overlooking them he can turn to That and see.

8. But how shall we find the way? What method can we devise? How can one see the "inconceivable beauty" which stays within in the holy sanctuary and does not come out where the profane may see it? Let him who can, follow and come within, and leave outside the sight of his eyes and not turn back to the bodily splendours which he saw before. When he sees the beauty in bodies he must not run after them; we must know that they are images, traces, shadows, and hurry away to that which they image. For if a man runs to the image and wants to seize it as if it was the reality (like a beautiful reflection playing on the water, which some story somewhere, I think, said riddlingly a man wanted to catch and sank down into the stream and disappeared) then this man who clings to beautiful bodies and will not let them go, will, like the man in the story, but in soul, not in body, sink down into the dark depths where intellect has no delight, and stay blind in Hades, consorting with shadows there and here. This would be truer advice "Let us fly to our dear country." What then is our way of escape, and how are we to find it? We shall put out to sea, as Odysseus did, from the witch Circe or Calypso—as the poet says (I think with a hidden meaning)—and was not content to stay though he had delights of the eyes and lived among much beauty of sense. Our country from which we came is there, our Father is there. How shall we travel to it, where is our way of escape? We cannot get there on foot; for our feet only carry us everywhere in this world, from one country to another. You must not get ready a carriage, either, or a boat. Let all these things go, and do not look. Shut your eyes, and change to and wake another way of seeing, which everyone has but few use.

9. And what does this inner sight see? When it is just awakened it is not at all able to look at the brilliance before it. So that the soul must be trained, first of all to look at beautiful ways of life then at beautiful works, not those which the arts produce, but the works of men who have a name for goodness: then look at the souls of the people who produce the beautiful works. How then can you see the sort of beauty a good soul has? Go back into yourself and look; and if you do not yet see yourself beautiful, then, just as someone making a statue which has to be beautiful cuts away here and polishes there and makes one part smooth and clears another till he has given his statue a beautiful face, so you too must cut away excess and straighten the crooked and clear the dark and make it bright, and never stop "working on your statue" till the divine glory of virtue shines out on you, till you see "self-mastery enthroned upon its holy seat." If you have become this, and see it, and are at home with yourself in purity, with nothing hindering you from becoming in this way one, with no inward mixture of anything else, but wholly yourself, nothing but true light, not measured by dimensions, or bounded by shape into littleness, or expanded to size by unboundedness, but everywhere unmeasured, because greater than all measure and superior to all quantity; when you see that you have become this, then you have become sight; you can trust yourself then; you have already ascended and need no one to show you; concentrate your gaze and see.

This alone is the eye that sees the great beauty. But if anyone comes to the sight bleary-eyed with wickedness, and unpurified, or weak and by his cowardice unable to look at what is very bright, he sees nothing, even if someone shows him what is there and possible to see. For one must come to the sight with a seeing power made akin and like to what is seen. No eye ever saw the sun without becoming sunlike, nor can a soul see beauty without becoming beautiful. You must become first all godlike and all beautiful if you intend to see God and beauty. First the soul will come in its ascent to intellect and there will know the Forms, all beautiful, and will affirm that these, the Ideas, are beauty; for all things are beautiful by these, by the products and essence of intellect. That which is beyond this we call the nature of the Good, which holds beauty as a screen before it. So in a loose and general way of speaking the Good is the primary beauty; but if one distinguishes the intelligibles [from the Good] one will say that the place of the Forms is the intelligible beauty, but the Good is That which is beyond, the "spring and origin" of beauty; or one will place the Good and the primal beauty on the same level. In any case, however, beauty is in the intelligible world.

*   *   *

ENNEAD V, TRACTATE 1: ON THE THREE PRIMARY HYPOSTASES

1. What is it, then, which has made the souls forget their father, God, and be ignorant of themselves and him, even though they are parts which come from his higher world and altogether belong to it? The beginning of evil for them was audacity and coming to birth and the first otherness and the wishing to belong to themselves. Since they were clearly delighted with their own independence, and made great use of self-movement, running the opposite course and getting as far away as possible, they were ignorant even that they themselves came from that world; just as children who are immediately torn from their parents and brought up far away do not know who they themselves or their parents are. Since they do not any more see their father or themselves, they despise themselves through ignorance of their birth and honour other things, admiring everything rather than themselves, and, astonished and delighted by and dependent on these [earthly] things, they broke themselves loose as far as they could in contempt of that from which they turned away; so that their honour for these things here and their contempt for themselves is the cause of their utter ignorance of God. For what pursues and admires something else admits at the same time its own inferiority; but by making itself inferior to things which come into being and perish and considering itself the most contemptible and the most liable to death of all the things which it admires it could not possibly have any idea of the nature and power of God. One must therefore speak in two ways to men who are in this state of mind, if one is going to turn them round to what lies in the opposite direction and is primary, and to lead them up to that which is highest, one, and first. What, then, are these two ways? One shows how contemptible are the things now honoured by the soul, and this we shall develop more amply elsewhere, but the other teaches and reminds the soul how high its birth and value are, and this is prior to the other one and when it is clarified will also make the other obvious. This is what we must speak about now; it is close to the subject of our investigation and will be useful for that other discourse. For that which investigates is the soul, and it should know what it is as an

investigating soul, so that it may learn first about itself, whether it has the power to investigate things of this kind, and if it has an eye of the right kind to see them, and if the investigation is suitable for it. For if the objects are alien, what is the point? But if they are akin, the investigation is suitable and discovery is possible.

2. Let every soul, then, first consider this, that it made all living things itself, breathing life into them, those that the earth feeds and those that are nourished by the sea, and the divine stars in the sky; it made the sun itself, and this great heaven, and adorned it itself, and drives it round itself, in orderly movement; it is a nature other than the things which it adorns and moves and makes live; and it must necessarily be more honourable than they, for they come into being or pass away when the soul leaves them or grants life to them, but soul itself exists for ever because "it does not depart from itself." This is how soul should reason about the manner in which it grants life in the whole universe and in individual things. Let it look at the great soul, being itself another soul which is no small one, which has become worthy to look by being freed from deceit and the things that have bewitched the other souls, and is established in quietude. Let not only its encompassing body and the body's raging sea be quiet, but all its environment: the earth quiet, and the sea and air quiet, and the heaven itself at peace. Into this heaven at rest let it imagine soul as if flowing in from outside, pouring in and entering it everywhere and illuminating it: as the rays of the sun light up a dark cloud, and make it shine and give it a golden look, so soul entering into the body of heaven gives it life and gives it immortality and wakes what lies inert. And heaven, moved with an everlasting motion by the wise guidance of soul, becomes a "fortunate living being" and gains its value by the indwelling of soul; before soul it was a dead body, earth and water, or rather the darkness of matter and non-existence, and "what the gods hate," as a poet says. The power and nature of soul will become still clearer and more obvious if one considers here how it encompasses the heaven and drives it by its own acts of will. For soul has given itself to the whole magnitude of heaven, as far as it extends, and every stretch of space both great and small, is ensouled; one body lies in one place and one in another, and one is here and another there; some are separated by being in opposite parts of the universe, and others in other ways. But soul is not like this and it is not by being cut up that it gives life, by a part of itself for each individual thing, but all things live by the whole, and all soul is present everywhere, made like to the father who begat it in its unity and its universality. And by its power the heaven is one, though it is multiple with one part in one place and one in another, and our universe is a god by the agency of this soul. And the sun also is a god because it is ensouled, and the other heavenly bodies, and we, if we are in any way divine, are so for this reason: for "corpses are more throwable away than dung." But that which is for the gods the cause of their being gods must necessarily be a divinity senior to them. But our soul is of the same kind, and when you look at it without its accretions and take it in its purified state you will find that very same honourable thing which [we said] was soul, more honourable than everything which is body. For all bodily things are earth; and even if they are fire, what would its burning principle be [but soul]? And the same is true of all things compounded of these, even if you add water to them, and air as well. But if the bodily is worth pursuing because it is ensouled, why does one let oneself go and pursue another? But by admiring the soul in another, you admire yourself.

3. Since the soul is so honourable and divine a thing, be sure already that you can attain God by reason of its being of this kind, and with this as your motive ascend to him: in all certainty you will not look far; and the stages between are not many. Grasp then the soul's upper neighbour, more divine than this divine thing, after which and from which the soul comes. For, although it is a thing of the kind which our discussion

has shown it to be, it is an image of Intellect; just as a thought in its utterance is an image of the thought in soul, so soul itself is the expressed thought of Intellect, and its whole activity, and the life which it sends out to establish another reality; as fire has the heat which remains with it and the heat which it gives. But one must understand that the activity on the level of Intellect does not flow out of it, but the external activity comes into existence as something distinct. Since then its existence derives from Intellect soul is intellectual, and its intellect is in discursive reasonings, and its perfection comes from Intellect, like a father who brings to maturity a son whom he begat imperfect in comparison with himself. Soul's establishment in reality, then, comes from Intellect and its thought becomes actual in its seeing of Intellect. For when it looks into Intellect, it has within it and as its own what it thinks in its active actuality. And we should call these alone activities of the soul, all it does intellectually and which spring from its own home; its inferior activities come from elsewhere and belong to a soul of this inferior kind. Intellect therefore makes soul still more divine by being its father and by being present to it; for there is nothing between but the fact that they are different, soul as next in order and as the recipient, Intellect as the form; and even the matter of Intellect is beautiful, since it has the form of Intellect and is simple. But what Intellect is like is clear from this very fact that it is superior to soul which is of such great excellence.

4. But one might see this also from what follows: if someone admires this perceptible universe, observing its size and beauty and the order of its everlasting course, and the gods in it, some of whom are seen and some are invisible, and the spirits, and all animals and plants, let him ascend to its archetypal and truer reality and there see them all intelligible and eternal in it, in its own understanding and life; and let him see pure Intellect presiding over them, and immense wisdom, and the true life of Kronos, a god who is fullness and intellect. For he encompasses in himself all things immortal, every intellect, every god, every soul, all for ever unmoving. For why should it seek to change when all is well with it? Where should it seek to go away to when it has everything in itself? But it does not even seek to increase, since it is most perfect. Therefore all things in it are perfect, that it may be altogether perfect, having nothing which is not so, having nothing in itself which does not think; but it thinks not by seeking but by having. Its blessedness is not something acquired, but all things are in eternity, and the true eternity, which time copies, running round the soul, letting some things go and attending to others. For around Soul things come one after another: now Socrates, now a horse, always some one particular reality; but Intellect is all things. It has therefore everything at rest in the same place, and it only is, and its "is" is for ever, and there is no place for the future for then too it is—or for the past—for nothing there has passed away—but all things remain stationary for ever, since they are the same, as if they were satisfied with themselves for being so.

But each of them is Intellect and Being, and the whole is universal Intellect and Being, Intellect making Being exist in thinking it, and Being giving Intellect thinking and existence by being thought. But the cause of thinking is something else, which is also cause of being; they both therefore have a cause other than themselves. For they are simultaneous and exist together and one does not abandon the other, but this one is two things, Intellect and Being and thinking and thought, Intellect as thinking and Being as thought. For there could not be thinking without otherness, and also sameness. These then are primary, Intellect, Being, Otherness, Sameness; but one must also include Motion and Rest. One must include movement if there is thought, and rest that it may think the same; and otherness, that there may be thinker and thought; or else, if you take away otherness, it will become one and keep silent; and the objects of thought, also, must have otherness in relation to each other. But one must include sameness, because it is one with itself, and all have some common unity; and the distinctive quality of each is otherness. The fact that there are several of these primaries makes number and quantity; and the particularity of each makes quality, and from these as principles everything else comes.

5. This god, then, which is over the soul, is multiple; and soul exists among the intelligible realities in close unity with them, unless it wills to desert them. When it has come near then to him and, in a way, become one with him, it lives for ever. Who is it, then, who begat this god? The simple god, the one who is prior to this kind of multiplicity, the cause of this one's existence and multiplicity, the maker of number. For number is not primary: the One is prior to the dyad, but the dyad is secondary and, originating from the One, has it as definer, but is itself of its own nature indefinite; but when it is defined, it is already a number, but a number as substance; and soul too is a number. For masses and magnitudes are not primary: these things which have thickness come afterwards, and sense-perception thinks they are realities. Even in seeds it is not the moisture which is honourable, but what is unseen: and this is number and rational principle. Therefore what is called number in the intelligible world and the dyad are rational principles and Intellect; but the dyad is indefinite when one forms an idea of it by what may be called the substrate, but each and every number which comes from it and the One is a form, as if Intellect was shaped by the numbers which came to exist in it; but it is shaped in one way by the One and in another by itself, like sight in its actuality; for intellection is seeing sight, and both are one.

6. How then does it see, and whom does it see? And how did it come into existence at all and arise from the One so as to be able to see? For the soul now knows that these things must be, but longs to answer the question repeatedly discussed also by the ancient philosophers, how from the One, if it is such as we say it is, anything else, whether a multiplicity or a dyad or a number, came into existence, and why it did not on the contrary remain by itself, but such a great multiplicity flowed from it as that which is seen to exist in beings, but which we think it right to refer back to the One. Let us speak of it in this way, first invoking God himself, not in spoken words, but stretching ourselves out with our soul into prayer to him, able in this way to pray alone to him alone. The contemplator, then, since God exists by himself as if inside the temple, remaining quiet beyond all things, must contemplate what correspond to the images already standing outside the temple, or rather that one image which appeared first; and this is the way in which it appeared: everything which is moved must have some end to which it moves. The One has no such end, so we must not consider that it moves. If anything comes into being after it, we must think that it necessarily does so while the One remains continually turned towards itself. When we are discussing eternal realities we must not let coming into being in time be an obstacle to our thought; in the discussion we apply the word "becoming" to them in attributing to them causal connection and order, and must therefore state that what comes into being from the One does so without the One being moved: for if anything came into being as a result of the One's being moved, it would be the third starting from the One, not the second, since it would come after the movement. So if there is a second after the One it must have come to be without the One moving at all, without any inclination or act of will or any sort of activity on its part. How did it come to be then, and what are we to think of as surrounding the One in its repose? It must be a radiation from it while it remains unchanged, like the bright light of the sun which, so to speak, runs round it, springing from it continually while it remains unchanged. All things which exist, as long as they remain in being, necessarily produce from their own substances, in dependence on their present power, a surrounding reality directed to what

is outside them, a kind of image of the archetypes from which it was produced: fire produces the heat which comes from it; snow does not only keep its cold inside itself. Perfumed things show this particularly clearly. As long as they exist, something is diffused from themselves around them, and what is near them enjoys their existence. And all things when they come to perfection produce; the One is always perfect and therefore produces everlastingly; and its product is less than itself. What then must we say about the most perfect? Nothing can come from it except that which is next greatest after it. Intellect is next to it in greatness and second to it: for Intellect sees it and needs it alone; but it has no need of Intellect; and that which derives from something greater than Intellect is intellect, which is greater than all things, because the other things come after it: as Soul is an expression and a kind of activity of Intellect, just as Intellect is of the One. But soul's expression is obscure—for it is a ghost of Intellect—and for this reason it has to look to Intellect; but Intellect in the same way has to look to that god, in order to be Intellect. But it sees him, not as separated from him, but because it comes next after him, and there is nothing between, as also there is not anything between soul and Intellect. Everything longs for its parent and loves it, especially when parent and offspring are alone; but when the parent is the highest good, the offspring is necessarily with him and separate from him only in otherness.

7. But we say that Intellect is an image of that Good; for we must speak more plainly; first of all we must say that what has come into being must be in a way that Good, and retain much of it and be a likeness of it, as light is of the sun. But Intellect is not that Good. How then does it generate Intellect? Because by its return to it it sees: and this seeing is Intellect. For that which apprehends something else is either sense-perception or intellect; (sense-perception is a line etc.) but the circle is of a kind which can be divided; but this [intellectual apprehension] is not so. There is One here also, but the One is the productive power of all things. The things, then, of which it is the productive power are those which Intellect observes, in a way cutting itself off from the power; otherwise it would not be Intellect. For Intellect also has of itself a kind of intimate perception of its power, that it has power to produce substantial reality. Intellect, certainly, by its own means even defines its being for itself by the power which comes from the One, and because its substance is a kind of single part of what belongs to the One and comes from the One, it is strengthened by the One and made perfect in substantial existence by and from it. But Intellect sees, by means of itself, like something divided proceeding from the undivided, that life and thought and all things come from the One, because that God is not one of all things; for this is how all things come from him, because he is not confined by any shape; that One is one alone: if he was all things, he would be numbered among beings. For this reason that One is none of the things in Intellect, but all things come from him. This is why they are substances; for they are already defined and each has a kind of shape. Being must not fluctuate, so to speak, in the indefinite, but must be fixed by limit and stability; and stability in the intelligible world is limitation and shape, and it is by these that it receives existence. "Of this lineage" is this Intellect of which we are speaking, a lineage worthy of the purest Intellect, that it should spring from nowhere else but the first principle, and when it has come into existence should generate all realities along with itself, all the beauty of the Ideas and all the intelligible gods; and it is full of the beings which it has generated and as it were swallows them up again, by keeping them in itself and because they do not fall out into matter and are not brought up in the house of Rhea; as the mysteries and the myths about the gods say riddlingly that Kronos, the wisest god, before the birth of Zeus took back and kept within himself all that he begat, and in this way is full and is Intellect in satiety; and after this they say he begat Zeus who is then his Koros [that is,

boy and satiety]; for Intellect generates soul, since it is perfect Intellect. For since it was perfect it had to generate, and not be without offspring when it was so great a power. But its offspring could not be better than it (this is not so even here below) but had to be a lesser image of it, and in the same way indefinite, but defined by its parent and, so to speak, given a form. And the offspring of Intellect is a rational form and an existing being, that which thinks discursively; it is this which moves round Intellect and is light and trace of Intellect and dependent on it, united to it on one side and so filled with it and enjoying it and sharing in it and thinking, but, on the other side, in touch with the things which came after it, or rather itself generating what must necessarily be worse than soul; about these we must speak later. This is as far as the divine realities extend.

8. This is the reason why Plato says that all things are threefold "about the king of all"—he means the primary realities—and "the second about the second and the third about the third." But he also says that there is a "father of the cause," meaning Intellect by "the cause": for Intellect is his craftsman; and he says that it makes Soul in that "mixing-bowl" he speaks of. And the father of Intellect which is the cause he calls the Good and that which is beyond Intellect and "beyond being." And he also often calls Being and Intellect Idea: so Plato knew that Intellect comes from the Good and Soul from Intellect. And [it follows] that these statements of ours are not new; they do not belong to the present time, but were made long ago, not explicitly, and what we have said in this discussion has been an interpretation of them, relying on Plato's own writings for evidence that these views are ancient. And Parmenides also, before Plato, touched on a view like this, in that he identified Being and Intellect and that it was not among things perceived by the senses that he placed Being, when he said "Thinking and Being are the same." And he says that this Being is unmoved—though he does attach thinking to it—taking all bodily movement from it that it may remain always in the same state, and likening it to "the mass of a sphere," because it holds all things in its circumference and because its thinking is not external, but in itself. But when he said it was one, in his own works, he was open to criticism because this one of his was discovered to be many. But Parmenides in Plato speaks more accurately, and distinguishes from each other the first One, which is more properly called One, and the second which he calls "One-Many" and the third, "One and Many." In this way he too agrees with the doctrine of the three natures.

9. And Anaxagoras also, when he says that Intellect is pure and unmixed, posits that the first principle is simple and that the One is separate, but he neglects to give an accurate account because of his antiquity. Heraclitus also knows that the one is eternal and intelligible: for bodies are always coming into being and flowing away. And for Empedocles Strife divides, but Love is the One—he too makes it incorporeal—and the elements serve as matter. Later, Aristotle makes the first principle separate and intelligible, but when he says that it knows itself, he goes back again and does not make it the first principle; and by making many other intelligible realities, as many as the heavenly spheres, that each particular intelligible may move one particular sphere, he describes the intelligible world in a different way from Plato, making a probable assumption which has no philosophical necessity. But one might doubt whether it is even probable: for it would be more probable that all the spheres, contributing their several movements to a single system, should look to one principle, the first. And one might enquire whether Aristotle thinks that the many intelligibles derive from one, the first, or whether there are many primary principles in the intelligible world; and if they derive from one, the situation will clearly be analogous to that of the heavenly spheres in the sense-world, where each contains the other and one, the outermost, dominates; so that there too the first would contain the others and there will be an intelligible universe; and, just as here in the sense-world the spheres are not empty, but

the first is full of heavenly bodies and the others have heavenly bodies in them, so there also the moving principles will have many realities in them, and the realities there will be truer. But if each is primary principle, the primary principles will be a random assembly; and why will they be a community and in agreement on one work, the harmony of the whole universe? And how can the perceptible beings in heaven be equal in number to the intelligible movers? And how can the intelligibles even be many, when they are incorporeal, as they are, and matter does not divide them? For these reasons those of the ancient philosophers who took up positions closest to those of Pythagoras and his successors (and Pherecydes) held closely to this nature; but some of them worked out the idea fully in their own writings, others did not do so in written works but in unwritten group discussions, or left it altogether alone.

10. It has been shown that we ought to think that this is how things are, that there is the One beyond being, of such a kind as our argument wanted to show, so far as demonstration was possible in these matters, and next in order there is Being and Intellect, and the nature of Soul in the third place. And just as in nature there are these three of which we have spoken, so we ought to think that they are present also in ourselves. I do not mean in [ourselves as] beings of the sense-world—for these three are separate from the things of sense—but in [ourselves as] beings outside the realm of senseperception; "outside" here is used in the same sense as those realities are also said to be "outside" the whole universe: so the corresponding realities in man are said to be "outside," as Plato speaks of the "inner man." Our soul then also is a divine thing and of a nature different [from the things of sense], like the universal nature of soul; and the human soul is perfect when it has intellect; and intellect is of two kinds, the one which reasons and the one which makes it possible to reason. Now this reasoning part of the soul, which needs no bodily instrument for its reasoning, but preserves its activity in purity in order that it may be able to engage in pure reasoning, one could without mistake place, as separate and unmixed with body, in the primary intelligible realm. I or we should not look for a place in which to put it, but make it exist outside all place. For this is how it is by itself and outside and immaterial, when it is alone and retains nothing from the nature of body. This is the reason why Plato says of the universe also that the craftsman wrapped the soul round it "from outside," indicating the part of the soul which remains in the intelligible; and he said obscurely about us that the soul is "on top in the head." And his exhortation to separate ourselves is not meant in a spatial sense—this [higher part] of soul is naturally separated—but refers to our not inclining to the body, and to our not having mental images, and our alienation from the body—if by any chance one could make the remaining form of soul ascend, and take along with us to the heights that of it which is established here below, which alone is the craftsman and modeller of the body and is actively concerned with it.

11. Since, then, there exists soul which reasons about what is right and good, and discursive reasoning which enquires about the rightness and goodness of this or that particular thing, there must be some further permanent rightness from which arises the discursive reasoning in the realm of soul. Or how else would it manage to reason? And if soul sometimes reasons about the right and good and sometimes does not, there must be in us Intellect which does not reason discursively but always possesses the right, and there must be also the principle and cause and God of Intellect. He is not divided, but abides, and as he does not abide in place he is contemplated in many beings, in each and every one of those capable of receiving him as another self, just as the centre of a circle exists by itself, but every one of the radii in the circle has its point in the centre and the lines bring their individuality to it. For it is with something of this sort in ourselves that

we are in contact with god and are with him and depend upon him; and those of us who converge towards him are firmly established in him.

12. Why then, when we have such great possessions, do we not consciously grasp them, but are mostly inactive in these ways, and some of us are never active at all? They are always occupied in their own activities, Intellect, and that which is before Intellect, always in itself, and soul, which is in this sense "ever-moving." For not everything which is in the soul is immediately perceptible, but it reaches us when it enters into perception; but when a particular active power does not give a share in its activity to the perceiving power, that activity has not yet pervaded the whole soul. We do not therefore yet know it, since we are accompanied by the perceptive power and are not a part of soul but the whole soul. And further, each soul-part, since it is always living, always exercises its own activity by itself; but the discovery of it comes when sharing with the perceptive power and conscious awareness takes place. If then there is to be conscious apprehension of the powers which are present in this way, we must turn our power of apprehension inwards, and make it attend to what is there. It is as if someone was expecting to hear a voice which he wanted to hear and withdrew from other sounds and roused his power of hearing to catch what, when it comes, is the best of all sounds which can be heard; so here also we must let perceptible sounds go (except in so far as we must listen to them) and keep the soul's power of apprehension pure and ready to hear the voices from on high.